CONFEDERATES
OF
ELMWOOD

A Compilation of Information Concerning
Confederate Soldiers and Veterans
Buried at Elmwood Cemetery
Memphis, Tennessee

Expanded Edition

John W. Cothern

HERITAGE BOOKS
2019

HERITAGE BOOKS

AN IMPRINT OF HERITAGE BOOKS, INC.

Books, CDs, and more—Worldwide

For our listing of thousands of titles see our website
at
www.HeritageBooks.com

Published 2019 by
HERITAGE BOOKS, INC.
Publishing Division
5810 Ruatan Street
Berwyn Heights, Md. 20740

Copyright © 2019 John W. Cothern

Heritage Books by the author:

Confederates of Elmwood: A Compilation of Information Concerning Confederate Soldiers and Veterans Buried at Elmwood Cemetery, Memphis, Tennessee (2001)

Confederates of Elmwood: A Compilation of Information Concerning Confederate Soldiers and Veterans Buried at Elmwood Cemetery, Memphis, Tennessee (Expanded Edition)

Front Cover: Confederate Monument. Confederate Soldiers Rest. Elmwood Cemetery.
Courtesy: Ed McCarver Postcard Collection, Mississippi Valley Collection,
University of Memphis. All rights reserved.

International Standard Book Number
Paperbound: 978-0-7884-5879-8

Confederate Dead

"Fame shall keep the records of your immortal deeds, and honor point the hallowed spot where your dust so proudly sleeps. The heroic soil of this proud land you baptized with your blood shall ever proudly claim the ashes of her braves as the rich spoils of war. Generations yet unborn shall come in laughing June, with opening flowers, to honor thy tombs. Never shall you lie neglected, forgot, nor your names perish from the lips of love."

The Memphis Daily Appeal, Thursday, June 6, 1878, page 4, column 7
(Quotation at end of article "Our Dead Heroes" on the unveiling of the Confederate Monument and decoration of the graves of the Southern Soldiers in Elmwood)

TABLE OF CONTENTS

PREFACE AND INDEX NOTE

The purpose of this expanded edition is to update and make corrections to the original 2001 edition and add new information and individual sketches. The updated and new information is from further research and information provided by many descendants and other researchers to whom my personal thanks is hereby expressed. Many records have been and continue to be digitalized that along with the many new and enhanced online sources, i.e., federal and state archives and libraries, newspapers, ancestry/genealogy websites and graves listings, were immensely helpful with additional, new and corrected information and new research leads for this work.

As stated in the original edition, this compilation was started as a personal project. The initial goal was to just compile a simple list of the soldiers buried in Confederate Soldiers Rest. This was desired because my maternal great-great-grandfather Francis M. Ross, Private Companies K, B & I, 7th Tennessee Cavalry Regiment, on whose record my son and I had joined the Sons of Confederate Veterans, is buried there. The project was later expanded in more detail when the Nathan Bedford Forrest Camp 215, Sons of Confederate Veterans, took on the project of helping secure a government grave stone for each soldier. It was further expanded to include Confederate soldiers and veterans buried outside of Confederate Soldiers Rest as well as other individuals, although not serving in the Confederate military, who served an important part in the Confederate Cause.

Initially and many times over, the Elmwood records were reviewed. This review included the Cemetery Daily Burial Record, Alpha, Single Grave and Section books. Then, the compiled service records of the soldiers whose unit could be identified were reviewed. This was necessary in order to verify the soldier's military service unit. Many of the units identified in the Elmwood records were only local designations and were quite often not the final or official designations or even the only unit in which the soldier served. Further, many days were spent walking the grounds to read headstones and monuments that led to identifying others for inclusion herein.

A compiled service record was not found on many of the soldiers. There are several reasons for this, including, but not limited to, the soldier dying before the unit was mustered into Confederate service, proper records of service not being made, records were lost or destroyed, or records were so vague that it was not possible to determine the correct name of the soldier or the unit in which the soldier served.

As this compilation is intended to be a memorial and lasting record to the Confederate soldiers buried at Elmwood, it is also hoped that it may be of some assistance to anyone researching their Confederate ancestor whether buried at Elmwood or not. However, this edition should not be considered a total and complete compilation of the records and other information on the respective soldiers and other individuals listed herein or the other subjects briefly discussed. Just like any research text, this compilation is intended to be an additional tool. Anyone researching a specific soldier or individual should review all pertinent records that can be found and not just rely solely on this work.

Once again, this book could not have been possible without the immeasurable assistance and cooperation of the Elmwood Cemetery Association and the Elmwood Cemetery staff. For this edition I want to especially acknowledge and thank Kimberly Bearden, Executive Director, Bob Barnett, Assistant Director, Kelly Sowell, Historian/Visitor Services & Volunteer Coordinator, and Michael Davis, Superintendent.

Lastly, I want to again thank my family, especially my wife Deborah Cothern, for their support for this project.

INDEX NOTE - Soldiers, veterans and others included in this work are listed in alphabetical order in the chapters with sketches and there is no separate index. Care should be taken to consider spelling variations as the surname spelling found in official records, if such was found, and other sources are not necessarily the spelling in the Cemetery records (Daily Burial Record, Alpha, Single Grave and Section books) and computer database index. Variations are generally noted in the sketches. There is a chapter on Confederate Soldiers Rest Name Spelling Variations.

John W. Cothern, Compiler

ELMWOOD CEMETERY
AND
CONFEDERATE SOLDIERS REST

Elmwood Cemetery was established August 28, 1852, and is the oldest active cemetery in Memphis. There are more than 70,000 burials presently at Elmwood. It is the burial place of mayors of Memphis and South Memphis, Tennessee governors, including Isham G. Harris who headed the state government when the War between the States broke out in 1861, United States senators, War generals and many others historic figures and public officials.

Elmwood may best be known as the cemetery of Confederate soldiers, especially the generals. Nineteen Confederate generals are listed in the "Touring Historic Elmwood Cemetery" Brochure (January 2000) and that brochure's predecessor "Touring historic Elmwood Cemetery" (Brochure and Map of Historic Gravesites) lists eighteen Confederate generals. Nathan Bedford Forrest, who died in 1877, was first buried at Elmwood but was removed to Forrest Park in 1904. There are two Union generals, William J. Smith and Milton T. Williamson (see Note 2 at end of "Generals" chapter, page 239), buried at Elmwood.

Confederate Soldiers Rest is located in the Fowler Section. More than 1000 Confederate soldiers and veterans are buried there. Many others are buried throughout Elmwood as well. Union soldiers were also buried at Elmwood during the War in a specially designated section but were removed to the Memphis National Cemetery, then known as Mississippi River National Cemetery, in May 1868. There are a few Union veterans buried throughout Elmwood.

Elmwood Cemetery donated a lot for Soldiers Rest per the following article in the September 25, 1861, *Memphis Daily Appeal*, Local Matters, page 4, column 1: "Elmwood Cemetery. –This Company, at the commencement of the War, very liberally donated and set apart a lot of ground for the purpose of burying, free of charge, all soldiers who may die honorably in defense of our liberties. We learn from Captain Lenow, the President of the Company, that he has enlarged the ground by changing one of the drives, which is a great improvement to it, and it is now ample for the purpose. In the center of the lot is a circle of twelve feet in diameter, for the erection of a monument, which our patriotic citizens will no doubt raise to the memory of the brave soldiers who have fallen in defense of our country. The grounds at Elmwood are continually receiving substantial improvements, and they are beautified and adorned in so handsome a manner that it reflects credit upon the taste and untiring industry of the President of the Company, who devotes so much time and attention to it."

The Tuesday, June 18, 1861, *Memphis Daily Appeal*, page 3, column 2, printed a report from Mrs. S. C. Law, President, Southern Mothers, that there was an intermit on Sunday (June 16, 1861 sic actually Monday, June 17, 1861), at Elmwood Cemetery with the Cemetery donating a lot and Flaherty (Funeral Home) donating a coffin and services. The Thursday, June 27, 1861, *Memphis Daily Appeal*, page 1, reported that a lot was donated at Elmwood Cemetery for burial of Thomas Gallagher (see sketch) of the Crockett Rangers who died after receiving a gunshot wound accidentally June 14, 1861, at Camp Randolph. Per Daily Burial Record Book William Gallagher was buried in Lot 159 Fowler Section Grave #20 on June 17, 1861, with Remarks: accidentally shot at Randolph. H.S.M. (Southern Mothers Hospital). Lot #159 became part of Soldiers Rest as there is no Lot 159 Fowler Section in the Fowler Book or on the Cemetery Plat. The Fowler Section lots skip from Lot #152/153 to Lot #162. Thus, he was the first burial in Confederate Soldiers Rest.

The last burial was John Frank Gunter on April 1, 1940. There is one female buried in Confederate Soldiers Rest, Mary Boddie, an unmarried school teacher, who was buried on May 30, 1908. Also, eight-year-old Charles G. Alford is buried (doubled) with his father, J. L. Alford.

Per an article in the March 14, 1886, *Memphis Daily Appeal*, page 2, the Confederate Historical Association collected funds to improve the Confederate lot at Elmwood. This included a substantial curbing, 7 x 9 inches and 710 feet long on a brick foundation around the lot, and 945 headstones placed at the head of the graves. Other improvements were contemplated, including a walk five feet square with curbing and ornamental posts around the monument and two brass guns at the entrance.

In addition to the Confederates soldiers and veterans, many other individuals are buried in the Cemetery who, although not serving in the Confederate military, served an important part in the Confederate Cause are included in this work.

CONFEDERATE MONUMENT

The monument in Confederate Soldiers Rest was unveiled on June 5, 1878. Per the article "Our Dead Heros" in the June 6, 1878, *Memphis Daily Appeal,* page 4, column 3, some four or five thousand people were present. Efforts to erect the monument was initially started by the Ladies Confederate Memorial Association. Per the article "Monument to the Memory of the Confederate Dead" in the April 28, 1866, *Memphis Daily Appeal,* page 4, column 1, a committee was appointed April 26, 1866, following the first decoration of graves of Confederate soldiers at Elmwood Cemetery on that date, for the purpose of soliciting contributions for the erecting a monument to the memory of the Confederate dead of Memphis. The project was completed by the Confederate Relief and Historical Association, later known as Confederate Historical Association. The total cost was $5,000.00.

Per the aforesaid June 6, 1878, article the following is the detailed description of the monument: A molded base, five feet six inches square, one foot ten inches high. On the front of the same are cut, in raised, polished letters, the words "Confederate Dead." On the back of the same is the following inscription: *"Illis Victoriam Non Immortatitatem Fata Negaverunt"* (The Fates Which Refused Them Victory Did Not Deny Them Immortality). On the base rests a molded base, four feet four inches square and eleven inches high, with column plinths at the angles. Then comes a die, three feet two inches square and two feet three inches high, recessed at the corners for the shafts. The faces of the die are highly polished - polished shafts, carved capitals and molded bases. The upper portion of the die is four feet two inches square and two feet five inches high, with a Gothic arch and panel on each side, and with a carved wreath in relief. On each spandrel the four corners are molded. Then comes a molded and carved cap, five feet square and one foot three inches high. Above this cap is a molded column base, three feet nine inches square and one foot eight inches high, with the Tennessee State and the Confederate States arms in high relief. Above these coats-of-arms and beneath the trophy are the words *"Deo Vindice"* (God Being the Vindicator), in relief. The shaft is three feet square at the bottom and two feet two inches square at the top, and sixteen feet long, with a trophy of flags and arms at the base of the shaft in high relief, and garlands in low relief - all polished. The frieze is molded, and has stars in full relief between the moldings. On top of all this is the capital, three feet four inches square and one foot seven inches high, richly carved. Surmounting all is a finial two feet two inches square and two feet eight high, composed of cannon balls.

The laying of the monument corner stone was officially held on Saturday, May 7, 1870, as the concluding portion of the annual floral tribute to the memory of the Confederate dead who lie in Elmwood Cemetery. Per the article "ELMWOOD. — Grand and Imposing Ceremonies of Commemoration Day." in the Sunday, May 8, 1870, *Memphis Daily Appeal*, page 4, column 2, those who wished to deposit mementos under the corner stone, were invited to come forward and do so. In response, Mr. Henry Moode (see sketch page 181) stepped forward and presented an envelope containing the following articles deposited in behalf of the ladies of Mississippi—specimens of Confederate and Mississippi money, a miniature Confederate battleflag, a photograph of President Davis and his cabinet, a photograph of General Lee, a roll of the Mississippi dead buried in Elmwood, and an autographed letter of Jefferson Davis. The following articles were also deposited by different persons: A copy of each of the daily papers of Memphis of the latest date; a copy of the August 24, 1863, *Memphis Daily Appeal* printed at Atlanta, Georgia; an envelope printed in red, white and red (being one of the first "Confederate envelopes" manufactured in Memphis); and a copy of General Albert Pike's exquisite song, "A Lament for Dixie." Additionally, numerous ladies dropped sprigs of evergreen into the little casket; and one, Miss Mattie E. Crowe, deposited a sprig of lilac in memory of Alabama braves.

The "Programme of the Commemoration Ceremonies" was reported in the article "The Confederate Dead" in the Friday, May 6, 1870, *Memphis Daily Appeal,* page 4, column 8.

Per the article "Monumental" in the June 6, 1874, *Memphis Daily Appeal,* page 4, column 5, Mr. Cook designed the Monument.

Dedication and description reported in *Frank Leslie's Illustrated Newspaper*, Supplement, January 11, 1879, page 347, and illustration of the monument on page 348.

Listed in "Touring Historic Elmwood Cemetery" Brochure (January 2000) #13.

CONFEDERATE SOLDIERS REST BURIALS

This is a list of Confederate soldiers and veterans buried in the Confederate Soldiers Rest Section at Elmwood Cemetery. After each name is the burial date, the lot/division (1 is the north part, 2 is the south part, and no lot/division for name stones), the grave/space number as recorded in the Cemetery records and the plat number as shown on the plat indicating the location of the grave. The numbers used on the plat are the actual numbers on the stones that were placed over each grave and the number assigned (ex N1) to the stones that had only a name on them. The name stones did not have a lot/division or a grave/space number indicated in the Cemetery records. See also Explanation of Grave/Space, Lot/Division and Grave Stone/Plat Numbers.

The regiment/unit identified, if any, for the soldier is what was indicated in the Elmwood records or other sources, including but not limited to, official compiled service records, grave stones, newspaper obituaries and unit articles, *Confederate Veteran*, descendants and individuals who knew of this research, and research materials on file in archives and libraries. The compiled service records of the soldiers whose unit could be identified were reviewed. This was necessary in order to verify the individual's service unit. Many of the units identified in the Elmwood records were only local designations and were quite often not the final or official designations or even the only unit in which served. A compiled service record was not found on many of the soldiers. Personal information is what was found in newspaper obituaries, pension files and other sources.

Adams, A. H.   Buried May 12, 1862   Lot/Division 2, #171   Plat Number 721
Arkansas 20 (King's) Infantry Regiment Private (Kelly's) Company K; enlisted March 6, 1862 Lafayette County, Arkansas; per March 6 to May 2, 1862 Muster Roll Remarks: Left at Fort Pillow sick April 26, 1863 (sic); per March 6 to June 30, 1862 Muster Roll Remarks: Died in Hospital, date not ascertained; died Overton Hospital typhoid fever and pneumonia per Daily Burial Record Book.

Adams, A. J.   Buried April 30, 1862   Lot/Division 1, #523   Plat Number 523
Arkansas 17 (Lemoyne's) Infantry Regiment Private Company A; enlisted October 7, 1861 Lewisburg, Arkansas; per Register of Soldiers who were killed in battle or who died of wounds or disease: Died April 29, 1862 at Fort Pillow; died Overton Hospital, Herly's Company (no Captain Herly found Arkansas 17 Infantry) and from Fort Pillow per Daily Burial Record Book; no record found under Arkansas 21 Infantry which was formed May 15, 1862 by consolidation of four companies from Arkansas 14 (McCarver's) Infantry and six companies of 17 (Lemoyne's) Infantry.

Adams, Anderson   Buried September 17, 1861   Lot/Division 1, #8   Plat Number 8
Arkansas 11 Infantry Regiment Private Company E "Falcon Guards"; name appears on Company Muster-in Roll with Muster-in Date of July 18, 1861; no other information in compiled service record; died measles age 25 camp per Daily Burial Record Book.

Adams, James   Buried May 23, 1862   Lot/Division 2, #259   Plat Number 809
Company B and died Overton Hospital typhoid and pneumonia per Daily Burial Record Book.

Adams, W. J.   Buried March 17, 1862   Lot/Division 1, #338   Plat Number 338
Arkansas 12 Infantry Regiment Private Company F; enlisted July 26, 1861 Arkadelphia, Arkansas; per Muster Roll Remarks: Died in Memphis March 1862; per Overton Hospital March 1862 Register of Deaths initials "J. W." and died March 16, 1862 with complaint of parotitis; per Register of Claims on Soldiers Who Died George Adams, father, made a claim.

Adams, W. T.   Buried May 14, 1862   Lot/Division 2, #203   Plat Number 753
Arkansas 20 (King's) Infantry Regiment Private (Kelly's) Company K; enlisted March 6, 1862 Lafayette County, Arkansas age 22; per March 6 to June 30, 1862 Muster Roll Remarks: Left at Fort Pillow in Hospital as Nurse; per March 6 to June 30, 1862 Muster Roll Remarks: Absent sick in Hospital; per September & October 1862 Muster Roll Remarks: Died of disease June 1862, Died at Hospital age 22; per Overton Hospital March 31, 1862 Register of Sick and Wounded admitted March 5, 1862 with complaint of pneumonia; per Daily Burial Record Book died typhoid fever and pneumonia.

Adams, Walter W.   Buried March 31, 1905   Lot/Division 1, #535   Plat Number 535
Mississippi 21 Infantry Regiment Private Company A; enlisted May 15, 1861 Vicksburg, Mississippi, age 20; severely wounded and captured at Cedar Creek October 19, 1864, shot in upper thigh; took Oath of Allegiance age 24 at Armory Square USA General Hospital Washington, DC, discharged from service August 7, 1865; per Tennessee Confederate Pension (S6343) born Warren County, Mississippi August 1840; per widow's (Lizzie C Clayton) Tennessee Confederate Pension (W2861) born August 20, 1840 and died March 28, 1905; per Daily Burial Record Book remarks grave 2nd row east side.

Adams, William J.   Buried May 15, 1862   Lot/Division 2, #214   Plat Number 764
Arkansas 18 (Carroll's) Infantry Regiment Private Company B; enlisted March 1, 1862 Princeton, Arkansas; per March to June 1862 Muster Roll Remarks: Died in Memphis May 12, 1862; died Overton Hospital congestive fever per Daily Burial Record Book.

Adams, William J.   Buried March 6, 1862   Lot/Division 1, #288   Plat Number 288
Arkansas 9 Infantry Regiment Private Company G; enlisted July 27, 1861 Pine Bluff, Arkansas; per March 1 to May 1, 1862 Muster Roll Remarks: Died March 7 at Memphis, Tennessee typhoid fever; per November 1, 1861 to June 30, 1862 Muster Roll Remarks: Died March 7, 1862 Memphis; per list of those who died at Overton General Hospital at Memphis during the month of March 1862 initial "W. T.," died March 5 of pneumonia and Private Arkansas 9 Regiment Company G; per Daily Burial Record Book Company C and died typhoid fever and pneumonia.

Akers, John E.   Buried May 20, 1862   Lot/Division 2, #248   Plat Number 798
Arkansas 23 (Adams') Infantry Regiment Private Company A; enlisted February 26, 1862 Poinsett County, Arkansas; per February 26 to June 30, 1862 Muster Roll Remarks: Died May 1862; died Irving Hospital typhoid fever and pneumonia per Daily Burial Record Book; per Irving Hospital Record admitted May 3, 1862 with complaint of typhoid pneumonia and died May 18, 1862.

Akins, Jasper L.   Buried September 14, 1861   Lot/Division 1, #9   Plat Number 9
Arkansas 9 Infantry Regiment Sergeant (Dunlap's) Company D; enlisted July 25, 1861 Pine Bluff, Arkansas; per November 1861 to June 1862 Muster Roll Remarks: Died on the 14 September at Memphis, Tennessee; died typhoid fever camp and name spelled "Aiken" per Daily Burial Record Book.

Aldrige, Thomas Hadden   Buried May 2, 1862   Lot/Division 2, #15   Plat Number 565
Arkansas Rivers' (Provence's/Arkansas First Light Artillery Company) Battery Private; enlisted October 26, 1861 Fort Smith, Arkansas; per March & April 1862 Muster Roll Remarks: Died Memphis, Tennessee April 30, 1862; name spelled "Aldridge" in Daily Burial Record Book; not listed in Cemetery Alpha or Single Grave books.

Alexander, S. R.   Buried April 30, 1862   Lot/Division 2, #4   Plat Number 554
Texas 9 (Sim's) Cavalry Regiment (Duncan's) Company F per Daily Burial Record Book; no compiled service record found.

Alford, Charles G.   Buried February 1, 1879   Lot/Division 2, #377   Plat Number 927
Eight (8) year old son of J. L. Alford; buried with father in Lot 2, Grave #377; died of diphtheria per Daily Burial Record Book; not listed in Cemetery Single Grave Book.

Alford, J. L.   Buried June 12, 1872   Lot/Division 2, #377   Plat Number 927
Listed in Elmwood 1874 book as Confederate soldier buried in Elmwood who was citizen of Memphis or vicinity; no unit indicated and died of consumption age 35 per Daily Burial Record Books; grave stone: 1837 1872.

Anderson, Eli   Buried March 5, 1862   Lot/Division 1, #285   Plat Number 285
Louisiana 12 Infantry Regiment Private Company I; enlisted August 13, 1861 Camp Moore, Louisiana; present on rolls to October 1861.

Andrews, H. J.   Buried March 31, 1862   Lot/Division 1, #401   Plat Number 401
Louisiana 12 Infantry Regiment Private (Steven's) Company F; no enlistment on single muster roll card in compiled service record dated March 17, 1862 Memphis age 27; Regiment organized at Camp Moore, Louisiana August 13, 1861.

Antrim, Henry   Buried May 7, 1862   Lot/Division 2, #108   Plat Number 658
Missouri 4 Infantry Regiment (Missouri 1 Brigade) Private (Walker's) Company A; per Company Muster Roll dated February 11, 1862, enlisted January 25, 1862, at Forsyth, Missouri, age 17; per Company Muster Roll dated December 7, 1861, to June 30, 1862, remarks: Died at Memphis May 4; per undated Company Muster Roll remarks: Died at Memphis May 8, 1862; per Company Muster Roll dated December 7, 1861, to June 30, 1862, remarks: Died at Memphis May 4; name appears on a Register of Officers and Soldiers of the Army of the Confederate States Who Were Killed in Battle, or Who Died of Wounds or Disease indicating died May 20, 1862, at Memphis, Tennessee; per Register containing a record of the Property of Deceased Confederate Soldiers died at Memphis May 4, 1862; died Overton Hospital per Daily Burial Record Book; name "Antrum" in Daily Burial Record Book and both "Antrum" and "Antwine" in Cemetery computer index.

Arnold, William   Buried August 29, 1865   Lot/Division 2, #360   Plat Number 910
Mississippi 11 Regiment and died congestive chill age 16 per Daily Burial Record Book; no compiled service record found.

Arondale, Anthony   Buried April 20, 1862   Lot/Division 1, #470   Plat Number 470
Missouri 1 Regiment Company I and died Overton Hospital typhoid fever and pneumonia per Daily Burial Record Book; no compiled service record found; name spelled "Avondale" in Cemetery computer index; not found either spelling in Missouri 1 Infantry Regiment compiled service record rolls; not listed in the First Missouri Battle of Shiloh casualty report in *Memphis Daily Appeal* April 23, 1862, page 2, column 2.

Arrington, Edmund A.   Buried April 30, 1862   Lot/Division 2, #3   Plat Number 553
Arkansas 2 (Locke's) Mounted Rifles Private (Hemby's) Company C; enlisted November 1, 1861 Camp on Flat Creek, Missouri age 43; per July & August 1862 Muster Roll Remarks: Absent sick, left at Hospital at Memphis; per July & August 1863 Muster Roll Remarks: Absent at Hospital at Memphis April 1862, supposed to be dead; per September & October 1863 Muster Roll Remarks: to be dropped from the Roll, Private at Memphis, Tennessee April 1862 and not since heard from; died Overton Hospital and Company B per Daily Burial Record Book.

Ashley, James Dan   Buried August 20, 1861   Lot/Division 1, #84   Plat Number 84
Missouri 1 Infantry Regiment Private (Captain Averill) Company K; per Company Muster-in Roll dated June 27, 1861, near Memphis, enlisted June 22, 1861, Memphis age 21; per Historic Roll (undated) enlisted June 27, 1861, age 24, at Memphis, native of Missouri, Gayoso, Pemiscot County, and Farmer and Remarks: Deserted August 22, 1861; listed on report of August 1861 Deaths at Southern Mothers Hospital in September 10, 1861, *Memphis Daily Appeal*, page 3, column 3; per report: Captain Avent's (sic) Company, from Humphreys County, Tennessee and died August 20, 1861, congestive fever.

Aust, L. F.   Buried November 28, 1861   Lot/Division 1, #226   Plat Number 226
Arkansas 9 Infantry Regiment Private Company K; enlisted August 9, 1861 Camp Lee, Arkansas; per November 1861 to June 1862 Muster Roll Remarks: Died 28 November 1861; died Southern Mothers Hospital enteritis per Daily Burial Record Book; name spelled "Anst" in Cemetery computer index.

Avery, Jesse N.   Buried October 24, 1861   Lot/Division 1, #132   Plat Number 132
Arkansas 15 (Josey's) Infantry Regiment Private Company H; enlisted July 23, 1861 Camp Yell Pittman's Ferry; present on July to August 31, 1861 Muster Roll; no other information in compiled service record; unit Arkansas 1 Regiment Company G and died Southern Mothers Hospital congestive fever age 18 per Daily Burial Record Book.

Baber, W. C.   Buried May 13, 1862   Lot/Division 2, #195   Plat Number 745
Texas 32 (Crump's Battalion) Cavalry Regiment Private Company H; enlisted February 19, 1862 Boston, Texas; per February 19 to August 31, 1862 Muster Roll Remarks: Private at Memphis; per September & October 1862 Muster Roll Remarks: Left at Memphis sick April 20; per May & June 1863 Muster Roll Remarks: Died at Memphis, Tennessee; died Overton Hospital per Daily Burial Record Book.

Bable (Babb?), A. E. L.   Buried May 9, 1862   Lot/Division 2, #122   Plat Number 672
No unit indicated or other information in Daily Burial Record Book; not found Confederate general index either spelling.

Bagley, Humphrey   Buried May 6, 1862   Lot/Division 2, #78   Plat Number 628
Miller's Battalion (Harris') Company and died Overton Hospital per Daily Burial Record Book; no compiled service record found; unit believed to be Arkansas 1 or 8 (not found) Infantry Battalion or 35 or 38 Infantry Regiment; there are only three Bagleys in Confederate general index and none are this soldier; not found Mississippi 1 (Miller's) Cavalry Battalion.

Baird, Felix   Buried April 10, 1862   Lot/Division 1, #434   Plat Number 434
Tennessee 1 (Jones') Heavy Artillery Private Companies D/F; enlisted August 5, 1861 Memphis age 26; per May & June 1862 Muster Roll Remarks: Left at Fort Pillow Detachment on Gun not since reported; from Country per Daily Burial Record Book.

Baker, Alex F.   Buried May 14, 1862   Lot/Division 2, #205   Plat Number 755
Arkansas 19 (Dockery's) Infantry Regiment Private Company I; enlisted March 3, 1862 Union County, Arkansas; per March 3 to June 30, 1862 Muster Roll Remarks: Left at CS Hospital Memphis, Tennessee sick 30th April; name appears on a Register of Claims on Deceased Soldiers (not dated) by widow, Elizabeth J. Baker, February 24, 1863 with indication that died Memphis, Tennessee; died Overton Hospital typhoid fever and pneumonia per Daily Burial Record Book.

Baker, Charles W.   Buried October 19, 1861   Lot/Division 1, #113   Plat Number 113
Confederate Cavalry Wood's Regiment (Mississippi Wirt Adams' Cavalry Regiment - Mississippi 1 Cavalry Regiment) Private 1 Company G; enlisted August 30, 1861 Memphis age 35; name appears on an undated muster roll at Vicksburg, Mississippi of Captain Klein's Cavalry Company (Company G of Wood's Confederate Cavalry Regiment); Colonel Adams' Regiment Company A and died Southern Mothers Hospital enteritis per Daily Burial Record Book.

Baker, Daniel   Buried September 15, 1861   Lot/Division 1, #24   Plat Number 24
Arkansas 11 (Smith's) Infantry Regiment and died Southern Mothers Hospital measles age 18 per Daily Burial Record Book.

Baker, Peter   Buried June 3, 1862   Lot/Division 2, #282   Plat Number 832
Tennessee 3 (Memphis Battalion) Infantry Battalion Private Company B; enlisted March 12, 1862 Memphis; present on March to May 1862 Muster Roll but no other information in compiled service record; see Notes of Interest "Memphis Battalion - Tennessee 3 (Memphis Battalion) Infantry Battalion"; died of amputation effects per Daily Burial Record Book; 1830 inscribed on grave stone.

Baker, T. R.   Buried March 29, 1862   Lot/Division 1, #391   Plat Number 391
Arkansas 12 Infantry Regiment Sergeant Company F; enlisted July 26, 1861 Arkadelphia, Arkansas; per July to October 1862 Muster Roll Remarks: Died at Memphis; per Overton Hospital March 1862 Register of Deaths initials "T. C." and died March 27 with complaint of pneumonia; second initial "K" per Daily Burial Record Book.

Baldin, J.   Buried May 7, 1862   Lot/Division 2, #98   Plat Number 648
Arkansas 15 Infantry Regiment and died Overton Hospital per Daily Burial Record Book; no compiled service record found; not James Balding, Arkansas 15 (Josey's) Infantry Regiment, Private/Musician Company H.

Ball, J. N.   Buried May 25, 1862   Lot/Division 2, #265   Plat Number 815
Arkansas Adams Regiment Company C; no service record found; unit per Daily Burial Record Book; J. M. Ball, Arkansas 5 Infantry, indicated on grave stone but compiled service records for J. M. Ball, Arkansas 5 Infantry Regiment, Private Company E, indicates that he was listed on Muster Roll in 1864 and paid; died Irving Hospital pneumonia per Daily Burial Record Book; second initial "N" in Cemetery Single Grave Book; initials "I. N." in Cemetery computer index; there is a "John H. Ball" listed in Elmwood 1874 book as Confederate soldier buried in Elmwood who was citizen of Memphis or vicinity; in Irving Hospital records there is a "J. N. Ball," Private Adams Regiment Company C admitted May 3, 1862 with complaint of diarrhea and died May 25, 1862; possibly Newton Ball, Arkansas (Adams) Infantry Regiment Private Company C, enlisted February 25, 1862 St. Francis County, Arkansas and indicated dead on October 31 to December 31, 1862 Muster Roll; does not appear to be James Ball, Arkansas 23 Adams' Infantry Regiment Private Company C, who was reported missing at Battle of Corinth, Mississippi October 3 to 5, 1862.

Bullard, St. Clare   Buried May 7, 1862   Lot/Division 2, #95   Plat Number 645
Missouri 1 Infantry Battalion Private Company C (Captain Kelsey's Company Jeff Thompson's Command); per May & June 1862, Company Muster Roll enlisted March 14, 1862, Pocahontas, Arkansas by Major W. F. Rapley with Remarks: Died May 5, 1862, Memphis Hospital; Company was at Fort Pillow during May 1862, and operated as marines aboard Confederate defense fleet gunboats; Company became Company K, Missouri 6 Infantry Regiment, in August 1862, but no record found in that unit's compiled service records; died Overton Hospital per Daily Burial Record Book; name "Ballard, St. Clair" in both Daily Burial Record Book and computer index.

Barclay, James   Buried May 15, 1862   Lot/Division 2, #218   Plat Number 768
Arkansas 18 (Carroll's) Infantry Regiment Private Company H; enlisted March 3, 1862 Little Rock, Arkansas; per March to June 1862 Muster Roll Remarks: Supposed to be dead; died Overton Hospital and name spelled "Barkley" per Daily Burial Record Book.

Barentine, William   Buried May 20, 1862   Lot/Division 2, #250   Plat Number 800
Arkansas 23 (Adams') Infantry Regiment Private (Pennington's) Company H; enlisted March 6, 1862 Arkadelphia, Arkansas; per March 6 to June 30, 1862 Muster Roll Remarks: Sent to Hospital Memphis, Tennessee April 18, 1862, supposed to be dead; per June 30 to August 31, 1862 Muster Roll Remarks: Left at Overton Hospital Memphis May the 7, not heard from since; died Overton Hospital and name spelled "Barrington" per Daily Burial Record Book.

Barham, John A.   Buried July 15, 1861   Lot/Division 1, #17   Plat Number 17
Tennessee 13 (Wright's) Infantry Regiment Private Company I; enlisted May 30, 1861 Jackson, Tennessee; per April 6, 1863 Muster Roll Remarks: Died in Hospital at Memphis, Tennessee July 19, 1861; died age 22 per Daily Burial Record Book; see comments herein under Bell, John K., Tennessee 13 Infantry Regiment.

Barker, James L.   Buried November 13, 1861   Lot/Division 1, #190   Plat Number 190
Tennessee 38 (Looney's) Infantry Regiment Private Company K; enlisted September 9, 1861 Memphis; present on September 1861 Muster Roll; no other information in compiled service record.

Barker, William A.   Buried August 19, 1866   Lot/Division 1, #32½
Died of congestion age 23 and buried Soldiers #1 Lot, Fowler Section Single Grave 32½ per Daily Burial Record Book; name listed both "Barker" (Confederate Section) and "Baker" (Lot 2) in Cemetery computer index; no grave stone found.

Barnes, John P.   Buried December 17, 1861   Lot/Division 1, #45   Plat Number 45
Tennessee 7 Cavalry Regiment Private (Taylor's) Company A; enlisted May 16, 1861 Memphis age, 25; per statement of mother, Mahala Barnes, in compiled service record died December 15, 1861 Camp Desha, Moscow, Kentucky; first enlisted Tennessee 6 (Logwood's) Cavalry Battalion (also known as Tennessee 1 Cavalry Battalion, which is unit indicated in Daily Burial Record Book); died before Tennessee 7 Cavalry Regiment organized (April 1862); funeral notice in December 17, 1861 *Memphis Daily Appeal*; member Memphis Light Dragoons; note that there two burials records for Grave #45, Division 1 (Frank Lyons September 11, 1861) but only one stone; no indication found in Cemetery records that he was ever removed.

Barnes, Joseph   Buried March 10, 1862   Lot/Division 1, #309   Plat Number 309
Texas 9 (Young's/Maxey's) Infantry Regiment Musician Company I; enlisted January 7, 1862; per Overton Hospital Register of Sick and Wounded admitted February 10, 1862 with complaint of rubella; per Overton Hospital March 1862 Register of Deaths admitted February 10, 1862 and died March 10 of rubella; name spelled "Barns" in Cemetery records.

Barnes, William   Buried May 6, 1862   Lot/Division 2, #83   Plat Number 633
Arkansas 17 Infantry Regiment Company F and died Overton Hospital per Daily Burial Record Book; no service record found.

Barnes, William C.   Buried May 10, 1862   Lot/Division 2, #155   Plat Number 705
Arkansas 18 (Carroll's) Infantry Regiment Private Company I; enlisted March 15, 1862 Camden, Arkansas; per March to June 1862 Muster Roll Remarks: Absent sick; per August to December 1862 Muster Roll Remarks: Missing, dropped from roll by order; died Irving Hospital measles per Daily Burial Record Book.

Barnett, Miles R.   Buried October 13, 1862   Lot/Division 2, #304   Plat Number 854
Mississippi 26 Infantry Regiment Private Company A; enlisted September 5, 1861 Iuka, Mississippi, age 23; per October 31, 1861 to July 31, 1862 Muster Roll Remarks: Private in Prison; per July 31 to October 31, 1862 Muster Roll Remarks: Died at Memphis, Tennessee September 4, 1862; captured at Fort Donelson, Kentucky February 16, 1862 and sent to Camp Morton, Indianapolis, Indiana; on Roll of Prisoners dated August 24, 1862; Parole - On Honor to Proceed to Vicksburg, Mississippi dated September 3, 1862; per Record of Organization enlisted August 19, 1861, Iuka, Mississippi, born Mississippi, occupation farmer, residence (nearest post office at enlistment) Iuka, Mississippi, age 26 (note age difference), single and died in Prison 1862; from Iuka, Mississippi and first name "Wiley" per Daily Burial Record Book.

Barradall, Norborne D.   Buried January 29, 1906   Lot/Division 1, #532   Plat Number 532
Virginia 19 Battalion Heavy Artillery Private Company A; enlisted April 29, 1861 Suffolk, Virginia; per January 29, 1906, *The Commercial Appeal* Memphis was a doctor and died January 28, 1906; died age 60y/9m/27d per Daily Burial Record Book.

Barteau, Clark Russell   Buried February 12, 1900   Lot/Division 1, #544   Plat Number 544
Tennessee 22 (Barteau's) Cavalry Regiment Colonel Field & Staff; enlisted October 17, 1861 as a Private in Company D Tennessee 7 Cavalry Battalion; June 12, 1862 elected Lieutenant Colonel of Tennessee 2 Cavalry (original designation of 22 Cavalry); appointed Colonel June 8, 1863; April 7, 1835 February 10, 1900 on grave stone; second initial "E" in Cemetery computer index; died age 65 per Daily Burial Record Book; member Confederate Historical Association and sketch in Mathes book; per sketch born April 7, 1835 Cuyahoga County, near Cleveland, Ohio; per Daily Burial Record Book remarks grave North Part #544; biography in *Confederate Military History*, *Extended Edition*, Volume X Tennessee, page 368.

Bass, S. H.   Buried April 26, 1871   Lot/Division 2, #372   Plat Number 922
Tennessee 14 (Neely's) Cavalry Regiment Private/Corporal Company D; enlisted June 20, 1863 Dancyville, Tennessee; per undated Return of Killed and Wounded in 1 Brigade, 1 Division, Forrest's Cavalry, during August 1864 wounded severely (killed) in left side Memphis August 21 (this was during Forrest's Raid into Memphis); per Daily Burial Record Book moved to Elmwood from Cane Creek; 1842 1864 on grave stone; initials "L. H." in Cemetery computer index; listed in Elmwood 1874 book as Confederate soldier buried in Elmwood who was citizen of Memphis or vicinity.

Bazar, Jacob   Buried August 8, 1861   Lot/Division 1, #86   Plat Number 86
Louisiana Captain Cole's Company Cavalry (Louisiana Mounted Rangers) Bugler, per Company Muster Roll dated October 30, 1861, enlisted July 23, 1861, East Baton. Rouge, Louisiana and remarks that "Died of dysentery in Memphis army hospl Aug 18"; name spelled "Bezar" in Daily Burial Record Book and "Bezer" in Single Grave Book.

Beard, P. L.   Buried March 19, 1862   Lot/Division 1, #348   Plat Number 348
Baker's Regiment Company F per Daily Burial Record Book; no compiled service record found; unit; per Overton Hospital March 1862 Register of Deaths initials "P. S." and died March 15 of pneumonia; not found Confederate 4 Infantry or Alabama 54 Infantry.

Beard, Thomas   Buried December 2, 1862   Lot/Division 2, #320   Plat Number 870
Tennessee 19 Infantry Regiment Private Company D; enlisted May 29, 1861 Knoxville, Tennessee; per May 12, 1861 Muster Roll Remarks: Discharged on Account of Disability; admitted to USA General Hospital Nashville September 18, 1862; returned to Duty November 20, 1862; amputation noted; unit not indicated in Cemetery Daily Burial Record or Single Grave books.

Beavers, Levi J.   Buried May 2, 1862   Lot/Division 2, #16   Plat Number 566
Texas 27 (Whitfield's Legion) Cavalry Regiment Private Company A; mustered into service 7 February 1862, at Daingerfield, Texas; per May & June 1862, Company Muster Roll died April 28, 1862, at Memphis, Tennessee; died Overton Hospital pneumonia per Daily Burial Record Book and name "Levi G. Bearen" in Daily Burial Record Book and computer index; born about 1834 in Tennessee, married Salina Lindsey 11 October 1860, in Cass County, Texas and only child was John Levi Beavers born 2 August 1861, in Cass County, Texas; information to correctly identify this soldier provided by family descendant, Georgia Daniel Cavanaugh.

Beasley, J. R.   Buried September 7, 1912   Plat Number N15
Tennessee 154 Senior Infantry Regiment Corporal/Private Company D; enlisted at Randolph, Tennessee May 14, 1861, age 19; per remarks on September & October 1863 Company Muster Roll wounded at battle of Chickamauga and at hospital in Atlanta; received Arkansas Confederate Pension (#12699); per Shelby County, Tennessee Burial Permit #25126 born in Richmond, Virginia 1842 (August per 1900 St. Francis County, Arkansas Census), a lawyer and resident of Forrest City, Arkansas and died St. Joseph Hospital, Memphis on September 6, 1912; died age 67 per Daily Burial Record Book.

Bell, G. W.   Buried May 5, 1862   Lot/Division 2, #61   Plat Number 611
Smead's Regiment Company F; no compiled service record found for Arkansas 19 Dockery/Smead's Infantry Regiment; unit and died Overton Hospital per Daily Burial Record Book; possibly Bell, George W., Private Company F, Arkansas 17 (Lemoyne's) Infantry Regiment (note reference card only in this record) that became Company E of Arkansas 21 Infantry Regiment who enlisted December 28, 1861 Yell County, Arkansas and who per April 28, 1862 Muster Roll Remarks was sick at Fort Pillow and per December 1861 to June 1862 Muster Roll Remarks died at Memphis May 2, 1862.

Bell, George   Buried April 26, 1914   Plat Number N22
No unit indicated and died age 72 per Daily Burial Record Book.

Bell, Henry F.   Buried April 20, 1862   Lot/Division 1, #471   Plat Number 471
Tennessee 9 Infantry Regiment Private Company H; enlisted January 1, 1862 Jackson, Tennessee; per January to May 1862 Muster Roll Remarks: Died April 23, 1862 from wounds at Battle of Shiloh; per Battle of Shiloh casualty list for unit reported in April 23, 1862, *Memphis Daily Appeal* was wounded in Battle; died Irving Hospital per Daily Burial Record Book; grave stone: 1839 1862.

Bell, John K.   Buried July 27, 1861   Lot/Division 1, #16   Plat Number 16
Tennessee 13 Infantry Regiment Private (Ross') Company I; enlisted May 30, 1861 Jackson, Tennessee; per April 6, 1863 Muster Roll Remarks: died in Hospital at Memphis, Tennessee August 1, 1861; died pneumonia age 20 per Daily Burial Record Book; per July 28, 1861 *Memphis Daily Appeal* died July 27, 1861 age 20 at residence of Mary E. Pope, Secretary of Southern Mothers, Memphis, of typhoid fever and was resident of Henderson County, Tennessee (now Chester County); July 30, 1861 *Memphis Daily Appeal* reprinted letter of W. B. Dickinson, Jr., Tennessee 13 Regiment, Colonel Wright, dated July 25, 1861 to Southern Mothers thanking them and especially Mary E. Pope, Secretary of the Southern Mothers Hospital, for care given to Messrs. Barham and Bell who she had taken into her home.

Bellows, John W.   Buried April 24, 1862   Lot/Division 1, #485   Plat Number 485
Missouri Windsor Guards - General Price's Escort; no compiled service record found; unit and died age 21 pneumonia per Daily Burial Record Book; unit should be Missouri 2 Cavalry Regiment Company I (also called H and K), which was known as the "Windsor Guards" and "Price's Escort" and per notations on company compiled service cards: "Note: This company has acted as escort to Maj. Gen'l Sterling Price ever since its organization, January 26, 1862, Springfield, Mo." and "This company was successively designated as Captain Smith's Company, Missouri Cavalry; Captain Smith's Company, Captain Collins' Company, (Old) Company H, (New) Company I, and (3d) Company K, 2d Regiment Missouri Cavalry" and "The 4th (also called 1st) Battalion Missouri Cavalry was organized in compliance with S. O. No. 66, Headquarters Army of the West, dated Memphis, April 26, 1862; and by S.O. No. 5, same Headquarters, dated Priceville, July 2, 1862, the battalion was increased to a regiment, and the regiment so formed was the 2d Regiment Missouri Cavalry."; per *Confederate Military History, Extended Edition*, Volume XV Texas, page 659, Captain Paul Fitzhugh Thornton (Missouri 2nd Cavalry Regiment Private 3rd Company K) joined Windsor Guards, a fine company organized in Henry County, Missouri, they served during 1861 in the Missouri State Guard, under General Sterling Price, afterward enlisted in Confederate Army and campaigned as Price's Body Guard; per *The History of Henry and St. Clair Counties, Missouri*, National Historical Company, St. Joseph, Missouri, 1883, page 314, "One company raised at or near Windsor, was General Price's body guard. But the record of those who went into the war on the Confederate side is not to be found."; based on 1860 Federal Census for Benton County, Missouri, which is adjacent to Henry County, possibly John Bellows, age 20; per a Bellows family history in the Fannin County TXGenWEB "Fannin County Folks & Facts," page 106, John Bellows (his father) was born in Kentucky in 1814 and moved to Missouri and married Margaret Brown in 1837 and they "... had four sons: John William (1839); Robert Clark (1841) were Confederate soldiers who died in the war, ..."; Company F Arkansas 29 Infantry (Trans-Mississippi 1 Regiment) that was accepted into Confederate service on June 6, 1862 and renamed (reorganized) as Arkansas 37 Infantry Regiment in the summer of 1862 was also known as Windsor Guards but no record found in those units or in any Arkansas compiled service records rolls.

Bennett, J. W.   Buried April 30, 1862   Lot/Division 1, #522   Plat Number 522
Texas 27 (Whitfield's Legion) Cavalry Regiment (Lewis') Company and died Overton Hospital pneumonia per Daily Burial Record Book; no compiled service record found and no Captain Lewis in unit.

Benson, Frederick A.   Buried May 6, 1862   Lot/Division 2, #74   Plat Number 624
Arkansas 18 (Carroll's) Infantry Regiment Sergeant Company B; enlisted March 1, 1862 Princeton, Arkansas; per March to June 1862 Muster Roll Remarks: Died in Memphis May 5, 1862; died Overton Hospital rubella per Daily Burial Record Book.

Benson, Joseph N.   Buried October 22, 1861   Lot/Division 1, #126   Plat Number 126
Arkansas 12 Infantry Regiment Private Company E; enlisted July 20, 1861 Arkadelphia, Arkansas; per July to October 1862 Muster Roll Remarks: Died October 18, 1861 Memphis; died age 18 measles camp per Daily Burial Record Book; grave stone: 1843 1861.

Benton, William   Buried November 4, 1861   Lot/Division 1, #164   Plat Number 164
Arkansas 12 Infantry Regiment Private Company E; enlisted July 20, 1861 Arkadelphia, Arkansas; per July to October 1862 Muster Roll Remarks: Died November 25, 1861 at Memphis; died camp per Daily Burial Record Book.

Biggs, David   Buried April 7, 1862   Lot/Division 1, #423   Plat Number 423
Arkansas 12 Infantry Regiment Private Company G; enlisted July 27, 1861 Arkadelphia, Arkansas; per Overton Hospital March 31, 1862 Register admitted March 23, 1862 with no death noted; compiled service record includes a card indicating at Camp Douglas, Illinois Prison Hospital July 1862 (possibly a misfiled card); died Overton Hospital pneumonia per Daily Burial Record Book.

Black, Henry L.   Buried May 5, 1862   Lot/Division 2, #57   Plat Number 607
Texas 10 (Locke's) Cavalry Regiment Private Company C; enlisted September 25, 1861 Quitman, Texas, age 32; per March to August 1862 Muster Roll Remarks: Died May 1, 1862; claim by mother, Clarinda Black, in record; died Overton Hospital pneumonia per Daily Burial Record Book; 1829 1862 on grave stone.

Black, William E.   Buried September 13, 1861   Lot/Division 1, #23   Plat Number 23
Arkansas 9 Infantry Regiment Private Company D; enlisted July 27, 1861 Pine Bluff, Arkansas; per July 25 to November 1, 1861 Muster Roll Remarks: Died at the Hospital at Memphis, Tennessee 13 September 1861; died Southern Mothers Hospital per Daily Burial Record Book.

Blackburn, Marion   Buried March 18, 1862   Lot/Division 1, #341   Plat Number 341
Arkansas 17 (Griffith's) Infantry Regiment Private Company G; enlisted November 22, 1861 Fayetteville, Arkansas, age 24; per January/February 1862 Muster Roll Remarks: Absent Sick; name appears on List of Prisoners of War for Exchange May 1862 with remark that sick; per Overton Hospital March 1862 Register of Deaths for "M. Blackburn" unit indicated as Arkansas 11 Infantry Private Company G and died March 17, 1862 of pneumonia (note the compiled service card for this Overton Hospital Register entry was found in compiled service record for T. M. Blackman, Arkansas 11 Infantry Private Company G (enlisted July 23, 1861 Little Rock) who died March 10, 1862 per January 1 to September 22, 1862 muster roll); unit indicated as Arkansas 11 Infantry in Daily Burial Record Book; first name "Morrison" in Cemetery Single Grave Book; the Arkansas 11 and 17 Infantry Regiments consolidated about December 1862 or January 1863 but no record found for either in consolidated records.

Blackwell, B. M.   Buried May 13, 1862   Lot/Division 2, #184   Plat Number 734
Texas 32 (Crump's Battalion) Cavalry Regiment Private Company I; enlisted February 22, 1862 Linden, Texas; per February to August 1862 Muster Roll Remarks: Died Memphis, Tennessee May 10, 1862; died Overton Hospital typhoid fever per Daily Burial Record Book.

Blackwell, J. T.   Buried September 3, 1861   Lot/Division 1, #56   Plat Number 56
Arkansas 13 Infantry Regiment (Johnson's) Company and died age 23 per Daily Burial Record Book; no compiled service record found; note no Captain Johnson in the unit.

Blake, Garret   Buried March 31, 1862   Lot/Division 1, #398   Plat Number 398
Tennessee 15 Infantry Regiment Private Company D; enlisted May 24, 1861 Jackson, Tennessee age 25; per Overton Hospital March 31, 1862 Register of Deaths died March 30 of typhoid fever; name spelled "Garrett" in Daily Burial Record Book; grave stone: 1836 1862.

Blake, William   Buried September 9, 1861   Lot/Division 1, #57   Plat Number 57
No unit indicated or other information in Daily Burial Record Book.

Blakely, John W.   Buried April 13, 1862   Lot/Division 1, #440   Plat Number 440
Arkansas 11 Infantry Regiment Private Company I; Enlisted October 29, 1861 Little Rock, Arkansas, age 24; per October 29, 1861 to September 23, 1862 Muster Roll Remarks: Absent sick at Memphis when the Regiment surrendered (this would have been surrender at Island 10 April 8, 1862); per Overton Hospital March 31, 1862 Register of Sick and Wounded admitted March 20.

Bland, James Wesley   Buried May 15, 1862   Lot/Division 2, #219   Plat Number 769
Arkansas 19 (Dockery/Smead's) Infantry Regiment Corporal Company A; enlisted February 26, 1862 Lewisville, Arkansas; per February 25 to June 30, 1862 Muster Roll Remarks: Died Memphis, Tennessee May 12, 1862; died Overton Hospital per Daily Burial Record Book; grave stone: 1839 1862.

Bledsoe, T. G.   Buried December 23, 1861   Lot/Division 1, #250   Plat Number 250
Arkansas 12 Infantry Regiment Private Company F; enlisted July 26, 1861 Arkadelphia, Arkansas; per July to October 1862 Muster Roll Remarks: Died at Memphis November 1861; second initial "H" in Daily Burial Record Book; first initial "J" in Cemetery Single Grave Book; name "T. H. Beldsoe" in Cemetery computer index.

Blevins, Jasper   Buried April 18, 1862   Lot/Division 1, #469   Plat Number 469
Arkansas 18 (Carroll's) Infantry Regiment Private (Parrish's) Company H; enlisted March 3, 1862 Little Rock, Arkansas; per March to June 1862 Muster Roll Remarks: Supposed Dead; died Overton Hospital erysipelas and name spelled "Blivens" in Daily Burial Record Book.

Blocker, James Alfred Ralph   Buried May 31, 1911   Plat Number N13
South Carolina 1 Cavalry Regiment Private Company I; enlisted April 3, 1862, Parker's Ferry, St. Paul's Parish, South Carolina; per Certificate of Disability for Discharge dated July 18, 1864 born Colleton District, South Carolina, age 24, farmer, unfit for duty because of phthisis pulmonalis; per Surgeon Certificate dated July 20, 1864 tubercular phthisis; member Confederate Historical Association; per Confederate Historical Association application born May 8, 1844, Colleton, South Carolina, enlisted May 1, 1861 Private Company I Marion Scouts, 1 South Carolina Cavalry; died age 67 per Daily Burial Record Book.

Blockman, S. W.   Buried May 12, 1862   Lot/Division 2, #167   Plat Number 717
Miller's Arkansas Battalion and died pneumonia per Daily Burial Record Book; unit believed to be Arkansas 8 (Miller's) Infantry Battalion but no record found; name listed both "Blackman" and "Blockmon" in Cemetery computer index.

Blunt, Thomas E.   Buried May 12, 1862   Lot/Division 2, #178   Plat Number 728
Arkansas 15 (Northwest) Infantry Regiment Private Company K; enlisted February 15, 1862 Ozark, Arkansas; December 31, 1862 to February 28, 1863 Muster Roll Remarks: Sick East of Mississippi River (all other muster roll cards state same); Companies A and B of Williamson's Battalion Arkansas Infantry were transferred to 15 Regiment and became Companies I and K; Williamson's Regiment Griders Company and died Overton Hospital per Daily Burial Record Book.

Boddie, Mary   Buried May 30, 1908   Plat Number N63
Unmarried School Teacher; died May 23, 1908, per newspaper articles; per Daily Burial Record Book first placed in a Receiving Tomb May 24, 1908, and interred in Confederate Lot (Rest) May 30, 1908, reason unknown; Receiving Tomb Book has name as "Mrs. Mary Boddie"; per May 24, 1908, the *Memphis Press Scimitar*, page 16, born Jackson, Mississippi and moved to Memphis when Federals desolated her home; per article her first experience as a teacher was in the family of Mr. and Mrs. Minor Meriwether, when she acted as governess for three sons of the family; in 1869 began teaching in public schools; for last eighteen years taught at St. Paul School; died age 68.

Boggs, Caldwell   Buried May 24, 1915   Plat Number N24
Arkansas 23 Infantry Regiment Private Company K; enlisted May 1, 1862 Harrisburg, Poinsett County, Arkansas; per Muster & Descriptive Roll of Prisoners of War surrendered May 11, 1865, enlisted Harrisburg, age 30, born North Carolina, 5' 8," blue eyes and light hair; per Tennessee Confederate Pension (S11645) born Cleveland County, North Carolina 1831; per widow's (Mary Jane Albert) Tennessee Confederate Pension (W5949) died May 23, 1915 age 83; C. Bogg on original Cemetery stone with no date.

Boliner, Patrick McHenry   Buried February 21, 1898   Lot/Division 1, #541A   Plat Number 541A
Texas 9 (Sim's) Cavalry Regiment Private Company E; enlisted October 14, 1861 Camp Reeves, Texas, age 27; per sketch in Mathes book enlisted May 1861 and born September 14, 1831 in Virginia; member Confederate Historical Association; second initial "A." in Daily Burial Record Book and name spelled "Boliver" in Cemetery computer index; original grave stone actually has number 541A on it; no stone number 541 found.

Bonds, T. S.   Buried April 4, 1862   Lot/Division 1, #416   Plat Number 416
Arkansas Captain Thomasson's Company per Daily Burial Record Book; Arkansas 9th Infantry Regiment Company B (new), the "Confederate Grays," was commanded by Captain Simon B. Thomasson but no compiled service record found.

Bonner, Benjamin F.   Buried May 13, 1862   Lot/Division 2, #180   Plat Number 730
Arkansas 23 (Adams') Infantry Regiment Private Company E; enlisted March 20, 1862 Phillips County, Arkansas; per March 20 to June 30, 1862 Muster Roll Remarks: Died May 10 at Memphis, Tennessee; died Irving Hospital diarrhea per Daily Burial Record Book; per Irving Hospital Record admitted April 30, 1862 with complaint of diarrhea and died May 11, 1862.

Bostick, Samuel   Buried May 27, 1862   Lot/Division 2, #272   Plat Number 822
Louisiana 19 Regiment and died Overton Hospital per Daily Burial Record Book; no compiled service record found and not found Booth Louisiana Book; per Booth Louisiana Book there was a soldier named S. R. Bostick, Private Company D Louisiana 3 Infantry, enlisted May 17, 1861 New Orleans, Louisiana; Muster Roll Remarks: Deserted at Little Rock June 3, 1861.

Boyd, Carter M.   Buried April 11, 1929   Plat Number N53
Mississippi 3 Cavalry (E. Q. Withers) Company per widow pension; no unit indicated in Daily Burial Record Book; not found in Mississippi 3 Cavalry records or in Mississippi index rolls; per widow's (Mary Tamer Wade) Tennessee Confederate Pension (W9576) born March 17, 1845 Marshall County, Mississippi and died April 10, 1929 in Memphis, Tennessee; per statement in application served in Company commanded by Captain E. Q. Withers, Lieutenant Gordon Smith and Moore; note E. Q. Withers was 2 Lieutenant of Company E, enlisted April 25, 1864 at age 18 at Oxford, Mississippi and surrendered at Grenada, Mississippi May 19, 1865 when indicated residence as Marshall County, Mississippi; no Lieutenant Smith or Moore found in this regiment; also per letter in pension file from Charles DeSaussure, Commander, Camp 28, United Confederate Veterans, Member of Confederate Historical Association (not found in Mathes book); per second letter in pension file from Charles DeSaussure dated July 12, 1929 Captain E Q Withers (sketch in Mathes book as R. Q. Withers indicating born Marshall County, Mississippi and enlistment in Mississippi 3 Cavalry) was up to time of his death a member of Camp 28, Memphis and per his camp record "E. Q. Withers, Captain, 3 Mississippi Cavalry, Chalmers' Brigade, Forrest's Division, surrendered at Gainesville, Alabama April 2, 1865"; pension file also includes a restatement of his Mississippi pension indicating enlisted January 1863 Marshall County, Mississippi, living in DeSoto County, Mississippi, (P. O. Olive Branch, Mississippi) and signed application August 26, 1922; died age 84 per Daily Burial Record Book.

Boyle, Robert   Buried April 20, 1862   Lot/Division 1, #473   Plat Number 473
Mississippi 44 (Blythe's 1 Battalion) Infantry Regiment Private Company B; enlisted June 11, 1861 Memphis age 27; per March & April 1862 Muster Roll Remarks: Died April 17, 1862 from wounds received at Battle of Shiloh; died Irving Hospital per Daily Burial Record Book; per Irving Hospital Record admitted April 10, 1862 with complaint of right heel and died April 19, 1862.

Boyle, Thomas   Buried November 18, 1861   Lot/Division 1, #200   Plat Number 200
Tennessee 2 (Walker's) Infantry Regiment 1 Sergeant Company H; enlisted April 26, 1861 Memphis; per August to October 1861 Muster Roll Remarks: Died Memphis Hospital November 25, 1861 (note date difference with Daily Burial Record Book); per Certified Captain's Statement in compiled service record: Born Ireland and enlisted May 13, 1861 Nashville age 37; died State Hospital per Daily Burial Record Book; 1835 1861 on grave stone; note marker dates do not agree with age in record.

Bradberry, James   Buried May 10, 1862   Lot/Division 2, #145   Plat Number 695
Arkansas 18 (Carroll's) Infantry Regiment Private Company C; enlisted March 8, 1862 Des Arc, Arkansas; per March to June 1862 Muster Roll Remarks: Died at Fort Pillow April 24, 1862; died Overton Hospital and first name "Joseph" per Daily Burial Record Books.

Bradburg, Thomas R.   Buried April 29, 1862   Lot/Division 1, #517   Plat Number 517
Missouri Gaines Artillery and died Overton Hospital pneumonia per Daily Burial Record Book; no compiled service record found; no Captain Gaines found for any Missouri artillery unit.

Bradley, Mitchell   Buried October 21, 1861   Lot/Division 1, #123   Plat Number 123
Arkansas 9 Infantry Regiment Private Company A; enlisted July 21, 1861, Pine Bluff; per July 25 to November 1861, Muster Roll Remarks: Died at Southern Mothers Home October 21, 1861; name appears on a Register of Soldiers Who Died of Wounds or Disease indicating born Arkansas and died October 21, 1861, Memphis; died Southern Mothers Hospital pneumonia per Daily Burial Record Book.

Bradshaw, A.   Buried April 7, 1862   Lot/Division 1, #422   Plat Number 422
Tennessee Bankhead's Battery (Tennessee Scott's Light Artillery); no service record found; unit and died Overton Hospital pneumonia per Daily Burial Record Book; name appears on Overton Hospital March 31, 1862 Register of Sick and Wounded.

Bradshaw, J. H.   Buried May 6, 1862   Lot/Division 2, #67   Plat Number 617
Texas 27 (Whitfield's Legion) Cavalry Regiment Private Company K; compiled service record found under J. A. Bradshaw; enlisted March 20, 1862 Polk County, Arkansas; per May & June 1862 Muster Roll Remarks: Died at Memphis May 4, 1862; Company A and died Overton Hospital pneumonia per Daily Burial Record Book.

Bradshaw, J. W.   Buried April 4, 1862   Lot/Division 1, #414   Plat Number 414
Tennessee 5 Infantry Regiment Sergeant Company A; enlisted May 20, 1861 Paris, Henry County, Tennessee, age 28; per February to July 1862 Muster Roll Remarks: Died April 7, 1862; per May 13, 1863 Muster Roll Remarks: Died in Memphis, Tennessee April 6, 1862; per January 20, 1864 Muster Roll Remarks: Died April 1862; died Overton Hospital typhoid fever per Daily Burial Record Book; grave stone: 1831 1862.

Breuer, Martin V.   Buried May 15, 1862   Lot/Division 2, #212   Plat Number 762
Arkansas 23 (Adams') Infantry Regiment Private (Black's) Company E; enlisted March 20, 1862 Phillips County, Arkansas; per March 20 to June 30, 1862 Muster Roll Remarks: Left in Hospital in Memphis; per June 30 to August 31, 1862 Muster Roll Remarks: Died in Hospital at Memphis June 1; died pneumonia and rubisills and name spelled "Brewer" in Daily Burial Record Book.

Brewster, J. J.   Buried August 28, 1861   Lot/Division 1, #21   Plat Number 21
Tennessee Bibb's Company Artillery Private (Memphis Guerillas); enlisted August 5, 1861 Memphis, age 33; died age 31 per Daily Burial Record Book (note age difference between records); grave stone: 1828 1861.

Brewton, James J.   Buried May 9, 1862   Lot/Division 2, #119   Plat Number 669
Arkansas 17 (Lemoyne's) Infantry Regiment Private Company E; reference card only in 17 Lemoyne's Infantry compiled service records; records found under Arkansas 21 Infantry, Private Company I that was successor of Company E of 17 Infantry; enlisted December 21, 1861 Dardanelle, Arkansas; per April 28, 1862 Muster Roll Remarks: Absent Memphis May 1, 1862; died Overton Hospital per Daily Burial Record Book.

Broach, Redding   Buried June 25, 1862   Lot/Division 2, #298   Plat Number 848
South Carolina 10 Infantry Regiment Private Company F; enlisted July 19,1861, at age 29 at White's Bridge (Camp Marion near Georgetown, South Carolina); per regimental returns: left in Mississippi and sent to Hospital from Corinth May 20, 1862; Name appears on a Register of Claims of deceased Officers and Soldiers from South Carolina, which were filed for settlement in the Office of the Confederate States Auditor for the War Department, claim filed by widow Mary Broach October 9, 1863, Memphis, Tennessee indicated where died; name spelled "Braach" and died State Hospital typhoid fever per Daily Burial Record Book.

Bronhors, A.   Buried February 1, 1863   Lot/Division 2, #336   Plat Number 886
Mississippi 17 Regiment Company B per Daily Burial Record Book; no compiled service record found.

Brooks, Jackson   Buried November 24, 1861   Lot/Division 1, #216   Plat Number 216
Arkansas 12 Infantry Regiment Private Company E; enlisted July 20, 1861 Arkadelphia, Arkansas; per July to October 1862 Muster Roll Remarks: Died November 23, 1861 at Memphis.

Brooks, Kosisco   Buried November 26, 1861   Lot/Division 1, #220   Plat Number 220
Arkansas 9 Infantry Regiment Private Company F; enlisted July 25, 1861 Pine Bluff, Arkansas; per November & December 1861 Muster Roll Remarks: Died in Memphis, Tennessee November 26, 1861; died Southern Mothers Hospital enteritis age 19 per Daily Burial Record Book; November 24, 1861 on grave stone; first name spelled "Kosciusko" in Cemetery computer index.

Broom, William   Buried August 16, 1861   Lot/Division 1, #85   Plat Number 85
Arkansas 13 (Tappan's) Infantry Regiment per Daily Burial Record Book; no compiled service records found although several Brooms in the Regiment; listed in report of August 1861 Deaths at Southern Mothers Hospital in September 10, 1861, *Memphis Daily Appeal*, page 3, column 3; per report: Captain Walker's Company (no Captain Walker in this unit), from Jonesboro, Arkansas and died August 15, 1861, pneumonia; name spelled "Broome" in Cemetery Daily Burial Record and Alpha books and "Brown" in Cemetery Single Grave Book.

Broombly, David T.   Buried October 25, 1861   Lot/Division 1, #136   Plat Number 136
Arkansas 12 Infantry Regiment Private Company G; no enlistment in compiled service record; per Register of Soldiers Killed or Died in Battle Remarks: Died October 25, 1861 Camp Johnson (Memphis); no other information; died camp measles age 28 and name spelled "Bromley" per Daily Burial Record Book.

Brown, Benjamin   Buried March 15, 1862   Lot/Division 1, #333   Plat Number 333
Arkansas 10 Regiment Company B per Daily Burial Record Book; no compiled service record found; per Overton Hospital March 1862 Register of Deaths initials "B. C.," Company D and died March 13 of pneumonia.

Brown, Benjamin   Buried May 10, 1862   Lot/Division 2, #140   Plat Number 690
Missouri H M Bledsoe's Company Light Artillery Private; enlisted April 27, 1862 Memphis; per Muster Roll Remarks: Left in Hospital in Memphis May 5, 1862; occupation farmer; died Irving Hospital catarrhal fever per Daily Burial Record Book; per Irving Hospital record admitted May 1, 1862 with complaint of catarrhal fever and died May 7,1862.

Brown, George   Buried March 19, 1862   Lot/Division 1, #350   Plat Number 350
Louisiana 13 Infantry Regiment Private Company B; enlisted September 11, 1861 Camp Moore, Louisiana; per Muster Roll Remarks: Absent Sick since March 1862; sent from Columbus, Kentucky to Memphis Hospital by order of Dr. Langenbecker; per Overton Hospital March 1862 Register of Sick admitted February 26, 1862, and died March 18, 1862, from rubella; note Daniel W. Brown, Sergeant Company G Louisiana 13 Infantry Regiment also died March 18, 1862, from diarrhea per the Overton Hospital March 1862 Register of Sick but not found buried at Elmwood.

Brown, Hiram Reeves   Buried March 13, 1927   Plat Number N46
Tennessee 22 (Barteau's) Cavalry Regiment Private Company K; enlisted October 1, 1862 Oxford, Mississippi; per Tennessee Confederate Pension (S13120) enlisted October 1, 1862, in Tennessee 2 Cavalry Company K, which later became Tennessee 22 Barteau's Cavalry; born 1845 Obion County, Tennessee; per Tennessee Questionnaire of Civil War Veterans enlisted October 1862

Dyersburg, Tennessee and will be 77 on October 2, 1922; per March 13, 1927 *The Commercial Appeal* Memphis (Section I, page 9, column 1) died March 12, 1927, age 81 and had come to Memphis from home in Union City, Tennessee a year ago; no sketch in Mathes book.

Brown, John F.   Buried May 9, 1862   Lot/Division 2, #139   Plat Number 689
Arkansas Miller's Battalion Company E unit and died Overton Hospital rubella per Daily Burial Record Book; no compiled service record found; second initial "J" in Cemetery computer index; possibly Arkansas 12 Infantry Company E (John F. Brown, Private Company E, who enlisted July 26, 1861 Arkadelphia, Arkansas and who per July to October 1862 Muster Roll Remarks died January 1862 at New Madrid, Missouri) or Arkansas 8 Infantry Battalion Company E (Henry H. S. Brown, Private Company E, whose name appears on a list of mechanics dated July 1862 with trade of shoemaker but no other information in compiled service records).

Brown, John H.   Buried March 10, 1862   Lot/Division 1, #308   Plat Number 308
Confederate 4 (Baker's) Infantry Regiment Private Company K; per Company Muster Roll for December 31, 1861, to September 27, 1862, enlisted December 27, 1861, at Fort Pillow, Tennessee and remarks: Absent on furlough when surrendered April 8, 1862, not since heard from; regiment (also known as 1st Alabama, Tennessee and Mississippi Infantry) was formed about December 9, 1861, with ten companies: four from Alabama, two from Mississippi, and four from Tennessee; captured at Island 10 April 8, 1862, and after exchange in September, 1862, the companies were reorganized and transferred to other commands; Company K became 2nd Company D of the Tennessee 42nd Infantry Regiment but no record for this regiment as died before transfer; died Overton Hospital per Daily Burial Record Book.

Brownelle, E. L.   Buried April 17, 1862   Lot/Division 1, #463   Plat Number 463
Tennessee 154 Senior Infantry Regiment Private Company L; enlisted March 7, 1862 Memphis; per May 6, 1863 Muster Roll Remarks: Killed Battle of Shiloh; on Register of Soldiers Killed in Battle with note that died April 20, 1862 Shiloh; on report dated October 30, 1863 of unit deaths as died April 20, 1862 at Memphis of wound and enlisted March 8, 1862 Memphis; wounded at Battle of Shiloh and arrived at Irving Hospital on April 15, 1862 per April 16, 1862 *Memphis Daily Appeal*; name spelled "Brownell" on grave stone, in Cemetery computer index, in *Memphis Daily Appeal* and per Lindsley's Annals; second initial "S" in Cemetery record; 1839 1862 on grave stone; per Irving Hospital record E. F. Brownell was admitted April 15, 1861 with complaint of left side and died April 16, 1862.

Brownfield, J. G.   Buried March 14, 1862   Lot/Division 1, #329   Plat Number 329
Texas 9 (Young's/Maxey's) Infantry Regiment Private Company E; enlisted September 26, 1861 Sanders Creek, Lamar County, Texas, age 20; per March 1862, Regimental Returns died of pneumonia near Memphis; name appears on Overton Hospital February & March 1862, Registers of Sick and Wounded; admitted February 9, 1862; per Overton Hospital March 1862 Register of Deaths name "I. G. Broomfield" and died March 14 of rubella.

Bruce, T. M.   Buried April 17, 1862   Lot/Division 1, #462   Plat Number 462
Tennessee 154 Senior Infantry Regiment Private Company F; enlisted May 4, 1861 age 20; per January to July 1862, Muster Roll Remarks: Wounded Battle of Shiloh and since died; per May 6, 1863, Muster Roll Remarks: Died in Overton Hospital Memphis and $50 Bounty due him; per Battle of Shiloh casualty list for unit reported in April 24, 1862, *Memphis Daily Appeal* was wounded in Battle; first initial "F" in Cemetery record; per Hospital Record admitted April 11, 1862, with complaint of side and arm and died April, 1862.

Brumley, Joseph   Buried May 11, 1862   Lot/Division 2, #157   Plat Number 707
Arkansas 23 (Adams') Infantry Regiment Private (Pennington's) Private Company H; enlisted March 6, 1862 Arkadelphia, Arkansas; per March 6 to June 30, 1862 Muster Roll Remarks: Died May 10, 1862 Memphis, Tennessee, relapse from measles; name appears on Register of Claims indicating that claim was filed April 25, 1863 by widow Rebecca Brumley with indication that died at Memphis, Tennessee; died Mansfield's and name spelled "Bromley" in Cemetery record.

Bryan, James   Buried February 13, 1862   Lot/Division 1, #263   Plat Number 263
Texas 9 (Young's/Maxey's) Infantry Regiment Private Company K; enlisted September 28, 1861 Tollet's Prairie, Texas, age 27; per Overton Hospital February 28, 1862, Register of Sick died February 12, 1862; name spelled "Bryant" and died Overton Hospital pneumonia per Daily Burial Record Book.

Bryant, J. W.   Buried March 7, 1862   Lot/Division 1, #296   Plat Number 296
Mississippi 25 Infantry Regiment Private Company H "Wigfall Guards"; enlisted August 10, 1861, Memphis, age 19 (no other information); unit indicated as Mississippi 2 Regiment, no initials and died State Hospital per Daily Burial Record Book.

Bryant, Jackson J.   Buried October 15, 1861   Lot/Division 1, #36   Plat Number 36
Arkansas 12 Infantry Regiment Private Company F; enlisted July 26, 1861 Arkadelphia, Arkansas; per July to October 1862 Muster Roll Remarks: Died at Memphis October 14, 1861; died age 21 camp pneumonia per Daily Burial Record Book.

Buckner, Jasper W.   Buried March 18, 1862   Lot/Division 1, #339   Plat Number 339
Arkansas 12 Infantry Regiment Company B per Daily Burial Record Book; no compiled service record found; per Overton Hospital March 1862 Register of Deaths died March 17 of pneumonia.

Buford, Smith   Buried October 22, 1899   Lot/Division 1, #543   Plat Number 543
Assistant Surgeon; per General and Staff records appointed April 21, 1865 from Mississippi and May 31, 1865 Confederate 5 Regiment (no record found this unit either cavalry or infantry); also served in Mississippi 17 (Steede's) Cavalry Battalion Assistant Surgeon; single card in record on a requisition for medicine dated July 24, 1863; originally enlisted Mississippi 15 Infantry Regiment Private Company F May 26, 1861 Corinth, Mississippi; captured at Fishing Creek January 19, 1862 and was a prisoner at Johnson's Island, Ohio; sent to Camp Chase May 24, 1862; sent to Vicksburg November 22, 1862; per May/June 1863 Muster Roll Remarks: Promoted to Assistant Surgeon April 15, 1863 and so dropped from roll, discharged; sketch in Mathes book (original edition) indicates enlisted in Company F Mississippi 13 (sic) Infantry early in 1861; sketch in Mathes book (enlarged edition) indicates enlisted in Company F Mississippi 15 Infantry then entered Medical Department as Assistant Surgeon and assigned to Steede's (Mississippi 17) Cavalry Battalion and afterwards served in Georgia 8 Battalion, Howell's Georgia Battery (no record found these units), and the last twelve months in the Confederate 5 Regiment, Granberry's Brigade, Cleburne's Division; member Confederate Historical Association and Company A United Confederate Veterans; per Daily Burial Record Book died age 61 and remarks Grave #543 North Division and this grave is on east-line next to drive; not Buford, S., Assistant Surgeon, Georgia 40 Infantry Battalion Company A and Georgia 40 Infantry Regiment Company H.

Bugg, William C.   Buried May 5, 1862   Lot/Division 2, #64   Plat Number 614
Arkansas 20 (King's 22) Infantry Regiment Private (Lindsey's) Company D; enlisted March 1, 1862, at Little Rock, Arkansas; per remarks on the March 1 to June 30, 1862, Company Muster Roll died in Memphis about 3rd of May; second initial "T" and died Overton Hospital pneumonia per Daily Burial Record Book.

Bull, Cicero B.   Buried February 27, 1862   Lot/Division 1, #273   Plat Number 273
Arkansas 15 (Johnson's) Infantry Regiment Private Company F; enlisted December 19, 1861 Lafayette, Arkansas; per December 1861 to October 1862 Muster Roll Remarks: Died at Memphis, Tennessee Hospital February 20, 1862; per Overton Hospital Register of Sick dated February 28, 1862: Died February 26, 1862; died Overton Hospital per Daily Burial Record Book.

Burch, A. D.   Buried November 5, 1861   Lot/Division 1, #166   Plat Number 166
Arkansas 6 Infantry Regiment Private Company D Old; enlisted July 26, 1861 Pocahontas age 27; name appears on a Register of Claims filed February 12, 1863 by father W H Burch indicating that died Memphis, Tennessee; died Southern Mothers Hospital and Company C per Daily Burial Record Book.

Burk, John H.   Buried May 17, 1862   Lot/Division 2, #230   Plat Number 780
Arkansas 2 Regiment Company B and died Irving Hospital pneumonia per Daily Burial Record Book; no compiled service record found; in Irving Hospital record unit indicated as Arkansas 19 Infantry Regiment Company B (but not found that unit and may be mistake as Richard Burk of Arkansas 19 Infantry was also admitted the same day) and admitted April 30, 1862, with complaint of measles and died May 16, 1862; does not appear to be J. H. Burk, Arkansas 2 Cavalry who took Oath of Allegiance April 18, 1864, and who indicated residence of Hots Springs, Arkansas, age 21 with remarks that deserted February 13, 1864.

Burkett, Andrew J.   Buried April 1, 1903   Lot/Division 1, #538   Plat Number 538
Arkansas 15 (Josey's) Infantry Regiment Private Company E; enlisted July 23, 1861 Camp Hardee, Pitman Ferry, Arkansas; per death notice in April 1, 1903 *The Commercial Appeal* Memphis was from Pensacola, Arkansas; name spelled "Burket" and died age 59y/8m/15d per Daily Burial Record Book.

Burks, William   Buried April 3, 1862   Lot/Division 1, #412   Plat Number 412
Confederate 1 (King's Battalion) Cavalry Regiment Private (Gray's) 2 Company F; enlisted January 10, 1862 Memphis age 18; per March & April 1862, Muster Roll Remarks: Died; died pneumonia per Daily Burial Record Book; name spelled "Burke" in Daily Burial Record Book, computer index and on grave stone; Craig's Company indicated Cemetery Single Grave Book.

Burnett, George W.   Buried May 16, 1873   Lot/Division 2, #379   Plat Number 929
Listed in Elmwood 1874 book as Confederate soldier buried in Elmwood who was citizen of Memphis or vicinity; no unit indicated in Daily Burial Record Book; possibly Tennessee 4 Infantry Regiment Private Company D, enlisted May 10, 1861, Germantown, Tennessee age 22 and took Oath of Allegiance April 1865, age 26; died age 36 chronic diarrhea per Daily Burial Record Book; government stone does not appear to be right - Private CS Army 1839 1862 (#879).

Burton, J. B.   Buried October 18, 1861   Lot/Division 1, #110   Plat Number 110
Arkansas 8 Regiment and died State Hospital per Daily Burial Record Book; no compiled service record found.

Cage, John F.   Buried May 1, 1868   Lot/Division 1, #525   Plat Number 525
Heth's Division Captain & Assistant Quartermaster General & Staff Officers; first enlisted Tennessee 7 Infantry, Private Company

E on May 26, 1861 Gallatin, Tennessee; per August 13, 1861 Muster Roll Remarks: On Extra Duty as Clerk for Commissary; per January to December 1862 Muster Roll Remarks: On Extra Duty as Brigade Wagon Master; per Muster Roll dated December 31, 1863 Remarks: Detailed as Division Quartermaster and served as that until October 16, 1863 when appointed Captain Adjutant & Quartermaster; name appears on a Record of Paroled Prisoners, Provost Marshall's Office Middle Military Department dated April 25, 1865 indicating captured or surrendered Appomattox Court House and took Oath April 24, 1865 at Fort Monroe, former residence of Nashville which was destination; name appears on a Register of Appointments, CSA, State of Tennessee, indicating date of appointment October 23, 1863, confirmed June 14, 1864, and to take rank October 16, 1863; Muster Roll dated March 31, 1864 near Orange Court House, Virginia indicates age as 26; second initial "T" and died age 31 per Daily Burial Record Book; listed in Elmwood 1874 book as Confederate soldier buried in Elmwood who was citizen of Memphis or vicinity and second initial "T."

Cahill, Edward Buried September 10, 1861 Lot/Division 1, #10 Plat Number 10
Tennessee 2 (Walker's) Infantry Regiment Private Company D; enlisted May 11, 1861 Memphis; per August to November 1861 Muster Roll Remarks: Died in Hospital in Memphis September 10, 1861; July 17, 1863 Muster Roll Remarks: died July 17, 1861; 1840 1861 on grave stone.

Caldwell, John Buried October 14, 1861 Lot/Division 1, #68 Plat Number 68
Arkansas 13 Infantry Regiment Company E; no compiled service record found; unit and died Southern Mothers Hospital enteritis per Daily Burial Record Book; not John W Caldwell, Confederate 3 Infantry (formerly Arkansas 18 Marmaduke's Infantry Regiment) Private Company E who was taken prisoner in the Battle of Murfreesboro, Tennessee December 31, 1862.

Callahan, David Buried October 20, 1861 Lot/Division 1, #116 Plat Number 116
Arkansas 8 Infantry Regiment Private New Company A; enlisted September 10, 1861 Camp Price, Arkansas age 18; per October 31, 1861 Muster Roll Remarks: Died - Absent at Memphis about 15 October; died State Hospital per Daily Burial Record Book.

Callaway, Levi A. Buried October 27, 1861 Lot/Division 1, #140 Plat Number 140
Arkansas 9 Infantry Regiment Private Company E; enlisted July 27, 1861 Pine Bluff, Arkansas; per July 27 to November 1, 1861 Muster Roll Remarks: Died 26 October in Memphis; Hospital per Daily Burial Record Book died Southern Mothers Hospital enteritis, age 22; name spelled "Calloway" in Daily Burial Record Book and computer index.

Cameron, John S. Buried October 6, 1861 Lot/Division 1, #101 Plat Number 101
Tennessee 40 (Walker's) Infantry Regiment Private Company H; enlisted September 4, 1861, Montgomery, Alabama age 22; per November 1, 1861, Muster Roll Remarks: Died October 6, 1861; per affidavit with claim filed by mother, Malinda Cameron, died October 5, 1861 at Camp Johnson, Memphis; died camp flux age 23 per Daily Burial Record Book; Walker's Regiment indicated as an Arkansas unit in Daily Burial Record Book.

Camper, John M. Buried May 5, 1862 Lot/Division 2, #53 Plat Number 603
Arkansas 19 (Dockery/Smead's) Infantry Regiment Private Company I; enlisted March 3, 1862 Union County, Arkansas; per March 3 to June 30, 1862 Muster Roll Remarks: Died 1 May 1862 at C S Hospital Memphis, Tennessee; died Overton Hospital per Daily Burial Record Book.

Capps, Thomas J. Buried March 19, 1862 Lot/Division 1, #344 Plat Number 344
Arkansas 11 Infantry Regiment Private Company D; enlisted December 3, 1861 Hot Springs, Arkansas; per November 1, 1861 to September 27, 1862 Muster Roll Remarks: Died at Memphis, Tennessee sometime in March 1862; per Overton Hospital March 1862 Register of Deaths died March 18 of pneumonia; second initial "G" in Daily Burial Record Book.

Carle, Everett Buried October 27, 1861 Lot/Division 1, #141 Plat Number 141
Adams' Regiment; unit and died Southern Mothers Hospital enteritis, age 20 and name spelled both "Carle" and "Carti" in Cemetery computer index; not found Confederate Cavalry Wood's Regiment (Mississippi Wirt Adams' Cavalry Regiment - Mississippi 1 Cavalry Regiment) or Arkansas 23 Adams' Infantry Regiment; not E. B. Carle Arkansas 19 (Dawson's) Infantry Regiment Private Company E or Charles Carl Arkansas 23 (Adams) Infantry Regiment.

Carlin, Dr. Robert F. Buried July 30, 1874 Lot/Division 2, #382 Plat Number 932
Surgeon Field and Staff 9 Confederate Infantry (5 Confederate Infantry, 5 Confederate Regiment Tennessee Infantry) that was formed by the consolidation of the 2 (Walker's) Regiment Tennessee Infantry and the 21 Regiment Tennessee Infantry and finally 3 Consolidated Regiment Tennessee Infantry; name (Robert F. Carlin, Surgeon 5 Regiment Confederate States Infantry) appears as signature to an Oath of Allegiance to the United States, subscribed and sworn to at Nashville, Tennessee, May 31, 1865, surrendered at Macon, Georgia, May 25, 1865, and Fulton County, Tennessee as place of residence; see also CARLIN, ROBERT F., Surgeon, appointed by Secretary of War, August 25, 1863, to rank from June 30, 1862. December 31, 1862, 5th Confederate, Harrodsburg, April 30, 1863, 3d and 5th Confederate Regiments, April 17, 1863, ordered to report to E. A. F., Medical Director, June 30, 1863. July 31, 1863, 3d and 5th Confederate Regiments. Passed Board at Columbus, Mississippi, June 30, 1862. August 30, 1863, December 31, 1863, January 31, 1864, 3d and 5th Confederate Regiments. Senior Surgeon Brigade listed in *Roster of*

the Medical officers of the Army of Tennessee. During the Civil War between the Northern and Southern States, 1861-1865. consolidated from the original Medical-Director's Records by Joseph Jones, M. D., L. L. D and found in the *Southern Historical Society Papers*, Volume XXII, Chapter XXIV, Page182; Doctor and died age 46 per Daily Burial Record Book but no unit indicated; death (July 29, 1874) reported in the July 30, 1874, *Memphis Daily Appeal*, page 1, column 8.

Carman, Samuel M. Buried May 6, 1862 Lot/Division 2, #68 Plat Number 618
Missouri 1 Infantry Battalion Brevet 2 Lieutenant Company B (Thompson's Brigade); per Company Muster Roll for March 5 to April 30, 1862, enlisted February 6, 1862, Clarkton, Missouri with Remarks: elected March 5, 1862; May & June 1862, Muster Roll Remarks: Died 3 of May 1862; Company was at Fort Pillow during May 1862, and operated as marines aboard Confederate defense fleet gunboats; August 1862, Company B consolidated with Company A to form Company K, Missouri 5 Infantry Regiment, but no record found that unit's compiled service record; died Irving Hospital pneumonia per Daily Burial Record Book; per Irving Hospital record admitted April 26, 1862, with complaint of pneumonia and died May 3, 1862.

Carrick, George Buried March 18, 1862 Lot/Division 1, #343 Plat Number 343
Confederate 1 (King's Battalion) Cavalry Regiment Private (Gray's) 2 Company F; enlisted January 10, 1862 Memphis, age 20; per March & April 1862 Muster Roll Remarks: Died; name appears on Overton Hospital March 1862 Register of Deaths with unit as King's Battalion, Gray's Company, complaint of rubella and died March 18; died pneumonia, Overton Hospital and Craig's Company King's Battalion per Daily Burial Record Book; there is no Craig's Company in unit.

Carrick, John (George) Buried March 11, 1862 Lot/Division 1, #320 Plat Number 320
Confederate 1 (King's Battalion) Cavalry Regiment Private (Gray's) 2 Company F; enlisted January 10, 1862 Memphis age 27; per March & April 1862 Muster Roll Remarks: Died; first name "George," died Overton Hospital and Craig's Company per Daily Burial Record Book; note: Daily Burial Record Book has two George Carricks for Craig's Company with different dates of death but there is only one George Carrick in unit records; based on March 18, 1862, date of death of George Carrick (see sketch next above), it is believed that this John Carrick; not found on Overton Hospital Registers; no Craig's Company in unit..

Carter, Robert D. Buried September 14, 1861 Lot/Division 1, #58 Plat Number 58
Arkansas 9 Infantry Regiment Private (Wallace's) Company G; enlisted July 27, 1861 Pine Bluff, Arkansas; per July 27 to November 1,1861 Muster Roll Remarks: Died September 13 typhoid fever at Memphis, Tennessee; died Southern Mothers Hospital typhoid fever per Daily Burial Record Book.

Carter, Thomas Jefferson Buried September 26, 1926 Plat Number N44
Mississippi 7 Cavalry Regiment Private Company F; enlisted April 20, 1864 Pontotoc, Mississippi; appears on a Prisoner of War register at Memphis, Tennessee dated November 28, 1864 age 18 (note age difference with other record below), when took oath and indicated place of residence Lafayette County, Mississippi; appears on a Roll of Prisoners of War paroled at Grenada, Mississippi May 20, 1865; per widow Mary Carter's Tennessee Confederate Pension (W10066), born in Carroll County, Mississippi October 10, 1839, joined April 15, 1861, Vaiden, Mississippi and paroled August 10, 1865; per letter in file from War Department dated February 26, 1931 to Tennessee Pension Board T. J. Carter, Private Company F, 7 Regiment Mississippi Cavalry, enlisted April 20, 1864 at Pontotoc, Mississippi, Oath of Allegiance sworn at Memphis November 28, 1864 and name appears on List of Prisoners of War surrendered at Citronelle, Alabama May 4, 1865 and paroled at Grenada, Mississippi May 29, 1865; per statement in file received Mississippi pension then moved to Tennessee and applied but had not lived in Tennessee long enough and died September 25, 1926; Mary Carter's maiden name was Odom, born Tallahatchie, Mississippi December 1859 and died June 29, 1948; per Mississippi Pension Index Book T. J. Carter applied for a pension in 1909 indicating served in 1 Mississippi Cavalry and Mrs. T. J. Carter, husband T. J. Carter 1 Mississippi Cavalry, applied for a pension in 1927, both indicated residence of Oktibbeha County, Mississippi; per single muster roll card in Mississippi 1 Cavalry Regiment record dated April 30 to October 31, 1862 enlisted August 1, 1861 Memphis and Private Company A (note on card indicates this company formerly served as Company K, 1 (Miller's) Battalion Mississippi Cavalry, and was transferred to this regiment when Battalion was disbanded about June 1862); per Mississippi 1 Battalion (Miller's) Cavalry enlisted August 16, 1861 at Memphis age 21 and Battalion disbanded about June 1862 and this company became Company A Mississippi 1 Cavalry Regiment; died age 87 and no unit indicated in Daily Burial Record Book.

Carwile, Flemuel Buried March 25, 1862 Lot/Division 1, #376 Plat Number 376
Tennessee Bankhead's Battery (Tennessee Scott's Light Artillery) Harris' Company and died of pneumonia per Daily Burial Record Book ; no compiled service record found; per Overton Hospital March 1862 Register of Deaths first name "Flemming," Company B and died March 24 of rubella; name spelled "Flemnel" in Cemetery computer index; note there are two grave stones #376; one is in short row north side of Monument and the other is at north end of row along Road of Honor Drive; only this burial record found.

Castinere, Antonio Buried March 26, 1862 Lot/Division 1, #383 Plat Number 383
Tennessee Bankhead's Battery (Tennessee Scott's Light Artillery) Harris' Company per Daily Burial Record Book; no compiled service record found; per Overton Hospital March 1862 Register of Sick name "Antonia Castenero," Company B Bankhead Regt and died March 25 of bronchitis; name also found spelled "Castineve."

Castleberry, Joel   Buried November 24, 1862   Lot/Division 2, #314   Plat Number 864
Arkansas 2 Infantry Regiment Private Company I; enlisted May 3, 1862; per December 30, 1862, to February 1863, Muster Roll Remarks: Died at Memphis, Tennessee 20 December; name spelled "Castlebury" in compiled service records and Daily Burial Record Book and not found in Alpha Book; spelling confirmed by descendant Mrs. Nancy Castleberry Harris via email March 3, 2003.

Chadwick, Frank   Buried May 17, 1862   Lot/Division 2, #233   Plat Number 783
Daily Burial Record Book indicates regiment and company not known and died Overton Hospital measles; possibly P. F. Chadwick, Arkansas 18 (Carroll's) Infantry Regiment Private Company B; per Company Muster Roll for March to June 30, 1862, enlisted March 2, 1862 Princeton, Arkansas with Remarks: Died in Memphis 16 May 1862.

Chamberland, Rufus   Buried November 11, 1861   Lot/Division 1, #184   Plat Number 184
Tennessee 21 (Pickett's) Infantry Regiment Private Company H (Advance Guard); enlisted May 15, 1861 Memphis; per November & December 1861 Muster Roll Remarks: Killed at Belmont November 7, 1861; name spelled "Chamberlain" and killed age 18 per Daily Burial Record Book; name also spelled "Chamberlin" in compiled service record and "Chambern" in the list of casualties at Battle of Belmont, Missouri reported in the November 13, 1861, *Memphis Daily Appeal*, page 2, column 5.

Chapman, Thomas   Buried April 1, 1862   Lot/Division 1, #405   Plat Number 405
Tennessee 4 Infantry Regiment Private Company G; enlisted May 15, 1861 Ripley, Tennessee age 22; per Overton Hospital March 31, 1862 Register of Deaths died March 31 of congestion; 1840 1862 on grave stone; initials "T. E. C. H." in compiled service record.

Chapman, William F.   Buried May 12, 1862   Lot/Division 2, #175   Plat Number 725
Arkansas 23 (Adams') Infantry Regiment Private (Harris') Company F; enlisted March 27, 1862 Jacksonport, Arkansas; per March 27 to June 30, 1862 Muster Roll Remarks: Died May 15, 1862 Memphis; died Scorbutus, Captain Swayer noted and second initial "T" per Daily Burial Record Book.

Charles, John H.   Buried April 3, 1862   Lot/Division 1, #413   Plat Number 413
Tennessee 5 Infantry Regiment Private Company C; enlisted May 20, 1861 Paris, Henry County, Tennessee; died typhoid fever per Daily Burial Record Book.

Chisp, John   Buried February 14, 1863   Lot/Division 2, #339   Plat Number 889
No unit indicated in Daily Burial Record Book.

Christenham, Peter   Buried March 25, 1862   Lot/Division 1, #378   Plat Number 378
Tennessee 21 Regiment and name spelled "Christenhorn" in Daily Burial Record Book; no compiled service record found; per Overton Hospital March 1862 Register of Deaths Died March 25 of pneumonia.

Christopher, Matthew   Buried March 7, 1862   Lot/Division 1, #293   Plat Number 293
Arkansas 11 Infantry Regiment Private Company I; enlisted January 12, 1862 Hot Springs, Arkansas; per October 29, 1861 to September 23, 1862 Muster Roll Remarks: Died in Hospital at Memphis in March 1862 date unknown; per Overton Hospital March 1862 Register of Deaths died March 6 of pneumonia.

Clair, John   Buried March 19, 1862   Lot/Division 1, #345   Plat Number 345
Louisiana 21 Infantry Regiment Private Company E; enlisted August 6, 1861 New Orleans, Louisiana; name appears on Overton Hospital March 1862, Register of Sick as admitted February 28 with complaint of asthma and died March 17, 1862.

Clark, Simpson H.   Buried October 29, 1861   Lot/Division 1, #145   Plat Number 145
Arkansas 12 Infantry Regiment Private Company E; enlisted July 27, 1861 Arkadelphia, Arkansas; per July to October 1862 Muster Roll Remarks: Died October 28, 1861 at Memphis; died camp measles per Daily Burial Record Book; first name "Sanford" in Arkansas Soldiers index; name spelled "Clarke" in Cemetery computer index.

Clark, William M.   Buried March 20, 1862   Lot/Division 1, #357   Plat Number 357
Tennessee 1 Heavy Artillery Regiment (Rucker's Battery) 2 Lieutenant; per Captain Edward W. Rucker, Confederate Artillery March 26, 1862, Report (Report Number 34 in Official Record, Volume 8) William M. Clark was killed at Island 10 on March 17, 1862; several other references to his death in other reports in Official Record Volume 8; per unit history in *Tennesseans in the Civil War Part 1*, page 120, and article "Bombardment of Island 10" in the March 21, 1862, *Memphis Daily Appeal*, page 1, column 1, Lieutenant Clark (no initials or first name) was killed during bombardment by Federal Fleet; per article "Lieut. Clarke" under Local Matters in the March 22, 1862, *Memphis Daily Appeal*, page 2, column 6, was a nephew of Captain Hailman of this city, age 18, from Kaskaska, Illinois, and when he joined the army he brought with him eighteen young men from his neighborhood and the vicinity of Cape Girardeau.

Clarke, Robert J.   Buried August 15, 1869   Lot/Division 2, #363   Plat Number 913
Tennessee 154 Senior Infantry Regiment Private 2 Company B; enlisted May 20, 1861 Somerville, Tennessee; wounded Battle of Murfreesboro; per Certificate of Disability for Discharge dated May 26, 1863 born Haywood County, Tennessee, age 20 and was a farmer; name also found spelled "Clark" in compiled service record; name "James R. Clark" in Cemetery records and as listed in Elmwood 1874 book as Confederate soldier buried in Elmwood who was citizen of Memphis or vicinity.

Clay, T. G.   Buried November 22, 1861   Lot/Division 1, #212   Plat Number 212
Arkansas 7 Infantry Regiment Private Company B; enlisted July 26, 1861 Camp Shaver, Arkansas; per September & October 1861 Muster Roll Remarks: Sick in Columbus Hospital; per December 31, 1861 Muster Roll Remarks: Absent on Furlough; per Discharge Paper in compiled service record to be paid to November 22, 1861; first initial "F" and died State Hospital per Daily Burial Record Book.

Clements, Augustus   Buried March 10, 1862   Lot/Division 1, #310   Plat Number 310
Arkansas 13 Infantry Regiment Private Company B; no enlistment in compiled service record; only card in record is Overton Hospital March 1862 Register of Deaths that indicates died March 9 of pneumonia.

Clifton, T. J.   Buried May 14, 1862   Lot/Division 2, #211   Plat Number 761
Texas 32 (Crump's Battalion) Cavalry Regiment Private Company D; enlisted January 20, 1862 S Springs, Texas; per January to August 1862 Muster Roll Remarks: Died May 15, 1862; from Darron's per Daily Burial Record Book.

Clinch, John E.   Buried November 21, 1861   Lot/Division 1, #209   Plat Number 209
Tennessee 40 (Walker's) Infantry Regiment Private Company K; enlisted October 20, 1861 Camp Johnson near Memphis age 24; per November & December 1861 Muster Roll Remarks: Died on 21 November 1861; per Register of Deaths born Dekalb County, Alabama and died November 21, 1861 Memphis, Tennessee measles; died Southern Mothers Hospital enteritis and name spelled "Clynch" per Daily Burial Record Book.

Clinton, Alexander M.   Buried March 11, 1917   Plat Number N28
Tennessee 38 Infantry Regiment Private 2 Company A; enlisted March 2, 1862 Camp Abington, Tennessee; per several rolls of Prisoners of War captured Sweetwater, Tennessee December 3, 1863; took Oath of Allegiance June 5, 1865 at Memphis age 23; per widow's (Mildred Rigsby) Tennessee Confederate Pension application (W6763) died March 10, 1917; 1842 on grave stone; died age 76 per Daily Burial Record Book.

Cloud, Joseph F.   Buried October 28, 1923   Plat Number N39
Mississippi 17 Infantry Regiment Sergeant Major Company F; compiled service record found under James F. Cloud; enlisted May 29, 1861 Corinth, Mississippi, age 21; per Tennessee Confederate Pension application #5560 born July 17, 1839 Marshall County, Mississippi; per Confederate Historical Association, Camp 28, Bivouac 18, application born July 1, 1839 Lafayette County, Mississippi; no sketch in Mathes book; died age 84 per Daily Burial Record Book.

Cobb, H. J.   Buried November 6, 1861   Lot/Division 1, #168   Plat Number 168
Arkansas 12 Infantry Regiment Company C and died camp per Daily Burial Record Book; no compiled service record found; there was a T. S. Cobb, Private Company B Arkansas 12 Infantry Regiment, who was captured July 9, 1863, and paroled July 12 and 13, 1863, at Port Hudson, Louisiana.

Coffman, John H.   Buried May 31, 1862   Lot/Division 2, #277   Plat Number 827
Texas 10 (Locke's) Cavalry Regiment Private Company C; compiled service record found under John H. Kaufman; enlisted October 31, 1861 Taos, Texas, age 26; per March to August 1862 Muster Roll Remarks: Died May 1, 1862; claim by father, James Coffman, in record indicates died at Memphis, Tennessee; at Fall's per Daily Burial Record Book.

Coffman, Warren   Buried May 2, 1862   Lot/Division 2, #24   Plat Number 574
Texas 9 (Sim's) Cavalry Regiment Private Company E; enlisted Camp Reeves, age 19 (no date indicated); per March & April 1862 Muster Roll Remarks: at Memphis sick; per May & June 1862 Muster Roll Remarks: Died at Memphis May 3, 1862; died erysipelas and Stewart's per Daily Burial Record Book.

Coggin, B. F.   Buried October 16, 1861   Lot/Division 1, #34   Plat Number 34
Arkansas 12 Infantry Regiment Company C and died camp measles age 23 per Daily Burial Record Book; no compiled service record found.

Cohn, Harvey H.   Buried July 5, 1861   Lot/Division 1, #91   Plat Number 91
Arkansas 2 (Hindman's) Infantry Regiment Private Company B; enlisted May 30, 1861, Helena; per June 20 to August 31, 1861, Muster Roll Remarks: Died at Memphis July 5, 1861; name spelled "Conn" in Daily Burial Record Book.

Cole, J. C.   Buried September 4, 1869   Lot/Division 2, #365   Plat Number 915
Colonel and died congestion of brain age 35 per Daily Burial Record Book; not listed in Cemetery Single Grave Book; possibly James C. Cole Lieutenant Colonel 9 Confederate Infantry (5 Confederate Infantry, 5 Confederate Regiment Tennessee Infantry) that was formed by the consolidation of the 2 (Walker's) Regiment Tennessee Infantry and the 21 Regiment Tennessee Infantry and finally 3 Consolidated Regiment Tennessee Infantry.

Cole, John B.   Buried January 2, 1870   Lot/Division 2, #366   Plat Number 916
Kentucky 2 (Duke's) Cavalry Regiment 3 Lieutenant Company K, letter in record from Colonel Joseph T. Taylor, Kentucky 11 Cavalry Regiment, which regiment was with General John Hunt Morgan, recommending him for a promotion to Captain Company B and in which letter he also states that J. B. Cole was originally a Lieutenant in Kentucky 2 Cavalry and was transferred in March 1863; originally enlisted July 13, 1861, at Camp Boone, Tennessee as a Private in Company B Kentucky 2 Mounted Infantry and remark on August 1 to October 31, 1862, Camp Muster Roll that promoted to 1 Lieutenant in Morgan's Cavalry (note there was a second John B. Cole in this regiment but he died July 5, 1862, while in prison at Camp Douglas, Illinois); listed in Elmwood 1874 book as Confederate soldier buried in Elmwood who was citizen of Memphis or vicinity; died typhoid pneumonia age 25 but no unit indicated in Daily Burial Record Book; per death notice in the January 2, 1870, *Memphis Daily Appeal*, page 1, column 9, formerly of Georgetown, Kentucky and a member of the Second Kentucky Regiment (Confederate).

Cole, Porter   Buried May 10, 1862   Lot/Division 2, #147   Plat Number 697
Arkansas 18 (Carroll's) Infantry Regiment Private Company G; enlisted March 2, 1862 Little Rock, Arkansas age 27; per September to December 1862 Muster Roll Remarks: Left at Memphis sick May 29, supposed dead; per March & April 1863, Muster Roll Remarks: Died, sent to General Hospital May 29, 1862 from Corinth, very sick, supposed to be dead; died Overton Hospital erysipelas and initials "E. P. C." per compiled service record.

Collier, T. W.   Buried April 1, 1862   Lot/Division 1, #407   Plat Number 407
Tennessee 40 (Walker's) Infantry Regiment Private (Bibb's) Company E; enlisted October 18, 1861, Athens (Mooresville), Alabama, age 34; per Register of Deaths (no date) born Alabama and died March 26, 1862, Island No. 10 chronic diarrhea; first initial "F" in some compiled Cemetery lists; not found in Lindsley's Annals 39 & 40 Consolidated Infantry Regiment Official Memorial Roll.

Collins, Dennis   Buried March 1, 1862   Lot/Division 1, #275   Plat Number 275
Tennessee 15 Infantry Regiment Private Company C; enlisted May 21, 1861 Memphis age 20; per January 1 to April 30, 1862 Muster Roll Remarks: Wounded Battle of Belmont, Missouri November 7, 1861 and died in Hospital; name appears on Overton Hospital Register of Sick and Wounded for December 31, 1861, January 31, 1862, and February 28, 1862; per Overton Hospital Register died February 25, 1862 from effects of wounds; 1840 1861 on grave stone.

Collins, James   Buried May 5, 1862   Lot/Division 2, #50   Plat Number 600
Arkansas 18 (Carroll's) Infantry Regiment Private Company D; enlisted March 1, 1862, Pine Bluff, Arkansas; per July 1, 1862, Muster Roll Remarks: Died April 30, 1862; died Irving Hospital typhoid fever and pneumonia per Daily Burial Record Book; per Irving Hospital record Company G, admitted May 1, 1862, with complaint of typhoid fever and died May 3, 1862.

Collins, John J.   Buried October 20, 1861   Lot/Division 1, #118   Plat Number 118
Arkansas 12 Infantry Regiment Private Company B; single card in compiled service record on Register of Claims for Deceased Soldiers by father, Joseph Collins, filed July 12, 1863; died camp measles age 21 per Daily Burial Record Book.

Collins, John W.   Buried May 10, 1862   Lot/Division 2, #151   Plat Number 701
Arkansas 17 (Lemoyne's) Infantry Regiment Private Company B; enlisted January 1, 1862, East Fork, Arkansas; no other information in compiled service records; no record found under Arkansas 21 Infantry that was successor of Arkansas 17 Infantry; died Overton Hospital typhoid fever and pneumonia per Daily Burial Record Book.

Collins, Thomas   Buried March 25, 1862   Lot/Division 1, #379   Plat Number 379
Louisiana 13 Regiment Company H per Daily Burial Record Book; no compiled service record found and not found Booth Louisiana Book; per Overton Hospital March 1862 Register of Deaths Company I and died March 25 of pneumonia.

Colloway, Nathaniel C.   Buried May 7, 1862   Lot/Division 2, #102   Plat Number 652
Arkansas 23 (Adams') Infantry Regiment Private (Pennington's) Company H; enlisted March 6, 1862, Arkadelphia; per March 6 to June 30, 1862, Muster Roll Remarks: Died May 7, 1862, Memphis, Tennessee typhoid fever; died at Mansfield's and name spelled "Calloway" per Daily Burial Record Book.

Comstock, Joseph L.   Buried May 3, 1862   Lot/Division 2, #32   Plat Number 582
Arkansas 19 (Dockery/Smead's) Infantry Regiment Private Company E; enlisted March 1, 1862, Hot Springs, Arkansas; per March 1 to June 30, 1862, Muster Roll Remarks: Died May 6, 1862; died Overton Hospital pneumonia per Daily Burial Record Book.

Cone, Elijah Merrill   Buried December 19, 1861   Lot/Division 1, #248   Plat Number 248
Arkansas 12 Infantry Regiment Private Company G; per Company Muster Roll for July 27, 1861, to October 1, 1862, enlisted July 27, 1861, at Arkadelphia; per Register of Soldiers who were killed in battle or died of wounds or disease died December 18, 1861, in Memphis; name spelled "McCone" and died Edgewood Hospital in Daily Burial Record Book; name spelled "McCone," "McCove," and "Cone" in Cemetery computer index; corrected spelling provided by great-grandson Noble Roberts; grave stone: October 28, 1834 December 19, 1861.

Conn, John S.   Buried October 21, 1861   Lot/Division 1, #121   Plat Number 121
Arkansas 12 Infantry Regiment Company H; no enlistment in compiled service record; on Register of Soldiers who died with remarks that died October 19, 1861, Camp Johnson, Memphis.

Conn, William   Buried May 9, 1862   Lot/Division 2, #132   Plat Number 682
CSS General Beauregard Seaman; enlisted April 5, 1862; gunboat participated in and was sank during the Battle of Memphis June 6, 1862; died Overton Hospital dropsy per Daily Burial Record Book; name written as "Wm Cole (Conn)" in Daily Burial Record Book; name indicated as "Cole or Conn" Alpha Book; name spelled "Cole" in Cemetery computer index.

Connelly, John   Buried May 17, 1862   Lot/Division 2, #234   Plat Number 784
Daily Burial Record Book indicates regiment and company not known and died Overton Hospital measles; possibly John Connelly, Tennessee 40 Infantry Regiment Sergeant Company G, enlisted September 23, 1861, Tyddersdale, Arkansas age 20; captured Island 10 April 8, 1862, and sent to Camp Butler, Springfield, Illinois and then to Vicksburg for exchange September 23, 1862 (possibly died on way to Vicksburg).

Conner, Z. M.   Buried April 16, 1862   Lot/Division 1, #458   Plat Number 458
Arkansas 20 (King's) Infantry Regiment Private (Beebe's) Company F; enlisted April 83, 1862, Perryville and per March 3 to May 2, 1862, Muster Roll Remarks: Died in Memphis; Beans Company per Daily Burial Record Book but no Captain Bean found; name spelled "Connor" in Cemetery records.

Connor, M. E.   Buried March 23, 1862   Lot/Division 1, #369   Plat Number 369
Texas 9 (Young's/Maxey's) Infantry Regiment Private Company G; enlisted October 8, 1861 Tarrant, Texas, age 21; per March 1862, Regimental Returns: Died March 26, 1862, Memphis, Tennessee pneumonia; died Overton Hospital pneumonia per Daily Burial Record Book.

Cook, J. E.   Buried May 10, 1862   Lot/Division 2, #154   Plat Number 704
Arkansas 19 (Dockery/Smead's) Infantry Regiment Private Company H; enlisted March 3, 1862, Caney, Arkansas (Marsh's Store, Arkansas); per March 3 to June 30, 1862 Muster Roll Remarks: Died in Memphis, Tennessee May 15, 1862; died Irving Hospital measles per Daily Burial Record Book; per Irving Hospital record admitted April 30, 1862 with complaint of measles and died May 10, 1862.

Cook, James   Buried March 13, 1862   Lot/Division 1, #324   Plat Number 324
Arkansas 11 Infantry Regiment Private Company E; name appears on a muster-in roll with muster-in date of July 18, 1862; per Overton Hospital March 1862 Register of Deaths died March 11 pneumonia.

Cook, Joseph   Buried April 24, 1862   Lot/Division 1, #491   Plat Number 491
Texas 3 Regiment Company K and died Irving Hospital congestive fever per Daily Burial Record Book; no compiled service record found; per Irving Hospital record admitted April 21, 1862, with complaint of congestive fever and died April 24, 1862.

Cook, S. P. C.   Buried February 12, 1862   Lot/Division 1, #262   Plat Number 262
Maxey's Regiment Company D and died Overton Hospital lung congestion per Daily Burial Record Book; no compiled service record found in Texas 9 (Young's/Maxey's) Infantry Regiment.

Cook, T. H.   Buried May 4, 1862   Lot/Division 2, #46   Plat Number 596
Arkansas 18 (Carroll's) Infantry Regiment Private (Lynch's) Company G; enlisted March 2, 1862, Little Rock, Arkansas age 21; per March to June 1862, Muster Roll Remarks; Died at Memphis May 5, 1862; died Overton Hospital typhoid fever and pneumonia per Daily Burial Record Book.

Cooley, Robert N.   Buried May 3, 1903   Lot/Division 1, #537   Plat Number 537
Tennessee 11 Infantry Regiment Private Company A; enlisted May 10, 1861, Nashville, Tennessee; grave stone: 1841 1903; died age 62 per Daily Burial Record Book; died May 2, 1903, Memphis, Tennessee per *Confederate Veteran*, Volume XI, November 1903, page 517, indicating had left three children in Desha, Arkansas when came to the hospital.

Cooper, James Alexander   Buried April 18, 1862   Lot/Division 1, #468   Plat Number 468
Missouri 5 (McCown's) Infantry Regiment Private Company A; enlisted January 1, 1862, Springfield, Missouri; per July & August

1862 Muster Roll Remarks: Died at Memphis, Tennessee April 15, 1862; per Historic Roll: Native of Ash County, North Carolina, age 30, Carpenter, and resident of Warrensberg, Johnson County, Missouri when enlisted and remarks that he participated in campaign in Arkansas and taken sick and died at Memphis, Tennessee April 15, 1862, Company I, McCowan's Regiment Company I, and died Overton Hospital pneumonia per Daily Burial Record Book.

Cooper, Thomas   Buried October 14, 1861   Lot/Division 1, #105   Plat Number 105
Arkansas 13 Infantry Regiment Company E and died Southern Mothers Hospital pneumonia per Daily Burial Record Book; no compiled service record found.

Copeland, Thomas W.   Buried October 7, 1861   Lot/Division 1, #66   Plat Number 66
Arkansas 9 Infantry Regiment Private Old Company I; enlisted July 27, 1861, Pine Bluff, Arkansas; per July 27 to November 1, 1861, Muster Roll Remarks: Died in Memphis the 9 October 1861; died Southern Mothers Hospital per Daily Burial Record Book.

Corder, Phillip T., Sr.   Buried April 14, 1862   Lot/Division 1, #446   Plat Number 446
Tennessee 15 Infantry Regiment Corporal Company G; enlisted June 5, 1861 Union City, Tennessee; per January to May 1862 Muster Roll Remarks: Wounded Battle of Shiloh April 6, 1862, and died April 13, 1862; wounded at Shiloh per Daily Burial Record Book; Cemetery record indicates "Jr." but compiled service record for P. T. Corder, Jr., 1 Sergeant Company G Tennessee 15 Infantry Regiment, indicates January 1 to May 1, 1862, Muster Roll Remarks: Present, May/June 1862 Muster Roll Remarks: Present, July/August 1862, Muster Roll Remarks: Deserted, and September/October 1862 Muster Roll Remarks: Dropped.

Cothran, Samuel M.   Buried April 5, 1862   Lot/Division 1, #417   Plat Number 417
Arkansas 11 Infantry Regiment Wagoner Company E; enlisted July 18, 1861 Benton, Arkansas; record contains a claim by mother, Mary W. Cothran, dated December 24, 1863; per Overton Hospital March 31, 1862, Register of Sick and Wounded admitted March 23; died Overton Hospital typhoid fever and pneumonia and Company C per Daily Burial Record Book.

Cottingham, Jeff   Buried April 29, 1862   Lot/Division 1, #519   Plat Number 519
Arkansas 20 (King's) Infantry Regiment Captain Company E; enlisted March 1, 1862 Washington, Arkansas; per March 1 to May 2, 1862, Muster Roll Remarks: Died at Memphis April 29, 1862; name appears on Register of Claims indicating that filed by Attorney G. D. Royston, January 20, 1863, with indication that died in Memphis, Tennessee; affidavit in record indicating that left widow and five children.

Cotton, James Richard   Buried November 15, 1909   Plat Number N6
Mississippi 9 Infantry Regiment Private (Old) Company K/Sergeant (New) Company K; enlisted February 19, 1861, Horn Lake, Mississippi, age 20; per Tennessee Confederate Pension application S9549 born Shelby County, Tennessee 1839; per widow's (Mary V. Hinds Cotton) Tennessee Confederate Pension W2990 died November 14, 1909; died age 68 per Daily Burial Record Book.

Cottrell, George   Buried May 2, 1862   Lot/Division 2, #19   Plat Number 569
Arkansas 23 (Adams') Infantry Regiment Private Company I; enlisted March 12, 1862, Jonesboro, Arkansas; per March 12 to June 30, 1862, Muster Roll Remarks: Died of measles at Memphis, Tennessee the 2nd day of May 1862; name spelled "Cotrell" in Daily Burial Record Book.

Cowan, Samuel S.   Buried April 17, 1862   Lot/Division 1, #465   Plat Number 465
Tennessee 154 Senior Infantry Regiment Private Company H; enlisted April 26, 1861 age 35; per January to July 1862, Muster Roll Remarks: Died in Memphis April 14 of wounds received at the Battle of Shiloh; per Register of Soldiers Killed in Battle Born in Georgia; per Battle of Shiloh casualty list for unit reported in April 24, 1862, *Memphis Daily Appeal*, page 1, column 5, wounded; 1826 1862 on grave stone; per Irving Hospital record admitted April 10, 1862, with complaint of left arm and died April 17, 1862.

Craft, Moses M.   Buried June 5, 1862   Lot/Division 2, #285   Plat Number 835
Texas 32 (Crump's Battalion) Cavalry Regiment Private (Bennett's) Company G; enlisted August 5, 1861, Lamar County, Texas; per February 28 to August 31, 1862, Muster Roll Remarks: Private in Memphis, Tennessee; per January & February 1863, Muster Roll Remarks: Private at Memphis, Tennessee April 1862, and not heard from since; unit Bennett's Company, Miller or Jones Battalion and died Overton Hospital pneumonia per Daily Burial Record Book; per Overton and Irving Hospital Register 1861 – 1862 admitted April 26, 1862, with complaint of diarrhea.

Crawford, Charles M.   Buried February 17, 1862   Lot/Division 1, #267   Plat Number 267
Arkansas 1 (Colquitt's) Infantry Regiment Private Company B; enlisted May 6, 1861, Little Rock, Arkansas age 31 Blacksmith.

Creason, William R.   Buried November 13, 1861   Lot/Division 1, #189   Plat Number 189
Tennessee 40 (Walker's) Infantry Regiment Private Company I; enlisted September 10, 1861, Madison, Arkansas age 18; per November & December 1861, Muster Roll Remarks: Died on the 12 of November 1861, at Memphis; per September 23, 1861, to October 5, 1862, Muster Roll Remarks: Died at Camp Johnson near Memphis in November; died camp congestive chill per Daily

Burial Record Book; Walker's Regiment indicated as an Arkansas unit in Daily Burial Record Book.

Creel, J. C.   Buried October 1, 1861   Lot/Division 1, #28   Plat Number 28
Died Southern Mothers Hospital per Daily Burial Record Book and no unit indicated; not James Creel Arkansas 4 Battalion Infantry or James C. Creel Arkansas 7 Cavalry Regiment as both were alive after 1861 per compiled service records.

Crittenden, E. A.   Buried October 19, 1861   Lot/Division 1, #114   Plat Number 114
Arkansas 12 Infantry Regiment Company B and died camp measles age 19 per Daily Burial Record Book; no service record found.

Crofford, John Alexander   Buried April 6, 1925   Plat Number N59
Tennessee 3 (Forrest's) Cavalry Regiment (McDonald's Battalion) Private Company D; enlisted August 25, 1863, Chattanooga; per Tennessee Questionnaire of Civil War Veterans #15240 filed July 2, 1917, born June 21, 1846; died age 78 per Daily Burial Record Book; removed to Confederate Soldiers Rest February 25, 1932, from Chapel Hill Lot 650/771 so location appears out of place based on the sequence of dates of burials of name stones but location is correct based on date moved to Confederate Soldiers Rest; widow (Kate Hill Crofford) filed for a Tennessee Confederate Pension (W8354); member Confederate Historical Association; sketch in Mathes book, pages 72 and 245.

Crook, T. W.   Buried April 14, 1862   Lot/Division 1, #445   Plat Number 445
No unit indicated in Daily Burial Record Book; possibly T. K. Crook Tennessee 28 Infantry Private Company E who was killed April 6, 1862, at the Battle of Shiloh.

Crouse, Franklin   Buried May 6, 1862   Lot/Division 2, #81   Plat Number 631
Arkansas 18 (Carroll's) Infantry Regiment Private Company B; enlisted March 1, 1862 Princeton, Arkansas; per March to June 1862, Muster Roll Remarks: Died in Memphis about May 5, 1862; died Overton Hospital per Daily Burial Record Book.

Crow, John M.   Buried September 30, 1861   Lot/Division 1, #62   Plat Number 62
Arkansas 9 Infantry Regiment Private Company A; enlisted July 25, 1861, Pine Bluff, Arkansas; per July 25 to November 1, 1861, Muster Roll Remarks: Died at Southern Mothers Home September 30, 1861, Memphis, Tennessee; died Southern Mothers Hospital lung congestion age 21 per Daily Burial Record Book.

Culberson, John Hugh   Buried October 9, 1927   Plat Number N47
South Carolina 3 Infantry Battalion Private Company C; enlisted March 22, 1862, Columbia, South Carolina; per Tennessee Confederate Pension application #14852 died October 8, 1927; per widow's (Mary Lizette Lavrez) Tennessee Confederate Pension application #8888 dated November 4, 1927, born February 14, 1848, Marietta, Georgia, enlisted December 1861, at Laurens, South Carolina in Company C South Carolina 3 Infantry, discharged April 26, 1865 at Greensboro, North Carolina and died October 8, 1927, Memphis; per application for Membership in Confederate Historical Association, Camp 28, Bivouac 18, United Confederate Veterans, Memphis, born February 14, 1848, Cobb County, Georgia; per sketch in Mathes book enlisted March 1864 as Private Company C South Carolina 3 Cavalry (note actually Infantry); died age 79 per Daily Burial Record Book.

Culpepper, Henry J.   Buried October 14, 1861   Lot/Division 1, #104   Plat Number 104
Arkansas 9 Infantry Regiment Private Company G; enlisted July 27, 1861, Pine Bluff, Arkansas; per July 27 to November 1, 1861, Muster Roll Remarks: Died October 13, relapse of measles, Southern Mothers Memphis; died Southern Mothers Hospital enteritis per Daily Burial Record Book.

Culpepper, John W.   Buried September 5, 1861   Lot/Division 1, #82   Plat Number 82
Arkansas 9 Infantry Regiment Private (Wallace's) Company G; enlisted July 27, 1861, Pine Bluff, Arkansas; per July 27 to November 1, 1861, Muster Roll Remarks: Died September 4 typhoid fever Southern Mothers Memphis; died age 24 per Daily Burial Record Book.

Cummins, Isaac A.   Buried November 22, 1861   Lot/Division 1, #211   Plat Number 211
Arkansas 13 Regiment and died age 28 per Daily Burial Record Book; no compiled service record found; believed to be the J. A. Cummings, Sergeant 13th Arkansas Company F, listed in the Overton Hospital Register 1861 – 186, indicting admitted 11th November with compliant – buttocks and died November 21, 1861, from erysepleatious (sic erysipelatous) inflammation; also listed with same name and information in the "Deaths at Overton Hospital" reported in the November 24, 1861, *Memphis Daily Appeal*, page 4, column 1; name "Isaac A." may be a mistake since the soldier listed just above him in Daily Burial Record Book is "Isaac A. Dean"; name spelled "Cummings" in Cemetery computer index.

Cunningham, D. C.   Buried May 3, 1862   Lot/Division 2, #28   Plat Number 578
Texas 27 (Whitfield's Legion) Cavalry Regiment Private Company F; compiled service record found under David J. Cunningham; enlisted March 7, 1862 Clarksville, Texas; per May & June 1862, Company Muster Roll Remarks: Dead, 15th May, 1862, near Memphis, Tennessee; second initial "E" and died Overton Hospital pneumonia per Daily Burial Record Book; second initial "E" and grave indicated as 38 in Cemetery computer index.

Cupp, Nathan J.   Buried May 3, 1862   Lot/Division 2, #42   Plat Number 592
Arkansas 21 Infantry Regiment Private Company C; enlisted November 18, 1861 Clarksville, Arkansas; per December 1861 to June 1862 Muster Roll Remarks: Placed in Hospital at Memphis April 26, 1862; per September & October 1862 Muster Roll Remarks: Supposed to have died at Memphis, placed there April 26, 1862 and never heard of since; name spelled "Cub" and from Dr. Baily per Daily Burial Record Book and computer index.

Curry, James D.   Buried May 10, 1862   Lot/Division 2, #149   Plat Number 699
Louisiana 12 Infantry Regiment Private Company D; enlisted February 10, 1862 Montgomery, Alabama; per compiled service record died Fort Pillow, Tennessee; per Daily Burial Record Book died Overton Hospital typhoid fever and Company K; May 8, 1862 on grave stone.

Curtic, J. R.   Buried February 27, 1862   Lot/Division 1, #272   Plat Number 272
Arkansas 10 Infantry Regiment Company C; enlisted July 24, 1861 Springfield, Arkansas; no rank in compiled service record; per Muster Roll Remarks: Died Memphis, Tennessee February 28, 1862; per Overton Hospital February 28, 1862 Register: Died 26 February 1862; name "J. C. Curtin" in Daily Burial Record Book and computer index.

Dalton, Daniel Webster "Kit"   Buried April 5, 1920   Plat Number N35
Captain; no compiled service record found and not found in Confederate general index; per his book *Under the Black Flag*. Lockard Publishing Company, Memphis, TN, 1914, page 10, born January 23, 1843, in Logan County, Kentucky near the Red River; also per his Book, page 12, while visiting uncle in Huntington (Huntingdon), Tennessee joined Company G, Seventh Tennessee, Captain Aiden (Aden) in Command; per article in April 4, 1920, *The Commercial Appeal* Memphis died April 3, 1920, at age 77 but age 78 indicated in death notice in same paper; further per newspaper joined Forrest forces at beginning of War and Forrest made him a Captain; when troops in Kentucky, given a furlough, failed to return and joined guerrillas because of abuse to family by Federals and outlaws; see also "Past Times" article in January 19, 1995, *The Commercial Appeal* Memphis; after War was a member of James Gang; spouse Amanda Ellison Dalton; per Kentucky Military records a D. and B. F. Dalton (not Kit) from Logan County, Kentucky served as privates in Company I Kentucky 8 Infantry Regiment; 1843 1920 on tombstone; listed in Roster of Guerrillas Who, at One Time or Another, Rode with William Clarke Quantrill in Carl W Breihan's Book *Quantrill and His Civil War Guerrillas* (Promontory Press, New York City, 1959); not found Missouri compiled service rolls for Quantrill's Company; listed in "Touring historic Elmwood Cemetery" (Brochure and Map of Historic Gravesites) #68; listed in "Touring Historic Elmwood Cemetery" Brochure (January 2000)#14; sketch #7 in Elmwood *Civil War Tour* booklet (2012).

Daly, William L.   Buried April 9, 1862   Lot/Division 1, #430   Plat Number 430
Louisiana 25 Infantry Regiment Private Company H; enlisted March 19, 1862, New Orleans, Louisiana; died Overton Hospital pneumonia, name spelled "Daily" and Company D per Daily Burial Record Books; name spelled "Daley" on grave stone and on one card in compiled service record; February 8, 1862, date of death on grave stone.

Dardenno, Andrew   Buried April 7, 1862   Lot/Division 1, #425   Plat Number 425
Arkansas 18 (Carroll's) Infantry Regiment Private (Owen's) Company K; enlisted February 22, 1862, at Pine Bluff, Arkansas and died at Overton Hospital Memphis April 10, 1862, per March 9 to June 23, 1862, Muster Roll; name spelled "Dirdan" and died Overton Hospital per Daily Burial Record Book and computer index.

Davenport, Jesse D.   Buried May 11, 1862   Lot/Division 2, #166   Plat Number 716
Texas 32 (Crump's Battalion) Cavalry Regiment Private Company I; enlisted February 22, 1862 Linden, Texas; per February 22 to August 31, 1862 Muster Roll Remarks: Left at Hospital in Memphis; per January & February 1863 Muster Roll Remarks: Died at Memphis, Tennessee June 20, 1862 (note difference); unit Crump's Arkansas Regiment and at Markam's rubella per Daily Burial Record Book; second initial "C" in Cemetery computer index.

Davenport, Moses   Buried May 11, 1862   Lot/Division 2, #165   Plat Number 715
Texas 32 (Crump's Battalion) Cavalry Regiment Private Company I; enlisted February 22, 1862 Linden, Texas; per February 22 to August 31, 1862 Muster Roll Remarks: Left at Hospital in Memphis; per January & February 1863 Muster Roll Remarks: Died June 21, 1862 (note difference); unit Crump's Arkansas Regiment and at Markam's of rubella per Daily Burial Record Book.

Davidson, J. F.   Buried October 1, 1861   Lot/Division 1, #63   Plat Number 63
Arkansas 13 Infantry Regiment and died Southern Mothers Hospital typhoid fever per Daily Burial Record Book; no compiled service record found.

Davidson, W. C.   Buried May 12, 1862   Lot/Division 2, #172   Plat Number 722
Texas 32 (Crump's Battalion) Cavalry Regiment Private Company I; enlisted February 22, 1862 Linden, Texas; per February 22 to August 31, 1862 Muster Roll Remarks: Left at Hospital Memphis, Tennessee; died Overton Hospital congestive fever per Daily Burial Record Book.

Davidson, W. M.   Buried November 1, 1861   Lot/Division 1, #155   Plat Number 155
Arkansas 8 Infantry Regiment Private New Company D; enlisted September 10, 1861 Camp Price, Arkansas age 22; no information in compiled service record on death, last record card dated September 1861; died State Hospital per Daily Burial Record Book.

Davis, Clarence W.   Buried April 28, 1862   Lot/Division 1, #513   Plat Number 513
J. B. Clark's Battalion Captain Steven Casper's Company and died Overton Hospital pneumonia per Daily Burial Record Book; no compiled service record found.

Davis, Nathan   Buried May 13, 1862   Lot/Division 2, #186   Plat Number 736
Arkansas 23 (Adams') Infantry Regiment Private (Harris') Company F; enlisted March 27, 1862 Jacksonport, Arkansas; per March 27 to June 30, 1862 Muster Roll Remarks: Died May 16, 1862 at Memphis; Company J in Daily Burial Record Book.

Davis, Samuel T.   Buried August 22, 1861   Lot/Division 1, #12   Plat Number 12
Mississippi 44 (Blythe's 1 Battalion) Infantry Regiment Private (Du Berry's) Company C; enlisted July 11, 1861, Memphis, age 21; per August 8 to November 1861, Muster Roll Remarks: Died at Mothers Home, Memphis, Tennessee, August 21, 1861; listed in report of August 1861, Deaths at Southern Mothers Hospital in September 10, 1861, *Memphis Daily Appeal*, page 3, column 3; per report: Captain Dewberry's (sic Du Berry) Company Blythe's Mississippi Battalion, from Calhoun County, Mississippi and died August 21, 1861, congestive fever; funeral reported in August 23, 1861, *Memphis Daily Appeal*, page 4, column 1; died age 21 per Daily Burial Record Book.

Davis, W. G.   Buried March 12, 1862   Lot/Division 1, #321   Plat Number 321
Arkansas 9 Infantry Regiment Private Company C; records found as "Glen/Glenn W. Davis"; enlisted December 25, 1861 Pine Bluff; Remarks on all compiled service records cards state absent on sick furlough but no death information and last muster roll card dated March 1 to May 1, 1862; no "W. G." or any variation in this regiment records; per Overton Hospital March 1862 Register of Deaths initials "W. G." and died March 11 of pneumonia; died of typhoid fever per Daily Burial Record Book.

Davis, William M.   Buried April 8, 1862   Lot/Division 1, #428   Plat Number 428
Texas 9 (Young's/Maxey's) Infantry Regiment Private Company G; enlisted October 8, 1862, Tarrant, Texas, age 18; per March 1862 Regimental Returns: Private at Memphis, Tennessee March 8, 1862; per Overton Hospital March 31, 1862 Register of Sick and Wounded admitted March 6, 1862; per April 1862 Regimental Returns: Died of pneumonia April 18, 1862 in camp; died Overton Hospital pneumonia per Daily Burial Record Book.

Dawes, John   Buried October 14, 1861   Lot/Division 1, #73   Plat Number 73
Arkansas 12 (Gant's) Regiment and died camp age 32 per Daily Burial Record Book; believed to be John Davis, Arkansas 12 (Gantt's) Infantry Regiment Private Company F, who per July 29, 1861 to October 1, 1862, Muster Roll died at Memphis and his father, Isaacs Davis, filed a claim pursuant to his death.

Dean, Isaac A.   Buried November 22, 1861   Lot/Division 1, #210   Plat Number 210
Arkansas 6 Regiment Company F and died Southern Mothers Hospital phthisis pulmonalis age 26 per Daily Burial Record Book; no Isaac A. Dean found in Arkansas 6 Infantry Regiment but there was a J. A. Dean, Arkansas 6 Infantry Regiment Private Old Company F, who per Muster Roll dated September 12, 1861, at Pitman Ferry enlisted May 30, 1861, at Little Rock and remarks that sick at Pitman Ferry - Absent; name "Isaac A." may be a mistake since the soldier listed just after him in Daily Burial Record Book is "Isaac A. Cummins."

Dempsey, John J.   Buried November 28, 1861   Lot/Division 1, #228   Plat Number 228
Tennessee 2 (Walker's) Infantry Regiment Private Company D; enlisted April 26, 1861, Memphis; per March & April 1862, Muster Roll Remarks: Died November 28, 1861, from wounds received at Belmont, Missouri; per January 1862, Muster Roll Remarks: Died December 1, 1861; per November 29, 1861, *Memphis Daily Appeal*, Local Matters, page 4, column 1, died November 28, 1861, Overton Hospital; included in list of deaths at Overton Hospital in the December 1, 1861, *Memphis Daily Appeal*, page 4, column 1; per Daily Burial Record Book died Southern Mothers Hospital enteritis with unit indicated as Arkansas 9 Infantry in Cemetery Single Grave Book and computer index; per Overton Hospital record admitted November 15, 1861, with complaint of head (fractured skull) and died November 28, 1861.

Demuth, George   Buried August 11, 1918   Plat Number N31
Alabama 13 Infantry Regiment Private Company A; enlisted April 25, 1861 Bridgeport, Alabama; captured at Gettysburg July 1, 1863; prisoner at Fort Delaware; released May 16, 1865; died age 85 per Daily Burial Record Book.

Denton, Frank Desha   Buried January 5, 1926   Plat Number N41
Arkansas 8 Infantry Regiment (Desha's Battalion) Sergeant/2 Lieutenant New Company H; enlisted July 1861 per one compiled service record card and November 6, 1861 Pocahontas, Arkansas per another; per Tennessee Confederate Pension application #14830 born November 23, 1841 Independence County, Arkansas; per Tennessee Questionnaire of Civil War Veterans enlisted in Arkansas 7 Infantry Battalion organized by uncle, F. W. Desha, which was consolidated with Arkansas 8 Infantry Regiment in

May 1862; per January 6, 1926 *The Commercial Appeal* Memphis died January 5, 1926, age 84, born Batesville, Independence County, Arkansas November 23, 1841 and husband of Martha Lewis Denton; member of Confederate Historical Association, Camp 28, Bivouac 18, Memphis; no sketch in Mathes book.

Denton, John B.   Buried April 26, 1862   Lot/Division 1, #501   Plat Number 501
Texas 27 (Whitfield's Legion) Cavalry Regiment Private Company K; enlisted March 20, 1862 Polk County, Arkansas; per March 20 to April 30, 1862 Muster Roll Remarks: Died in Hospital at Memphis April 25; died Overton Hospital pneumonia per Daily Burial Record Book.

Deny, James A.   Buried July 19, 1915   Plat Number N25
No unit indicated and died age 76 per Daily Burial Record Book.

Dickinson, Henry   Buried June 9, 1862   Lot/Division 2, #287   Plat Number 837
Arkansas 30 Regiment Company C and died State Hospital per Daily Burial Record Book; no compiled service record found.

Dickson, Barton   Buried January 17, 1909   Plat Number N5
Alabama 16 Infantry Regiment Captain Company A; enlisted July 11, 1861, Cherokee, Alabama; per widow's (Nillie Mayes) Tennessee Confederate Pension application (W2325) born October 31, 1836, Franklin County, Alabama and died January 15, 1909; died age 72 per Daily Burial Record Book; member Confederate Historical Association; sketch in Mathes book, page 84; death (January 15, 1909) mentioned in *Confederate Veteran* Volume X, October 1909, page 520 in "Death List of Memphis Historical Society" between January 1, 1909, and July 1, 1909.

Dickson, James R.   Buried August 1, 1861   Lot/Division 1, #87   Plat Number 87
Tennessee 7 Cavalry Regiment Private (White's) Company (Logwood's 6 Cavalry Battalion); enlisted June 14, 1861, Memphis; died prior to Tennessee 7 Cavalry Regiment formal organization on April 1, 1862; died Overton Hospital per Daily Burial Record Book; not listed in the Letter to the Editor, *Memphis Daily Appeal*, April 1, 1887, page 9, column 2, that list the original members of the Tennessee Mounted Rifles.

Dier, Andrew J.   Buried March 16, 1862   Lot/Division 1, #336   Plat Number 336
Arkansas 12 Infantry Regiment Private Company J; enlisted July 24, 1861, Arkadelphia, Arkansas; per July to October 1862, Muster Roll Remarks: Died at Memphis (day and month illegible) 1862; per Overton Hospital March 1862 Register of Deaths died March 15, 1862, with complaint of pneumonia; name spelled "Dyer" on Overton Hospital Register, Daily Burial Record Book and computer index, grave stone and some muster roll entries in compiled service record.

Dierman, Daniel   Buried August 6, 1861   Lot/Division 1, #50   Plat Number 50
Hindman's Regiment per Daily Burial Record Book; not found Arkansas 2 (Hindman's) Infantry Regiment; does not appear to be Rueben Dearman Arkansas 2 (Hindman's) Infantry Regiment Private Company H who enlisted June 10, 1861, at Helena, Arkansas age 39 and per June 10 to August 31, 1861, Company Muster Roll remarks sick at Camp Hardee and per Register of Payment to Discharged Soldiers discharged August 19, 1861, and paid September 11, 1861.

Ditchler, G. W.   Buried April 28, 1862   Lot/Division 1, #514   Plat Number 514
Missouri 2 Regiment Company C and died Overton Hospital pneumonia per Daily Burial Record Book; no compiled service record found; no "Ditchler" found in Confederate general index.

Dixon, Claiborne   Buried November 2, 1861   Lot/Division 1, #159   Plat Number 159
Tennessee 40 (Walker's) Infantry Regiment Private Company C; enlisted September 13, 1861 Montgomery, Alabama; per November & December 1861, Muster Roll Remarks: Died November 1, 1861, at Camp Johnson near Memphis; died camp per Daily Burial Record Book; not found in Lindsley's Annals 39 & 40 Consolidated Infantry Regiment Official Memorial Roll.

Dobbs, Benjamin O.   Buried May 1, 1862   Lot/Division 2, #7   Plat Number 557
Arkansas 19 (Dockery/Smead's) Infantry Regiment Sergeant Company G; enlisted March 1, 1862 Hillsboro, Arkansas; per March 1 to June 30, 1862 died May 5, 1862, at Memphis, Tennessee; second initial "M" in Cemetery computer index.

Doherty, James   Buried April 25, 1862   Lot/Division 1, #494   Plat Number 494
Arkansas 1 (Colquitt's) Infantry Regiment Private Company D; enlisted May 1, 1961 Pine Bluff, Arkansas age 23; on list dated April 28, 1862, near Corinth of men in Regiment who lost their arm in the engagement of April 6 & 7, 1862, at Shiloh; per Register of Killed & Missing at Battle of Shiloh wounded April 6, 1862 in arm severely; wounded Battle of Shiloh and died Irving Hospital per Daily Burial Record Book; name listed in Irving Hospital report in April 15, 1862, *Memphis Daily Appeal*; per Irving Hospital record admitted April 13, 1862, with complaint of right arm and died April 24, 1862.

Donnell, A. L.   Buried May 25, 1862   Lot/Division 2, #266   Plat Number 816
Missouri 6 Regiment Company H, Federal and died Overton Hospital erysipelas per Daily Burial Record Book; no compiled service

record found; not listed in Cemetery Alpha Book; not found either Confederate or Union general indexes or Confederate or Union Missouri 6 Infantry compiled service record rolls; spelling variation checked but not found; possibly Alexander Leo Donnell who was born October 6, 1837, in Wilson County, Tennessee, and who was living in Hickory County, Missouri when 1850 census was taken and the brother of Lemuel Amzi Donnell who served in the Missouri State Guard and Missouri 11 Infantry Regiment and who stated in a short sketch in the *Reminiscences of the Boys in Gray 1861-1865* Volume 1 (Sketches of several hundred Confederate veterans, residing in Texas, giving particulars of their war service) that was compiled by Miss Mamie Yeary and published for the author by Smith & Lamar, Publishing House M.E. Church, South, Dallas, Texas, 1912, that his brother died in Memphis just after the battle of Shiloh.

Donohoe, Thomas   Buried April 14, 1862   Lot/Division 1, #447   Plat Number 447
Tennessee 2 (Walker's) Infantry Regiment Private Company I; enlisted April 26, 1861 Memphis; per undated Muster Roll Remarks: Died at Memphis January 1862; per August to November 1861 Muster Roll Remarks: enlisted May 12, 1861 Fort Harris; per Reports in April 10,1862 and April 13, 1862 *Memphis Daily Appeal* wounded Battle of Shiloh; per April 15, 1862 *Memphis Daily Appeal* Irving Hospital report right leg shattered by a shot and died April 13, 1862; per Irving Hospital record admitted April 10, 1862 with complaint of right leg and died April 14, 1862; name crossed out in Daily Burial Record Book and name not listed in Cemetery Alpha Book, Single Grave Book or computer index.

Dorr, Frederick   Buried December 23, 1861   Lot/Division 1, #251   Plat Number 251
Vol. Co. M. Artillery Corps in Daily Burial Record Book; Mo. Vol. Artillery Corps in original list prepared by Cemetery Office; no compiled service record found; not found Confederate general index.

Dorrough, John G.   Buried May 7, 1862   Lot/Division 2, #91   Plat Number 641
Arkansas 18 (Carroll's) Infantry Regiment Private Company H; enlisted March 3, 1862 Little Rock, Arkansas; per March to June 1862 Muster Roll Remarks: Died May 3, 1862; name spelled "Dunrough" Hospital in Daily Burial Record Book and computer index and died Overton per Daily Burial Record Book.

Douglas   Buried February 7, 1863   Lot/Division 2, #338   Plat Number 888
No first name, unit or other information in Daily Burial Record Book.

Dowdy, John T.   Buried June 4, 1862   Lot/Division 2, #283   Plat Number 833
Jeff Thompson's Command (McDonald's) Company; Str National noted in Daily Burial Record Book; believed to be John T. Dowdy, Private, Captain McDonald's Company, Missouri Light Artillery who enlisted March 13, 1862, at Camp Defiance and per Company Muster Roll dated May & June 1862, died at Randolph; this Company was part of the General Jeff Thompson's command prior to and at the Battle of Memphis June 6, 1862; the Confederate Transport *New National* was captured by the Union at the Battle of Memphis.

Downey, J. M.   Buried November 19, 1861   Lot/Division 1, #202   Plat Number 202
Tennessee 13 Infantry Regiment Private Company G; enlisted May 24, 1861, Jackson, Tennessee age 21; per May 2, 1863, Muster Roll Remarks: mortally wounded at Battle of Belmont November 7, 1861; wounded Battle of Belmont, Missouri per casualty list reported in November 13, 1861, *Memphis Daily Appeal*; per report in November 15, 1861, *Memphis Daily Appeal* arrived at Overton Hospital November 4, 1861; per Overton Hospital report in November 20, 1861, *Memphis Daily Appeal*, page 4, column 1, died November 19, 1861, with note that was wounded near the hip and died from lock jaw caused by the wound; died November 19, 1862, and Company A per list of deaths at Overton Hospital in November 24, 1861, *Memphis Daily Appeal*; per Overton Hospital record admitted November 15, 1861, with complaint of tetanus and died November 19, 1861; 1840 1861 on grave stone.

Downs, E. G.   Buried May 17, 1862   Lot/Division 2, #229   Plat Number 779
Arkansas 4 Infantry Battalion Private Company E; enlisted March 1, 1862 El Paso, Arkansas/Olive Creek, Arkansas; per March 1 to April 30, 1862 Muster Roll Remarks: Left in Memphis at hospital April 29, 1862; per December 31, 1862 to February 28, 1863 Muster Roll Remarks: Left at Memphis hospital sick April 29, 1862, not returned; per February 13 to April 30, 1863 Muster Roll Remarks: Dropped from the roll cause absent without leave considered a deserter; died typhoid fever per Daily Burial Record Book.

Doyle, Wiley   Buried November 11, 1861   Lot/Division 1, #180   Plat Number 180
Tennessee 2 (Walker's) Infantry Regiment Private Company E; enlisted May 11, 1861 Camp Walker; per Muster Roll Remarks: Killed November 7, 1861 Battle of Belmont, Missouri; wounded at Battle of Belmont, Missouri per casualty report in November 13, 1861 *Memphis Daily Appeal*; 1839 1861 on grave stone.

Dozier, D. M.   Buried November 15, 1861   Lot/Division 1, #193   Plat Number 193
Arkansas 12 Infantry Regiment Company A and died State Hospital per Daily Burial Record Book; no compiled service record found.

Drake, John B.   Buried August 21, 1875   Lot/Division 2, #383   Plat Number 933
Tennessee 3 (Forrest's) Cavalry Regiment Private Company A; originally enlisted Tennessee 154 Senior Infantry Regiment Private Company B May 14, 1861, at Randolph, Tennessee age 24 and present on August 14-November 1, 1861, Muster Roll; per Tennessee 3 (Forrest's) Cavalry (McDonald's Battalion) Regiment record enlisted May 4, 1861, at Randolph, Tennessee, captured near Raleigh January 1, 1864, sent to Military Prison Alton, Illinois, transferred to Camp Douglas August 23, 1864, and released May 11, 1865; per August 21, 1875, *Memphis Daily Appeal* died August 20, 1875, aged 39; died age 40 per Daily Burial Record Book; member Confederate Historical Association; per sketch in Mathes book born Shelby County, Tennessee, descendant of General James Robertson (the Father of Tennessee), enlisted April 16, 1861, died August 20, 1875, and buried in the Confederate Lot in Elmwood Cemetery; listed in *Reminiscences of the Civil War* by John Hallum, Tunnah & Pittard, printers, 1903, as member of Bluff City Grays; listed in June 6, 1878, *Memphis Daily Appeal* article "OUR DEAD HEROES" covering the unveiling of the Confederate Monument and Decoration of Graves at Elmwood as then one of twenty-eight members of the Bluff City Grays, Company B of the 154 Senior Infantry Regiment and Company A of Forrest's Old (Third) Cavalry Regiment buried at Elmwood; listed as one of the "comrades who sleep at Elmwood cemetery" in the article "Veterans in Council" in *Memphis Daily Appeal*, May 12, 1881, page 4, column 4, concerning the meeting of the surviving members in the city of the old Bluff City Grays to appoint the necessary committees for the purpose of making special decoration on the graves of their dead comrades at Elmwood and Calvary cemeteries on Sunday next, Memorial Day; listed in "A COMPLETE ROSTER OF THE BLUFF CITY GREYS" located in the Memphis Room of the Memphis/Shelby County Public Library and Information Center Central Library with notation "Prisoner of War. Died at Memphis" and buried in Elmwood; see Notes of Interest - Bluff City Grays.

Duffo, Stephen M.   Buried March 30, 1862   Lot/Division 1, #394   Plat Number 394
Tennessee Captain Shelton's Company Volunteers per Cemetery record; no compiled service record found.

Dumas, John C.   Buried May 5, 1862   Lot/Division 2, #51   Plat Number 601
Arkansas 25 (Turnbull's) Infantry Regiment Private Company E; enlisted March 10, 1862 Jacksonport, Arkansas; per March 10 to June 30, 1862 Muster Roll Remarks: left in hospital in Memphis, Tennessee; per May 1 to June 30, 1862 Muster Roll Remarks: Private Memphis April 1863 (sic), never paid; died Overton Hospital pneumonia per Daily Burial Record Book.

Dunn, John C.   Buried September 29, 1861   Lot/Division 1, #5   Plat Number 5
Mississippi 22 (Bonham's) Infantry Regiment Private Company E; enlisted August 12, 1861 Iuka, Mississippi age 24; per August to November 1861 Muster Roll Remarks: Died Memphis September 27, 1861 of measles; died State Hospital per Daily Burial Record Book.

Dunn, T. J.   Buried March 21, 1862   Lot/Division 1, #362   Plat Number 362
Arkansas 11 Infantry Regiment Private Company A; enlisted November 7, 1861 Saline County, Arkansas; per November 1, 1861 to September 21, 1862 Muster Roll Remarks: Absent at capture of Island 10, present locality unknown; per Overton Hospital March 1862 Register of Deaths died March 20 of pneumonia; see also Arkansas 11/17 Consolidated Infantry Regiment.

Dunn, W. O.   Buried March 8, 1862   Lot/Division 1, #304   Plat Number 304
Arkansas 10 Infantry Regiment Private Company D; no enlistment in compiled service record; per March & April 1862 Muster Roll Remarks: Private in Nashville February, no report; per Overton Hospital February 28, 1862 Register admitted February 24, 1862 with no complaint noted; died Overton Hospital per Daily Burial Record Book.

Dunnigan, James   Buried December 2, 1862   Lot/Division 2, #319   Plat Number 869
No unit or other information in Daily Burial Record Books; name spelled both "Dunnigan" and "Dunningan" in Cemetery computer index.

Dupuy, John J.   Buried December 1, 1898   Lot/Division 1, #542   Plat Number 542
Tennessee 4 Infantry Regiment Private/Lieutenant Company A; enlisted June 14, 1861, Randolph, Tennessee; appointed Adjutant Arkansas 12 Infantry April 7, 1863; on list of wounded at Battle of Shiloh reported in April 16, 1862 *Memphis Daily Appeal*; death notice in November 30, 1898 *The Commercial Appeal* Memphis, page 3, indicating that died November 29, 1898 in his office; also per November 30, 1898 article a Virginian by birth, born 1838, educated at Hampden-Sidney College and post graduate work at Cumberland University at Lebanon, Tennessee, at outbreak of War enlisted in Shelby County Grays of Memphis (Company A Tennessee 4 Infantry Regiment), after War settled in Bolivar, Hardeman County, Tennessee and took up the practice of law, 1870 elected as Attorney General for the District, served two eight year terms, at end of second term moved to Memphis, was a member of the Confederate Historical Association and took an active part in its meetings; funeral notice on page 5 of December 1, 1898 *The Commercial Appeal* Memphis indicating to be buried in Elmwood Cemetery Confederate Lot; died November 28, 1898 per *Confederate Veteran* Volume 38, page 207 or Volume 7, page 172; name spelled "Dupray" in Cemetery record books and "Duhuy" in computer index; member Confederate Historical Association and sketch in Mathes book; died suddenly November 28, 1898 per Mathes enlarged edition Introduction; died age 56 per Daily Burial Record Book; per article in November 28, 1868, *Memphis Daily Appeal*, page 2, John J. Dupuy of Bolivar, Tennessee married Sarah C. Baskerville on November 24 at her father's (Colonel Charles Baskerville) residence in Noxubee County, Mississippi.

Dutton, Peter   Buried June 17, 1862   Lot/Division 2, #293   Plat Number 843
Texas 2 (Moore's) Infantry Regiment Private Company C; enlisted August 13, 1861 Camp McCraven, Texas; per March & April 1862 Muster Roll Remarks: Absent sick in Hospital and wounded Shiloh April 7; per July & August 1862 Muster Roll Remarks: Wounded at Shiloh, sent to Hospital and not heard from since; per September & October 1862 Muster Roll Remarks: General Hospital Houston, Texas; per January & February 1863 Muster Roll Remarks: Sent to Corinth Hospital, not since heard from and dropped from the roll January 10, 1863; wounded and died State Hospital per Daily Burial Record Book.

Dyal, G. W.   Buried October 1, 1861   Lot/Division 1, #98   Plat Number 98
Tennessee 4 Infantry Regiment Private Company G; enlisted May 15, 1861, Ripley, Tennessee Age 24; per January 20, 1864, Muster Roll Remarks: Died August 15, 1861, at Memphis; died Southern Mothers Hospital marasmus per Daily Burial Record Book; name spelled "Dial" in Daily Burial Record Book and computer index, *Tennesseans in the Civil War* Part 2, on grave stone and one card in compiled service record.

Earwin, J. C.   Buried April 1, 1862   Lot/Division 1, #406   Plat Number 406
Tennessee 42 Regiment and from Bolivar, Tennessee per Daily Burial Record Book; no compiled service record found; J. C. Erwin Private Company H Tennessee Cavalry 1834 1862 on grave stone; not J. C. Erwin, Tennessee 2 (Ashby's) Cavalry Regiment, Private Company H, as he was still living in 1865 when troops were surrendered; name spelled both "Earwin" and "Erwin" in Cemetery computer index.

Easley, James C.   Buried May 9, 1862   Lot/Division 2, #134   Plat Number 684
Arkansas 23 (Adams') Infantry Regiment Private Company H; enlisted March 6, 1862 Arkadelphia, Arkansas; per March 6 to June 30, 1862, Muster Roll Remarks: Died May 9, 1862 Memphis.

Eckles, Benjamin E.   Buried August 1, 1923   Plat Number N38
Tennessee 38 Infantry Regiment Private/Corporal Company D; enlisted October 11, 1861, Camp Abington, Tennessee; per Daily Burial Record Book died age 80; 1849 1923 on grave stone (note age difference with Cemetery record); name spelled "Ekels" in Cemetery computer index.

Edgecomb, Melvin   Buried November 25, 1861   Lot/Division 1, #218   Plat Number 218
Tennessee 2 (Walker's) Infantry Regiment Private Company H; enlisted April 26, 1861, Memphis; per Muster Roll Remarks: Killed Accidentally Columbus, Kentucky; per December 1, 1861, *Memphis Daily Appeal*, page 4, column 1, died November 24, 1861, Overton Hospital and no second "E" in last name; per notice in November 26, 1861, *Memphis Daily Appeal* died November 25, 1861, Overton Hospital and had skull fractured by a refractory mule; per Hospital record admitted November 15, 1861, with complaint of head (from Waggon (sic) running over him) and died November 24, 1861; first name "Alvin" in Daily Burial Record Book and computer index; 1839 1861 on grave stone; record found Tennessee 2 (Walker's) Infantry Regiment and not Tennessee 2 Infantry Battalion as indicated in *Tennesseans in the Civil War*; there is also a William Edgecomb in compiled service records of Tennessee 2 (Walker's) Infantry Regiment Private Company H with same enlistment and muster roll remark that died in Memphis in hospital November 24, 1861; only William Edgecomb found in Lindsley's Annals, therefore possibly the same individual.

Edwards, James J.   Buried May 6, 1862   Lot/Division 2, #73   Plat Number 623
Arkansas 19 (Dockery/Smead's) Infantry Regiment Private (Clayton's) Company E; enlisted March 1, 1862, Hot Springs County by Captain Clayton; per March 1 to June 30, 1862, Muster Roll Remarks: Absent sick; per September & October 1862, Muster Roll Remarks: Sent to Hospital April 24, 1862, never heard from since; per January & February 1863 Muster Roll Remarks: Died or deserted, sent to Hospital April 24, 1862, never heard from since; King's Regiment Clayton's Company and died Overton Hospital per Daily Burial Record Book; per company regiment compiled service record cards Clayton's Company E was formerly Company I King's Regiment Arkansas Infantry.

Edwards, William B.   Buried October 6, 1861   Lot/Division 1, #31   Plat Number 31
Arkansas 9 Infantry Regiment Private (Gantt's) Old Company I; enlisted July 27, 1861, Pine Bluff, Arkansas; per July 27 to November 1, 1861, Muster Roll Remarks: Died in Memphis the 9 October 1861; died Southern Mothers Hospital chronic diarrhea per Daily Burial Record Book; second initial "R" in Daily Burial Record Book and computer index.

Ehretsman, Joseph   Buried May 1, 1862   Lot/Division 2, #8   Plat Number 558
Gallimard's Company Sappers & Miners 2 Sapper; enlisted May 17, 1861, New Orleans, Louisiana; per Muster Roll Remarks: Absent sick in Memphis Hospital April 29, 1862; from Fort Pillow per Daily Burial Record Book.

Elam, W. S.   Buried October 24, 1911   Plat Number N12
Kentucky 2 Cavalry Regiment (2 Battalion Mounted Riflemen) Private Companies A/I; enlisted October 21, 1862, Floyd County, Kentucky age 21; captured near Buffington, Ohio July 19, 1863, (this was during General Morgan's famous raid through Indiana and Ohio); sent to Prison at Camp Morton, Indiana; released April 4, 1865; per Tennessee Confederate Pension application #12869 born October 24, 1842, McCracken County, Kentucky; died age 70 per Daily Burial Record Book; 1841 1911 on grave stone (note birth year difference); member Confederate Historical Association (joined July 17, 1895)and active member of Company A, United

Confederate Veterans; per sketches in Mathes book (both editions) enlisted November 18, 1861, in Jones Battery of Memphis and served at Columbus, Island 10 and Corinth and was in the second day's fight at Shiloh; was transferred to Waters' Battery, and was with Bragg's Army in Kentucky, after Battle of Perryville transferred to Company I, 2 Kentucky Cavalry, Morgan's Old Squadron.

Elliott, Mark L.   Buried December 4, 1861   Lot/Division 1, #238   Plat Number 238
Arkansas 12 Infantry Regiment Private Company F; enlisted July 26, 1861, Arkadelphia; per July to October 1862, Muster Roll Remarks: Died Memphis; per Register on Claims of Deceased Soldiers father, H. H. Elliott, made claim that indicated died at Memphis, Tennessee but no date indicated; died camp per Daily Burial Record Book.

Ellis, William   Buried July 10, 1861   Lot/Division 1, #90   Plat Number 90
Claiborne's Regiment; not found Confederate 7 Cavalry (Claiborne's Regiment Partisan Rangers) or Confederate 1 Cavalry (Claiborne's Regiment Confederate Cavalry) or Arkansas 15 (Cleburne's-Polk's-Josey's) Infantry Regiment which was organized at Mound City, Arkansas in May 1861, and first called 1 (Cleburne's) Regiment when organized for State service.

Elmore, James L.   Buried May 3, 1862   Lot/Division 2, #41   Plat Number 591
From G. Falls per Daily Burial Record Book; possibly James Elmore Tennessee 22 Infantry Regiment who enlisted July 22, 1861, Trenton, Tennessee age 19 and who per March & June 1862, Muster Roll Remarks was absent sick in hospital.

Embree, William   Buried May 7, 1862   Lot/Division 2, #101   Plat Number 651
General Steins' (possibly Brigadier General Alexander E. Steen, Missouri State Guard) Bodyguard (Cooper's) Company and died typhoid fever and Bailey's per Daily Burial Record Book.

Embry, Mitchell A.   Buried December 21, 1895   Lot/Division 1, #538   Plat Number 538
Confederate Cavalry Wood's Regiment Sergeant Company E; enlisted October 14, 1861, Memphis age 21; detailed as Hospital Nurse; died age 56 per Daily Burial Record Book; name spelled "Emory" in Daily Burial Record Book and computer index; unit also known as Mississippi 1 Cavalry Regiment and Wirt Adams' Cavalry Regiment; grave stone: January 12, 1840 December 12, 1895.

Emmerson, Thomas J   Buried September 27, 1861   Lot/Division 1, #61   Plat Number 61
Arkansas 9 Infantry Regiment Private (Haseslip's) Company F; enlisted July 25, 1861 Pine Bluff, Arkansas; per July 25 to November 1, 1861, Muster Roll Remarks: Died September 27, 1861, Memphis, Tennessee; died typhoid fever age 27 per Daily Burial Record Book.

Erkridge, George C.   Buried May 3, 1862   Lot/Division 2, #39   Plat Number 589
Arkansas 19 (Dockery/Smead's) Infantry Regiment Private Company A; enlisted February 26, 1862 Lewisville, Arkansas; per February 25 to June 30, 1862 Muster Roll Remarks: Died at Memphis, Tennessee May 6, 1862; name spelled "Eskridge" in Daily Burial Record Book and computer index; died Overton Hospital per Daily Burial Record Book.

Eubank, Richard Presley   Buried August 26, 1864   Lot/Division 2, #350   Plat Number 900
Missouri 2 Cavalry Regiment Private Company A; per Historic Roll for the unit dated April 24, 1865, farmer and age 25 when enlisted May 1, 1863, at Panola, Missouri, native of Cooper County, Missouri, with remarks: "Was member of Cole's Company, Brown's Regiment, 6 Division Missouri State Guard. Participated in battle Boonville, Missouri, Carthage, Lexington. He returned to Missouri aided in raising and organizing a company of which he was a Lieutenant of. When he reached the army of the Trans-Mississippi Department, he resigned and came to this Regiment. He participated in the battle of Salem, Collierville, Tennessee, Wyatt, Mississippi, Collierville, Tennessee, Moscow, Tennessee, Senatobia (2nd), Fort Pillow, Tennessee, Harrisburg, Abbeville, Mississippi and was mortally wounded in the attack on Memphis, Tennessee 21 August 1864, fell into the hand of the enemy, who recognized him, was supposed to have murdered him, as his head was badly cut up with sabers"; "R Eubanks" and killed but unit not indicated in Daily Burial Record Book; name indicated as "R. P. Ebrams" in Cemetery Single Grave Book; listed ("R. P. Eubank") in Elmwood 1874 book as Confederate soldier buried in Elmwood who was citizen of Memphis or vicinity, which may not be correct as 1860 Cooper County, Missouri census shows Richard P. Eubank, age 24, as resident along with two of his brothers, Joseph James Eubank and John Robert Eubank (killed near Collierville, Tennessee August 15, 1863), who also served in Missouri 2 Cavalry Regiment Company A.

Evans, Caleb J.   Buried April 15, 1862   Lot/Division 1, #450   Plat Number 450
Arkansas 14 (McCarver's) Infantry Regiment Private Company C; enlisted September 1, 1861 Pocahontas, Arkansas; no death noted in record; last muster roll dated November 1, 1861, to January 31, 1862, with remarks that present; wounded per Cemetery Daily Burial Record Book; per card in Arkansas 21 Infantry records, Private Company A, enlisted September 7, 1861 Pocahontas and per May & June 1862 Muster Roll Remarks: Died April 14, 1862; Arkansas 21 Infantry was formed by consolidation of four companies from 14 (McCarver's) Infantry Regiment and six Companies from Arkansas 17 (Lemoyne's) Infantry Regiment.

Evans, Crawford L.   Buried October 9, 1861   Lot/Division 1, #102   Plat Number 102
Arkansas 9 Infantry Regiment Private Company C; enlisted July 25, 1861 Pine Bluff, Arkansas; per July 25 to November 1, 1861

Muster Roll Remarks: Died October 8 at Mothers Home Memphis, Tennessee; died Southern Mothers Hospital pneumonia, age 21 and Company I per Daily Burial Record Book.

Evans, Ezekiel   Buried October 1, 1861   Lot/Division 1, #40   Plat Number 40
Arkansas 9 Infantry Regiment Corporal Company D; enlisted July 27, 1861, Pine Bluff, Arkansas; per July 25 to November 1, 1861 Muster Roll Remarks: Died on the 1 October State Hospital Memphis, Tennessee; died State Hospital per Daily Burial Record Book.

Evans, N.   Buried May 25, 1862   Lot/Division 2, #264   Plat Number 814
South Carolina 10 Regiment Private (Miller's) Company F; enlisted July 19,1861, at age 49 at White's Bridge (Camp Marion near Georgetown, South Carolina); per regimental returns: left in Mississippi and sent to Hospital from Corinth May 20, 1862; initials "J. M." in Daily Burial Record Book and computer index; died age 49 per Daily Burial Record Book.

Evans, John B.   Buried October 31, 1861   Lot/Division 1, #152   Plat Number 152
Hailman's Company and died Southern Mothers Hospital lung congestion age 20 per Daily Burial Record Book; should be Tennessee Bibb's Company Artillery ("Memphis Guerillas") but no compiled service records found and per report from the Camp of Returned Prisoners, Jackson, Mississippi, dated October 3, 1862, all the books and papers belonging to the Company were destroyed at the time the battery's capture at Island 10 April 8, 1862 (see *Tennesseans in the Civil War Part 1*, page 126).

Everett, Francis M.   Buried October 18, 1861   Lot/Division 1, #112   Plat Number 112
Arkansas 8 Infantry Regiment Private New Company B; enlisted September 10, 1861 Camp Price, Northeast Arkansas age 24; per October 31, 1861 Muster Roll Remarks: Sent to General Hospital Memphis (no other information in compiled service record); died State Hospital per Daily Burial Record Book.

Farris, Miles H.   Buried October 22, 1913   Plat Number N19
Georgia 1 Regiment Local Troops, Infantry (Augusta, Georgia) Private Companies D, E & B (Captain George T. Jackson), record found under "Ferris", per Company D Muster Roll for August 15, 1863, to February 29, 1864, enlisted January 20, 1864, at Augusta, Georgia age 31 and remarks that transferred to Company E same regiment and transferred from Augusta Factory, per Company B Muster Roll for May & June, 1864, transferred (assigned) June 29, 1864; Unassigned listed in *Tennesseans in the Civil War Part 2* (Machinist and Pistol Factory); no Tennessee compiled service record found; per Deposition in Tennessee Confederate Pension application(S13729) "… I will state upon corporal oath, that I served the Confederate Government from the beginning of the war between the States; first because I was an expert mechanic, I was set to work in the pistol and sword factory at Columbus, Ga. where I served till we were called out to enlist, in Aug. 1864. I enlisted in "Company D"; George T. Jackson's Augusta Battalion, Wright's Brigade, Hardee's Corp; Capt. Carmichael commanded the company. … (battalion) was disbanded without any formal discharge or parole. …"; letter in pension file from War Department to Tennessee Pension Board dated October 5, 1912, stating that no record of service found; also per pension application born Oglethorpe County, Georgia (no date indicated) and per letter in file died October 23, 1913; per widow's (Mary Rosalie McGinnis) Tennessee Confederate Pension application (W5487), his birth stated as February 28, 1842, in letter dated July 10, 1923, in file from Mrs. J. C. Lovelace to Comptroller of the Treasury inquiring about her pension; died age 71 per Daily Burial Record Book.

Farris, Oliver Buckley   Buried January 3, 1909   Plat Number N4
Tennessee 22 (Barteau's) Cavalry Regiment Major/Captain Company K; enlisted October 1, 1862, Oxford, Mississippi; elected Captain October 1, 1863; recommended for Major May 15, 1864 and appointed February 23, 1865, to rank May 10, 1864; originally enlisted Tennessee 27 Infantry Regiment August 20, 1861, Camp Trenton, Tennessee, age 20, 2 Lieutenant Company C and discharged July 2, 1862, at Tupelo, Mississippi; Company K 22 Cavalry Regiment organized December 1, 1863, at Newbern, Dyer County, Tennessee of men from Obion County; see *Glory and Tears* Obion County, Tennessee 1860 - 1870 by Rebel C. Forrester, Second Edition 1990, Lanzer Printing, Union City, Tennessee: Chapter Six (pages 67 - 69) "Times of Tears" concerning the killing of State Senator Dr. Almon Case in September 1866, for possibly being involved in death of John Farris, brother of Oliver B. Farris, during War, believed July 1864, Company Histories (pages 121-122) on companies in 22 Cavalry Regiment raised, in whole or in part, in Lake and Obion counties, including Company K, and Muster Rolls (pages 137-138) for list of soldiers, including several Farris members, who served in Company K; per family information in personal file in Cemetery individual files born Obion County, Tennessee; information on Farris family and unit also found in Goodspeed's History on Obion County (Goodspeed's History of Tennessee, County Histories, The Goodspeed Publishing Company, Nashville, Tennessee 1887), pages 828, 948 and 949; 22 Cavalry Regiment originally and usually called 2 Cavalry Regiment and also 2 Cavalry Battalion; regiment improperly identified as 2 Infantry in the "Death List of Memphis Historical Society" concerning members who died between the dates January 1, 1909, and July 1, 1909, as reported in *Confederate Veteran* Volume XVII, August 1909 No. 8 page 424 and October 1909 No. 10 page 520; member Confederate Historical Association and sketch in Mathes book; October 8, 1842 January 2, 1909 on grave stone; died age 66 per Daily Burial Record Book; widow, Frances Townsend Farris, received Tennessee Confederate Pension (W2246).

Faust, J.   Buried September 16, 1861   Lot/Division 1, #80   Plat Number 80
Arkansas 9 Infantry Regiment and died State Hospital per Daily Burial Record Book; no compiled service record found; not Captain J. W. Faust Arkansas 33 Infantry Regiment.

Ferguson, Terrence   Buried September 24, 1861   Lot/Division 1, #42   Plat Number 42
Tennessee 2 (Walker's) Infantry Regiment Private Company D; enlisted May 11, 1861 Memphis; per August to November 1861, Muster Roll Remarks: Died in Hospital in Memphis September 20, 1861; died State Hospital per Daily Burial Record Book; note: compiled service record includes a card on a Francis Ferguson with a July 17, 1863, Muster Roll Remark that died August 17, 1861.

Ferguson, William B.   Buried May 7, 1862   Lot/Division 2, #378   Plat Number 928
Arkansas 7 Regiment Lieutenant per Daily Burial Record Book; no compiled service record found Arkansas 7 Infantry Regiment spelled Ferguson; moved to Confederate Rest October 30, 1872, from Chapel Hill Lot 659, Grave #72; name spelled "Farguson" and Grave #72, Lot 2 in Cemetery Single Grave Book; listed in Elmwood 1874 book as Confederate soldier buried in Elmwood who was citizen of Memphis or vicinity; possibly William B. Furgerson, Arkansas 17 (Lemoyne's) Infantry Regiment 2 Lieutenant Company D which has a reference card only in compiled service record rolls (no Fergusons); note Arkansas 17 Infantry Regiment Company D became Company H of Arkansas 21 Infantry Regiment; in Arkansas 21 Infantry Regiment, Ferguson, W. B., 2 Lieutenant Company H, enlisted November 3, 1861, Dardanelle, Arkansas and who per November 1861 to June 30, 1862, Muster Roll Remarks was discharged June 4, 1862, some cards reference 17 Infantry Regiment and both spellings found; there was a William F. Furgerson, Private Company C, Arkansas 7 Infantry Regiment who enlisted July 26, 1861, Camp Shaver, present/sick on July 26 to August 31, 1861, Muster Roll, December 31, 1861, Muster Roll Remarks indicate in Hospital in Nashville and reference card dated January 22, 1862, indicates died.

Fink, John W.   Buried October 6, 1861   Lot/Division 1, #75   Plat Number 75
Arkansas 12 (Gantt's) Infantry Regiment Private (Jones') Company E; enlisted July 20, 1861, at Arkadelphia, Arkansas; per July 20, 1861, to October 1, 1862, Company Muster Roll died October 5, 1861, at Memphis; per Register of claims on deceased soldiers Captain E. C. Jones filed a claim on January 20, 1863 (spelled "Funk" on the Register); per October 6, 1861, *Memphis Daily Appeal,* page 2, column 8, J. W. Funk died October 5, 1861, at residence of Mrs. S. R. Rembert and was member of Hot Springs Riflemen, Arkansas 12 under Command of E. W. Gantt; name spelled "Funk" in Daily Burial Record Book and computer index; died typhoid fever age 23 per Daily Burial Record Book.

Finley, C. M.   Buried May 6, 1862   Lot/Division 2, #69   Plat Number 619
Miller's Battalion Holmes' Company and died Overton Hospital per Daily Burial Record Book; no service record found; unit believed to be Arkansas 8 (Miller's) Infantry Battalion (Holmes') Company G; not found Mississippi 1 (Miller's) Cavalry Battalion.

Fisher, Joseph   Buried May 14, 1862   Lot/Division 2, #210   Plat Number 760
No information in Daily Burial Record Book.

Fitzgerald, T. R.   Buried March 21, 1888   Plat Number N1
No unit indicated, died age 60 and grave first north side of #676 Section 2 per Daily Burial Record Book; mentioned as a member of General Morgan's Kentucky Cavalry in the article "Loving Tributes." *Memphis Daily Appeal,* May 12, 1888, page 2, column 1, on that day's "Decorating the Confederate Graves." but no compiled service record found to confirm.

Fitzhugh, John M.   Buried May 3, 1862   Lot/Division 2, #31   Plat Number 581
Arkansas 20 (King's) Infantry Regiment Private Company D; enlisted March 1, 1862 Little Rock, Arkansas; per March 1 to May 2, 1862, Muster Roll Remarks: Sick in Hospital; per March 1 to June 30, 1862, Muster Roll Remarks: Died at Memphis about 1 May; name appears on Register of Soldiers who died of Wounds or Disease indicating died May 1, 1862, Memphis; died Overton Hospital typhoid fever per Daily Burial Record Book.

Flanigan, John D.   Buried January 24, 1931   Plat Number N56
Tennessee 51 Infantry Regiment Private Company G; compiled service record under J. D. Flancken in same unit; enlisted December 1861; captured at Battle of Missionary Ridge and sent to Louisville, Kentucky then to Rock Island Barracks, Illinois; per Tennessee Confederate Pension application #8935 born December 12, 1842, near Bolton College, Shelby County, Tennessee; per widow's (Epsie Lee Pollard) Tennessee Confederate Pension application (W10057) died January 20, 1931; 1843 1931 on grave stone; died age 88 per Daily Burial Record Book.

Fletcher, John N.   Buried June 2, 1862   Lot/Division 2, #281   Plat Number 831
Missouri 1 Cavalry Regiment Private Company D; enlisted December 24, 1861, Camden, Missouri age 22; per Muster Roll Remarks: Private in Memphis; died Overton Hospital erysipelas per Daily Burial Record Book; per Hospital record admitted May 19, 1862, with complaint of measles but no death indicated.

Florrence, J. H.   Buried November 24, 1862   Lot/Division 2, #313   Plat Number 863
Alabama 34 Infantry Regiment Private Company K; enlisted April 15, 1862 Salem, Alabama age 28; per Muster Roll Remarks: Left on road sick by Wagon Train October 18, 1862, and died November 23, 1862; name spelled "Florence" in Daily Burial Record Book and computer index.

Floyd, A. J.   Buried May 3, 1862   Lot/Division 2, #25   Plat Number 575
No unit indicated and died erysipelas per Daily Burial Record Book.

Fortune, Asa J.   Buried January 10, 1863   Lot/Division 2, #325   Plat Number 875
Mississippi 6 Infantry Regiment Private Company B; enlisted September 3, 1861, Brookhaven, Mississippi; per February 28 to June 30 1863, Muster Roll Remarks: Died in Tennessee, date not known.

Foster, John Thomas   Buried March 3, 1862   Lot/Division 1, #277   Plat Number 277
Mississippi 1 Cavalry Regiment Private Company E (Captain George Polk's Rangers); per Registers related to his death died in transit from Columbus to Memphis on Steamboat "Kentucky" March 1, 1862; father Thomas Foster made claim based on his death and received payment of $93.40; initials "T. J." in Daily Burial Record Book and computer index; died Overton Hospital per Daily Burial Record Book.

Foulk, Adam   Buried March 21, 1862   Lot/Division 1, #361   Plat Number 361
Tennessee 40 (Walker's) Infantry Regiment Private Company I; enlisted September 12, 1861, Madison, Arkansas age 22; per November & December 1861, Muster Roll Remarks: Discharged by Surgeon December 17, 1861, at Fort Pillow; per Overton Hospital March 1862, Register of Deaths died March 20 of pneumonia; name spelled "Fowlkes" in Daily Burial Record Book and computer index; not found in Lindsley's Annals 39 & 40 Consolidated Infantry Regiment Official Memorial Roll.

Fount, James   Buried April 15, 1862   Lot/Division 1, #455   Plat Number 455
Tennessee 2 Regiment per Cemetery Daily Burial Record Book; no compiled service record found in Tennessee Walker's or Robison's 2 Infantry Regiments; not listed in the casualties at the battles of Shiloh April 6 & 7 of the Tennessee 2 Regiment as submitted by Colonel J. Knox Walker and reported in the April 13, 1862, *Memphis Daily Appeal*.

Fox, Peter   Buried October 4, 1861   Lot/Division 1, #100   Plat Number 100
Louisiana Volunteers (Dreper's – possibly Dresser's) Company and died Southern Mothers Hospital chronic dysentery per Daily Burial Record Book; no compiled service record found and not found Booth Louisiana Book; unit; may be Union as Cemetery Alpha Book indicates moved (no date indicated) which appears to be "National" (not found Memphis National Cemetery records) but could be "Louisiana"; no Captain Dreper found in either Confederate or Union general indexes; no Peter Fox found Union Louisiana general index; no record of a second burial in grave #100; not "Fox, Peter" Louisiana 1 Cavalry Regiment Adjutant and General & Staff 1 Lieutenant Adjutant and does not appear to be "Fox, Peter C." Louisiana Militia Continental Regiment (Louisiana Continental Infantry Regiment, Militia).

Frail, Henry   Buried November 8, 1861   Lot/Division 1, #174   Plat Number 174
Warner's Southern Artillery (Tennessee Sterling's Company Heavy Artillery) and died age 26 per Cemetery Daily Burial Record Book; no compiled service record found.

Franklin, William   Buried October 3, 1871   Lot/Division 2, #375   Plat Number 925
No unit indicated and died ulceration of bowels age 37 per Cemetery Daily Burial Record Book.

Freeland, W. J.   Buried May 9, 1862   Lot/Division 2, #128   Plat Number 678
Texas 10 (Locke's) Cavalry Regiment Private Company F; enlisted October 31, 1861 Taos, Texas, age 26; per March & August 1862 Muster Roll Remarks: Died at Memphis, Tennessee June 7, 1862; claim by father in record; per Captain statement in record born Maury County, Tennessee; died Overton Hospital per Cemetery Daily Burial Record Book.

French, J. G.   Buried April 3, 1862   Lot/Division 1, #411   Plat Number 411
Texas 2 (Moore's) Infantry Regiment Private Company K; enlisted October 12, 1861 Galveston, Texas; per March & April 1862 Muster Roll Remarks: Sick in Hospital Memphis since March 31, 1862; per May & June 1862 Muster Roll Remarks: Died in Hospital April 1, 1862; died pneumonia per Cemetery Daily Burial Record Book.

Friar, John   Buried April 22, 1862   Lot/Division 1, #478   Plat Number 478
Arkansas 15 Infantry Regiment Company B and died from pneumonia Overton Hospital per Cemetery Daily Burial Record Book; no compiled service record found.

Fuller, E. R.   Buried May 14, 1862   Lot/Division 2, #201   Plat Number 751
Texas 32 (Crump's Battalion) Cavalry Regiment Private (Bennett's) Company G; enlisted February 26, 1862 Arkansas; per February 28 to August 31, 1862 Muster Roll Remarks: Died at Memphis; died Irving Hospital measles per Cemetery Daily Burial Record Book; per Irving Hospital record admitted April 21, 1862 with complaint of measles and died May 13, 1862.

Galbreath, James   Buried October 13, 1861   Lot/Division 1, #37   Plat Number 37
Arkansas 12 (Gantt's) Infantry Regiment and died camp pneumonia age 25 per Daily Burial Record Book; no service record found.

Galey, Oliver   Buried October 6, 1861   Lot/Division 1, #65   Plat Number 65
Captain Gregory's Company and died State Hospital per Daily Burial Record Book; no compiled service record found.

Gallagher, Thomas   Buried June 17, 1861   Lot/Division 1, #20   Plat Number 20
Tennessee 154 Senior Infantry Regiment Private Company H; per May 6, 1863, Company Muster Roll enlisted April 26, 1861, Memphis, age 25, and remarks: Died of wounds received accidentally May (sic) 12, 1861; per Daily Burial Record Book first name "William," buried Lot 159 Fowler Section Grave #20 and accidentally shot at Randolph HSM (Southern Mothers Hospital); Lot 159 Fowler Section became part of Soldiers Rest as there is no Lot 159 Fowler Section in the Fowler Book or on Cemetery Plat; Fowler Section lots skip from Lot #152/153 to #162; thus he was first burial in Soldiers Rest; death reported in the Sunday, June 16, 1861, *Memphis Daily Appeal*, page 2, column 5, with note was member of Crockett Guard now at Randolph (Camp Randolph near Memphis and later known as Fort Wright); the June 17, 1861, *Avalanche* (Memphis) reported sad occurrence at Randolph — During the drilling of a company of soldiers at Randolph on Friday June 14, 1861, (note date difference between compiled service record and other reports on death), as the men were taking up their guns, which had been grounded, one of them improperly left cocked, went off. The ball entered the neck of the man in front and striking the vertebrae below the back of the head, killed him. He was a young Irishman named Thomas Gallagher and was buried in the City yesterday. His remains were escorted to the grave by several companies of the Home Guard; Tuesday, June 18, 1861, *Memphis Daily Appeal*, page 3, column 2, printed a report from Mrs. S. C. Law, President, Southern Mothers, that there was an intermit on Sunday (June 16, 1861 sic actually Monday June 17, 1861), at Elmwood Cemetery with the Cemetery donating a lot and Flaherty (Funeral Home) donating a coffin and services; June 27, 1861, *Memphis Daily Appeal* reported that a lot was donated at Elmwood Cemetery for burial of Thomas Gallagher of the Crockett Rangers (note difference of company name with earlier article) who died at house of friend J. M. Patrick after receiving a gunshot wound accidentally June 14, 1861, at Camp Randolph; Lindsley's Annals Official Memorial Roll for Tennessee 154 Senior Infantry Company H (The Crockett Rangers) lists Gallagher, Thomas killed May 12, 1861; not listed in Cemetery Single Grave Book.

Gantron, Jack   Buried March 26, 1862   Lot/Division 1, #384   Plat Number 384
Louisiana 21 Regiment Company H unit and died Overton Hospital per Daily Burial Record Book; no compiled service record found and not found Booth Louisiana Book; name spelled "Gantrion" in Cemetery computer index; possibly J. Grandsir, Private Company D Louisiana 21 (Kennedy's) Infantry Regiment, enlisted July 31, 1861, New Orleans, Louisiana, July 31 to October 31, 1861 Muster Roll Remarks Absent Sick in Hospital Memphis; per list of those who died at Overton General Hospital at Memphis during the month of March 1862, "Grantham, Jack" died March 26 of diarrhea and Private Louisiana 21 Regiment Company H.

Garlington, W. H. C.   Buried May 10, 1862   Lot/Division 2, #142   Plat Number 692
Arkansas 19 (Dockery/Smead's) Infantry Regiment Lieutenant Company A; enlisted February 26, 1862 Lewisville, Arkansas; per February 25 to June 30, 1862 Muster Roll Remarks: Died at Memphis, Tennessee May 10, 1862; rank was Junior 2 Lieutenant; died Overton Hospital typhoid fever per Daily Burial Record Book.

Garner, John L.   Buried June 2, 1862   Lot/Division 2, #280   Plat Number 830
Arkansas 19 (Dockery/Smead's) Infantry Regiment Private Company E; enlisted March 1, 1862, Hot Springs, Arkansas; per March 1 to June 30, 1862, Muster Roll Remarks: Absent sick; per September & October 1862, Muster Roll Remarks: Sent to Hospital from Fort Pillow April 24, 1862, never heard from since; per January & February 1862, Muster Roll Remarks: Died or deserted, sent to Hospital April 24, 1862, not heard from since; died Overton Hospital spinal affects per Daily Burial Record Book.

Gentry, C. W.   Buried February 19, 1900   Lot/Division 1, #545   Plat Number 545
No unit indicated and died age 60 and grave north part Number 545 per Daily Burial Record Book.

Gentry, G.   Buried April 25, 1862   Lot/Division 1, #495   Plat Number 495
Whitfield's Texas Rangers Company I and died Overton Hospital pneumonia per Daily Burial Record Book; no compiled service record found; not Green Gentry, Private Company B Texas 27 (Whitfield's Legion) Cavalry Regiment who enlisted February 18, 1862 Fayetteville, Arkansas, and per March & April 1862 Muster Roll Remarks killed in action at Elkhorn March 6, 1862.

Gentry, J. A.   Buried May 13, 1862   Lot/Division 2, #187   Plat Number 737
Lieutenant Jeff Thompson's Brigade Kelsey's Company per Daily Burial Record Book; based on date of death unit should be Missouri 1 Battalion Infantry (Alvah George Kelsey's) Company C, which was at Fort Pillow during May 1862, and operated as marines aboard Confederate defense fleet gunboats; Company C became Company K (Captain Alvah G. Kelsey), Missouri 6 Infantry Regiment, about August 23, 1862, but no record found in either units' compiled service records; soldiers enlisted in Missouri 1 Battalion Infantry (Alvah George Kelsey's) Company C in Pocahontas, Randolph County, Arkansas in March 1862 by Major W. F. Rapley; possibly John A. Gentry whose estate was probated in Randolph County, Arkansas on August 18, 1862, with Hiram Kelsey (brother of Alvah George Kelsey based on genealogy research) as administrator.

Gerris, David   Buried November 22, 1861   Lot/Division 1, #213   Plat Number 213
Arkansas 9 Regiment and died State Hospital per Daily Burial Record Book; no compiled service record found.

Gibson, Samuel   Buried May 14, 1862   Lot/Division 2, #197   Plat Number 747
Miller's Battalion (Jones') Company and died Irving Hospital typhoid fever per Daily Burial Record Book; unit believed to be Arkansas 8 Infantry Battalion (Jones') Company C but no compiled service record found; per Irving Hospital record admitted May 1, 1862 with complaint of typhoid fever and died May 12, 1862.

Giles, Franklin M. J.   Buried August 9, 1861   Lot/Division 1, #49   Plat Number 49
Arkansas 2 (Hindman's) Infantry Regiment Private Company G; enlisted June 10, 1861 Helena age 23; per June 10 to August 31, 1861 Muster Roll Remarks: Deserted, left at Memphis on sick furlough, not since heard of; died age 24 per Daily Burial Record Book.

Giles, G. Y.   Buried November 4, 1861   Lot/Division 1, #162   Plat Number 162
Arkansas 2 Infantry Regiment per Daily Burial Record Book; no compiled service record found; there was a Giles, Franklin M. J., Private Company D, Arkansas 2 Infantry Regiment, who at age 23 enlisted June 6, 1861 at Helena, Arkansas and who per June 10 to August 31, 1861, Company Muster Roll remarks: Deserted, left at Memphis on sick furlough and not since heard of.

Gilliland, Robert S.   Buried May 6, 1862   Lot/Division 2, #76   Plat Number 626
Texas 27 (Whitfield's Legion) Cavalry Regiment Private Company L; enlisted March 21, 1862 Clarksville, Texas; per May & June Muster Roll Remarks: Died about April 30, 1862 in Hospital Memphis, Tennessee; died Overton Hospital pneumonia per Daily Burial Record Book.

Gish, H. H.   Buried May 2, 1862   Lot/Division 2, #21   Plat Number 571
Arkansas 18 Infantry Regiment Private Company C; enlisted March 8, 1862 Des Arc, Arkansas; per March to June 1862 Muster Roll Remarks: Died at Memphis May 2, 1862.

Gleason, Michael   Buried April 14, 1862   Lot/Division 1, #448   Plat Number 448
Tennessee 2 (Walker's) Infantry Regiment Private Company D; enlisted May 11, 1861 Memphis; per March & April 1862 Muster Roll Remarks: Died April 12, 1862 of wounds; per July 17, 1863 Muster Roll Remarks: Deserted May 10, 1862 Corinth, Mississippi; wounded dangerously in neck at the battles of Shiloh April 6 & 7 per the casualties' report of Colonel J. Knox Walker and published in the April 13, 1862, *Memphis Daily Appeal*.

Godwin, B. F.   Buried March 11, 1862   Lot/Division 1, #315   Plat Number 315
Arkansas 11 Infantry Regiment Private Company I; enlisted January 12, 1862 Hot Springs, Arkansas; per October 29, 1861 to September 23, 1862 Muster Roll Remarks; died in Memphis in March 1862 day unknown; believed to be the "Godfrey, Benj." listed on the list of those who died at Overton General Hospital at Memphis during the month of March 1862 which indicates died March 10 of rheumatism and Private Arkansas 11 Regiment Company I; name spelled "Goodman" in Daily Burial Record Book and computer index; died Overton Hospital pneumonia and per Daily Burial Record Book.

Goforth, William   Buried December 1, 1861   Lot/Division 1, #232   Plat Number 232
Arkansas 13 Infantry Regiment Company C and gunshot wound per Daily Burial Record Book; no compiled service record found; died November 30, 1861, Overton Hospital per List of Deaths in December 1, 1861, *Memphis Daily Appeal*, Local Matters, page 4, column 1; per Hospital record admitted November 20, 1862, with complaint of an arm, amputated and died November 30, 1862, and remark Elliott Street; not Alfred Goforth of this unit who died in General Hospital Macon, Georgia April 1, 1862.

Golden, George W.   Buried November 22, 1862   Lot/Division 2, #309   Plat Number 859
Georgia 56 Infantry Regiment (also called 55th Regiment) Private Company E; per Pay Roll showing payment of bounty dated June 13, 1862, enlisted May 1, 1862, Atlanta; per Register of Prisoners of War taken at Harrodsburg, Kentucky shipped to Vicksburg November 12, 1862; appears on a Receipt for Confederate prisoners of war received on board Steamer Metropolitan near Vicksburg, Mississippi December 4, 1862, indicating captured October 11, 1862, at Harrodsburg, Kentucky, age 22, with Remarks: Died November 20, 1862.

Golding, John   Buried May 10, 1862   Lot/Division 2, #148   Plat Number 698
Arkansas 17 (Lemoyne's) Infantry Regiment Private Company H; reference card only in 17 Lemoyne's Infantry compiled service records; records found under Arkansas 21 Infantry, Private Company G that was successor of Company H of 17 Infantry; enlisted February 15, 1862 Prairie County, Arkansas; per April 28, 1862, Muster Roll Remarks: Sick Memphis Hospital and left April 27, 1862; per September & October 1862, Muster Roll Remarks: Died place and date unknown; died Overton Hospital rubella per Daily Burial Record Book.

Goodman, C. B.   Buried September 30, 1861   Lot/Division 1, #27   Plat Number 27
Arkansas 13 Infantry Regiment and from Steamer Key West per Daily Burial Record Book; no compiled service record found.

Goodwin, J. H.   Buried April 15, 1862   Lot/Division 1, #456   Plat Number 456
Arkansas 9 Infantry Regiment Private (Thomasson's) New Company B; enlisted December 18, 1861 Monticello; per December 18, 1861 to March 1, 1862 Muster Roll Remarks: Died at Overton Hospital Memphis April 11, 1862; died pneumonia per Daily Burial Record Book; first name "James" and grave #455 in computer index.

Gowans, Daniel   Buried May 13, 1862   Lot/Division 2, #181   Plat Number 731
Arkansas Miller's Battalion Wilson's Company and died Overton Hospital per Daily Burial Record Book; unit believed to be Arkansas 8 Infantry Battalion (Wilson's) Company F but no compiled service record found.

Gowen, William   Buried April 27, 1862   Lot/Division 1, #505   Plat Number 505
D. W. Carroll's Regiment Company B and died Overton Hospital pneumonia per Daily Burial Record Book; unit should be Arkansas 18 (D. W. Carroll's) Infantry Regiment no compiled service record found.

Gowns, William   Buried April 26, 1862   Lot/Division 1, #500   Plat Number 500
Arkansas 18 (Carroll's) Infantry Regiment Private (Lynch's) Company G; enlisted March 2, 1862 Little Rock, Arkansas age 30; per March to June 1862 Muster Roll Remarks: Died Memphis April 15, 1862; name spelled "Goins" in Daily Burial Record Book and computer index; died Overton Hospital pneumonia per Daily Burial Record Book.

Graden, John   Buried October 31, 1861   Lot/Division 1, #151   Plat Number 151
Phressen's Battalion Company D and died Southern Mothers Hospital enteritis per Daily Burial Record Book; no compiled service record found; name spelled "Grayden" in Single Grave Book and both spelling in Cemetery computer index.

Graham, A. H.   Buried February 11, 1862   Lot/Division 1, #261   Plat Number 261
DeShea's Battalion Company F and died Overton Hospital pneumonia per Daily Burial Record Book; possibly William A. H. Graham, Private New Company B Arkansas 8 Infantry Regiment who originally enlisted age 22 in Arkansas 7 (Desha) Battalion Infantry July 21, 1861, at Jacksonport, Arkansas, detailed as musician per October 31, 1861, Muster-in Roll and deserted May 11, 1862, at Corinth, Mississippi per February 28 to April 30, 1862, Company Muster Roll; Arkansas 7 (Desha) Battalion Infantry consolidated with the Arkansas 8 Infantry Regiment after the Battle of Shiloh; record found in compiled service records of Arkansas 8 Infantry Regiment; Arkansas 7 (Desha) Battalion Infantry was in Memphis in February, 1862.

Graves, Riley   Buried October 8, 1861   Lot/Division 1, #3   Plat Number 3
Captain Gregory's Company and died State Hospital per Daily Burial Record Book; no compiled service record found.

Gray, A. B.   Buried November 21, 1868   Lot/Division 2, #362   Plat Number 912
Captain, Confederate Soldier and moved from Vault Lot 1 Chapel Hill per Cemetery Alpha Book but not found in Chapel Hill Section Book, Daily Burial Record Book or Single Grave Book; believed to be Captain Andrew Belcher Gray, Captain of Infantry and Topographical Engineer, April 1, 1861, ordered to report to General Leonidas Polk at Memphis, Tennessee and served on his staff as Engineering Officer (see *Confederate Staff Officers 1861 -1865* by Joseph H. Crute, Jr., Derwent Books 1982), assigned the task of completing a series of land batteries at Number 10 July 1, 1861, April 1862, killed within the works of Fort Pillow when detailed to reconnaissance the River for the most favorable points for defensive works southward of Fort Pillow and north of Port Hudson (see General G. T. Beauregard's September 24, 1862, correspondence , Official Record, Series 1, Volume 15, Serial No. 21, page 810); per death notice in the April 19, 1862, *Memphis Daily Appeal*, page 1, column 7,"On the 16th instant, at Fort Pillow, Captain A. B. Grey, Engineer corps, C.S. He was killed by the accidental discharge of a gun in the hands of a soldier."; possibly moved to Cemetery after War.

Gray, Columbus D.   Buried November 18, 1861   Lot/Division 1, #198   Plat Number 198
Arkansas 11 Infantry Regiment Company E; name appears on a Company Muster-in Roll with Muster-in Date of July 18, 1861, and remarks "gun D. B. Shot gun"; no other information in compiled service record; died Southern Mothers Hospital congestive chill and Reverend per Daily Burial Record Book.

Graydon, G. W. A.   Buried October 29, 1861   Lot/Division 1, #147   Plat Number 147
Tennessee Bibb's (Hailman's) Company Artillery Corporal; enlisted August 5, 1861 Memphis age, 32; died Southern Mothers Hospital mania a potu and name spelled "Graden" in Daily Burial Record Book and "Grayden" in Cemetery computer index

Green, Joseph   Buried May 26, 1862   Lot/Division 2, #270   Plat Number 820
Tennessee 154 Senior Infantry Regiment Private Company G; enlisted June 3, 1861 Memphis; per May 6, 1863 Muster Roll Remarks: Died May 20, 1862; per Report of Deaths dated October 30, 1863 born North Carolina, died Corinth from wound received at Battle of Shiloh; name spelled "Grew" in Battle of Shiloh casualty list for unit reported in April 24, 1862 *Memphis Daily Appeal*; per Lindsley's Annals died May 20, 1862; per Daily Burial Record Book died May 20, 1862 pneumonia Corinth, Mississippi.

Greer, A. Sidney   Buried May 10, 1862   Lot/Division 2, #143   Plat Number 693
Arkansas 19 (Dockery/Smead's) Infantry Regiment 4 Sergeant Company H; enlisted March 3, 1862 Caney, Arkansas; per March

3 to June 30, 1862 Muster Roll Remarks: Died in Memphis, Tennessee May 9, 1862; died Overton Hospital per Daily Burial Record Book.

Greer, James   Buried April 30, 1862   Lot/Division 2, #2   Plat Number 552
Texas 10 (Locke's) Cavalry Regiment Private Company B; enlisted September 25, 1861 Quitman, Texas, age 51; per March to August 1862 Muster Roll Remarks: Died May 1, 1862; per wife's, Margaret Greer, claim in compiled service record died in Memphis; died Overton Hospital typhoid fever per Daily Burial Record Book.

Gregory, Edward   Buried April 1, 1862   Lot/Division 1, #403   Plat Number 403
Kentucky 7 Mounted Infantry Regiment Private Company K; originally enlisted Arkansas 13 Infantry Regiment Company E October 4, 1861 Desha County, Arkansas; Company transferred to Kentucky 7 Infantry April 1862; per Overton Hospital Register admitted February 28, 1862 and died March 31, 1862; died of chronic diarrhea per Daily Burial Record Book; 1840 1862 inscribed on grave stone.

Griffith, Silvester   Buried May 9, 1862   Lot/Division 2, #117   Plat Number 667
Arkansas 25 (Turnbull's) Infantry Regiment Private Company D; enlisted March 26, 1862 Pocahontas, Arkansas; per March 25 to June 30, 1862 Muster Roll Remarks: Left in Memphis at the Hospital sick; per September & October 1862 Muster Roll Remarks: Sent to the hospital sick April 10 Memphis, Tennessee; first name spelled "Sylvester" on March & April 1863 Muster Roll and afterwards; name spelled "Griffin," Company B and died Overton Hospital in Daily Burial Record Book and both "Griffith" and "Griffin" in Cemetery computer index; not listed in Cemetery Alpha or Single Grave books.

Grimmett, Robert W.   Buried March 18, 1862   Lot/Division 1, #340   Plat Number 340
Arkansas 11 Infantry Regiment Private Companies B/I; enlisted October 29, 1861, Little Rock, Arkansas, age 38; per Overton Hospital March 1862 Register of Deaths name spelled "Grimet, R." and died March 18 of pneumonia; per Arkansas 11/17 Consolidated Infantry Regiment Company A Muster Roll for August 1 to December 31, 1862, remarks: Absent at capture of Island 10. Supposed to be dead.

Griswold, D. B.   Buried June 9, 1876   Lot/Division 2, #385   Plat Number 935
Obituary in *Memphis Daily Appeal*, Saturday June 10, 1876, under Local Paragraphs, page 14, column 2, indicating that he died suddenly on Wednesday night (June 7, 1876), was a Confederate soldier in General Chalmers's command during the late war between the States and that he raised a company and was elected captain and afterwards promoted to the rank of major; per Mortuary Report in *Memphis Daily Appeal*, Sunday June 11, 1876, died age 46 dysentery, name spelled "Griswell"; no compiled service record found for a Major D. B. Griswold but there was a Captain D. B. Griswold, 13 Battery Missouri Light Artillery, and a Lieutenant D. B. Griswold, Lieutenant Flynn's Company Sappers and Miners; D. B. Griswold, Lieutenant 48th Infantry, listed in the *Tennesseans in the Civil War, Part 2*, but no record found; died flux per Daily Burial Record Book.

Grooms, J. C.   Buried April 1, 1862   Lot/Division 1, #402   Plat Number 402
Confederate 1 (King's Battalion) Cavalry Regiment Private (Gray's) 2 Company F; per Company Muster-in Roll dated February 9, 1862, at Memphis enlisted January 10, 1862 Memphis, age 18; per March & April 1862, Muster Roll Remarks: Died; per Daily Burial Record Book died erysipelas; name appears on Overton Hospital's March 31, 1862 Register of Sick and Wounded with second initial "G"; per list of those who died at Overton General Hospital at Memphis during the month of March 1862 died March 31 of erysipelas and Private Grays Company.

Guard, William   Buried April 9, 1862   Lot/Division 1, #429   Plat Number 429
Tennessee 15 Infantry Regiment Captain Genette's Company and died typhoid fever and pneumonia age 24 per Daily Burial Record Book; no compiled service record found; possibly William R. Griffith Private Company B Tennessee 15 Infantry Regiment, enlisted May 17, 1861 Memphis age 27, January to March 1862 Muster Roll Remarks killed by the cars coming from Columbus, Kentucky March 2, 1862, July & August 1862 Muster Roll Remarks killed at Moscow Kentucky (which is south of Columbus, Kentucky); not found Lindsley's Annals; not listed in Cemetery Single Grave Book.

Gunn, Charles H.   Buried August 13, 1868   Lot/Division 1, #34A
Tennessee 154 Senior Infantry Regiment Private Company E; enlisted May 14, 1861 at Randolph, Tennessee; per May 15, 1863 Muster Roll (age 25) Remarks in hospital Rome, Georgia; paroled at Greensboro, NC May 1, 1865; unit not indicated in Daily Burial Record Book but identified in a notice in the *Public Ledger* (Memphis), August 14, 1868, page 3, column 2, under Locals in Brief: "One of the few survivors of the old 154th Tennessee, Mr. Chas. H. Gunn, was buried yesterday."; died consumption age 31 and buried Fowler Section Grave No. 34A per Daily Burial Record Book with Remarks: first division Confederate Interments; not listed in Cemetery Single Grave Book; no grave stone found; listed in Elmwood 1874 book as Confederate soldier buried in Elmwood who was citizen of Memphis or vicinity.

Gunter, John Franklin   Buried April 1, 1940   Plat Number N66
Mississippi 7 Infantry Regiment Private Company A; enlisted August 12, 1861 Franklin County, Mississippi; mustered-in September 27, 1861, Bay St Louis, Mississippi; per June 1862 Regimental Returns: Absent sick since May 25, 1862 at Hazlehurst

Hospital on Post Surgeon Certification; no other information in compiled service record; per March 31, 1940 *The Commercial Appeal* Memphis had 100 Birthday March 29, 1940 and died March 30, 1940; native of Amite, County, Mississippi and lived there much of his life after the War; moved to Memphis six years before his death; see also Mississippi 44 Infantry Regiment Company K; per Daily Burial Record Book grave 4 north of Stone #654; original grave stone deep underground.

Guyton, T. B.   Buried September 15, 1861   Lot/Division 1, #94   Plat Number 94
Arkansas 10 Regiment Jennings's Company and died Southern Mothers Hospital per Daily Burial Record Book; no compiled service record found; note L. B. Jennings was Captain of Company C of Arkansas 10 Infantry Regiment; name spelled "Guyon" in Daily Burial Record Book and Single Grave books and "Gunyon" in Cemetery computer index.

Hackett, John   Buried April 12, 1862   Lot/Division 1, #436   Plat Number 436
Tennessee 154 Senior Infantry Regiment Private Company C; enlisted May 18, 1861 age 28; per May & June 1862 Muster Roll Remarks: Got sick and furloughed March 1, 1862; per May 5, 1863 Muster Roll Remarks: Sent to Hospital February 1862 and deserted; 1833 1862 on grave stone; not found in Lindsley's Annals.

Hackleburn, L. D.   Buried November 16, 1861   Lot/Division 1, #195   Plat Number 195
Arkansas 13 Regiment per Daily Burial Record Book; no compiled service record found.

Haifleigh, Augustus   Buried March 9, 1862   Lot/Division 1, #306   Plat Number 306
Louisiana 13 Infantry Regiment Private Company G; enlisted June 5, 1861 Wax Bayou, Louisiana; present on Roll to October 1861; per Overton Hospital March 1862 Register of Deaths died March 8 of diarrhea and named spelled "Hufleigh, Gus"; name "Hailleigh" in Cemetery computer index.

Haley, David G.   Buried May 15, 1862   Lot/Division 2, #220   Plat Number 770
Arkansas 18 (Carroll's) Infantry Regiment Private (Parrish's) Company H; enlisted March 3, 1862 Little Rock, Arkansas; per March to June 1862 Muster Roll Remarks: Died May 6, 1862; died Overton Hospital typhoid fever per Daily Burial Record Book.

Hall   Buried June 11, 1862   Lot/Division 2, #290   Plat Number 840
Died State Hospital per Daily Burial Record Book.

Hall, James   Buried March 4, 1862   Lot/Division 1, #281   Plat Number 281
Texas 9 (Young's/Maxey's) Infantry Regiment Private Company C; compiled service record under Joseph Hall; no enlistment in record; per March 1862 Regimental Returns: Died at Memphis, Tennessee of pneumonia; per Overton Hospital February 28, 1862 Register of Sick and Wounded admitted February 10, 1862; per Overton Hospital March 1862 Register of Deaths died March 4 of pneumonia; first name "Joseph" in Overton Hospital Registers.

Hall, James O.   Buried April 14, 1862   Lot/Division 1, #444   Plat Number 444
Tennessee 3 (Forrest's) Cavalry Regiment Private Company C; enlisted September 1, 1861 Memphis; per March to June 1862 Muster Roll Remarks: Killed Battle of Shiloh April 7, 1862; per April 15, 1862 *Memphis Daily Appeal* J. O. Hall died April 13, 1862 in Irving Hospital and belonged to Forrest Cavalry; per Irving Hospital record admitted April 12, 1862 with complaint of legs and died April 13, 1862; name spelled "Hail" in Lindsley's Annals.

Hall, Jesse H.   Buried May 7, 1862   Lot/Division 2, #93   Plat Number 643
Arkansas 17 (Lemoyne's) Infantry Regiment Private Company E; enlisted December 21, 1861 Dardanelle, Arkansas; per April 28, 1862 Muster Roll Remarks: Died at Fort Pillow April 26, 1862; died Overton Hospital, from Fort Pillow and name spelled "Haile" in Daily Burial Record Book and computer index; no record found under Arkansas 21 Infantry that was successor of Arkansas 17 Infantry.

Hall, John W.   Buried March 29, 1862   Lot/Division 1, #393   Plat Number 393
Tennessee 5 Infantry Regiment Corporal 2 Company C; enlisted May 20, 1861 Paris, Henry County, Tennessee, age 19; died Overton Hospital per Daily Burial Record Book; 1842 1862 on grave stone.

Hall, Lucilius Marion   Buried April 29, 1862   Lot/Division 1, #518   Plat Number 518
Arkansas 17 (Lemoyne's) Infantry Regiment Private Company E; per Company Muster Roll dated April 28, 1862, enlisted December 21, 1861, Dardanelle, Arkansas, with Remarks: Left sick at Fort Pillow 26 April 1862; no record found under Arkansas 21 Infantry that was successor of Arkansas 17 Infantry (there was a William M. Hall, Arkansas 21 Infantry, Private Company H who enlisted November 3, 1861, Dardanelle, Arkansas and who per November 1861 to June 1862 Muster Roll Remarks died at Memphis May 4, 1862); Company G, died Overton Hospital pneumonia and from Fort Pillow per Daily Burial Record Book.

Halley, A. B.   Buried May 31, 1862   Lot/Division 2, #278   Plat Number 828
Arkansas Keep's Regiment Company G and died Overton Hospital typhoid fever per Daily Burial Record Book; no compiled service record found including none found in Confederate 3 Infantry or Arkansas 18 (Marmaduke's) Captain H. V. Keep's

Company H ; possibly A. F. Halley Arkansas 9 Infantry Regiment or A. B. Hales Arkansas 19 (Dockery's) Infantry Regiment, Private Company C who enlisted February 27, 1862 Columbia County, Arkansas and per February 27 to June 30, 1862 Muster Roll Remarks died at West Point May 5, 1862.

Halton, James R.   Buried June 5, 1862   Lot/Division 2, #284   Plat Number 834
Carroll's Regiment and from Bird Springs per Daily Burial Record Book; no compiled service record found; name spelled "Hallton" in Daily Burial Record Book and computer index.

Hamilton, Isiah   Buried October 15, 1918   Plat Number N32
Mississippi 25 (Martin's) Infantry Regiment (1 Mississippi Valley Infantry Volunteers) Private Company F (Captain Benjamin O'Haver's Company, Martin's Regiment of Volunteers), per Company Muster-in Roll dated August 10, 1861, at Memphis enlisted August 10, 1861, at Memphis, age 26; January 31, 1862, Company became Company F Confederate 2 Infantry Regiment which disbanded May 8, 1862, then Company F consolidated with Company K to form (New) Company C Missouri 1 Infantry; no record found under Confederate 2 Infantry but under Missouri 1 Infantry same enlistment and per July & August 1862, Company Muster Roll remarks absent, wounded and missing since Battle of Shiloh (no other information in record); applied for Tennessee Confederate pension September 9, 1908, (S10507), and indicated wounded and captured at Shiloh and when exchanged joined Kentucky 1 Cavalry but captured again and held prisoner to end of the War and took oath of allegiance at Fort Delaware, per statement in the application file from George T. O'Haver, Memphis Chief of Police and son of Captain Benjamin O'Haver, he knew him in army and in his father's company and saw him when he was shot in legs after Shiloh, in application states that he was born May 5, 1835, in Clark County, Indiana; Kentucky 1 Cavalry Regiment Private Company B, per Company Muster Roll dated January 1 to April 30, 1863, enlisted November 11, 1862, at Chattanooga, Tennessee, captured in Sequatchie Valley, Tennessee October 2, 1863, first sent to Nashville, Tennessee, then Military Prison, Louisville, Kentucky, then Camp Morton, Indianapolis, Indiana, and lastly to Fort Delaware, Delaware where took Oath of Allegiance on June 9, 1865, and released, on oath form stated he was from Shelby County, Tennessee; died age 83 per Daily Burial Record Book; name spelled "Isaiah" in most records.

Hampton, Wade   Buried May 14, 1862   Lot/Division 2, #206   Plat Number 756
Arkansas 23 (Adams') Infantry Regiment Private Company A; enlisted February 26, 1862 Craighead County, Arkansas; per February 26 to June 30, 1862 Muster Roll Remarks: Died May 1862; died Irving Hospital remittent fever per Daily Burial Record Book; per Irving Hospital record admitted May 3, 1862 with complaint of remittent fever and died May 14, 1862.

Hankins, William Wright   Buried December 5, 1861   Lot/Division 1, #239   Plat Number 239
Arkansas 13 (Tappan's) Infantry Regiment Private Company A and died Overton Hospital per Daily Burial Record Book and newspaper reports; no compiled service records found; per December 6, 1861, *Memphis Daily Appeal* died December 5, 1861, Overton Hospital after having received a gunshot wound to elbow shattering the bone to pieces; per December 6, 1861, *Memphis Daily Appeal*, Local Matters, W. R. Hankins, Arkansas 13 Regiment Company A, died December 5, 1861, Overton Hospital; name spelled both "Hankins" and "Hawkins" in Cemetery computer index.

Hannberger, Wiley W.   Buried September 25, 1861   Lot/Division 1, #26   Plat Number 26
Arkansas 11 Regiment and died Southern Mothers Hospital inflammation of lungs age 24 per Daily Burial Record Book; no compiled service record found.

Hanrahan, James   Buried August 31, 1861   Lot/Division 1, #92   Plat Number 92
Mississippi 22 (Bonham's) Infantry Regiment Private Company C; enlisted June 25, 1861 Vicksburg, Mississippi age 28; per July & August 1861 Muster Roll Remarks: Died Memphis August 30, 1861.

Hardee, George W.   Buried April 27, 1862   Lot/Division 1, #509   Plat Number 509
Louisiana 12 Regiment Company K and from a Boat per Daily Burial Record Book; no compiled service record found and not found Booth Louisiana Book; name spelled "Harder" in Cemetery computer index.

Hardeman, Elbert   Buried May 13, 1862   Lot/Division 2, #189   Plat Number 739
Arkansas 19 Infantry Regiment Company B and died Overton Hospital congestive fever per Daily Burial Record Book; no compiled service record found.

Hardin, Powell   Buried May 8, 1862   Lot/Division 2, #113   Plat Number 663
Arkansas 17 Infantry Regiment Company A and died Irving Hospital remittent fever per Daily Burial Record Book; no compiled service record found.

Hardin, William   Buried May 7, 1862   Lot/Division 2, #100   Plat Number 650
Miller's Battalion (Holmes') Company; unit and died Overton Hospital per Daily Burial Record Book; no compiled service record found; unit believed to be Arkansas 8 (Miller's) Infantry Battalion (Holmes) Company G; Wilson's Battalion in Cemetery Single Grave Book (M. R. Wilson became Major of Arkansas 8 Infantry Battalion upon resignation Major John Miller August 8, 1862); not found Mississippi 1 (Miller's) Cavalry Battalion.

Hare, Elijah L.   Buried May 6, 1862   Lot/Division 2, #66   Plat Number 616
Arkansas 19 (Dockery/Smead's) Infantry Regiment Private Company H; enlisted March 3, 1862 Caney, Arkansas; per March 3 to June 30, 1862 Muster Roll Remarks: Died in Memphis, Tennessee May 15, 1862; died Irving Hospital measles and pneumonia per Daily Burial Record Book; per Irving Hospital record admitted April 30, 1862 with complaint of measles and died May 4, 1862.

Harper, James J   Buried April 25, 1862   Lot/Division 1, #489   Plat Number 489
Tennessee 3 (Forrest's) Cavalry Regiment Private Company D "May's Avengers"; enlisted February 27, 1862, Memphis; per March to June 1862 Muster Roll Remarks: Died at Memphis April 24, 1862; initials "J.G." in Daily Burial Record Book and computer index; wounded and died Irving Hospital per Daily Burial Record Book.

Harper, John   Buried November 8, 1862   Lot/Division 2, #307   Plat Number 857
Georgia 34 Infantry Regiment Private Company D; originally enlisted Georgia 8 Infantry Regiment; enlisted Georgia 34 Infantry Regiment May 14, 1862, Chattanooga, Tennessee; captured Wild Cat , Kentucky; shipped to Cairo, Illinois November 18, 1862; per muster roll remarks: died on or about November 8, 1862, as prisoner in Tennessee while on way to Vicksburg, Mississippi; per separate muster roll remarks: died October 25, 1862; prisoner died on his way to Vicksburg per Daily Burial Record Book; died November 7 per list of the prisoners of war who died on board the Federal transport Maria Denning, en route for Vicksburg prepared by Charles Boyd, A. A. Surgeon U.S.N., in charge of sick en route for Vicksburg.

Harper, T. J.   Buried May 10, 1862   Lot/Division 2, #150   Plat Number 700
Colonel Adams' Arkansas Regiment Company I and died Overton Hospital per Daily Burial Record Book; no compiled service record found including not found Confederate Cavalry Wood's Regiment (Mississippi Wirt Adams' Cavalry Regiment - Mississippi 1 Cavalry Regiment) or Arkansas 23 Adams' Infantry Regiment.

Harper, William H.   Buried May 6, 1862   Lot/Division 2, #71   Plat Number 621
Arkansas 25 (Turnbull's) Infantry Regiment Private Company D; enlisted March 5, 1862 Pocahontas, Arkansas; per March 25 to April 30, 1862 Muster Roll Remarks: Is in the hospital in Memphis; per July & August 1862 Muster Roll Remarks: Private at hospital April 18, 1862 Memphis, Tennessee; per January & February 1864 Muster Roll Remarks: Absent Private in Memphis April 18, 1862; one card in record as appearing on a Register of Way Hospital, Meridian, Mississippi; died Overton Hospital pneumonia and initials "G. W." per Daily Burial Record Book; initials "G. W." in Daily Burial Record Book and computer index.

Harrington, William J.   Buried December 1, 1861   Lot/Division 1, #233   Plat Number 233
Tennessee 40 (Walker's) Infantry Regiment Private Company G; enlisted September 23, 1861 Tyddesdale, Arkansas age 20: per November & December 1861 Muster Roll Remarks: Died November 30, 1861 Camp Johnston disease measles and pneumonia; father Andrew J. Harrington filed a claim for settlement in the Office of the Confederate States Auditor for the War Department for pay due at time of death; died measles and pneumonia and from Ferguson's per Daily Burial Record Book; grave stone: 1840 1861.

Harris, Andrew J.   Buried September 3, 1912   Plat Number N14
Mississippi 19 Infantry Regiment Private Company I; enlisted May 25, 1861 Marshall County, Mississippi, age 21; per Tennessee Confederate Pension application #11015 born Marshall County, Mississippi February 23, 1840; per widow's (Lillie Sophonia Harris) Tennessee Confederate Pension application (W4565) died September 2, 1912; died age 72 per Daily Burial Record Book.

Harris, John W.   Buried November 11, 1861   Lot/Division 1, #181   Plat Number 181
Tennessee 13 Infantry Regiment Private Company C "The Secession Guards"; enlisted May 16, 1861, Shelby County, Tennessee; per May 5, 1863, Muster Roll Remarks: Killed Battle of Belmont November 7, 1861; per casualty report born Tennessee; killed at Battle of Belmont, Missouri per casualty report in November 13, 1861, *Memphis Daily Appeal* with second initial "C"; killed per Daily Burial Record Book.

Harris, Joseph   Buried May 8, 1862   Lot/Division 2, #111   Plat Number 661
Missouri 1 Regiment Company H and died Overton Hospital enteritis per Daily Burial Record Book; no compiled service record found; first name "James" in Cemetery computer index; does not appear to be J. E. Harris, Missouri 1 Infantry Regiment, Private Company H, who per Roll of Prisoners of War was captured at Helena, Arkansas July 4, 1863, and sent to General Hospital at Memphis, Tennessee on US Steamer R. C. Wood (no other Harris in Company H).

Harrison, Thomas   Buried September 26, 1861   Lot/Division 1, #41   Plat Number 41
Mississippi 22 (Bonham's) Infantry Regiment Private Company K; enlisted July 28, 1861, Lafayette County, Mississippi; per August to October 1861, Muster Roll Remarks: Died at Memphis, Tennessee September 24; died State Hospital per Daily Burial Record Book.

Harrison, W. B.   Buried May 17, 1862   Lot/Division 2, #228   Plat Number 778
Texas 10 (Locke's) Cavalry Regiment Private Company D; enlisted September 25, 1861 Quitman, Texas; per March to August

1862, Muster Roll Remarks: Private at Memphis, Tennessee; per July & August 1862, Muster Roll Remarks: Private at Memphis April 25, 1862.

Hart, C. F.   Buried May 9, 1862   Lot/Division 2, #129   Plat Number 679
Missouri State Guard (Gant's) Company and died Overton Hospital pneumonia per Daily Burial Record Book; no compiled service record found; there was a Captain S. Gant, Company B, Missouri State Guard Cavalry.

Hartsfield, W. H.   Buried May 9, 1862   Lot/Division 2, #121   Plat Number 671
Arkansas 19 (Dockery/Smead's) Infantry Regiment Company C and died Overton Hospital rubella per Daily Burial Record Book; no "W. H. Hartsfield" found Arkansas 19 (Dockery/Smead's) Infantry Regiment but found "V. S. Hartsfield" Private Company C who enlisted February 27, 1862, Columbia County, Arkansas and who per February 27 to June 30, 1862, Muster Roll Remarks died at Corinth, Mississippi May 23, 1862.

Harwell, Washington   Buried March 17, 1862   Lot/Division 1, #337   Plat Number 337
Confederate 4 (Baker's) Infantry Regiment Private Company F (Captain Joshua Morse's Company "Andy Moore Guard"); per Company Muster-in Roll dated October 15, 1861, at Camp near Memphis, Tennessee enlisted September 8, 1861, at Butler, Alabama age 52; per Overton Hospital March 1862, Register of Sick died March 16, 1862, of pneumonia; per Register of Officers and Soldiers who died of wounds or disease died March 25, 1862, (note date difference with interment) in Memphis of chronic diarrhea; widow Rachael Abney Harwell claimed and received his pay and commutation due him; regiment (also known as 1st Alabama, Tennessee and Mississippi Infantry) was formed about December 9, 1861, with ten companies: four from Alabama, two from Mississippi, and four from Tennessee; captured at Island 10 April 8, 1862, and after exchange in September, 1862, the companies were reorganized and transferred to other commands; Company F became Company F of the Alabama 54th Infantry Regiment but no record for this regiment as died before transfer; name spelled "Hartwell" in Daily Burial Record Book, computer index.and grave stone; grave in short row north side of Monument.

Hatton, W. H.   Buried March 7, 1862   Lot/Division 1, #290   Plat Number 290
Confederate 1 (King's Battalion) Cavalry Regiment Private (Gray's) 2 Company F; enlisted February 5, 1862, Memphis, age 22; per March & April 1862, Muster Roll Remarks: Died; per Overton Hospital March 1862 Register of Deaths died March 6 of typhoid fever.

Hawkins, James J.   Buried May 3, 1862   Lot/Division 2, #30   Plat Number 580
Arkansas 20 (King's) Infantry Regiment Private Company G; enlisted February 17, 1862, Little Rock, Arkansas; per February 17 to May 2, 1862, Muster Roll Remarks: Left at Fort Pillow sick; per February 17 to June 30, 1862, Muster Roll Remarks: Died Memphis 1 May; name appears on Register of Claims indicating that claim filed January 19, 1863, by widow Elizabeth Hawkins; died Overton Hospital pneumonia and Company B per Daily Burial Record Book.

Hawkins, William L. C.   Buried April 23, 1862   Lot/Division 1, #483   Plat Number 483
Tennessee 4 Infantry Regiment Private Company A; enlisted 15 May 1861 Germantown, Tennessee age 21; per April to June 1862, Muster Roll Remarks: Died April 23, 1862, from wound to right leg received at Battle of Shiloh; on List of Wounded at Battle of Shiloh Reported in April 16, 1862 *Memphis Daily Appeal*; initials "W. S." in list of Shelby Grays in *The Commercial Appeal* Memphis May 15, 1909; not listed in list of Shelby Grays reported in December 7, 1861 *Memphis Daily Appeal*; died Irving Hospital per Daily Burial Record Book; per Irving Hospital record admitted April 14, 1862 with complaint of right thigh and died April 23, 1862; 1839 1862 on grave stone.

Hawthorn, Augustus   Buried March 26, 1862   Lot/Division 1, #381   Plat Number 381
Arkansas 11 Infantry Regiment Private Company D; enlisted December 3, 1861 Bradley County, Arkansas; per November 1, 1861 to September 27, 1862, Muster Roll Remarks: Absent Sick at the time of surrender (this would have been surrender at Island 10 April 8, 1862), present locality not known; per Overton General Hospital March 1862 Register of Deaths initials "M. A." and died March 24 of pneumonia; name spelled "Hathorn" in Daily Burial Record Book and computer index.

Hays, William A.   Buried May 17, 1862   Lot/Division 2, #231   Plat Number 781
Texas 9 (Sim's) Cavalry Regiment Private Company I; enlisted October 14, 1861, Camp Reeves, Texas, age 22; per May & June Muster Roll Remarks: Left in Hospital at Memphis April 25, not heard from since; per September & October 1862, Muster Roll Remarks: Dropped from Roll, left in Hospital at Memphis April 25; name spelled "Haze" in Daily Burial Record Book and computer index; died Overton Hospital per Daily Burial Record Book.

Hefferon, Thomas   Buried February 20, 1930   Plat Number N55
Missouri Snider's Cavalry Battalion Company E; enlisted August 1, 1862, Boone County, Missouri age 37; per Tennessee Confederate Pension application (S16474) first enlisted in Porter's Missouri Cavalry (Missouri 1 NE Cavalry) which was dismounted to become Missouri 9 Infantry (record not found under this unit) and born 1844 New Orleans, Louisiana; per February 20, 1930, *The Commercial Appeal* Memphis died February 19, 1930, age 85 and served under General Sterling Price.

Henderson, Jesse Montgomery　　　Buried March 8, 1862　　　　Lot/Division 1, #300　　　Plat Number 300
Texas 9 (Young's/Maxey's) Infantry Regiment Private Company G; per Company Muster-in Roll dated December 1, 1861, at Camp Rusk, Lamar County, Texas enlisted October 8, 1862, at Tarrant, Texas, age 18; per March 1862, Regimental Returns: Died Memphis, Tennessee pneumonia; per Overton General Hospital, March 1862, Register of Sick died March 7, 1862, of pneumonia.

Henderson, John W.　　　Buried October 15, 1861　　　　Lot/Division 1, #72　　　Plat Number 72
Confederate 4 (Bakers') Infantry Regiment Private Company B (Captain Jonas Griffin's Rifles); per Company Muster-in Roll enlisted August 10, 1861, at Montgomery, Alabama age 24; per Company Muster Roll dated October 31, 1861, remarks: Died of Typhoid Fever at the Southern Mothers Home in Memphis, Tennessee on the 15th of October, 1861; regiment (also known as 1st Alabama, Tennessee and Mississippi Infantry) was formed about December 9, 1861, with ten companies: four from Alabama, two from Mississippi, and four from Tennessee; captured at Island 10 April 8, 1862, and after exchange in September, 1862, the companies were reorganized and transferred to other commands; Company B became Company C of the Alabama 54th Infantry Regiment but no record for this regiment as died before transfer; died Southern Mothers Hospital enteritis and typhoid fever per Daily Burial Record Book.

Henderson, Thomas　　　Buried April 26, 1862　　　　Lot/Division 1, #503　　　Plat Number 503
Captain Warren's Company Price's Division and died camp per Daily Burial Record Book; no compiled service record found.

Hendrix, Daniel　　　Buried April 10, 1862　　　　Lot/Division 1, #431　　　Plat Number 431
Confederate 4 (Baker's) Infantry Regiment Private Company D (Captain Henry Laird's Company "Gulf Rangers"); per Company Muster-in Roll enlisted September 14, 1861, at Montgomery, Alabama age 22; per Overton General Hospital, Memphis, Tennessee Register of Sick dated March 31, 1862, (name spelled "Hendricks") admitted March 27, 1862, but no other information; per Register of Claims of deceased Officers and Soldiers from Alabama which were filed for settlement in the Office of the Confederate States Auditor for the War Department Amy Hendrix (mother per census records) filed claim July 16, 1863, indicating died Memphis, Tennessee (no date or cause indicated); regiment (also known as 1st Alabama, Tennessee and Mississippi Infantry) was formed about December 9, 1861, with ten companies: four from Alabama, two from Mississippi, and four from Tennessee; captured at Island 10 April 8, 1862, and after exchange in September, 1862, the companies were reorganized and transferred to other commands; Company B became Company C of the Alabama 54th Infantry Regiment but no record for this regiment as died before transfer; name spelled "Hendricks" in Daily Burial Record Book and computer index; died Overton Hospital typhoid fever per Daily Burial Record Book; brother Charles served in the same company and he died July 7, 1862, in prison at Camp Douglas, Illinois; two other brothers (Wesley and Samuel) served in the Alabama 33rd Infantry Regiment and died during the War; there is a government stone with death year 1863 for him in the Wesley Chapel United Methodist Church Cemetery in Geneva County, Alabama where his mother is buried but may be memorial as there are also stones for his brothers and others who were probably cousins who served in the War in the cemetery as well; no record of ever being removed from Elmwood.

Henley, J.　　　Buried October 18, 1861　　　　Lot/Division 1, #111　　　Plat Number 111
Arkansas 13 Infantry Regiment and died Southern Mothers Hospital per Daily Burial Record Book; no service record found.

Henly, James M.　　　Buried April 12, 1862　　　　Lot/Division 1, #438　　　Plat Number 438
Missouri 1 Infantry Regiment Private Company I; enlisted August 17, 1861 New Madrid Missouri; per Historic Roll card: age 25, native of New Madrid, Missouri, farmer; per March & April 1862, Muster Roll Remarks: Died Memphis April of wounds received at Shiloh April 6; wounded Battle of Shiloh per Daily Burial Record Book; listed in Battle of Shiloh casualty report for Missouri 1 Infantry, Company I, in April 23, 1862, *Memphis Daily Appeal* as wounded and since died; name spelled "Hanly" in Daily Burial Record Book and computer index.

Henson, John　　　Buried October 2, 1861　　　　Lot/Division 1, #29　　　Plat Number 29
Arkansas 13 Infantry Regiment Company C and died Southern Mothers Hospital pneumonia per Daily Burial Record Book; no compiled service record found.

Henson, W. H.　　　Buried March 7, 1862　　　　Lot/Division 1, #297　　　Plat Number 297
Louisiana 12 Regiment and died Southern Mothers Hospital per Daily Burial Record Book; no compiled service record found and not found Booth Louisiana Book; per Booth Louisiana Book there was a soldier named W. H. Henson, Private Company B, Louisiana 17 Infantry, enlisted September 30, 1861 Camp Moore, Louisiana; per September to November 1861 Muster Roll Remarks: Present, Regimental Return for November 1861 Remarks died November 5, 1861 at Camp Chalmette, Louisiana; per remark in Cemetery record grave in short row north side of Monument.

Higgins, S. S.　　　Buried November 25, 1862　　　　Lot/Division 2, #317　　　Plat Number 867
Florida 7 Regiment per Daily Burial Record Book; no compiled service record found and not found Confederate index or Florida regiments books.

High, Edward Durantz　　　Buried January 21, 1937　　　　　　　Plat Number N64
Georgia Cobb's Legion Cavalry Battalion Company D; enlisted August 10, 1861 Albany, Georgia; captured June 3, 1864; sent to

Elmira, New York July 12, 1864; exchanged October 29, 1864; per Tennessee Confederate Pension application #10421 born October 22, 1843 Anson County, North Carolina; per January 21, 1937 *The Commercial Appeal* Memphis died January 20, 1937, age 97 and born Phelm, Georgia (note birth location difference); per Confederate Historical Association, Camp 28, Bivouac 18, Memphis, application served as Body Escort to General A. P. Hill; no sketch in Mathes book; first name also found as "Edmond"; per Cemetery record grave 2 north of Stone #654.

Hill, Allen L.   Buried May 13, 1862   Lot/Division 2, #193   Plat Number 743
Arkansas 17 (Lemoyne's) Infantry Regiment Private Company C; reference card only in 17 Lemoyne's Infantry compiled service records; records found under Arkansas 21 Infantry, Private Company C that was successor of Company C of 17 Infantry; enlisted March 24, 1862 Pocahontas, Arkansas; per December 1861 to June 1862 Muster Roll Remarks: Placed in hospital at Memphis April 28, 1862; per September & October 1862 Muster Roll Remarks: Died at Memphis hospital May 11, 1862; died Overton Hospital per Daily Burial Record Book; second initial "A" in Daily Burial Record Book and computer index; second initial "S" in Arkansas 21 Infantry compiled service record.

Hill, Benjamin   Buried December 19, 1861   Lot/Division 1, #247   Plat Number 247
Arkansas 12 Infantry Regiment Private Company G; enlisted July 27, 1861; per July to October 1862, Muster Roll Remarks: Died at Memphis December 17, 1861; died Edgewood Hospital age 20 per Cemetery record.

Hill, James   Buried March 29, 1862   Lot/Division 1, #392   Plat Number 392
Tennessee Bankhead's Battery (Tennessee Scott's Light Artillery) and died Overton Hospital per Daily Burial Record Book; no compiled service record found; not James Hill in Scott's Company compiled service records who lived after this soldier's death; may be the "J. W. Hill" on the list of those who died at Overton General Hospital at Memphis during the month of March 1862, indicating died March 29 of diarrhea and Private Bankhead's.

Hill, M. H.   Buried October 21, 1861   Lot/Division 1, #125   Plat Number 125
Arkansas 12 Infantry Regiment Company B and died camp measles age 18 per Daily Burial Record Book; no service record found.

Hogan, John   Buried November 26, 1861   Lot/Division 1, #222   Plat Number 222
Tennessee 8 Regiment per Daily Burial Record Book; no compiled service record found; grave stone: J E Hogan Co C 8 Regt Tenn Cav 1830 1861 but not J. E. Hogan Tennessee 8 Cavalry 2 Lieutenant Company C as he was alive after November 1861; not John Hogan Tennessee 2 (Walker's) Infantry Regiment Company C included in November 15, 1861, *Memphis Daily Appeal* report of November 4, 1861, arrivals at Overton Hospital or two other John Hogans in Tennessee 2 Infantry as records indicate all were alive after November 1861.

Holbert, F. S.   Buried October 26, 1861   Lot/Division 1, #137   Plat Number 137
Arkansas 11 Infantry Regiment Company F and died Southern Mothers Hospital enteritis per Daily Burial Record Book; no compiled service record found; there is a George M. Holbert in this unit (see also 11/17 Consolidated Infantry Regiment) with single card in compiled service record that indicates captured at Island 10 (that would have been April 8, 1862, which was after this soldier's death).

Holcombe, William H.   Buried November 1, 1861   Lot/Division 1, #158   Plat Number 158
Arkansas 7 Infantry Regiment Private Company H; enlisted July 26, 1861 Camp Shaver, Arkansas age 19; per September & October 1861 Muster Roll Remarks: in the hospital Memphis, Tennessee; per December 31, 1861, Muster Roll Remarks: Died in hospital Memphis, Tennessee November 1, 1861; died Southern Mothers Hospital enteritis age 21 per Daily Burial Record Book; name spelled "Holcomb" in Daily Burial Record Book and computer index.

Holden, G. W.   Buried March 8, 1862   Lot/Division 1, #303   Plat Number 303
Kentucky 7 Mounted Infantry Regiment Private (Stubblefield's) Company G; enlisted October 10, 1861, Camp Burnett, Kentucky age 25; per Overton Hospital March 1862 Register Sheffield's Company, admitted February 28, 1862 and died March 7 of rubella; 1837 1862 on grave stone.

Holden, John   Buried November 15, 1861   Lot/Division 1, #35   Plat Number 35
Confederate 4 (Baker's) Infantry Regiment Private Company F (Captain Joshua Morse's Company "Andy Moore Guard"); per Company Muster-in Roll dated October 15, 1861, at Camp near Memphis, Tennessee enlisted September 8, 1861, Butler, Alabama age 19; per Register of Officers and Soldiers who died of wounds or disease died November 14, 1861, of measles in Memphis, Tennessee; regiment (also known as 1st Alabama, Tennessee and Mississippi Infantry) was formed about December 9, 1861, with ten companies: four from Alabama, two from Mississippi, and four from Tennessee; captured at Island 10 April 8, 1862, and after exchange in September, 1862, the companies were reorganized and transferred to other commands; Company F became Company F of the Alabama 54th Infantry Regiment but no record for this regiment as died before transfer.

Hollinsworth, A. W.   Buried March 20, 1862   Lot/Division 1, #353   Plat Number 353
Arkansas 11 Infantry Regiment Private Company B; enlisted July 13, 1861, Benton, Arkansas; per November 1, 1861 to September

23, 1862, Muster Roll Remarks: Sent off sick from Island 10 March 14, 1862, learn he is dead; per Overton Hospital March 1862 Register of Deaths name spelled "Hollingsworth, A.," died March 19 and Company B; Company A in Daily Burial Record Book; second initial "N" and name spelled "Hollingsworth" with a "g" in Daily Burial Record Book and computer index; see also 11/17 Arkansas Consolidated Infantry Regiment.

Hollinsworth, Matthew   Buried April 30, 1862   Lot/Division 1, #520   Plat Number 520
Arkansas 19 Infantry Regiment Company B and died Overton Hospital per Daily Burial Record Book; no service record found.

Holsonback, John R.   Buried May 1, 1862   Lot/Division 2, #14   Plat Number 564
Arkansas 31 (McCray's) Infantry Regiment Private Company B; enlisted December 30, 1861, Van Buren County age 19; per October 30, 1861, to August 31, 1862, Muster Roll Remarks: Died May 1, 1862, in Hospital; McRae's Battalion and died Irving Hospital typhoid fever per Daily Burial Record Book; name spelled "Holsenbach" in Daily Burial Record Book and computer index; per Irving Hospital record name spelled "Holsomback" McRae's Battalion, admitted April 23, 1862, with complaint of typhoid pneumonia and died April 30, 1862.

Honeycut, Francis M.   Buried April 28, 1862   Lot/Division 1, #512   Plat Number 512
Arkansas 23 (Adams') Infantry Regiment Private Company I; enlisted March 15, 1862, Jonesboro, Arkansas; per March 12 to June 30, 1862, Muster Roll Remarks: Died at Memphis April 25, 1862, congestive chill; died camp per Daily Burial Record Book; name spelled both "Honeycut" and "Honeycutt" in Cemetery computer index.

Hopkins, Henry   Buried November 19, 1861   Lot/Division 1, #204   Plat Number 204
Tennessee Crain's Artillery and died Southern Mothers Hospital per Daily Burial Record Book; no compiled service record found; per unit history in *Tennesseans in the Civil War, Part 1*, page 129, no muster rolls found for Crain's Battery and date and place of organization not known (see Notes of Interest on Crain's Artillery).

Horn, D. W.   Buried April 26, 1871   Lot/Division 2, #369   Plat Number 919
Missouri 2 Cavalry Regiment Sergeant Company E; enlisted March 10, 1862, Clarkston, Missouri; per undated muster roll remarks: Wounded at Memphis and since died about September 5, 1864, (this would have been during Forrest's August 21, 1864, raid into Memphis); moved to Elmwood Cemetery from Cane Creek per Daily Burial Record Book; name spelled "Horne" in Cemetery Daily Burial Record and Alpha books and "Mone" in computer index; listed as "E. W. Horne" in Elmwood 1874 book as Confederate soldier buried in Elmwood who was citizen of Memphis or vicinity.

Horton, A. J.   Buried February 17, 1862   Lot/Division 1, #266   Plat Number 266
Texas 9 (Young's/Maxey's) Infantry Regiment Private Company K; enlisted Tollet's Prairie, Texas, age 46 (no date indicated); per Overton Hospital Register of Deaths died February 16, 1862; died Overton Hospital per Daily Burial Record Book.

Horton, Thomas A.   Buried February 22, 1862   Lot/Division 1, #268   Plat Number 268
Texas 9 (Young's/Maxey's) Infantry Regiment Private Company G; enlisted October 8, 1862, Tarrant, Texas, age 28; per March 1862 Regimental Returns: Died Memphis, Tennessee pneumonia; per Overton Hospital Register of Deaths Died February 21, 1862; first initial "J" in Cemetery computer index and "F" in Cemetery Single Grave Book and initials "T. A" in Cemetery Daily Burial Record and Alpha books.

Howell, W. B.   Buried April 15, 1862   Lot/Division 1, #454   Plat Number 454
Arkansas 18 (Carroll's) Infantry Regiment Private (Lynch's) Company G; enlisted March 2, 1862, Little Rock, Arkansas age 20; per March to June 1862, Muster Roll Remarks: Died Memphis April 9, 1862.

Howell, William   Buried April 14, 1862   Lot/Division 1, #449   Plat Number 449
No unit indicated and from Cenotaph (which means empty tomb or War Memorial) per Cemetery record.

Hudson, Henry   Buried November 28, 1861   Lot/Division 1, #227   Plat Number 227
Arkansas 9 Infantry Regiment Private (Henry's) Company C; enlisted July 25, 1861, Pine Bluff, Arkansas; per November 1861 to January 1, 1862, Muster Roll Remarks: Died December 1, 1861, at Memphis, Tennessee; died Southern Mothers Hospital per Daily Burial Record Book.

Hulsey, H. C.   Buried October 27, 1861   Lot/Division 1, #142   Plat Number 142
Arkansas 12 Infantry Regiment Private Company G; per July 27 to October 1, 1862, Company Muster Roll enlisted July 27, 1861, Arkadelphia, Arkansas and Remarks: Died at Memphis November 5, 1861; died camp measles and name spelled "Hulcy" in Daily Burial Record Book and "Huley" in Cemetery computer index.

Hunter, James   Buried March 11, 1862   Lot/Division 1, #314   Plat Number 314
Louisiana 21 Regiment Company I and died pneumonia per Daily Burial Record Book; Overton Hospital March 1862 Register of Deaths indicates died March 9 of rheumatism and Company H; no compiled service record found.

Hunter, John P.   Buried November 12, 1861   Lot/Division 1, #188   Plat Number 188
Tennessee 40 (Walker's) Infantry Regiment Corporal Company K; enlisted October 2, 1861, Camp Johnson near Memphis age 21; per November & December 1861, Muster Roll Remarks: Died November 11, 1861; name appears on Register of Soldiers Killed in Battle or Died of Wounds or Disease that indicates born York District, South Carolina and died November 12, 1861, at Fort Pillow; widow Elizabeth Hunter filed a claim April 20, 1863; Walker's Regiment indicated as an Arkansas unit in Daily Burial Record Book ; died camp measles per Daily Burial Record Book.

Husbands, Henry L.   Buried April 23, 1862   Lot/Division 1, #482   Plat Number 482
Kentucky 3 Mounted Infantry Regiment Private Company D; enlisted July 15, 1861, Camp Boone, Kentucky age 17; per April 16, 1862, *Memphis Daily Appeal* wounded severely at Shiloh; died Overton Hospital and from Paducah, Kentucky per Daily Burial Record Book; first name "Harry" in Cemetery computer index.

Hutto, James   Buried January 9, 1863   Lot/Division 2, #324   Plat Number 874
Alabama 37 Infantry Regiment Company A per Daily Burial Record Book; not Hutto (Hutte), Private Company A, Alabama 37 Infantry who took Oath September 26, 1865; possibly James Hutts, Company ___, Alabama 37 Infantry, with note in compiled service record concerning small pox, G H (General Hospital), Memphis, Tennessee, no other information.

Hutto, Thomas   Buried May 1, 1862   Lot/Division 2, #12   Plat Number 562
Louisiana 25 Infantry Regiment Private Company H; enlisted March 19, 1862, New Orleans, Louisiana age 28; per Muster Roll Remarks: Died Memphis in Hospital of Disease; two dates stated: about April 14, 1862 and April 15, 1862; 1834 1862 on grave stone; not found in Booth Louisiana Book.

Hyden, Matthew Handley   Buried May 14, 1862   Lot/Division 2, #196   Plat Number 746
Arkansas 20 (King's) Infantry Regiment Private Company E; enlisted March 1, 1862, Washington (Hempstead County), Arkansas; per March 1 to May 2, 1862, Muster Roll Remarks: Left at Hospital in Memphis April 1862; last card in compiled service record January & February 1863, Muster Roll with same remark; died Overton Hospital lung congestion per Daily Burial Record Book; 1835 1862 on grave stone; name "William H." in Cemetery computer index, "Wm. H." in Daily Burial Record Book and "W. H." or "M. H." in Alpha Book; per great-grandson, Bill R. Hyden, lived in Hempstead County, Arkansas, left home March 23, 1862, to join Confederate Army with brother and friends, and wife, Jane never knew his fate and waited twelve years before remarrying; Bill R. Hyden along with Gene Hyden wrote in the HEYDON-HAYDEN-HYDEN FAMILIES Quarterly (Volume VI, No. 1, January 1984) the article "He just didn't come back..." about him joining the Army, dying and being buried in Memphis without his family knowing it and his wife having said many times that "he just didn't come back"; granddaughter Ruby Hyden Flowers wrote poem *Ballad of 1862* that she published in 1976 in her book *A Walk in the Garden* (see poem herein) about his fate; obviously family did later found out his fate.

Hyman, S. C.   Buried October 25, 1861   Lot/Division 1, #135   Plat Number 135
Arkansas 7 Regiment Company H, died Southern Mothers Hospital lung congestion and name spelled Hymen in Daily Burial Record Book; no compiled service record found; possibly Samuel Himer Arkansas 7 Infantry Regiment Private Company E who enlisted July 26, 1861, Camp Shaver, Arkansas age 32 and who per December 31, 1861, muster roll remarks died in hospital at Memphis, Tennessee October 25, 1861.

Ing, Richard   Buried September 12, 1919   Plat Number N34
Missouri Farris' Battery Light Artillery (Clark Artillery) Sergeant/Private; enlisted January 10, 1862, Green(e) County, Missouri age 33; per undated Muster Roll Remarks: Deserted near Grenada, Mississippi November 1862, and Preacher from London, England; per Tennessee Confederate Pension application (S3268) enlisted Missouri Clark's Battery and transferred to Colonel Richardson's Staff Tennessee 12 Cavalry; no record found that verifies this but possibly is the Richard Inge, Tennessee 1 Cavalry who was captured near Germantown, Tennessee July 29, 1863, and sent to Provost Marshall Memphis, Tennessee, on Overton Hospital Register of Wounded as admitted August 8, 1863, deserted February 18, 1864, shot while attempting to escape from Hospital February, 1864, claimed British protection and was prisoner previous spring; see also *Medical and Surgical History of the Civil War*, Volume X, pages 525-526, which discusses surgery of wound received August 8, 1863, gunshot fracture (wound) to right shoulder joint and a note on letter he wrote dated March 25, 1874, from Williston, Fayette County, Tennessee to Surgeon General Barnes advising that operation at Overton Hospital was a complete success (note indicates that he was a native of London); per pension application born London, England January 15, 1839, lived at Mason, Tipton County, Tennessee and died September 11, 1919; name spelled "Inge" in Daily Burial Record Book and computer index; died age 84 per Daily Burial Record Book.

Irwin, G. W.   Buried March 27, 1862   Lot/Division 1, #385   Plat Number 385
Arkansas 11 Infantry Regiment Private Company I; enlisted January 15, 1862, Hot Springs, Arkansas; per October 29, 1861, to September 23, 1862, Muster Roll Remarks: Absent sick at Memphis at the time his company was surrendered (this would have been the surrender at Island 10 April 8, 1862); per Overton Hospital March 1862 Register of Deaths died March 26 of rubella; name spelled "Erwin" in Overton Hospital Register, Daily Burial Record Book and computer index and on grave stone.

Irwin, G. W.   Buried December 13, 1861   Lot/Division 1, #246   Plat Number 246

Arkansas 2 Regiment and died State Hospital per Daily Burial Record Book; no compiled service record found; not G. T. (G. S.) Irwin, Arkansas 2 Hindman's Infantry Regiment Private Company I who was captured at Stone's River (Battle of Murfreesboro, Tennessee December 30, 1862) and died January 13, 1863.

Irwin, Thomas   Buried November 7, 1861   Lot/Division 1, #170   Plat Number 170

Arkansas 2 Infantry Regiment and died State Hospital per Daily Burial Record Book; no compiled service record found.

Ivy, J. C.   Buried October 27, 1862   Lot/Division 2, #305   Plat Number 855

Tennessee 42 Infantry Regiment Company G and from Jackson County, Alabama per Daily Burial Record Book; no compiled service record found; possibly James L. Ivy, Corporal 1 Company I, Tennessee 42 Infantry Regiment who enlisted November 13, 1861, at Camp Cheatham, Tennessee, captured Fort Donelson February 16, 1862, sent to Camp Douglas (Chicago), Illinois, Prison Roll dated September 4, 1862, indicates "Sick in Hospital," Prison Roll dated September 29, 1862, indicates "Dead," Register of Soldiers who died indicates born at Jackson County, Alabama and died November 25, 1862, in Arkansas on his way from prison, and note in compiled service record indicates died at Helena, Arkansas 25 November 1862; there was a "John C. Ivey" listed in Jackson County, Alabama Land Record Book; not found in Lindsley's Annals; grave stone "CO H 4 REGT 8 TENN CAV" (Tennessee 8 Smith's Cavalry does not appear to be correct as per compiled service record absent sick in Chattanooga August 1863, and regiment mustered in the field as the 4th Murray's Regiment but officially designated as the 8th Smith's Regiment Cavalry).

Jackson, A. M.   Buried October 20, 1861   Lot/Division 1, #115   Plat Number 115

Arkansas 12 Infantry Regiment Private Company G; enlisted July 27, 1861, Arkadelphia, Arkansas; per July to October 1862, Muster Roll Remarks: Died at Memphis October 19, 1861; died camp per Daily Burial Record Book.

Jackson, J. A.   Buried May 7, 1862   Lot/Division 2, #110   Plat Number 660

Missouri 1 Regiment Company B and died Overton Hospital pneumonia per Daily Burial Record Book; no compiled service record found; there was a Jackson, C. H., Missouri 1 Infantry Regiment, Company C, enlisted August 6, 1861, Memphis, May & June 1862, Muster Roll Remarks: died 30 May of wounds received Battle Shiloh; not listed in Battle of Shiloh casualty report for Missouri 1 Infantry in April 23, 1862, *Memphis Daily Appeal*, page 2, column 2.

Jackson, J. C.   Buried May 5, 1862   Lot/Division 2, #62   Plat Number 612

Arkansas 19 (Dockery/Smead's) Infantry Regiment Company E/F; enlisted March 1, 1862, El Dorado; per March 1 to June 30, 1862, Muster Roll Remarks: Died at Hernando 12 May; no rank in record; died Overton Hospital per Daily Burial Record Book.

Jackson, Reuben   Buried November 17, 1861   Lot/Division 1, #197   Plat Number 197

Tennessee 2 (Walker's) Infantry Regiment Private Company B; enlisted May 11, 1861, Memphis; per August to November 1861, Muster Roll Remarks: Wounded Battle of Belmont, Missouri November 7, 1861, and died November 17, 1861; wounded at Battle of Belmont, Missouri per casualty report in November 13, 1861, *Memphis Daily Appeal*; died November 17, 1861, at Overton Hospital per list of deaths in November 24, 1861, *Memphis Daily Appeal*; per hospital record admitted November 11, 1861, with complaint of hip (amputated hip joint November 16, 1861) and died November 17, 1862; not found in Lindsley's Annals.

Jackson, Salathiel P.   Buried October 26, 1861   Lot/Division 1, #138   Plat Number 138

Arkansas 12 Infantry Regiment Private Company H; compiled service record found under "A. P. Jackson"; per July to October 1862, Company Muster Roll enlisted July 26, 1861, Arkadelphia, Arkansas, and Remarks: Died at Memphis October 20, 1861; per Register of Soldiers killed in battle or died of wounds or disease: died October 26, 1861, Memphis Tennessee; died camp measles per Daily Burial Record Book.

Jackson, William   Buried October 4 1861   Lot/Division 1, #4   Plat Number 4

Tennessee 42 Infantry Regiment Private (Barbiere's) 2 Company I; enlisted August 10, 1861, Memphis, age 20; per October 21, 1863, Muster Roll Remarks: Died Memphis, Tennessee September 21, 1861; died State Hospital per Daily Burial Record Book; note: "Jackson, W." died June 12, 1862, per Lindsley's Annals (possibly mistake or second soldier with same name but only one by this name in compiled service records for this unit).

Jackson, William S.   Buried October 21, 1861   Lot/Division 1, #120   Plat Number 120

Arkansas 12 Infantry Regiment Private Company H; enlisted July 29, 1861, Arkadelphia, Arkansas; per July to October 1862, Muster Roll Remarks: Died at Memphis October 25, 1861; per Register of Soldiers Killed in Battle or who died of Wounds or Disease: Died October 19, 1861, at Memphis, Tennessee.

James   Buried January 19, 1863   Lot/Division 2, #330   Plat Number 880

"Confederate Soldier James" in Daily Burial Record Book Name Column; listed under "J's" in Cemetery Alpha Book; listed as "James" under Unknowns in Cemetery Single Grave Book.

James, Isaacs   Buried May 3, 1862   Lot/Division 2, #26   Plat Number 576
Arkansas 23 (Adams') Infantry Regiment Private Company A; enlisted February 26, 1862, Missouri; per February 26 to June 30, 1862, Muster Roll Remarks: Died May 1862; A Ross ("Rofs") under Remarks in Daily Burial Record Book; first name spelled "Isaac" in Daily Burial Record Book and computer index.

January, W. W.   Buried October 15, 1897   Lot/Division 1, #540   Plat Number 540
Forrest 's Scouts, CSA Private Harvey's Company Scouts; no enlistment in compiled service record; single card that "Appears on a Roll of Prisoners of War of Captain A. Harvey Scouts, CSA, commanded by Lieutenant George Harvey, surrendered at Citronelle, Alabama, by Lieutenant General R. Taylor, CSA, to Major General E. R. S. Canby, USA, May 4, 1865, and paroled at Jackson, Mississippi, May 13, 1865," with residence stated as Claiborne County, Mississippi; Harvey's Scouts and 1850 1897 on grave stone; member Confederate Historical Association and sketch in Mathes book; per sketch "enlisted January 15, 1864, as a private in Harvey's Scouts and served in General W. H. Jackson's Division. These scouts were not attached to any regiment; paroled at Canton, Miss., April 1865. Admitted to this Association January 14, 1896."; per narrative for Kizer's Tennessee Cavalry in *Tennesseans in the Civil War, Part I*, on December 2, 1864, General Forrest ordered: "There are four regularly organized and recognized Companies of scouts for this command: Captain Henderson's, Harvey's, Kizer's and Cobb's. None others will be recognized."; note that the compiled service record card for Forrest 's Scouts, C.S.A. indicated that "The following companies served at various times as part of this command: Capt. Joseph T. Cobb's Company, Capt. Thomas W. Elliott's Company, Capt. Addison Harvey's Company, Capt. Thomas Henderson's Company, Capt. Thomas N. Kizer's Company, and Captain _____ Sanders' Company"; died age 47 per Daily Burial Record Book; listed in the article "Harvey's Scouts. Roster of a Famous Confederate Organization." by J. L. Goodloe (Harvey's Scout veteran also buried at Elmwood, see sketch) that was cut from a newspaper (paper name and date not shown) and submitted in support of Mattie S. Lorance's application for a Tennessee Confederate Pension (W3571) based on her deceased husband's (John Lorance, Private Harvey Scouts) service; listed in the Correction, page 24, of *A Sketch, Harvey's Scouts, formerly of Jackson's Cavalry Division, Army of Tennessee*. J. F. H. Claiborne, Starkville, Miss., 1885.

Jeffery, Jesse L.   Buried May 19, 1862   Lot/Division 2, #240   Plat Number 790
Captain Rice's Arkansas Artillery and died Overton Hospital typhoid pneumonia per Daily Burial Record Book; no compiled service record found as an Arkansas unit; possibly J. S. Jeffries, Private Missouri Captain O. W. Barret's Company Light Artillery (formerly Captain D. A. Rice's Company Missouri Light Artillery and also known as the 10th Missouri Battery), per Company Muster Roll dated October 11, 1862, enlisted March 18, 1862, at Pocahontas, Arkansas by Captain Rice; per Company Muster Roll for September 30 to December 31, 1862, Remarks: Left sick in Memphis, Tennessee May 8, 1862, when the Battery marched; per Company Muster Roll for September & October 1863, Remarks: Supposed to have deserted from Hospital. Has not been heard from by Captain Barret for nearly two (2) years; listed as Jeffrey, Jepe L. in computer index, which may be from misreading the double "s" in "Jesse" as written old style in Daily Burial Record Book.

Jeffus, Needham H.   Buried September 9, 1861   Lot/Division 1, #93   Plat Number 93
Arkansas 11 Infantry Regiment Private Company G and died age 28 per Daily Burial Record Book; no compiled service record found; August 11, 1836 August 9, 1861 on grave stone.

Jennings, John W.   Buried March 14, 1916   Plat Number N26
Mississippi 11 Infantry Regiment Private Company K; enlisted April 29, 1861, Carrollton, Mississippi, age 18; wounded Seven Pines May 3, 1862, Gettysburg July 3, 1863, and Weldon Railroad August 19, 1864; per Oath of Allegiance document residence was Carroll County, Mississippi; per Tennessee Confederate Pension application (S14920) born September 16, 1844, Lowndes County, Mississippi; member Confederate Historical Association, Camp 28, Bivouac 18, Memphis; no sketch in Mathes book; second initial "M" in Cemetery computer index; died age 72 per Daily Burial Record Book.

Jewerls, J. W.   Buried May 9, 1862   Lot/Division 2, #126   Plat Number 676
Arkansas 31 (McCray's) Infantry Regiment Private (Barnes') Company H; enlisted March 1, 1862, Byoudeview, Arkansas; per undated Muster Roll age 20, native of Alabama, farmer and enlisted March 27, 1862, Jackson County, Arkansas; per January 1 to February 28, 1862, Muster Roll Remarks: Absent sick since April 28, 1862, Memphis; per December 1863 to February 1864, Muster Roll Remarks: Absent sick since May 8, 1862, have not heard from since; name "M. Jerald" and died Overton Hospital per Daily Burial Record Books; name "W. Jerald" in Cemetery computer index.

Johnekin, John E.   Buried March 3, 1862   Lot/Division 1, #279   Plat Number 279
Arkansas 15 (Johnson's) Infantry Regiment Private Company C; per October 22, 1861, to October 6, 1862, Company Muster Roll enlisted October 22, 1861, Camden, Arkansas and Remarks: Sent off from Donelson before surrender and whereabouts unknown; per Overton Hospital March 1862, Register of Sick admitted February 18, 1862, with complaint of pneumonia and died March 3, 1862; name spelled "Jonakin" in Daily Burial Record Book.

Johnson, Isaiah Woody   Buried October 2, 1926   Plat Number N45
Texas 2 (Moore's) Infantry Regiment Private Company G; compiled service record found under J. W. Johnson; enlisted September 7, 1861, Houston, Texas; captured at Vicksburg, Mississippi July 4, 1863; took Oath of Allegiance at Vicksburg, Mississippi at

Exchange July 7, 1863; Parole of Honor July 1, 1865; per Tennessee Confederate Pension application (S12556) born June 17, 1845, Decatur County, Georgia; per widow's (Lillie Charlotte Sheet) Tennessee Confederate Pension application #W8553 died October 1, 1926; per Tennessee Questionnaire of Civil War Veterans first name "Isaiah"; member Confederate Historical Association, Camp 28, Bivouac 18, Memphis; no sketch in Mathes book; died age 81 per Daily Burial Record Book.

Johnson, J. R. M.   Buried June 8, 1873   Lot/Division 2, #380   Plat Number 930
Listed in Elmwood 1874 book as Confederate soldier buried in Elmwood who was citizen of Memphis or vicinity; died consumption age 43 per Daily Burial Record Book; per obituary in *Memphis Daily Appeal*, June 9, 1873, page 5, column 7, age 43 and born in Tuscumbia, Alabama; grave number indicated as 280 in Daily Burial Record Book and computer index but 380 is correct grave based on date of burial sequence; John L. Garner (buried June 2, 1862) is buried in Division 2, Grave # 280.

Johnson, Jack   Buried June 11, 1862   Lot/Division 2, # 291   Plat Number 841
Mississippi 31 Infantry Regiment Company I and died State Hospital erysipelas per Daily Burial Record Book; no Jack Johnson found in Company I; there were a number of Johnsons in unit with one in Company I, but none appear to be him.

Johnson, Matthew   Buried November 4, 1861   Lot/Division 1, #165   Plat Number 165
Tennessee & Alabama 1 Regiment (Heath's) Company and died camp per Daily Burial Record Book; no compiled service record found and no Captain Heath found in Alabama, Tennessee or Confederate units.

Johnson, Morgan   Buried October 20, 1861   Lot/Division 1, #117   Plat Number 117
Arkansas 2 Infantry Regiment and died State Hospital per Daily Burial Record Book; no compiled service record found; unit indicated as Arkansas 20 in Cemetery Single Grave Book.

Johnson, R. B.   Buried April 26, 1862   Lot/Division 1, #498   Plat Number 498
Captain Jones' Company and died Overton Hospital brain congestion per Daily Burial Record Book.

Johnson, Thomas S.   Buried May 9, 1862   Lot/Division 2, #137   Plat Number 687
Arkansas 17 (Griffith's) Infantry Regiment Private Company G; enlisted November 22, 1861, Fayetteville, Arkansas, age 18; per January & February 1862, Muster Roll Remarks: Absent (no other information); Company H and died Overton Hospital typhoid fever per Daily Burial Record Book.

Johnston, James J.   Buried March 20, 1862   Lot/Division 1, #351   Plat Number 351
Arkansas 11 Infantry Regiment Private Company K; enlisted December 21, 1861, Saline County, Arkansas; per December 21, 1861 to September 23, 1862, Muster Roll Remarks: Died; died Overton Hospital pneumonia at age 21 per Daily Burial Record Book.

Jones   Buried January 29, 1863   Lot/Division 2, #335   Plat Number 885
Captain Jones and no initials, unit or other information in Daily Burial Record Book.

Jones, Andrew J.   Buried March 22, 1862   Lot/Division 1, #365   Plat Number 365
Arkansas 11 Infantry Regiment Private Company K; compiled service record found under "J. Jones"; enlisted December 21, 1861, Pulaski County, Arkansas; per December 21, 1861 to September 23, 1862, Muster Roll Remarks: Died March 1862; per Overton Hospital March 1862 Register of Sick died March 21 of erysipelas; widow, Mary T. Jones, filed a claim for settlement in the Office of the Confederate States Auditor for the War Department; unit indicated as Arkansas 10 Infantry in Daily Burial Record Book.

Jones, George P.   Buried October 16, 1861   Lot/Division 1, #71   Plat Number 71
Arkansas 12 Infantry Regiment Private Company F; enlisted July 26, 1861 Arkadelphia, Arkansas; per July to October 1862 Muster Roll Remarks: Died at Memphis October 16, 1861; per affidavit with claim by father, James F. Jones, died of pneumonia; died camp measles age 17 per Daily Burial Record Book.

Jones, George Washington   Buried November 12, 1929   Plat Number N54
Obituary in November 12, 1929, *The Commercial Appeal* Memphis, page 7, indicating Confederate Veteran died suddenly at home November 11, 1929, served in Polk's Corps (no unit indicated), was with General Joseph E. Johnston's Command from 1863 to time of capture, imprisoned at Camp Chase, Ohio until close of War, wounded during fighting around Atlanta, native of Sumter County, Alabama, moved to Mississippi then Arkansas, and to Memphis five years ago to live with daughter; per General and Staff records George W. Jones, Major and Quartermaster, Captain reported to Alabama 4 Infantry Regiment and promoted to Major Assistant Quartermaster April 27, 1861, (record indicates Quartermaster and enlisted May 7, 1861, Lynchburg, Virginia); appointed Quartermaster, Major, September 14, 1861, on the staff of Brigadier General William H. C. Whiting per *Confederate Staff Officers 1861-1865* by Joseph H. Crute, Jr., Derwent Books 1982, page 210; not the George W. Jones who served in Mississippi Stanford's Company Light Artillery who died August 20, 1924, in Memphis (buried in Grenada, Mississippi) and whose wife filed for Tennessee Confederate Pension (W8556); does not appear to be the G. W. Jones (George W. Jones on some cards) Mississippi 39 Infantry Regiment Private Company D, enlisted December 31, 1862, Decatur, Mississippi, captured near Allatoona, Georgia

October 5, 1864, first sent to Louisville Military Prison then to Camp Chase October 24, 1864, Oath of Allegiance dated May 15, 1865, when indicates residence of _ ton (?) County, Mississippi, age 19; no unit indicated in Daily Burial Record Book.

Jones, J. W.   Buried February 27, 1862   Lot/Division 1, #270   Plat Number 270
Captain Jones' Company; not Arkansas 2 Cavalry Private Company G.

Jones, James L.   Buried September 23, 1861   Lot/Division 1, #7   Plat Number 7
Mississippi 22 (Bonham's) Infantry Regiment Private (Lester's) Company K; enlisted July 28, 1861, Lafayette County, Mississippi; per August to October 1861, Muster Roll Remarks: Died at Memphis, Tennessee September 26; died State Hospital measles age 19 per Daily Burial Record Book.

Jones, N. L.   Buried March 10, 1862   Lot/Division 1, #312   Plat Number 312
Captain Jones' Heavy Artillery and died State Hospital per Daily Burial Record Book; not found Tennessee 1 Heavy Artillery.

Jones, R.   Buried May 10, 1862   Lot/Division 2, #144   Plat Number 694
Missouri Clark's Infantry Regiment Private (Wright's) Company C; enlisted July 28, 1861, Crawford County, Arkansas; per Muster Roll Remarks: Sick in Hospital Little Rock, Arkansas; died Overton Hospital per Daily Burial Record Book.

Jones, William D.   Buried December 3, 1861   Lot/Division 1, #236   Plat Number 236
Arkansas 10 Infantry Regiment Private Company C; enlisted July 24, 1861, Springfield, Arkansas; per January to April 1862, Muster Roll Remarks: Died Memphis, Tennessee December 1861, not reported dead before; second initial as "B" on father's claim filed December 16, 1863, in compiled service record and in Daily Burial Record Book and computer index; died Overton Hospital Enteritis per Daily Burial Record Book.

Jones, William P.   Buried May 12, 1862   Lot/Division 2, #169   Plat Number 719
Arkansas 17 (Lemoyne's) Infantry Regiment Private Company E; reference card only in 17 Lemoyne's Infantry compiled service records; records found under Arkansas 21 Infantry, Private Company E (I), that was successor of 17 Infantry; enlisted December 21, 1861, Dardanelle, Arkansas; per December 21, 1861 to June 30, 1862, Muster Roll Remarks: Sick in Hospital at Memphis; per April 28, 1862, Muster Roll Remarks: Sick at Hospital at Memphis April 1, 1862; per July & August 1862, Muster Roll Remarks: Deserted being seven days absent without leave, left at Memphis in Hospital; died Overton Hospital per Daily Burial Record Book.

Jones, William Rutledge   Buried February 5, 1918   Plat Number N27
Tennessee Cavalry Private Company I; no compiled service record found; unit per grave stone; no information found to verify which of the several William or William R. Jones found in Tennessee cavalry regiments; based on Company I on marker very possibly William Jones Private Company I Tennessee 19 (Biffle's) Cavalry; name spelled "Johnes" and 1837 1918 on grave stone; per February 5, 1918, *The Commercial Appeal* Memphis died February 4, 1918, age 72; per February 7, 1918, *The Commercial Appeal* Memphis died from hypostatic pneumonia and influenza; died age 72 per Daily Burial Record Book.

Jones, Willis   Buried April 27, 1862   Lot/Division 1, #504   Plat Number 504
Arkansas 2 Mounted Rifles Regiment Private Company I; enlisted December 20, 1861, age 18, Cantonment Bee, Arkansas and per March & April 1862, Muster Roll Remarks absent sick and no other information; per Overton Hospital Record Willis Jones, Private Company I Arkansas 2 Regiment admitted April 22, 1862, with complaint of typhoid pneumonia and died April 26, 1862; Company J, first name "Willey" and died Overton Hospital per Daily Burial Record Book; first name "Wiley" in Cemetery computer index.

Jordan, John   Buried May 3, 1862   Lot/Division 2, #40   Plat Number 590
Texas 3 (Greer's) Cavalry Regiment Private (Chisum's') Company F; enlisted June 3, 1861 Kaufman County, Texas; per May & June 1862 Muster Roll Remarks: Died at Memphis from disease May 1, 1862; died Overton Hospital pneumonia per Daily Burial Record Book.

Josey, William H.   Buried March 11, 1862   Lot/Division 1, #316   Plat Number 316
Tennessee Bankhead's Battery (Tennessee Scott's Light Artillery) and died pneumonia per Daily Burial Record Book; no compiled service record found; per Overton Hospital March 1862 Register of Deaths died March 10 of jaundice and Harris Company.

Joyce, T. S.   Buried May 9, 1862   Lot/Division 2, #138   Plat Number 688
Arkansas 17 (Griffith/Rector's) Infantry Regiment Company G per Daily Burial Record Book; no service record found.

Julian, John R.   Buried March 19, 1862   Lot/Division 1, #349   Plat Number 349
Arkansas 11 Infantry Regiment Private Company K; enlisted December 20, 1861 Saline County, Arkansas; per December 21, 1861 to September 23, 1862 Muster Roll Remarks: Died March 1862; per Daily Burial Record Book died Overton Hospital.

Kearney, J. R.   Buried March 10, 1910   Plat Number N7
Tennessee 21 Infantry Regiment Private Company A; compiled service records found under J. R. Kerney; enlisted June 11, 1861

Memphis; name appears on list dated June 3, 1862, Booneville, Mississippi of prisoners taken at Booneville, Mississippi and deserters who delivered themselves up, forwarded to rear to General Headquarters; record also found "R. Kerney" Tennessee 3 (Forrest's) Cavalry Private Company B with only one card that states appears on a Report of Prisoners of War Paroled at Memphis, Tennessee for five days ending May 25, 1865; per Tennessee Confederate Pension application (S10176) born Warren County, Mississippi August 24, 1839; per March 10, 1910 *The Commercial Appeal* Memphis died March 9, 1910; member Confederate Historical Association and sketch in Mathes book; per sketch and March 10, 1910 *The Commercial Appeal* Memphis, page 4, J. Robert Kearney enlisted May 16, 1861 Company A Tennessee Infantry Colonel Pickett and left on a parole when member of McDonald Battalion, Forrest Cavalry 1865; died age 72 per Daily Burial Record Book; death reported "The Last Roll" section *Confederate Veteran* Volume IXX, April 1911, page 174.

Kearns, Thomas   Buried December 2, 1861   Lot/Division 1, #234   Plat Number 234
Tennessee 21 Infantry Regiment Sergeant Company B; enlisted June 10, 1861 Memphis; per November & December 1861 Muster Roll Remarks: Died at Memphis December 2, 1861 of wounds received at Battle of Belmont; gunshot wound and died December 2, 1861 Overton Hospital per Daily Burial Record Book; name spelled "Karns" on list of casualties at Battle of Belmont, Missouri reported in November 13, 1861 *Memphis Daily Appeal*; name spelled "Karnes" on list of arrivals at Overton Hospital on November 4, 1861 reported in November 15, 1861 *Memphis Daily Appeal*; name spelled "Carnes" in Daily Burial Record Book and computer index and in report of death in December 3, 1861 *Memphis Daily Appeal.*

Keith, John T.   Buried May 3, 1862   Lot/Division 2, #27   Plat Number 577
Arkansas 19 (Dockery/Smead's) Infantry Regiment Lieutenant Company D; per March 1 to June 30, 1862, Company Muster Roll enlisted March 1, 1862, Rock Port and Remarks: Died May 1, 1862; second initial "W" in compiled service record; died Overton Hospital per Daily Burial Record Book.

Keller, Wesley M.   Buried March 25, 1862   Lot/Division 1, #380   Plat Number 380
Bankhead Battalion and died Overton Hospital per Daily Burial Record Book; unit should be Tennessee Scott's Light Artillery, but no compiled service record found; per list of those who died at Overton General Hospital at Memphis during the month of March 1862 name "McKeller, J. W.," died March 25 of rubella and Private Bankhead's Company B.

Kelley, James A.   Buried April 23, 1862   Lot/Division 1, #484   Plat Number 484
Missouri 6 (Hedgpeth's Battalion) Infantry Regiment Corporal (A. G. Kelsey's) Company K; per July & August 1862, Company Muster Roll enlisted March 11, 1862, Pocahontas, Arkansas by Major W. F. Rapley; September & August 1862, Muster Roll Remarks: Was killed in charge on Corinth, Mississippi October 3, 1862; appears on a Historic Roll (not dated) indicating age 19 when enlisted, native of Tennessee, Murry (sic) County, enlisted January 1, 1862, Pocahontas, Arkansas with Remarks: Was in Battles Fort Pillow May 10, 1862, Iuka, Corinth where he was instantly killed when shot through temples; record also found in Missouri 1 Battalion Infantry Corporal Company C ("Kelly") with same enlistment and which Company became Company K, Missouri 6 Infantry Regiment, in August 1862; died camp per Daily Burial Record Book; name spelled "Kell" in both Daily Burial Record Book and computer index; not listed in Single Grave Book.

Kelly, James   Buried February 27, 1929   Plat Number N51
No unit indicated and died age 82 per Daily Burial Record Book; first name "John" with no initial on Tennessee, Shelby County, Death Certificate with age 82 indicated; PVT CO A 2ND TENN INF 1837 1929 on grave stone; possibly P. J. Kelly who has a sketch in Mathes book, page 135, Tennessee 2 Infantry Company A (Patrick Kelly, Tennessee 2 Infantry Private (Strocky's - spelled Shockery in Mathes sketch) Company A), enlisted June 3, 1861, Randolph, March & April 1862, Muster Roll Remarks absent wounded, undated Muster Roll Remarks discharged on account of wound received at Battle of Shiloh and joined April 26, 1861, (no age indicated in record); per sketch born in County Clare, Ireland June, 1842, and moved to Memphis in 1858.

Kelly, John H.   Buried June 22, 1871   Lot/Division 2, #376   Plat Number 926
Listed in Elmwood 1874 book as Confederate soldier buried in Elmwood who was citizen of Memphis or vicinity; no unit indicated and died congestion age 43 per Daily Burial Record Book; not listed in Cemetery Single Grave Book.

Kimbrough, James P.   Buried October 25, 1920   Plat Number N37
Alabama 34 Infantry Regiment Private Company F; enlisted February 26, 1862; per Daily Burial Record Book died age 84; 1836 1920 on grave stone; died October 24, 1920 per *The Commercial Appeal* Memphis October 25, 1920 page 5, no mention of Confederate service; per descendant (Emma Lee) he was visiting stepson-in-law in Memphis at time of death and was from Texas where moved after the War and that widow (second wife) gave wrong age as was born 1839.

King, Andy   Buried May 7, 1862   Lot/Division 2, #92   Plat Number 642
Arkansas 20 (King's) Infantry Regiment Private Company K; enlisted March 6, 1862 Lafayette County, Arkansas; per March 6 to May 2, 1862 Muster Roll Remarks: Left at Fort Pillow Hospital; per March 6 to June 30, 1862 Muster Roll Remarks: Died in Hospital, date not ascertained; Company B, from Fort Pillow and died Overton Hospital per Cemetery records; name "Andrew" in Daily Burial Record Book and computer index.

King, S. M.   Buried November 4, 1861   Lot/Division 1, #163   Plat Number 163
Hailman's Guerillas and died Southern Mothers Hospital per Daily Burial Record Book; unit should be Tennessee Bibb's Company Artillery ("Memphis Guerillas") but no compiled service records found as its papers and books were destroyed at the time of the battery's capture at Island 10 April 8, 1862; not listed in Cemetery Single Grave Book.

Knowles, Hardy   Buried May 14, 1862   Lot/Division 2, #202   Plat Number 752
Arkansas 17 Infantry Regiment Company H and from W. D. Ferguson's per Daily Burial Record Book; no service record found.

Knox, William M.   Buried January 17, 1862   Lot/Division 1, #256   Plat Number 256
Arkansas 12 Infantry Regiment per Daily Burial Record Book; no compiled service record found.

LaVelle, James   Buried December 28, 1905   Lot/Division 1, #534   Plat Number 534
No unit indicated in Daily Burial Record Book or newspaper; possibly James Lavelle, Private Company B Louisiana 6 Infantry Regiment who enlisted July 1, 1861 Fairfax, Virginia, present on rolls to October 1861, per July & August 1862 Muster Roll discharged since last report to Lynchburg, per record copied from Memorial Hall New Orleans, Louisiana born New Orleans, laborer, age 17 and never heard from since December 1861; not J. Lavelle, Private Company K, Louisiana 13 Infantry who died May 1, 1863; name spelled "LaVells" and "Lavener" in Cemetery computer index; died age 67 per Daily Burial Record Book; died December 28, 1905 per December 29, 1905 *The Commercial Appeal* Memphis.

Lackey, William   Buried May 6, 1862   Lot/Division 2, #77   Plat Number 627
Arkansas 17 (Lemoyne's) Infantry Regiment Private Company A; enlisted October 7, 1861 Lewisburg, Arkansas; no other information in compiled service records; no records found under Arkansas 21 Infantry that was successor of Arkansas 17 Infantry; not the William Lackey of Company D of 17 Infantry and Company H of 21 Infantry; died Overton Hospital pneumonia per Daily Burial Record Book.

Laird, Miles F.   Buried May 8, 1862   Lot/Division 2, #114   Plat Number 664
Arkansas 19 (Dockery/Smead's) Infantry Regiment Private Company D; enlisted March 1, 1862 Rock Port; per March 1 to June 30, 1862 Muster Roll Remarks: Absent sick; appointed Corporal from March 1 to June 5, 1862; per September & October 1862 Muster Roll Remarks: Died May 30, 1862; died Overton Hospital lung congestion per Daily Burial Record Book.

Lamb, Asa   Buried May 14, 1862   Lot/Division 2, #209   Plat Number 759
Barrett's Battery, Van Dorn's Division and died State Hospital per Daily Burial Record Book; no compiled service record found; not found Missouri Captain Barret's Company Light Artillery.

Lamb, Samuel F.   Buried May 15, 1862   Lot/Division 2, #215   Plat Number 765
Arkansas 25 (Turnbull's) Infantry Regiment Private (Peirs') Company D; enlisted March 5, 1862 Pocahontas, Arkansas; per March 25 to April 30, 1862 Muster Roll Remarks: Was left near Memphis sick; per July & August 1862 Muster Roll Remarks: Private at private (House) April 18, 1862 Memphis, Tennessee; per March & April 1863 Muster Roll Remarks: Private at private House in Memphis April 12, 1862; died Overton Hospital per Daily Burial Record Book; unit indicated as Carroll's Arkansas Regiment in Single Grave Book.

Lambert, Joel   Buried June 26, 1925   Plat Number N40
Alabama 27 Infantry Regiment Corporal Company I; enlisted January 10, 1862 Florence, Alabama; per Muster Roll Remarks: Captured at Fort Donelson February 16, 1862; Tennessee Confederate Pension application (S2533) indicates born 1840 in Lauderdale County, Alabama; per wife's (Martha C (Griffis) Lambert) Tennessee Confederate Pension application (W8344) he was born 1840 in Rogersville, Alabama, she was born July 24, 1851 in Lincoln County, Tennessee, and they were married May 8, 1869 in Lincoln County, Tennessee; Alabama 11 Cavalry Private Company K written on pension file card in widow's pension record; per Alabama 11 Cavalry rolls Private Company K, one card indicates enlisted February 29, 1964 and another card indicates enlisted May 1864 at Tuscumbia and that Alabama 11 Cavalry Company K had previously been Company K Alabama 10 Cavalry; per Tennessee Questionnaire of Civil War Veterans born Rogersville, Alabama (age 82 when completed Questionnaire); per June 25, 1925 *The Commercial Appeal* Memphis died June 24, 1925 age 85; original grave stone underground and broken with name only partially legible; 1840 1925 on grave stone.

Lambright, Lewis T.   Buried March 5, 1862   Lot/Division 1, #286   Plat Number 286
Louisiana 12 Infantry Regiment Private Company I; enlisted August 13, 1861 Camp Moore, Louisiana; present on rolls to October 13, 1861.

Land, William T.   Buried March 24, 1862   Lot/Division 1, #371   Plat Number 371
Louisiana 12 Regiment (not organized) and died State Hospital per Daily Burial Record Book; no compiled service record found and not found Booth Louisiana Book; 1844 1863 on grave stone; there was a soldier named William T. Land, Private Company F Louisiana 12 Infantry Regiment whose record has date of death April 19, 1863 (not found that date in Cemetery records) and other information that conflicts with this burial.

Lane, Morris   Buried March 10, 1862   Lot/Division 1, #311   Plat Number 311
CSS Steamer Ponchatrain and died Overton Hospital per Daily Burial Record Book; no records found Navy and Marine rolls; in Cemetery Alpha and Single Grave books there is a "Cane, M." for same grave but only "Morris Lane" in Daily Burial Record Book for the date of death; per list of those who died at Overton General Hospital at Memphis during the month of March 1862 died March 9 of vul sclop(?).

Langford, Jordan H.   Buried May 3, 1862   Lot/Division 2, #37   Plat Number 587
Missouri 1 Infantry Regiment Sergeant Company H; enlisted June 22, 1861 Memphis age 35; per Muster Roll Remarks: Wounded Battle of Shiloh and died Memphis May 15, 1862; per Battle of Shiloh casualty list for unit reported in April 23, 1862 *Memphis Daily Appeal* was wounded in Battle; died Irving Hospital per Daily Burial Record Book; per Irving Hospital record admitted April 10, 1862 with complaint of right leg and died May 1, 1862.

Lassiter, Amos A.   Buried January 21, 1862   Lot/Division 1, #257   Plat Number 257
Confederate 4 (Baker's) Infantry Regiment Private Company F (Captain Joshua Morse's Company "Andy Moore Guard"); per Company Muster-in Roll dated October 15, 1861, at Camp near Memphis, Tennessee enlisted September 8, 1861, Butler, Alabama age 21; per Company Muster Roll dated October 31, 1861, remarks: Sick, Chills and fever; regiment (also known as 1st Alabama, Tennessee and Mississippi Infantry) was formed about December 9, 1861, with ten companies: four from Alabama, two from Mississippi, and four from Tennessee; captured at Island 10 April 8, 1862, and after exchange in September, 1862, the companies were reorganized and transferred to other commands; Company F became Company F of the Alabama 54th Infantry Regiment but no record for this regiment as died before transfer; per Daily Burial Record Book Marsh Walker's Regiment (no record found) and died Charleston House Hotel; grave #259 in Cemetery computer index; not listed in Cemetery Single Grave Book.

Latham, Charles   Buried November 12, 1861   Lot/Division 1, #187   Plat Number 187
Tennessee 40 (Walker's) Infantry Regiment Private Company E; enlisted September 25, 1861 Mooresville, Alabama age 45; per November & December 1861, Muster Roll Remarks: Died of Disease at Camp Johnson November 11, 1861; per Register of Soldiers Killed in Battle or Died of Wounds or Disease died November 13, 1861, Camp Johnson measles; per Lindsley's Annals died November 11, 1861; per Daily Burial Record Book died camp flux; Walker's Regiment indicated as an Arkansas unit in Daily Burial Record Book.

Lax, Joseph G.   Buried March 23, 1862   Lot/Division 1, #370   Plat Number 370
Arkansas 1 (Colquitt's) Infantry Regiment Private Company G; record found mixed in compiled service record of Joel T. Lax (who enlisted May 5, 1861 Jacksonport, Arkansas age 25 farmer); died Overton Hospital.

Lay, James A.   Buried May 16, 1876   Lot/Division 2, #384   Plat Number 934
No unit indicated and died pneumonia age 45 per Daily Burial Record Book.

Leary, D.   Buried October 8, 1861   Lot/Division 1, #38   Plat Number 38
Captain Barbiere's Company per Daily Burial Record Book; no service record found; died before regiment formally organized; Joseph Barbiere was 1 Lieutenant of "The Gayoso Guards" per June 5, 1861 *Memphis Daily Appeal*; per August 1, 1861 *Memphis Daily Appeal*, Captain Barbiere was authorized to raise a regiment; per *Tennesseans in the Civil War, Part 1*, "The Gayoso Guards" was Company A Tennessee 39 (Avery's) Infantry Regiment but regiment officially organized as Alabama-Tennessee-Mississippi 1 Infantry Regiment (Confederate 4 Infantry); after unit's capture at Island 10 in April 1862 and exchange Company became 2 Company I Tennessee 42 Infantry Regiment; per September 26, 1861 the *Avalanche Memphis*, Colonel Avery's Regiment - the Gayoso Guard Captain Barbiere and one or two other companies belonging to Colonel W. T. Avery's Regiment will leave today for their rendezvous in the vicinity of Germantown; not found in Lindsley's Annals 39 & 40 Consolidated Infantry Regiment Official Memorial Roll.

Lee, Jesse   Buried May 5, 1862   Lot/Division 2, #59   Plat Number 609
Arkansas Miller's Battalion Company E and died Overton Hospital typhoid fever and pneumonia per Daily Burial Record Book; unit believed to be Arkansas 8 Infantry Battalion Company E but no service record found.

Lee, Richard   Buried April 1, 1862   Lot/Division 1, #404   Plat Number 404
Louisiana 12 Regiment per Daily Burial Record Book; no compiled service record found.

Lefebere, John   Buried May 19, 1862   Lot/Division 2, #241   Plat Number 791
Louisiana 25 Infantry Regiment Private (Scarborough's) Company K; enlisted March 20, 1862 Providence, Louisiana, age 40; per March 2 to June 30, 1862 Muster Roll Remarks: Deceased about May 20, 1862; name appears on a list of soldiers who were Killed in Battle or who Died of Wounds or Disease that indicates died May 18, 1862 at Memphis and cause unknown; died Overton Hospital mania a potu per Daily Burial Record Book; name spelled "Lefene" in Daily Burial Record Book and computer index; in hospital record there is a John Lefebre, Private Orleans Guard Company B, admitted April 11, 1862 with complaint of groin and on furlough April 13, 1862, however, may not be same soldier as Orleans Guard was part of Louisiana 30 Battalion/Regiment.

Leggett, William T.   Buried October 3, 1861   Lot/Division 1, #64   Plat Number 64
Arkansas 10 Infantry Regiment Company D and died Southern Mothers Hospital per Daily Burial Record Book; no service record found.

Leland, Charles F.   Buried June 1, 1917   Plat Number N29
Tennessee 4 Infantry Regiment Drummer Company H; enlisted May 15, 1861; per Muster Roll Remarks: Discharged because of age; per Tennessee Confederate Pension application #15035 born 1846 Hennepin County, Minnesota; member Confederate Historical Association, Camp 28, Bivouac 18, Memphis; no sketch in Mathes book; 1843 1917 on grave stone; died age 70 per Daily Burial Record Book.

Lendwell, William D.   Buried May 11, 1862   Lot/Division 2, #164   Plat Number 714
Arkansas 12 Infantry Regiment Private Company H; enlisted July 29, 1861 Arkadelphia, Arkansas; per July to October 1862 Muster Roll Remarks: Escaped from Island 10 (no other information); name spelled "Lewdwell" in Daily Burial Record Book and computer index.

Letlow, Isham H.   Buried May 10, 1862   Lot/Division 2, #156   Plat Number 706
Arkansas 18 (Carroll's) Infantry Regiment Private Company A; record found under "J. H. Letlow"; initials "I. H." on other cards in record; enlisted February 25, 1862 Jefferson County, Arkansas age 28; per muster roll card for February 25 to June 30, 1862 left at Memphis sick; per Regiment web page (researched by Byran R. Howerton) enlisted at Byrd Springs, Arkansas February 25, 1862, died in hospital at Memphis, Tennessee, May 1862, and born c 1834; name spelled "Detlow" in Daily Burial Record Book and computer index; died Irving Hospital measles per Daily Burial Record Book; per Irving Hospital record "Ludlow, Isham," Carroll's Arkansas Regiment, Private Company A, admitted May 2, 1862 with complaint of measles and died May 9, 1862.

Leverett, Martin M.   Buried September 21, 1861   Lot/Division 1, #43   Plat Number 43
Mississippi 22 (Bonham's) Infantry Regiment Private Company K; enlisted July 28, 1861 Lafayette County, Mississippi; per August to October 1861 Muster Roll Remarks: Died at Memphis, Tennessee September 24; name "W. M. Leverit" in Daily Burial Record Book and computer index.

Lewis, Jacob   Buried March 12, 1862   Lot/Division 1, #323   Plat Number 323
Confederate 4 (Baker's) Infantry Regiment Private Company D (Captain Henry Laird's Company "Gulf Rangers"); per Company Muster-in Roll enlisted September 14, 1861, at Montgomery, Alabama age 35; appears on Overton General Hospital, Memphis, Tennessee Register of Sick dated December 31, 1861, but no other information; per Register of Claims of Deceased Officers and Soldiers from Alabama, which were filed for settlement in the Office of the Confederate States Auditor for the War Department, Margaret Lewis filed claim July 16, 1863, indicating died Memphis, Tennessee (no date or cause indicated); regiment (also known as 1st Alabama, Tennessee and Mississippi Infantry) was formed about December 9, 1861, with ten companies: four from Alabama, two from Mississippi, and four from Tennessee; captured at Island 10 April 8, 1862, and after exchange in September, 1862, the companies were reorganized and transferred to other commands; Company D became Company E of the Alabama 54th Infantry Regiment but no record for this regiment as died before transfer; died State Hospital per Daily Burial Record Book.

Lewis, Lindsey   Buried February 18, 1878   Lot/Division 2, # 390   Plat Number 940
Died Heart Disease age 30 per Cemetery record; name "Lewis Lindsey" in Cemetery Single Grave Book; first name spelled "Lindsay" in Cemetery computer index; per Shelby Register of Deaths Linsey Lewis died February 16, 1878, single, age 28, heart disease, occupation clerk and Missouri nativity; 1874 Boyle-Chapman Memphis City Directory: Lewis, Lindsay C., clerk; possibly Lindsey Lewis Arkansas 25 Infantry Regiment Corporal Company B, enlisted March 1862 (no age) and per March 1 to May 1, 1862 Muster Roll Remarks sent to Hospital Little Rock, Arkansas April 6, 1862 and no other information; possibly Linsey C. Lewis, Arkansas 36 Infantry Regiment Private Company H, no enlistment in record, name appears on Register of Payments on Descriptive Lists as paid Bounty June 18, 1863 and name on receipt roll for clothing issued August 5, 1863.

Lindsay, John H.   Buried November 23, 1861   Lot/Division 1, #215   Plat Number 215
Arkansas 9 Infantry Regiment Private Company H; enlisted July 27, 1861 Pine Bluff, Arkansas; per November 1, 1861 to January 1, 1862 Muster Roll Remarks: Died at Memphis 23 November 1861; from Steamer per Daily Burial Record Book.

Lindsey, W. P.   Buried May 20, 1862   Lot/Division 2, #244   Plat Number 794
Texas 10 (Locke's) Cavalry Regiment Private Company A; enlisted September 25, 1861 Quitman, Texas, age 18; per March to August 1862 Muster Roll Remarks: Died at Memphis, Tennessee June 25, 1862; unit Texas 4 per Cemetery Single Grave Book; unit Tennessee 4 and died at W. B. Nelson's per Daily Burial Record Book; Texas 10 Cavalry Company A 1843 1862 on grave stone; per Overton Hospital record Private Company A Texas 4 Regiment and admitted April 21, 1862 with complaint of pneumonia and died May 19, 1862.

Lingo, George   Buried May 21, 1862   Lot/Division 2, #255   Plat Number 805
Miller's Regiment Company G and died Dr. Fraim's per Daily Burial Record Book; no compiled service record found; unit believed

to be Arkansas 8 Infantry Battalion Company G but no compiled service record found; not George Lingo Arkansas 35 Infantry or G. Lingo Arkansas 38 Infantry; not found Mississippi 1 (Miller's) Cavalry Battalion.

Loftin, William   Buried May 14, 1862   Lot/Division 2, #204   Plat Number 754
Arkansas 18 (Carroll's) Infantry Regiment Private (McLenders') Company B; enlisted March 21, 1862 Little Rock, Arkansas; per March to June 1862 Muster Roll Remarks: Sick at Memphis, Tennessee; per September to December 1862 Muster Roll Remarks: Died at Memphis, Tennessee about May 1, 1862 (exact date unknown); died Overton Hospital typhoid fever and pneumonia per Daily Burial Record Book; name spelled "Lofton" in Daily Burial Record Book and computer index and on some compiled service record cards.

Long, Adam L.   Buried September 19, 1861   Lot/Division 1, #96   Plat Number 96
Arkansas 9 Infantry Regiment 1st Sergeant Company A; enlisted July 25, 1861 Pine Bluff, Arkansas; per Muster Roll dated July 25 to November 1, 1861 Remarks: Died Memphis September 18, 1861 typhoid fever; died camp typhoid fever age 26 per Daily Burial Record Book.

Loomis, J. J.   Buried March 21, 1862   Lot/Division 1, #363   Plat Number 363
Arkansas 11 Infantry Regiment Company F and died State Hospital pneumonia per Daily Burial Record Book; no compiled service record found; per list of those who died at Overton General Hospital at Memphis during the month of March 1862 name "Tooms, J. J." died March 20 of pneumonia and Private Arkansas 11 Regiment Company F.

Loud, Curty   Buried May 19, 1862   Lot/Division 2, #242   Plat Number 792
Walker's Regiment, shot by sentry and died Overton Hospital per Daily Burial Record Book; believed to be "Louth, Christopher" Tennessee 2 (Walker's) Infantry Regiment, Private Company A (Captain F. A. Strocky), enlisted April 26, 1861, Memphis, remarks on an undated muster roll "Killed in Memphis May 1862" and first name "Christy" on two cards in compiled service record; *Memphis Daily Appeal*, May 20, 1862, page 2, column 7, reported in a Local Matters article "SHOT BY A SENTINEL -- On Sunday night, between 9 and 10 o'clock, a soldier, of Capt. Sherwin's company, named Christopher Lowery, who was passing up Poplar street at the end of Brinkley's avenue, the eastern boundary of the city, was challenged by the guard who, finding he had no pass, directed him to go into the city and get one. This he refused to do, and continued to insist on passing. Lieut. Priest came up and informed him that he must submit to the rule that was applied to all without discrimination. After the officer was gone away, Lowery swore no man should prevent his passing and he seized the sentinel's gun. The sentinel pulled the trigger and the unfortunate man fell in corpse. Citizens and others desiring to go out of the city in any direction must provide themselves with passports; the guards on duty have strict orders which they cannot disobey."; the *Avalanche* Memphis May 20, 1862, reported in a Local Matters article "A Sudden Death -- An old and honest citizen at Memphis, a brave member of the 2d Tennessee regiment, was shot, night before last, while attempting it is said, to pass the eastern terminus of Poplar street. Persons wishing to pass the corporate limits should procure themselves a pass. The neglect of so doing has, in the instance above recorded, cost Memphis an industrious citizen, the Confederacy a good soldier, and many a warm-hearted Irishman a good friend, true as steel and brave as a lion. The formality of an inquest was regularly gone through, but even in the Coroner's inquest the name of the sentinel who shot the poor fellow does not appear, at least in a public print."; Tennessee 2 (Walker's) Infantry Regiment consolidated with Tennessee 21 Infantry Regiment July 21, 1862, to form the Confederate 9 Infantry Regiment that was also called Confederate 5 Infantry Regiment but not found listed for those units in Confederate Index Book or in compiled service record rolls under any spellings; "Louth, Christopher" Tennessee 2 (Walker's) Infantry Regiment is only "Louth" in Confederate Index Book and not found any "Lowery" spelling in the index book for a Tennessee unit; per *Tennesseans in the Civil War, Part 2*, Christopher Sherwin listed as Captain Company A Harman's Infantry Regiment (organized in Memphis March 8, 1862) (no record found on him in this unit's compiled service record) that was later Company F Confederate 1 Infantry Battalion (not found in Confederate Index Book for this unit under any spelling or compiled service record), Captain Company I 154 Senior Infantry Regiment, and 1 Lieutenant Company A 3 (Forrest's) Cavalry Regiment; not found in Lindsley's Annals; first name "Courty" in Single Grave Book; found as "Land, Curty" in Cemetery computer index and also found same burial date in computer index as "Lond, Courtney."

Love, Nathan   Buried May 12, 1862   Lot/Division 2, #174   Plat Number 724
Arkansas 18 (Carroll's) Infantry Regiment Private Company C; enlisted March 8, 1862 Des Arc, Arkansas; per March to June 1862 Muster Roll Remarks: Died at Memphis May 12, 1862; Major Foute's noted in Daily Burial Record Book.

Lowe, G. H.   Buried November 29, 1861   Lot/Division 1, #231   Plat Number 231
Tennessee 154 Senior Infantry Regiment Private Company G "The Beauregards"; enlisted June 10, 1861 Memphis age 30; per Report of Deaths dated October 30, 1863 Notations: Enlisted Memphis (no date stated), born Memphis and died December 1861 on way to Memphis of pneumonia; per Register of Soldiers Killed in Battle Remarks: Died May (note month discrepancy) 1861 on way to Memphis; died December 20, 1861 per Lindsley's Annals; 1831 1861 on grave stone.

Lowe, Samuel C.   Buried November 10, 1861   Lot/Division 1, #178   Plat Number 178
Arkansas 9 Infantry Regiment Private Company H; enlisted July 27, 1861 Pine Bluff, Arkansas; per July 25 to November 1, 1861 Muster Roll Remarks: Absent, left at Mathers House (possibly Southern Mothers Home) Memphis cause sickness; per Muster Roll to May 1, 1862 Remarks: Died November 9, 1861; name "S. C. Len" in Daily Burial Record Book and computer index.

Loyd, Wiley H.   Buried May 5, 1862   Lot/Division 2, #58   Plat Number 608
Arkansas 25 (Turnbull's) Infantry Regiment Private Company D; enlisted March 26, 1862 Pocahontas, Arkansas; per March 25 to April 30, 1862 Muster Roll Remarks: Is in Memphis sick; died Overton Hospital per Daily Burial Record Book; name spelled "Lloyd" in Daily Burial Record Book and computer index.

Ludlow, S.   Buried March 31, 1862   Lot/Division 1, #400   Plat Number 400
Bankhead's Battery per Daily Burial Record Book; unit should be Tennessee Scott's Light Artillery but no compiled service record found; per list of those who died at Overton General Hospital at Memphis during the month of March 1862 name "Ledlow, A.," died March 31 of rubella and Private Bankhead's.

Luther, Calvin   Buried May 2, 1862   Lot/Division 2, #18   Plat Number 568
Arkansas 31 (McCray's) Infantry Regiment Private Company G; enlisted March 5, 1862 Conway, Arkansas; per March to August 1862 Muster Roll Remarks: Died April 30, 1862 sick; Descriptive List in record indicates born Missouri, age 19 and farmer; died Irving Hospital pneumonia and unit McRae's Battalion per Daily Burial Record Book; per Irving Hospital record admitted April 23, 1862 with complaint of measles and pneumonia and died May 1, 1862.

Luther, Jackson   Buried May 21, 1862   Lot/Division 2, #256   Plat Number 806
Arkansas 31 (McCray's) Infantry Regiment Private Company G; enlisted March 5, 1862 Conway, Arkansas; per September 1 to October 31, 1862 Muster Roll Remarks: Absent since April 20, 1862 sick; Descriptive List in record indicates born Missouri, age 21 and farmer; McRae's Regiment per Daily Burial Record Book.

Lynch, R.   Buried April 21, 1862   Lot/Division 1, #477   Plat Number 477
Arkansas 18 (Carroll's) Infantry Regiment (Parrish's) Company H and died Overton Hospital per Daily Burial Record Book; no compiled service record found; possibly Lynch, Archibald, Private Company H, Arkansas 18 Infantry Regiment, enlisted March 3, 1862 Little Rock, Arkansas and who per all muster rolls was absent sick but no other information.

Lynn, Thomas   Buried May 26, 1862   Lot/Division 2, #269   Plat Number 819
Arkansas 2 Mounted Rifles Regiment Private Company A; enlisted October 25, 1861 Camp on Otter Creek age 22; per November & December 1862 Muster Roll Remarks: Private in Memphis in April 1862, not since heard from; per May & June 1863 Muster Roll Remarks: Dropped from Roll - Private at Hospital Memphis, Tennessee, not since heard from; died Irving Hospital per Daily Burial Record Book; per Irving Hospital record admitted April 22, 1862 with complaint of diarrhea and died May 26, 1862.

Lyons, Frank   Buried September 11, 1861   Lot/Division 1, #45   Plat Number 45
Tennessee 2 (Walker's) Infantry Regiment Private Company I; enlisted May 12, 1861 Fort Harris (Memphis); per August to November 1861 Muster Roll Remarks: Died September 15, 1861 in Hospital in Memphis; per undated Muster Roll Remarks: Died August 1861; died Memphis September 15, 1861 and name spelled "Lyon" per Lindsley's Annals; note that there two burials records for Grave #45, Division 1 (Barnes, John P. December 17, 1861) but only one stone; no indication found in Cemetery records that Lyons was ever removed since he was the first buried.

Macomb, N.   Buried November 7, 1861   Lot/Division 1, #169   Plat Number 169
Arkansas 1 Infantry Regiment Company E and died Southern Mothers Hospital per Daily Burial Record Book; no compiled service record found; name spelled "Macolnb" in Daily Burial Record Book, "McComb" in Alpha Book and both "Macomb" and "Macolmb" in Cemetery computer index.

Macon, Richard T.   Buried October 7, 1863   Lot/Division 2, #342   Plat Number 892
Arkansas 1 (Dobbins') Cavalry Regiment Private Company H (Walker's Brigade); no enlistment in compiled service record; per Register of Prisoners of War in custody of Provost Marshall, Memphis, Tennessee: Received September 17, 1863 and sent to Hospital September 30, 1863; per Register of Sick and Wounded Prisoners at Overton Hospital admitted October 1863 with complaint of diarrhea and died October 6, 1863; per undated Muster Roll Card: Captured near Helena, Arkansas September 3, 1863 and died in Hospital October 7, 1863; died age 30 per Daily Burial Record Book.

Maddox, L. H.   Buried May 13, 1862   Lot/Division 2, #185   Plat Number 735
Texas 10 (Locke's) Cavalry Regiment Private Company C; enlisted March 18, 1862 Jacksonport, Arkansas; per March to August 1862 Muster Roll Remarks: Died May 1, 1862; name spelled "Maddux", died pneumonia and R P Walt per Daily Burial Record Book; name spelled "Maddun" in Cemetery computer index.

Mahaffie, H. Alexander   Buried May 10, 1862   Lot/Division 2, #146   Plat Number 696
Texas 11 (Young's) Cavalry Regiment Company E; enlisted October 2, 1861 Camp Reeves, Texas; per August 31 to December 31, 1862 Muster Roll Remarks: Left at Memphis sick April 24; name "Mahaffey" and died Overton Hospital pneumonia and typhoid fever per Daily Burial Record Book.

Malin, John   Buried June 21, 1862   Lot/Division 2, #297   Plat Number 847
CSS Colonel Lovell and died dropsy per Daily Burial Record Book; no compiled service record found Confederate Navy and Marine rolls; possibly John Mallon, Grand Master, who was found listed on a Colonel Lovell Payroll List; Gunboat participated in and was sank during Battle of Memphis June 6, 1862.

Mansell, James   Buried May 1, 1862   Lot/Division 2, #5   Plat Number 555
Texas 10 (Locke's) Cavalry Regiment Private (Martin's) Company I; enlisted October 31, 1861 Taos, Texas, age 23; per March to August 1862 Muster Roll Remarks: Died April 28, 1862; Wiggins' Company and died pneumonia per Daily Burial Record Book.

Mantequis, Jules   Buried December 6, 1861   Lot/Division 1, #240   Plat Number 240
Watson's Battery and died Southern Mothers Hospital per Daily Burial Record Book; no compiled service record found; in compiled service records for Louisiana Watson's Battery (Captain Daniel Beltzhoover's) there was a soldier by the name of "T. E. Mantegues" (possibly same soldier or relative) with single compiled service record card (no enlistment indicated) indicating Soldier signed a Petition in Missouri dated October 13, 1861, protesting against transfer to the Army of Tennessee and requesting to continue in State Service, for which purpose it was originally intended; September 18, 1861, the *Avalanche* (Memphis) under Local Matters reported that the celebrated Watson's Battery from New Orleans, with 147 men and 75 horses arrived here yesterday; unit participated in Battle of Belmont, Missouri November 7, 1861; unit referenced in a letter from Columbus, Kentucky in November 10, 1861, *Memphis Daily Appeal* (page 2, column 3); not listed in the List of the Killed, Wounded and Missing at the Battle Belmont as Wounded in the November 13, 1861, *Memphis Daily Appeal*, page 2, column 6; not listed in Cemetery Single Grave Book.

Marcus, G. M.   Buried July 28, 1861   Lot/Division 1, #51   Plat Number 51
Missouri 1 Infantry Regiment Private Company K; enlisted June 20, 1861 Memphis age 23; per Muster Roll Remarks: Died Memphis; died congestive chill age 23 per Daily Burial Record Book.

Marsh, Richard   Buried January 10, 1878   Lot/Division 2, #389   Plat Number 939
No unit indicated and died typhoid pneumonia age 41 per Daily Burial Record Book.

Marsh, William   Buried November 16, 1861   Lot/Division 1, #194   Plat Number 194
Tennessee 40 (Walker's) Infantry Regiment Private Company H; enlisted September 4, 1861 Montgomery, Alabama age 18; per September 4, 1861 to January 1, 1862 Muster Roll Remarks: Died November 15, 1861; per Register of Soldiers Killed in Battle or Died of Wounds or Disease died November 17, 1861 measles Memphis; Needham Marsh, father, filed a claim March 11, 1863; died November 15, 1861 and name spelled "Marst" in Lindsley's Annals 39 & 40 Consolidated Infantry Regiment Official Memorial Roll.

Marshall, William A.   Buried October 4, 1861   Lot/Division 1, #76   Plat Number 76
Tennessee 13 Infantry Regiment Private Company H; enlisted June 4, 1861, Germantown, Tennessee age 24; per May 5, 1863, Muster Roll Remarks: age 26 and died October 8, 1861, (note date difference with Cemetery record); died in Memphis of measles per Report of Deaths in unit records; died State Hospital measles per Daily Burial Record Book; died October 3, 1861, per October 5, 1861, *Memphis Daily Appeal* with unit identified as Yancy Rifles; died October 8, 1861, per Lindsley's Annals; possibly the "young Marshall" mentioned by Dr. S. H. Ford in his address on the occasion to commemorate (Confederate Memorial Day) Confederates buried at Elmwood on April 26, 1866, (see article "Honors To The Memory Of The Hero Dead" in the April 27, 1866, *Memphis Daily Appeal*, page 3, column 1).

Martin, Alfred   Buried August 3, 1861   Lot/Division 1, #15   Plat Number 15
Martin's Regiment Ray's Company; no compiled service record found; listed in report of August 1861 deaths at Southern Mothers Hospital in September 10, 1861, *Memphis Daily Appeal*, page 3, column 3; per report: Captain Ray's Company, Colonel Martin's Regiment, from Columbus, Kentucky and died August 2, 1861 pneumonia; died age 43 per Daily Burial Record Book; unit believed to be Mississippi 25 (Colonel John D. Martin) Infantry (Captain C. P. Ray) Company C; Company C later became Company K, Kentucky 7 Mounted Rifles (Company from Kentucky); not found in Kentucky Confederate books or compiled service records for the unit; Mississippi 25 Infantry Regiment by Special Order No. 25 dated January 21, 1862 became Confederate 2 Infantry Regiment but that unit disbanded about May 8, 1862; no record found under Confederate 2 Infantry Regiment; per August 15, 1861 the *Avalanche* Memphis Colonel Martin's Regiment (Ray listed as a Captain) left the City Wednesday August 14, 1861; there is no Alfred Martin in Mississippi 25 Infantry Regiment compiled service records but an Alexander Martin, Private Company C, who enlisted August 10, 1861 at Memphis, age 19, but no death indicated and no later records; grave stone: Co C 25 Miss Inf 1818 1861.

Martin, Henry R.   Buried November 16, 1861   Lot/Division 1, #196   Plat Number 196
Arkansas 7 Infantry Regiment Private Company A; enlisted July 26, 1861 Camp Shaver; per July 26 to August 31, 1861 Muster Roll Remarks: Sick; per August 31 to October 31, 1861 Muster Roll Remarks: Left at Columbus 13 October in Hospital; per December 31, 1861 Muster Roll Remarks: Private at Columbus, Kentucky October 12, now at Memphis, Tennessee.

Martin, James   Buried October 16, 1861   Lot/Division 1, #107   Plat Number 107
Tennessee 21/22 Cavalry Regiment Private Company G; no enlistment stated in compiled service record; name appears on Roll of Deserters and Absentees Without Leave dated March 1, 1865 with note as born Tishomingo County, Mississippi (would appear as never dropped from rolls); died Southern Mothers Hospital chronic diarrhea per Daily Burial Record Book.

Martin, John   Buried May 28, 1862   Lot/Division 2, #274   Plat Number 824
Arkansas 23 (Adams') Infantry Regiment Private (Harris') Company F; enlisted March 27, 1862 Jacksonport, Arkansas per March 27 to June 30, 1862 Muster Roll with remarks that discharged from service May 15, 1862 at Corinth, Mississippi (no other information in record); died Irving Hospital lung congestion per Daily Burial Record Book; not listed in Single Grave Book.

Martin, M. M.   Buried March 14, 1862   Lot/Division 1, #327   Plat Number 327
Baker's Alabama-Tennessee-Mississippi Regiment and died State Hospital per Daily Burial Record Book; no compiled service record found; unit should be 1st Alabama-Tennessee-Mississippi Infantry Regiment that after capture at Island 10 in April 1862 and exchange in Vicksburg, Mississippi in September, 1862, the six Alabama and Mississippi companies became known as Confederate 4 Infantry Regiment (soon to become the 54th Alabama Infantry Regiment) and the four Tennessee companies merged into the 42nd Tennessee Regiment but no compiled service record found in those regiments records.

Mason, Frank Y.   Buried September 1, 1931   Plat Number N58
Tennessee 7 Cavalry Regiment Private Companies B/K; enlisted March 18, 1862 Company K, Mason Depot, Tennessee; transferred to Company B August 18, 1862; discharged October 18, 1862 for being a minor (under 18); re-enlisted in Company B April 1, 1863 at Benton, Mississippi; per Tennessee Confederate Pension application #12634 born Mason, Fayette County, Tennessee December 2, 1844; per September 1, 1931 *The Commercial Appeal* Memphis, page 7, died August 31, 1931 age 86; died age 87 per Daily Burial Record Book.

Massey, George   Buried April 24, 1862   Lot/Division 1, #486   Plat Number 486
Tennessee 9 Infantry Regiment Private Company E; enlisted July 2, 1861 Union City, Tennessee; per Muster Roll Remarks: Died Hospital; died Private House per Daily Burial Record Book; not in Battle of Shiloh casualty list for unit reported in April 23, 1862, *Memphis Daily Appeal*; died April 25, 1862 per Lindsley's Annals.

Matheus, Samuel   Buried May 18, 1862   Lot/Division 2, #236   Plat Number 786
Arkansas 19 (Dockery/Smead's) Infantry Regiment Private Company A; enlisted February 25, 1862 Lewisville, Arkansas; per February 25 to June 30, 1862 Muster Roll Remarks: Absent sick; per September 1 to October 31, 1862 Muster Roll Remarks: Deserted. This man was sent to Memphis Hospital May 1 and he has never been heard of since; name spelled "Matthews" in Daily Burial Record Book and computer index; died at Mrs. Mecham's per Daily Burial Record Book.

Mathews, John W.   Buried May 10, 1862   Lot/Division 2, #152   Plat Number 702
Arkansas 19 (Dockery/Smead's) Infantry Regiment Private Company A; enlisted February 25, 1862 Lewisville, Arkansas; per February 25 to June 30, 1862 Muster Roll Remarks: Died at Memphis, Tennessee May 15, 1862; died Overton Hospital congestion per Daily Burial Record Book.

Mathis, Andrew J.   Buried April 17, 1862   Lot/Division 1, #461   Plat Number 461
Arkansas 17 (Lemoyne's) Infantry Regiment Private Company F; reference cards only with spelling as "Mathis" in 17 Lemoyne's Infantry and 21 Infantry Regiments compiled service records; records found under name "Mathews, A. J.," Arkansas 21 Infantry Regiment, Private Company E that was successor of Companies F and G of 17 Infantry; card with name "Mathews, A. J." indicates enlisted December 28, 1861 Wilson's Store and per muster roll for the period December 28, 1861 to June 30, 1862 died at Memphis April 20, 1862; card with name as "Mathis, Andrew J.," Private Company F Arkansas 17 Infantry muster roll dated April 28, 1862 for the period December 28, 1861 to January 27, 1862 indicates died at Memphis Hospital April 17, 1862; name spelled "Matthews" in Daily Burial Record Book and computer index; died April 14, 1862 dysentery per Daily Burial Record Book.

Mathis, B. B.   Buried May 3, 1862   Lot/Division 2, #34   Plat Number 584
Arkansas 25 (Turnbull's) Infantry Regiment Private Company E; enlisted March 10, 1862 Jacksonport, Arkansas; per March 10 to April 30, 1862 Muster Roll Remarks: Left in Hospital in Memphis, Tennessee; per Muster Roll dated May 1, 1862 died in Hospital Memphis, Tennessee; died camp, name spelled "Mathew" in Daily Burial Record Book and computer index; Company A in Daily Burial Record Book.

Matthews, Daniel S.   Buried May 20, 1862   Lot/Division 2, #245   Plat Number 795
Texas 9 (Sim's) Cavalry Regiment Private Company E; enlisted October 14, 1861 Camp Reeves, Texas, age 19; per March & April 1862 Muster Roll Remarks: at Memphis, sick; per September & October 1863 Muster Roll Remarks: Private at Memphis, Tennessee March 1862; Died C. R. Stuart's per Daily Burial Record Book.

Matthews, John B.   Buried March 12, 1862   Lot/Division 1, #322   Plat Number 322
Mississippi Graves' Company Light Artillery (Issaquena Battery); Graves Battery Ky in Daily Burial Record Book but records

found under Mississippi; enlisted October 12, 1861 Bowling Green, Kentucky in Captain R. E. Graves' Company Light Artillery (2 Division Army of Central Kentucky); unit captured at Fort Donelson, Tennessee February 1862, and exchanged at Vicksburg August 1862; also found listed as member of Graves Battery Artillery, Kentucky in *Report of The Adjutant General of the State of Kentucky, Confederate Kentucky Volunteers War 1861-65*; died Overton Hospital per Daily Burial Record Book.

Mauldin, Jesse A.   Buried March 20, 1862   Lot/Division 1, #358   Plat Number 358
Arkansas 8 Infantry Regiment Private New Company C; enlisted September 10, 1861 Camp Price Northeast Arkansas age 17; per April 30 to June 30, 1862 Muster Roll Remarks: Absent Sick; per December 31, 1862 to February 28, 1863 Muster Roll Remarks: Absent Sick December 1861, Surgeon; per October 31 to December 31, 1863 Muster Roll Remarks: Died in Hospital; per Overton Hospital March 1862 Register of Deaths died March 19 of pneumonia and name "J. A. Maudling," Private Company H Arkansas 8 Regiment; Company H per Daily Burial Record Book; New Company E of Arkansas 8 Infantry Regiment formed from consolidation of Old Companies E & H.

May, Leander   Buried May 16, 1862   Lot/Division 2, #225   Plat Number 775
Arkansas 23 (Adams') Infantry Regiment Private Company C; enlisted February 22, 1862 St Francis County, Arkansas; per March 13 to June 30, 1862 Muster Roll Remarks: Died May 17, 1862; first name spelled "Lauder" and died Irving Hospital measles in Daily Burial Record Book; first name spelled both "Lauder/Lander" in Cemetery computer index; per Irving Hospital Record admitted May 7, 1862 with complaint of measles and died May 15, 1862; not listed in Cemetery Single Grave Book.

May, William H.   Buried August 31, 1861   Lot/Division 1, #46   Plat Number 46
Arkansas 9 Infantry Regiment Private Company G; enlisted July 27, 1861 Pine Bluff, Arkansas; per July 27 to November 1, 1861 Muster Roll Remarks: Died August 30 from congestive chill Memphis, Tennessee; died congestive chill age 23 per Daily Burial Record Book.

Maynard, John H.   Buried April 2, 1862   Lot/Division 1, #409   Plat Number 409
Tennessee 5 Infantry Regiment Private Company C; enlisted May 20, 1861 Paris, Henry County, Tennessee, age 25; per Muster Roll Remarks: Died April 1862 Memphis Hospital; 1836 1862 on grave stone; died April 20, 1862 per Lindsley's Annals.

McAnulty, S. H.   Buried May 6, 1862   Lot/Division 2, #65   Plat Number 615
Arkansas 19 (Dockery/Smead's) Infantry Regiment Private Company G; enlisted March 1, 1862 Union County, Arkansas; per March 1 to June 30, 1862 Muster Roll Remarks: Absent sick; per August 31 to October 31, 1862 Muster Roll Remarks: Absent sick since 1 May, not since heard from; per November & December 1862 Muster Roll Remarks: Sent to Hospital, not heard from since 1 May 1862; per January & February 1863 Muster Roll Remarks: Sent to Hospital at Memphis 28 April 1862, believed to be dead; name spelled "McAnally" in Daily Burial Record Book and computer index; died Overton Hospital per Daily Burial Record Book.

McCaghren, James   Buried October 16, 1861   Lot/Division 1, #108   Plat Number 108
Louisiana 12 Infantry Regiment Private Company A; enlisted August 18, 1861 Camp Moore, Louisiana; per Muster Roll Remarks: Absent on furlough for sickness since October 13, 1861; died Southern Mothers Hospital enteritis, name spelled "McCaghan" in Daily Burial Record Book and computer index; Company I per Daily Burial Record Book.

McCammon, Columbus D.   Buried October 31, 1861   Lot/Division 1, #153   Plat Number 153
Arkansas 5 Infantry Regiment Private (Green's) Company C; enlisted June 10, 1861 Little Rock, Arkansas; present on July & August 1861 Muster Roll; no other information in compiled service record; died pneumonia age 21 per Cemetery record; name spelled "McCommon" in Cemetery computer index.

McCance, R. M.   Buried March 21, 1862   Lot/Division 1, #364   Plat Number 364
Arkansas 11 Infantry Regiment Private Company K per Daily Burial Record Book; no compiled service record found; per Overton Hospital March 1862 Register of Sick died March 20 of pneumonia; not listed in Cemetery Single Grave Book.

McCardy, George Robert   Buried July 21, 1861   Lot/Division 1, #52   Plat Number 52
Missouri 1 Regiment Volunteers and died congestive chill age 22 per Daily Burial Record Book; no compiled service record found; second initial "P" in Cemetery Single Grave Book; not found Missouri 1 Infantry Regiment compiled service record rolls, which had organized June 22, 1861, at Camp Calhoun near Memphis.

McCarty, William E.   Buried May 4, 1862   Lot/Division 2, #44   Plat Number 594
Arkansas 20 (King's) Infantry Regiment Private Company C; enlisted February 28, 1862 Warren, Bradley County, Arkansas; per February 28 to May 2, 1862 Muster Roll Remarks: Died at Hospital in Memphis April 30, 1862; per February 28 to June 30, 1862 Muster Roll Remarks: Died May 1 at Memphis; died Overton Hospital typhoid fever per Daily Burial Record Book; name spelled "McCarthy" in Daily Burial Record Book and computer index.

McClanahan, W. P.   Buried March 13, 1862   Lot/Division 1, #325   Plat Number 325
Louisiana 21 Regiment Company D per Daily Burial Record Book; no compiled service record found; per Overton Hospital March 1862 Register of Sick died March 12 of rubella and name W. P. McCallahan, Louisiana 21 Regiment Private Company D; Overton Hospital February 28, 1862 Register of Sick and Wounded indicates unit as Kennedy D. (J. B. G. Kennedy was Colonel of Louisiana 21 Infantry Regiment).

McClintock, Edwin Morgan   Buried October 22, 1861   Lot/Division 1, #127   Plat Number 127
Pheister's Battalion Company E per Daily Burial Record Book; no compiled service record found; not found Arkansas 6 Battalion Cavalry (Phifer's Battalion); full name per descendant Marian Frye who worked in the Elmwood Cemetery Office.

McLure, R. H.   Buried March 7, 1862   Lot/Division 1, #291   Plat Number 291
Arkansas 11 Infantry Regiment Private Company E per Daily Burial Record Book; no compiled service record found.

McClure, Jere   Buried March 20, 1862   Lot/Division 1, #352   Plat Number 352
Tennessee 7 Cavalry Regiment Private (White's) Company (Logwood's 6 Cavalry Battalion); enlisted June 14, 1861, Memphis; died prior to Tennessee 7 Cavalry Regiment formal organization on April 1, 1862; died Overton Hospital per Daily Burial Record Book; may be the Paggy McClure listed in the Letter to the Editor ("The Tennessee Rifles"), *Memphis Daily Appeal*, April 10, 1887, page 9, column 2, that list the original members of the Tennessee Mounted Rifles.

McClusky, W. P.   Buried March 13, 1862   Lot/Division 1, #326   Plat Number 326
Louisiana 21 Regiment Company D and died State Hospital per Daily Burial Record Book; no compiled service record found.

McCollum, John W.   Buried May 11, 1862   Lot/Division 2, #158   Plat Number 708
Arkansas 23 (Adams') Infantry Regiment Private (Pennington's) Company H; enlisted March 6, 1862 Arkadelphia, Arkansas; per March 6 to June 30, 1862 Muster Roll Remarks: Died May 10, 1862 Memphis typhoid fever; Mansfield's noted in Daily Burial Record Book; name spelled "McCallum" in Daily Burial Record Book and computer index.

McCool, Andrew J.   Buried January 27, 1862   Lot/Division 1, #258   Plat Number 258
Arkansas 11 (Smith's) Infantry Regiment Private Company A; enlisted January 9, 1862, at Benton, Arkansas; per November 1, 1861 to September 21, 1862 Muster Roll Remarks: Discharged January 25, 1862; per Register of Claim filed for settlement in the Office of the Confederate States Auditor for the War Department: father, Andrew McCool, filed a claim May 8, 1863, indicating that died at Memphis, Tennessee (date not stated) and due $56.16; affidavit by father also in file indicates death on or about January 24, 1862, at Memphis, Tennessee; name spelled "McCove" in Daily Burial Record Book and both "McCove" and "McCone" in Cemetery computer index and "McCone" on grave stone.

McCormic, Patrick   Buried March 24, 1862   Lot/Division 1, #375   Plat Number 375
Louisiana 11 Infantry Regiment Private Company B; enlisted August 19, 1861 Camp Moore, Louisiana; per Overton Hospital March 1862 Register of Deaths died March 24 of pneumonia and name "McCormick"; name spelled "McCormick" in Daily Burial Record Book and computer index; per Cemetery record grave in short row north side of Monument.

McCulloch, James   Buried November 11,1861   Lot/Division 1, #179   Plat Number 179
Arkansas 2 Regiment Hindman Legion and died State Hospital per Daily Burial Record Book; not found Arkansas 2 Hindman's Infantry Regiment; does not appear to be J. McCullah, Arkansas 2 Hindman's Infantry Regiment Company G, as compiled service record indicates captured at Vicksburg, Mississippi July 4, 1863.

McCullough, Alexander   Buried July 1, 1876   Lot/Division 2, #386   Plat Number 936
Tennessee 154 Senior Infantry Regiment Private Company A; enlisted May 14, 1861 Randolph age 28; paroled May 10, 1865 at Meridian, Mississippi; died congestion age 45 per Daily Burial Record Book; possibly "Alexander McCulloch" who is listed in Mathes book as one time a member of Confederate Historical Association but no sketch; burial reported under "Local Paragraphs" in *Memphis Daily Appeal*, July 2, 1876, page 4, column 2, which indicated that members of the Hundred-fifty-fourth regiment and other military companies attended the funeral.

McCurdy, William P.   Buried November 28, 1861   Lot/Division 1, #229   Plat Number 229
Arkansas 9 Infantry Regiment Private Company K; enlisted August 9, 1861, Camden, Arkansas; per November 1, 1861 to January 1, 1862 Muster Roll Remarks: Died November 28, 1861; died Southern Mothers Hospital enteritis per Daily Burial Record Book.

McDaniel, Daniel   Buried March 3, 1862   Lot/Division 1, #280   Plat Number 280
Mississippi 44 (Blythe's 1 Battalion) Infantry Regiment Private Company K; enlisted December 27, 1861 Natchez, Mississippi; per March & April 1862 Muster Roll Remarks: Died in Hospital Memphis, Tennessee, March 3, 1862; per Report of Deaths of Organization dated December 8, 1863 indicates born Amite County, Mississippi and died from disease in Memphis, Tennessee March 15, 1862; name spelled "McDaniels" in Daily Burial Record Book and computer index; died Overton Hospital per Daily Burial Record Book; not listed in Cemetery Single Grave Book.

McDonnel, John C.   Buried April 21, 1862   Lot/Division 1, #476   Plat Number 476
Arkansas 21 Infantry Regiment Private Company K; enlisted March 16, 1862 Pocahontas, Arkansas; per February to June 1862 Muster Roll Remarks: Left at Memphis in Hospital April 14, 1862; unit Arkansas 17 Regiment Company (not found Arkansas 17 Lemoyne's Infantry Regiment Company D that was predecessor of Arkansas 21 Infantry Regiment Company K), died Overton Hospital pneumonia per Daily Burial Record Book; name spelled "McDonald" in Daily Burial Record Book and computer index.

McFarland, Andrew J.   Buried April 29, 1862   Lot/Division 1, #516   Plat Number 516
Missouri 4 Infantry (Major Johnson's Battalion, also known as 1st Battalion) Regiment Private Company H, per Company Muster Roll for January 1 to June 30, 1862, enlisted February 10, 1862, at Springfield, Missouri with remarks: Died of congestive chill in Memphis April 28, company roll cards have initials both as "A. J." and "J. A." and name "Andrew" on a Historic Roll with remarks that had served in 8th Division, Missouri State Guard, Missouri 4 Infantry Regiment was organized April 28, 1862, at Memphis, Tennessee by the consolidation Major Waldo Porter Johnson's 1st Battalion with Major Archibald MacFarlane's Battalion and Captains Jeptha Feagan's and George Bates' Missouri State Guard companies; only initial "J" in Daily Burial Record Book and computer index; died camp per Daily Burial Record Book.

McFarland, John N.   Buried September 23, 1861   Lot/Division 1, #79   Plat Number 79
Tennessee 15 Infantry Regiment Private Company A; enlisted June 6, 1861 Jackson, Tennessee; per August 15, 1861 Muster Roll Remarks: Absent Sick August 11, 1861; per August to November 1861 Muster Roll Remarks: Reported dead at Hospital at Memphis but unofficial; not found in Lindsley's Annals.

McGill, J. T.   Buried May 16, 1862   Lot/Division 2, #221   Plat Number 771
Texas 27 (Whitfield's Legion) Cavalry Regiment Private Company H; enlisted March 10, 1862 Clarksville, Texas; per March 10 to April 30, 1862 Muster Roll Remarks: Absent sick and reduced to rank at Memphis, Tennessee April 24, 1862 (no death indicated); from Red River County per Daily Burial Record Book.

McGowen, John   Buried December 3, 1861   Lot/Division 1, #237   Plat Number 237
Tennessee 21 Infantry Regiment Private Company G; enlisted June 9, 1861 Vicksburg, Mississippi; per November & December 1861 Muster Roll Remarks; wounded at Belmont and died December 12, 1861; name spelled "McGowan," gunshot wound, Company B and died Overton Hospital per Daily Burial Record Book; per Overton Hospital Record name spelled "McGowan," admitted November 15, 1861 with complaint of ancle (sic) and died December 3, 1861; listed as "John McGown Company G" in Report of Wounded in November 15, 1861 *Memphis Daily Appeal* that arrived at Overton Hospital on November 4, 1861; in December 4, 1861 *Memphis Daily Appeal* listed on Overton Hospital Report of Deaths on December 3, 1861, Company A and name spelled "McCowan"; not listed in Cemetery Single Grave Book.

McGuire, Rufus   Buried October 16, 1861   Lot/Division 1, #33   Plat Number 33
Arkansas 13 Infantry Regiment Company I and died Southern Mothers Hospital dysentery per Daily Burial Record Book; no compiled service record found.

McGuire, Thomas   Buried July 11, 1861   Lot/Division 1, #18   Plat Number 18
From Vicksburg, Mississippi per Daily Burial Record Book; possibly Thomas McGuire, Arkansas 2 Infantry Regiment Private Company B, who enlisted May 23, 1861 Helena, Arkansas age 32 and who per Muster Roll dated June 20, 1861 was at camp near Memphis and per May to August 1861 Muster Roll Remarks present but no other information in compiled service record.

McIntush, King   Buried November 3, 1861   Lot/Division 1, #160   Plat Number 160
Tennessee 40 (Walker's) Infantry Regiment Private Company H; enlisted September 4, 1861 Montgomery, Alabama age 19; per November 1, 1861 Muster Roll Remarks: Sick in Hospital; per September 4, 1861 to January 1, 1862 Muster Roll Remarks: Died November 3, 1861; per Register of Soldiers Killed in Battle or Died of Wounds or Disease born Green County, Alabama and died November 9, 1861 Memphis measles; name spelled "McIntosh" in Daily Burial Record Book and computer index; died camp per Daily Burial Record Book; name "R. McIntosh" indicated in Lindsley's Annals 39 & 40 Consolidated Infantry Regiment Official Memorial Roll.

McKay, Michael   Buried April 14, 1862   Lot/Division 1, #443   Plat Number 443
Arkansas 18 (Carroll's) Infantry Regiment (Lynch's) Company G and died Overton Hospital pneumonia per Daily Burial Record Book; no compiled service record found for McKay but may be Michael McCoy, Private Company G who enlisted March 2, 1862, at Little Rock, Arkansas age 45 and who per Company Muster Roll dated September 1 to December 31, 1862, remarks died in Memphis; not listed in Cemetery Single Grave Book.

McKinney, John   Buried October 29, 1861   Lot/Division 1, #146   Plat Number 146
Arkansas 9 Infantry Regiment Private Company E; enlisted July 27, 1861 Pine Bluff, Arkansas; per July 27 to November 1, 1861 Muster Roll Remarks: Died October 18, 1861 in Memphis, Tennessee; died Southern Mothers Hospital enteritis and Company D per Daily Burial Record Book.

McKinney, L. R.   Buried April 20, 1862   Lot/Division 1, #472   Plat Number 472
Arkansas 18 (Carroll's) Infantry Regiment Private Company C; enlisted March 8, 1862 Des Arc, Arkansas; per March to June 1862 Muster Roll Remarks: Died in Hospital Memphis April 14, 1862; died Overton Hospital per Daily Burial Record Book; not listed in Cemetery Single Grave Book.

McLellan, William   Buried April 27, 1862   Lot/Division 1, #506   Plat Number 506
Tennessee 154 Senior Infantry Regiment Private Company H; enlisted April 26, 1861 Memphis age 22; per January to June 1862 Muster Roll Remarks: Died in Memphis April 22, 1862 of wounds received at Shiloh; per May 6, 1863 Muster Roll Remarks: Died in Memphis April 22, 1862 of wounds received in Battle of Shiloh April 6, 1862; per Register of Soldiers Killed in Battle: born Ohio, deceased April 25, 1862 at Memphis; listed on Report of Deaths dated October 30, 1863; name also found spelled "McClellan" in compiled service record; name spelled "McLelland" in Lindsley's Annals; name spelled "McClelland" in Daily Burial Record Book and computer index ; died State Hospital per Daily Burial Record Book; reported as wounded in unit casualty list for Battle of Shiloh reported in April 24, 1862 *Memphis Daily Appeal*.

McMullen, John   Buried November 18, 1861   Lot/Division 1, #199   Plat Number 199
Tennessee 21 Infantry Regiment Private Company C; enlisted June 1, 1861 Pocahontas, Mississippi; per November & December 1861 Muster Roll Remarks: Killed Battle of Belmont November 7, 1861; on list of casualties from Battle of Belmont, Kentucky as reported in November 13, 1861 *Memphis Daily Appeal*; arrived at Overton Hospital November 4, 1861 per November 15, 1861 *Memphis Daily Appeal*; died November 17, 1861 per November 24, 1861 *Memphis Daily Appeal*; died Overton Hospital per Daily Burial Record Book; per Overton Hospital record admitted November 15, 1861 with complaint of leg but no date of death indicated.

McMaury, Hezekiah E.   Buried November 19, 1861   Lot/Division 1, #203   Plat Number 203
Arkansas 12 (Gantt's) Infantry Regiment (Wyatt's) Company F, per Company Muster Roll dated July 26, 1861, to October 1, 1862, enlisted July 26, 1861, at Arkadelphia, Arkansas, and remarks: Died at Memphis November, 1861, per Register of Claim filed for settlement in the Office of the Confederate States Auditor for the War Department: father, Sam McMurry, filed a claim March 12, 1863, indicating that died at Memphis, Tennessee (date not stated); name spelled "McMurray" in Daily Burial Record Book and computer index; died age 22 per Daily Burial Record Book.

McWright, W. D.   Buried May 3, 1862   Lot/Division 2, #33   Plat Number 583
No unit indicated and died Overton Hospital pneumonia per Daily Burial Record Book.

Meek, Joseph C.   Buried May 9, 1862   Lot/Division 2, #133   Plat Number 683
Arkansas 23 (Adams') Infantry Regiment Private (Harris') Company F; enlisted March 27, 1862 Jacksonport, Arkansas; per March 27 to June 30, 1862 Muster Roll Remarks: Died May 14, 1862 at Memphis; initials "J. A." in Daily Burial Record Book and computer index; not listed in Cemetery Single Grave Book.

Mehan, Martin   Buried December 26, 1861   Lot/Division 1, #252   Plat Number 252
No unit indicated and died Overton Hospital per Daily Burial Record Book; not listed in Cemetery Single Grave Book.

Melton, John   Buried May 7, 1862   Lot/Division 2, #99   Plat Number 649
Missouri 1 Infantry Battalion Private Company C; per May & June 1862, Company Muster Roll enlisted March 11, 1862, Pocahontas, Arkansas by Major W. F. Rapley with Remarks: Died May 6, 1862, Memphis Hospital, Kelsey's Company, which was at Fort Pillow during May 1862, and operated as marines aboard Confederate defense fleet gunboats; Company became Company K, 6th Regiment Missouri Infantry, about August 23, 1862, but no record found in that unit's compiled service records; Rapsley's Arkansas Battalion Company B and died Overton Hospital typhoid pneumonia in Daily Burial Record Book; name "Milton" in Daily Burial Record Book and computer index; not listed in Single Grave Book.

Merrit, B.   Buried January 17, 1863   Lot/Division 2, #326   Plat Number 876
Alabama 1 Regiment Company B per Daily Burial Record Book; no compiled service record found.

Middleton, C. H.   Buried November 27, 1861   Lot/Division 1, # 225   Plat Number 225
Tennessee 13 Infantry Regiment Private Company F; enlisted May 13, 1861, Jackson, Tennessee age 22; per May 2, 1863, Muster Roll Remarks: Killed at Battle of Belmont; per Report of Deaths born Virginia and killed in action November 7, 1861, at Belmont; wounded at Battle of Belmont, Missouri per casualty report in November 13, 1861, *Memphis Daily Appeal*; arrived at Overton Hospital November 4, 1861, per November 15, 1861, *Memphis Daily Appeal*; shot in face at Battle of Belmont, Missouri and unit 12 Infantry per November 28, 1861, *Memphis Daily Appeal*, page 4, column 1; died Overton Hospital per Daily Burial Record Book; per Overton Hospital Record admitted November 15, 1861, with complaint of shoulder and face and died November 27, 1861; 1839 1862 on grave stone.

Miller, H.   Buried March 19, 1862   Lot/Division 1, #346   Plat Number 346
Arkansas 11 Infantry Regiment Private Company B; compiled service record found under Harden Miller, Private Company B, who

was captured at Island 10 April 8, 1862; per Overton Hospital February 28, 1862 Register of Sick and Wounded admitted February 23 (no other information); died Overton Hospital per Daily Burial Record Book; not Harden Miller, Arkansas 11/17 Consolidated Infantry Regiment Color Corporal Companies A & B who was present in 1863 per compiled service records.

Miller, R. B.   Buried December 28, 1902   Lot/Division 1, #549   Plat Number 549
Tennessee 18 Cavalry Regiment Private Company K; enlisted April 10, 1864 Jackson, Tennessee; per May & June 1864 Muster Roll Remarks: Absent since May 28, 1864 and left at Jackson, Tennessee; died age 76 per Daily Burial Record Book; 1826 1902 on grave stone.

Miller, Robert   Buried March 11, 1862   Lot/Division 1, #318   Plat Number 318
Arkansas 12 Infantry Regiment Private Company H; enlisted July 29, 1861 Arkadelphia, Arkansas; per July to October 1862 Muster Roll Remarks: Died at Memphis March 1862; per Overton Hospital March 1862 Register of Deaths died March 11 of pernio.

Miller, Van   Buried April 24, 1862   Lot/Division 1, #487   Plat Number 487
Arkansas 25 Infantry Regiment Sergeant (McKay's) Company I; no enlistment in compiled service record; per March 19 to April 30, 1862 Muster Roll Remarks: Died at Overton Hospital April 23, 1862; died Overton Hospital and McCoy's Regiment Company E per Daily Burial Record Book.

Millner, Robert   Buried August 8, 1865   Lot/Division 2, #359   Plat Number 909
No unit indicated in Daily Burial Record Book; R. Milner in Cemetery Alpha Book; Miller, B. and "killed when Forrest came into Memphis" indicated in Cemetery Single Grave Book; may be the William Miller listed in Elmwood 1874 book as Confederate soldier buried in Elmwood who was citizen of Memphis or vicinity (see sketch in chapter "Confederates Buried Outside of Soldiers Rest"); also may be the "Billy Miller" who per sketch in "Historic Elmwood Walking Tour" Volume I, April 22, 1995, pages 12-16, compiled by Malcolm Gary Hood (copy on file in Cemetery Office), was a Private in the "Wigfall Grays, assigned to Company E, Seventh Tennessee Cavalry fightin' with Generals Forrest and Chalmers" and killed when he tried to rescue his girlfriend (Ginny (name Jenny in Cemetery record) McGhee who had died unbeknownst to him January 24, 1864) from the Irving Block Prison during Forrest's Raid on Memphis August 21, 1864; possibly B. Milner, Private Company D, 3 Tennessee Cavalry who enlisted December 24, 1862, Middleburg, Tennessee and per November/December 1862, Muster Roll Remarks captured at Parkers Crossroads December 31, 1862, but no other information in record; not R. B. Miller Tennessee 7 Cavalry Regiment; cannot tell if any of the Milners in Tennessee 3 Cavalry Regiment; note "Wigfall Grays" was Company C 4th (Neely's) Tennessee Infantry Regiment, which was not part of the Forrest Raid on Memphis.

Mims, John Thomas   Buried October 21, 1861   Lot/Division 1, #124   Plat Number 124
Confederate 4 (Bakers') Infantry Regiment Private Company B (Captain Jonas Griffin's Rifles); per Company Muster-in Roll enlisted August 10, 1861, at Montgomery, Alabama age 17; per Company Muster Roll dated October 31, 1861, remarks: Died of Typhoid Fever at the Southern Mothers Home in Memphis, Tennessee on the 21st of October, 1861; regiment (also known as 1st Alabama, Tennessee and Mississippi Infantry) was formed about December 9, 1861, with ten companies: four from Alabama, two from Mississippi, and four from Tennessee; captured at Island 10 April 8, 1862, and after exchange in September, 1862, the companies were reorganized and transferred to other commands; Company B became Company C of the Alabama 54th Infantry Regiment but no record for this regiment as died before transfer; died Southern Mothers Hospital typhoid fever age 17 per Daily Burial Record Book and name spelled "Minnis" in Daily Burial Record Book and computer index.

Mineace, J. J.   Buried May 7, 1862   Lot/Division 2, #107   Plat Number 657
Arkansas 17 Infantry Regiment and died Overton Hospital per Daily Burial Record Book; no compiled service record found.

Mitchell, John   Buried June 9, 1862   Lot/Division 2, #288   Plat Number 838
Flarney's Company and died State Hospital per Daily Burial Record Book; no compiled service record found; see Smith, N. D. (Grave# 286) who was buried same date and unit name appears to be the same in the Daily Burial Record Book but transcribed differently in other Cemetery records.

Mitchell, William   Buried April 23, 1862   Lot/Division 1, #481   Plat Number 481
Arkansas 1 Infantry Regiment Company D; wounded and died Irving Hospital per Daily Burial Record Book; possibly W. R. Mitchell, Arkansas 1 Mounted Rifles, Private Company E who enlisted June 9, 1861 Fort Smith, Arkansas and who per January & February 1862 Muster Roll Remarks was Private at Corinth Hospital April 24, 1862 and per March & April 1862 Muster Roll Remarks not heard from since April 1862 and supposed to be dead.

Montgomery, G. W.   Buried May 13, 1862   Lot/Division 2, #194   Plat Number 744
Texas 6 (Stone's) Cavalry Regiment Company C; enlisted September 10, 1861 Dallas, Texas, age 22; per March & April 1862 Muster Roll Remarks: Absent sick in Hospital at Memphis, Tennessee from April 25; per May & June 1862 Muster Roll Remarks: died of disease May 12, 1862; died Overton Hospital typhoid fever per Daily Burial Record Book.

Montjoie, P. T.   Buried July 13, 1861   Lot/Division 1, #89   Plat Number 89
Pettus Flying Artillery per Daily Burial Record Book (Mississippi Hoole's Company Light Artillery (Hudson's), which mustered into service in May 1861, at Eureka, Mississippi and sent to Memphis June 28, 1861, and then to New Madrid, Missouri); no compiled service record found; per article in July 14, 1861, *Memphis Daily Appeal* died Southern Mothers Hospital; inquest on death reported in July 15, 1861, the *Avalanche* Memphis.

Moore, Edward   Buried March 20, 1862   Lot/Division 1, #354   Plat Number 354
Texas 9 (Young's/Maxey's) Infantry Regiment Private Company A; enlisted September 26, 1861 Paris, Texas; per Descriptive List: age 18, born Tennessee, farmer, died March 26, 1862 of disease in Overton Hospital, Memphis, Tennessee and has received no pay; per Overton Hospital March 1862 Register of Deaths admitted February 9 and died March 19 of rubella.

Moore, Frank   Buried March 21, 1862   Lot/Division 1, #360   Plat Number 360
Texas 9 (Young's/Maxey's) Infantry Regiment Company A and died Overton Hospital per Daily Burial Record Book; no compiled service record found; not F. L. Moore in same unit as he survived the War per his service record; not listed in Single Grave Book.

Moore, Peter   Buried May 3, 1862   Lot/Division 2, #38   Plat Number 588
Arkansas 15 (Josey's) Infantry Regiment Private Company C; enlisted July 23, 1861 Camp Hardee Pittmans Ferry; per February 28 to June 30, 1862 Muster Roll Remarks: Died of wounds in Hospital at Memphis April 21; per November & December 1862 Muster Roll Remarks Died in Hospital at Memphis of a wound received at Shiloh; unit Arkansas 1 Regiment in Daily Burial Record Book; Arkansas 15 Josey's Infantry originally called 1 Cleburne's Regiment; wounded and died Irving Hospital per Daily Burial Record Book; not listed in Cemetery Single Grave Book.

Moore, William   Buried May 18, 1862   Lot/Division 2, #239   Plat Number 789
Arkansas 2 Infantry Regiment Private Company B; enlisted May 23, 1861 Helena, Arkansas age 28; per May 23 to August 31, 1861, Muster Roll Remarks: Deserted in Memphis July 31, 1861 (no other information); died Irving Hospital diarrhea and pneumonia per Daily Burial Record Book; per Irving Hospital record admitted April 22, 1862 with complaint of diarrhea and died May 18, 1862.

Moore, William H.   Buried May 3, 1862   Lot/Division 2, #36   Plat Number 586
Arkansas 19 (Dockery/Smead's) Infantry Regiment Private Company D/E; enlisted March 1, 1862 Rock Port; per March 1 to June 30, 1862 Muster Roll Remarks: Died May 1, 1862; died Overton Hospital pneumonia per Daily Burial Record Book; per compiled service record full initials "W. H. H."

Morfels, Henry   Buried March 8, 1862   Lot/Division 1, #299   Plat Number 299
Memphis Appeal Battery per Daily Burial Record Book but no compiled service record found; unit later became Arkansas 5 Battery Light Artillery (Appeal Battery) and also known as Captain Bryan's, Hogg's and Scott's Arkansas Light Artillery; died before unit officially organized in April 1862; not listed in Cemetery Single Grave Book.

Morgan, Charles A.   Buried October 26, 1861   Lot/Division 1, #139   Plat Number 139
Tennessee 40 (Walker's) Infantry Regiment Private Company F; enlisted October 5, 1861 Memphis age 17; per October 31, 1861 Muster Roll Remarks: Died October 24, 1861; died camp measles per Daily Burial Record Book; died October 2, 1861 per Lindsley's Annals 39 & 40 Consolidated Infantry Regiment Official Memorial Roll.

Morris, John   Buried May 5, 1862   Lot/Division 2, #54   Plat Number 604
Arkansas 3 (Borland's) Cavalry Regiment Private (Blackwell's) Company B; enlisted March 6, 1862 Perryville, Arkansas; per January 31 to April 30, 1862 Muster Roll Remarks: Sick in Hospital since April 23, 1862; per May & June 1862 Muster Roll Remarks: Left in Hospital at Memphis since April 23, 1862 reported dead date not known; name appears on a Register of Soldiers who died of Wounds or Disease indicating died May 3, 1861 (sic) in Memphis; name appears on a Register Containing a Record of the Property of Deceased Confederate Soldiers dated September 8, 1862 indicating died at Memphis May 3, 1862; Balland's Cavalry and died Overton Hospital pneumonia per Daily Burial Record Book.

Morris, Richard   Buried October 2, 1861   Lot/Division 1, #99   Plat Number 99
Martin's Regiment Company G and died Southern Mothers Hospital pneumonia and dysentery age 15 per Daily Burial Record Book; no compiled service record found; unit believed to be Mississippi 25 Infantry based on Alfred Martin's death information but not found that unit or Confederate 2 Infantry or Arkansas 9 Infantry, which were subsequent designations for the Mississippi 25 Infantry Regiment Company G (Captain Charles Bowen, Osceola Hornets).

Morris, Thomas   Buried March 13, 1914   Plat Number N21
Mississippi 1 (Johnston's) Infantry Regiment Private Company K; enlisted November 15, 1864 Tuscumbia, Alabama; captured at Nashville, Tennessee December 15, 1864, sent to Military Prison Louisville, Kentucky, transferred to Camp Douglas, Illinois December 20, 1864; name appears on Roll of Prisoners at Camp Douglas applying for Oath of Allegiance January 1865, claims to have been loyal, was conscripted into the Rebel Army and deserted to avail himself of the Amnesty Proclamation; per widow's

(Mary A. Kelly) Tennessee Confederate Pension application (W5469) born October 1835 Nashville, Tennessee and died March 11, 1914; 1830 (note birth year difference with widow's pension application) 1914 on grave stone; died age 84 per Daily Burial Record Book.

Mowatt, James   Buried October 5, 1861   Lot/Division 1, #39   Plat Number 39
Captain Barbiere's Company per Daily Burial Record Book; no compiled service record found; not found Confederate general index; died before regiment formally organized; Joseph Barbiere was 1 Lieutenant of "The Gayoso Guards" per June 5, 1861, *Memphis Daily Appeal*; per August 1, 1861 *Memphis Daily Appeal*, Captain Barbiere was authorized to raise a regiment; per *Tennesseans in the Civil War* Part 1, "The Gayoso Guards" was Company A Tennessee 39 (Avery's) Infantry Regiment but regiment officially organized as 1 Alabama-Tennessee-Mississippi Infantry Regiment (Confederate 4 Infantry); after unit's capture at Island 10 in April 1862 and exchange Company became 2 Company I Tennessee 42 Infantry Regiment; per September 26, 1861, the *Avalanche* Memphis Colonel Avery's Regiment - the Gayoso Guard Captain Barbiere and one or two other companies belonging to Colonel W. T. Avery's Regiment will leave today for their rendezvous in the vicinity of Germantown; not found in Lindsley's Annals 39 & 40 Consolidated Infantry Regiment Official Memorial Roll.

Mullins, Albert A.   Buried May 20, 1862   Lot/Division 2, #243   Plat Number 793
Arkansas 2 Infantry Regiment Private Company K; enlisted June 18, 1861 Memphis, age 21; per April 30 to June 30, 1862 Muster Roll Remarks: Wounded and sent to Hospital; per October 31 to December 31, 1862 Muster Roll Remarks: Sent to Hospital wounded and not present since the Shiloh fight; J. Moon's noted in Daily Burial Record Book; arrived at Irving Hospital April 15, 1862 per April 16, 1862 *Memphis Daily Appeal*, Local Matters.

Murphree, Anderson   Buried June 7, 1901   Lot/Division 1, #548   Plat Number 548
Mississippi 8 Cavalry Regiment Private Company C; enlisted August 17, 1863 Concord, Mississippi; per undated Historic Roll of Regiment age 42, native of Tennessee, occupation mechanic; residence (nearest Post Office at enlistment) Air Mount, Yalobusha County, Mississippi and on extra duty as blacksmith; name spelled "Murphy" and died age 77y/5m/23d per Daily Burial Record Book; 1823 1901 on grave stone.

Music, Richard   Buried May 7, 1862   Lot/Division 2, #96   Plat Number 646
Arkansas 17 (Lemoyne's) Infantry Regiment Private Company A; enlisted October 7, 1861 Lewisburg, Arkansas; no other information in service records; no record found under Arkansas 21 Infantry that was successor of Arkansas 17 Infantry; died Overton Hospital pneumonia per Daily Burial Record Book; name spelled "Musick" in Daily Burial Record Book and computer index.

Myers, J. A.   Buried March 15, 1862   Lot/Division 1, #331   Plat Number 331
Arkansas 8 Infantry Regiment (Desha's Battalion Company E) Private New Company K; enlisted November 16, 1861 Pocahontas by Major F. W. Desha; per April 30 to June 30, 1862 Muster Roll Remarks: Absent Sick; per February 28 to April 30, 1863 Muster Roll Remarks: Absent sick, left in Hospital at Memphis, Tennessee February 8, 1862 (note some cards indicate left February 6 and 20, 1862); per December 31, 1863 Muster Roll Remarks: Died in Hospital in Memphis, Tennessee; per Overton Hospital March 1862 Register of Deaths died March 15 of rubella, Deaheas (sic) Battalion Company E.

Nairon, Green V.   Buried March 8, 1862   Lot/Division 1, #302   Plat Number 302
Tennessee 5 Infantry Regiment Private Company A; enlisted May 20, 1861 Paris, Tennessee, age 20 per Muster Roll dated August 9, 1861; Age 18 indicated on Muster Roll dated May 13, 1862 with remark died in March 1862; per Overton Hospital March 1862 Register of Deaths died March 7 of congestive fever and Cooks Company; name "M. G. Naaron" in Overton Hospital Register and Daily Burial Record Book and "N. G. Naaron" in Cemetery Alpha Book; name spelled "Nairan" and 1841 1862 on grave stone; not found in Lindsley's Annals; first name "Green," born November 25, 1841, brother of Hampton V. Naron of same unit but not related to A. V. Nairon of same unit per great nephew Joe Nairon.

Nall, William   Buried March 30, 1862   Lot/Division 1, #395   Plat Number 395
Tennessee Bankhead's Battery (Tennessee Scott's Light Artillery) Harris' Company per Daily Burial Record Book; no service record found.

Nash, Abner W.   Buried April 26, 1871   Lot/Division 2, #371   Plat Number 921
Missouri 2 Cavalry Regiment Private Company G; enlisted March 15, 1863, Charleston, Missouri; residence at enlistment: Glasgow, Howard County, Missouri; per Historic Roll dated January 1, 1865, at Mobile, Alabama Remarks: Wounded in thigh August 21, 1864, at Memphis rendering amputation necessary and died from effects on the 3rd day. He was a brave and good soldier and participated in nearly every engagement this Company and Regiment have been in from his enlistment to his death. He was killed in the midst of the enemy; per Daily Burial Record Book moved to Elmwood from Cane Creek; tombstone (not government marker) indicates date of death as August 22, 1864 age 24; unit participated in the Forrest raid into Memphis August 21, 1864; listed in Elmwood 1874 book as Confederate soldier buried in Elmwood who was citizen of Memphis or vicinity; large upright tombstone located between grave numbers 897 and 898 at south end of rows.

Neal, William   Buried April 24, 1862   Lot/Division 1, #488   Plat Number 488
Arkansas 1 Mounted Rifles (Harper's) Regiment Private Company H; enlisted November 10, 1861 Fayetteville, Arkansas age 17; per March & April 1862 Muster Roll Remarks: Died April 23, 1862 at Memphis; wounded Shiloh, name spelled "Neil" in Daily Burial Record Book and computer index; died Overton Hospital pneumonia per Daily Burial Record Book; listed in Dr. Robert H Dacus' book ...*Reminiscences... of Company "H" First Arkansas Mounted Rifles* (Dardanelle, Arkansas August 1, 1897, Post-dispatch Print, Dardanelle, Arkansas); also stated in Dacus Book that "Neal, William, died sometime in April 1862. He was not related to the Neal family who has lived so long in this County, near Chickalah."

Nearce, H. J.   Buried May 14, 1862   Lot/Division 2, #198   Plat Number 748
Arkansas 18 (Carroll's) Infantry Regiment Company A and died Irving Hospital measles per Daily Burial Record Book; no service record found.

Neely, Calvin H.   Buried May 1, 1862   Lot/Division 2, #13   Plat Number 563
Arkansas 23 (Adams') Infantry Regiment 1st Lieutenant Company I; enlisted March 12, 1862 Jonesboro, Arkansas; per March 12 to June 30, 1862 Muster Roll Remarks: Died at Memphis, Tennessee April 29, 1862 congestive chill; Company J in Daily Burial Record Book but no Company J in unit.

Neely, Huron   Buried October 10, 1861   Lot/Division 1, #67   Plat Number 67
Arkansas 13 Infantry Regiment Company H and died Southern Mothers Hospital pneumonia age 17 per Daily Burial Record Book; no compiled service record found; name "Hermann" in one entry of Cemetery computer index, "Hurom" in Daily Burial Record Book and not found in Alpha Book.

Neighbours, Thomas J.   Buried May 7, 1862   Lot/Division 2, #109   Plat Number 659
Arkansas McRea's Regiment Company G and died Overton Hospital per Daily Burial Record Book; unit may be Arkansas 15 (Northwest) Infantry Regiment that was originally known as McRae's 3 Battalion Arkansas Infantry but no compiled service record found; possibly Neighbors, Thomas, Private Company H Arkansas 31 (McCray's) Infantry Regiment who per an undated muster roll name spelled "Nabors" enlisted March 27, 1862, Jackson County, Arkansas age 20, farmer and native of Arkansas and per Company Muster Roll for March 1 To August 31, 1862, enlisted March 1, 1862, at Bayou de View, Arkansas with remarks that Died in (Tennessee) Memphis 10 May 1862; name spelled "Neighbors" in Cemetery computer index.

Nelson, C.   Buried March 11, 1862   Lot/Division 1, #319   Plat Number 319
Louisiana 21 Regiment Company A and died Overton Hospital pneumonia per Daily Burial Record Book; no service record found either Kennedy's or Patton's 21 Infantry Regiment; per list of those who died at Overton General Hospital at Memphis during the month of March 1862 died March 4 of typhoid fever and Private Louisiana 13 Regiment Company H but no record found that unit.

Nelson, Irvin   Buried April 27, 1862   Lot/Division 1, #507   Plat Number 507
Confederate 2 Infantry Regiment Private Company G; enlisted August 10, 1861 Memphis; per April 11, 1862 Muster Roll Remarks: Wounded at Shiloh slightly and missing; wounded, died Irving Hospital per Daily Burial Record Book; first name "Irving" in Daily Burial Record Book and computer index; per Irving Hospital record admitted April 12, 1862 with complaint of side and died April 26, 1862; not found in Lindsley's Annals.

Nelson, William   Buried October 28, 1862   Lot/Division 2, #306   Plat Number 856
No unit or other information in Daily Burial Record Book with Remark "regt unknown"; article in Saturday Evening, November 1, 1862, *Memphis Daily Appeal*, page 1, column 7, "Kind Sympathy--Yesterday the remains of a young man named William Nelson, of Arkansas, a Confederate soldier, who was taken at the battle of Perryville, and died on reaching this city Monday, was buried in Elmwood cemetery, by a number of friends. His remains were put off on the levee in a box, and would have been left there probably to decay, had it not been for the kind sympathy of Mrs. Susan Henderson, Mrs. Porter and Mrs. Curtis, who kindly had the corpse take to Mrs. Henderson's and gave it a decent burial. The young man had a brother on board the boat, a prisoner, who was not allowed to come ashore and see his brother buried. It will be some consolation to the friends and relatives of the deceased, to know that young Nelson was buried by kind friends in Elmwood cemetery, and every attention shown his remains. The friends and relatives of the deceased may rest assured that all was done for him that could be done. —*Memphis Argus*, 29th."

Newberry, William   Buried May 2, 1862   Lot/Division 2, #23   Plat Number 573
Texas 10 (Locke's Rangers) Cavalry Regiment (Winston's) Company and died Overton Hospital per Daily Burial Record Book; no compiled service record found; no Captain Winston found Texas 10 (Locke's) Cavalry Regiment.

Newman, B. S.   Buried May 17, 1862   Lot/Division 2, #232   Plat Number 782
Arkansas 23 (Adams') Infantry Regiment Private Company C; enlisted February 2, 1862 St Francis County, Arkansas; per March 13 to June 30, 1862 Muster Roll Remarks: Died May 15, 1862; died Irving Hospital pneumonia per Daily Burial Record Book; per Irving Hospital Record admitted May 7, 1862, complaint of pneumonia and died May 17, 1862; second initial "I" in computer index.

Newman, Martin   Buried April 22, 1862   Lot/Division 1, #479   Plat Number 479
Arkansas 25 (Turnbull's) Infantry Regiment Private Company E; enlisted March 10, 1862 Jacksonport, Arkansas; per March 10 to April 30, 1862 Muster Roll Remarks: Died in Hospital at Memphis, Tennessee April 22, 1862; Company A and died Overton Hospital per Daily Burial Record Book; unit indicated as Stramhalls(?) in Cemetery Single Grave Book.

Nicholson, Daniel R.   Buried May 6, 1862   Lot/Division 2, #82   Plat Number 632
Homers Artillery Price's Division and died Overton Hospital pneumonia per Daily Burial Record Book; no compiled service record found; first name "David" in Cemetery Single Grave Book.

Nicholson, John D.   Buried March 9, 1891   Plat Number N68
Tennessee 42 Infantry Regiment Private Company G; enlisted October 24, 1861 Camp Cheatham, Tennessee; captured at Fort Donelson, Tennessee February 16, 1862; sent to Prison Camp Douglas, Illinois; released June 1862; died age 60 and grave first on north side of #919 (Division 2) per Daily Burial Record Book; 1837 1891 on grave stone.

Nixon, William Christopher   Buried December 23, 1912   Plat Number N16
Tennessee 4 Infantry Regiment Lieutenant Company G; enlisted May 13, 1861, Ripley, Tennessee age 18; wounded Battle of Shiloh and at Murfreesboro, Tennessee; took Oath May 18, 1865; on list of wounded at Battle of Shiloh reported in April 16, 1862, *Memphis Daily Appeal*; per Tennessee Confederate Pension application #S8876 born Montgomery County, Tennessee August 1843 (note 1842 on grave stone); per widow's (Hattie Benton) Tennessee Confederate Pension application #4953 born August 8, 1845, (note birth year differences) Clarksville (Montgomery County), Tennessee and died December 22, 1912; died age 68 per Daily Burial Record Book.

Nolan, David C.   Buried June 11, 1863   Lot/Division 2, #341   Plat Number 891
Arkansas 20 (King's) Infantry Regiment Private Company E; enlisted March 1, 1862 Washington, Arkansas; per March 1 to May 2, 1862 Muster Roll Remarks: Private in Hospital in Memphis; appears on a Register of Sick and Wounded Confederate Prisoners at US Military Hospitals, Memphis, Tennessee - Complaint of G S (gunshot) wound, admitted May 31, 1863, treated in Overton and remarks that on furlough June 1.

Noonan, John   Buried March 16, 1862   Lot/Division 1, #334   Plat Number 334
Confederate 1 (King's Battalion) Cavalry Regiment Private (Gray's) 2 Company F; enlisted December 6, 1861 Memphis age 25; per Muster Roll Remarks: Died Memphis February 1862; per list of those who died at Overton General Hospital at Memphis during the month of March 1862 name "Newman, Jno," died March 16 of pneumonia and Private Grays Company; died State Hospital and Craig's Company per Daily Burial Record Book; per Cemetery record grave in short row north side of Monument.

Northup, A. J.   Buried May 7, 1862   Lot/Division 2, #104   Plat Number 654
Missouri 1 Regiment Company C and died Overton Hospital per Daily Burial Record Book; no compiled service record found; name spelled "Northrup" in Cemetery computer index; not listed in Cemetery Single Grave Book; no "Northup," "Northrup" or "Northrop" found in Missouri 1 Infantry Regiment compiled service record rolls.

Norton, Peter   Buried July 5, 1862   Lot/Division 2, #300   Plat Number 850
Tennessee 2 (Walker's) Infantry Regiment Private Company D; enlisted May 11, 1861 Memphis; per March & April 1862 Muster Roll Remarks: Absent sick of wounds; per July 17, 1863 Muster Roll Remarks: Died from wounds received at Battle of Shiloh; name spelled "Worton" in Daily Burial Record Book and computer index; knee cap broke per unit casualty report in April 13, 1862 *Memphis Daily Appeal*; note: there are two burial records for Division 2 Grave #300 (Stephen Pratt) but no information in Cemetery records of either being moved; not found in Lindsley's Annals.

Nowell, A. J.   Buried March 26, 1862   Lot/Division 1, #382   Plat Number 382
Arkansas 4 Infantry Battalion Private Company E; enlisted March 1, 1862 El Paso, Arkansas; per March 1 to April 30, 1862 Muster Roll Remarks: Left on work boat near Tiptonville March 15, 1862; per February 28 to April 30, 1863 Muster Roll Remarks: Dropped from the roll cause absent without leave considered a deserter; Company D and died Overton Hospital pneumonia per Daily Burial Record Book; believed to be the "Lowell, A. J.," on the list of those who died at Overton General Hospital at Memphis during the month of March 1862 which indicates died March 25 of pneumonia and Private Terry's Battery.

Null, John B.   Buried January 17, 1862   Lot/Division 1, #255   Plat Number 255
Arkansas 18 (Marmaduke's) Infantry Regiment Private (Robertson's) Company K; enlisted December 19, 1861 Little Rock, Arkansas age 29; per Claim for Settlement filed by widow, Linda Null, on October 15, 1863 died Memphis, Tennessee but no date indicated; died Overton Hospital age 26 per Daily Burial Record Book.

Obors, James M.   Buried May 17, 1862   Lot/Division 2, #235   Plat Number 785
Daily Burial Record Book indicates regiment and company not known and died Overton Hospital measles.

O'Day, Roger   Buried March 11, 1862   Lot/Division 1, #317   Plat Number 317
Tennessee 21 Infantry Regiment Private Company F; enlisted May 25, 1861 Memphis; appears on a Register of Sick in Overton General Hospital Memphis, Tennessee indicating admitted February 27, 1862 with complaint of phthisis and died March 9; on the list of those who died at Overton General Hospital at Memphis during the month of March 1862 which indicates died March 9 of phthisis; name "Day, Roger O." in Daily Burial Record Book and computer index; died Overton Hospital diarrhea per Daily Burial Record Book.

Odell, James   Buried March 11, 1862   Lot/Division 1, #313   Plat Number 313
Arkansas 11 Infantry Regiment Private Company I; enlisted January 13, 1862 Hot Springs, Arkansas; per October 29, 1861 to September 23, 1862 Muster Roll Remarks: Died at Memphis at Hospital date unknown; per Overton Hospital March 1862 Register of Deaths died March 10 of rubella and Company F; died heart disease per Daily Burial Record Book.

Ortner, D. M.   Buried May 7, 1862   Lot/Division 2, #106   Plat Number 656
Arkansas 20 (King's) Infantry Regiment Private Company G; enlisted February 17, 1862, Little Rock, Arkansas; per February 17 to May 2, 1862, Muster Roll Remarks: Left at Fort Pillow Sick; per February 17 to June 30, 1862, Muster Roll Remarks: Died at home 5 May 1862; Company A and died Overton Hospital enteritis, per Daily Burial Record Book; name spelled "Ortney" in Daily Burial Record Book and computer index.

Osborne, William W.   Buried December 26, 1903   Lot/Division 1, #536   Plat Number 536
Tennessee 26 Infantry Regiment Private Company C; enlisted June 27, 1861 Camp Cummings near Knoxville age 23; died age 70 per Daily Burial Record Book; 1838 1903 on grave stone.

Overton, William G.   Buried September 14, 1861   Lot/Division 1, #451   Plat Number 451
Kentucky 2 (Woodward's) Cavalry Regiment 3 Sergeant Company E; only one card in record indicating enlisted August 22, 1861 Memphis age 20; per note on record card "This company (Company E) was organized in Memphis, Tenn., August 22, 1861, and was successively designated as Company A, Forrest's (Old) Regiment Tennessee Cavalry; Company A, 3d Regiment Tennessee Cavalry; Company F, 18th Battalion (Balch's) Tennessee Cavalry; and Company E, 2d Regiment (Woodward's) Kentucky Cavalry."; "Boone Rangers Colonel Forrest" and died Southern Mothers Hospital age 19 Flux per Daily Burial Record Book; "Boone Rangers" organized in Brandenburg, Meade County, Kentucky, J. F. Overton, Captain (possible relative who had same enlistment age 30; there was also a "R. B. Overton" Private Company E with same enlistment age 18), and later John Crutcher, Captain, and was Company A of the first organization of what became Tennessee 3 (Forrest's) Cavalry Regiment (no compiled service record found that unit), then Company F of the 18 (Balch's) Cavalry Battalion that was one of the two battalions of the Forrest Cavalry Regiment (McDonald's Battalion was the other battalion) and December 1862 became Company E of Kentucky 2 (Woodward's) Cavalry Regiment; Kentucky 2 (Woodward's) Cavalry Regiment indicated as Kentucky 15 Regiment Cavalry in Kentucky Adjutant General's Office *Report of the Adjutant General of the State of Kentucky: Confederate Kentucky Volunteers, War 1861-1865* (Frankfort: State Journal Company Printers, 2 Vols., 1915-1918; reprinted 1980-1990 by McDowell Publications, Utica, KY) but not found in roster for the unit in this publication; originally buried Chapel Hill Section, Lot 89, Grave #3; date moved to Confederate Rest not indicated but would have been after May 4, 1867 when the remains of Parker Dunnico, who was originally buried in Grave #451, Lot #1, was removed and sent to St. Louis, Missouri.

Owen, E.   Buried November 20, 1861   Lot/Division 1, #206   Plat Number 206
Avery's Regiment per Daily Burial Record Book; no compiled service record found; died before regiment organized; per *Tennesseans in the Civil War Part 1*, Tennessee 39 (Avery's) Infantry Regiment was organized December 1861 but regiment officially organized as 1 Alabama-Tennessee-Mississippi Infantry Regiment (records under Confederate 4 Infantry); unit disbanded after unit's capture at Island 10 in April 1862 and parole in Vicksburg, Mississippi in September 1862, and the four Tennessee companies merged into the 42nd Tennessee Regiment as 2 Company I; per September 26, 1861 the *Avalanche* Memphis Colonel Avery's Regiment - the Gayoso Guard Captain Barbiere and one or two other companies belonging to Colonel W. T. Avery's Regiment will leave today for their rendezvous in the vicinity of Germantown.

Owen, F. M.   Buried September 28, 1861   Lot/Division 1, #97   Plat Number 97
Mississippi 44 (Blythe's 1 Battalion) Infantry Regiment Private (Humphries') Company B; enlisted June 11, 1861 Memphis, age 27; per August 7 to November 1, 1861 Muster Roll Remarks: Died September 27, 1861; per Report of Deaths for Organization dated December 4, 1863: Born Mississippi and died September 20, 1861 Memphis Hospital, typhoid fever; died Southern Mothers Hospital per Daily Burial Record Book.

Owen, Thomas Henderson   Buried December 29, 1914   Plat Number N23
Tennessee 13 Infantry Regiment Private Company B; per Company Muster-in Roll dated August 14, 1861, at camp near New Madrid, Missouri enlisted May 28, 1861, at Jackson, Tennessee age 20; per Company Muster Roll for July and August 1862, remarks: Absent sick since 10 August 1862; per Company Muster Roll dated May 29, 1863, remarks absent without leave; name appears on a register of Prisoners of War at Memphis, Tennessee – Deserted from rebel army dated March 17, 1865; name appears on an Oath of Allegiance to the United States, sworn at Memphis, Tennessee, from March 15 to April 1, 1865, dated March 17, 1865, age 22 and place of residence Memphis, Tennessee; Tennessee 15 Cavalry Regiment (Consolidated) 2 Sergeant Company I,

per single card in file for Company Muster Roll dated May 12, 1864, enlisted July 12, 1862, in Shelby County; per Tennessee Confederate Pension application S6714 born June 8, 1842, Fayette County, Tennessee and living in Memphis when joined the army and was left at hospital when Bragg went to Kentucky, received a furlough and after recovery joined Tennessee 15 Cavalry Regiment under Forrest, later captured and taken to Memphis; widow's (Jennie Lee Baker) Tennessee Confederate Pension application W9245; per Shelby County, Tennessee death certificate died December 28, 1914, age 73; member of the Confederate Relief and Historical Association of Memphis (*Record of Ex-Confederate Soldiers and Sailors, Members of the Confederate Relief and Historical Association of Memphis* - Original Tennessee State Library and Archives holding - Manuscript Microfilm #1276, Reel 5, Oversize Volume 8), which was the forerunner of the West Tennessee Historical Society; the Association subsequently became known as the Confederate Historical Association, which passed a Resolution in his honor at his death, however, no sketch in Mathes book; died age 73 per Daily Burial Record Book; *Find A Grave*, database and images (https://www.findagrave.com), memorial page for Pvt Thomas H. Owen (8 Jun 1842–28 Dec 1914), Find A Grave Memorial no. 59519194, citing Elmwood Cemetery, Memphis, Shelby County, Tennessee, USA; Maintained by Cousins by the Dozens (contributor 46904925); note there is a grave marker on the grave for Thomas H. Owen, Capt Co E 37 Regt Tenn, 1830 1914 (*Find A Grave*, database and images (https://www.findagrave.com), memorial page for Thomas H. Owen (1830–1914), Find A Grave Memorial no. 8566069, citing Elmwood Cemetery, Memphis, Shelby County, Tennessee, USA; Maintained by Anonymous (contributor 46573565)), however, based on age in death certificate and Cemetery record, this would be incorrect; per 37 Tennessee Infantry Regiment Company E Muster-in Roll dated November 1, 1861, at Camp Hayes Captain Thomas H. Owen enlisted October 8, 1861, at Paint Rock, Alabama at age 31; per various narratives written about Madison County, Alabama Confederate Army units "The New Madison Guards," Company E, 37th Tennessee Infantry Regiment, was formed by Owen in April 1861 of men from the New Hope and Owen's Crossroads area, was intended for David C. Humphreys' regiment, joined a Tennessee regiment when Alabama could not accept them, which according to tradition, the company was at Madison Station when a train arrived carrying the Tennessee troops (Regiment was enroute from its own organization site at Camp Ramsey, near Knoxville, Tennessee to Camp Sam Hayes, Germantown, Shelby County, Tennessee) and Captain Owen asked if they could use another company and with the answered being in the affirmative, the Alabamians clambered aboard; John Grayson replaced Owen as captain in May 1862; possibly he is T. H. Owen, 2 Sergeant Company F, 4 Alabama (Russell's) Cavalry Regiment, who per Company Muster-in Roll dated September 22, 1862, enlisted September 8, 1862, at Huntsville, Alabama at age 33; per *Find A Grave*, database and images (https://www.findagrave.com), memorial page for Sgt Thomas H Owen (5 Apr 1829–15 Dec 1868), Find A Grave Memorial no. 61365516, citing New Hope Cemetery, New Hope, Madison County, Alabama, USA ; Maintained by Vicki Mandeville-Trezise (contributor 47450049) he is buried in New Hope Cemetery, Madison County, Alabama, however, note that the Memorial states "This man should not be confused with Capt Thomas Owen of Company E 37th Tennessee Infantry. Capt Owen has a memorial marker at New Hope Cemetery (*Find A Grave*, database and images (https://www.findagrave.com), memorial page for Thomas H Owen (5 Apr 1829–15 Dec 1868), Find A Grave Memorial no. 59465138, citing New Hope Cemetery, New Hope, Madison County, Alabama, USA; Maintained by grammy (contributor 47124087)) but he is buried at Elmwood in Memphis."

Owens, D. F.   Buried May 2, 1862   Lot/Division 2, #22   Plat Number 572
Campbell's Battalion (Wright's) Company and died Overton Hospital pneumonia per Daily Burial Record Book.

Owens, T. L.   Buried October 25, 1861   Lot/Division 1, #134   Plat Number 134
Arkansas 12 Infantry Regiment Company C and died camp measles age 19 per Daily Burial Record Book; no compiled service record found; not listed in Single Grave Book.

Palmer, Edward G.   Buried June 12, 1866   Lot/Division 2
Tennessee 3 (Forrest's) Cavalry Corporal Company B, enlisted March 10, 1862 Memphis; listed in Elmwood 1874 book as Confederate soldier buried in Elmwood who was citizen of Memphis or vicinity; article in the *Daily Memphis Avalanche*, June 12, 1866, page 3, indicates born in Missouri, spring 1862 left St. Joseph, Missouri, made his way to Memphis, reported to Captain McDonald who was raising a company for Forrest's Regiment, and late of Captain Barbour's Company, McDonald's Battalion (Tennessee 3 Cavalry Regiment); died effects of morphine and buried Soldiers #2 Lot, Fowler Section but no grave number indicated in Daily Burial Record Book; Confederate Section but no grave number indicated in Cemetery computer index; no grave stone found; not found Lindsley's Annals.

Palmer, Green M.   Buried December 7, 1861   Lot/Division 1, #242   Plat Number 242
Arkansas 9 Infantry Regiment Ordnance Sergeant Company G; enlisted June 27, 1861 Pine Bluff, Arkansas; per November 1, 1861 to January 1, 1862 Muster Roll Remarks: Died on the 7 December at Memphis; died Southern Mothers Hospital per Daily Burial Record Book.

Palmer, J. M.   Buried March 21, 1862   Lot/Division 1, #359   Plat Number 359
Arkansas 11 Infantry Regiment Private Company K; enlisted December 22, 1861 Saline Company, Arkansas; per Muster Roll (date unclear) Remarks: Died; per Overton Hospital March 1862 Register of Deaths died March 19 of rubella; initial "M" only in Daily Burial Record Book and computer index; in Alpha Book there is a notation of having been moved to Turley Section Lot 1410 & 11 on December 19, 1906, however, that is incorrect as notation should have been for Lucius Porter on previous page of Alpha Book per notation with Lucius Porter (October 18, 1860) in Daily Burial Record Book and per listing in Turley Book.

Palmer, John   Buried April 16, 1862   Lot/Division 1, #457   Plat Number 457
Alabama 21 Infantry Regiment Private Company I; enlisted October 13, 1861 age 34; per Muster Roll Remarks: Left in Memphis and heard of death on June 26, 1862; widow Elizabeth was paid $139.53; first name "Jackson" in Daily Burial Record Book and computer index; unit indicated as Louisiana in Cemetery Single Grave Book.

Parker, William Lacey   Buried May 13, 1862   Lot/Division 2, #192   Plat Number 742
Texas 9 (Sim's Rangers) Cavalry Regiment Private Company A; enlisted March 1, 1862, Slidell, Arkansas; per March & April 1862 Muster Roll Remarks: Sick in Hospital in Memphis; per July & August 1862 Muster Roll Remarks: Private in Hospital at Memphis, not since heard; per September & October 1862 Muster Roll Remarks: Died of disease in Memphis after it was evacuated, date not reported; initials "W. F." only in Daily Burial Record Book and computer index; died Overton Hospital typhoid fever and pneumonia per Daily Burial Record Book.

Parks, John   Buried June 18, 1862   Lot/Division 2, #295   Plat Number 845
Arkansas 18 (Carroll's) Infantry Regiment Sergeant (Peel's) Company A; enlisted February 25, 1862 Jefferson County, Arkansas age 33; per February to June 1862 Muster Roll Remarks: Died May 16, 1862; died State Hospital chronic diarrhea per Daily Burial Record Book; per Overton and Irving Hospitals records there was a John Parks, Private Carroll's Regiment Company who was admitted May 2, 1862 with complaint of dysentery and put on leave to Galloways Switch May 3, 1862 that was extended 15 days but death indicated.

Parsley, Amsi   Buried May 26, 1862   Lot/Division 2, #268   Plat Number 818
Arkansas 25 (Turnbull's) Infantry Regiment Private Company G; enlisted March 13, 1862 Pocahontas, Arkansas; per March 13 to April 30, 1862 Muster Roll Remarks: At the Hospital in Memphis, Tennessee sick; per Muster Roll dated June 30, 1862 died at Memphis, Tennessee about May 28, 1862; died Overton Hospital pneumonia and Company E per Daily Burial Record Book.

Parton, D. L.   Buried November 24, 1861   Lot/Division 1, #217   Plat Number 217
Arkansas 6 Regiment Captain Jones' Company and died State Hospital per Daily Burial Record Book; no compiled service record found Arkansas 6 Infantry Regiment (also no Captain Jones in this unit); possibly D. L. Parton, Arkansas 8 Infantry Regiment, Private (Jones') Company D New (also known as Old Company F), enlisted September 10, 1861 Camp Price, Arkansas but no other information in records.

Pate, Wiley A.   Buried May 9, 1862   Lot/Division 2, #127   Plat Number 677
Arkansas 19 (Dockery/Smead's) Infantry Regiment Private Company G; enlisted March 1, 1862 Hillsboro, Arkansas; per March 1 to June 30, 1862 Muster Roll Remarks: Died May 9, 1862 at Memphis; died Overton Hospital per Daily Burial Record Book.

Patrick, Dan   Buried February 10, 1862   Lot/Division 1, #260   Plat Number 260
Arkansas 9 Infantry Regiment Private (Thomasson's) New Company B; enlisted December 18, 1861 Monticello; per December 18, 1861 to March 1, 1862 Muster Roll Remarks: Died at State Hospital Memphis February 14, 1862; died State Hospital per Daily Burial Record Book.

Patterson, Charles E.   Buried May 21, 1862   Lot/Division 2, #254   Plat Number 804
Arkansas 2 Infantry Regiment Lieutenant Colonel; no enlistment date indicated in service record; Special Order 84/5 dated June 29, 1861 reads 1 Lieutenant C. E. Patterson, Infantry, will report at Memphis to Colonel T. C. Hindman as Adjutant of his Regiment of Arkansas Volunteers; per War Department statement in compiled service record appointed Lieutenant June 26, 1861 and later promoted Lieutenant Colonel (date not known), severely wounded in arm Battle of Shiloh April 6, 1862 and other records show died that day; body escorted to Memphis; per Sunday April 20, 1862, *Memphis Daily Appeal*, page 2, column 7, "Died-on the 16 instant half past five o'clock p. m. at Corinth, Lieutenant Colonel Charles E. Patterson of the 2 Arkansas Regiment. He was seriously wounded in the Battle of the 6 instant. His remains were brought to this City and deposited in Elmwood Cemetery yesterday."

Patterson, Martin D.   Buried February 11, 1926   Plat Number N42
Alabama 11 Cavalry Regiment Company H; no compiled service record found; unit per Tennessee Confederate Pension application #15746 which indicates joined Rand's Company, Williams Battalion, which became 11 Alabama, December 1863 and born Morgan County, Alabama (no date indicated) and moved to Franklin (now Colbert) County; per Confederate Historical Association, Camp 28, Bivouac 18, Memphis, application born June 16, 1847 Franklin (now Colbert) Company, Alabama; widow Annie L. (Price) Patterson received Tennessee pension (File #8432); per her file he was born in Decatur (Morgan County), Alabama June 16, 1846, she was born March 5, 1852 in South Florence, Alabama, they were married December 21, 1870 in Tuscumbia, Colbert County, Alabama, and he died February 9, 1926; note differences of dates and places in files; died age 79 per Daily Burial Record Book; no sketch in Mathes book; original grave stone underground south of Shivers and death date on stone but broken.

Patterson, William S.   Buried August 30, 1870   Lot/Division 2, #367   Plat Number 917
Tennessee 7 Cavalry Regiment Private (Logwood's/Taylor's) Company A ("The Memphis Light Dragoons"); enlisted May 16, 1861, Memphis age, 32; first enlisted Tennessee 6 (Logwood's) Cavalry Battalion (also known as Tennessee 1 Cavalry Battalion); Tennessee 7 Cavalry Regiment organized April 1862; per Company Muster Roll for July & August 1863 detailed Assistant

Quartermaster April 1, 1861; name (W. S. Patterson, Sgt. Company A, 7 Tennessee Cavalry) appears on a Roll of Prisoners of War of men detailed in Commissary and Quartermaster Departments and paroled at Columbus, Mississippi, May, 1865; funeral notice in September 3, 1870, *Memphis Daily Appeal*, page 1, column 4, "On Monday last (August 29, 1870), in this city, Captain William S. Patterson" and indicates that states he was a native of North Carolina but lived in Memphis for more than twenty years, was a cotton salesman and book-keeper, and served four years in the Confederate army; article under "Local News" August 30, 1870, *Memphis Daily Appeal*, page 4, column 2, indicating that Captain Patterson first enlisted in a company of light dragoons, commanded by Captain, afterwards Colonel Logwood, Patterson himself became a Captain (this rank not indicated in compiled service record), his health failed and was assigned to post duty, however, followed his (Dibbrell's) brigade and became connected with the commissary or Q. M. Department, born in Hillsboro, North Carolina, died in the 37th (sic) year of age and an Odd Fellow; listed in Elmwood 1874 book as Confederate soldier buried in Elmwood who was citizen of Memphis or vicinity; initials "W. L." in Young's *Seventh Tennessee Cavalry* book; unit not indicated and died congestion per Daily Burial Record Book; not listed in Single Grave Book.

Patton, Lucius Elmer   Buried March 9, 1931   Plat Number N57
Kentucky 2 (Duke's) Cavalry Regiment Private Company C; enlisted September 25, 1861 Green River, Kentucky; captured Madisonville, Tennessee December 3, 1863; per Tennessee Confederate Pension application #16503 born September 12, 1848 Wood County, Virginia (now West Virginia); per widow's (Martha W. Bunch, third wife) Tennessee Confederate Pension application #10102 discharged October 18, 1862 (note discrepancy with capture date) and died March 8, 1931 age 82; Captain per Daily Burial Record Book that was based on his ownership and captain of a steamboat.

Peak, T. J.   Buried April 7, 1862   Lot/Division 1, #426   Plat Number 426
Louisiana 25 Infantry Regiment Private Company H; enlisted March 19, 1862 New Orleans, Louisiana; died State Hospital disease per Daily Burial Record Book; initials "J. T." in Daily Burial Record Book and computer index.

Pearce, Andrew J.   Buried May 20, 1862   Lot/Division 2, #249   Plat Number 799
Arkansas 17 (Lemoyne's) Infantry Regiment Private Company E; reference card only in compiled service record; record found under Arkansas 21 Infantry, Private Company I that was successor of Company E of 17 Infantry; enlisted December 21, 1861 Dardanelle, Arkansas; per April 28, 1862 Muster Roll Remarks: Left in Memphis in Hospital May 1, 1862; name spelled "Pierce" in Daily Burial Record Book and computer index; died Overton Hospital per Daily Burial Record Book.

Pearcy, C. C.   Buried April 18, 1862   Lot/Division 1, #467   Plat Number 467
Arkansas 18 (Carroll's) Infantry Regiment Private Company K; enlisted February 22, 1862 Pine Bluff, Arkansas; per March & April 1862 Muster Roll Remarks: Died Overton Hospital Memphis April 1862; died Overton Hospital pneumonia per Daily Burial Record Book.

Pearson, N. D.   Buried March 30, 1862   Lot/Division 1, #396   Plat Number 396
Louisiana 12 Infantry Regiment Private (Steven's) Company F; no enlistment in compiled service record with single muster roll card dated March 17, 1862 Memphis age 20; unit organized Camp Moore, Louisiana August 13, 1861; 1842 1862 on grave stone.

Pearson, S. W.   Buried October 14, 1861   Lot/Division 1, #69   Plat Number 69
Walker's Regiment (McLean's) Company and died Southern Mothers Hospital typhoid fever per Daily Burial Record Book; no service record found; McClain's Company was Tennessee 40 (Walker's) Infantry Regiment Company F and subsequently Company E Arkansas 15 (Johnson's) Infantry Regiment; Walker's Regiment indicated as an Arkansas unit in Daily Burial Record Book.

Pentecost, F. J.   Buried March 5, 1862   Lot/Division 1, #284   Plat Number 284
Kentucky 7 Mounted Infantry Regiment Private Company K; enlisted October 19, 1861 Desha County, Arkansas; per Overton Hospital March 1862 Register admitted February 28, 1862, complaint of pneumonia and died March 4; first initial "T" in Daily Burial Record Book and computer index.

Peoples, John W.   Buried March 3, 1862   Lot/Division 1, #278   Plat Number 278
Louisiana 12 Infantry Regiment Private Company C; enlisted August 18, 1861 Camp Moore, Louisiana; present on muster rolls to October 13, 1861; died Overton Hospital per Daily Burial Record Book; name spelled "Peeples" in Daily Burial Record Book and computer index.

Perkins, Enos S.   Buried August 22, 1864   Lot/Division 2, #343   Plat Number 893
Tennessee 12 Cavalry Regiment Private Company C; per Company Muster Roll for October 18, 1862, to May 14, 1864, enlisted March 5, 1861, Jackson City, Arkansas; name appears on undated Return of Killed and Wounded, 1 Brigade, 1 Division, Forrest's Cavalry, during the Month of August 1864, with remarks: killed August 21 at Memphis; mentioned in "Forrest Raid Into Memphis" by W. B. Stewart, Arlington, Tennessee, *Confederate Veteran*, Volume XI, November 1903, pages 503-504; killed Irving Block Memphis per Cemetery Alpha Book and killed in the City per Daily Burial Record Book; not found in Lindsley's Annals.

Perkins, G. W.   Buried November 13, 1861   Lot/Division 1, #191   Plat Number 191
Arkansas 7 Infantry Regiment Private Company F; enlisted July 26, 1861 Camp Shaver, Arkansas age 36; per December 31, 1861 Muster Roll Remarks: Absent Sick at Memphis; 1823 1861 inscribed on grave stone.

Perkins, T. J.   Buried May 11, 1862   Lot/Division 2, #162   Plat Number 712
Arkansas 7 Regiment Company B and died Charleston House per Daily Burial Record Book; first initial "F" in Cemetery Single Grave Book; no compiled service record found.

Permenter, J. R.   Buried May 8, 1862   Lot/Division 2, #112   Plat Number 662
Arkansas 19 (Dockery's) Infantry Regiment Private Company H; enlisted March 3, 1862 Caney, Arkansas; per March 3 to June 30, 1862 Muster Roll Remarks: Died in Memphis, Tennessee May 15, 1862; died Irving Hospital measles per Daily Burial Record Book; per Irving Hospital record admitted April 30, 1862 with complaint of measles and died May 7, 1862.

Pettigrew, James L.   Buried February 1, 1929   Plat Number N50
Mississippi 2 Infantry Regiment Private Company C; enlisted March 1, 1862 Verona, Mississippi; per Tennessee Confederate Pension application #S4763 born May 11, 1846 Butler County, Alabama; per January 31, 1929 *The Commercial Appeal* Memphis, page 7, born Richmond, Mississippi (note birth place difference) and died January 30, 1929 age 83; member Confederate Historical Association, Camp 28, Bivouac 18, Memphis; admitted January 8, 1895; sketch in Mathes book.

Philip, Lewis   Buried March 4, 1862   Lot/Division 1, #282   Plat Number 282
Tennessee 21 Infantry Regiment Private Company G; enlisted June 6, 1861 Vicksburg, Mississippi; per November & December 1861 Muster Roll Remarks: Deserted (no other information); name spelled "Phillips" in Daily Burial Record Book and computer index and "Philips" in Cemetery Alpha Book; 1837 1862 on grave stone.

Phillips, David P.   Buried March 1, 1862   Lot/Division 1, #274   Plat Number 274
Arkansas 3 Infantry Regiment Corporal/Sergeant Company D; enlisted June 20, 1861 Selma, Arkansas; per February 18 to April 30, 1862 Muster Roll Remarks: Died at Memphis, Tennessee while on furlough at Overton Hospital February 27, 1862; name on a Register of Sick in Overton General Hospital, Memphis, Tennessee dated February 28, 1862 indicating died February 27, 1862; died Overton Hospital per Daily Burial Record Book.

Phillips, G. W.   Buried November 27, 1861   Lot/Division 1, #224   Plat Number 224
Arkansas 13 Infantry Regiment Company D and died Southern Mothers Hospital phthisis pulmonalis per Daily Burial Record Book; no compiled service record found and not G. B. Phillips Company C of this unit who was alive in 1864 per service record.

Phillips, James   Buried April 25, 1862   Lot/Division 1, #493   Plat Number 493
Missouri 1 (Bowen's) Infantry Regiment Sergeant Company D; enlisted June 25, 1861 New Orleans, Louisiana; per Muster Roll Remarks: Wounded both hips Battle of Shiloh and died; per Battle of Shiloh casualty list for unit reported in April 23, 1862 *Memphis Daily Appeal* was wounded in Battle and member of Company A; born Ireland.

Phillips, John C.   Buried May 22, 1862   Lot/Division 2, #258   Plat Number 808
Texas 14 (Johnson's) Cavalry Regiment Sergeant (Hamilton's) Company D; single compiled service record card dated February 15, 1862 Camp Likens, Texas age 26 with no enlistment date indicated.

Pickering, J. E.   Buried May 26, 1862   Lot/Division 2, #267   Plat Number 817
Arkansas 13 Infantry Regiment (Gand's) Company and died Overton Hospital brain inflammation per Daily Burial Record Book; no compiled service record found and no Captain Gand in the unit.

Pilcher, S. C.   Buried March 24, 1862   Lot/Division 1, #372   Plat Number 372
Tennessee 40 Infantry Regiment Private Company C; enlisted September 13, 1861 Montgomery, Alabama; per November & December 1861 Muster Roll Remarks: Sick in State Hospital at Memphis, Tennessee; name appears on list of sick in State Hospital dated December 31, 1861; per January 1 to October 5, 1862 Muster Roll Remarks: Private at Fort Pillow, Tennessee and not heard from since; died Overton Hospital pneumonia per Daily Burial Record Book; 1837 1862 on grave stone; not found in Lindsley's Annals 39 & 40 Consolidated Infantry Regiment Official Memorial Roll.

Pinnell, A. N.   Buried April 13, 1862   Lot/Division 1, #439   Plat Number 439
Missouri 1 Infantry Regiment Private (Phillip's) Company I; enlisted August 25, 1861 near New Madrid, Missouri; record indicates wounded Battle of Shiloh and died Memphis April 12, 1862; per Battle of Shiloh casualty list for unit reported in April 23, 1862 *Memphis Daily Appeal* was wounded in Battle and since died; second initial "M" in Cemetery computer index.

Pitman, W. Thomas   Buried May 5, 1862   Lot/Division 2, #49   Plat Number 599
Arkansas 20 (King's) Infantry Regiment Private Company E; enlisted March 1, 1862 Washington, Arkansas; per March 1 to May 2, 1862 Muster Roll Remarks: Private in Hospital at Memphis; per March 1 to June 30, 1862 Muster Roll Remarks: Died at

Memphis 3 May; died Overton Hospital typhoid fever and pneumonia and name "Pittman" in Cemetery computer index.

Pittman, P. P.   Buried March 8, 1862   Lot/Division 1, #301   Plat Number 301
Arkansas 13 Infantry Regiment Private Company F; no enlistment in compiled service record; per Overton Hospital Register of Sick dated February 28, 1862: Admitted February 26, 1862 (no other information); died Overton Hospital per Daily Burial Record Book.

Pitts, James Francis Martin   Buried March 2, 1929   Plat Number N52
Arkansas 5 Infantry Regiment Private Company B; enlisted June 12, 1861, Wittsburg, Arkansas; per Tennessee Confederate Pension application #9355 born July 30, 1830 (application also indicates born 1840 Meriwether County, Georgia); per March 2, 1929 *The Commercial Appeal* Memphis, page 9, full name "James Francis Martin (Marion) Pitts" and enlisted June 10, 1861 Company B Arkansas 5 Infantry, elected Captain, later Private; died age 98 per Daily Burial Record Book; Tennessee Questionnaire of Civil War Veterans has same information; member Confederate Historical Association, Company A, United Confederate Veterans; sketch in Mathes book indicates born July 29, 1840 Meriwether County, Georgia and "M." second initial.

Pope, Jacob Jasper   Buried May 16, 1862   Lot/Division 2, #224   Plat Number 774
Arkansas 19 (Dockery's) Infantry Regiment Private Company K; enlisted March 8, 1862 Columbia County, Arkansas; per March 8 to June 30, 1862, Muster Roll Remarks: Died on the 20th May at Memphis Hospital; initials "A. J." and died Overton Hospital typhoid fever per Daily Burial Record Book; grave stone: April 19, 1837 May 16, 1862.

Pope, Riley   Buried March 25, 1862   Lot/Division 1, #377   Plat Number 377
Arkansas 12 Infantry Regiment Company D and died typhoid fever per Daily Burial Record Book; no compiled service record found; per Overton Hospital March 1862 Register of Deaths died March 24 of pneumonia; there was a Riley Pope, Arkansas 11 Infantry Regiment Private Company D, who enlisted December 17, 1861 Hots Springs, Arkansas and who per November 1861 to September 1862 Muster Roll Remarks was absent sick at time of surrender (Regiment was captured at Island 10 April 8, 1862) with present locality unknown.

Porter, E. V.   Buried May 15, 1862   Lot/Division 2, #213   Plat Number 763
Arkansas 20 (King's) Infantry Regiment Private Company E; enlisted March 1, 1862 Washington, Arkansas; per March 1 to May 2, 1862 Muster Roll Remarks: Private in Hospital at Memphis; per January & February 1863 Muster Roll Remarks: Absent sick, left Memphis April 1862; name appears on Register of Claims indicating that claim filed February 13, 1863 by mother Sarah Porter indicating died Memphis, Tennessee; died Overton Hospital typhoid and pneumonia per Daily Burial Record Book; believed to be Elijah V. Porter, mother Sarah (McLain) Porter, who lived near Washington, Arkansas per great great grandnephew Jim Porter.

Porter, William C.   Buried January 22, 1863   Lot/Division 2, #332   Plat Number 882
Tennessee 30 Infantry Regiment Private Company G; enlisted October 22, 1861 Red Springs, Tennessee; name appears of a Roll of prisoners of War at camp Butler, Springfield, Illinois that indicates captured Fort Donaldson February 16, 1862; exchanged September 23, 1862; per Company Muster Roll for March 1 to June 30, 1863, remarks: Was left December 1, 1862, on the retreat from tipper forde and has not been heard from since; per Company Muster Roll dated March 8, 1864 at Dalton, Georgia age 28 and Remarks: Captured by enemy and died; 1834 1863 on grave stone; not found in Lindsley's Annals.

Posten, William   Buried June 23, 1861   Lot/Division 1, #55   Plat Number 55
Arkansas Regiment; "9th" crossed out in Daily Burial Record Book but is in Single Grave Book; Cemetery Computer Index does not include first name "Wm." that is in Daily Burial Record Book; not found in any Arkansas index.

Potter, Pleasant B.   Buried May 18, 1862   Lot/Division 2, #237   Plat Number 787
Arkansas 23 (Adams') Infantry Regiment Private Company I; enlisted March 15, 1862 Jonesboro, Arkansas; per March 12 to June 30, 1862 Muster Roll Remarks: Died at Memphis May 18, 1862 measles.

Powell, Thomas J.   Buried March 24, 1862   Lot/Division 1, #373   Plat Number 373
Tennessee 31 (Bradford's) Infantry Regiment Private Company D; enlisted September 29, 1861 Trenton, Tennessee; per March 12, 1863 Muster Roll Remarks: Died March 20, 1862 in Hospital; per Daily Burial Record Book died pneumonia; died May 11, 1862 per Lindsley's Annals; per Cemetery record grave in short row north side of Monument.

Pratt, Stephen   Buried June 28, 1862   Lot/Division 2, #300   Plat Number 850
Arkansas McRae's Infantry Regiment Company B and died State Hospital per Daily Burial Record Book; no compiled service record found; note: there are two burials for Division 2 Grave #300 (Peter Norton) but no record found of either being removed.

Price, Haisten T.   Buried November 29, 1861   Lot/Division 1, #230   Plat Number 230
Texas Watts Cameron's Company Infantry; enlisted September 15, 1861 Jefferson, Texas age 37; per November 18 to December 31, 1861 Muster Roll Remarks: Died at Memphis, Tennessee November 27, 1861 at Southern Mothers Hospital; Watts Cameron's Texas Company Infantry was attached to Kentucky 5 Infantry Regiment by Special Order No. 247 dated December 1, 1861;

Regiment was later designated as Kentucky 9 Mounted Infantry Regiment by Special Order No. 10 dated October 4, 1862; compiled service record also found under this unit as "Hasten Trezan Price" Private Company H with same enlistment information; second initial "F" in Daily Burial Record Book and computer index; died lung congestion per Daily Burial Record Book .

Prince, James   Buried October 16, 1861   Lot/Division 1, #70   Plat Number 70
Arkansas 13 Infantry Regiment Company C and died Southern Mothers Hospital chronic dysentery per Daily Burial Record Book; no James Prince found this unit but a John N. Prince with no enlistment or other information except a card with written note indicating that was "taken prisoner at Belmont" and to see personal papers of J. R. Brown of this unit that includes a list dated November 8, 1861, of soldiers taken prisoner at Battle of Belmont that includes John N. Prince.

Prince, John   Buried November 19, 1861   Lot/Division 1, #201   Plat Number 201
Arkansas Captain Holmes' Company G and from Steamer per Daily Burial Record Book; no compiled service record found; believed to be Arkansas 8 Infantry Battalion, Captain Holmes Company G, but not found in that unit records.

Pringle, W.   Buried February 3, 1863   Lot/Division 2, #337   Plat Number 887
Mississippi 4 Regiment Company K unit per Daily Burial Record Book; no compiled service record found; no Pringle Company K found in Confederate general index; possibly William Pringle, Mississippi 1 (Johnston's) Infantry Regiment Company D, enlisted August 24, 1861 Hernando, Mississippi age 30 and whose compiled service record last entry indicates captured Fort Donelson February 16, 1862.

Pryor, W. J.   Buried October 24, 1861   Lot/Division 1, #133   Plat Number 133
Arkansas 12 Infantry Regiment Company C and died camp measles age 36 per Daily Burial Record Book; no service record found.

Pyburn, John   Buried March 6, 1862   Lot/Division 1, #289   Plat Number 289
Louisiana 21 Regiment Company G per Daily Burial Record Book; no compiled service record found; per Overton Hospital March 1862 Register of Deaths died March 5 of rubella.

Quinn, William   Buried July 7, 1861   Lot/Division 1, #54   Plat Number 54
Arkansas 2 (Hindman's) Infantry Regiment Private Company F; enlisted June 10, 1861 Memphis, age 18; per June 5 to August 31, 1861 Muster Roll Remarks: Died at Memphis, Tennessee July 6; McCullough Rifles and died congestive chill age 21 per Daily Burial Record Book.

Ragland, J. W.   Buried March 7, 1862   Lot/Division 1, #292   Plat Number 292
Tennessee Bankhead's Battery (Tennessee Scott's Light Artillery) per Daily Burial Record Book; no compiled service record found; per Overton Hospital March 1862 Register of Deaths died March 6 of rubella (pneumonia per list of those who died at Overton General Hospital at Memphis during the month of March 1862) Harris Company.

Railey, L.   Buried November 10, 1861   Lot/Division 1, #176   Plat Number 176
Walker's Regiment (Aaron's) Company per Daily Burial Record Book; Aaron's Company was an Arkansas Company that enrolled September 23, 1861, as Company G Tennessee 40 (Walker's) Infantry Regiment and subsequently became Company D Arkansas 15 (Johnson's) Infantry Regiment; no compiled service record found as L Railey but there is a Beloved Raley (Railey on some cards) in this Company who per Company Muster Roll dated October, 1861, enlisted September 23, 1861, at Tyddersdale, Arkansas at age 18, per Company Muster Roll for November and December, 1861, remarks died November 9, 1861, at Camp Johnston, Tennessee from measles and pneumonia and father Zebulon Raley filed for a claim for settlement April 9, 1863; spelling "Railey" in 1860 Magnolia, Columbia County, Arkansas census with Beloved Railey age given as 17; based on information from researching this company "Tyddersdale" is a common misreading of "Liddesdale" or "Lydesdale" in Columbia County, Arkansas; not listed in Single Grave Book.

Rains, William J.   Buried April 27, 1862   Lot/Division 1, #510   Plat Number 510
Arkansas 25 (Turnbull's) Infantry Regiment Private Company C; enlisted Charles, Arkansas (no date indicated); per February 22 to April 30, 1862 Muster Roll Remarks: Died at Memphis, Tennessee April 27,1862; name appears on a Register of Claims indicating that claim filed May 16, 1863 by father C. M. Rains indicating died Memphis, Tennessee; died Overton Hospital pneumonia per Daily Burial Record Book; name spelled "Raines" in Cemetery computer index.

Raney, Marcus G.   Buried May 21, 1862   Lot/Division 2, #253   Plat Number 803
Arkansas 1 Mounted Rifles (Harper's) Regiment Private Company A; enlisted October 25, 1861 Camp Harris age 18; per May & June 1862 Muster Roll Remarks: Died at Memphis May 1862; name spelled "Rainey" in Daily Burial Record Book and computer index.

Ray, Mark R.   Buried May 14, 1862   Lot/Division 2, #208   Plat Number 758
Arkansas 19 (Dockery/Smead's) Infantry Regiment Private (Perry's) Company K; enlisted March 8, 1862 Columbia County, Arkansas; per March 8 to June 30, 1862 Muster Roll Remarks: Died on the 10 May at Memphis Hospital; died Overton Hospital

typhoid fever per Daily Burial Record Book; name "Clay" written in parenthesis in Daily Burial Record Book.

Rayburn, M.   Buried May 6, 1862   Lot/Division 2, #75   Plat Number 625
Arkansas 17 Infantry Regiment Bonner's Company and died Overton Hospital per Daily Burial Record Book; no compiled service record found and no Captain Bonner found Arkansas units.

Rasor, John W.   Buried May 12, 1862   Lot/Division 2, #177   Plat Number 727
Arkansas 2 Infantry Regiment Private Company A; enlisted May 26, 1861, at Helena, Arkansas age 35; per Company Muster Roll dated April 30 to June 30, 1862, remarks on furlough wounded in action April 6, 1862 (Battle of Shiloh); per Company Muster Roll dated January & February 1863, remarks absent from wound received on April 6, 1862, last heard from Memphis; name spelled "Razor" in Daily Burial Record Book and computer index; "at D. S. Wrights" per Daily Burial Record Book remark.

Read, A. E.   Buried March 18, 1862   Lot/Division 1, #342   Plat Number 342
Tennessee 7 Cavalry Regiment Private Company I (6 Logwood's Cavalry Battalion); no enlistment in compiled service record; appears on Roll of Prisoners of War who were paroled May 11, 1865 (apparently never dropped from rolls); per that roll residence Baton Rouge, Louisiana; no death information in compiled service record; died before 7 Cavalry Regiment formally organized in April, 1862; not found in Lindsley's Annals or Young's Book; per Daily Burial Record Book died State Hospital.

Reams, Levi E.   Buried May 1, 1862   Lot/Division 2, #11   Plat Number 561
Arkansas 19 (Dockery/Smead's) Infantry Regiment Private Company D/E; enlisted March 1, 1862 Rock Port; per March 1 to June 30, 1862 Muster Roll Remarks: Died May 1, 1862; died pneumonia and name spelled "Reames" per Daily Burial Record Book.

Redding, Benjamin J.   Buried May 25, 1862   Lot/Division 2, #263   Plat Number 813
Price's Division and "died at Mt. Markings" per Daily Burial Record Book; no compiled service record found.

Redwine, Dr. Rufus E.   Buried December 11, 1862   Lot/Division 2, #322   Plat Number 872
Texas 10 (Locke's) Cavalry Regiment Private (Redwine's) Company E; enlisted October 31, 1861 Taos, Texas, age 26; per List of Rebel Prisoners of War dated November 18, 1862, captured Camp Dick Robinson, Kentucky October 25, 1862; per undated Register of Prisoners of War sent to Vicksburg, Mississippi November 29, 1862; per August 31 to December 31, 1862 Muster Roll Remarks: Died on Boat between Cairo, Illinois and Vicksburg, Mississippi; per Certification by W. J. Young, 2 Lieutenant, soldier was a physician; Rusk Company Texas, and "died on Street Madison City" per Daily Burial Record Book remarks.

Reeves, E. L.   Buried May 7, 1862   Lot/Division 2, #87   Plat Number 637
Arkansas 19 (Dockery/Smead's) Infantry Regiment Company F; enlisted March 1, 1862 El Dorado; per March 1 to June 30, 1862 Muster Roll Remarks: Died in Hospital at Memphis May 10, 1862; no rank in compiled service record; died Overton Hospital diarrhea per Daily Burial Record Book.

Reeves, M. L.   Buried October 30, 1861   Lot/Division 1, #149   Plat Number 149
Arkansas 5 Regiment per Daily Burial Record Book; no service record found; possibly Reaves, Mathew L., Arkansas 5 Infantry Regiment, Private Company C who enlisted June 30, 1861 Little Rock, Arkansas but no information after being reported present on the Company Muster Roll dated July 27 to May 31, 1861; grave stone two spaces south side of Stone (Space) 222, Division 1.

Reeves, Stephen C.   Buried November 5, 1861   Lot/Division 1, #167   Plat Number 167
Arkansas 8 Infantry Regiment Private New Company E; enlisted September 10, 1861 Camp Price age 22; per October 31, 1861 Muster Roll Remarks: in the Hospital at Memphis but no other information; died State Hospital per Daily Burial Record Book.

Reynolds, E.   Buried May 13, 1862   Lot/Division 2, #188   Plat Number 738
Jones' Battalion (Love's) Company and died Overton Hospital pneumonia per Daily Burial Record Book; no compiled service record found; there was a Captain N. S. Love's Company A, Arkansas 8 Battalion (Lieutenant Colonel Jones) Infantry but not found in that unit.

Reynolds, E. T.   Buried March 27, 1862   Lot/Division 1, #386   Plat Number 386
Tennessee 5 Infantry Regiment Private Company F; enlisted May 20, 1861 Paris, Tennessee; per March & April 1862 Muster Roll Remarks: Died of disease March 22, 1862; per undated Muster Roll Remarks: at Memphis; per January 20, 1864 Muster Roll Remarks: Died at Memphis March 25, 1862; per Overton Hospital March 1862 Register of Deaths died March 24 of congestion and Company E; per Daily Burial Record Book died March 22, 1862 Overton Hospital, typhoid fever and Company I; March 24, 1862 on grave stone; died April 27, 1862 per Lindsley's Annals.

Rhine, George   Buried February 5, 1862   Lot/Division 1, #259   Plat Number 259
Arkansas Volunteers Captain Gray's Company and died Overton Hospital age 22 per Daily Burial Record Book; no service record found.

Rhodes, Charles C.   Buried April 12, 1862   Lot/Division 1, #437   Plat Number 437
Arkansas 18 (Carroll's) Infantry Regiment Private Company K; enlisted February 22, 1862 Pine Bluff, Arkansas; per March to June 1862 Muster Roll Remarks: Died Overton Hospital Memphis April 10, 1862; died pneumonia per Daily Burial Record Book.

Rhodes, M.   Buried April 26, 1871   Lot/Division 2, #370   Plat Number 920
Listed in Elmwood 1874 book as Confederate soldier buried in Elmwood who was citizen of Memphis or vicinity; "moved from Cane Creek" per Daily Burial Record Book remark; possibly Tennessee 16 (Logwood's) Cavalry Regiment, enlisted November 1, 1863 Tipton County, Tennessee (no other information).

Rhodes, Morgan G.   Buried November 4, 1861   Lot/Division 1, #161   Plat Number 161
Arkansas 12 Infantry Regiment Private Company H; enlisted July 29, 1861 Arkadelphia, Arkansas; per July to October 1862 Muster Roll Remarks: Died at Memphis November 1, 1861.

Rhodes, William H.   Buried November 15, 1861   Lot/Division 1, #192   Plat Number 192
Arkansas 9 Infantry Regiment Private (Henry's) Company C; enlisted July 25, 1861 Pine Bluff; per November 1, 1861 to January 1, 1862 Muster Roll Remarks: Discharged 11 November 1861; no death indicated in service record; died State Hospital typhoid fever and pneumonia per Daily Burial Record Book; two burial records found for Grave #192 (J. A. Woodward) but only one stone found.

Richardson, James   Buried April 30, 1862   Lot/Division 1, #521   Plat Number 521
Arkansas Rivers' (Provence's/Arkansas First Light Artillery Company) Battery Private; enlisted October 26, 1861 Fort Smith, Arkansas and per March/April 1862 Muster Roll Remarks: Died at Memphis, Tennessee April 28, 1862; per Daily Burial Record Book first name "John," died Overton Hospital pneumonia and unit "Provines Artillery Co - Harpers Ark Regt"; not John S. Richardson, Arkansas 1 (Harper's) Mounted Rifles, Private Company K who enlisted June 9, 1861 Fort Smith, Arkansas age 25 and discharged September 21, 1862 age 26 per September/October 1862 muster roll remarks.

Richmond, Charles W.   Buried June 26, 1919   Plat Number N33
No unit indicated and died age 70 per Daily Burial Record Book; believed to be Charles W. Richmond who applied for membership in Confederate Historical Association, Camp 28, Bivouac 18, Memphis; no unit indicated but indicated born September 24, 1856 (?) New Orleans, Louisiana; no record of actual membership found and no sketch in Mathes book; small death notice in June 26, 1919 *The Commercial Appeal* Memphis indicating second initial "W," died June 24, 1919, aged 67 and to be buried in Confederate Plot at Elmwood but no Confederate service unit indicated.

Ricketts, John C.   Buried October 6, 1862   Lot/Division 2, #303   Plat Number 853
Mississippi 26 Infantry Regiment Private Company C; enlisted August 24, 1861 Iuka, Mississippi, age 26; captured at Fort Donelson, Kentucky February 16, 1862, sent to Camp Morton, Indianapolis, Indiana; Parole - On Honor to Proceed to Vicksburg, Mississippi dated September 3, 1862; per July 31 to October 31, 1862 Muster Roll Remarks: Left on return from Prison in Hospital at Memphis; per November & December 1862 Muster Roll Remarks: Private at Memphis on return from Prison, supposed to be dead, date not known; from Tishomingo County, Mississippi per Daily Burial Record Book.

Rigney, Henry   Buried September 17, 1861   Lot/Division 1, #25   Plat Number 25
Arkansas 9 Infantry Regiment 2nd Lieutenant Company H; no enlistment in compiled service record; per Roster of Commissioned Officers died September 16, 1861; died Southern Mothers Hospital pneumonia age 35 per Daily Burial Record Book.

Riley, William   Buried April 30, 1862   Lot/Division 2, #1   Plat Number 551
Arkansas 17 Infantry Regiment Company E per Daily Burial Record Book; no compiled service record found.

Roark, W. T.   Buried March 27, 1862   Lot/Division 1, #388   Plat Number 388
Confederate 1 (King's Battalion) Cavalry Regiment Private (Gray's) 2 Company F; enlisted January 10, 1862 Memphis age 22; per March & April 1862 Regimental Return Remarks: Died; per Overton Hospital March 1862 Register of Deaths died March 27 of chronic dysentery.

Roberts, John S. Baxter   Buried May 17, 1862   Lot/Division 2, #226   Plat Number 776
Arkansas 17 (Lemoyne's) Infantry Regiment Private Company E; reference Card only in 17 Lemoyne's Infantry compiled service records; records found under Arkansas 21 Infantry, Private Company I that was successor of Company E of 17 Infantry; enlisted December 21, 1861 Dardanelle, Arkansas; per April 28, 1862 Muster Roll Remarks: Sick at Memphis May 1, 1862; per July & August 1862 Muster Roll Remarks: Left at Memphis in Hospital; from Mrs. Wilson's per Daily Burial Record Book.

Robertson, Augustus   Buried December 2, 1861   Lot/Division 1, #235   Plat Number 235
Arkansas 9 Infantry Regiment Private Company D; records found under "Arthur Robinson"; enlisted July 1861 Pine Bluff, Arkansas; per July to November 1861 Muster Roll Remarks: Sick at Columbus, Kentucky; per November 1861 to January 1862 Muster Roll Remarks: Died at Memphis, Tennessee on December 1, 1861; died Southern Mothers Hospital enteritis per Daily

Burial Record Book; not listed in Cemetery Single Grave Book.

Robinson, John   Buried May 13, 1862   Lot/Division 2, #190   Plat Number 740
No unit indicated and died Overton Hospital per Daily Burial Record Book.

Robinson, Wallace   Buried October 27, 1861   Lot/Division 1, #143   Plat Number 143
Arkansas Regiment Company I and died Southern Mothers Hospital enteritis age 18 per Daily Burial Record Book; not W. W. Robinson, Arkansas 27 Infantry, Private Company I, who per records deserted about December 20, 1862.

Roden, George   Buried August 30, 1910   Plat Number N8
Mississippi 1 Cavalry Regiment Private Company H; enlisted June 11, 1862 Poplar Springs; per July/August 1863 Muster Roll Remarks: Absent without leave since August 1863; per May/June 1864 Muster Roll Remarks: Deserted April 1, 1864; first enlisted in Mississippi 1 (Miller's) Cavalry Battalion Private Company A (Captain F. A. Montgomery's Company) June 13, 1861 at Memphis (Company A after battalion disbanded about June 1862 became Company H Mississippi 1 Cavalry Regiment); died age 70 per Daily Burial Record Book; member Confederate Historical Association, Camp 28, Bivouac 18, United Confederate Veterans of Tennessee, Company A; per sketch in Mathes book born 1842 in County Calvin, Ireland, winter of 1863 the Company was furloughed to go home and re-equip, cut off by Sherman's raid up the Yazoo, reported to General Wirt Adams, assigned to Headquarters of Scouts under Captain W. A. Montgomery where served to end of war and was surrendered at Gainesville, Alabama May 12, 1865; per Mississippi Captain Montgomery's Company of Scouts records G. W. Roden enlisted September 10, 1864 Issaquena, Mississippi and paroled May 12, 1865 at Gainesville, Alabama; note Mississippi 1 Cavalry Regiment is not the same as Wirt Adams' Cavalry Regiment, which was also known as 1 Regiment Mississippi Cavalry, and that was later officially known as Confederate Wood's Cavalry Regiment so no record found in these units; death reported in *Confederate Veteran,* Volume XIX, April 1911, page 174, "The Last Roll" Deaths of Confederates in Memphis, Tennessee who died during 1910 and were members of the Confederate Historical Association, Camp 28, U. C. V., Bivouac 18, C. V. of Memphis, Tennessee; per sketch in Mathes book joined Confederate Historical Association 1893 and became a member of Company A.

Rodgers, C. M.   Buried June 12, 1862   Lot/Division 2, #292   Plat Number 842
Tennessee 31 Infantry Regiment Company I; enlisted September 17, 1861 Trenton, Tennessee; per May & June 1862 Muster Roll Remarks: Sent to Hospital at Memphis from Corinth; per May 12, 1863 Muster Roll Remarks: age 20 and died August 1862; per Overton and Irving Hospital records Company J, admitted May 20, 1862 with complaint of intermittent fever but no death indicated; first initial "D" in Daily Burial Record Book and computer index; died State Hospital measles per Daily Burial Record Book; died August 1862 indicated in Lindsley's Annals.

Rodgers, John   Buried April 8, 1862   Lot/Division 1, #427   Plat Number 427
Tennessee Bankhead's Battery (Tennessee Scott's Light Artillery) Harris' Company and died Overton Hospital typhoid fever per Daily Burial Record Book; no service record found.

Rodgers, R. B.   Buried June 29, 1865   Lot/Division 2, #358   Plat Number 908
Arkansas C. S. A. (possibly Art C.S.A. but not clear in Daily Burial Record Book) and died consumption age 25 per Daily Burial Record Book; Cemetery computer index also lists burial as June 29, 1863, but only June 29, 1865, in Daily Burial Record Book; possibly Rueben B. Rodgers, Arkansas 1 Cavalry Battalion, Private Company I (not found Arkansas 1 Stirman's Cavalry Battalion).

Rogers, Oliver G.   Buried October 16, 1861   Lot/Division 1, #109   Plat Number 109
Louisiana 12 Infantry Regiment Private Company C; enlisted August 8, 1861 Camp Moore, Louisiana; per Muster Roll Remarks: Absent on furlough since October 13, 1861 for sickness; letter in record states died Memphis on or about October 20, 1861 with no wife or child; died Overton Hospital enteritis and Company I per Daily Burial Record Book.

Romine, Henry   Buried May 7, 1862   Lot/Division 2, #85   Plat Number 635
Missouri 2 Cavalry Regiment Private Company G; enlisted February 26, 1862 Cove Creek, Arkansas; per Muster Roll Remarks: Died Memphis May 6, 1862; unit Missouri 1 Cavalry, died typhoid fever, at Mrs. Turley's and age 19 per Daily Burial Record Book.

Roof, William C.   Buried October 28, 1861   Lot/Division 1, #144   Plat Number 144
Tennessee 4 Infantry Regiment Private (Sutherland's) Company G; enlisted May 5, 1861 Ripley, Tennessee, age 23; died Southern Mothers Hospital enteritis age 24 per Daily Burial Record Book; name spelled "Roph" in Cemetery Daily Burial Record, Alpha and Single Grave books and "Rolph" in computer index; not found in Lindsley's Annals.

Ros, A. William   Buried October 21, 1861   Lot/Division 1, #122   Plat Number 122
Arkansas 13 Infantry Regiment Company I and died Southern Mothers Hospital congested fever per Daily Burial Record Book; no compiled service record found; name spelled "Ross" in Cemetery computer index.

Rose, M. K.   Buried October 31, 1861   Lot/Division 1, #150   Plat Number 150
Arkansas 12 Infantry Regiment Company A and died camp per Daily Burial Record Book; no compiled service record found; grave stone three spaces south side of Stone (Space) 222, Division 1.

Ross, Francis M.   Buried May 3, 1910   Plat Number N9
Tennessee 7 Cavalry Regiment Private Company I; enlisted Company K March 18, 1862, Mason Depot, Tennessee; served as Teamster in Quartermaster Department for most of War; born March 16, 1837, Fayette County, Tennessee where resided after War until moved to Memphis in 1907; died May 2, 1910, Memphis age 73; obituary on front page of May 5, 1910, *The Commercial Appeal* Memphis; Tennessee Confederate Pension S5550.

Ross, William R.   Buried November 11, 1861   Lot/Division 1, #183   Plat Number 183
Tennessee 40 (Walker's) Infantry Regiment Private Company D; enlisted October 5, 1861, Jonesboro, Arkansas age 20; per November & December 1861, Muster Roll Remarks: Died November 10, 1861, at Camp Johnston, Tennessee; per Written Inventory Statement: Died of measles November 10, 1861, at Camp Johnston, Tennessee; died measles per Daily Burial Record Book; not listed in Cemetery Single Grave Book.

Rowan, G. W.   Buried May 9, 1862   Lot/Division 2, #131   Plat Number 681
Texas 27 (Whitfield's Legion) Cavalry Regiment Sergeant/Private Company K; enlisted March 20, 1862, Polk County, Texas; 5 Sergeant at enlistment; per May & June 1862, Muster Roll Remarks (rank Private): Died at Memphis May 9, 1862; Doctor and died Overton Hospital per Daily Burial Record Book; name spelled "Roman" in Cemetery Single Grave Book.

Rowe, E. A.   Buried June 8, 1871   Lot/Division 2, #374   Plat Number 924
Listed in Elmwood 1874 book as Confederate soldier buried in Elmwood who was citizen of Memphis or vicinity; no unit indicated and died age 53 consumption per Daily Burial Record Book; not listed in Cemetery Single Grave Book.

Russel, Oliver   Buried March 15, 1862   Lot/Division 1, #332   Plat Number 332
Arkansas 11 Infantry Regiment Private Company A; enlisted December 14, 1861 Saline County, Arkansas; per November 1, 1861 to September 1, 1862 Muster Roll Remarks: Died March 10, 1862; died Overton Hospital per Daily Burial Record Book; name spelled "Russell" in Daily Burial Record Book and computer index; not listed in Cemetery Single Grave Book.

Rutherford, Felix   Buried November 1, 1936   Plat Number N62
Tennessee 19 (Biffle's) Cavalry Regiment Private Company L; compiled service record found under "F. Retherford"; enlisted July 11, 1862 Jackson, Tennessee; appears on a Report of Absentees Without Leave dated March 1, 1865 with remarks that residence was Madison County, Tennessee and may be found at home; per Tennessee Confederate Pension application (S10729) born Haywood County, Tennessee; lived Raleigh Springs, Tennessee; died October 30, 1936 age 91; original grave stone underground with name and date of death.

Ryan, A. K.   Buried August 7, 1892   Plat Number N2
No unit indicated and died age 58 per Daily Burial Record Book with comment first grave north of Grave #540 (believed Grave #540 of southern part); no grave stone found.

Sackett, James   Buried February 13, 1862   Lot/Division 1, #264   Plat Number 264
Arkansas 9 Infantry Regiment Private (Thomasson's) New Company B; enlisted December 18, 1861 Monticello; per December 18, 1861 to March 1, 1862 Muster Roll Remarks: Died at State Hospital Memphis February 25, 1862; died State Hospital per Daily Burial Record Book.

Saddler, C. G.   Buried May 7, 1862   Lot/Division 2, #90   Plat Number 640
Arkansas 2 Mounted Rifles Regiment Private Company A; enlisted October 1, 1861 Camp Holloway age 19; per May & June 1862 Muster Roll Remarks: Dead, died at Memphis April 1862; name appears on a Register of Soldiers who died of Wounds or Disease with indication of deceased April 18, 1862; died Irving Hospital measles per Daily Burial Record Book; name spelled "Sadler" in Daily Burial Record Book and computer index.

Samples, J. W.   Buried March 28, 1900   Lot/Division 1, #547   Plat Number 547
No unit or other information in Daily Burial Record Book; possibly J. W. Sample, Arkansas 25 Infantry Regiment, Private Company E, enlisted March 10, 1862 Jacksonport, Arkansas with last record entry as sick in Hospital August 1863.

Sanders   Buried May 7, 1862   Lot/Division 2, #89   Plat Number 639
Arkansas 4 Regiment and died Overton Hospital pneumonia per Daily Burial Record Book; no first name in Daily Burial Record Book or computer index; several Sanders in the Arkansas 4 Infantry Regiment but cannot tell from rolls which one this would be and some records stop before this soldier's date of death; Issac Sanders, Jr. died January 10, 1862.

Sanders, George Henry   Buried November 30, 1935   Plat Number N61
Tennessee 3 (Forrest's) Cavalry Regiment; listed as 3 Cavalry in *Tennesseans in the Civil War Part 2*; per Tennessee Confederate Pension application S16627 enlisted summer 1862 Colonel Logan's Cavalry (Captain M. D. Logan, 1st Company G, Tennessee 3 Cavalry and became 2nd Company I Kentucky 7 Cavalry Regiment but no compiled service record found either unit) and born July 1, 1831, Woodstock, Ontario, Canada; per November 29, 1935, *The Commercial Appeal* Memphis, page 13, died November 28, 1935, Lauderdale County, Tennessee, age 105, married twice and oldest soldier receiving Tennessee Confederate pension at time; government stone has wrong date of death November 24, 1935; original grave stone underground.

Sanders, John B.   Buried May 13, 1862   Lot/Division 2, #183   Plat Number 733
Arkansas 10 Infantry Regiment Sergeant Company D; no enlistment in compiled service record; per March & April 1862 Muster Roll Remarks: Promoted from Private to 2 Sergeant March 21, 1862 and detailed to accompany two wounded men home to White, Arkansas; died Irving Hospital erysipelas per Daily Burial Record Book; name spelled "Saunders" in Daily Burial Record Book and computer index.

Sarat, William   Buried March 28, 1862   Lot/Division 1, #390   Plat Number 390
Arkansas 11 Infantry Regiment Company C and died Overton Hospital pneumonia per Daily Burial Record Book; no compiled service record found; per Overton Hospital March 1862 Register of Deaths died March 27 of pneumonia and name W. S. (L.) Serratt, Arkansas 11 Private Company C; does not appear to be Sirratt (also spelled Seratt), N. M., Private Company C, Arkansas 11 Infantry (see also 11/17 Consolidated Infantry Regiment) who was captured at Island 10 April 8, 1862.

Saunders, J. C.   Buried May 10, 1862   Lot/Division 2, #153   Plat Number 703
Arkansas 19 (Dockery/Smead's) Infantry Regiment Private Company G; enlisted March 1, 1862 Hillsboro, Arkansas; per March 1 to June 30, 1862 Muster Roll Remarks: Died May 10, 1862 at Memphis; name appears on a Register of Claims on Deceased Soldiers by father R. B. Saunders filed on April 3, 1862 with indication that died in Memphis, Tennessee; died typhoid fever per Daily Burial Record Book; name spelled "Sanders" in Daily Burial Record Book and computer index.

Saunders, William H.   Buried September 6, 1861   Lot/Division 1, #22   Plat Number 22
Arkansas 9 Infantry Regiment Private (Henry's) Company C; enlisted July 25, 1861 Pine Bluff, Arkansas age 25; per July 25 to November 1, 1861 Muster Roll Remarks: Died September 6, 1861 Mothers Home Memphis; name spelled "Sanders" in Daily Burial Record Book and computer index; died age 25 per Daily Burial Record Book; appears to be the soldier by name of "Saunders" who died Southern Mothers Hospital and funeral reported in September 8, 1861, *Memphis Daily Appeal*.

Saxon, Irving   Buried May 11, 1862   Lot/Division 2, #163   Plat Number 713
Missouri 1 Infantry Battalion Private (Kelsey's) Company C; per May & June, 1862, Company Muster Roll enlisted March 4, 1862, at Pocahontas, Arkansas by Major W. F. Raply with Remarks: Died May 15, 1862, at Memphis, Kelsey's Company, which was at Fort Pillow during May 1862, and operated as marines aboard Confederate defense fleet gunboat; Company became Company K, 6th Regiment Missouri Infantry, about August 23, 1862, but no record found in that unit's compiled service records; Jeff Thompson's Command Captain A. G. Kelsey and died at Sims in Daily Burial Record Book; name "Ervin Savon " in Daily Burial Record Book, Single Grave Book and computer index.

Scales, William M.   Buried May 17, 1864   Lot/Division 2, #381   Plat Number 931
Mississippi 5 Cavalry Regiment Captain Company D; enlisted September 28, 1863, Grenada, Mississippi; per undated roster of unit captured by enemy at Collierville, Tennessee November 3, 1863; per Register of Prisoners of War in the custody of Provost Marshall, Memphis, Tennessee received February 26, 1864, and sent to Overton Hospital; name appears on Register of the sick and wounded prisoners at Overton Hospital, Memphis, Tennessee with complaint of sprained ankle, captured at Collierville, Tennessee November 3, 1863, admitted November 4, 1863, and returned to duty February 26, 1864, and with remarks captured at Collierville, Tennessee November 3, 1863, and transferred to the care of Provost Marshall; name appears on a register of Prisoners of War in custody of Provost Marshall, Memphis, Tennessee, with disposition remarks that sent to Johnson's Island, Ohio March 3, 1864; name appears on Descriptive Roll of Prisoners of War at Camp Chase, Ohio that indicates arrested at Collierville, Tennessee, November 3, 1863, received at Camp Chase March 7, 1864, from Memphis, Tennessee and date of departure April 9, 1864, with remarks died; name appears on undated Military Prison (prison not indicated) Record that indicates died April 9, 1864 from erysipelas and buried in Grave 133, 1/3 MSCC; per Register of Confederate Soldiers, Sailors, and Citizens who Died in Federal Prisons and Military Hospitals in the North, 1861-1865, Camp Chase (not in compiled service records) died April 9, 1864, and buried Grave 133 with notation RMD (removed); per Daily Burial Record Book died consumption age 30; originally buried Chapel Hill Section, Lot 491 and moved to Confederate Rest May 9, 1874.

Scherbe, A.   Buried April 21, 1862   Lot/Division 1, #474   Plat Number 474
Appeal Battery Bryan's Company and died Overton Hospital per Daily Burial Record Book; unit later Arkansas 5 Battery Light Artillery (Appeal Battery) but no compiled service record found.

Schinon, E. H.   Buried May 27, 1862   Lot/Division 2, #271   Plat Number 821
McNair's Regiment Company E unit and died Overton Hospital typhoid fever per Daily Burial Record Book; name spelled "Schinou" in Cemetery computer index; no compiled service record found in Arkansas 4 McNair's Infantry Regiment.

Scott, Alfred M.   Buried March 19, 1862   Lot/Division 1, #347   Plat Number 347
Texas 9 (Young's/Maxey's) Infantry Regiment Private Company A; enlisted September 26, 1861 Paris, Texas, age 21; per March 1862 Regimental Return: Sick in Hospital in Memphis; per April 1862 Regimental Return: Died Memphis pneumonia; record includes an affidavit by father making a claim on what might be due his son; per Descriptive List age 21, born Texas, farmer, and died of disease in Overton Hospital, Memphis, Tennessee March 17, 1862; per Overton Hospital March 1862 Register of Deaths died March 18 of pneumonia; died of typhoid fever per Daily Burial Record Book.

Scrouse, J.   Buried May 14, 1862   Lot/Division 2, #207   Plat Number 757
Arkansas 18 (Carroll's) Infantry Regiment Company H and died Overton Hospital typhoid fever per Daily Burial Record Book; no compiled service record found; name spelled "Scronse" in Cemetery computer index.

Seabrook, John Thomas   Buried February 27, 1867   Lot/Division 1, #69½   Plat Number 69½
Tennessee 4 Infantry Regiment Private Company A; enlisted May 15, 1861, Germantown, Tennessee age 19; age 20 per April 25 to June 30, 1862, Company Muster Roll with Remarks: died April 16, 1862, from wounds received at Shiloh; on list of wounded at Battle of Shiloh reported in April 16, 1862, *Memphis Daily Appeal*, page 1, column 2; "J. T. Seabrook, Jr." killed Shiloh per Tennessee 4 Infantry Regiment Memorial Roll in Lindsley's Annals page 193; died from wounds age 21 and buried Fowler Section Single Grave 69½ per Daily Burial Record Book with Remarks: Confederate Interment 1st Division; 1848 1862 inscribed on grave stone; Carlisle Page, President of Elmwood Cemetery and nephew of Seabrook, advised on January 22, 1994, that he just put grave marker where it is as he did not know where Seabrook is actually buried; listed in Elmwood 1874 book as Confederate soldier buried in Elmwood who was citizen of Memphis or vicinity; see Seabrook papers in the Carroll file in the Elmwood Cemetery Office.

Seton, William   Buried January 24, 1863   Lot/Division 2, #333   Plat Number 883
Tennessee 20 Company K and per Daily Burial Record Book; Texas 20 Regiment indicated in Cemetery Single Grave Book; not found Tennessee 20 Infantry Regiment rolls or in McMurray's History of the 20 Tennessee Regiment Volunteers Infantry CSA; not William Seton, Union Tennessee 2 Mounted Infantry; does not appear to be any of the "Seatons" in Tennessee units.

Sewell, J. B.   Buried May 12, 1862   Lot/Division 2, #170   Plat Number 720
Arkansas 19 (Dockery/Smead's) Infantry Regiment Company B; no "J. B. Sewell" found in unit but several other Sewells; possibly James H. Sewell, Private Company A who enlisted February 25, 1862, Lewisville, Arkansas, absent sick per February 25 to June 30, 1862, Company Muster Roll Remarks, and deserted - was sent to Memphis Hospital and has never returned or reported per September 1 to October 31, 1862, Company Muster Roll Remarks; died Overton Hospital per Daily Burial Record Book.

Sewell, John   Buried May 5, 1862   Lot/Division 2, #52   Plat Number 602
Arkansas 19 (Dockery/Smead's) Infantry Regiment Private (Johnson's) Company A; enlisted February 25, 1862, Lewisville, Arkansas; per February 25 to June 30, 1862, Company Muster Roll Remarks: Died at Memphis, Tennessee May 5, 1862; died Overton Hospital typhoid fever and pneumonia per Daily Burial Record Book.

Shackleford, L. A.   Buried April 10, 1862   Lot/Division 1, #433   Plat Number 433
Arkansas 12 Infantry Regiment Company A and died Overton Hospital typhoid fever and pneumonia per Daily Burial Record Book; no compiled service record found.

Shadrick, J. M.   Buried May 2, 1862   Lot/Division 2, #20   Plat Number 570
Arkansas King's Regiment Wheeler's Company and died Overton Hospital typhoid fever and pneumonia per Daily Burial Record Book; unit should be Arkansas 20 (King's) Infantry Regiment (Wheeler's) Company H but not found in that unit records.

Shanault, A. S.   Buried April 4, 1862   Lot/Division 1, #415   Plat Number 415
Arkansas 11 Infantry Regiment Company B and died Overton Hospital typhoid fever per Daily Burial Record Book; no service record found.

Shanberger, George W.   Buried May 7, 1862   Lot/Division 2, #88   Plat Number 638
Arkansas 20 (King's) Infantry Regiment Private Company G; enlisted February 17, 1862 Little Rock, Arkansas; per February 17 to May 2, 186, Company Muster Roll Remarks: Left at Fort Pillow sick; per February 17 to June 30, 1862, Company Muster Roll Remarks: Sick at Memphis Hospital 1st May, last heard of him; per January 1 to February 28, 1863, Company Muster Roll Remarks: Supposed to be dead and dropped from rolls; died Overton Hospital per Daily Burial Record Book; name spelled "Schaumberger" in Daily Burial Record Book and computer index.

Shanks, M. C.   Buried March 24, 1862   Lot/Division 1, #374   Plat Number 374
Arkansas 9 Infantry Regiment Private (Thomasson's) New Company B; only a single Company Muster Roll card dated December 18, 1861 to March 18, 1862, in compiled service record indicating enlisted December 18, 1861, Monticello; died State Hospital per Daily Burial Record Book and grave in short row north side of Monument.

Shanks, M. O.   Buried October 20, 1861   Lot/Division 1, #119   Plat Number 119
Arkansas 12 Infantry Regiment; no compiled service record found; unit and died measles age 23 per Daily Burial Record Book.

Sharpling, Lemuel   Buried April 2, 1862   Lot/Division 1, #408   Plat Number 408
Louisiana 1 Regiment Company G and died phthisis pulmonalis per Daily Burial Record Book; no compiled service record found.

Shaw, C. M.   Buried January 17, 1863   Lot/Division 2, #327   Plat Number 877
Mississippi 24 Regiment per Daily Burial Record Book; several Shaws in regiment but no compiled service found.

Shea, Michael   Buried November 9, 1861   Lot/Division 1, #175   Plat Number 175
Tennessee 2 (Walker's) Infantry Regiment Private Company A; enlisted April 26, 1861, Memphis; per March & April 1862, Muster Roll Remarks: Absent Sick; per undated muster roll remarks: Died in Hospital July 1862 (note date difference with Cemetery record); died State Hospital per Daily Burial Record Book; name spelled "Sheer" in Cemetery computer index; not found in Lindsley's Annals.

Shean, John   Buried August 20, 1861   Lot/Division 1, #48   Plat Number 48
Tennessee 2 Regiment Volunteers per Daily Burial Record Book; no compiled service record found Tennessee 2nd (Walker's or Robison's) Infantry Regiments.

Sheffield, Mark   Buried May 21, 1862   Lot/Division 2, #252   Plat Number 802
Arkansas 4 (McNair's) Infantry Regiment Private (Tyson's) Company D; enlisted December 28, 1861 Rondo, Arkansas; per February 28 to June 30, 1862 Muster Roll Remarks: Sent to hospital sick; per September & October 1862 Muster Roll Remarks: Absent at hospital age 18; per January & February 1864 Muster Roll Remarks: Sent to hospital from Memphis April 29, 1862; died Overton Hospital per Daily Burial Record Book.

Sheffield, William   Buried April 26, 1862   Lot/Division 1, #499   Plat Number 499
Missouri Landis' Company Light Artillery; enlisted December 8, 1861 St. Clair County, Missouri; per muster roll remarks: Died Memphis April 21, 1862; died Overton Hospital pneumonia per Daily Burial Record Book.

Shelton, George B.   Buried April 23, 1862   Lot/Division 1, #480   Plat Number 480
Arkansas 23 (Adams') Infantry Regiment Private (Hillis') Company A; enlisted February 26, 1862, Craighead County, Arkansas; per February 26 to June 30, 186,2 Muster Roll Remarks: Died April 1862; "Boat" noted in Daily Burial Record Book Remarks.

Shelton, Jesse F.   Buried May 8, 1862   Lot/Division 2, #115   Plat Number 665
Arkansas 23 (Adams') Infantry Regiment Private Company A; enlisted February 26, 1862, Poinsett County, Arkansas; per February 26 to June 30, 1862, Muster Roll Remarks: Died April 1862; died Irving Hospital congestive fever per Daily Burial Record Book; per Irving Hospital record admitted May 4, 1862, with complaint of congestive fever and died May 5, 1862.

Shelton, John   Buried November 12, 1861   Lot/Division 1, #185   Plat Number 185
Tennessee 40 (Walker's) Infantry Regiment Private Company G; enlisted September 23, 1861 Camp Tyddersdale, Arkansas, age 18; per November & December 1861 Muster Roll Remarks: Died November 12, 1861 Camp Johnston, Tennessee disease measles and pneumonia; died camp measles age 17 per Daily Burial Record Book; Walker's Regiment indicated as an Arkansas unit in Daily Burial Record Book.

Sheppard, James H.   Buried September 19, 1861   Lot/Division 1, #60   Plat Number 60
Arkansas 9 Infantry Regiment Private (Blankenship's) Company E; enlisted July 27, 1861 Pine Bluff, Arkansas; per July 27 to November 1, 1861 Muster Roll Remarks: Died 18 September; died Southern Mothers Hospital and name "William Shepherd" in Daily Burial Record Book but no record found that name.

Sheridan, Michael   Buried September 15, 1861   Lot/Division 1, #44   Plat Number 44
Confederate Marines Captain Hays and died State Hospital per Daily Burial Record Book; no compiled service record found; there was a Captain Andrew J. Hays of Confederate Marine Corps; per book the *Confederate States Marine Corps*, by Ralph W. Donnelly, 1989, White Mane Publishing Company, Inc., page 22, "During the months of August, September, and October (1861), efforts had been made by Captain Andrew J. Hays to recruit a Company D for the Marine Corps at the Mississippi Port Memphis, Tennessee."; brief sketch as Appendix II in the thesis written by Donald Ray Gardner entitled "The Confederate Corps of Marines" (1973) presented to the Faculty of the Graduate School Memphis State University in partial fulfillment of the requirements for the degree Master of Arts with first name as "Wick" that is just a misreading of his handwritten name in the Single Grave Book.

Sherman, Dr. S. B.   Buried March 14, 1862   Lot/Division 1, #330   Plat Number 330
Arkansas 1 Infantry Regiment Company E, doctor and died Overton Hospital per Daily Burial Record Book; not George W. Sherman, Surgeon Arkansas 10 Infantry; Dr. S. B. Sherman found Arkansas 1860 Census, Little Rock, Pulaski County, page 58, age 24, Physician, and born in Tennessee.

Sherwood, Jonathan   Buried December 10, 1861   Lot/Division 1, #244   Plat Number 244
Tennessee 22 Infantry Regiment Private Company E; enlisted July 22, 1861 Trenton, Tennessee age 30; per December 11, 1861 *Memphis Daily Appeal* unit was Tennessee 2 Infantry Regiment (possibly Battalion which was later known as 22 Regiment) and died December 9, 1861, Overton Hospital after leg amputated due to gunshot wounds to thigh and leg; Company I per Daily Burial Record Book; killed at Belmont per Lindsley's Annals; per Irving Hospital record Private Company J, admitted November 15, 1861 with complaint of ancle (sic), remarks that leg amputated November 30, 1861, and died December 9, 1981, with remark leg amputated November 30, 1861, and pneumonia supervened.

Shields, S. J.   Buried November 22, 1861   Lot/Division 1, #214   Plat Number 214
Arkansas 12 Infantry Regiment Private Company G; enlisted July 27, 1861 Arkadelphia, Arkansas; per July to October 1862 Muster Roll Remarks: Died at Memphis October or November 1861.

Shik, John   Buried January 28, 1863   Lot/Division 2, #334   Plat Number 884
Texas 4 Regiment per Daily Burial Record Book; no compiled service record found.

Shivers, James Norborn   Buried March 11, 1926   Plat Number N43
Tennessee 4 Infantry Regiment Private Company B; enlisted May 15, 1861 Germantown, Tennessee age 16; per Casualty Report dated April 10, 1862 Corinth, Mississippi: Wounded severely in ankle at Battle of Shiloh; per April to June 1862 Muster Roll Remarks: Wounded and absent since May 28, 1862; per November 14, 1862 Muster Roll Remarks: Discharged July 3, 1962 (papers signed July 9, 1862); on list of wounded at Battle of Shiloh reported in April 16, 1862 *Memphis Daily Appeal*; per Tennessee Confederate Pension application S13824 born October 23, 1844 Shelby County, Tennessee; per widow's (Virginia Albany Bennett) Tennessee Confederate Pension application W8967 died March 10, 1926; original grave stone underground with name and date of death.

Simmons, John B.   Buried May 16, 1862   Lot/Division 2, #222   Plat Number 772
Arkansas 23 (Adams') Infantry Regiment Private Company I; enlisted March 15, 1862, Jonesboro, Arkansas; per March 12 to June 30, 1862, Company Muster Roll Remarks: Died at Memphis May 15, 1862 measles; Company C per Daily Burial Record Book.

Simmons, John C.   Buried May 2, 1862   Lot/Division 2, #17   Plat Number 567
Arkansas 18 (Carroll's) Infantry Regiment Private Company H; enlisted March 3, 1862 Little Rock, Arkansas; per March to June 1862 Muster Roll Remarks: Died April 29, 1862; died Overton Hospital pneumonia per Daily Burial Record Book; second initial "T" in Daily Burial Record Book and computer index; grave number indicated as 16 in Cemetery computer index.

Simmons, T. J.   Buried October 31, 1861   Lot/Division 1, #154   Plat Number 154
Tennessee 40 (Walker's) Infantry Regiment Private Company H; enlisted September 4, 1861 Montgomery, Alabama age 24; per November & December 1861 Muster Roll Remarks: Died October 30, 1861; per Register of Soldiers Killed in Battle or Died of Wounds or Disease died October 15, 1861 Memphis measles; died measles age 25 per Daily Burial Record Book.

Simpson, John F.   Buried March 7, 1862   Lot/Division 1, #295   Plat Number 295
Louisiana 5 Battalion Company G per Daily Burial Record Book; no compiled service record found; per Overton Hospital March 1862, Register of Deaths died March 6 of chronic diarrhea; Louisiana 5th Battalion became part of Louisiana 21st (Kennedy's) Infantry Regiment on February 9, 1862, but Regiment disbanded July 28, 1862, by order of General Braxton Bragg.

Simpson, Thomas P.   Buried May 4, 1862   Lot/Division 2, #43   Plat Number 593
Arkansas 20 (King's) Infantry Regiment Private (Swaggerty's) Company G; enlisted February 17, 1862 Little Rock, Arkansas; per February 2, to May 2, 1862, Muster Roll Remarks: Absent sick and left at Fort Pillow; per February 17 to June 30, 1862, Muster Roll Remarks: Died Memphis May 1, 1862; compiled service record found Thomas Simpson but there is also a "Thomas P. Simpson" in same Company and who was captured and died; died Overton Hospital per Daily Burial Record Book.

Sims, G. W.   Buried April 7, 1862   Lot/Division 1, #420   Plat Number 420
Louisiana 25 Infantry Regiment Private Company H; enlisted March 19, 1862 New Orleans, Louisiana; two dates of death noted in compiled service record: April 5, 1862, and April 10, 1862; April 12, 1862, on grave stone; "S. W. Sims" on one card of compiled service record; died Overton Hospital pneumonia per Daily Burial Record Book; name spelled "Simms" in Daily Burial Record Book and computer index.

Sims, William Henry   Buried November 10, 1861   Lot/Division 1, #177   Plat Number 177
Tennessee 40 (Walker's) Infantry Regiment Private (Bush's) Company D; enlisted September 19, 1861 Jonesboro, Arkansas age 21; per November & December 1861 Muster Roll Remarks: Died November 9, 1861 Camp Johnson; per Register of Soldiers Killed in Battle or Died of Wounds or Disease died November 9, 1861 Camp Johnston, Tennessee; statement in compiled service record indicates died of measles.

Skeggs, James M.   Buried February 24, 1862   Lot/Division 1, #269   Plat Number 269
Texas 9 (Young's/Maxey's) Infantry Regiment Private Company E; enlisted January 11, 1862 Clarksville, Texas; per Overton Hospital February 1862 Register of Deaths Died February 22, 1862; name spelled "Skaggs" in Daily Burial Record Book and both spellings in Cemetery computer index; Captain Thompson's Company indicated in Cemetery Single Grave Book.

Skinner, John   Buried March 23, 1862   Lot/Division 1, #368   Plat Number 368
Tennessee 40 Infantry Regiment Private Company I; enlisted September 20, 1861 Madison, Arkansas age 19; per September 3, 1861 to October 5, 1862 Muster Roll Remarks: Discharged by Surgeon November 1, 1861; per Overton Hospital March 1862 Register of Deaths died March 22 of pneumonia; 1842 1862 on grave stone; not found in Lindsley's Annals 39 & 40 Consolidated Infantry Regiment Official Memorial Roll.

Sledge, Washington M.   Buried April 15, 1862   Lot/Division 1, #452   Plat Number 452
Arkansas 9 Infantry Regiment Corporal (Hawley's) Company A; enlisted July 25, 1861, Pine Bluff, Arkansas; per July 25 to November 1, 1861, Muster Roll Remarks: Sick at Memphis and left at State Hospital about September 15; per March 1 to April 30, 1862, Muster Roll Remarks: Died at Memphis April 17, 1862; per Overton Hospital Register dated March 31, 1862, admitted March 29, 1862; wounded per Daily Burial Record Book; listed in Elmwood 1874 book as Confederate soldier buried in Elmwood who was citizen of Memphis or vicinity.

Smedley, Henry H.   Buried February 17, 1862   Lot/Division 1, #265   Plat Number 265
Texas 9 (Young's/Maxey's) Infantry Regiment Private Company H; enlisted October 14, 1861 Bonham, Texas age 22; per Overton Hospital February 1862, Register died February 16, 1862, with no cause indicated.

Smith, Armstrong B.   Buried October 9, 1861   Lot/Division 1, #32   Plat Number 32
Confederate 4 (Bakers') Infantry Regiment Private Company B (Captain Jonas Griffin's Rifles); per Company Muster-in Roll enlisted August 10, 1861, at Montgomery, Alabama age 21; per Company Muster Roll dated October 31, 1861, remarks: Died of Typhoid Fever at the Southern Mothers Home in Memphis, Tennessee on the 9th of October, 1861; compiles service record under "A. P. Smith"; regiment (also known as 1st Alabama, Tennessee and Mississippi Infantry) was formed about December 9, 1861, with ten companies: four from Alabama, two from Mississippi, and four from Tennessee; captured at Island 10 April 8, 1862, and after exchange in September, 1862, the companies were reorganized and transferred to other commands; Company B became Company C of the Alabama 54th Infantry Regiment but no record for this regiment as died before transfer; per Daily Burial Record Book died Southern Mothers Hospital typhoid fever age 21.

Smith, B. A.   Buried March 27, 1862   Lot/Division 1, #387   Plat Number 387
Louisiana 12 Infantry Regiment Private Company K; enlisted May 13, 1861 Camp Moore, Louisiana; per Muster Roll Remarks: Absent since December 1861; on Pay Record July 16, 1862; died State Hospital per Daily Burial Record Book; not found in Booth Louisiana Books but compiled service record found.

Smith, C. C.   Buried May 9, 1862   Lot/Division 2, #123   Plat Number 673
Arkansas 19 (Dockery/Smead's) Infantry Regiment Private Company B; enlisted February 26, 1862 Columbia County, Arkansas; no remarks on muster rolls; note in compiled service record to Oklahoma Board of Pension Committee confirming information on enlistments with indication that name may be "Calvin"; died Overton Hospital congestion per Daily Burial Record Book.

Smith, George B.   Buried May 14, 1862   Lot/Division 2, #199   Plat Number 749
Arkansas 18 (Carroll's) Infantry Regiment Private Company H; enlisted March 3, 1862 Little Rock, Arkansas; per all Muster Roll Remarks: Absent sick but no other information; died Irving Hospital pneumonia per Daily Burial Record Book; per Irving Hospital record admitted May 1, 1862 with complaint of typhoid fever and died May 12, 1862.

Smith, J. L.   Buried December 9, 1910   Plat Number N10
No unit indicated and died age 75 per Daily Burial Record Book; per *The Commercial Appeal* Memphis December 10, 1910, page 4, Confederate Soldier (no unit identified) and first buried in Potter's Field by mistake and moved to Elmwood December 9, 1910 after Ladies Confederate Memorial Association, Confederate Historical Association and J. Harvey Mathes Chapter United Daughters of the Confederacy raised funds to move him.

Smith, James   Buried May 23, 1862   Lot/Division 2, #260   Plat Number 810
Bruce's Battalion Company A and died Overton Hospital typhoid fever per information in the Daily Burial Record Book; no compiled service record or other information found on a Bruce's Battalion; per *Find A Grave*, database and images

(https://www.findagrave.com), memorial page for James William Smith (1829–1862), Find A Grave Memorial no. 127386176, citing Elmwood Cemetery, Memphis, Shelby County, Tennessee, USA, maintained by Kay Bazemore (contributor 47629412), born 1829 in Tennessee, in 1847 married Martha Mary Jane Tate, lived much of his life in Itawamba, and Tippah, Mississippi, September of 1861 enlisted in the 23rd Mississippi Infantry, Company E, wounded at the Battle of Shiloh in 1862, taken to the Corinth, Mississippi Hospital, his wife Martha, with 2 slaves came and moved him to a hospital in Memphis, where he died of his wounds and Typhoid Fever on May 23,1862; per single card for Company Muster Roll for September 12, 1861, to September 12, 1862, in Mississippi 23rd Infantry Regiment compiled service records (William Smith) enlisted in Company E as a Private September 12, 1861, at Iuka, Mississippi, age 33; no information in service record on injury or death.

Smith, Joel Henry   Buried September11, 1928   Plat Number N48
Mississippi 26 Infantry Regiment Private/Musician Company F; enlisted September 1, 1861 Iuka, Mississippi, age 17; per Record of Organization born Mississippi, occupation saddler, residence (nearest Post Office at enlistment) Corinth, age 17 and single; captured Fort Donelson, Kentucky February 16, 1862; captured at Vicksburg, Mississippi July 4, 1863; released from Point Lookout, Maryland June 19, 1865; per Tennessee Confederate Pension application (S9348) born Tippah County, Mississippi February 5, 1844; per widow's (Victoria Brooks Smith) Tennessee Confederate Pension application (W9199) born February 13, 1844, Corinth, Alcorn County, Mississippi (note differences) and died September 9, 1928; admitted March 12, 1910, Confederate Historical Association, Camp 28, Bivouac 18, United Confederate Veterans; brick mason after War per Confederate Historical Association application; no sketch in Mathes book; died age 84 per Daily Burial Record Book.

Smith, John   Buried September 24, 1938   Plat Number N65
Per September 23, 1938 *The Commercial Appeal* Memphis born Missouri and died September 22, 1938 age 100; newspaper also indicated that due to there being so many John Smiths never got a pension, was a cobbler, fought some but mostly made shoes for other soldiers, and faced burial in Potters Field; per September 24, 1938 *The Commercial Appeal* Memphis was saved from the Potter's Field when the United Daughters of the Confederacy made arrangements for burial in Confederate Veterans' Rest at Elmwood Cemetery; per Cemetery record grave 3 north of Stone #654; government grave stone (original stone underground).

Smith, John F.   Buried May 7, 1862   Lot/Division 2, #105   Plat Number 655
Tennessee 4 Infantry Regiment Private Company E; enlisted May 15, 1861 Germantown, Tennessee age 20; per April to June 1862, Muster Roll Remarks: Died Memphis May 7, 1862; per casualty report on unit dated April 10, 1862 at Corinth, Mississippi: Wounded severely in side and arm at Battle of Shiloh April 6 & 7, 1862; on list of wounded at Overton Hospital in April 11, 1862 *Memphis Daily Appeal*; on casualty list reported in April 16, 1862, *Memphis Daily Appeal* for Battle of Shiloh as having been severely wounded arm and side; died Overton Hospital per Daily Burial Record Book.

Smith, Levi   Buried November 25, 1862   Lot/Division 2, #318   Plat Number 868
Texas 10 (Locke's) Cavalry Regiment Private Company H; enlisted October 31, 1861 Taos, Texas, age 21; per August 1 to December 31, 1862 Muster Roll Remarks: Died at Memphis, Tennessee November 25, 1862.

Smith, N. D.   Buried June 9, 1862   Lot/Division 2, #286   Plat Number 836
Flannery's Company regiment unknown and died State Hospital per Daily Burial Record Book; originally no first name or initials in Daily Burial Record Book but "Hal(?)" was later written in pencil; initials "N. D." in Cemetery Alpha Book; listed both ways in Cemetery index; see Mitchell, John (Grave# 288) who was buried same date and unit name appears to be the same in the Daily Burial Record Book but transcribed differently in other Cemetery records.

Smith, Robert   Buried April 7, 1862   Lot/Division 1, #424   Plat Number 424
Louisiana 25 Infantry Regiment Private Company E; compiled service record has two enlistments: March 7, 1862 Union Parrish, Louisiana and March 7, 1862 Monroe, Louisiana; name on May & June 1862 Muster Roll with Remarks: Died April 12, 1862 (note date difference with Cemetery record) Overton Hospital disease.

Smith, Robert J.   Buried May 20, 1862   Lot/Division 2, #246   Plat Number 796
Texas 6 (Stone's) Cavalry Regiment Private Company G; enlisted September 7, 1861 Dallas, Texas, age 23; per July & August 1862, Muster Roll Remarks: Private at Memphis April 22, nothing has been heard from him since; per January & February 1863 Muster Roll Remarks: Supposed to have died at Memphis about May 10, 1862.

Smith, S. C.   Buried June 17, 1862   Lot/Division 2, #294   Plat Number 844
Died State Hospital pneumonia per Daily Burial Record Book.

Smith, W. S.   Buried October 13, 1861   Lot/Division 1, #2   Plat Number 2
Arkansas 13 Infantry Regiment Company G and died Southern Mothers Hospital lung congestion per Daily Burial Record Book; no service record found.

Smith, William S.   Buried May 6, 1862   Lot/Division 2, #84   Plat Number 634
Arkansas 8 (Miller's) Infantry Battalion Private Company C; enlisted March 15, 1862 Little Rock, Arkansas; per March 15 to April

30, 1862, Company Muster Roll Remarks: Died from disease at Fort Pillow, Tennessee on April 26; wife, Elizabeth J. Smith, filed a claim for settlement in the Office of the Confederate States Auditor for the War May 15, 1863; died Overton Hospital and second initials "W. J." in Daily Burial Record Book and computer index.

Smutherman, Green A.   Buried May 6, 1862   Lot/Division 2, #70   Plat Number 620
Arkansas 25 (Turnbull's) Infantry Regiment Private Company G; enlisted March 13, 1862 Pocahontas, Arkansas age 22; per March 13 to April 30, 1862 Muster Roll Remarks: at the Hospital in Memphis, Tennessee sick; per July 7 to August 1862 Muster Roll Remarks: Supposed to be dead and ordered to be dropped from the roll; name spelled "Smotherman" and died Overton Hospital typhoid fever per Daily Burial Record Book.

Snead, Thomas   Buried May 9, 1862   Lot/Division 2, #130   Plat Number 680
Arkansas 19 Infantry Regiment Company __ and died Overton Hospital per Daily Burial Record Book; no service record found.

Sorralls, James R.   Buried May 1, 1862   Lot/Division 2, #9   Plat Number 559
Arkansas 18 (Carroll's) Infantry Regiment Private Company A; enlisted February 25, 1862 Jefferson County, Arkansas age 25; per February to June 1862 Muster Roll Remarks: Died April 30, 1862; name spelled "Sorrells" in Daily Burial Record Book and computer index.

South, N. M.   Buried May 5, 1862   Lot/Division 2, #56   Plat Number 606
Young's Regiment Company D and died Overton Hospital pneumonia per Daily Burial Record Book; no compiled service record found; possibly William M. South, Private Company D, Texas 11 (Young's Regiment, Third Cavalry) Cavalry Regiment who enlisted October 2, 1861, at Camp Reeves, Texas, and per October 2 to December 31, 1861, Company Muster Roll remarks absent sick but no other information in service record.

Southerland, James M.   Buried November 21, 1861   Lot/Division 1, #208   Plat Number 208
Tennessee 40 (Walker's) Infantry Regiment Private Company K; enlisted November 3, 1861, Camp Johnston near Memphis, Tennessee age 22; per November & December 1861,, Muster Roll Remarks: Died November 21, 1861; per Register of Soldiers Killed in Battle or Died of Wounds or Disease with name spelled "Sutherlin:" Born Georgia and died November 21, 1861, at Fort Pillow, Tennessee of pneumonia; name spelled "Sutherland" and died Southern Mothers Hospital pneumonia per Daily Burial Record Book; name spelled "Sutherlin" in Lindsley's Annals 39 & 40 Consolidated Infantry Regiment Official Memorial Roll.

Southerland, Peter   Buried May 16, 1862   Lot/Division 2, #223   Plat Number 773
Arkansas 23 (Adams') Infantry Regiment Private Company I; enlisted March 12, 1862, Jonesboro, Arkansas; per March 12 to June 30, 1862, Muster Roll Remarks: Died at Memphis May 14, 1862, measles; name spelled "Sutherland" in Cemetery computer index.

Spencer, Benjamin   Buried July 1, 1861   Lot/Division 1, #19   Plat Number 19
From Mississippi per Daily Burial Record Book; not B. C. Spencer or B. E. Spencer Mississippi 8 Cavalry Regiment as they enlisted after his death; not Benjamin F. Spencer Mississippi 31 Infantry Regiment as executed for desertion April 25, 1864.

Spillman, Robert Bowman   Buried May 27, 1906   Lot/Division 1, #223   Plat Number 223
Tennessee 154 Senior Infantry Regiment Private Company L; enlisted March 7, 1862, Memphis; per November 1862, to February 1863, Muster Roll Remarks: Wounded Murfreesboro, Tennessee and left there; per undated List of Casualties: Severely wounded at Battle of Murfreesboro, Tennessee December 31, 1862; per Roll of Prisoners of War at Camp Morton, in captured at Stone River; first name "Robert" on one card in compiled service record but only found as "R. P." on all other records reviewed; per Daily Burial Record Book died age 74 and grave eight feet from south side of walk around Monument; member Confederate Historical Association; elected Association Vice President 1885; per Mathes book was an early Member of Association, at all times active and was especially efficient upon Annual Memorial occasions when the Graves of Confederates were strewn with flowers at Elmwood; per *Confederate Military History, Extended Edition*, Volume X Tennessee, page 726, Robert Bowman Spillman, native Orange County, Virginia, Vice President of Confederate Historical Association 1885-87 and became President upon the death of Colonel C. W. Frazer; article in *The Commercial Appeal* Memphis, May 27, 1906, page 5, column 3, refers to him as Colonel R. B. Spillman and indicates was native of Virginia but lived in Memphis since before the War; Captain, born 1833, and died May 26, 1906, inscribed on "In Memory Of" stone located in walk around Confederate Soldiers Rest Monument; note there is a second burial Grave #223 - William Woodward who is buried in the grave at the North end of the row in front of the Monument.

Stacy, L.   Buried May 23, 1862   Lot/Division 2, #261   Plat Number 811
Arkansas Colonel Adams Regiment and died at W. P. Deadricks per Daily Burial Record Book; not found Arkansas 23 Adams' Infantry Regiment or Confederate Cavalry Wood's Regiment (Wirt Adams' Cavalry Regiment - Mississippi 1 Cavalry Regiment).

Starrett, F. C.   Buried May 30, 1862   Lot/Division 2, #275   Plat Number 825
Texas 32 (Crump's Battalion) Cavalry Regiment Private Company D; per January to August 1862 Muster Roll Remarks: Enlisted age 21, Camp Crump, Marion County, Texas and died May 31, 1862; Company A and died at Dr. Taylor's per Daily Burial Record Book.

Steaphuns, John M.   Buried May 9, 1862   Lot/Division 2, #125   Plat Number 675
Arkansas 23 (Adams') Infantry Regiment Company H (no rank in record); enlisted March 6, 1862 Arkadelphia, Arkansas; per March 6 to June 30, 1862 Muster Roll Remarks: Died Memphis, Tennessee Overton Hospital typhoid May 9, 1862; died Overton Hospital pneumonia per in Daily Burial Record Book; name spelled "Stephens" in Daily Burial Record Book and computer index.

Steiner, J. P.   Buried May 18, 1862   Lot/Division 2, #364   Plat Number 914
CSS Colonel Lovell Clerk/Purser; appointed Clerk March 25, 1862; per Irving Hospital Record admitted May 17, 1862, with complaint of chronic diarrhea and died May 17, 1862; originally buried Chapel Hill Lot 252, Grave #3 and moved to Confederate Rest August 18, 1869; gunboat participated in and was sank during Battle of Memphis June 6, 1862; listed in Elmwood 1874 book as Confederate soldier buried in Elmwood who was citizen of Memphis or vicinity with rank of Lieutenant.

Stephens, Felix   Buried May 31, 1862   Lot/Division 2, #279   Plat Number 829
Missouri 6 Infantry Private Company K (Jeff Thompson's Command); per July & August 1862, Company Muster Roll enlisted January 5, 1862, New Madrid, Missouri and Remarks: absent sick near Memphis, Tennessee April 20, 1862; appears on Regimental Return for the month of August, 1862, with notation "Absent Memphis April 20. left sick."; September & October 1862, Company Muster Roll Remarks: left sick Memphis, Tennessee April 21, 1862; November & December 1862 Muster Roll Remarks: left sick Hospital Memphis, Tennessee April 21, 1862; May & June 1863 Muster Roll Remarks: Sent to Hospital Memphis June 21, 1862 (incorrect as already died); per Historic Roll (not dated) native of New Madrid, Missouri, farmer and age 20 when enlisted and remarks indicating in Fort Pillow May 10, 1862, and deserted on the evacuation of Memphis, Tennessee (incorrect as already died); record also found Missouri 1 Infantry Battalion Private (Kelsey's) Company C with same enlistment and Remarks: absent sick in hospital, Memphis, Tennessee, and which Company became Company K, Missouri 6 Infantry Regiment, in August 1862; died at A. N. Edward's of consumption in Daily Burial Record Book; name spelled "Stevens" in Daily Burial Record Book and computer index.

Stephens, J. J.   Buried May 9, 1862   Lot/Division 2, #118   Plat Number 668
Arkansas 19 (Dockery/Smead's) Infantry Regiment Sergeant Company B; enlisted February 26, 1862 Columbia County, Arkansas; per March 26 to June 30, 1862 Muster Roll Remarks: Absent sick at Memphis; no other information in record; died Overton Hospital per Daily Burial Record Book.

Stewart, E.   Buried May 2, 1912   Plat Number N11
No unit indicated and died age 60 per Daily Burial Record Book.

Stewart, Jerry F.   Buried September 16, 1862   Lot/Division 2, #301   Plat Number 851
Alabama 1 Infantry Regiment Private Company C; no enlistment in service record; per Muster Roll Remarks: Captured at Island 10 April 8, 1862, and died on Hospital Boat September 14, 1862; from Benton-Lowndes County per Daily Burial Record Book.

Stickney, Horace N.   Buried May 13, 1877   Lot/Division 2, #388   Plat Number 938
No unit indicated and died consumption age 45 per Daily Burial Record Book.

Stocks, James   Buried June 27, 1862   Lot/Division 2, #299   Plat Number 849
Sharpshooter from White River and died State Hospital per Daily Burial Record Book; not found Confederate Stirman's Regiment, Sharpshooters, Arkansas 12 Battalion Sharpshooters or Arkansas 1 (Stirman's) Battalion Cavalry.

Stockton, George M.   Buried October 10, 1868   Lot/Division 2, #361   Plat Number 911
Tennessee 154th Senior Infantry Regiment Corporal/1 Lieutenant Company E ("The Hickory Rifles"), per Company Muster Roll for August 14 to October 21,1861, enlisted May 14, 1861, at Randolph, Tennessee, per Company Muster Roll for May & June 1862, elected Lieutenant at reorganization 3 May 1862, captured twice - first at Perryville, Kentucky, October 12,1862, and exchanged in Vicksburg, Mississippi, October 12,1862, at age 28, and second outside Memphis, Tennessee on April 29, 1863, and sent to Military Prison, Alton, Illinois, and paroled at Johnson's Island, Ohio, and transferred to City Point February 24,1865; death reported (George W. Stockton) under Coroner's Inquest in *Memphis Daily Appeal*, October 10, 1868, page 3, column 2, "A Man Found Drowned in Wolf River" (Supposed Suicide); "IN MEMORIAM" in *Memphis Daily Appeal*, October 12, 1868, page2, column 4, "Alas! our friend and comrade, George M. Stockton has gone, and sleeps now quietly and calmly beneath the shades of Elmwood, where, surrounded by those with whom he had braved the storms of battle, ... and of his high soldierly qualities, his comrades of the of the old 154th are willing witnesses."; listed in Elmwood1874 book as Confederate soldier buried in Elmwood who was citizen of Memphis or vicinity; no unit indicated and drowned age 30 per Daily Burial Record Book; not listed in Cemetery Single Grave Book.

Stokes, James E.   Buried November 12, 1861   Lot/Division 1, #186   Plat Number 186
Tennessee 40 (Walker's) Infantry Regiment Private Company D; enlisted September 19, 1861 Monticello, Arkansas age 22; per November & December 1861 Muster Roll Remarks: Died November 11, 1861 at Camp Johnson; per written statement by Captain in compiled service record died of typhoid fever November 11, 1861 in Camp; died camp measles age 21 per Daily Burial Record

Book; name spelled "Tokes" in one entry of Cemetery computer index and "Stockes" in Alpha Book; Walker's Regiment indicated as an Arkansas unit in Daily Burial Record Book.

Stone, M. F.   Buried May 14, 1862   Lot/Division 2, #200   Plat Number 750
Texas 10 (Locke's) Cavalry Regiment Private Company G; compiled service record found under W. F. Stone; enlisted October 31, 1861 Taos, Texas, age 44; per March to August 1862 Muster Roll Remarks: Died at Memphis May 12, 1862; died Irving Hospital pneumonia per Daily Burial Record Book; per Irving Hospital record admitted May 3, 1862 with complaint of pneumonia and died May 13, 1862.

Strickland, William V.   Buried March 8, 1918   Plat Number N30
Mississippi 19 Infantry Regiment Private Company F; enlisted May 15, 1861, Oxford, Mississippi, age 15; captured Battle of Gettysburg, Pennsylvania July 3, 1863, (July 5, 1863, on some cards); per Oath of Allegiance, place of residence Lafayette, Mississippi, released May 10, 1865, from Fort Delaware, Delaware; per Tennessee Confederate Pension application S14163 born 1846 Lafayette County, Mississippi; died March 7, 1918, age 73 per Daily Burial Record Book; member Confederate Historical Association, Camp 28 United Confederate Veterans, Bivouac 18, Memphis; per Association application born February 13, 1846, Lafayette County, Mississippi; born February 7, 1845, per Tennessee, Shelby County, Death Certificate; no sketch in Mathes book.

Strussell, Thomas   Buried April 16, 1862   Lot/Division 1, #459   Plat Number 459
Harmon's Regiment (Sherman's) Company per Daily Burial Record Book which is believed to be Tennessee Harman's Infantry Regiment, Sherwin's Company A; no compiled service record found under "Strussell"; Colonel B. Desha Harman was authorized to recruit a regiment at Memphis by Secretary of War about January 1862; three companies were mustered in prior to March 1862, and one prior to April 1, 1862; regiment never completed organization and original four companies combined into one company about July 1862, and assigned to Confederate 1 Battalion Infantry as Company F (not found either spelling in this unit records); there is a soldier in the Harman compiled service record rolls name "T. Trussell" with a single card in the record on a muster roll dated March 8, 1862, at Memphis indicating enlisted March 8, 1862, Memphis age 40 by Captain John Adams for the War but no other information.

Sullivan, George   Buried October 9, 1861   Lot/Division 1, #74   Plat Number 74
Walker's Regiment Company H and died State Hospital per Daily Burial Record Book; regiment believed to be Tennessee 40 (Walker's) Infantry Regiment Company H that later became Company A Alabama 54th Infantry Regiment but no record found.

Swindle, William   Buried April 28, 1862   Lot/Division 1, #511   Plat Number 511
Alabama 50 (26) Infantry Regiment Company K (service record cards has unit as Company K, 26 Regiment Alabama Infantry; W. F. Swindle); enlisted September 25, 1861, at Camp Abington, Fayette County, Tennessee; per March and April Muster Roll remarks: wounded severely in the shoulder in the battle of Shiloh; Appears on a Register containing a Report of the Killed, Wounded and Missing of the Second Corps, Army of Mississippi, at the Battle of Shiloh, April 6 and 7, 1862, with Time and place of wound April 6, 8 pm and Nature of wound Shoulder dangerously; Name appears on a Register of Claims of deceased Officers and Soldiers from Alabama which were filed for settlement in the Office of the Confederate States Auditor for the War Department and which claim was filed by Pernnina Swindle, Widow, May 21, 1863, for amount due of $119.72; 26th Alabama Regiment Captain Hutto's Company, wounded and died Irving Hospital per Daily Burial Record Book; "26th Alabama – Wm. Swinde, Hutto's comp'y" reported as wounded in the Irving Hospital in *Memphis Daily Appeal* April 11, 1862; per Irving Hospital records admitted April 10, 1862, with complaint of left shoulder and died April 27, 1862; per unit service record cards "This Company was designated at various times as Company K, 38th Regiment Tennessee Infantry; Company K, 26th Regiment (Coltart's) Alabama Infantry; and Company K, 50th Regiment Alabama Infantry." and "Golladay's Battalion and Chadick's Battalion Alabama Vols. were consolidated by S. O. No. 27, dated Headquarters 2d Corps, A. M., April 3, 1862, to form the 26th Regiment (Coltart's) Alabama Vols, and this designation was changed to the 50th Regiment Alabama Vols. by S. O. No. 135, dated A. & I. G. O. June 6, 1863."; per narrative in Tennesseans in the Civil War: A Military History of Confederate and Union Units with Available Rosters of Personnel. Nashville, Tennessee: Civil War Centennial Commission, 1964, Part 1, the 38th Tennessee Infantry Regiment (also called 8th (Looney's) Tennessee Infantry) organized September 23, 1861, at Camp Abington, Fayette County, Tennessee and John C. Hutto, Company "K" transferred to Golladay's 5th Alabama Battalion in March, 1862 and later 26th/50th Alabama Infantry Regiment; the designation was changed to 50th in June, 1863, when it was learned that another 26th Infantry was already serving in Virginia; thus he would have originally mustered into Hutto's Company K 38th Regiment Tennessee Infantry at Camp Abington when he enlisted on September 25, 1861 and transferred with the company to Golladay's 5th Alabama Infantry Battalion in April, 1862, before the battle of Shiloh and his death occurred before the 50th designation, which confirms why his service record cards indicate 26 Regiment Alabama Infantry; great-great nephew, Kent Faith, who researched his Swindle ancestry advised that he was born 1 September 1839, Walker County, Alabama, and his parents were Daniel and Jerusha Caroline Robertson Swindle; he also secured a VA government marker for his grave: William Swindle, Co K 50 Ala Infantry, Confederate States Army, Sep 1 1839 Apr 27 1862 and organized a Marker Dedication Ceremony that was held at the grave site on 20 May 2016.

Swink, Drew L.   Buried April 11, 1862   Lot/Division 1, #435   Plat Number 435
Arkansas 18 (Carroll's) Infantry Regiment Private (Lynch's) Company G; enlisted March 2, 1862 Little Rock, Arkansas age 24; per March to June 1862 Muster Roll Remarks: Died Memphis April 8, 1862; name spelled "Swenk" in Cemetery computer index.

Tate, J. L.   Buried October 23, 1861   Lot/Division 1, #130   Plat Number 130
Arkansas 12 Infantry Regiment Company A and died camp measles per Daily Burial Record Book; does not appear to be J. L. Tate, private Company D, who enlisted July 28, 1861, at Arkadelphia, Arkansas, per July to October 1862 Muster Roll Remarks: Escaped from Island 10, and name appears on Roll of Prisoners of War that indicates captured Port Hudson, Louisiana July 9, 1863.

Tate, R. H.   Buried September 16, 1861   Lot/Division 1, #95   Plat Number 95
Tennessee 11 Regiment and died Southern Mothers Hospital per Daily Burial Record Book; no compiled service record found and not found in Lindsley's Annals; Tennessee 11 Infantry Regiment was in East Tennessee at the time of his death.

Taylor, G. W.   Buried November 20, 1861   Lot/Division 1, #205   Plat Number 205
Arkansas 13 Infantry Regiment Company B and died Southern Mothers Hospital dysentery age 18 per Daily Burial Record Book; no compiled service record found.

Taylor, Joseph   Buried April 7, 1862   Lot/Division 1, #421   Plat Number 421
Tennessee 5 Infantry Regiment Private Company K; enlisted June 25, 1861 Camp Brown, Union City, Obion County, Tennessee, age 25; per Overton Hospital Registers dated February 28, 1862 and March 31, 1862 admitted February 19, 1862; per Muster Roll Remarks: Sent to Hospital from Columbus, Kentucky and supposed to have died in Hospital in Memphis April 1862; died Overton Hospital and first name "James" in Daily Burial Record Book and computer index; not found in Lindsley's Annals.

Taylor, William   Buried August 28, 1861   Lot/Division 1, #83   Plat Number 83
Mississippi 22 (Bonham's) Infantry Regiment Private Company C; enlisted July 4, 1861 Vicksburg, Mississippi age 25; per July to November 1861 Muster Roll Remarks: Killed on the Memphis & Charleston Railroad en route for Memphis from Iuka August 18, 1861; per Daily Burial Record Book run over by cars and age 27.

Terigaltoo, Salrater   Buried March 27, 1863   Lot/Division 2, #340   Plat Number 890
No unit or other information in Daily Burial Record Book; name spelled "Teridallon" in Single Grave Book and "Salrath Terigalto" in computer index; not found in Confederate general index.

Terry, James G.   Buried April 26, 1862   Lot/Division 1, #497   Plat Number 497
Arkansas 17 (Lemoyne's) Infantry Regiment Private (Perry's) Company C; reference card only in 17 Lemoyne's Infantry compiled service records; records found under Arkansas 21 Infantry, Private Company C that was successor of Company C of 17 Infantry; enlisted November 18, 1861 Clarksville, Arkansas; per December 1861 to June 1862 Muster Roll Remarks: Died at Memphis April 18, 1862; died Overton Hospital diarrhea per Daily Burial Record Book.

Teufel, Fred   Buried July 25, 1861   Lot/Division 1, #88   Plat Number 88
Mississippi Volunteers Captain Dockery and died pneumonia per Daily Burial Record Book; no compiled service record found; James B. Dockery was Captain of Company D Mississippi 44 Infantry Regiment but not found that unit; name spelled "Tenfel" in Cemetery computer index.

Thomas, George   Buried May 3, 1862   Lot/Division 2, #35   Plat Number 585
Texas 10 (Locke's) Cavalry Regiment Private Company C; enlisted September 25, 1861 Quitman, Wood County, Texas, age 27; per March to August 1862 Muster Roll Remarks: Died May 1, 1862; died Irving Hospital pneumonia per Daily Burial Record Book; per Irving Hospital record George Thomas, Texas 4 Private Company C, was admitted April 21, 1862 with complaint of pneumonia and died May 1, 1862; not listed in Cemetery Single Grave Book.

Thomas, John P.   Buried March 10, 1913   Plat Number N18
Mississippi 23 Infantry Regiment Private/Corporal Company E; enlisted August 4, 1861, age 19 at Baldwin, Mississippi, captured twice during the War, first at Fort Donelson, Tennessee on February 16, 1862, sent to Camp Douglas, Illinois and then to Vicksburg, Mississippi for exchange and second near Nashville, Tennessee December 15, 1864, and sent to Camp Douglas, Illinois where took Oath of Allegiance March 1865; Mississippi 3 Infantry Regiment indicated on Confederate Historical Association application, admitted July 12, 1906, born April 22, 1844, Ripley, Pontotoc County, Mississippi, enlisted Mississippi 3 Infantry Company E June 28, 1861, but no record found Mississippi 3 Infantry Regiment State Troops or Mississippi 3 Infantry Army of 10,000) and died May 9, 1910 (sic); unit identified from Arkansas Confederate Pension application, living in Clarksdale, Crittenden County, Arkansas when applied and widow, Iberia Thomas, applied after his death; per Shelby County, Tennessee Death Record Book 13, page 346, died March 9, 1913, died at Clarksdale, Arkansas, age 72.

Thomas, W. H.   Buried April 5, 1862   Lot/Division 1, #418   Plat Number 418
Confederate 1 (King's Battalion) Cavalry Regiment Private (Gray's) 2 Company F; per Company Muster-in Roll dated February 9, 1862, at Memphis enlisted January 10, 1862, Memphis, age 17; per March & April 1862, Muster Roll Remarks: Died; per Daily Burial Record Book died Overton Hospital typhoid fever.

Thompson, Andrew J. R.   Buried October 22, 1861   Lot/Division 1, #128   Plat Number 128
Arkansas 9 Infantry Regiment Private Company D; enlisted July 25, 1861 Pine Bluff, Arkansas; per July 27, to November 1, 1861 Muster Roll Remarks: Died at State Hospital Memphis 21 October 1861; died State Hospital per Daily Burial Record Book.

Thompson, John F.   Buried October 15, 1861   Lot/Division 1, #106   Plat Number 106
Arkansas 9 Infantry Regiment Private Company E; enlisted July 27, 1861, Pine Bluff, Arkansas; per July 27 to November 1, 1861, Muster Roll Remarks: Died 15 October 1861, in Memphis, Tennessee; died Southern Mothers Hospital enteritis and second initial "T" per Daily Burial Record Book.

Thompson, Maston   Buried November 11, 1861   Lot/Division 1, #182   Plat Number 182
Tennessee 40 (Walker's) Infantry Regiment Private Company H; enlisted September 4, 1861 Montgomery, Alabama age 28; per November & December 1861 Muster Roll Remarks: Died November 10, 1861; died camp typhoid pneumonia per Daily Burial Record Book; first name spelled "Marston" in Cemetery computer index and Lindsley's Annals 39 & 40 Consolidated Infantry Regiment Official Memorial Roll.

Thompson, Thomas   Buried April 3, 1862   Lot/Division 1, #410   Plat Number 410
Confederate 1 (King's Battalion) Cavalry Regiment Private (Gray's) 2 Company F; per Company Muster-in Roll dated February 9, 1862, at Memphis enlisted January 10, 1862 Memphis, age 24; per March & April 1862, Muster Roll Remarks: Died; died pneumonia per Daily Burial Record Book.

Thompson, W. J.   Buried October 23, 1861   Lot/Division 1, #129   Plat Number 129
Mississippi Blythe's Rifles per Daily Burial Record Book; no compiled service record found; Blythe's Rifles was Company D, Mississippi 44 Infantry Regiment, part of which included the Mississippi 1st (Blythe's) Battalion Infantry; not William P. Thompson Company F Mississippi 44 Infantry Regiment who was killed at Battle of Shiloh April 6, 1862.

Thompson, W. M.   Buried November 7, 1861   Lot/Division 1, #171   Plat Number 171
Arkansas 2 Infantry Regiment Company D and died State Hospital per Daily Burial Record Book; no compiled service record found.

Thompson, William   Buried May 6, 1862   Lot/Division 2, #72   Plat Number 622
Captain Wood's Company and died Winchester House per Daily Burial Record Book.

Thornton, A. L.   Buried November 26, 1861   Lot/Division 1, #221   Plat Number 221
Died enteritis age 20 per Daily Burial Record Book; possibly Austin L. Thornton Arkansas 11 Infantry Private Company E, per single card in compiled service record name appears on a Company Muster-in Roll with Muster-in Date July 18, 1861.

Thornton, W. B.   Buried March 22, 1862   Lot/Division 1, #367   Plat Number 367
Tennessee 5 Regiment Company M per Daily Burial Record Book; Overton Hospital March 1862 Register of Sick indicates died March 21, 1862, of congestion; possibly B. F. Thornton, Tennessee 5 Infantry Regiment, Private 2 Company H (Company was known at various times as Captain Winfrey's Company; Captain Fry's Company; Company M and 2nd Company H), enlisted September 10, 1861, Mayfield, Kentucky; per February to July 1862, Muster Roll Remarks: Died March 20, 1862; per May 13, 1863 Muster Roll Remarks: Died Memphis March 28, 1862; per January 20, 1864, Muster Roll Remarks: Enlisted Camp Brown June 4, 1861, and died at Memphis March 10, 1862.

Thornton, William   Buried May 15, 1862   Lot/Division 2, #216   Plat Number 766
Arkansas 23 Infantry Regiment (Hughes' Battalion) Private Robinson's Company G; enlisted March 27, 1862 Jacksonport; June 30 to August 31, 1862 Muster Roll Remarks: Left at Overton Hospital Memphis; died Overton Hospital per Daily Burial Record Book.

Thrailkille, James M.   Buried May 7, 1862   Lot/Division 2, #94   Plat Number 644
Arkansas 17 (Lemoyne's) Infantry Regiment Private Company H; reference card only in 17 Lemoyne's Infantry compiled service records; records found under Arkansas 21 Infantry, J. M. Thurlkeld, Private Company G that was successor of Company H of 17 Infantry; enlisted February 15, 1862 Prairie County, Arkansas; per April 28, 1862, Muster Roll Remarks: Sick at Fort Pillow and left April 26, 1862; per March To June 1862, Muster Roll Remarks: Died in Memphis Hospital May 5, 1862; died Overton Hospital per Daily Burial Record Book; name spelled "Thurlket" in Cemetery books and "Thrilket" in computer index.

Tidwell, John L.   Buried November 8, 1861   Lot/Division 1, #173   Plat Number 173
Tennessee 40 (Walker's) Infantry Regiment Corporal (Aaron's) Company G; enlisted September 23, 1861, Tyddersdale, Arkansas age 20; rank Corporal in compiled service record but private in *Tennesseans in the Civil War Part 2*; per November & December 1861 Muster Roll Remarks: Died November 7, 1861 at Camp Johnston, Tennessee disease measles; father Darling Tidwell filed a claim; died camp per Daily Burial Record Book.

Timberlake, William H.   Buried April 11, 1868   Lot/Division 1, #524   Plat Number 524
Listed in Elmwood 1874 book as Confederate soldier buried in Elmwood who was citizen of Memphis or vicinity; died brain concussion age 34 per Daily Burial Record Books; possibly William H. Timberlake, Corporal, Company H, Missouri 11 Infantry Regiment, enlisted June 20, 1862, Fort Smith, Arkansas, appointed Corporal November 28, 1862, per April 30 to August 31, 1863 Muster Roll Remarks wounded in knee at Helena, per List of Wounded Soldiers who were wounded at Battle of Helena, Arkansas July 4, 1863 wounded severely, per casualty list dated May 9, 1864 at Camp Harris wounded severely in arm at Battle of Jenkins' Ferry, Arkansas April 30, 1864.

Timmons, Jordan   Buried May 9, 1862   Lot/Division 2, #120   Plat Number 670
Texas 10 Cavalry Regiment Private Company I; enlisted October 31, 1861 Taos, Texas age 29; per March to August 1862 Muster Roll Remarks: Private at Memphis; per January & February 1863 Muster Roll Remarks: Died May 20, 1862; wife, Nancy Timmons, made claim June 1863; name spelled "Jourdan Timmins" and died Irving Hospital pneumonia per Daily Burial Record Book; per Irving Hospital record Texas 4 Regiment Private Company I, admitted April 21, 1862 with complaint of pneumonia and died May 6, 1862.

Tinsley, W. D.   Buried January 14, 1906   Lot/Division 1, #533   Plat Number 533
Per January 14, 1906 *The Commercial Appeal* Memphis died Saturday January 13, 1906 at home age 67; no unit or other information in Daily Burial Record Book.

Tippett, Zachariah   Buried May 5, 1862   Lot/Division 2, #60   Plat Number 610
Missouri Priest's Regiment (Hughes') Company and died at Taylor's of congestive chill per Daily Burial Record Book; no compiled service record found; listed in book *1883 History of Howard and Chariton Counties, Missouri*, page 531-532, indicating "(O)n the same date, October 10, 1861, a third company, which was raised in the neighborhood of the present town of Salisbury, was enlisted in the State Guards. This is Company B...."; most listed who could be found in Confederate index served in Missouri Infantry 3 Battalion and its successor Missouri 6 Infantry Regiment but not found in the records on the same; Colonel John W. Priest's Regiment (5 Battalion Missouri State Guard) was part of the Army of the West, Price's Division, that was headquartered in Memphis April 29, 1862; per great-great-granddaughter, Sue Apgar, he was born about 1828 in Madison County, Kentucky, in about 1858 married Laura Brewer Bills, they had two children, William Robert and Mary Evan (her great-grandmother), he also served in the war with Mexico, and Thomas Tippett, who is also listed in the 1883 book, was his brother but no records found for him either; VA grave stone "PVT HUGHES CO MO STATE GDS 1828 1862."

Tomberland, William H.   Buried January 9, 1863   Lot/Division 2, #323   Plat Number 873
Florida 6 Infantry Regiment Private Company B; enlisted March 12, 1862 Quincy, Florida age 25; per Muster Roll Remarks: Private in Hospital in Lexington, Kentucky September 7, 1862; captured October 17, 1862; shipped to Vicksburg, Mississippi November 12, 1862; per Florida Roster born 1837, 5' 6," Black Eyes, Light Hair & Skin and exchanged near Vicksburg December 1862 (note in roster: Watkins; Florida Pension #24045).

Tomlinson, Felix G.   Buried March 31, 1862   Lot/Division 1, #397   Plat Number 397
Arkansas 12 Infantry Regiment Private Company D; enlisted July 28, 1861 Arkadelphia, Arkansas; per July to October 1862 Muster Roll Remarks: Died unknown; per Register of Claims for Settlement by mother, Amanda Tomlinson, died Memphis, Tennessee but no date indicated; per Overton Hospital March 1862 Register of Deaths died March 29 of capillary congestion.

Trammell, George W.   Buried May 12, 1862   Lot/Division 2, #173   Plat Number 723
Arkansas 8 (Miller's) Infantry Battalion Private Company C; enlisted March 15, 1862 Little Rock, Arkansas; per March 13 to April 30, 1862 Muster Roll Remarks: on detached service at Fort Pillow in Hospital April 24; Company E, died Overton Hospital rubella and first name "Philip" per Daily Burial Record Book.

Tribble, Alfred L.   Buried September 25, 1861   Lot/Division 1, #6   Plat Number 6
Arkansas 9 Infantry Regiment Private Old Company B (Cut-Off Guard Drew County, Arkansas); enlisted July 25, 1861 Pine Bluff, Arkansas; per July 25 to November 1, 1861 Muster Roll Remarks: Died September 25, 1861 at Memphis, Tennessee; died State Hospital and name spelled "Trible" in Daily Burial Record Book and computer index.

Trible, C. B.   Buried May 4, 1862   Lot/Division 2, #47   Plat Number 597
Arkansas 19 (Dockery/Smead's) Infantry Regiment Private (Cook's) Company H; enlisted March 3, 1862 Caney, Arkansas; per March 3 to June 30, 1862 Muster Roll Remarks: Died in Memphis, Tennessee May 2, 1862; died Overton Hospital pneumonia, name spelled "Tribble" and second initial "W" in Daily Burial Record Book and computer index.

Trimble, M. R.   Buried October 30, 1861   Lot/Division 1, #148   Plat Number 148
Arkansas 7 Infantry Regiment Private Company H; enlisted July 26, 1861 Camp Shaver, Arkansas Age 24; per December 31, 1861 Muster Roll Remarks: Died in Hospital Memphis, Tennessee November 2, 1861; first name "William" in Daily Burial Record Book and computer index; died Southern Mothers Hospital typhoid fever per Daily Burial Record Book; grave stone south side of Stone (Space) 222, Division 1.

Truite, Lafayette   Buried May 9, 1862   Lot/Division 2, #135   Plat Number 685
Arkansas McRea's (sic) Battalion Company B and died Overton Hospital per Daily Burial Record Book; no service record found; name spelled "Tristle" in one entry of Cemetery computer index; unit believed to be Arkansas 15 Northwest Infantry Regiment that was originally known as McRae's Battalion but no record found in that unit's compiled service records; Arkansas 21 (McRae's) Infantry Regiment was organized July 1861 as Arkansas 3 Infantry Battalion and later became Arkansas 15 Northwest Infantry.

Tuck, W. L.   Buried May 15, 1862   Lot/Division 2, #217   Plat Number 767
Texas 32 (Crump's Battalion) Cavalry Regiment Private (Weaver's) Company D; enlisted November 4, 1861 Camp Crump, Marion County, Texas, age 29; per January to August 1862 Muster Roll Remarks: Died May 20, 1862; died Overton Hospital per Daily Burial Record Book; second initial "T." in Cemetery computer index but not clear in Daily Burial Record Book.

Tucker, Adolphus Fenton   Buried March 2, 1913   Plat Number N17
Mississippi 1 Infantry Battalion Company A; no compiled service record found Mississippi 1 Battalion Sharp Shooters; record in Mississippi 25 Infantry Regiment, Private Company I, enlisted August 10, 1861, Memphis age 18; record in Confederate 2 Infantry Regiment, Private Company I with single card on Register of Payments to Discharged Soldiers that Discharged May 15, 1862; unit per widow's pension file and Mathes sketch; per widow's (Cara L. Jewel) Tennessee Confederate Pension application W4994 born Panola County, Mississippi and died March 1, 1913; letter in pension files indicates joined July 1861, Company A Mississippi 1 Battalion; died age 69 per Daily Burial Record Book; member Confederate Historical Association, Camp 28, Bivouac 18, Memphis, joined September 15, 1891; Memorial Statement in Confederate Historical Association application file that indicates born Panola County, Mississippi 1845, enlisted Como Avengers, Company I of Mississippi 1 Infantry Battalion, discharged after Shiloh then enlisted Mississippi 2 Cavalry Company D (Captain James D. Ruffin); single card in Mississippi 2 Cavalry record on Prisoner of War indicating residence Senatobia, DeSoto County, Mississippi and surrendered Columbus, Mississippi May 16, 1865.

Tuder, Benjamin F.   Buried April 17, 1862   Lot/Division 1, #464   Plat Number 464
Texas 9 (Young's/Maxey's) Infantry Regiment Private Company K; enlisted September 28, 1861, Tollet's Prairie, Texas, age 21; per July/August 1862, Muster Roll Remarks: Private in Memphis February 13, 1862; per March /April 1863, Muster Roll Remarks: Died date unknown; per Overton Hospital March 31, 1862 Register of Sick and Wounded admitted February 11, 1862 but no complaint or death indicated; name spelled "Tutod" and wounded per Daily Burial Record Book and both "Tutod" and "Tudod" in Cemetery computer index.

Turner, G. W.   Buried May 22, 1862   Lot/Division 2, #257   Plat Number 807
Arkansas 15 (Northwest/McRae's Battalion) Infantry Regiment Private Tweedy's Company I; enlisted May 5, 1862; per February 8, 1862 Muster Roll Remarks: Died May 21, 1862 (no place indicated); died Irving Hospital brain fever per Daily Burial Record Book; per Irving Hospital record admitted May 19, 1862 with complaint of remittent and brain fever and died May 19, 1862.

Unknown   Buried July 12, 1861   Lot/Division 1, #53   Plat Number 53
May be unknown soldier subject of inquest reported in July 12, 1861, *Memphis Daily Appeal*.

Unknown   Buried August 8, 1861   Lot/Division 1, #14   Plat Number 14
Died Overton Hospital per Daily Burial Record Book; from State Hospital per Cemetery Single Grave Book.

Unknown   Buried September 16, 1861   Lot/Division 1, #59   Plat Number 59

Unknown   Buried March 14, 1862   Lot/Division 1, #328   Plat Number 328

Unknown   Buried March 20, 1862   Lot/Division 1, #355   Plat Number 355
From a boat and died Overton Hospital per Daily Burial Record Book.

Unknown   Buried March 20, 1862   Lot/Division 1, #356   Plat Number 356
From a boat and died Overton Hospital per Daily Burial Record Book.

Unknown   Buried April 16, 1862   Lot/Division 1, #460   Plat Number 460
In Room 114 (location not stated), from Pope County, Arkansas and died pneumonia per Daily Burial Record Book.

Unknown   Buried April 26, 1862   Lot/Division 1, #502   Plat Number 502
Died Overton Hospital in Room 29 per Daily Burial Record Book.

Unknown   Buried May 3, 1862   Lot/Division 2, #29   Plat Number 579

Unknown   Buried May 4, 1862   Lot/Division 2, #48   Plat Number 598
Not listed in Cemetery Single Grave Book.

Unknown	Buried May 7, 1862	Lot/Division 2, #97	Plat Number 647

Died Overton Hospital per Daily Burial Record Book.

Unknown	Buried May 9, 1862	Lot/Division 2, #124	Plat Number 674
Unknown	Buried May 13, 1862	Lot/Division 2, #182	Plat Number 732
Unknown	Buried May 24, 1862	Lot/Division 2, #262	Plat Number 812

From a Boat per Daily Burial Record Book.

Unknown	Buried May 27, 1862	Lot/Division 2, #273	Plat Number 823

Died Overton Hospital per Daily Burial Record Book; not listed in Cemetery Single Grave Book.

Unknown	Buried November 22, 1862	Lot/Division 2, #310	Plat Number 860
Unknown	Buried November 22, 1862	Lot/Division 2, #311	Plat Number 861
Unknown	Buried November 22, 1862	Lot/Division 2, #312	Plat Number 862
Unknown	Buried November 24, 1862	Lot/Division 2, #315	Plat Number 865
Unknown	Buried November 24, 1862	Lot/Division 2, #316	Plat Number 866
Unknown	Buried December 2, 1862	Lot/Division 2, #321	Plat Number 871
Unknown	Buried January 18, 1863	Lot/Division 2, #329	Plat Number 879
Unknown	Buried January 19, 1863	Lot/Division 2, #331	Plat Number 881

Texas 6 Rangers; no other information in Daily Burial Record Book.

Unknown	Buried August 26, 1864	Lot/Division 2, #344	Plat Number 894

Killed per Daily Burial Record Book; possibly killed during Forrest's Raid into Memphis.

Unknown	Buried August 26, 1864	Lot/Division 2, #345	Plat Number 895

Killed per Daily Burial Record Book; possibly killed during Forrest's Raid into Memphis.

Unknown	Buried August 26, 1864	Lot/Division 2, #346	Plat Number 896

Killed per Daily Burial Record Book; possibly killed during Forrest's Raid into Memphis.

Unknown	Buried August 26, 1864	Lot/Division 2, #347	Plat Number 897

Killed per Daily Burial Record Book; possibly killed during Forrest's Raid into Memphis.

Unknown	Buried August 26, 1864	Lot/Division 2, #348	Plat Number 898

Killed per Daily Burial Record Book; possibly killed during Forrest's Raid into Memphis.

Unknown	Buried August 26, 1864	Lot/Division 2, #349	Plat Number 899

Killed per Daily Burial Record Book; possibly killed during Forrest's Raid into Memphis.

Unknown	Buried August 26, 1864	Lot/Division 2, #351	Plat Number 901

Killed per Daily Burial Record Book; possibly killed during Forrest's Raid into Memphis.

Unknown	Buried August 26, 1864	Lot/Division 2, #352	Plat Number 902

Killed per Daily Burial Record Book; possibly killed during Forrest's Raid into Memphis.

Unknown	Buried August 26, 1864	Lot/Division 2, #353	Plat Number 903

Killed per Daily Burial Record Book; possibly killed during Forrest's Raid into Memphis.

Unknown	Buried August 26, 1864	Lot/Division 2, #354	Plat Number 904

Killed per Daily Burial Record Book; possibly killed during Forrest's Raid into Memphis.

Unknown   Buried August 26, 1864   Lot/Division 2, #355   Plat Number 905
Killed per Daily Burial Record Book; possibly killed during Forrest's Raid into Memphis.

Unknown   Buried August 26, 1864   Lot/Division 2, #356   Plat Number 906
Killed per Daily Burial Record Book; possibly killed during Forrest's Raid into Memphis.

Unknown   Buried August 26, 1864   Lot/Division 2, #357   Plat Number 907
Killed per Daily Burial Record Book; possibly killed during Forrest's Raid into Memphis.

Unknown   Buried April 26, 1871   Lot/Division 2, #373   Plat Number 923
Moved in from Cane Creek per Daily Burial Record Book; not listed in Cemetery Single Grave Book.

Unknown   Lot/Division 1, #108   Plat Number 108
Second Grave Stone #108 found but no burial record found; not listed in Cemetery computer index.

Unknown   Lot/Division 1, #109   Plat Number 109
Second Grave Stone #109 found but no burial record found; not listed in Cemetery computer index.

Unknown   Lot/Division 1, #298   Plat Number 298
Second Grave Stone #298 found but no burial record found; not listed in Cemetery computer index.

Unknown   Lot/Division 1, #376   Plat Number 376
Second Grave Stone #376 found but no burial record found; not listed in Cemetery computer index.

Unknown   Lot/Division 1, #526   Plat Number 526
Grave stone found but no burial record found; not listed in Cemetery computer index.

Unknown   Lot/Division 1, #527   Plat Number 527
Grave stone found but no burial record found; not listed in Cemetery computer index.

Unknown   Lot/Division 1, #528   Plat Number 528
Grave stone found but no burial record found; not listed in Cemetery computer index.

Unknown   Lot/Division 1, #529   Plat Number 529
Grave stone found but no burial record found; not listed in Cemetery computer index.

Unknown   Lot/Division 1, #530   Plat Number 530
Grave stone found but no burial record found; not listed in Cemetery computer index.

Unknown   Lot/Division 1, #531   Plat Number 531
Grave stone found but no burial record found; not listed in Cemetery computer index.

Unknown   Lot/Division 1, #537   Plat Number 537
Second Grave Stone #537 found but no burial record found; not listed in Cemetery computer index.

Unknown   Lot/Division 1, #538   Plat Number 538
Third Grave Stone #538 found but no burial record found; not listed in Cemetery computer index.

Unknown   Lot/Division 1, #539   Plat Number 539
Grave stone found but no burial record found; not listed in Cemetery computer index.

Unknown   Lot/Division 1, #546   Plat Number 546
Grave stone found but no burial record found; not listed in Cemetery computer index.

Unknown   Lot/Division 1, #550   Plat Number 550
Grave stone found but no burial record found; not listed in Cemetery computer index.

Van Horn, J. W.   Buried June 9, 1862   Lot/Division 2, #289   Plat Number 839
Texas 3 Cavalry Teamster and died Apperson's per Daily Burial Record Book; no compiled service record found.

Vandever, G. W.   Buried October 12, 1861   Lot/Division 1, #103   Plat Number 103
Arkansas 13 Infantry Regiment Company G and died Southern Mothers Hospital enteritis per Daily Burial Record Book; no service

record found; first initial "A" in Cemetery computer index.

Varnell, William P.   Buried August 29, 1861   Lot/Division 1, #11   Plat Number 11
Arkansas 9 Infantry Regiment Private Company G; enlisted July 27, 1861 Pine Bluff, Arkansas; per July 27 to November 1, 1861 Muster Roll Remarks: Died August 28, 1861 typhoid fever State Hospital Memphis; name spelled "Vernell" in Daily Burial Record Book and computer index.

Vevers, J.   Buried March 7, 1862   Lot/Division 1, #298   Plat Number 298
Louisiana 12 Regiment and died State Hospital per Daily Burial Record Book; no compiled service record found; per remark in Cemetery record grave in short row north side of Monument.

Waggoner, Hugh N.   Buried November 21, 1861   Lot/Division 1, #207   Plat Number 207
Tennessee 13 Infantry Regiment Private (Crook's) Company I; enlisted May 30, 1861, Jackson, Tennessee; per April 6, 1863, Muster Roll Remarks: Killed Battle of Belmont, Missouri November 7, 1861; gunshot wound and died Overton Hospital age 22 per Daily Burial Record Book; per Overton Hospital record H. A. Waggener, Tennessee 13 Private Company J, admitted November 15, 1861, with complaint of hip amputated and died November 21, 1861; name "Hugh M. Waggener" in Cemetery Alpha Book, "Hugh M. Waginer" in Daily Burial Record Book, and "Hugh M. Wagner" in Cemetery computer index; name "Wagner" and 1839 1861 on grave stone; name "Hugh N. Wagner" and wounded at Battle of Belmont, Missouri per casualty report in the November 13, 1861 *Memphis Daily Appeal*, page 2, column 5; arrived at Overton Hospital November 4, 1861 per report in November 15, 1861 *Memphis Daily Appeal*, with name written as "M. N. Waggener"; per Overton Hospital List of Deaths in November 24, 1861, *Memphis Daily Appeal*, page 4, column 1 second initial "A" and died November 21, 1861.

Wagnon, Clarence   Buried May 4, 1862   Lot/Division 2, #45   Plat Number 595
Arkansas 17 (Lemoyne's) Infantry Regiment Private Company H; reference card only in 17 Lemoyne's Infantry compiled service records; records found under Arkansas 21 Infantry, Private Company G that was successor of Company H of 17 Infantry; enlisted February 15, 1862 Prairie County, Arkansas; per Muster Roll Card for Company H, 17 Lemoyne Infantry in the 21 Infantry rolls dated April 28, 1862 Remarks: Sick in Memphis Hospital and left April 27, 1862; per January & February 1863 Muster Roll Remarks: Detailed as Ordnance Train Guard; name appears on Roll of Prisoners of War Paroled at Vicksburg, Mississippi July 7, 1863 with date of capture of July 4, 1863; appears to be mix up of two different soldiers; name spelled "Waginer" and died Overton Hospital erysipelas per Daily Burial Record Book; name spelled "C. Wagner" in Cemetery Single Grave Book and "Waginer" in Cemetery computer index.

Waits, Dempsey   Buried April 27, 1862   Lot/Division 1, #508   Plat Number 508
Arkansas 23 Infantry Regiment (Hughes' Battalion) Private (Robinson's) Company G; enlisted March 27, 1862 Jacksonport, Arkansas; per March 26 to June 30, 1862 Remarks: Died April 26, 1862; died Overton Hospital per Daily Burial Record Book.

Waldrop, William L.   Buried May 9, 1862   Lot/Division 2, #136   Plat Number 686
Arkansas Miller's Battalion Company D and died Overton Hospital per Cemetery; unit believed to be Arkansas 8 Infantry Battalion Company D but no compiled service record found

Walker, James A.   Buried February 27, 1862   Lot/Division 1, #271   Plat Number 271
Louisiana 12 Infantry Regiment Private Company D; enlisted August 18, 1861 Camp Moore, Louisiana; per August 18 to October 13, 1861 Muster Roll Remarks: Present; name appears on Pay Record for June 1862.

Walker, John T.   Buried September 13, 1861   Lot/Division 1, #81   Plat Number 81
Arkansas 9 Infantry Regiment Corporal (Armstrong's) Company H; enlisted July 25, 1861 Pine Bluff, Arkansas; per July 25 to November 1, 1861 Muster Roll Remarks: Died September 11, 1861; per Roster of Killed Soldiers died December 1, 1861; per Property Record of Deceased Soldiers died September 10, 1861 at Memphis; died State Hospital per Daily Burial Record Book; second initial "W" in Daily Burial Record Book and computer index.

Wallace, A. M.   Buried May 11, 1862   Lot/Division 2, #160   Plat Number 710
Arkansas 19 (Dockery/Smead's) Infantry Regiment Private Company A; enlisted February 25, 1862 Lewisville, Arkansas; per February 25 to June 30, 1862 Muster Roll Remarks: Died at Memphis, Tennessee May 9, 1862; died Overton Hospital typhoid pneumonia per Daily Burial Record Book.

Wallace, J.   Buried March 16, 1862   Lot/Division 1, #335   Plat Number 335
Tennessee Bankhead's Battery (Tennessee Scott's Light Artillery) and died Overton Hospital per Daily Burial Record Book; no compiled service record found; initial "S" in Cemetery computer index; grave in short row north side of Monument.

Wallace, R. J.   Buried March 31, 1862   Lot/Division 1, #399   Plat Number 399
Confederate 4 (Bakers') Infantry Regiment Private Company B (Captain Jonas Griffin's Rifles); per Company Muster-in Roll enlisted August 10, 1861, at Montgomery, Alabama age 40; per Overton Hospital March 1862, Register of Sick died March 30,

1862, of pneumonia; name appears on a Register of Officers and Soldiers of the Army of the Confederate States Who Were Killed in Battle, or Who Died of Wounds or Disease that deceased April 5, 1862, at Memphis, Tennessee; regiment (also known as 1st Alabama, Tennessee and Mississippi Infantry) was formed about December 9, 1861, with ten companies: four from Alabama, two from Mississippi, and four from Tennessee; captured at Island 10 April 8, 1862, and after exchange in September, 1862, the companies were reorganized and transferred to other commands; Company B became Company C of the Alabama 54th Infantry Regiment but no record for this regiment as died before transfer; died Overton Hospital pneumonia per Daily Burial Record Book.

Wallace, Robert   Buried October 15, 1861   Lot/Division 1, #1   Plat Number 1
Arkansas 6 Regiment per Daily Burial Record Book; no compiled service record found Arkansas 6 Infantry Regiment; possibly R. N. Wallace, Arkansas 6 Cavalry Battalion, Company C (no rank), name appears on a Descriptive List of the Members of the Crittenden Rangers mustered into the service of the State of Arkansas on June 3, 1861, birthplace Tennessee, born 1841, 5' 7" and farmer, also one reference card in record indicates admitted Hospital November 28, 1861; died State Hospital per Daily Burial Record Book.

Walters, Robert A.   Buried July 9, 1907   Plat Number N3
Tennessee 5 Infantry Regiment Private 2 Company I (company was known at various times as Captain Fowler's Company; Captain Peeples' Company; (1st) Company G and (2nd) Company I), per Company Muster-in Roll dated August 9, 1861, at Camp Brown, Tennessee enlisted age 19 at Paris, Tennessee May 20, 1861, remarks on card: On furlough sick with measles, per Company Muster Roll dated January 20, 1864, near Dalton Georgia remarks: Discharged December 10, 1861, at Columbus, Kentucky; widow, Margaret A. Walters, when living in Poinsett County, Arkansas, filed for an Arkansas Confederate Pension (#16764) on August 4, 1909, on application she stated that she was the widow of R. A. Walters who served in Company G, 5th Tennessee Volunteer Infantry and he was honorably discharged (paroled or released) on or about the 1st of December, 1861, and that he died on July 8, 1907, the proof of service was a sworn statement from J. P. Harman and W. L. Hagler, both living in Henry County, Tennessee, and who served in same company with him and stated that he served from May 20, 1861, to about December 1, 1861, and was honorably discharged, her application was not approved due to insufficient proof of indigency; when living in Craighead County, Arkansas she again applied on September 29, 1910, furnishing another statement from his comrades, J. P. Harman and W. L. Hagler, and a sworn statement from her son, R. A. Walters, that she does not own property to the amount of $400 and that she has no income whatever from any source, and her application was approved; first name "Robert" in 1880 Carroll County, Tennessee Census and 1900 Weakley County, Tennessee Census; birth December 1842, in Tennessee per 1900 Census; second initial "E" in Daily Burial Record Book and computer index; died age 64 per Daily Burial Record Book; second initial "E" ("C" in index) and died age 64 from diabetes mellitus on July 9, 1907, per Tennessee Death Certificate (note statement by doctor on Certificate that he attended deceased from July 7, 1907, to July 8, 1907, and last saw him alive on July 8, 1907, and that death occurred on the date stated above at about 8 pm).

Walton, Tilman   Buried September 25, 1861   Lot/Division 1, #78   Plat Number 78
Mississippi 22 (Bonham's) Infantry Regiment Private Company I; enlisted June 26, 1861 Greenville, Mississippi, age 38; July to October 1861 Muster Roll Remarks: Died at Memphis September 24, 1861; died State Hospital per Daily Burial Record Book.

Warburg, Edward   Buried July 7, 1876   Lot/Division 2, #387   Plat Number 937
Death notice in the *Memphis Daily Appeal,* July 7, 1876, page 1, column 8, indicates a native of Hamburg, Germany, died July 6, 1876, and aged 40 years and 12 days; suicide age 40 per Daily Burial Record Book and Shelby County Mortuary Report in the July 9, 1876, *Memphis Daily Appeal*, page 7, column 9; no unit indicated in Cemetery record; possibly Edward Warburg, Captain and Adjutant, Missouri 16 (some cards indicate 7) Infantry Regiment, (reference card also found Missouri 7 Cavalry Regiment); wounded and taken prisoner at Helena, Arkansas, July 4, 1863, sent to General Hospital in Memphis, left leg below knee amputated, was supposed to be exchanged September, 1863, but no record found to confirm that, still on Prisoner of War roll at Memphis Hospital April 30, 1864, under treatment, on Register of sick and wounded at Irving Military Prison Hospital, Memphis indicating admitted June 15, 1864, with complaint of amputation, expressed desire to take Oath of Allegiance May 31, 1864; age on some records cards would fit with his age at death.

Ward, Isaac L.   Buried October 23, 1861   Lot/Division 1, #131   Plat Number 131
Arkansas 12 Infantry Regiment Private Company K; no record found for Isaac L. Ward but records found for J. S. Ward Private Company K who enlisted July 29, 1861 Arkadelphia, Arkansas and who per July to October 1862 Muster Roll Remarks died October 10, 1861 at Memphis; died camp measles per Daily Burial Record Book.

Ward, Isaac Newton   Buried May 17, 1862   Lot/Division 2, #227   Plat Number 777
Missouri Ross' Regiment (Waddell's) Company per Daily Burial Record Book; no compiled service record found; possibly "A. Ward" Missouri 5 Infantry Regiment, Private Company A, who per Historic Roll card enlisted age 15, from Johnson County, Missouri, farmer, Warrensburg, Missouri, and remarks that was wounded in Battle Elkhorn and died at Memphis April 28, 1862; Owen A. Waddell was a Captain/Major of Missouri 5 Infantry Regiment.

Warner, W. E.   Buried May 20, 1862   Lot/Division 2, #238   Plat Number 788
Arkansas 19 Infantry Regiment and died measles at Mrs. Norton's per Daily Burial Record Book; no service record found.

Warren, J. H. Buried November 8, 1862 Lot/Division 2, #308 Plat Number 858
Tennessee 9 Infantry Regiment Private Company K; per Company Muster Roll for July & August, 1862, enlisted June 5, 1861, Jackson with Remarks: Captured Perryville (since died); prisoner died on his way to Vicksburg per Daily Burial Record Book; name spelled "Warner "in both Daily Burial Record Book and computer index; died November 7 per list of the prisoners of war who died on board the Federal transport Maria Denning, en route for Vicksburg prepared by Charles Boyd, A. A. Surgeon U.S.N., in charge of sick en route for Vicksburg;); not found in Lindsley's Annals.

Warwick, W. L. Buried May 8, 1862 Lot/Division 2, #116 Plat Number 666
Missouri 14 Cavalry State Guard Company C and died camp per Daily Burial Record Book; no compiled service record found; Missouri 14 Cavalry State Guard Company C was in the 8 Division Captain William Y. Bronaugh.

Washburn, John M. Buried May 5, 1862 Lot/Division 2, #55 Plat Number 605
Arkansas 25 (Turnbull's) Infantry Regiment Private Company K; enlisted February 22, 1862 St Charles, Arkansas; per February 22 to April 30, 1862 Muster Roll Remarks: Was left at Hospital Memphis, Tennessee April 25, 1862; per May & June 1862 Muster Roll Remarks: Died at Memphis, Tennessee on the 5 May 1862; died Overton Hospital per Daily Burial Record Book.

Watkins, J. W. Buried April 15, 1862 Lot/Division 1, #453 Plat Number 453
Arkansas 17 Regiment per Daily Burial Record Book; no compiled service record found; does not appear to J. W. Watkins, Arkansas 7 Infantry Regiment, Private Company K, who enlisted August 6, 1861, Camp Dean, age 19, per Company Muster Roll for March & April 1862, remarks died about first of April 1862 at Atlanta, Georgia, per Company Muster Roll dated December 31, 1861, remarks sick in Nashville, Tennessee and Company station on December 31, 1862, was Bowling Green, Kentucky.

Watkins, Robert Buried May 6, 1862 Lot/Division 2, #80 Plat Number 630
No unit indicated or other information in Daily Burial Record Book.

Watson, William J. Buried August 26, 1861 Lot/Division 1, #47 Plat Number 47
Carroll's Regiment per Daily Burial Record Book; no compiled service record found; not found Arkansas 18 (Carroll's) Infantry Regiment; listed in report of August 1861 deaths at Southern Mothers Hospital in September 10, 1861, *Memphis Daily Appeal*, page 3, column 3; per report in Captain Lambert's Company (there is a Captain Lambert in Arkansas 13 Infantry Company A, but not found that unit), from Helena, Arkansas and died August 18, 1861 congestive fever.

Waymack, Joel S. Buried April 21, 1862 Lot/Division 1, #475 Plat Number 475
Arkansas 18 (Carroll's) Infantry Regiment Private (Parrish's) Company H; enlisted March 3, 1862 Little Rock, Arkansas; per March to June 1862 Muster Roll Remarks: Absent Sick; died Overton Hospital typhoid fever and pneumonia per Daily Burial Record Book; name spelled "Warmack" in Cemetery books and "Wamach" in computer index.

Webb, George Buried May 7, 1862 Lot/Division 2, #103 Plat Number 653
Missouri Goram's Artillery in Cemetery Daily Burial Book (Gormon's Missouri Regiment in Cemetery lists) and died pneumonia Overton Hospital per Daily Burial Record Book; unit believed to be Captain J. C. Gorham's Company of Missouri Artillery that became the Missouri 3 Field Battery Light Artillery but no compiled service record found in that unit.

Webb, James Buried September30, 1862 Lot/Division 2, #302 Plat Number 852
No unit indicated or other information in Daily Burial Record Book.

Webb, Theophilius S. T. Buried March 28, 1862 Lot/Division 1, #389 Plat Number 389
Arkansas 11 Infantry Regiment Private Company K; enlisted December 21, 1861, Saline County, Arkansas; per December 28, 1861 to September 23, 1862, Company Muster Roll Remarks: Absent sick when 11 Arkansas was captured locality unknown; per Overton Hospital March 1862 Register of Sick died March 26, 1862, of rubella.

Wehrle, Fred Buried April 13, 1862 Lot/Division 1, #442 Plat Number 442
Tennessee 3 (Forrest's) Cavalry Regiment Private Company A and Tennessee 154 Senior Infantry Regiment Private 1 Company B "Bluff City Grays" (name spelled "Wehler"); per Tennessee 154 Senior Infantry Regiment Company Muster-in Roll dated August 13,1861, enlisted May 14, 1861, Randolph, Tennessee age 34; per Tennessee 3 (Forrest's) Cavalry Regiment Company Muster Roll for January 1 to July 1, 1861, enlisted May 4, 1861, Randolph, Tennessee and remarks: Killed at Shiloh; wounded per "List of the Dead and Wounded of Shelby County" per article concerning battle of Shiloh reported in the April 10, 1862, *Memphis Daily Appeal*, page 2, column 3; funeral notice in April 13, 1862, M*emphis Daily Appeal*, page 1, column 7; found in Lindsley's Annals under McDonald's Battery (sic Battalion) Company A name spelled "Frederick Wehrh" and killed in action at Shiloh April 6, 1862; listed ("Wherle") in June 6, 1878, *Memphis Daily Appeal*, page 4, column 3, article "OUR DEAD HEROES" covering the unveiling of the Confederate Monument and Decoration of Graves at Elmwood as then one of twenty-eight members of the Bluff City Grays, Company B of the 154 Senior Infantry Regiment and Company A of Forrest's Old (Third) Cavalry Regiment buried at Elmwood; listed (Wherle) as one of the "comrades who sleep at Elmwood cemetery " in the article "Veterans in Council" in

Memphis Daily Appeal, May 12, 1881, page 4, column 4, concerning the meeting of the surviving members in the city of the old Bluff City Grays to appoint the necessary committees for the purpose of making special decoration on the graves of their dead comrades at Elmwood and Calvary cemeteries on Sunday next, Memorial Day; see also Notes of Interest - Bluff City Grays; listed ("Wehrle") as member of Bluff City Grays in *Reminiscences of the Civil War* by John Hallum, Tunnah & Pittard printers, 1903; listed ("Wherle") in "A COMPLETE ROSTER OF THE BLUFF CITY GREYS" located in the Memphis Room of the Memphis/Shelby County Public Library and Information Center Central Library with notation Died of wound at Shiloh April 6, 1862, and buried in Elmwood with location noted; per Register of Deaths in the City of Memphis (name spelled "Wherle) died April 12, 1862, age 30, Soldier, Gun Shot Shiloh.

Welch, William   Buried March 9, 1862   Lot/Division 1, #307   Plat Number 307
Arkansas 12 Infantry Regiment Company A per Daily Burial Record Book; no compiled service record found; per Overton Hospital March 1862 Register of Deaths died March 8 of congestion; 1843 1862 on grave stone.

Weldon, Columbus   Buried May 31, 1862   Lot/Division 2, #276   Plat Number 826
Arkansas 4 Infantry Regiment Private Company F; enlisted August 17, 1861 Camp near Mt Vernon, Missouri; per Certificate of Disability for Discharge enlisted August 17, 1861, born in Bell County, Texas, 17 years old, 5' 6," farmer, unfit for duty 60 days for last 2 months and discharged 13 Day of May 1862; died Overton Hospital typhoid fever per Daily Burial Record Book.

Wells, G. L.   Buried October 5, 1861   Lot/Division 1, #30   Plat Number 30
Arkansas 9 Infantry Regiment and died Southern Mothers Hospital per Daily Burial Record Book; possibly George W. Wells, Arkansas 9 Infantry Regiment Private Company D but one card in compiled service record indicates Prisoner of War captured Champion Hill, Mississippi May 16, 1863, and sent to Memphis, Tennessee May 25, 1863.

Wells, Julius Theodore   Buried June 14, 1920   Plat Number N36
Tennessee 4 Infantry Regiment Private Company D Musician/Drummer; enlisted May 16, 1861 Germantown, Tennessee age 20; per Tennessee Confederate Pension application #14537 born June 21, 1841 Raleigh, Shelby County, Tennessee; died age 79 per Daily Burial Record Book; grave stone: 1840 1920.

Welsh, John   Buried May 13, 1862   Lot/Division 2, #179   Plat Number 729
CSS General Bragg; Naval record indicates was transferred from Alabama 1 Battalion Artillery (no record found that unit); gunboat participated in and was captured during the Battle of Memphis June 6, 1862; died Overton Hospital pneumonia per Daily Burial Record Book.

Wheeler, George   Buried April 25, 1862   Lot/Division 1, #496   Plat Number 496
Missouri 1 Infantry Regiment Private Company K; enlisted June 22, 1861 Memphis age 27; per Muster Roll Remarks: Wounded Battle of Shiloh; per Battle of Shiloh casualty list for unit reported in April 23, 1862 *Memphis Daily Appeal* was wounded in Battle; died State Hospital and Company G per Daily Burial Record Book.

Wheeler, James William   Buried January 7, 1929   Plat Number N49
Tennessee Phillips' Company Light Artillery Private; enlisted October 15, 1861, Jackson, Tennessee, age 23; per November & December 1862 Muster Roll Remarks: Discharged October 6, 1862; per Certificate of Disability for Discharge was found incapable of performing duties of a soldier because of an accidental gunshot wound to right hand causing loss of two fingers; per Tennessee Confederate Pension application #12898 born Cumberland County, Virginia and home Fayette County, Tennessee at death; died age 87 on January 6, 1929, from Terminal Broncho-pneumonia per State of Tennessee Death Certificate; per January 7, 1929, *The Commercial Appeal* Memphis joined Forrest Cavalry and served two years, five months when suffered loss of right hand and discharged at rank of Sergeant; born Richmond, Henrico County, Virginia (note birth location difference) and moved to Jackson, Tennessee at age 12; possibly "W. Wheeler" who is listed in Mathes book as one time a member of Confederate Historical Association but no sketch.

Wheeler, John   Buried May 7, 1862   Lot/Division 2, #86   Plat Number 636
Arkansas 17 Infantry Regiment Company E and died Overton Hospital per Daily Burial Record Book; no service record found.

Whitaker, Alfred H.   Buried September 28, 1861   Lot/Division 1, #77   Plat Number 77
Arkansas 9 Infantry Regiment Private (Isom's) Old Company B; enlisted July 25, 1861 Pine Bluff, Arkansas; per July 25 to November 1, 1861 Muster Roll Remarks: Died September 27, 1861 Memphis, Tennessee; died State Hospital per Daily Burial Record Book.

White, Andrew J.   Buried January 12, 1871   Lot/Division 2, #368   Plat Number 918
Listed in Elmwood 1874 book as Confederate soldier buried in Elmwood who was citizen of Memphis or vicinity; no unit indicated and died ulceration of bowels age 37 per Daily Burial Record Book; not listed in Cemetery Single Grave Book; possible Andrew Jackson White listed in the 1868-69 Memphis City Directory with occupation indicated as Carpenter.

White, J. F.   Buried August 17, 1861   Lot/Division 1, #13   Plat Number 13
Mounted Battalion (Foot's) Company and died congestion age 30 per Daily Burial Record Book; no compiled service record found; not found in record on Mississippi Captain Foote's Mounted Men or Mississippi 1 Cavalry or 17 Infantry each of which had a Captain Foote with soldiers named White.

White, John H.   Buried January 12, 1862   Lot/Division 1, #254   Plat Number 254
Tennessee 40 Infantry Regiment Private Company K; enlisted October 28, 1861 Camp Johnson age 26; per November & December 1861 Muster Roll Remarks: Sick at Memphis; name appears on Overton Hospital December 31, 1861 Register of Sick and Wounded; died Overton Hospital age 26 per Daily Burial Record Book; initials "J. C. H." in Cemetery computer index; not found in Lindsley's Annals 39 & 40 Consolidated Infantry Regiment Official Memorial Roll.

White, S. W.   Buried November 1, 1861   Lot/Division 1, #156   Plat Number 156
Carver's Regiment and died State Hospital per Daily Burial Record Book; no Colonel Carver found in Confederate general index.

White, William   Buried November 8, 1861   Lot/Division 1, #172   Plat Number 172
Tennessee 40 (Walker's) Infantry Regiment Private (Bush's) Company D; enlisted September 19, 1861 Jonesboro, Arkansas age 19; per November & December 1861 Muster Roll Remarks: Died November 8 at Camp Johnson, Tennessee; died November 8, 1861 per Lindsley's Annals; died camp per Daily Burial Record Book.

Whitehead, William   Buried March 3, 1862   Lot/Division 1, #276   Plat Number 276
Arkansas 12 Infantry Regiment and died Overton Hospital per Daily Burial Record Book but no service record found.

Whitescarver, F W.   Buried April 17, 1862   Lot/Division 1, #466   Plat Number 466
Louisiana 25 Infantry Regiment Private Company E; compiled service record has two enlistments: February 26, 1862 Union Parrish, Louisiana and March 7, 1862 Monroe, Louisiana; per Muster Roll Remarks: Died Memphis with two dates of death: April 1, 1862 and April 15, 1862; died Overton Hospital pneumonia per Daily Burial Record Book; name spelled "Whitecarver" (no "s") in Cemetery Alpha Book, Single Grave Book and computer index.

Whitney, George   Buried April 13, 1862   Lot/Division 1, #441   Plat Number 441
Arkansas Miller's Battalion (Murray's) Company per Daily Burial Record Book; unit believed to be Arkansas 8 Infantry Battalion Company D but no compiled service record found.

Whittington, C. M.   Buried April 10, 1862   Lot/Division 1, #432   Plat Number 432
Texas 2 (Moore's) Infantry Regiment Private Company K; enlisted October 12, 1861 Galveston, Texas; per March & April 1862 Muster Roll Remarks: Sick in Hospital since March 31, 1862; per May and June 1862 Muster Roll Remarks: Died in Hospital April 15, 1862; died Overton Hospital pneumonia per Daily Burial Record Book.

Wicklin, Louis W.   Buried April 28, 1862   Lot/Division 1, #515   Plat Number 515
Texas 27 (Whitfield's Legion) Cavalry Regiment Private Company D/M; enlisted January 1, 1862 Hallettsville, Texas; per April 14 to April 30, 1862, Muster Roll Remarks: Transferred to Company M April 14, 1862, and died April 24, 1862; first name also spelled "Lewis" in compiled service record; died Overton Hospital per Daily Burial Record Book.

Wicks, George D.   Buried December 7, 1861   Lot/Division 1, #241   Plat Number 241
Tennessee 2 (Walker's) Infantry Regiment Private Company B; enlisted May 11, 1861, Memphis; per August to November 1861, Muster Roll Remarks: Resigned as Sergeant and died October 23, 1861, in Hospital in Memphis; per note under Local Matters in December 8, 1861, *Memphis Daily Appeal* died at Overton Hospital on December 7, 1861, after being wounded in hip; name "Nicks" in Daily Burial Record Book and computer index; died Overton Hospital per Daily Burial Record Book; per Overton Hospital record admitted November 15, 1861, with complaint of hip and died December 7, 1861; not found in Lindsley's Annals.

Wiginton, W. J.   Buried March 7, 1862   Lot/Division 1, #294   Plat Number 294
Arkansas 12 Infantry Regiment Private Company F; enlisted July 26, 1861 Arkadelphia, Arkansas; per July to October 1862 Muster Roll Remarks: Died at Memphis March 1862; per Overton Hospital March 1862 Register of Deaths name spelled "Wiggington," died March 6 of pneumonia and unit Arkansas 12 Private Company F; name spelled "Wigginton" in Daily Burial Record Book and computer index; Arkansas 11 Infantry per Daily Burial Record Book.

Wilder, H. H.   Buried March 9, 1862   Lot/Division 1, #305   Plat Number 305
Mississippi 10 Infantry Regiment (Crook's) Company and died Overton Hospital per Daily Burial Record Book; no service record found.

Wilkerson, George   Buried December 7, 1861   Lot/Division 1, #243   Plat Number 243
Mississippi 3 Regiment Company E and died Southern Mothers Hospital per Daily Burial Record Book; no compiled service record

found; there was a G. L. Wilkinson Private Company B (company previously Company E) Mississippi 3 Infantry with Muster Roll Card dated September 29, 1861 indicating present.

Williams, J. W.   Buried May 11, 1862   Lot/Division 2, #161   Plat Number 711
Texas 9 Regiment Company H and died Overton Hospital typhoid fever per Daily Burial Record Book; possibly J. P. Williams, Texas 9 (Sim's) Cavalry Regiment Captain Company K who enlisted October 14, 1861, at Camp Reeves, Texas age 32; per March & April 1862 Muster Roll Remarks: Sick in Memphis; per May & June 1862 Muster Roll Remarks: Not elected and discharged May 20, 1862; per Inspection Report at Camp New Corinth, Mississippi May 3, 1862 Remarks: Absent sick at Memphis.

Williams, Robert   Buried January 18, 1863   Lot/Division 2, #328   Plat Number 878
No unit or other information in Daily Burial Record Book.

Williams, Samuel J.   Buried May 21, 1862   Lot/Division 2, #251   Plat Number 801
Arkansas 23 (Adams') Infantry Regiment Private Company A; enlisted February 26, 1862 Poinsett County, Arkansas; February 26 to June 30, 1862 Muster Roll Remarks: Died May 1862; died Overton Hospital typhoid fever and pneumonia per Daily Burial Record Book.

Williams, Thomas   Buried May 12, 1862   Lot/Division 2, #176   Plat Number 726
Arkansas Captain Murray's Company Green's Company and died Overton Hospital typhoid per Daily Burial Record Book; no compiled service record found; not found Arkansas 8 Battalion rolls (G.S. Murray Captain Company D).

Williams, William   Buried April 25, 1862   Lot/Division 1, #492   Plat Number 492
Arkansas 11 Infantry Regiment Private Company D; enlisted December 7, 1861 Hot Springs County, Arkansas; per Form No. 58 signed by Captain April 23, 1863, born in Hot Springs County, Arkansas, age 35, farmer, enlisted December 17, 1861, and died April 24, 1862 of sickness contracted in camp at New Madrid, Missouri; claim of widow Angelina Williams in compiled service record; died at Mrs. Duke's House per Daily Burial Record Book.

Williamson, J. J.   Buried May 6, 1862   Lot/Division 2, #79   Plat Number 629
Arkansas (King's) 20 Infantry Regiment Private Company H/B, per Company Muster Roll (Company B) dated February 28 to May 2, 1862, enlisted March 23, at Little Rock with Remarks: In Memphis at Hospital; per Company Muster Roll (Company H) for February 28 to June 30, 1862, enlisted February 28, 1862, at Warren, Arkansas with Remarks: Died May 6; there was also J. Williams, Private Company F, who per Company Muster Roll (Company D) dated March 3 to May 2, 1862, enlisted April 1, 1862, at Perryville with remarks: died at Memphis, Tennessee, and per Company Muster Roll (Company F) dated March 3 to June 30, 1862, remarks: died the 29 April 1862; and John B. Williams, Private Company G who per Company Muster Roll dated February 17 to May 2, 1862, enlisted February 17, 1862, at Little Rock with remarks: left at Fort Pillow sick, and per Company Muster Roll dated February 17 to June 30, 1862, remarks: left at Memphis hospital sick, not heard from since; and Company B and died Overton Hospital phthisis pulmonalis per Daily Burial Record Book; name spelled "Williams" in Daily Burial Record Book and computer index.

Williford, David Judson, Sr.   Buried March 22, 1934   Plat Number N60
North Carolina 17 Infantry Regiment (1 Organization) Private Company D; enlisted May 22, 1861 Murfreesboro, North Carolina age 19; teacher; captured at Hatteras and paroled; per Tennessee Confederate Pension application (S16615) born April 30, 1842 Hartford County, North Carolina; pension application indicates joined North Carolina 7 Infantry Company I but record found under 17 Infantry Company D; died March 20, 1934; widow (Eula D. Robinson) applied for Tennessee Confederate Pension (W10806); died age 92 per Daily Burial Record Book; grave stone: April 30, 1842 March 20, 1934.

Willis, W. L.   Buried March 22, 1862   Lot/Division 1, #366   Plat Number 366
Arkansas 1 Infantry Regiment Company H and died erysipelas Overton Hospital per Daily Burial Record Book; no compiled service record found; per Overton Hospital March 1862 Register of Sick died March 21, 1862, of erysipelas and Private Company H 1 Regiment and appears to indicate Tennessee as state but no record found Tennessee.

Wilson, J. R.   Buried May 13, 1862   Lot/Division 2, #191   Plat Number 741
Arkansas 19 (Dockery/Smead's) Infantry Regiment Private Company C; enlisted February 27, 1862 Columbia County, Arkansas; per February 27 to June 30, 1862 Muster Roll Remarks: Died at Memphis May 11, 1862; died Overton Hospital congestive fever per Daily Burial Record Book; first initial "F" in Cemetery computer index.

Winters, James C.   Buried May 12, 1862   Lot/Division 2, #168   Plat Number 718
Arkansas 8 (Miller's) Infantry Battalion Private (Franklin's) Company C; enlisted March 15, 1862 Little Rock, Arkansas; per March 15 to April 30, 1862 Muster Roll Remarks: Private in Hospital in Fort Pillow, Tennessee April 24, 1862; died William Hill's per Daily Burial Record Book.

Wirt, William   Buried November 25, 1861   Lot/Division 1, #219   Plat Number 219
Arkansas 7 Infantry Regiment Private Company D; enlisted July 26, 1861 Camp Shaver, Arkansas age 22; per September & October 1861 Muster Roll Remarks: Sick in Hospital Columbus, Kentucky; December 31, 1861 Muster Roll Remarks: Sick in Hospital Memphis, Tennessee.

Womac, John A.   Buried December 12, 1861   Lot/Division 1, #245   Plat Number 245
Arkansas 9 Infantry Regiment Private Company H; enlisted July 27, 1861, Pine Bluff, Arkansas; present on July 25 to November 1, 1861, muster rolls and no other information in compiled service record; died Southern Mothers Hospital enteritis age 18 per Daily Burial Record Book; name spelled "Warmack" in Daily Burial Record Book and computer index.

Womack, William Dento   Buried March 4, 1914   Plat Number N20
Tennessee 35 Infantry Regiment Private Company A; enlisted September 6, 1861 Camp Smartt (near McMinnville), Tennessee age 18; died age 71 per Daily Burial Record Book; 1841 1914 on grave stone.

Wood, Edward   Buried May 1, 1862   Lot/Division 2, #6   Plat Number 556
Missouri 1 Infantry Battalion Private Company C; per May & June 1862, Company Muster Roll enlisted March 17, 1862, Pocahontas, Arkansas by Major W. F. Rapley with Remarks: Died May 2, 1862, at Memphis, Kelsey's Company, which was at Fort Pillow during May 1862, and operated as marines aboard Confederate defense fleet gunboats; Company became Company K, 6th Regiment Missouri Infantry, about August 23, 1862, but no record found in that unit's compiled service records; Rapley's Arkansas Regiment Kelsie's Company in Daily Burial Record Book.

Wood, P. Q.   Buried May 17, 1889   Plat Number N67
Died age 51 per Daily Burial Record Book; grave first North side of #720 per Cemetery Single Grave Book but not stated in Daily Burial Record or Alpha books); possibly P. O. Wood Tennessee 3 (Forrest's) Cavalry Private Company B, enlisted January 3, 1862, Memphis, and paroled per undated Report of Prisoners of War; not listed in Cemetery computer index.

Woods, S. K.   Buried March 6, 1862   Lot/Division 1, #287   Plat Number 287
McCown's Brigade Company H per Daily Burial Record Book; no service record found; per Overton Hospital March 1862 Register of Sick died March 5, 1862, of rubella; the Brigade was at New Madrid and Island Ten during March 1862, as the Battle of Island Number Ten was an engagement at the New Madrid or Kentucky Bend on the Mississippi River from February 28 to April 8, 1862.

Woodson, James Monroe   Buried March 4, 1862   Lot/Division 1, #283   Plat Number 283
Arkansas 8 Infantry Regiment Private New Company K; enlisted November 16, 1861, Pocahontas by Major F. W. Desha; per April to June 1862, Muster Roll Remarks: Absent Sick; per October 31 to December 31 1862, Muster Roll Remarks: Died at Hospital March 1862; per Overton Hospital March 1862 Register of Deaths died March 3 of phthisis and Desheas Battalion (believed to be Desha who was Lieutenant Colonel of Arkansas 7 Infantry Battalion); note: Arkansas 8 Infantry New Company K was formed by consolidation of Companies A & E of Arkansas 7 Infantry Battalion; Derbin's Regiment Company E in Daily Burial Record Book but no Colonel Derbin found Confederate general index.

Woodward, J. A.   Buried February 22, 1862   Lot/Division 1, #192   Plat Number 192
Texas 9 (Young's/Maxey's) Infantry Regiment Corporal Company G; per Company Muster-in Roll dated December 1, 1861, enlisted October 8, 1861, Tarrent, Texas, age 25; per March 1862 Regimental Returns: Died pneumonia Memphis, Tennessee; per Overton Hospital Register died February 21, 1862; some compiled service record cards have initials as "A. J."; initials "A. S." in Daily Burial Record Book; name spelled "Woodard" in Cemetery computer index; initials "J. T." on VA grave stone; grave originally designated as #269 in Daily Burial Record Book but crossed out with #192 written above the 269; grave listed as #192 in Cemetery Alpha Book; two burial records found for Grave #192 (William H. Rhodes) but only one stone found.

Woodward, Jason   Buried April 24, 1862   Lot/Division 1, #490   Plat Number 490
Arkansas 18 (Carroll's) Infantry Regiment Private Company I; enlisted March 15, 1862 Camden, Arkansas; per March to June 1862, Muster Roll Remarks: Died at Memphis April 20, 1862; died Overton Hospital pneumonia per Daily Burial Record Book.

Woodward, William F.   Buried November 26, 1861   Lot/Division 1, #223   Plat Number 223
Arkansas 9 Infantry Regiment Private Old Company I; enlisted July 27, 1861, Pine Bluff, Arkansas; per November & December 1861, Muster Roll Remarks: Died Columbus, Kentucky 26 November 1861; died Southern Mothers Hospital per Daily Burial Record Book; note there is a second burial Grave #223, Division 1 - R. B. Spillman (buried May 27, 1906) who is buried eight feet from the south side of the walk around the Monument per Daily Burial Record Book.

Woody, J. M.   Buried May 5, 1862   Lot/Division 2, #63   Plat Number 613
Arkansas 6 Infantry Regiment Private Company C (Captain Cameron's Company, Dallas Rifles); per Muster Roll dated September 12, 1861, enlisted July 26, 1861, Pocahontas age 21; per February 28 to April 30, 1862, Company Muster Roll Remarks: Discharged 11 April 1862, on account of gun shot wound; wounded and died Overton Hospital per Daily Burial Record Book.

Workman, Amos   Buried April 5, 1862   Lot/Division 1, #419   Plat Number 419
Arkansas 11 Infantry Regiment Private Company K; enlisted December 18, 1861 Saline County, Arkansas; per December 28, 1861 to September 25, 1862, Muster Roll Remarks: Died March 1862; per Overton Hospital March 31, 1862, Register of Sick and Wounded admitted March 15, 1862; per Daily Burial Record Book died Overton Hospital typhoid fever and pneumonia.

Worsham, John   Buried December 20, 1861   Lot/Division 1, #249   Plat Number 249
Tennessee 2 (Walker's) Infantry Regiment Private Company G; enlisted September 27, 1861, Columbus, Kentucky age 23; per July 19, 1863 Muster Roll Remarks: Died at Memphis in Hospital; per August & September 1861, Muster Roll Remarks: Enlisted October 5, 1861, Columbus, Kentucky; died State Hospital per Daily Burial Record Book; 1831 1861 on grave stone.

Wray, T. J.   Buried May 10, 1862   Lot/Division 2, #141   Plat Number 691
Texas 27 (Whitfield's Legion) Cavalry Regiment Private Company F; per May & June 1862, Company Muster Roll enlisted March 7, 1862, Clarksville, Texas and Remarks: Dead, 15th May at Memphis, Tennessee; died Overton Hospital per Daily Burial Record Book; name spelled "Ray" in the Daily Burial Record Book and computer index.

Wren, Thomas   Buried June 18, 1862   Lot/Division 2, #296   Plat Number 846
Tennessee 2 (Walker's) Infantry Regiment Private Company F; per Company Muster Roll dated July 19, 1863, at Chattanooga enlisted December 7, 1862 (sic 1861), Columbus with Remarks: Discharged at Columbus, Kentucky; died State Hospital phthisis pulmonalis per Daily Burial Record Book.

Wright, Henry C.   Buried May 1, 1862   Lot/Division 2, #10   Plat Number 560
Texas 32 (Crump's Battalion) Cavalry Regiment Private Company D (Company A in Daily Burial Record Book); per Company Muster-in Roll dated November 4, 1861, enlisted November 4, 1861, Camp Crump, Marion County, Texas age 21; per January to August 1862, Company Muster Roll Remarks: Died May 1, 1862; no grave stone.

Wright, Thomas   Buried May 20, 1862   Lot/Division 2, #247   Plat Number 797
No unit indicated in Daily Burial Record Book but Remarks: "At Sam Davis – Vance Street."

Wynn, Newton M.   Buried May 11, 1862   Lot/Division 2, #159   Plat Number 709
Captain Wood's Company, from Craighead County, Arkansas and died Overton Hospital typhoid pneumonia per Daily Burial Record Book.

Yearger, Elias   Buried November 1, 1861   Lot/Division 1, #157   Plat Number 157
Confederate 4 (Bakers') Infantry Regiment Private Company B (Captain Jonas Griffin's Rifles); per Company Muster-in Roll enlisted August 10, 1861, at Montgomery, Alabama age 46; name appears on a Register of Officers and Soldiers of the Army of the Confederate States Who Were Killed in Battle, or Who Died of Wounds or Disease with Remarks: Died October 31, 1861, in Memphis of fever; J. C. Yager (sic) filed a claim on April 16, 1863, for settlement in the Office of the Confederate States Auditor for the War Department; regiment (also known as 1st Alabama, Tennessee and Mississippi Infantry) was formed about December 9, 1861, with ten companies: four from Alabama, two from Mississippi, and four from Tennessee; captured at Island 10 April 8, 1862, and after exchange in September, 1862, companies reorganized and transferred to other commands; Company B became Company C of the Alabama 54th Infantry Regiment but no record as died before transfer; died camp per Daily Burial Record Book.

Young, Thomas   Buried January 11, 1862   Lot/Division 1, #253   Plat Number 253
Arkansas 9 Infantry Regiment Private (Thomasson's) New Company B; enlisted December 18, 1861, Monticello; per December 18, 1861, to March 1, 1862, Muster Roll Remarks: Died at Overton Hospital Memphis January 12, 1862; died congestion age 18 per Daily Burial Record Book.

CONFEDERATE SOLDIERS REST NAME SPELLING VARIATIONS

The following is a list of surname spelling variations between the Confederate Soldiers Rest sketch spelling and the spelling found in the Cemetery records books and computer database index.

Cemetery Records	Sketch	Cemetery Records	Sketch	Cemetery Record	Sketch
Aiken	Akins	Dupray	Dupuy	Lofton	Loftin
Aldridge	Aldrige	Dunnica	Dunnico	LaVells	LaVelle
Anst	Aust		(Removed)	Lavener	LaVelle
Antrum	Antrim	Dunningan	Dunnigan	Macolmb	Macomb
Avondale	Arondale	Dunrough	Dorrough	Maddun	Maddox
Baker	Barker	Dyer	Dier	Mahaffey	Mahaffie
Ballard	Bullard	Erwin	Earwin	Mathew	Mathis
Barkley	Barclay	Ebrams	Eubank	Matthews	Matheus
Barns	Barnes	Ekels	Eckles	Matthews	Mathis
Barrington	Barentine	Emory	Embry	McAnally	McAnulty
Bearen	Beavers	Eskridge	Erkridge	McCaghan	McCaghren
Beldsoe	Bledsoe	Erwin	Irwin	McCallum	McCollum
Bezar/Bezer	Bazar	Eubanks	Eubank	McCarthy	McCarty
Blackman	Blockman	Farguson	Ferguson	McClelland	McLellan
Blockmon	Blockman	Florence	Florrence	MacColmb	Macomb
Blivens	Blevins	Fowlkes	Foulk	MacColnb	Macomb
Boliver	Boliner	Funk	Fink	McComb	Macomb
Braach	Broach	Gantrion	Gantron	McCommon	McCammon
Brewer	Breuer	Goins	Gowns	McCormick	McCormic
Bromley	Broombly	Goodman	Godwin	McCone/McCove	Cone
Bromley	Brumley	Graden	Graydon	McDaniels	McDaniel
Broome	Broom	Grayden	Graden	McDonald	McDonnel
Brown	Broom	Griffin	Griffith	McGowan	McGowen
Brownell	Brownelle	Gunyon	Guyton	McIntosh	McIntush
Bryant	Bryan	Guyon	Guyton	McMurray	McMaury
Burke	Burks	Haile	Hall	Miller	Millner
Burket	Burkett	Hailleigh	Haifleigh	Milton	Melton
Calloway	Colloway	Hallton	Halton	Minnis	Mims
Cane	Lane	Hanly	Henly	Mone	Horn
Carti	Carle	Harder	Hardee	Murphy	Murphree
Carnes	Kearns	Hartwell	Harwell	Musick	Music
Castenero	Castinere	Hathorn	Hawthorn	Naaron	Nairon
Castlebury	Castleberry	Hawkins	Hankins	Neighbors	Neighbours
Chamberlain	Chamberland	Haze	Hays	Neil	Neal
Christenhorn	Christenham	Hendricks	Hendrix	Nicks	Wicks
Clark	Clarke	Holcomb	Holcombe	Northrup	Northup
Clarke	Clair	Hollingsworth	Hollinsworth	Ortney	Ortner
Clarke	Clark	Holsenbach	Holsonback	Peeples	Peoples
Clay	Ray	Honeycutt	Honeycut	Philips/Phillips	Philip
Clynch	Clinch	Horne	Horn	Pierce	Pearce
Cole	Conn	Hulcy/Heley	Hulsey	Pittman	Pitman
Conn	Cohn	Hymen	Hyman	Raines	Rains
Connor	Conner	Inge	Ing	Rainey	Raney
Cotrell	Cottrell	Jeffrey	Jeffery	Razor	Rasor
Cub	Cupp	Jerald	Jewerls	Ray	Wray
Cummings	Cummins	Jonakin	Johnekin	Reames	Reams
Curtin	Curtic	Kell	Kelley	Rolph/Roph	Roof
Daily	Daly	Land	Loud	Roman	Rowan
Day	O' Day	Lefene	Lefebere	Ross	Ros
Detlow	Letlow	Len	Lowe	Russell	Russel
Dial	Dyal	Leverit	Leverett	Sadler	Saddler
Dirdan	Dardenno	Lewdwell	Lendwell	Sanders	Saunders
Duhuy	Dupuy	Lloyd	Loyd	Saunders	Sanders

Cemetery Records	Sketch	Cemetery Records	Sketch	Cemetery Record	Sketch
Savon	Saxon	Swenk	Swink	Waginer	Wagnon
Schaumberger	Shanberger	Tenfel	Teufel	Wagner	Waggoner
Schinou	Schinon	Terigalto	Terigaltoo	Wagner	Wagnon
Scronse	Scrouse	Thrilket	Thrailkille	Wamach	Waymack
Sheer	Shea	Thurlket	Thrailkille	Warmack	Waymack
Shepherd	Sheppard	Timmins	Timmons	Warmack	Womac
Simms	Sims	Tokes	Stokes	Warner	Warren
Skaggs	Skeggs	Tribble	Trible	Whitecarver	Whitescarver
Smotherman	Smutherman	Trible	Tribble	Wigginton	Wiginton
Sorrells	Sorralls	Tristle	Truite	Williams	Williamson
Stephens	Steaphuns	Tudod/Tutod	Tuder	Woodard	Woodward
Stevens	Stephens	Vernell	Varnell	Worton	Norton
Stocks	Stokes	Waggener	Waggoner		
Sutherland	Southerland	Waginer	Waggoner		

CONFEDERATE SOLDIERS REST
EXPLANATION OF GRAVE/SPACE, LOT/DIVISION
AND
GRAVE STONE/PLAT NUMBERS

General

Confederate Soldiers Rest grave numbers in the Daily Burial Record Book are listed in the "No. Grave" column. "Soldiers" (1st/north) or "Soldiers #2" (2nd/south) is indicated in the "No. Lot" column for most burials. "Confederate" or "Confederate Lot" is indicated for some burials, primarily after the War. The Confederate Soldiers Rest burials in the Cemetery Fowler Section Single Graves (Public Lot) Book are not listed in a public lot but in a separate listing specifically for Confederate Soldiers Rest.

Confederate Soldiers Rest

Confederate Soldiers Rest as indicated above is divided into two parts/divisions (1st - north; 2nd - south). In the Daily Burial Record Book, the 1st (north) division graves are numbered 1 through 549 and the 2nd (south) division graves are numbered 1 through 390.

The stones are numbered 1 through 940, with some duplications. Based upon that numbering, the 2nd (south) division burial number 390 in the Cemetery records should be stone number 940. If that is correct, then number 550 should be the last grave in the 1st (north) division (940 - 390 = 550) and number 551 should be grave number 1 of the 2nd (south) division. Although there is an actual stone number 550, there is not a burial listing for grave number 550 in the Cemetery records.

Initially, the 1st (north) division entries in the Daily Burial Record Book stopped with grave number 523 on April 30, 1862. Entries then began to be referenced as Soldiers #2 (2nd/south division) with the burial for grave number 1 also being on April 30, 1862. While the 2nd division burials were being made, only two (2) additional burials were made in the 1st division (burials numbers 524 on April 11, 1868 and 525 on May 1, 1868). The last burial entry for the 2nd division was number 390 on February 18, 1878. Thereafter, burials were recorded as either as a number between 526 and 549 in the 1st/north division or with "name" indicated in the number grave column with the soldier's name put on the stone. The "name" stone burials are located between the two sections and did not have a lot/division or a grave number indicated in the Cemetery records.

Anomalies

- grave burial record number 32½ 1st division for Baker, William A., August 19, 1866 but stone not found
- grave burial record number 34A 1st division for Gunn, Charles H., August 13, 1868 but stone not found
- grave burial record 2nd division for Palmer, Edward G., June 12. 1866, but no grave number indicated in Cemetery records and no stone found
- two (2) burial records number 45 1st division (Lyons, Frank, September 11, 1861 and Barnes, John, December 17, 1861) but only one (1) stone found; no record of Lyons possibly being moved
- grave burial record number 69½ 1st division for Seabrook, John T., February 27, 1867; death in compiled service record and on grave stone is 1862, so was moved to Elmwood; note, however, that Carlisle Page, President of Elmwood Cemetery and nephew of Seabrook, advised that he just put marker where it is as he did not know where Seabrook is actually buried
- two (2) stones number 108 1st division but only one burial record for McCaghren, James, October 16, 1861; that burial should be the 108 stone on the north end of the fourth row adjacent to the Road of Honor Drive in order to follow in date sequence with grave number 107 (October 16, 1861); and the other 108 stone should be the one at the south end of the third row (no burial record found)
- two (2) stones number 109 1st division but only one burial record for Rogers, Oliver, October 16, 1861; that burial should be the 109 stone on the north end of the fourth row adjacent to the Road of Honor Drive in order to follow in date sequence with grave number grave number 110 (October 18, 1861); and the other 109 stone should be the one at the south end of the third row (no burial record found)

- two (2) burial records number 192 1st division (Rhodes, William H., November 15, 1861 and Woodward, J. A., February 22, 1865) but only one stone found; no record of Rhodes possibly being removed
- two (2) burial records number 223; one with 1st division indicated for Woodward, William F., November 26, 1861 whose stone is found at north end of row in front of monument and one with no division indicated for Spillman, R. B., May 27, 1906, for whom the Daily Burial Record Book remarks indicate grave eight feet from walk around south side of monument
- two (2) stones 298 1st division but only one burial record for Vevers, J., March 7, 1862
- two (2) stones 376 1st division but only one burial record for Carwile, Flemuel, March 25, 1862
- no grave burial records numbered 526 - 531 1st division but stones found
- two (2) stones 537 1st division but only one burial record for Cooley, Robert N., May 3, 1903
- three (3) stones 538 1st division but only two (2) burials records (Embry, Mitchell A., December 21, 1895 and Burkes, A. J., April 1, 1903)
- no grave burial record number 539 1st division but stone found
- no 541 stone or burial record 1st division but a 541A stone and burial record for Boliner, P. N., February 1898, which fits into burial sequence dates
- no grave burial record number 546 1st division but stone found
- no grave burial record number 550 1st division but stone found
- two (2) grave burial records number 300 2nd division (Pratt, Stephen, June 28, 1862 and Norton, Peter, July 5, 1862) but only one stone (850) found; no record found of Pratt possibly being moved
- burial location (N59) of Crofford, John A., who was originally interred in Chapel Hill Lot 650/771 on April 6, 1925, appears to be out of place based on the sequence of dates of burials with "name" stones but location is correct based on the date moved from original burial location to Confederate Soldiers Rest on February 25, 1932

Plat Numbers

The numbers used on the plat are the actual numbers on the stones placed over each grave and the number assigned (ex N1) to the stones that only had a name on them. As indicated above, the numbered stones are numbered 1 through 940, with some duplications. There are 68 name stones.

Note: The following three individuals are listed in the Cemetery computer database index as buried in Confederate Soldiers Rest but are not believed to be since the grave number is entered in the "Single Grave" column in the Daily Burial Record Book and not in the "No. Grave" column where Confederate Soldiers Rest grave numbers are listed and nothing indicted in the "No. Lot" column as was when the burial was in Confederate Soldiers Rest, i.e. "Soldiers" (1st/north), or "Soldiers #2" (2nd/south), "Confederate" or "Confederate Lot":

1. Moore, Nathan M. - per database index buried "Confederate" Section, Lot "2 D2" but per Daily Burial Record Book buried Fowler Section, Single Grave "2d Div 2" (Single Grave Column), December 23, 1862, age 23.
2. Petty, J. C. - per database index buried "Confederate" Section, Lot "1" but per Daily Burial Record Book buried Fowler Section, Single Grave "2d Div 1" (Single Grave Column), December 27, 1862, age 23, with Remarks: "killed by robbers"; note: child age 2 buried in same grave August 11, 1864.
3. Trout, Dixon H. - per database index buried "Confederate" Section, Lot "376 D2" but per Daily Burial Record Book Kelly, John H. actually buried in this grave June 22, 1871; per Daily Burial Record Book Trout was buried in Fowler Section, Single Grave "376" (Single Grave Column), December 1, 1862, (name spelled "Frout" in Cemetery Alpha Book) with Remarks: "on Capt. Hamilton's coffin" - see sketch on S. H. D. Hamilton, Jr., buried January 2, 1862, Fowler Section, Single Grave "376" (Single Grave Column), in chapter Confederates Buried Outside of Soldiers Rest. No notation in Fowler Single Grave Book regarding Trout being buried in Hamilton grave. Note: There is a Trout, Dixon H. listed in the Quartermaster General's Office. *Roll of Honor. Names of Soldiers Who Died in Defense of the American Union. Interred in the National Cemeteries. Washington, D.C.: U.S. Government Printing Office, 1865-1871. Volume XXI*, Mississippi River National Cemetery, Near Memphis, Tennessee, page 209, with date of death November 30, 1862, and original place of interment Elmwood cemetery, Memphis. So, he should have been removed to National Cemetery in 1868.

Elmwood Cemetery
Confederate Soldiers Rest

Monument

GROUND WATER INSTITUTE
The University of Memphis

Special thanks to Drs. John Smith and Jerry Anderson and the students of the Ground Water Institute of The University of Memphis for their survey of the grave markers of Confederate Soldiers Rest and preparing this plat.

CONFEDERATE SOLDIERS REST
GRAVE STONE/PLAT NUMBERS LIST
WITH
LOT/DIVISION AND GRAVE/SPACE NUMBERS

The first column of numbers are the actual numbers on the stones placed over each grave and the number assigned (ex N1) to the stones that had only a name on them and are the numbers shown on the plat indicating the location of the graves. The second column is the lot/division per the Daily Burial Record Book with 1 being the north lot/division and 2 being the south lot/division. The third column is the grave/space number listed in the Cemetery records. The name stones did not have a lot/division or a grave/space number indicated in the Cemetery records. No location has been found for the first three listed.

STONE/ PLAT #	LOT/ DIV #	GRAVE/ SPACE #	SOLDIER	STONE/ PLAT #	LOT/ DIV #	GRAVE/ SPACE	SOLDIER
	1	32½	Barker, William A	45	1	45	Barnes, John P
	2	0	Palmer, Edward G	46	1	46	May, William H
	1	34A	Gunn, Charles H	47	1	47	Watson, William J
1	1	1	Wallace, Robert	48	1	48	Shean, John
2	1	2	Smith, W S	49	1	49	Giles, Franklin J
3	1	3	Graves, Riley	50	1	50	Dierman, Daniel
4	1	4	Jackson, William	51	1	51	Marcus, G M
5	1	5	Dunn, John C	52	1	52	McCardy, George R
6	1	6	Tribble, Alfred L	53	1	53	Unknown
7	1	7	Jones, James L	54	1	54	Quinn, William
8	1	8	Adams, Anderson	55	1	55	Posten, William
9	1	9	Akins, Jasper L	56	1	56	Blackwell, J T
10	1	10	Cahill, Edward	57	1	57	Blake, William
11	1	11	Varnell, William P	58	1	58	Carter, Robert D
12	1	12	Davis, Samuel T	59	1	59	Unknown
13	1	13	White, J F	60	1	60	Sheppard, James H
14	1	14	Unknown	61	1	61	Emmerson, Thomas J
15	1	15	Martin, Alfred	62	1	62	Crow, John M
16	1	16	Bell, John K	63	1	63	Davidson, J F
17	1	17	Barham, John A	64	1	64	Leggett, William T
18	1	18	McGuire, Thomas	65	1	65	Galey, Oliver
19	1	19	Spencer, Benjamin	66	1	66	Copeland, Thomas W
20	1	20	Gallagher, Thomas	67	1	67	Neely, Huron
21	1	21	Brewster, J J	68	1	68	Caldwell, John
22	1	22	Saunders, William H	69	1	69	Pearson, S W
23	1	23	Black, William E	69½	1	69½	Seabrook, John T
24	1	24	Baker, Daniel	70	1	70	Prince, James
25	1	25	Rigney, Henry	71	1	71	Jones, George P
26	1	26	Hannberger, Wiley W	72	1	72	Henderson, John W
27	1	27	Goodman, C B	73	1	73	Dawes, John
28	1	28	Creel, J C	74	1	74	Sullivan, George
29	1	29	Henson, John	75	1	75	Fink, John W
30	1	30	Wells, G L	76	1	76	Marshall, William A
31	1	31	Edwards, William B	77	1	77	Whitaker, Alfred H
32	1	32	Smith, Armstrong B	78	1	78	Walton, Tilman
33	1	33	McGuire, Rufus	79	1	79	McFarland, John N
34	1	34	Coggin, B F	80	1	80	Faust, J
35	1	35	Holden, John	81	1	81	Walker, John T
36	1	36	Bryant, Jackson J	82	1	82	Culpepper, John W
37	1	37	Galbreath, James	83	1	83	Taylor, William
38	1	38	Leary, D	84	1	84	Ashley, James D
39	1	39	Mowatt, James	85	1	85	Broom, William
40	1	40	Evans, Ezekiel	86	1	86	Bazar, Jacob
41	1	41	Harrison, Thomas	87	1	87	Dickson, James R
42	1	42	Ferguson, Terrence	88	1	88	Teufel, Fred
43	1	43	Leverett, Martin M	89	1	89	Montjoie, P T
44	1	44	Sheridan, Michael	90	1	90	Ellis, William
45	1	45	Lyons, Frank	91	1	91	Cohn, Harvey H

STONE/ PLAT #	LOT/ DIV #	GRAVE/ SPACE #	SOLDIER	STONE/ PLAT #	LOT/ DIV #	GRAVE/ SPACE #	SOLDIER
92	1	92	Hanrahan, James	152	1	152	Evans, John B
93	1	93	Jeffus, Needham H	153	1	153	McCammon, Columbus D
94	1	94	Guyton, T B	154	1	154	Simmons, T J
95	1	95	Tate, R H	155	1	155	Davidson, W M
96	1	96	Long, Adam L	156	1	156	White, S W
97	1	97	Owen, F M	157	1	157	Yearger, Elias
98	1	98	Dyal, G W	158	1	158	Holcombe, William H
99	1	99	Morris, Richard	159	1	159	Dixon, Claiborne
100	1	100	Fox, Peter	160	1	160	McIntush, King
101	1	101	Cameron, John S	161	1	161	Rhodes, Morgan G
102	1	102	Evans, Crawford L	162	1	162	Giles, G Y
103	1	103	Vandever, G W	163	1	163	King, S M
104	1	104	Culpepper, Henry J	164	1	164	Benton, William
105	1	105	Cooper, Thomas	165	1	165	Johnson, Matthew
106	1	106	Thompson, John F	166	1	166	Burch, A D
107	1	107	Martin, James	167	1	167	Reeves, Stephen C
108	1	108	McCaghren, James	168	1	168	Cobb, H J
108	1	108	Unknown	169	1	169	Macomb, N
109	1	109	Rogers, Oliver G	170	1	170	Irwin, Thomas
109	1	109	Unknown	171	1	171	Thompson, W M
110	1	110	Burton, J B	172	1	172	White, William
111	1	111	Henley, J	173	1	173	Tidwell, John L
112	1	112	Everett, Francis M	174	1	174	Frail Henry
113	1	113	Baker, C W	175	1	175	Shea, Michael
114	1	114	Crittenden, E A	176	1	176	Railey, L
115	1	115	Jackson, A M	177	1	177	Sims, William H
116	1	116	Callahan, David	178	1	178	Lowe, Samuel C
117	1	117	Johnson, Morgan	179	1	179	McCulloch, James
118	1	118	Collins, John J	180	1	180	Doyle, Wiley
119	1	119	Shanks, M O	181	1	181	Harris, John W
120	1	120	Jackson, William S	182	1	182	Thompson, Maston
121	1	121	Conn, John S	183	1	183	Ross, William R
122	1	122	Ros, A W	184	1	184	Chamberland, Rufus
123	1	123	Bradley, Mitchell	185	1	185	Shelton, John
124	1	124	Mims, John T	186	1	186	Stokes, James E
125	1	125	Hill, M H	187	1	187	Latham, Charles
126	1	126	Benson, Joseph N	188	1	188	Hunter, John P
127	1	127	McClintock, Edwin M	189	1	189	Creason, William R
128	1	128	Thompson, Andrew J	190	1	190	Barker, James L
129	1	129	Thompson, W J	191	1	191	Perkins, G W
130	1	130	Tate, J L	192	1	192	Rhodes, William H
131	1	131	Ward, Isaac L	192	1	192	Woodward, J A
132	1	132	Avery, Jesse N	193	1	193	Dozier, D M
133	1	133	Pryor, W J	194	1	194	Marsh, William
134	1	134	Owens, T L	195	1	195	Hackleburn, L D
135	1	135	Hyman, S C	196	1	196	Martin, Henry R
136	1	136	Broombly, David T	197	1	197	Jackson, Reuben
137	1	137	Holbert, F S	198	1	198	Gray, Columbus
138	1	138	Jackson, Salathiel P	199	1	199	McMullen, John
139	1	139	Morgan, Charles A	200	1	200	Boyle, Thomas
140	1	140	Callaway, Levi A	201	1	201	Prince, John
141	1	141	Carle, Everett	202	1	202	Downey, J M
142	1	142	Hulsey, H C	203	1	203	McMurray, Hezekiah
143	1	143	Robinson, Wallace	204	1	204	Hopkins, Henry
144	1	144	Roof, William C	205	1	205	Taylor, G W
145	1	145	Clark, Simpson H	206	1	206	Owen, E
146	1	146	McKinney, John	207	1	207	Waggoner, Hugh N
147	1	147	Graydon, G W A	208	1	208	Southerland, James M
148	1	148	Trimble, M R	209	1	209	Clinch, John E
149	1	149	Reeves, M L	210	1	210	Dean, Isaac A
150	1	150	Rose, M K	211	1	211	Cummins, Isaac A
151	1	151	Graden, John	212	1	212	Clay, T G

STONE/ PLAT #	LOT/ DIV #	GRAVE/ SPACE #	SOLDIER	STONE/ PLAT #	LOT/ DIV #	GRAVE/ SPACE #	SOLDIER
213	1	213	Gerris, David	274	1	274	Phillips, David P
214	1	214	Shields, S J	275	1	275	Collins, Dennis
215	1	215	Lindsay, John H	276	1	276	Whitehead, William
216	1	216	Brooks, Jackson	277	1	277	Foster, John Thomas
217	1	217	Parton, D L	278	1	278	Peoples, John W
218	1	218	Edgecomb, Melvin	279	1	279	Johnekin, John E
219	1	219	Wirt, William	280	1	280	McDaniel, Daniel
220	1	220	Brooks, Kosisco	281	1	281	Hall, James
221	1	221	Thornton, A L	282	1	282	Philip, Lewis
222	1	222	Hogan, John	283	1	283	Woodson, J M
223	1	223	Spillman, Robert B	284	1	284	Pentecost, F J
223	1	223	Woodward, William F	285	1	285	Anderson, Eli
224	1	224	Phillips, G W	286	1	286	Lambright, Lewis T
225	1	225	Middleton, C H	287	1	287	Woods, S K
226	1	226	Aust, L F	288	1	288	Adams, William J
227	1	227	Hudson, Henry	289	1	289	Pyburn, John
228	1	228	Dempsey, John J	290	1	290	Hatton, W H
229	1	229	McCurdy, William P	291	1	291	McLlure, R H
230	1	230	Price, Haisten T	292	1	292	Ragland, J W
231	1	231	Lowe, G H	293	1	293	Christopher, Matthew
232	1	232	Goforth, William	294	1	294	Wiginton, W J
233	1	233	Harrington, William J	295	1	295	Simpson, John F
234	1	234	Kearns, Thomas	296	1	296	Bryant, J W
235	1	235	Robertson, Augustus	297	1	297	Henson, W H
236	1	236	Jones, William D	298	1	298	Vevers, J
237	1	237	McGowen, John	298	1	298	Unknown
238	1	238	Elliott, Mark L	299	1	299	Morfels, Henry
239	1	239	Hankins, William W	300	1	300	Henderson, Jesse M
240	1	240	Mantequis, Jules	301	1	301	Pittman, P P
241	1	241	Wicks, George D	302	1	302	Nairon, Green V
242	1	242	Palmer, Green M	303	1	303	Holden, G W
243	1	243	Wilkerson, George	304	1	304	Dunn, W O
244	1	244	Sherwood, Jonathan	305	1	305	Wilder, H H
245	1	245	Womac, John A	306	1	306	Haifleigh, Augustus
246	1	246	Irwin, G W	307	1	307	Welch, William
247	1	247	Hill, Benjamin	308	1	308	Brown, John H
248	1	248	Cone, Elijah M	309	1	309	Barnes, Joseph
249	1	249	Worsham, John	310	1	310	Clements, Augustus
250	1	250	Bledsoe, T G	311	1	311	Lane, Morris
251	1	251	Dorr, Frederick	312	1	312	Jones, N L
252	1	252	Mehan, Martin	313	1	313	Odell, James
253	1	253	Young, Thomas	314	1	314	Hunter, James
254	1	254	White, John H	315	1	315	Godwin, B F
255	1	255	Null, John B	316	1	316	Josey, William H
256	1	256	Knox, William M	317	1	317	Day, Roger O
257	1	257	Lassiter, Amos A	318	1	318	Miller, Robert
258	1	258	McCool, Andrew J	319	1	319	Nelson, C
259	1	259	Rhine, George	320	1	320	Carrick, John
260	1	260	Patrick, Dan	321	1	321	Davis, W G
261	1	261	Graham, A H	322	1	322	Matthews, John B
262	1	262	Cook, S P C	323	1	323	Lewis, Jacob
263	1	263	Bryan, James	324	1	324	Cook, James
264	1	264	Sackett, James	325	1	325	McClanahan, W P
265	1	265	Smedley, Henry H	326	1	326	McClusky, W P
266	1	266	Horton, A J	327	1	327	Martin, M M
267	1	267	Crawford, Charles M	328	1	328	Unknown
268	1	268	Horton, Thomas A	329	1	329	Brownfield, J G
269	1	269	Skeggs, James M	330	1	330	Sherman, S B
270	1	270	Jones, J W	331	1	331	Myers, J A
271	1	271	Walker, James A	332	1	332	Russel, Oliver
272	1	272	Curtic, J R	333	1	333	Brown, Benjamin
273	1	273	Bull, Cicero B	334	1	334	Noonan, John

STONE/ PLAT #	LOT/ DIV #	GRAVE/ SPACE #	SOLDIER	STONE/ PLAT #	LOT/ DIV #	GRAVE/ SPACE #	SOLDIER
335	1	335	Wallace, J	396	1	396	Pearson, N D
336	1	336	Dier, Andrew J	397	1	397	Tomlinson, Felix G
337	1	337	Harwell, Washington	398	1	398	Blake, Garret
338	1	338	Adams, W J	399	1	399	Wallace, R J
339	1	339	Buckner, Jasper W	400	1	400	Ludlow, S
340	1	340	Grimmett, Robert W	401	1	401	Andrews, H J
341	1	341	Blackburn, Marion	402	1	402	Grooms, J C
342	1	342	Read, A E	403	1	403	Gregory, Edward
343	1	343	Carrick, George	404	1	404	Lee, Richard
344	1	344	Capps, Thomas J	405	1	405	Chapman, Thomas
345	1	345	Clair, John	406	1	406	Earwin, J C
346	1	346	Miller, H	407	1	407	Collier, T W
347	1	347	Scott, Alfred M	408	1	408	Sharpling, Lemuel
348	1	348	Beard, P L	409	1	409	Maynard, John H
349	1	349	Julian, John R	410	1	410	Thompson, Thomas
350	1	350	Brown, George	411	1	411	French, J G
351	1	351	Johnston, James J	412	1	412	Burks, William
352	1	352	McClure, Jere	413	1	413	Charles, John H
353	1	353	Hollinsworth, A W	414	1	414	Bradshaw, J W
354	1	354	Moore, Edward	415	1	415	Shanault, A S
355	1	355	Unknown	416	1	416	Bonds, T S
356	1	356	Unknown	417	1	417	Cothran, Samuel M
357	1	357	Clark, William M	418	1	418	Thomas, W H
358	1	358	Mauldin, Jesse A	419	1	419	Workman, Amos
359	1	359	Palmer, J M	420	1	420	Sims, G W
360	1	360	Moore, Frank	421	1	421	Taylor, Joseph
361	1	361	Foulk, Adam	422	1	422	Bradshaw, A
362	1	362	Dunn, T J	423	1	423	Biggs, David
363	1	363	Loomis, J J	424	1	424	Smith, Robert
364	1	364	McCance, R M	425	1	425	Dardenno, Andrew
365	1	365	Jones, Andrew J	426	1	426	Peak, T J
366	1	366	Willis, W L	427	1	427	Rodgers, John
367	1	367	Thornton, W B	428	1	428	Davis, William M
368	1	368	Skinner, John	429	1	429	Guard, William
369	1	369	Connor, M E	430	1	430	Daly, William L
370	1	370	Lax, Joseph G	431	1	431	Hendricks, Daniel
371	1	371	Land, William T	432	1	432	Whittington, C M
372	1	372	Pilcher, S C	433	1	433	Shackleford, L A
373	1	373	Powell, Thomas J	434	1	434	Baird, Felix
374	1	374	Shanks, M C	435	1	435	Swink, Drew L
375	1	375	McCormic, Patrick	436	1	436	Hackett, John
376	1	376	Carwile, Flemuel	437	1	437	Rhodes, Charles C
376	1	376	Unknown	438	1	438	Henly, James M
377	1	377	Pope, Riley	439	1	439	Pinnell, A N
378	1	378	Christenham, Peter	440	1	440	Blakely, John W
379	1	379	Collins, Thomas	441	1	441	Whitney, George
380	1	380	Keller, Wesley M	442	1	442	Wehrle, Fred
381	1	381	Hawthorn, Augustus	443	1	443	McKay, Michael
382	1	382	Nowell, A J	444	1	444	Hall, James O
383	1	383	Castinere, Antonio	445	1	445	Crook, T W
384	1	384	Gantron, Jack	446	1	446	Corder, Sr Phillip T
385	1	385	Irwin, G W	447	1	447	Donohoe, Thomas
386	1	386	Reynolds, E T	448	1	448	Gleason, Michael
387	1	387	Smith, B A	449	1	449	Howell, William
388	1	388	Roark, W T	450	1	450	Evans, Caleb J
389	1	389	Webb, T S	451	1	451	Overton, William G
390	1	390	Sarat, William	452	1	452	Sledge, Washington M
391	1	391	Baker, T R	453	1	453	Watkins, J W
392	1	392	Hill, James	454	1	454	Howell, W B
393	1	393	Hall, John W	455	1	455	Fount, James
394	1	394	Duffo, Stephen M	456	1	456	Goodwin, J H
395	1	395	Nall, William	457	1	457	Palmer, John

STONE/ PLAT #	LOT/ DIV #	GRAVE/ SPACE #	SOLDIER	STONE/ PLAT #	LOT/ DIV #	GRAVE/ SPACE #	SOLDIER
458	1	458	Conner, Z M	520	1	520	Hollinsworth, Matthew
459	1	459	Strussell, Thomas	521	1	521	Richardson, James
460	1	460	Unknown	522	1	522	Bennett, J W
461	1	461	Mathis, Andrew J	523	1	523	Adams, A J
462	1	462	Bruce, T M	524	1	524	Timberlake, William H
463	1	463	Brownelle, E L	525	1	525	Cage, John F
464	1	464	Tuder, Benjamin F	526	1	526	Unknown
465	1	465	Cowan, Samuel S	527	1	527	Unknown
466	1	466	Whitescarver, F W	528	1	528	Unknown
467	1	467	Pearcy, C C	529	1	529	Unknown
468	1	468	Cooper, James A	530	1	530	Unknown
469	1	469	Blevins, Jasper	531	1	531	Unknown
470	1	470	Arondale, Anthony	532	1	532	Barradall, Norborne D
471	1	471	Bell, Henry F	533	1	533	Tinsley, W D
472	1	472	McKinney, L R	534	1	534	LaVelle, James
473	1	473	Boyle, Robert	535	1	535	Adams, Walter W
474	1	474	Scherbe, A	536	1	536	Osborne, William W
475	1	475	Waymack, Joel S	537	1	537	Cooley, Robert N
476	1	476	McDonnel, John C	537	1	537	Unknown
477	1	477	Lynch, R	538	1	538	Embry, Mitchell A
478	1	478	Friar, John	538	1	538	Unknown
479	1	479	Newman, Martin	538	1	538	Burkett, Andrew J
480	1	480	Shelton, George B	539	1	539	Unknown
481	1	481	Mitchell, William	540	1	540	January, W W
482	1	482	Husbands, Henry L	541A	1	541A	Boliner, Patrick M
483	1	483	Hawkins, William L C	542	1	542	Dupuy, John J
484	1	484	Kelley, James A	543	1	543	Buford, Smith
485	1	485	Bellows, John W	544	1	544	Barteau, Clark R
486	1	486	Massey, George	545	1	545	Gentry, C W
487	1	487	Miller, Van	546	1	546	Unknown
488	1	488	Neal, William	547	1	547	Samples, J W
489	1	489	Harper, James J	548	1	548	Murphree, Anderson
490	1	490	Woodward, Jason	549	1	549	Miller, R B
491	1	491	Cook, Joseph	550	1	550	Unknown
492	1	492	Williams, William	551	2	1	Riley, William
493	1	493	Phillips, James	552	2	2	Greer, James
494	1	494	Doherty, James	553	2	3	Arrington, Edmund A
495	1	495	Gentry, G	554	2	4	Alexander, S R
496	1	496	Wheeler, George	555	2	5	Mansell, James
497	1	497	Terry, James G	556	2	6	Wood, Edward
498	1	498	Johnson, R B	557	2	7	Dobbs, Benjamin O
499	1	499	Sheffield, William	558	2	8	Ehretsman, Joseph
500	1	500	Gowns, William	559	2	9	Sorralls, James R
501	1	501	Denton, John B	560	2	10	Wright, Henry C
502	1	502	Unknown	561	2	11	Reams, Levi E
503	1	503	Henderson, Thomas	562	2	12	Hutto, Thomas
504	1	504	Jones, Willis	563	2	13	Neely, Calvin H
505	1	505	Gowen, William	564	2	14	Holsonback, John R
506	1	506	McLellan, William	565	2	15	Aldrige, Thomas H
507	1	507	Nelson, Irvin	566	2	16	Beavers, Levi J
508	1	508	Waits, Dempsey	567	2	17	Simmons, John C
509	1	509	Hardee, George W	568	2	18	Luther, Calvin
510	1	510	Rains, William J	569	2	19	Cottrell, George
511	1	511	Swindle, William	570	2	20	Shadrick, J M
512	1	512	Honeycut, Francis M	571	2	21	Gish, H H
513	1	513	Davis, Clarence W	572	2	22	Owens, D F
514	1	514	Ditchler, G W	573	2	23	Newberry, William
515	1	515	Wicklin, Louis W	574	2	24	Coffman, Warren
516	1	516	McFarland, J	575	2	25	Floyd, A J
517	1	517	Bradburg, Thomas R	576	2	26	James, Isaacs
518	1	518	Hall, Lucilius M	577	2	27	Keith, John T
519	1	519	Cottingham, Jeff	578	2	28	Cunningham, D C

STONE/ PLAT #	LOT/ DIV #	GRAVE/ SPACE #	SOLDIER	STONE/ PLAT #	LOT/ DIV #	GRAVE/ SPACE #	SOLDIER
579	2	29	Unknown	641	2	91	Dorrough, John G
580	2	30	Hawkins, James J	642	2	92	King, Andy
581	2	31	Fitzhugh, John M	643	2	93	Hall, Jesse H
582	2	32	Comstock, Joseph L	644	2	94	Thrailkille, James M
583	2	33	McWright, W D	645	2	95	Bullard, St Clare
584	2	34	Mathis, B B	646	2	96	Music, Richard
585	2	35	Thomas, George	647	2	97	Unknown
586	2	36	Moore, William H	648	2	98	Baldin, J
587	2	37	Langford, Jordan H	649	2	99	Melton, John
588	2	38	Moore, Peter	650	2	100	Hardin, William
589	2	39	Erkridge, George C	651	2	101	Embree, William
590	2	40	Jordan, John	652	2	102	Colloway, Nathaniel C
591	2	41	Elmore, James L	653	2	103	Webb, George
592	2	42	Cupp, Nathan J	654	2	104	Northup, A J
593	2	43	Simpson, Thomas P	655	2	105	Smith, John F
594	2	44	McCarty, William E	656	2	106	Ortner, D M
595	2	45	Wagnon, Clarence	657	2	107	Mineace, J J
596	2	46	Cook, T H	658	2	108	Antrim, Henry
597	2	47	Trible, C B	659	2	109	Neighbours, Thomas J
598	2	48	Unknown	660	2	110	Jackson, J A
599	2	49	Pitman, W T	661	2	111	Harris, Joseph
600	2	50	Collins, James	662	2	112	Permenter, J R
601	2	51	Dumas, John C	663	2	113	Hardin, Powell
602	2	52	Sewell, John	664	2	114	Laird, Miles F
603	2	53	Camper, John M	665	2	115	Shelton, Jesse F
604	2	54	Morris, John	666	2	116	Warwick, W L
605	2	55	Washburn, John M	667	2	117	Griffith, Silvester
606	2	56	South, N M	668	2	118	Stephens, J J
607	2	57	Black, Henry L	669	2	119	Brewton, James J
608	2	58	Loyd, Wiley H	670	2	120	Timmons, Jordan
609	2	59	Lee, Jesse	671	2	121	Hartsfield, W H
610	2	60	Tippett, Zachariah	672	2	122	Bable (Babb?), A E L
611	2	61	Bell, G W	673	2	123	Smith, C C
612	2	62	Jackson, J C	674	2	124	Unknown
613	2	63	Woody, J M	675	2	125	Steaphuns, John M
614	2	64	Bugg, William C	676	2	126	Jewerls, J W
615	2	65	McAnulty, S H	677	2	127	Pate, Wiley A
616	2	66	Hare, Elijah L	678	2	128	Freeland, W J
617	2	67	Bradshaw, J H	679	2	129	Hart, C F
618	2	68	Carman, Samuel M	680	2	130	Snead, Thomas
619	2	69	Finley, C M	681	2	131	Rowan, G W
620	2	70	Smutherman, Green A	682	2	132	Conn, William
621	2	71	Harper, William H	683	2	133	Meek, Joseph C
622	2	72	Thompson, William	684	2	134	Easley, James C
623	2	73	Edwards, James J	685	2	135	Truite, Lafayette
624	2	74	Benson, Frederick A	686	2	136	Waldrop, William L
625	2	75	Rayburn, M	687	2	137	Johnson, Thomas S
626	2	76	Gilliland, Robert S	688	2	138	Joyce, T S
627	2	77	Lackey, William	689	2	139	Brown, John F
628	2	78	Bagley, Humphrey	690	2	140	Brown, Benjamin
629	2	79	Williamson, J J	691	2	141	Ray, T J
630	2	80	Watkins, Robert	692	2	142	Garlington, W H C
631	2	81	Crouse, Franklin	693	2	143	Greer, A S
632	2	82	Nicholson, Daniel R	694	2	144	Jones, R
633	2	83	Barnes, William	695	2	145	Bradberry, James
634	2	84	Smith, William S	696	2	146	Mahaffie, H A
635	2	85	Romine, Henry	697	2	147	Cole, Porter
636	2	86	Wheeler, John	698	2	148	Golding, John
637	2	87	Reeves, E L	699	2	149	Curry, James D
638	2	88	Shanberger, George W	700	2	150	Harper, T J
639	2	89	Sanders	701	2	151	Collins, John W
640	2	90	Saddler, C G	702	2	152	Mathews, John W

STONE/PLAT #	LOT/DIV #	GRAVE/SPACE #	SOLDIER	STONE/PLAT #	LOT/DIV #	GRAVE/SPACE #	SOLDIER
703	2	153	Saunders, J C	765	2	215	Lamb, Samuel F
704	2	154	Cook, J E	766	2	216	Thornton, William
705	2	155	Barnes, William C	767	2	217	Tuck, W L
706	2	156	Letlow, Isham H	768	2	218	Barclay, James
707	2	157	Brumley, Joseph	769	2	219	Bland, James W
708	2	158	McCollum, John W	770	2	220	Haley, David G
709	2	159	Wynn, Newton M	771	2	221	McGill, J T
710	2	160	Wallace, A M	772	2	222	Simmons, John B
711	2	161	Williams, J W	773	2	223	Southerland, Peter
712	2	162	Perkins, T J	774	2	224	Pope, J J
713	2	163	Saxon, Irving	775	2	225	May, Leander
714	2	164	Lendwell, William D	776	2	226	Roberts, John B
715	2	165	Davenport, Moses	777	2	227	Ward, Isaac N
716	2	166	Davenport, Jesse D	778	2	228	Harrison, W B
717	2	167	Blockman, S W	779	2	229	Downs, E G
718	2	168	Winters, James C	780	2	230	Burk, John H
719	2	169	Jones, William P	781	2	231	Hays, William A
720	2	170	Sewell, J B	782	2	232	Newman, B S
721	2	171	Adams, A H	783	2	233	Chadwick, Frank
722	2	172	Davidson, W C	784	2	234	Connelly, John
723	2	173	Trammell, George W	785	2	235	Obors, James M
724	2	174	Love, Nathan	786	2	236	Matheus, Samuel
725	2	175	Chapman, William F	787	2	237	Potter, Pleasant B
726	2	176	Williams, Thomas	788	2	238	Warner, W E
727	2	177	Rasor, John W	789	2	239	Moore, William
728	2	178	Blunt, Thomas E	790	2	240	Jeffery, Jesse L
729	2	179	Welsh, John	791	2	241	Lefebere, John
730	2	180	Bonner, Benjamin F	792	2	242	Loud, Curty
731	2	181	Gowans, Daniel	793	2	243	Mullins, Albert A
732	2	182	Unknown	794	2	244	Lindsey, W P
733	2	183	Sanders, John B	795	2	245	Matthews, Daniel S
734	2	184	Blackwell, B M	796	2	246	Smith, Robert J
735	2	185	Maddox, L H	797	2	247	Wright, Thomas
736	2	186	Davis, Nathan	798	2	248	Akers, John E
737	2	187	Gentry, J A	799	2	249	Pearce, Andrew J
738	2	188	Reynolds, E	800	2	250	Barentine, William
739	2	189	Hardeman, Elbert	801	2	251	Williams, Samuel J
740	2	190	Robinson, John	802	2	252	Sheffield, Mark
741	2	191	Wilson, J R	803	2	253	Raney, Marcus G
742	2	192	Parker, William L	804	2	254	Patterson, Charles E
743	2	193	Hill, Allen L	805	2	255	Lingo, George
744	2	194	Montgomery, G W	806	2	256	Luther, Jackson
745	2	195	Baber, W C	807	2	257	Turner, G W
746	2	196	Hyden, Matthew H	808	2	258	Phillips, John C
747	2	197	Gibson, Samuel	809	2	259	Adams, James
748	2	198	Nearce, H J	810	2	260	Smith, James
749	2	199	Smith, George B	811	2	261	Stacy, L
750	2	200	Stone, M F	812	2	262	Unknown
751	2	201	Fuller, E R	813	2	263	Redding, Benjamin J
752	2	202	Knowles, Hardy	814	2	264	Evans, N
753	2	203	Adams, W T	815	2	265	Ball, J N
754	2	204	Loftin, William	816	2	266	Donnell, A L
755	2	205	Baker, Alex F	817	2	267	Pickering, J E
756	2	206	Hampton, Wade	818	2	268	Parsley, Amsi
757	2	207	Scrouse, J	819	2	269	Lynn, Thomas
758	2	208	Ray, Mark R	820	2	270	Green, Joseph
759	2	209	Lamb, Asa	821	2	271	Schinon, E H
760	2	210	Fisher, Joseph	822	2	272	Bostick, Samuel
761	2	211	Clifton, T J	823	2	273	Unknown
762	2	212	Breuer, Martin V	824	2	274	Martin, John
763	2	213	Porter, E V	825	2	275	Starrett, F C
764	2	214	Adams, William J	826	2	276	Weldon, Columbus

STONE/ PLAT #	LOT/ DIV #	GRAVE/ SPACE #	SOLDIER	STONE/ PLAT #	LOT/ DIV #	GRAVE/ SPACE #	SOLDIER
827	2	277	Coffman, John H	888	2	338	Douglas
828	2	278	Halley, A B	889	2	339	Chisp, John
829	2	279	Stephens, Felix	890	2	340	Terigaltoo, Salrater
830	2	280	Garner, John L	891	2	341	Nolan, David C
831	2	281	Fletcher, John N	892	2	342	Macon, Richard T
832	2	282	Baker, Peter	893	2	343	Perkins, Enos S
833	2	283	Dowdy, John T	894	2	344	Unknown
834	2	284	Halton, James R	895	2	345	Unknown
835	2	285	Craft, Moses M	896	2	346	Unknown
836	2	286	Smith, N D	897	2	347	Unknown
837	2	287	Dickinson, Henry	898	2	348	Unknown
838	2	288	Mitchell, John	899	2	349	Unknown
839	2	289	Van Horn, J W	900	2	350	Eubank, Richard P
840	2	290	Hall	901	2	351	Unknown
841	2	291	Johnson, Jack	902	2	352	Unknown
842	2	292	Rodgers, C M	903	2	353	Unknown
843	2	293	Dutton, Peter	904	2	354	Unknown
844	2	294	Smith, S C	905	2	355	Unknown
845	2	295	Parks, John	906	2	356	Unknown
846	2	296	Wren, Thomas	907	2	357	Unknown
847	2	297	Malin, John	908	2	358	Rodgers, R B
848	2	298	Broach, Redding	909	2	359	Millner, Robert
849	2	299	Stocks, James	910	2	360	Arnold, William
850	2	300	Pratt, Stephen	911	2	361	Stockton, George W
850	2	300	Norton, Peter	912	2	362	Gray, A B
851	2	301	Stewart, Jerry F	913	2	363	Clarke, Robert J
852	2	302	Webb, James	914	2	364	Steiner, J P
853	2	303	Ricketts, John C	915	2	365	Cole, J C
854	2	304	Barnett, Miles R	916	2	366	Cole, John B
855	2	305	Ivy, J C	917	2	367	Patterson, William S
856	2	306	Nelson, William	918	2	368	White, Andrew J
857	2	307	Harper, John	919	2	369	Horn, D W
858	2	308	Warren, J H	920	2	370	Rhodes, M
859	2	309	Golden, George W	921	2	371	Nash, Abner W
860	2	310	Unknown	922	2	372	Bass, S H
861	2	311	Unknown	923	2	373	Unknown
862	2	312	Unknown	924	2	374	Rowe, E A
863	2	313	Florrence, J H	925	2	375	Franklin, William
864	2	314	Castleberry, Joel	926	2	376	Kelly, John H
865	2	315	Unknown	927	2	377	Alford, Charles G
866	2	316	Unknown	927	2	377	Alford, J L
867	2	317	Higgins, S S	928	2	378	Ferguson, William B
868	2	318	Smith, Levi	929	2	379	Burnett, George W
869	2	319	Dunnigan, James	930	2	380	Johnson, J R
870	2	320	Beard, Thomas	931	2	381	Scales, William M
871	2	321	Unknown	932	2	382	Carlin, R F
872	2	322	Redwine, Rufus E	933	2	383	Drake, John B
873	2	323	Tomberland, William H	934	2	384	Lay, James A
874	2	324	Hutto, James	935	2	385	Griswold, D B
875	2	325	Fortune, Asa J	936	2	386	McCullough, Alexander
876	2	326	Merrit, B	937	2	387	Warburg, Edward
877	2	327	Shaw, C M	938	2	388	Stickney, Horace N
878	2	328	Williams, Robert	939	2	389	Marsh, Richard
879	2	329	Unknown	940	2	390	Lewis, Lindsey
880	2	330	James	N1			Fitzgerald, T R
881	2	331	Unknown	N2			Ryan, A K
882	2	332	Porter, William C	N3			Walters, R E
883	2	333	Seton, William	N4			Farris, Oliver B
884	2	334	Shik, John	N5			Dickson, Barton
885	2	335	Jones	N6			Cotton, James R
886	2	336	Bronhors, A	N7			Kearney, J R
887	2	337	Pringle, W	N8			Roden, George

STONE/ PLAT #	SOLDIER	STONE/ PLAT #	SOLDIER
N9	Ross, Francis M	N39	Cloud, Joseph F
N10	Smith, J L	N40	Lambert, Joel
N11	Stewart, E	N41	Denton, Frank D
N12	Elam, W S	N42	Patterson, Martin D
N13	Blocker, Ralph J	N43	Shivers, James N
N14	Harris, Andrew J	N44	Carter, Thomas J
N15	Beasley, J R	N45	Johnson, Isaiah W
N16	Nixon, William C	N46	Brown, Hiram R
N17	Tucker, Adolphus F	N47	Culberson, John H
N18	Thomas, John P	N48	Smith, Joel H
N19	Farris, Miles H	N49	Wheeler, James W
N20	Womack, W D	N50	Pettigrew, James L
N21	Morris, Thomas	N51	Kelly, James
N22	Bell, George	N52	Pitts, James F
N23	Owen, Thomas H	N53	Boyd, Carter M
N24	Boggs, Caldwell	N54	Jones, George W
N25	Deny, James A	N55	Hefferon, Thomas
N26	Jennings, John W	N56	Flanigan, John D
N27	Jones, William R	N57	Patton, Lucius E
N28	Clinton, Alexander M	N58	Mason, Frank Y
N29	Leland, Charles F	N59	Crofford, John A
N30	Strickland, William V	N60	Williford, Sr David J
N31	Demuth, George	N61	Sanders, George H
N32	Hamilton, Isiah	N62	Rutherford, Felix
N33	Richmond, Charles W	N63	Boddie, Mary
N34	Ing, Richard	N64	High, Edward D
N35	Dalton, Kit	N65	Smith, John
N36	Wells, Julius T	N66	Gunter, John F
N37	Kimbrough, James P	N67	Wood, P Q
N38	Eckles, Benjamin E	N68	Nicholson, John D

CONFEDERATES BURIED OUTSIDE OF SOLDIERS REST

This is a list of known Confederate soldiers and veterans, including a servant/slave Jack Shelton, buried at Elmwood Cemetery outside of Confederate Soldiers Rest as well as other individuals, although not serving in the Confederate military, who served an important part in the Confederate Cause. Individuals were identified from several sources, including but not limited to, review of Elmwood records and publications, grave stones, newspaper obituaries and unit articles, *Confederate Veteran*, descendants and individuals who knew of this research, research materials on file in archives and libraries and online sources. Obviously, there are many more Confederate soldiers and veterans buried at Elmwood Cemetery that are not listed but would have been if they had been identified or known. Therefore, this area is a continuing research project to identify and research other soldiers, veterans and individuals important to the Confederate Cause.

Adams, Charles W.   Buried September 10, 1878   South Grove 156, #5

Arkansas 23 (Adams') Infantry Regiment Colonel; per undated descriptive roll in compiled service record originally entered service as Colonel April 25, 1862, age 45 and born Massachusetts; per June 30 - August 31, 1862 Field and Staff muster roll: commissioned (elected) April 25, 1862 at Memphis; wrote General Smith on February 6, 1864 and asked for promotion to Brigadier General; in June 24, 1864 report from Northern Arkansas General Shelby mentions Adams as General Adams; no records found in General and Staff records; per sketch in *More Generals in Gray* born August 16, 1817 in Boston, Massachusetts, first served as Major and Quartermaster of Arkansas State Troops, after dissolution of the Army of Arkansas in late 1861 raised Arkansas 23 Infantry Regiment and elected Colonel April 23, 1862, Regiment disbanded in July 1863 and joined staff of Major General Thomas Hindman, in December 1863 returned to Arkansas, from 1864 to early 1865 served as Commander of Northern Subdistrict of Arkansas with rank of Acting Brigadier General, and died of yellow fever on September 9, 1878; not listed in the *Memorandum relative to the General Officers Appointed by the President in the Armies of the Confederate States - 1861-1865* compiled from Official Records by the Military Secretary's Office, U. S. War Department 1905; not listed in *Generals in Gray*; grandfather of Helen Keller; sketch, photograph, if available, and grave stone photograph in book *Quiet Places: The Burial Sites of Civil War Generals in Tennessee* by Buckner and Nathaniel C. Hughes, Jr., East Tennessee Historical Society (1992); grave stone (bronze): Brigadier General 23 Ark Regiment C.S.A. August 16, 1817 September 10, 1878; also listed in chapter on Generals; listed under Generals in "Touring historic Elmwood Cemetery" (Brochure and Map of Historic Gravesites) #1; listed in "Touring Historic Elmwood Cemetery" Brochure (January 2000) #82; sketch #28 in Elmwood *Civil War Tour* booklet (2012).

Adams, Reuben B.   Buried April 30, 1862   South Grove 11, #1

Louisiana 18 Regiment Company K and from Corinth, Mississippi per Daily Burial Record Book; no compiled service record found; first buried South Grove 17, #1 and moved to South Grove 11 (no date found when moved); grave stone born July 13, 18__ Tipton County, Tennessee (it appears) died April 18, 1862 and a member of 18 Louisiana Volunteers.

Adams, W. A.   Buried June 12, 1864   Fowler Public Lot 2, #73

"W. S. Adams" listed in Elmwood 1874 book as Confederate soldier buried in Elmwood who was citizen of Memphis or vicinity; believed to be "William A. Adams," Private Company H, Tennessee 7 Cavalry Regiment who was killed June 10, 1864 at Brice's Crossroad per memorial rolls in Lindsley's Annals; died age 30 "new monia" per Daily Burial Record Book.

Allin, Philip T.   Buried February 25, 1870   Chapel Hill Circle 65, #1

Tennessee 3 (Forrest's) Cavalry Regiment Lieutenant Colonel; listed in June 6, 1878 *Memphis Daily Appeal* article "OUR DEAD HEROES" covering the unveiling of the Confederate Monument and decoration of graves at Elmwood as then one of twenty-eight members of the Bluff City Grays, Company B of the 154 Senior Infantry Regiment and Company A of Forrest's Old (Third) Cavalry Regiment buried at Elmwood (see Notes of Interest - Bluff City Grays); per 154 Senior Infantry Regiment record enlisted 2 Lieutenant Company B May 14, 1861 Randolph, Tennessee age 24 and elected Captain May 3, 1862; per 3 Cavalry records enlisted May 4, 1861 Randolph, Tennessee, Captain of Captain P. T. Allin's Sharpshooters General Preston Smith Brigade, appointed Major October 8, 1863, Tennessee 26 Cavalry Battalion; single card Captain Company F in Tennessee 11(Holman's) Cavalry Regiment records; listed in Elmwood 1874 book as Confederate soldier buried in Elmwood who was citizen of Memphis or vicinity and sketch indicating rank of Major and died in Memphis 1869 about age 30; listed in *Reminiscences of the Civil War* by John Hallum, Tunnah & Pittard printers, 1903, as member of Bluff City Grays with name spelled "Allen"; listed in "A COMPLETE ROSTER OF THE BLUFF CITY GREYS" located in the Memphis Room of the Memphis/Shelby County Public Library and Information Center Central Library with notation that died Memphis and buried in Elmwood; per sketch in Mathes book proposed for Confederate Historical Association membership by James E. Beasley and elected February 3, 1870; sketch in Elmwood Cemetery 1874 book; name spelled "Allen," and died pneumonia age 35 per Daily Burial Record Book.

Ammon, D. C.   Buried March 26, 1872   Fowler 529, #1

Tennessee 3 (Forrest's) Cavalry Regiment Private Company B; enlisted May 27, 1862 Jacksonport, Arkansas; listed in Elmwood 1874 book as Confederate soldier buried in Elmwood who was citizen of Memphis or vicinity; died meningitis age 28 per Daily Burial Record Book; name spelled "Ammen" in Daily Burial Record Book, computer index and Confederate Soldiers who were citizens of Memphis and vicinity list in Elmwood 1874 book.

Anderson, Abram Keller   Buried April 26, 1918   Turley 395½, #5
Kentucky 5 Mounted Infantry Regiment 2 Lieutenant 3rd Company I; originally enlisted Kentucky 9 Mounted Infantry Regiment (Captain Jo Desha's Company of Infantry) 2 Lieutenant Company I, which Company subsequently became 3rd Company I Kentucky 5 Mounted Infantry; per Company Muster-in Roll dated September 28, 1862, enlisted July 1, 1862; wounded and captured during Atlanta Campaign August 27 to August 3, 1864, and exchanged September 19, 1864, at Rough and Ready, Georgia; sketch in Mathes: "Captain Company I, Fifth Kentucky Infantry, Hanson's Brigade; enlisted April, 1861, and served in the Army of Virginia; was discharged with First Kentucky Infantry at the expiration of enlistment at Camp Winder, near Richmond; re-enlisted June, 1862, and was transferred from the Ninth Kentucky to the Fifth Kentucky Infantry, Hanson's Brigade; was wounded at Chickamauga; captured at Jonesboro, Ga., September 1, 1864; exchanged September 22, 1864; was sent to Kentucky April, 1865, to recruit for the Kentucky Brigade; surrendered and was paroled at New Castle, Ky., May 21, 1865. Afterward married in Helena, Ark., and has since lived in Memphis, and been prominent in connection with local military and State affairs, and commanded the State forces during; the Coal Creek riots and troubles with a coolness and efficiency that gave him great distinction. He now holds (1896) a revenue appointment under President Cleveland, with headquarters in Memphis, but his duties extend over a wide field."; circle grave stone: Col. Keller Anderson Cynthiana, KY born Sept 21, 1842, and Memphis, Tenn Apr 24, 1918.

Anderson, Butler Preston   Buried September 3, 1878   Fowler 468, #3
Referred to as Colonel Butler P. Anderson, whose grave was handsomely decorated and located outside the Confederate grounds, in the May 17, 1881, *Memphis Daily Appeal*, page 2, column 3, article "OUR HEROIC DEAD" reporting on the Memorial Day ceremonies at Elmwood Cemetery on Sunday May 15, 1881; believed to have served in Tennessee 3 (Forrest's) Cavalry Regiment Private Company K, (only one card in record) name appears on a roll of Prisoners of War paroled May 24, 1865, at La Grange, Tennessee with notes that captured at La Grange May 24, 1865, and remarks that left his command at Spring Creek, Tennessee November 1864; as President of Howard Association went to Grenada, Mississippi to aid in yellow fever epidemic of 1878, contracted the disease and died (see Young's *Standard History of Memphis, Tennessee* page 175); yellow fever heroics also mentioned in *Confederate Veterans* magazine, Volume IX, No. 3, March 1901, page 108; grave stone: 1928 - 1878; died age 55 yellow fever per Daily Burial Record Book.

Anderson, George W.   Buried May 12, 1901   Fowler 62/64, #14
Tennessee 3 (Forrest's) Cavalry Regiment Private Company A "Bluff City Grays"; first enlisted in the Tennessee 154 Senior Infantry Regiment Private Company H, per Company Muster-in Roll dated August 13, 1861, at New Madrid, Missouri, enlisted on May 3, 1861, at Memphis age 27; per January 1 to July 1, 1862, Company Muster Roll remarks Detailed in Ordnance Department Columbus, Mississippi; per Tennessee 3 (Forrest's) Cavalry Regiment Company Muster Roll for October 31 to December 31, 1862 enlisted May 4, 1861, at Randolph; also Tennessee 3 (Forrest's) Cavalry Regiment compiled service record includes a card that appears on Roll of Prisoners of War paroled at Gainesville, Alabama May 11, 1865, resident of Memphis, Tennessee but note there is a compiled service record card in Tennessee 154 Senior Infantry Regiment records that appears on a roll of Prisoners of War received at Military Prison, Alton, Illinois, May 25, 1864, captured at Calhoun, Georgia, May 18, 1864, and discharged January 13, 1865, on Oath; (see Notes of Interest - Bluff City Grays); listed (initials "G. W.") in "A COMPLETE ROSTER OF THE BLUFF CITY GREYS" located in the Memphis Room of the Memphis/Shelby County Public Library and Information Center Central Library with notation that died Memphis 1901 but not listed as buried in Elmwood; not listed as member of Bluff City Grays in *Reminiscences of the Civil War* by John Hallum, Tunnah & Pittard printers, 1903; died age 62 years, 2 months and 22 days per Daily Burial Record Book; died interstitial nephritis per Shelby County Register of Death.

Anderson, Isaac M.   Buried November 4, 1872   Fowler 62, #9
Tennessee 3 (Forrest's) Cavalry Regiment Sergeant Company A "Bluff City Grays"; (initials "J. M." in compiled service record); first enlisted (initials "J. M.") in Company G of the 154 Senior Infantry Regiment on June 3, 1861, at Memphis, age 17; per September & October, 1862, Company Muster Roll remarks transferred to Captain Allin's Company Sharp Shooters; per Company Muster Roll dated May 5, 1863, at Shelbyville, Tennessee transferred to Bluff City Grays Edmondson Cavalry; paroled at Gainesville, Alabama, May 11, 1865; listed (initials "I. M.") in June 6, 1878, *Memphis Daily Appeal* article "OUR DEAD HEROES" covering the unveiling of the Confederate monument and decoration of graves of the southern soldiers at Elmwood as then one of twenty-eight members of the Bluff City Grays, Company B of the 154 Senior Infantry Regiment and Company A of Forrest's Old (Third) Cavalry Regiment buried at Elmwood (see Notes of Interest - Bluff City Grays); listed with initials "I. W." as one of the "comrades who sleep at Elmwood cemetery " in the article "Veterans in Council" in *Memphis Daily Appeal*, May 12, 1881, page 4, column 4, concerning the meeting of the surviving members in the city of the old Bluff City Grays to appoint the necessary committees for the purpose of making special decoration on the graves of their dead comrades at Elmwood and Calvary cemeteries on Sunday next, Memorial Day; note there is also a compiled service record found for J. M. Anderson 154 Senior Infantry Regiment Private 1st Company B who enlisted May 14, 1861, at Randolph, Tennessee age 24 and appears to have remain with 154 Senior Infantry Regiment and not transferred to Tennessee 3 (Forrest's) Cavalry Regiment as record contains cards that name appears on roll of non-commissioned officers and privates on extra duty 1863 & 1864 - by order of General Polk wagoner from May 16, 1863 to March 15, 1864 with remarks: 300 days @ 25 cents a day and on a register of Way Hospital, Meridian, Mississippi with complaint of disability and admitted January 29, 1865, but record also contains a copy of monthly pay sheet for I. M. Anderson, Private Bluff City Grays dated 14 February 1863, for the period of November 1, 1862 - January 1, 1863; this should be the J. M. Anderson listed in *Reminiscences of the Civil War* by John Hallum, Tunnah & Pittard, printers, 1903, as member of Bluff City Grays; note additionally that there was a second J. M. Anderson in Tennessee 3 (Forrest's) Cavalry Regiment records

Private Company C/A indicating enlisted March 10, 1862, Memphis by Colonel Forrest – this should be the J. W. Anderson who filed for a Tennessee Confederate Pension September 24, 1901, and indicated on his application that he enlisted in Forrest Regiment in March, 1862, Colonel N. B. Forrest, and was born in Haywood County, Tennessee in 1840, and witness P. A. Taylor stated that joined Company C; listed in Bluff City Grays roster list in Memphis library Memphis Room with initials "I. M"; died consumption age 29 per Daily Burial Record Book.

Anderson, James Patton   Buried September 22, 1872   Fowler 469, #1
Major General; appointed from Florida as Brigadier General February 10, 1862 (rank February 10, 1862) and promoted to Major General February 17, 1864 (rank February 17, 1864) per the *Memorandum relative to the General Officers Appointed by the President in the Armies of the Confederate States - 1861-1865* compiled from Official Records by the Military Secretary's Office, U. S. War Department 1905; December 1860 elected delegate from Jefferson County to a general convention of the State of Florida that passed the ordinance of secession on January 10, 1861; also served as Confederate Congressman (Florida) when as a member of the Florida convention of January 1861,was appointed delegate and attended sessions of the Provisional Congress for about three weeks when resigned April 8, 1861 to accept the colonelcy of the First Florida Infantry (see sketch in Warner's *Confederate Congress* book pages 5-6); elected Colonel 1 Florida Infantry Regiment March 26, 1861 per some records and April 5, 1861 per service record and autobiography; Florida 1 Infantry Regiment record found under Anderson, J. Patton and General and Staff record found under Anderson, Patton; almost killed by bullet in jaw at Chickamauga; listed (Anderson, Gen. J. Patton) in Elmwood 1874 book as Confederate soldier buried in Elmwood who was a citizen of Memphis or vicinity and sketch; died of pneumonia age 50 per Cemetery record; born Winchester, Franklin County, Tennessee February 16, 1822; February 16, 1822 September 20, 1872 on grave stone; biography in *Confederate Military History, Extended Edition*, Volume XVI Florida, page 195; see Mrs. J. P. Anderson (transcriber), "Autobiography of Gen. Patton Anderson, C.S.A.," *Southern Historical Society Papers*, Volume XXIV (1896), pages 57-70, and Anderson's autobiography in the *Biography Directory of the American Congress*; sketch in the PoliticalGraveyard.com; sketch, photograph, if available, and grave stone photograph in *Quiet Places: The Burial Sites of Civil War Generals in Tennessee* by Buckner and Nathaniel C. Hughes, Jr., East Tennessee Historical Society (1992); also listed in chapter on Generals; listed under Generals in "Touring historic Elmwood Cemetery" (Brochure and Map of Historic Gravesites) #2; listed in "Touring Historic Elmwood Cemetery" Brochure (January 2000) #15; sketch #11 in Elmwood *Civil War Tour* booklet (2012).

Anderson, Julius C.   Buried June 25, 1869   Fowler 62, #7
Tennessee 3 (Forrest's) Cavalry Regiment Private Company A "Bluff City Grays"; per Company Muster Roll dated November & December, 1863, enlisted December 1, 1862, in the field and detailed in M. D. Department; name appears on Roll of Prisoners of War paroled at Gainesville, Alabama May 11, 1865, resident of Memphis, Tennessee; listed (initials "J. C.") in June 6, 1878, *Memphis Daily Appeal* article "OUR DEAD HEROES" covering the unveiling of the Confederate monument and decoration of graves of the southern soldiers at Elmwood as then one of twenty-eight members of the Bluff City Grays, Company B of the 154 Senior Infantry Regiment and Company A of Forrest's Old (Third) Cavalry Regiment buried at Elmwood (see Notes of Interest - Bluff City Grays); listed in "A COMPLETE ROSTER OF THE BLUFF CITY GREYS" located in the Memphis Room of the Memphis/Shelby County Public Library and Information Center Central Library (first name "Jule" and enlisted December 1, 1863) with notation that died Memphis and buried in Elmwood; not found in 154 Senior Infantry Regiment compiled service records; not listed as member of Bluff City Grays in *Reminiscences of the Civil War* by John Hallum, Tunnah & Pittard printers, 1903; died age 42 pruperal(?) fever per Daily Burial Record Book.

Anderson, William Lindsley   Buried August 30, 1889   Lenow Circle 63, #2
Mississippi 1 Cavalry Regiment Sergeant Company K ("Pontotoc Dragoons"); per company muster rolls enlisted June 2, 1861, at Union City, Tennessee; per Company Muster Roll for January 1, 1863, to June 30, 1863, remarks wounded March 27, 1863, at Ponchatoula, Louisiana and never returned but present on later muster rolls; paroled May 17, 1865, at Columbus, Mississippi per Roll of Prisoners of War dated May 17, 1865, at Citronelle, Alabama with residence indicated as Pontotoc, Mississippi; died age 50 per Daily Burial Record Book; not listed in Cemetery alpha index.

Andrews, W. N.
Listed in Elmwood 1874 book as Confederate soldier buried in Elmwood who was citizen of Memphis or vicinity; possibly William H. Andrews, age 42, buried October 2, 1873, Chapel Hill 506, #3, no stone; or Dr. William R. Andrews, age 31, buried March 1, 1867, Fowler 76 and removed to Turley 964 April 10, 1889, and possibly served in Tennessee 7 Cavalry Regiment Private Company C, enlisted June 6, 1861, age 26, no stone.

Apperson, John Wesley   Buried April 10,1862   Turley 7, #4
Tennessee 3 (Forrest's) Cavalry Regiment Private 2 Company B; no enlistment in compiled service record; per register of deaths dated December 20, 1862, killed April 7, 1862, at Shiloh from cannon shot in charging a battery; killed Battle of Shiloh per report of casualties reported in April 10, 1862, *Memphis Daily Appeal* for McDonald's Cavalry and April 23, 1862, *Memphis Daily Appeal* for Forrest's Cavalry; funeral notice also in the April 10, 1862, *Memphis Daily Appeal*; per information in sketch on father Edmond Minetry Apperson in *Tennessee, The Volunteer State, 1769-1923*, Volume IV, page 759, born on the 31st of August, 1836, and obtained his more advanced education in the Kentucky Military Institute at Frankfort, in March, 1862 was appointed to General Harris' staff and promised the rank of captain, after which he joined the troops at the battle of Shiloh, Harris was not engaged in the initial fighting and Apperson was sitting on his horse when General Forrest was ordered out, in passing, General Harris said:

"Jack, fall in the last furrow. We need just such a fellow as you along." and in the conflict was struck by a cannon ball that took off both of his legs, General Harris, riding over the ground, called to him and, finding him still alive, had him placed in a tent, where he died the next morning--April 6; grave stone indicates born August 21, 1836, and died April 7, 1862, from wounds received on the 6 at the Battle of Shiloh; Lot 7 is Apperson lot with monument indicating son of E. M. (Edmond Minetry) & S. B. (Susan Brown Morecock) Apperson and died on the battlefield of Shiloh April 7, 1862; listed in Elmwood 1874 book as Confederate soldier buried in Elmwood who was citizen of Memphis or vicinity; mentioned by Dr. S. H. Ford in his address on the occasion to commemorate (Confederate Memorial Day) Confederates buried at Elmwood on April 26, 1866, (see articles "The Confederate Dead" in the *Public Ledger* (Memphis), April 27, 1866, page 3, column 2, and "Honors To The Memory Of The Hero Dead" in the April 27, 1866, *Memphis Daily Appeal*, page 3, column 1).

Armstrong, John W.
Listed in Elmwood 1874 book as Confederate soldier buried in Elmwood who was citizen of Memphis or vicinity; possibly John W. Armstrong, buried December 19, 1867, age 38, pneumonia, Chapel Hill 480.5 Division A #3; John Walton Armstrong died December 17, 1867, aged 38 years 7 months on family monument; died pneumonia per death notice in December 19, 1867, *Memphis Daily Appeal,* page 2, column 5, but no service information in newspaper.

Armstrong, William James   · Buried September 22, 1878   Evergreen 150-151, #2
Assistant Surgeon; per General and Staff record appointed from Tennessee April 4, 1863 at Lauderdale, Mississippi and took oath May 13, 1865 (Wil J. Armstrong on card); per War Department card in widow's (Louisa Charlotte Hanna Armstrong December 2, 1847 - September 20, 1924) Tennessee Confederate Pension file (W5449), record found as Will J. Armstrong, contract surgeon at Oxford, Mississippi May 8 - November 12, 1862 when appointed assistant surgeon C. S. Army, on duty at Enterprise, Mississippi 1863 & 1864, and at Lauderdale, Mississippi in February 1865; further per pension application he was born in Maury County, Tennessee July 24, 1839, enlisted from Medical College, Nashville, Tennessee, served about four years in Mississippi, and married at Columbus, Mississippi (marriage certificate Lowndes, County, Mississippi December 2, 1863); per article "The Life and Letters of Dr. William J. Armstrong" by Marshall Wingfield, *The West Tennessee Historical Society Papers,* IV (1950), pages 97-114, before War studied medicine under Dr. Joseph E. Dixon, which was probably the limit of his medical training, after War returned to Maury County, Tennessee, moved to Memphis in 1873, and died September 20, 1878 from yellow fever; small notice "Dr. W. J. Armstrong died yesterday afternoon." under Local Paragraphs in *Memphis Daily Appeal,* September 21, 1878, page 2; subject of Past Times articles by Perre Magness, *The Commercial* Appeal Memphis, Part 1 "Yellow fever's fearful toll recounted" June 13, 1996, and Part 2 "Doctor succumbs to fever horror" June 20, 1996, Section EM, Neighbors, page 2, which summarizes letters to his wife giving "an account of the terrible yellow fever epidemics that decimated Memphis in the 1870s"; excerpts of 1878 letters also published in article "The Epidemic As Seen Through the Eyes of an Attending Physician" in *ANSEARCHIN' NEWS*, Summer 1998, pages 11- 13; originally buried Fowler Lot 263, Howard Association Section, and moved March 9, 1896; grave stone: July 24, 1839 September 20, 1878; died age 39 per Daily Burial Record Book.

Arnold, Herman Frank   Buried April 12, 1927   Miller 14, #3
Orchestrated "Dixie" and it was played for the first time at the inauguration of Jefferson Davis, President of the Confederacy, Montgomery, Alabama, February 18, 1861; the original score of "Dixie" is inscribed on his grave stone; born October 6, 1837, Eilenburg, Prussia, Germany, and came to the United States in 1854; died April 10, 1927, Memphis, Tennessee; wife, Victoria Luciani Arnold (November 26, 1840 November 2, 1928); originally buried Chapel Hill 578½; article in the Spring 1990 *Elmwood Journal*; sketch 37 in Elmwood *Civil War Tour* booklet (2012).

Atkinson, Martin Van Buren   Buried May 28, 1910   Chapel Hill 915, #1
Tennessee 8 Infantry Regiment Private Company H (Atkisson, M. V.); per Company Muster Roll dated January 10, 1864, enlisted May 17, 1861, at Nashville, Tennessee age 20; paroled May 1, 1865, at Greensboro, North Carolina as Private Company D, 1st Consolidated Tennessee Infantry (Adkisson, M. V.); widow, Ellen Olivia Atkinson, filed for Tennessee Confederate Pension (W4199) October 4, 1911, name "Atkisson, Martin Vanburen"; date of birth in Pension file March 26, 1843, Jamestown, Fentress County, Tennessee; married E. O. Argo in Warren County, Tennessee May 9, 1870; died age 66 per Daily Burial Record Book; per May 28, 1910 *The Commercial Appeal* Memphis died May 27, 1910, age 67; originally buried Confederate Rest and moved November 19, 1911.

Avent, Dr. Benjamin Ward   Buried September 12, 1878   South Grove 149, #5
Surgeon; per General & Staff compiles service records rolls appointed from Tennessee July 19, 1861, from Murfreesboro, Tennessee and paroled in 1865; per obituary in the April 13, 1878, *Memphis Daily Appeal,* page 1, column 1, on medical staff of C.S.A. and died September 12, 1878, age 66; per Shelby County Funeral book from Alabama and died of yellow fever; circular stone around grave; died age 66 per Daily Burial Record Book.

Avery, William Thomas (Tecumseh)   Buried May 23, 1880   Chapel Hill 39, #1
Confederate 4 (Baker's) Infantry Regiment Lieutenant Colonel (originally indexed as Tennessee 39 (Avery's) Infantry Regiment Lieutenant Colonel – see *Tennesseans in the Civil War, Part 1*, pages 258-259); regiment (also known as 1st Alabama, Tennessee and Mississippi Infantry) was formed about December 9, 1861, with ten companies: four from Alabama, two from Mississippi, and four from Tennessee; captured at Island 10 April 8, 1862, and after exchange in September, 1862, the companies were reorganized

and transferred to other commands; companies A, G, H, and K became (2d) Companies I, A, C and D, respectively, of the Tennessee 42th Infantry Regiment; per Confederate 4 Infantry Regiment compiled service record captured April 7, 1862, at Island 10 and sent to Johnson's Island; per sketch in Mathes book originally Lieutenant Colonel 1 Regiment Alabama, Tennessee & Mississippi Infantry (subsequently Confederate 4 Infantry Regiment), afterward Superintendent of Post Office Department in Trans-Mississippi Department, proposed for Confederate Historical Association membership by Isham G. Harris and R. Dudley Frayser and elected March 20, 1870; served as U.S. Congress 1857-1861; born in Hardeman County, Tennessee November 16, 1819; drowned in Ten Mile Bayou, Crittenden County, Arkansas May 22, 1880; see *Biographical Directory of the Tennessee General Assembly*, Volume I, 1796-1861, page 22, Tennessee State Library and Archives, Nashville, 1975; per sketch in the PoliticalGraveyard.com accidentally drowned in Ten Mile Bayou, Arkansas May 22, 1880; drowned age 60 per Daily Burial Record Book; large family stone: born November 11, 1819 and died May 22, 1880; small grave stone: WM Thomas Avery 1819-1880; listed in "Touring historic Elmwood Cemetery" (Brochure and Map of Historic Gravesites) #59 and its successor "Touring Historic Elmwood Cemetery" Brochure (January 2000) #66 but not included in Elmwood *Civil War Tour* booklet (2012).

Bailey, Thomas F.   Buried July 24, 1907   Turley 24, 1907
Tennessee 3 (Forrest's Old) Cavalry Regiment Private 2 Company A and Tennessee 154 Senior Infantry Regiment Private 1 Company B "Bluff City Grays"; per Tennessee 154 Senior Infantry Regiment Company Muster-in Roll dated August 13,1861, enlisted May 25, 1861, Randolph age 20; per Tennessee 3 (Forrest's) Cavalry Regiment Company Muster Roll for January 1 to July 1, 1862, enlisted May 4, 1861, Randolph; name appears on Roll of Prisoners of War paroled at Gainesville, Alabama May 11, 1865, resident of Memphis, Tennessee; per sketch in Mathes book (page 36) joined Confederate Historical Association October 9, 1884; listed in "A COMPLETE ROSTER OF THE BLUFF CITY GREYS" located in the Memphis Room of the Memphis/Shelby County Public Library and Information Center Central Library; listed as member of Bluff City Grays in *Reminiscences of the Civil War* by John Hallum, Tunnah & Pittard printers, 1903; listed with indication "Died" in "Captain Thomas F. Pattison's History of the Bluff City Grays" with names as appeared on First Muster Roll and those who joined after September 1, 1861, to surrender, 1865, which document found in the Tennessee Confederate Pension Application (W10343) of Minnie Swayne Wilkins, widow of William G. Wilkins (see sketch infra); see also Notes of Interest - Bluff City Grays; died age 64 per Daily Burial Record Book.

Balch, Robert Monroe   Buried April 8, 1872   Fowler 606
Tennessee 3 (Forrest's) Cavalry Regiment Major F&S and Private C; per Company Muster-in Roll dated October 16,1861, enlisted September 1, 1861, Memphis age 28; per Company Muster Roll for March 1 to June 30, 1862, remarks elected major April 1, 1862; appears on a Register of Commissioned Officers as Lieutenant Colonel; Oath of Allegiance sworn to at Memphis from march 1 to 15, 1865 with residence indicated as Memphis and age 35; per article under "Local Paragraphs" in the April 7, 1872, M*emphis Daily Appeal*, page 4, column 2, he was shot in Crittenden county by the Sheriff when he refused to retire when being served a writ to remove him from possession of some land; per sketch in Mathes book (page 234) "BALCH, ROBERT LANGDON, born in Virginia; he was a son of Rev. Thomas Bloomer Balch, who married a first cousin of General Robert E. Lee, and was a grandson of Rev. Stephen Bloomer Balch of Georgetown, D. C, who was a captain in the Revolutionary war in Georgia, though a native of Maryland. R. L. Balch lived in Memphis before the war, and was a man of means; enlisted as a private in Forrest's old regiment; was elected major just before the battle of Shiloh, and served until September 1862, when Lieutenant-Colonel D. C. Kelley resigned and was succeeded by Major Balch. Major Rambaut, of General Forrest's staff, just before he died, spoke of Colonel Balch in the highest terms as a soldier and gentleman. In 1863 he was wounded in Middle Tennessee, lost health and spirits, was granted a leave of absence indefinitely, and dropped out of the service, as far as activity was concerned. After the war he was assassinated on his plantation, a few miles west of Memphis, in Crittenden county. Ark., when he was perhaps little over 40 years old. He never married."; "Gun shot Wound" noted in Daily Burial Record Book.

Ball, John H.   Buried February 25, 1866   Turley 121, #3
Tennessee 154 Senior Infantry Regiment Private Company E; enlisted May 14, 1861, Randolph, Tennessee age 30; reported present on January and February 1864, muster roll; last card in compiled service record on receipt roll for clothing dated March 1864; killed age 32 per Daily Burial Record Book; listed in Elmwood 1874 book as Confederate soldier buried in Elmwood who was citizen of Memphis or vicinity; per sheet in Elmwood Office files killed at Franklin, Tennessee November 1864, not found Lindsley's Annals; disinterred from the battlefield at an unknown date and reburied in Elmwood.

Bankhead, Smith Pyne   Buried April 1, 1867   Chapel Hill 67, #2
Trans-Mississippi Department Artillery Colonel; originally enlisted as Captain Tennessee Light Artillery Bankhead's/Scott's Company May 13, 1861, in Memphis at age 37; record also found Tennessee Artillery Corps (McCown's) Captain Company 6 with commission dated May 17, 1861; served as Colonel of Texas Cavalry Mann's Regiment which records has only one card that indicates name appears on a Return of Captain Peel's and Captain Bond's Detachment, Mann's Regiment, Texas Cavalry at Headquarters of Bankhead's Brigade dated June 21, 1864; per sketch in *More Generals in Gray* born August 28, 1823, at Fort Moultrie near Charleston, South Carolina, served in Mexican War, served as Captain of Artillery at Columbus, Kentucky, New Madrid and Fort Pillow, promoted Major of Artillery April 1, 1862, at Battle of Shiloh Chief of Artillery of Polk's Corps, after Shiloh served in Trans-Mississippi Department, promoted to Colonel November 13, 1862, Spring 1863 commanded San Antonio, Texas Post, assigned to command the Northern Sub-District of Texas as Acting Brigadier General on May 30, 1863, and after assignment rank reverted to Colonel which rank was not confirmed until January 14, 1865, to rank from June 15, 1864; not listed in the *Memorandum relative to the General Officers Appointed by the President in the Armies of the Confederate States - 1861-*

1865 compiled from Official Records by the Military Secretary's Office, U. S. War Department 1905; not listed in *Generals in Gray*; not listed in Elmwood 1874 book as Confederate soldier buried in Elmwood who was a citizen of Memphis or vicinity but sketch; called Acting Brigadier General in Official Record and General in Lindsley's Annals; murdered on Main Street March 30, 1867; died age 43 from effects of a blow on head per Daily Burial Record Book; grave stone: born Fort Moultrie, South Carolina August 28, 1823, and died March 31, 1867; also listed in chapter on Generals; listed under Generals in "Touring historic Elmwood Cemetery" (Brochure and Map of Historic Gravesites) #3; listed in "Touring Historic Elmwood Cemetery" Brochure (January 2000) #71; sketch #24 in Elmwood *Civil War Tour* booklet (2012).

Barbour, James G.   Buried December 8, 1891   Chapel Hill 481, #6
Tennessee 3 (Forrest's) Cavalry Regiment Captain Company B; enlisted March 10, 1862, Memphis; promoted to Captain June 15, 1863; single card found Tennessee 11 (Holman's) Cavalry Regiment indicating 1 Lieutenant Company A; per sketch in Mathes book Captain in McDonald's Battalion, entered service April 1861, remained four years, merchant after war, admitted to Confederate Historical Association upon own application July 15, 1870, removed to Mississippi and died in Yazoo City; service information on grave stone; Major per Daily Burial Record Book.

Barksdale, Robert E.   Buried April 15, 1862   Chapel Hill 606, #2
Arkansas 15 (Josey's) Infantry Regiment Private Company C; enlisted July 23, 1861, Pitman's ("Pitmans" historic) Ferry, Arkansas; per February 28 to June 30, 1862, muster roll remarks: died April 13, 1862, from wounds received at Battle of Shiloh; per *Memphis Daily Appeal* wounded Battle of Shiloh; died from effect of amputation per Daily Burial Record Book; born Rutherford County, Tennessee January 31, 1837; citizen of Helena, Arkansas; attorney; graduate of University of Mississippi; obituary in the April 19, 1862, *Memphis Daily Appeal*; name appears on copy of a roll dated July 23, 1861, of officers and privates of Company F (actually Company C "Yell Rifles") indicating enlisted April 27, 1861.

Barton, David H.   Buried May 8, 1862   Chapel Hill 659, #74
Tennessee 3 (Forrest's) Cavalry Regiment Private Company C; enlisted March 10, 1862, Memphis; per March to June 1862, muster roll remarks: died at Memphis May 6, 1862; funeral notice of Dr. D. H. Barton in the May 8, 1862, *Memphis Daily Appeal*; per Lindsley's Annals died at Memphis, Tennessee May 6, 1862; typhoid fever per Daily Burial Record Book; government grave stone: 1834 May 7, 1862.

Bateman, Morgan Magness   Buried April 24, 1870   Turley 213, #10
Arkansas 1 (Dobbin's) Cavalry Regiment Captain Company E; per Muster Roll for January & February 1864, enlisted October 1, 1862, Jacksonport; appears on a Muster and Descriptive Roll of prisoners of war paroled at Jacksonport, Arkansas, June 5, 1865, that indicates enlisted at Jacksonport, Arkansas and was born in Tennessee; death reported under Obituaries in the "River News" section of the April 24, 1870, *Memphis Daily Appeal*, page 1, column 3, which states "was a pioneer Boatman" and "(A)t the breaking out of the war he raised a company of cavalry at Jacksonport, Arkansas, and led them gallantly in many hard battles fought in the Trans-Mississippi Department."; died age 43 pneumonia per Daily Burial Record Book.

Bayliss, William H.   Buried July 13, 1861   Chapel Hill 175, #3
Tennessee 7 Cavalry Regiment Private (White's) Company (Logwood's 6 Cavalry Battalion); per Company Muster-in Roll dated August 20, 1861, enlisted June 11, 1861, Memphis with remarks: killed July 22 by fall from horse; died prior to Tennessee 7 Cavalry Regiment formal organization on April 1, 1862; listed (Balis, Wm) in the Letter to the Editor, *Memphis Daily Appeal*, April 1, 1887, page 9, column 2, that list the original members of the Tennessee Mounted Rifles; listed in Elmwood 1874 book as Confederate soldier buried in Elmwood who was citizen of Memphis or vicinity; per family monument member Company B 7 Tennessee Cavalry died July 12, 1861, in 21 year of age; not found in Lindsley's Annuals.

Beard, William Dwight   Buried December 9, 1910   Miller 3, #1
Quartermaster (QM), Major, Stewart's Corps Army of Tennessee; per General and Staff records Major QM Department, originally appointed to QM Department in April 1862, and gave Oath of Allegiance June 20, 1865, at Galveston, Texas; single record card also found Missouri miscellaneous rolls indicating Major of Cavalry and cards filed with General and Staff Officers; listed as Major, QM, on staff of General A. P. Stewart in Confederate Staff Officers 1861 -1865 by Joseph H. Crute, Jr., Derwent Books 1982, page 185; large monument: "In memoriam William Dwight Beard born October 25, 1835, departed this life December 7, 1910, an honored citizen, a brave Confederate soldier, an eminent jurist served sixteen years upon the supreme bench, one term as chief justice, beloved and revered by Tennessee"; per sketch in Mathes book born in Wilson County, Tennessee, joined Confederate army in May 1862, and assigned to staff of General A. P. Stewart as Brigade QM, later served with Bragg, transferred to Trans-Mississippi summer 1863, with General Price's command in Missouri in 1864, wounded at Battle of Westport, and paroled at Galveston, Texas June 1865; article in Friday December 9, 1911, *The Commercial* Appeal Memphis indicating Justice William Dwight Beard died suddenly in apartment in the Hotel Hermitage (Nashville) Wednesday Morning at 9 o'clock, born October 25, 1835, and once during War learned that wife was in St. Louis and put on citizen clothes and passed through lines, while there received a note from Colonel Crittenden, local Union commander, who he knew and had seen him, telling him that Federals were aware that he was there and to get out quickly which he did; sketch in Goodspeed's Shelby County History, page 925; "Judge and died age 75 per Daily Burial Record Book; death reported "The Last Roll" section *Confederate Veteran,* Volume XIX, April 1911, page 174 that indicates at time of death was Chief Justice of the Supreme Court of the State of Tennessee.

Beasley, James Edward Buried May 26, 1925 Fowler 606

Captain Aide de Camp staff of Brigadier General Otho F. Strahl; Tennessee 4 Infantry Regiment Private/Sergeant Major Company A ("Shelby Greys"); per Company Muster-in Roll dated August 16, 1861, enlisted May 15, 1861, Germantown age 22; per Muster Roll of Officers and men paroled at Greensboro, North Carolina May 1, 1865, rank given as Sergeant major; per sketch in Mathes book (page 36) "was born in the town of Plymouth, N. C, August 31, 1839; graduated at the University of North Carolina (Chapel Hill) June 2, 1859, and came to Memphis immediately afterward. Became a member of the Shelby Grays, a company organized in this city in February, 1861. This company became Company A of the Fourth Tennessee Infantry, was mustered into service by General W. H. Carroll of Germantown, on the 15th day of May, 1861. Served the last two years of the war in different positions at the Brigade Headquarters of Brigadier-General O. F. Strahl; was with General Strahl when he was killed, November 30, 1864, in the trenches at Franklin, Tenn.; was surrendered with General Johnston's army and paroled at Greensboro, N. C, April 26, 1865, and returned to Memphis to live, reaching here June 21, 1865. He was one of the original and most active members of the Association."; biography in *Confederate Military History, Extended Edition*, Volume X Tennessee, page 373; article in *Confederate Veteran* Volume XXXIII, September 1925, page 348; per *Confederate Staff Officers 1861-1865* by Joseph H. Crute, Jr. (Derwent Books 1982) Captain Aide de Camp, 1863, on the staff of Brigadier General Otho F. Strahl; prepared the list of members and history of the company reported in the May 15, 1909, *The Commercial Appeal* Memphis article "Forty=Eight Years Ago Today, The Shelby Greys Entered the Confederate Service—Record of a Famous Memphis Military Company."

Beaumont, G. T.

Listed in Elmwood 1874 book as Confederate soldier buried in Elmwood who was citizen of Memphis or vicinity; no Cemetery record found; possibly G. T. Beaumont, Tennessee 3 (Forrest's) Cavalry Private Company A, who is listed in Bluff City Grays roster list in Memphis and Shelby County Library Memphis Room; only card in compiled service record is name appears on roll of prisoners of war paroled at Gainesville, Alabama May 9, 1865; single miscellaneous compiled service record card found for G. T. Beaumont, Private, who appears on a tabular Statement of the Staff of Maj. Gen. N. B. Forrest, made in response to an order from his Headquarters at Tupelo, Miss., dated March 7, 1864, which form indicated was in Cavalry, serving as a clerk and order issued by Gen. Kirby Smith with remarks that was detailed by Gen, Kirby Smith at Richmond, KY; not found Tennessee 154 Senior Infantry Regiment rolls; not listed in *Reminiscences of the Civil War* by John Hallum, Tunnah & Pittard, printers, 1903, as member of Bluff City Grays; not listed in June 6, 1878, *Memphis Daily Appeal* article "OUR DEAD HEROES" covering the unveiling of the Confederate Monument and Decoration of Graves at Elmwood as then one of twenty-eight members of the Bluff City Grays, Company B of the 154 Senior Infantry Regiment and Company A of Forrest's Old (Third) Cavalry Regiment, buried at Elmwood (see Notes of Interest - Bluff City Grays); if Godfrey Thulus Beaumont, spouse, Imogene Beaumont, buried January 9, 1926, in Chapel Hill Lot 595,608.

Bedford, Hugh Lawson Buried December 24, 1915 Chapel Hill 360, #6

Confederate General Staff and Officer, Lieutenant Artillery and Ordnance Officer; identified as 1st Lieutenant Artillery Tennessee regiment when prisoner at Camp Chase March 1, 1862, after capture at Fort Donelson February 16, 1862, and paroled to Columbus, Ohio April 22, 1862; signed a parole of honor pledge at Camp Chase April 22, 1862; appears on roll of prisoners of war at Johnson's Island, Sandusky, Ohio September 1, 1861; per second card in record sent to Vicksburgh (sic) September 1, 1862; appears on a register of appointments 2 Lieutenant Artillery Tennessee, CSA, to report to Colonel J Gorgas, Artillery Officer, appointment October 6, 1863, confirmation June 10, 1864, and to rank May 2, 1863; signed parole of honor at Jackson, Mississippi May 14, 1865, after surrender; per sketch in Goodspeed's Shelby County History, page 927, born in Fayette County, Tennessee, June 11, 1836, raised on a plantation in Mississippi, had the finest education, graduated from the University of Mississippi, the Kentucky Military Institute and from the law department of the Cumberland University at Lebanon and practiced law three years in Memphis before the war; member of the Confederate Historical Association, Camp 28, Bivouac 18, United Confederate Veterans of Tennessee; per sketch in Mathes book was early member of the Confederate Historical Association, married Miss Louisa Mclean at Grenada, MS, May 23, 1867, who served as a President of the Ladies' Confederate Memorial Association of Memphis, which was organized as an auxiliary society of the Confederate Historical Association in 1889; large Monument stone with both names; Bedford engraved on lot stone, which lot per Cemetery List of Proprietors was purchased by his father, B. W. Bedford, Sr.; per Death Certificate died December 22, 1915 from Tuberculosis; listed "Col. H L Bedford" in Daily Burial Record Book and died age 72.

Beecher, Edward A. Buried January 21, 1873 Turley 326, #2

Quartermaster (QM), Major, Polk's Corps Army of Tennessee; per *Confederate Staff Officers 1861-1865* by Joseph H. Crute, Jr., Derwent Books 1982, appointed QM, Major, October 21, 1862, on the staff of Brigadier General Preston Smith (page 181), January 1, 1863, on the staff of Colonel Alfred J Vaughan, Jr. (page 199), and September 29, 1864, on the staff of General John B. Hood (page 90); listed in Elmwood 1874 book as Confederate soldier buried in Elmwood who was citizen of Memphis or vicinity with rank of Major; per sketch in Mathes book born state of New York 1834, came to Memphis about 1856, enlisted in McDonald's Dragoons (Tennessee 3 Forrest's Cavalry Regiment Company K and Tennessee 11 Holman's Cavalry Regiment Company A but no records found) in 1861, 1862 joined General Polk's staff as QM, joined the Confederate Historical Association September 9, 1869, and died of pneumonia 1873; sketch in Elmwood Cemetery 1874 book; per grave stone died January 19, 1873, aged 39 years; died pneumonia age 39 per Daily Burial Record Book.

Bell, Dr. William S.   Buried March 15, 1862   Turley Wheatley's Vault

Confederate States Army Surgeon & Medical Director; May 23, 1861, Surgeon, McCown's Corps of Artillery (Tennessee) joined for duty at this date. Appointed by Governor Isham G. Harris and confirmed by the Senate August 14, 1861. Station, New Madrid, Missouri; August 20, 1861. Surgeon, Medical Director, Pillow's Division; September 21, 1861. Surgeon, Medical Director, Pillow's Division; October 31, 1861. Surgeon, Medical Director, at Columbus Kentucky; November 7 1861. On duty at Battle of Belmont, Missouri; February 10 1862. Surgeon Bell writes to Major General Polk, stating that he has received no appointment in the Confederate. Service. On same date Major General Polk, commanding 1st Division Western Department, at Columbus, Kentucky, forwards this letter to Secretary of War (Benjamin) asking that the appointment be made - - to date from August 9, 1861, as Surgeon Bell has been employed in Confederate Service since that date; February 17, 1862. Appointed Surgeon, from Tennessee, to take rank August 9, 1861, to report to Surgeon General; March 12, 1862. Appointed Medical Director, 1st Grand Division, Army of the Mississippi (Polk); March 13, 1862. Killed at New Madrid, Missouri; death reported in the March 16, 1862, *Memphis Daily Appeal*, page 1, column 2, in the article "Latest from New Madrid": "Among the killed on our side was Dr. Bell, the medical director of the division, and well-known in Memphis. He was standing in the cabin of the Mohawk between Gen. McCown and the captain of the boat. The shot passed between the general's legs, cutting off both legs of Dr. Bell above the ankle and going out between the feet of the captain. Amputation being necessary, was performed by Dr. Gus Thornton; but the shock was too great, and Dr. Bell died at 5 a. m. on Friday evening. His loss is deeply lamented by the whole army, by whom he was so much loved, and who held him in the highest estimation. His body has been brought to this city."

Bill, Nelson A.   Buried March 4, 1912   Fowler 270, #13

Mississippi Captain John J. Gage's Company (Wigfall Guard) Private; per undated Company Muster Roll enlisted May 2, 1861, at Grenada; per notation on single card in record some of the members of this company subsequently served in Company H, 25th Regiment Mississippi Infantry; per Mississippi Civil War Regiments, Rosters and Muster Rolls "Captain John J. Gage's Company, the Wigfall Guards, mustered into State service May 2, 1861, and was probably not accepted for Confederate service. Some of the members of this Company subsequently served in Company H, 25th Mississippi Infantry (changed to the 2nd Regiment Confederate Infantry) which on May 8, 1862, became Company D, 1st Battalion, Mississippi Sharpshooters."; no service record found in any of these units; per City of Memphis Burial Permit died March 2, 1912, age 68 years, 5 months.

Black, H. M.   Buried May 13, 1862   Chapel Hill 252, #3

Tennessee 24 Infantry Regiment Private Company C; enlisted August 24, 1861, Camp Trousdale age 33; per December 13, 1861, to April 30, 1862, muster roll remarks: wounded Battle of Shiloh; per February to June 1862, muster roll remarks: died at Memphis, Tennessee day not known; per Overton Hospital record admitted April 16, 1862, with complaint of left knee and died May 12, 1862; *Tennesseans in Civil War, Part 2*, unit indicated as 13 Infantry but found only 24 Infantry; Grave #2 in Cemetery Daily Burial Record and Alpha books and computer index but Grave #3 in Chapel Hill book; possibly "H. W. Black" listed in Elmwood 1874 book as Confederate soldier buried in Elmwood who was citizen of Memphis or Vicinity.

Black, Robert J.   Buried November 8, 1910   Chapel Hill 709, #4

Tennessee 7 Cavalry Regiment Brevet 2 Lieutenant Company B; enlisted May 31,1861, Mason Depot, Tennessee, age 26; Private and elected 1 Lieutenant November 23, 1863; signed Parole of Honor May 11, 1865, at Gainesville, Alabama; per sketch in Mathes book, page 38, enlisted May 31, 1861, wounded three times, after War located in Memphis, Secretary of Confederate Historical Association and moved to St. Louis but will probably return to Memphis; sketch in Goodspeed's 1887 Biographical Sketches, Shelby County, page 930; died age 78 per Daily Burial Record Book; service sketch in *Confederate Veteran*, Volume VI, September 1898, page 435 that indicates born in Fayette County, Tennessee in 1841 and was Major, A. D. C. on staff of General A. J. Vaughan, commanding Tennessee Division, United Confederate Veterans; death reported in *Confederate Veteran*, Volume XIX, April 1911, page 174, "The Last Roll, Death of Confederates in Memphis, Tennessee" who died during 1910 and were members of the Confederate Historical Association, Camp 28, U.C.V., Bivouac 18, C.V., of Memphis, Tennessee; grave stone: R. J. Black, 2 LIEUT., 7 TENN. CAV. C.S.A., November 7, 1910.

Blount, Dr. Benjamin F.   Buried October 26, 1873   Turley 612 (Masonic Lot), #48

Alabama 17 Infantry Regiment Assistant Surgeon; per Roster Register dated April 14, 1864, appointed September 5, 1861; per October 27, 1873, Monday Evening *Public Ledger*, page 1, column 2, "The name of Dr. B. F. Blount is added to the list of noble physicians who have fallen victims to the destroyer in the mist of their usefulness and while striving successfully to save others. Dr. Blount died yesterday, after an illness of about ten days"; "Dr. Blunt" in Daily Burial Record Book and "Blunt" in computer index.

Borum, Joseph Beverly   Buried July 8, 1876   Chapel Hill 129, #10

Arkansas 38 Infantry (Shaver's) Regiment Captain, Company B inscribed on grave stone but no company nor enlistment in compiled service record, per Roll of Prisoners of War at Camp Douglas, Chicago, Illinois, received November 13, 1863, from Military Prison Columbus, Kentucky, captured in Arkansas October 19, 1863, and remark Guerilla, on a Roll of Prisoners of War paroled at Johnson's Island, Ohio and transferred to New Orleans, Louisiana for exchange January 9, 1865, on a Roll of rebel prisoners of war received from Johnson's Island, Ohio and exchanged at Red River Landing, Louisiana February 26, 1865, signed Parole of Honor June 8, 1865, at Shreveport, Louisiana and indicated residence as Mississippi County, Arkansas; per Obituary in the July 16, 1876, *Memphis Daily Appeal*, page 1, column 7, died at his residence in Mississippi County, Arkansas on Friday, July

7, 1867, born in Virginia in 1828, moved to Henderson, Kentucky at an early age and then to Mississippi County, Arkansas; died age 47 congestion of bowles (sic) per Daily Burial Record Book; grave stone: 1830 1876.

Bourne, Edward   Buried February 23, 1925   Chapel Hill 351
Confederate 3 Infantry Regiment Private Company B ("Young Guard" - see history in Lindsley's Annals, page 599, submitted by Edward Bourne); per sketch in Mathes book "was born June 23, 1846, in Memphis: and "drilled with the Young Guards under Captain John F. Cameron. Owing to his youth and delicate physique he was not accepted as a soldier for some time; was finally sworn into the same company when his brother Wm. F. Bourne became its captain in the latter part of 1863, when the army was in winter quarters at Dalton. This company (B) was then a part of the Third Confederate Regiment, and afterward, near the end, was consolidated with the First Arkansas Regiment. Private Bourne was in most of the fighting from Dalton to Atlanta, where his brother, Captain Bourne, was killed on the 22d of July, 1864, and Comrade Bourne buried him with the assistance of Sergeant Pixley on the battlefield."; April, 1865, regiment consolidated with other regiments to form Arkansas 1st Consolidated Infantry Regiment and surrendered and paroled with that designation in April, 1865, at Greensboro, North Carolina; after the War came home to Memphis and went into business and "served two years as President of Memphis Board of Underwriters, and was also President of the Memphis Salvage Corps.... In his time he has belonged to several local military companies and held offices. In the Inter-State drill given in Memphis in May, 1895, he was a member of the Military Committee."; per Death Certificate died February 21, 1925, at age 79 from Bright's Disease, occupation Insurance; circle grave stone: 1846-1925.

Boyle, Virginia Frazer   Buried December 14, 1938   Fowler 727,747, #5
"Poet Laureate of the Confederacy" per legend that Jefferson Davis gave her that designation on a visit with him in 1873; per article "Mrs. Boyle and Her Tribute to Forrest" in the *Confederate Veteran* Volume IX, June 1901, No. 6, wrote the poem "The Wizard of the Saddle" as tribute to General Forrest and the poem was read when the cornerstone of the monument of General Nathan Bedford Forrest in Forrest Park, Memphis, Tennessee, was laid during the May, 1901, UCV Reunion in Memphis; wrote the inscription on the base of the Forrest monument and the inscription on the monument of General Pat Cleburne at Helena, Arkansas; daughter of Charles Wesley Frazer, Confederate 5 Infantry Regiment Captain Company B and Major and Assistant Adjutant General (see his sketch infra); February 14, 1863 December 13, 1938 inscribed on grave stone; sketch #10 in Elmwood *Civil War Tour* booklet (2012).

Bradley, Thomas H.   Buried October 3, 1864   Chapel Hill 305, #1
Brigadier General Arkansas State Forces; per sketch in *More Generals in Gray* was named brigadier general of Arkansas state forces by the secession convention, Arkansas Military Board relieved him of duty in July 1861, took no further part in the War, and relocated to Memphis where died on September 30, 1864; not listed in the *Memorandum relative to the General Officers Appointed by the President in the Armies of the Confederate States - 1861-1865* compiled from Official Records by the Military Secretary's Office, U. S. War Department 1905; not listed in *Generals in Gray*; not found Confederate index books and no records found in General and Staff records; not listed in Elmwood 1874 book as Confederate soldier buried in Elmwood who was a citizen of Memphis or vicinity but sketch that indicates born Williamson County, Tennessee July 25, 1808, in 1842 became a citizen of Crittenden County, Arkansas, made a Brigadier General of the Confederacy but age and physical infirmities prevented very active service, and died September 1864; died age 62 per Daily Burial Record Book; sketch, photograph, if available, and grave stone photograph in book *Quiet Places: The Burial Sites of Civil War Generals in Tennessee* by Buckner and Nathaniel C. Hughes, Jr., East Tennessee Historical Society (1992); also listed in chapter on Generals; not listed in "Touring Historic Elmwood Cemetery" Brochure (January 2000) but listed as General in its predecessor "Touring historic Elmwood Cemetery" (Brochure and Map of Historic Gravesites) #3B; sketch #26 in Elmwood *Civil War Tour* booklet (2012).

Brady, James H.   Buried March 8,1862   Chapel Hill 214, #1
Louisiana 1 Cavalry Regiment Private Company C; enlisted September 12, 1861, Baton Rouge, Louisiana; per Overton Hospital Register admitted February 23, 1862; died State Hospital per Daily Burial Record Book.

Brett, James, Sr.   Buried October 27, 1917   Lenow Circle 29, #9
Tennessee 154 Senior Infantry Regiment Corporal/Private Company G (record found "Brett, James Jr."); per Company Muster-in Roll dated August 13, 1861, enlisted June 3, 1861, Memphis, age 23; February 13, 1862, Inspectors Report shows him as Volunteer Aide de camp to General W. H. Carroll and Absent under orders; per Company Muster Roll dated May 5, 1863, Deserted March 20, 1863, in Memphis, Tennessee; per Tennessee Death and Burial Index born 23 November 1838 in South Carolina, died 26 October 1917 in Memphis, Shelby, Tennessee, age 78, widowed, lawyer and residence Germantown, Tennessee and buried 27 October 1917 Elmwood Cemetery; per 1860 Census living in Monroe County, Tennessee age 22 and lawyer.

Bridges, William H.   Buried December 17, 1873   Chapel Hill Circle 58½, #3
Tennessee 3 (Memphis Battalion) Infantry Battalion Sergeant (Captain E. C. Kirk) Company E; per Company Muster Roll for March 12 to May 1, 1862, enlisted March 12, 1862; see Notes of Interest "Memphis Battalion - Tennessee 3 (Memphis Battalion) Infantry Battalion"; death announcement (column 1) and death notice (column 4) in the December 17, 1873, *Memphis Daily Appeal*, page 1; cause of death inflammation of stomach age 42 per Daily Burial Record Book.

Brooks, Albert J.   Buried May 10, 1862   Chapel Hill 180, #4
Arkansas 5 Battery Light Artillery (Appeal Battery) compiled service record found under "J. Brooks"; enlisted March 30, 1862, Memphis; per July and August 1862, muster roll remarks: killed by "r road" (railroad) May 8 (accidentally); Appeal Battery and killed by cars per Daily Burial Record Book.

Brown, Alfred H.   Buried December 31, 1914   Fowler 526, #2
Tennessee 13 Infantry Regiment Private Company B (Macon Grays); enlisted Corinth, Mississippi no date indicated per March 1 to July 1, 1862, Company Muster Roll and enlisted May 8, 1862, at Memphis per August 31 to December 31, 1862, Company Muster Roll; per September & October 1863, Company Muster Roll absent on furlough wounded at Chickamauga; per November & December 1863, Company Muster Roll furlough expired November 13, 1863; no other information in Tennessee 13 Infantry Regiment rolls; per Tennessee pension file #S9813 born Fayette County, Tennessee November 25, 1841, enlisted Corinth, Mississippi about 2 weeks after Shiloh and surrendered at Wittsburg, Arkansas about May 1, 1865, with General Dobbin's Cavalry Brigade; per letters in pension file lived in eastern Arkansas with mother when War started and when furloughed for wound went home and after wound healed joined General Dobbin's command because may not have been possible to rejoin command; per Arkansas 1 (Dobbin's) Cavalry compiled service record Private Company C, enlisted Augusta, Arkansas (no date indicated) age 23 and born Fayette County, Tennessee and appears on a muster and description roll when surrendered May 25, 1865, at Wittsburg, Arkansas; biography in *Confederate Military History, Extended Edition*, Volume X Tennessee, page 383; name "Alfred" inscribed on large grave stone and Born November 25, 1841, Reared at Macon, Tennessee, Member Macon Gray's Company B, husband of Sallie S. Hare, and died December 30, 1914; first name spelled "Alford" on death certificate and in Daily Burial Record Book and computer index; died age 73 per Daily Burial Record Book.

Brown, Joseph John   Buried September 28, 1918   Turley 1343, # 2
Tennessee Captain Phillips' Company Light Artillery (also known as Capt. Eldridge's, Capt. Wright's and Capt. Mebane's Co., L. Art'y) Sergeant; per Company Muster Roll for December 31 to April 30, 1862, enlisted October 15, 1861, at Jackson, Tennessee; appears on a Report of Prisoners of War surrendered May 27, 1865, at La Grange, Tennessee with remarks that left his command at Meridian, Mississippi April 20, 1865; per sketch in Mathes book, page 53: born in Hardeman County, Tennessee January 24, 1840, first joined a company of infantry in 1861, whose services were offered to the State but not accepted, as the quota desired was full, in November, 1861, enlisted in Eldridge's Battery, made up from Fayette, Hardin and Wayne counties, was in all the campaigns of his battery and in some awful close places, especially at Spanish Fort (one of the approaches to the city of Mobile, in April, 1865), where the Confederates were confronted by a force of perhaps ten to one, also the battles of Franklin and Nashville, Tennessee in November and December 1864, never wounded after many other engagements, after the evacuation of Mobile the battery went up to Demopolis, where the men were given muskets, having left their guns in the fort, were ordered over to Meridian, Mississippi where the company surrendered, ten of them not feeling disposed to do so, on that morning broke their muskets over a tree and left for Tennessee, reaching La Grange, Tennessee surrendered and received paroles in June, 1865, member of Confederate Historical Association, a member of Company A, Confederate Veterans, lived in Shelby county and home located at Buntyn area of Memphis; per Death Certificate died September 27, 1918, from Cancer of the face.

Brown, Thomas W.   Buried July 21, 1906   Fowler 231, #6
Tennessee Judge Advocate, Captain of Cavalry; appointed to General Leonida Polk Corps December 16, 1862; served in General William J. Hardee's Corps 1864 and 1865; appears om a Muster Roll of the Lieutenant General and officers of the Staff of Hardee's Corps, paroled in accordance with the terms of a Military Convention entered into the 26th day of April, 1865, between General Joseph E. Johnston, Commanding Confederate Army, and Major General W. T. Sherman, Commanding United States Army of in North Carolina, rolled dated Trinity College, N. C., April 27, 1865 and Paroled at Greensboro, N. C., May 1, 1865; per biography in *Confederate Military History, Extended Edition*, Volume X Tennessee, page 384: born in Henry county, Ky., March 4, 1828, reared in Shelby county, Ky., graduated with the honors of his class at Center college, Danville, in 1845, after acting one year as principal of the Bardstown Presbyterian male academy, enlisted for the Mexican war, and served in the regiment of Kentucky mounted infantry, under Col. Humphrey Marshall, with this command participated in the battle of Buena Vista, after his return prepared for admission to the bar, which occurred in 1849, and then engaged in the practice of law in Shelby county, Ky., until 1861, when moved to Memphis; per sketch in Mathes book, page 47: conspicuous in recovering the liberties of ex-Confederates from the reconstruction measures and joined the Confederate Historical Association April 12, 1884.

Browne, William Herndon   Buried December 15, 1921   Turley 95
Tennessee 154 Senior Infantry Regiment Private Company G (record found "William Brown"); per Company Muster-in Roll dated August 31, 1861, at New Madrid, Missouri enlisted June 3, 1861, at Memphis; per Company Muster Roll for August 13 to October 31, 1861, elected corporal October 1, 1861; per Company Muster Roll for January 1, to July 1, 1862 reduced to the ranks May 6, 1862, and detailed to the ordnance department; name appears on Pay Receipt Rolls in 1863, and 1864, indicating was a carpenter at Selma Arsenal; name appears on a register of prisoners of War at Memphis, Tennessee – Deserters from rebel army dated April 29, 1864; name appears as signature to an Oath of Amnesty subscribed and sworn to at Memphis, Tennessee April 1864; per Tennessee Confederate Pension file (S14089) filed June 26, 1913, born Fayette County, Tennessee August 18, 1838; per Shelby County, Tennessee Death Certificate died December 13, 1921, cause of death Chronic Nephritis and occupation retired lumberman and operated factory; grave stone: 1838-1921.

Bryan, William C.   Buried August 22, 1866   Chapel Hill 96, #4

Arkansas 5 Battery Light Artillery (Appeal Battery) Captain; authorized by General Polk March 7, 1862, to raise the company; compiled service record includes a letter dated August 28, 1862, from him to General Polk resigning due to health, suffered from gravel; per list compiled by Captain C. C. Scott (last Captain of Battery) captain Bryan resigned 1862; listed in Elmwood 1874 book as Confederate soldier buried in Elmwood who was citizen of Memphis or vicinity and sketch (name spelled "Bryant"); per sketch born (we believe) Lincoln County, Tennessee, dentist in Memphis, commanded a light artillery during the war, died August 21, 1866, and aged 51; notice in the November 15, 1861, *Memphis Daily Appeal* that W. C. Bryan, Captain of Artillery, leaving in the morning with two field pieces to join General Carroll's command in east Tennessee, recruits for active service wanted; recruit notice in the March 11, 1862, *Memphis Daily Appeal*, Dr. W. C. Bryan; died bilious fever age 51 per Daily Burial Record Book; grave #4 indicated in Daily Burial Record Book and computer index but listed in grave #3 in Chapel Hill book with "infant of W. C. Bryan" listed in grave #4.

Bullington, Richard Edward   Buried January 21, 1943   Miller Circle 288, #4

Mississippi 18 Cavalry Regiment Private Company F; enlisted September 20, 1864, Senatobia, Mississippi; paroled May 15, 1865, at Memphis; card in compiled service record dated January 12, 1942, indicating born September 2, 1847, and age 94 with note "Private Bullington, for 45 years a dentist in Memphis, Tennessee is still living and is in good health. He holds the position of honorary Commander-in-Chief for life of the United *Confederate Veteran,* address 205 Pasadena, Memphis, Tennessee" this note given by his close friend, Robert G. Bachman, Johnson City, Tennessee, who is doing research work in the Confederate records at this time, January 12, 1942; per sketch in Mathes book sketch born April (sic) 2, 1847, De Soto County, Mississippi; earned doctor medicine degree in 1872; became member of Confederate Historical Association June 13, 1894; received Tennessee Confederate pension (File #S16518) January 1930, for which he had originally filed September 9, 1929, but withdrew September 21, 1929, and later resubmitted; per pension application surrendered with command by General N. B. Forrest at Gainesville, Alabama and had served as a Commissioner of Confederate Pension Board; on staff (Aide de Camp) of General Bennett H. Young, Commander in Chief United Confederate Veterans, 1913, picture in *Confederate Veteran,* Volume XXIII, No. 6, June 1915, died January 20, 1943; sketch in Goodspeed's Shelby County History, page 934; died age 95 per Daily Burial Record Book; grave stone 1847-1943.

Buntyn, Dr. Geraldus Oscar   Buried February 19, 1880   Turley 50, #9

Tennessee 7 Cavalry Regiment Private Company A; per Company Muster-in Roll dated August 18, 1861, enlisted May 16, 1861, Memphis with remarks: Absent on furlough, sick; no other information in compiled service record; per Young's Seventh Tennessee Cavalry book wounded at Coldwater September 9, 1862; per article in the March 20, 1880, *Saturday Evening Public Ledger*, page 1, column 1, died in Nashville and will be buried under the direction of the Masonic fraternity with services to be conducted by Brother Bun. F. Price, of DeSoto lodge, and that "(A) wound he received during the war caused his death."; per article in the March 21, 1880, *Memphis Daily Appeal*, page 6, column 3, "Losing a leg during the war, his health became impaired there from, and his mind eventually gave way."; cause of death softening of brain age 50 per Daily Burial Record Book; on May 22, 1819, John Overton, James Winchester, and Andrew Jackson founded the City of Memphis and formed Shelby County on land secured through speculation and post-war grants and that same year Geraldus Oscar Buntyn from North Carolina and father of Dr. Buntyn was granted, as payment for his services in the War of 1812, a parcel of land approximately 10 miles east of the city, which land, in part, eventually became Buntyn Station on the Memphis-LaGrange Railroad line, Memphis Country Club and Audubon Park.

Buttinghaus, Frederick William   Buried September 10, 1888   Evergreen 209, #2

Tennessee 3 (Memphis Battalion) Infantry Battalion Captain Company F; per Company Muster-in Roll dated March 12, 1862, enlisted March 11, 1862, age 41; see Notes of Interest "Memphis Battalion - Tennessee 3rd (Memphis) Infantry Battalion"; the Battalion disbanded May, 1862; December 29, 1863, appointed Colonel of the 3rd Regiment, Enrolled Militia of the District of Memphis/West Tennessee, a Union Home Guard (see *Tennesseans in the Civil War, Part 1*, page 412); biography in *Colonel in Blue—Indiana, Kentucky and Tennessee: A Civil War Biographical Dictionary.* Roger D. Hunt. McFarland & Company, Inc., Publishers, Jefferson, North Carolina, and London, 2014., page 201; resigned per September 21, 1864, *Memphis Bulletin:* "It will be seen by an advertisement in another column that Col. F. W. Buttinghaus has resigned the command of the 3d Regiment of the Enrolled Militia, to the command of which General Buckland has appointed 1st Lieutenant M. T. Williamson (see sketch in "Generals" chapter), 73d (sic 72d) Regiment Ohio Infantry, with the rank of Colonel. It is proper to state that the resignation of Col. Buttinghaus was not induced by pique at not having the flags awarded as was generally anticipated they would by the regiment on last Monday [19th]. Other circumstances and the claims of his official duties necessitated his withdrawal. Col. Buttinghaus is a public spirited gentleman, and had taken a deep interest in the militia of Memphis, but some matters in the regiment have not been altogether harmonious, and he desired to devote his whole time to the Recordership, in which he is certainly a terror to evil doers. It is not at all unlikely that they may be a vacancy in another of the prominent positions in the militia."; died September 8, 1888, from Dysentery age 67 per Register of Death in the Taxing District (Memphis); originally buried Chapel Hill Single Grave Public Lot 2 Grave #1369 and removed to 209 Evergreen January 31, 1889, per Daily Burial Record Book.

Cameron, D. W.   Buried May 8, 1862   Chapel Hill 659, #73

Tennessee 154 Senior Infantry Regiment Corporal/Private Company F; enlisted May 14, 1861, Randolph, Tennessee age 31; per January to July 1862, muster roll remarks: wounded at the Battle of Shiloh and since died; per report of deaths dated December 31, 1863, died May 1862, in hospital Memphis, Tennessee from wound received at Battle of Shiloh, born Montreal, Canada and $50 bounty due him; per May 6, 1863, muster roll remarks: age 32, wounded severely at Battle of Shiloh and died at Memphis; per

Battle of Shiloh casualty list for unit reported in April 24, 1862, *Memphis Daily Appeal* wounded in battle; wounded per Daily Burial Record Book; grave stone: CSA 1830 May 7, 1862.

Cameron, John Frayser Buried March 11, 1882 Chapel Hill 53, #12
Confederate 3 Infantry Regiment Field & Staff Lieutenant Colonel; initially was part of the "Harris Zouave Cadets" in Memphis, Tennessee, but he and others withdrew from that company in April 1861, and organized the "Young Guard" (see history in Lindsley's Annals, page 599, submitted by Edward Bourne), as Captain John P. Cameron's independent company Tennessee infantry, and subsequently became Company F 15th Tennessee Infantry, Company M Arkansas 2 Infantry (Arkansas 1st Battalion), Company B Arkansas 18th (Marmaduke's) Infantry Regiment and by Special Order dated January 31, 1862, the designation changed to Confederate 3rd Infantry Regiment with him initially serving as Captain of Company B; April, 1865, regiment consolidated with other regiments to form Arkansas 1st Consolidated Infantry Regiment and surrendered and paroled with that designation in April, 1865, at Greensboro, North Carolina; after the War became Captain of the "Bluff City Grays" in Memphis that was a military competitive drill organization; died March 10, 1882, at age 41 from consumption; no grave stone.

Cannon, Henry E. Buried May 19, 1918 Fowler 121-127, #16
Tennessee 7 Cavalry Regiment, Private Company A; per Young's *Seventh Tennessee Cavalry* joined Company A May 16, 1861, and detailed with Captain Anderson October 16, 1862; per note in sketch for 7 Cavalry in *Tennesseans in the Civil War* in February 1865, Captain James A. Anderson's 2 Company D of the 2 Mississippi Partisan Rangers Regiment (also called Ballentine's Cavalry Regiment) was attached to the 7 Cavalry Regiment as 2 Company K; per sketch in Mathes book wounded while scouting around Lost Mountain and Powder Springs, Georgia, paroled May 11, 1865, and admitted to Confederate Historical Association June 1, 1895; per descendant Clark Doan also served in Mississippi 2 Partisan Rangers Company K, member of Camp A; sketch in Goodspeed's Shelby County History, page 948; listed on the 1912, list of Camp 28 United Confederate Veterans; stone: Died May 18, 1918, Aged 78; Tennessee Widow (Bessie Rembert Cannon) Pension #W9917; government stone: Henry E Cannon, PVT CO A & K 7 TENN CAV, Jul 5, 1840 May 18, 1918.

Cannon, Wynne Gay Buried March 1, 1924 Miller Circle 48, #3
Tennessee 154 Senior Infantry Regiment Captain Company D; per Company Muster-in Roll dated May 14, 1861, enlisted May 14, 1861, age 19, 2 Lieutenant; promoted to Captain August 30, 1862; signed Parole of Honor May 9, 1865, at Meridian, Mississippi; per biography in *Confederate Military History, Extended Edition*, Volume X Tennessee, page 393: born at Clarksville, Tenn., July 24, 1844, reared at Memphis from the age of ten years, and became a member and lieutenant of the Harris Zouave Cadets, which enrolled as Company D, One Hundred and Fifty-fourth (senior) regiment upon the organization of the State army in 1861, took part in the battles of Belmont and Shiloh, and the engagements about Corinth during the siege, and then, going into Kentucky with Kirby Smith, was in battle at Richmond, after which he was promoted to captain, at the age of eighteen years, commanded the company at Perryville and Murfreesboro, and in the latter battle, December 31, 1862, shot through the left lung, wound thought to be mortal and laid for three months in a private house near the field, finally regaining some strength, during this time under parole, and when able to walk sent to Fort Delaware as a prisoner of war, soon after his arrival at the latter place included in two ship loads of prisoners sent to City Point for exchange, was his misfortune to be one of the thirty-six officers who were left over, their fate being determined by drawing white and black beans, taken to Fortress Monroe and put aboard the Maple Leaf for transportation back to Fort Delaware, along with a number of prisoners from Arkansas, in route the Confederates, finding themselves in sufficient force, took possession of the boat, ran it to a point on Virginia Beach and escaped safely, though landed 160 miles inside the Federal lines, returning to his company fought at Chickamauga, Lookout Mountain, Resaca, Tilton, Kenesaw Mountain (dead angle), New Hope Church, Peachtree Creek, Atlanta, Jonesboro, Spring Hill, Franklin and Nashville, again captured, and taken to Johnson's Island, but made escape when taken to Sandusky City as a witness in a court martial, by wearing citizens clothes under his uniform and discarding the latter at a favorable opportunity while on way back to his regiment, the war came to an end and he surrendered at Meridian, Mississippi, and was brevetted lieutenant-colonel for his gallantry; grave stone: Captain Born July 24, 1844 Clarksville, Tenn. Died February 28, 1924.

Capers, Richard Samuel Buried June 6, 1913 South Grove 245 SW½, #5
Tennessee 3 (Forrest's) Cavalry Regiment Private Company F; only parole card in compiled service record indicating name appears on a Report of Prisoners of War paroled on terms as agreed upon for 5 days ending May 20, 1865, at Memphis, Tennessee; per sketch in Mathes book, page 237: at college at Clinton, Mississippi, when war began, came to Memphis and at the age of 14 years joined Forrest's old regiment under Captain Fred Rogers, went all through the war, and was in nearly all of Forrest's fights, wounded seriously in the shoulder at Shiloh and disabled for four months, also wounded at West Point and Tishomingo creek and at the battle of Franklin, captured thirty miles east of Memphis by Steger's command on a raid, but released on account of his youthful appearance, another time when came into Memphis to get a horse picked up on the streets and thrown into the Irving Block prison, released at the end of twenty-four hours through the influence of Mr. J. E. Merriman, a kind hearted and very influential Union man, at the close of the war paroled at Gainesville, Alabama, returned to Memphis and went to work the next day in the chancery court clerk's office, and remained in public service in the courthouse for thirty years with eight years of that time Clerk of the Criminal Court; per biography in *Confederate Military History, Extended Edition*, Volume X Tennessee, page 394: born in born in Haywood county, Tenn., June 21, 1847.

Carnes, James Alexander   Buried March 28, 1867   Chapel Hill 13, #1
Tennessee State Militia Brigadier General; per sketch in appendix in *More Generals in Gray* was Brigadier General of Tennessee Militia and his brigade was ordered into service to protect the City of Memphis in 1862 (see February 22, 1862, *Memphis Avalanche*); not listed in the *Memorandum relative to the General Officers Appointed by the President in the Armies of the Confederate States - 1861-1865* compiled from Official Records by the Military Secretary's Office, U. S. War Department 1905; not listed in *Generals in Gray*; no compiled service record found; not listed in Elmwood 1874 book as Confederate soldier buried in Elmwood who was a citizen of Memphis or vicinity but sketch that indicates made Major general of the State Militia in the first year of the late war, died during the war in Georgia (sic - see grave stone note), about age 50, and remains were transferred to Elmwood; died age 47 per Daily Burial Record Book; placed in personal vault Chapel Hill Lot 535 and moved September 17, 1867; father of William W. Carnes, Tennessee Carnes' Artillery; grave stone: Born Humphreys County, Tennessee March 9, 1818, and Died in Columbia, South Carolina May 14, 1864; also listed in chapter on Generals; listed in "Touring Historic Elmwood Cemetery" Brochure (January 2000) #53 but not listed as General in its predecessor "Touring historic Elmwood Cemetery" (Brochure and Map of Historic Gravesites); sketch #14 in Elmwood *Civil War Tour* booklet (2012).

Carnes, John Barnet   Buried June 23, 1884   Turley 170, #4
Captain Assistant Commissary of Subsistence (A.C.S.) Jackson's Cavalry Division (no other service record found); death notice in *Memphis Daily Appeal*, June 22, 1884, page 2, column 9: Carnes – At his residence in Tunica County, Mississippi, Saturday, June 21, 1884, Captain John B. Carnes; Captain and died age 55 in Daily Burial Record Book; born April 9, 1833 died June 21, 1884 on grave stone.

Carroll, Charles Montgomery   Buried December 10, 1899   Fowler 120 (IOOF), #D-54
Tennessee 15 Infantry Regiment Colonel; enlisted June 7, 1861 age 40 Jackson, Tennessee and appointed Colonel; subject of court martial November 8, 1861, for conduct prejudicial to good order and military discipline and conduct unbecoming an officer and gentleman for which received reprimand and returned to duty; per sketch in Mathes book native of Nashville, Tennessee, born 1821, and retired after Battle of Corinth 1862; died age 78 per Daily Burial Record Book; buried Odd Fellows (IOOF) Section.

Carroll, William Henry, Sr.   Buried September 7, 1869   Lenow Circle 57, #1
Brigadier General; appointed from Tennessee October 26, 1861, (rank October 26, 1861) and resigned February 1, 1863, per *Memorandum relative to the General Officers Appointed by the President in the Armies of the Confederate States - 1861-1865* compiled from Official Records by the Military Secretary's Office, U. S. War Department 1905; originally Brigadier General Provisional Army of Tennessee and entered Confederate service as Colonel Tennessee 37 Infantry Regiment; no compiled service record found but listed on first organization card in Tennessee 37 Infantry Regiment compiled service record rolls; per Elmwood "Touring historic Elmwood Cemetery" (Brochure and Map of Historic Gravesites) #4 son of governor, brother of mayor, postmaster before War and went to Canada after War where died; per sketch in *Generals in Gray* born in Nashville probably 1810 (sic see below), son of Tennessee Governor William Carroll, operated plantation in Panola County, Mississippi, moved to Memphis 1848, where was postmaster, entered Confederate service as Colonel Tennessee 37 Infantry Regiment, promoted to Brigadier General October 26, 1861, arrested on order of General Bragg, after Court of Inquiry resigned commission February 1, 1863, and went to Canada where family had migrated after occupation of Memphis by Federals, died in Montreal, Quebec, Canada, May 3, 1868, and remains moved to Elmwood the following years with headstone inaccurate as to years of his birth and death (1813-1866); per Bruce Allardice's article "In Search of ... General William Henry Carroll" in *West Tennessee Historical Society Papers*, XLVIII (1994), pages 60-72, he was actually born 1816 or 1817 based on ages listed in 1850 and 1860 U.S. Census returns for Shelby County, Tennessee; listed (Carroll, Gen. Wm. H.) in Elmwood 1874 book as Confederate soldier buried in Elmwood who was a citizen of Memphis or vicinity and sketch; per Lindsley's Annals, page 596, was Colonel and incorporator of Tennessee 154 Tennessee Infantry (Senior) when incorporated by Act of the Legislature March 22, 1860; biography in *Confederate Military History, Extended Edition*, Volume X Tennessee, page 300; removed from Canada per Daily Burial Record Book; originally buried Chapel Hill Lot 215, Grave #3; see Carroll file in the Elmwood Cemetery Office; sketch in *Tennessee, The Volunteer State, 1769-1923*, Volume II, page 86; sketch, photograph, if available, and grave stone photograph in book *Quiet Places: The Burial Sites of Civil War Generals in Tennessee* by Buckner and Nathaniel C. Hughes, Jr., East Tennessee Historical Society (1992); also listed in chapter on Generals; listed under Generals in "Touring historic Elmwood Cemetery" (Brochure and Map of Historic Gravesites) #4; listed in "Touring Historic Elmwood Cemetery" Brochure (January 2000) #41; sketch #29 in Elmwood *Civil War Tour* booklet (2012).

Carroll, William Henry, Jr.   Buried April 17, 1915   Turley 1080, #8
Tennessee 37 Infantry Regiment; possibly the William Carroll Private Company H who enlisted November 16, 1861, at Chattanooga, Tennessee and on muster rolls to August 1862, but remarks on rolls indicate deserted; appointed Captain Aid de Camp January 19, 1862, on staff of General William H. Carroll (his father) and appointed Captain Acting Assistant Adjutant General April 27, 1863, on staff of General James R. Chalmers per *Confederate Staff Officers 1861 -1865* by Joseph H. Crute, Jr., Derwent Books 1982, pages 31-32; per sketch in *Tennessee, The Volunteer State, 1769-1923*, Volume II, page 860, referred to as Colonel, son of General William Henry Carroll (see sketch herein), grandson of William Carroll who was six times governor of Tennessee, born in Panola County, Mississippi in 1842, a child when his parents removed with their family to Memphis, attended private schools and subsequently completed his literary education in the Western Military Institute at Nashville, in 1861, at age nineteen years enlisted in the Confederate army with his father, with whom went to Knoxville where drilled a regiment that his father had

there raised--the Thirty-seventh Tennessee, with his regiment went to Germantown and had his baptism of fire at the battle of Fishing Creek on the 19th of January, 1862, when General Chalmers took command of North Mississippi in 1863, reported to him and was assigned to duty as acting assistant adjutant general, while later was elected captain of Company C of the Eighteenth Mississippi Battalion under Colonel Alexander H. Cheatham, continued with that command until near the close of the war when his health failed and was discharged, afterward studied law and was admitted to the bar in 1875, following his admission to the bar first became associated in his practice with Senator Isham G. Harris and Colonel Casey Young (see sketches herein), had several other partnerships including one in 1894, with of General James R. Chalmers (see sketch herein) that was maintained until the death of General Chalmers in 1898, wedded Miss Mattie McKay, and died on the 15th of April, 1915; biography in *Confederate Military History, Extended Edition*, Volume X Tennessee, page 398; sketch in Mathes book page 238; obituary in *The Commercial Appeal* Memphis April 16, 1915, page 1, column 7, that indicates died April 15, 1915; grave stone: "Wm. H. Carroll, Born Feb. 18, 1842 Died April 14, 1915" (note date difference).

Carson, William Orval   Buried May 24, 1920   Fowler Public Lot 6, #2092
Mississippi 11(Perrin's) Cavalry Regiment Private Company C; enlisted March 20, 1864, Kosciusko, Mississippi; applied for Tennessee Confederate pension ("William Orville Carson" File #S15151) February 23, 1917, that was not approved as had not lived in Tennessee the required fourteen years before applying; in pension application unit identified as Mississippi 13 Cavalry, which was incorrect as there was not a Mississippi 13 Cavalry Regiment, but correctly identified his Captain James Buford; per pension application born Madison County, Mississippi, enlisted February 1864, at age 17 and paroled June 15, 1865, at Jackson, Mississippi; no confirmation on service from War Department in pension file; unit information on grave stone; initials "W. O." and died age 73 in Daily Burial Record Books; died May 23, 1920 aged 73 per death notice in May 24, 1920, *The Commercial Appeal* Memphis, page 7.

Certon, William
Listed in Elmwood 1874 book as Confederate soldier buried in Elmwood who was citizen of Memphis or vicinity but no Cemetery record found; possibly William L. Certain, 1 Lieutenant Tennessee 7 Cavalry Regiment Company A, enlisted May 16, 1861, Memphis age 25, elected 1 Lieutenant January 24, 1863, took Oath of Allegiance May 11, 1865, at Gainesville, Alabama; W. L. Certain found 1860, Memphis, Shelby County, Tennessee census age 25, Merchant and born Alabama; William L. Certain found in Halpin 1866 Memphis City Directory but not found other directories; William L. Certain found 1850, Huntsville, Madison County, Alabama census age 16 (Jacob father and Elizabeth mother); W. L. Certain death found May 24, 1866, Madison County, Alabama and buried in Maple Hill Cemetery, Huntsville, Alabama (birth July 22, 1843); No Certon or Certain found in the Index to Obituaries in *The Memphis Appeal* 1843-1894 compiled by Joyce McKibben, Research and Instruction Librarian, The University of Memphis.

Chalmers, James Ronald   Buried April 10, 1898   Evergreen 448, #1
Brigadier General; appointed from Mississippi February 13, 1862, (rank February 13, 1862) per *Memorandum relative to the General Officers Appointed by the President in the Armies of the Confederate States - 1861-1865* compiled from Official Records by the Military Secretary's Office, U. S. War Department 1905; first served in Mississippi 9 Infantry Regiment as Captain Old Company K and Colonel; enlisted February 17, 1861, Hernando, Mississippi age 30; elected Colonel April 11, 1861; assigned to command of brigade April 15, 1861; relieved of brigade command September 9, 1861, and resumed command of Regiment; prominent in Forrest command; grave stone: born Halifax County, Virginia January 11, 1831, and died April 9, 1898, Memphis; per sketch in Mathes book born Halifax County, Virginia January 11, 1831, March 1861, elected Colonel Mississippi 9 Infantry Regiment, February 12, 1862, made Brigadier General, ordered to North Mississippi in 1863, to command cavalry until Forrest arrived and then commanded First Division of Forrest's Cavalry which he held until end of War; per General and Staff record surrendered at Gainesville, Alabama May 10, 1865; elected to four terms of Congress (1876, 1878, 1880 and 1882); resident of Mississippi and had law office in Memphis; sketch in *Generals in Gray*; died age 67 per Daily Burial Record Book; biography in *Confederate Military History, Extended Edition*, Volume IX Mississippi, page 244; sketch in the PoliticalGraveyard.com; sketch, photograph, if available, and grave stone photograph in book *Quiet Places: The Burial Sites of Civil War Generals in Tennessee* by Buckner and Nathaniel C. Hughes, Jr., East Tennessee Historical Society (1992); also listed in chapter on Generals; listed under Generals in "Touring historic Elmwood Cemetery" (Brochure and Map of Historic Gravesites) #5; listed in "Touring Historic Elmwood Cemetery" Brochure (January 2000) #127; sketch #34 in Elmwood *Civil War Tour* booklet (2012).

Chambers, Henry Cousins   Buried May 13, 1871   Chapel Hill Circle 76, #4
Confederate Congressman (Mississippi); see sketch in Warner's Confederate Congress book pages 44-45; born Limestone County, Alabama July 26, 1823, graduated with honors from what is now Princeton University, moved to Rankin County, Mississippi to engage in planting, 1854 went to Coahoma County, also owned land in adjoining Bolivar County, sent to legislature in 1859, vied for a seat in the First Regular Confederate Congress and the race became so heated that on October 15, 1861, forced his opponent, William Augustus Lake, into a duel - rifles at fifty paces - at Hopefield, Arkansas and killed him, had no opposition when sought reelection to the Second Congress in 1863, after War returned to plantation in Bolivar County, and died May 1, 1871, at a Mississippi River steamboat landing known as Carson's in Bolivar County; sketch in the PoliticalGraveyard.com; died aged 47, rheumatism per Daily Burial Record Book; no grave stone.

Chilton, Thomas Harding   Buried December 12, 1911   Lenow Circle 25, #9
Mississippi 11 Infantry Regiment Company G; enlisted August 7, 1861, Manassas; clerk in Quartermaster (QM) Department; on original roll born Alabama, student of Oxford, Mississippi, age 19 when enlisted, detailed as clerk in QM Department; took Oath of Allegiance June 11, 1865, and per card resident of Lafayette, Mississippi; per sketch in Mathes book, page 73, born in Benton, now Calhoun County, Alabama, removed to Mississippi and grew up at Byhalia and Oxford, enlisted in Lamar Rifles under Captain Green in 1861, sworn in July 7, 1861, at age 18, served with unit throughout war, captured at Petersburg April 2, 1865, imprisoned at Fort Delaware and released June 11, 1865, arrived in Memphis June 27, walked to Oxford and was member of Confederate Relief and Historical Association and successor organization since the first organization; biography in *Confederate Military History, Extended Edition,* Volume X Tennessee, page 408; died age 68 per Daily Burial Record Book; grave #7 in Cemetery computer index; grave stone: born February 3, 1842 and died December 11, 1911.

Clapp, Jeremiah Watkins   Buried September 7, 1898   Chapel Hill 535, Vault
Confederate Congressman (Mississippi); see sketch in Warner's Confederate Congress book page 49; born September 24, 1814, in Abington, Virginia, educated at Hampden-Sydney College where graduated in law in 1836, after practicing in Abington for a time moved to Holly Springs, Mississippi in 1841, 1854 delegate to the Charleston convention, was member of Mississippi secession convention , elected to the First Regular Congress but defeated for reelection in1863 and from 1852 to 1867 trustee of the University of Mississippi; per sketch in Mathes book (enlarged edition) after War removed from Holly Springs, Mississippi to Memphis where stood in front of the bar for thirty years and died at Red Sulphur Springs, Hardin County, Tennessee September 1898, aged 84 years; sketch in Goodspeed's Shelby County History, page 939; mentioned in sketch on son (same name) in sketch in *Tennessee, The Volunteer State, 1769-1923,* Volume IV, page 113; sketch in the PoliticalGraveyard.com; judge, died age 84 per Daily Burial Record Book and interred in Donoho vault; September 24, 1814 September 5, 1898 on circle grave stone.

Claridge, John M.   Buried April 25, 1867   Turley 380, #3
Tennessee 154 Senior Infantry Regiment Private Company E (record found "Clarige, John W."); per Company Muster-in Roll dated August 13, 1861, enlisted May 14, 1861, Randolph, Tennessee; per Company Muster Roll for May & June, 1862, remarks: Deserted May 14, 1862, Dropped from Roll; per Company Muster Roll dated May 5, 1863, age 24, remarks: Deserted at Corinth, Mississippi, May 1862; per article "Bloody Affray Last Night, Policeman Killed—The Murderer Arrested" in the April 24, 1867, Saturday Evening *Public Ledger*, page 3, column 3, Claridge, a policeman, was killed when attempting to arrest the parties involved in a disturbance at the Cotton Plant salon; article stated "During the war he served in the 154th regiment."; murdered age 27 per Daily Burial Record Book.

Cochran, Francis Trigg   Buried March 26, 1872   South Grove 46, #1
Tennessee 3 (Forrest's) Cavalry Regiment Sergeant Company B; enlisted January 3, 1862, Memphis; listed in Elmwood 1874 book as Confederate soldier buried in Elmwood who was citizen of Memphis or vicinity and sketch; per sketch born Abington, Virginia, enlisted and served as a soldier under General Forrest and died on farm in Crittenden County, Arkansas in 1872, at age 45; died age 46 typhoid fever per Daily Burial Record Book; small grave stone 1827-1872; large grave stone "Robert Trigg Cochran" born 1827 died 1872.

Cochran, John W.   Buried January 15, 1899   Miller Circle 190, #1
Inspector General, Lieutenant, staff of General Joseph Wheeler March 1, 1864, relieved January 5, 1865 (see *Confederate Staff Officers* 1861 - 1865 by Joseph H. Crute, Jr., Derwent Books 1982); Tennessee 154 Senior Infantry Regiment 1 Lieutenant Company L; per Company Muster-in Roll dated March 8, 1862, enlisted 5 Sergeant March 7, 1862, Memphis; per Company Muster Roll dated May 6, 1863, elected 2 Lieutenant at reorganization; June 6, 1863, appointed Provost Marshal of General Preston Smith's Brigade; September 19-22, 1863, Lieutenant Provost Marshal to Colonel A. J. Vaughan, Jr., commanding Smith's Brigade (General Smith killed September 19, 1863); November 13 and December 31, 1863, Provost Marshall for Brigade; March 1, 1864, appointed Inspector General on Staff of Major General Joseph Wheeler, relieved January 5, 1865; signed Parole of Honor May 12, 1865, at Meridian, Mississippi; per sketch in Mathes book, page 240: born Abingdon, Va., came to Memphis before the war, left Memphis in 1861 in Captain McDonald's sixty-day company, served out his time with said company, returned to Memphis, joined Captain Cole's company, which afterward was attached to the One Hundred and Fifty-fourth Senior Tennessee Regiment just before the battle of Shiloh, remained with it for some three years, in all the engagements that it was in during that time, detailed on General Preston Smith's staff at Shelbyville, Tenn. and with him when he and two of his staff were killed at Chickamauga, afterward ordered to report to General Joseph Wheeler at Dalton, Ga., for staff duty, with rank of captain, and remained with him to the close of the war, and paroled at Gainesville, Ala., May, 1865; biography in *Confederate Military History, Extended Edition*, Volume X Tennessee, page 418; sketch in Goodspeed's Shelby County History, page 940; large grave stone: May 24, 1833 January 14, 1899; died age 65 years 8 months per Daily Burial Record Book; per *The Commercial Appeal* Memphis Bygone Days articles September 25, 1874, elected president of the Exposition Association and died at his residence January 15, 1899.

Cocke, John H.   Buried November 16, 1891   Turley 1095, #7
Texas Morgan's Cavalry Regiment Private Company I; per Company Muster Roll for April 30 to August 31, 1863 (only card in record), enlisted July 8, 1861, Marshall, Texas; October 1, 1844 November 14, 1891; died age 47 per Daily Burial Record Book.

Cole, Edmund Anderson   Buried December 18, 1909   Chapel Hill Circle 56, #6

Tennessee 154 Senior Infantry Regiment Captain Company L; per Company Muster-in Roll dated March 8, 1862, enlisted March 7, 1862, age 37; elected Captain May 3, 1862; submitted letter of resignation dated November 19, 1863, due to health problems; per sketch in Mathes book, page 71: licensed to practice law at age 21 but practiced only a short time before he served in war with Mexico and was one of the earliest members of the old Confederate Relief and Historical Association, but delicate health prevented him from taking an active part; biography in *Confederate Military History, Extended Edition*, Volume X Tennessee, page 420; per City of Memphis Burial permit born December 5, 1824 and died December 16, 1909.

Collier, William Armistead   Buried August 19, 1929   Miller Circle 152, #2

Tennessee 7 Cavalry Regiment Private/Corporal Company B; first enlisted in Confederate 1 Cavalry Regiment Company I March 7, 1862, at Memphis age 18 and per November 1, 1862 to April 30, 1863, muster roll remarks discharged and final statement given March 28; enlisted 7 Cavalry Regiment February 15, 1864, at Grenada, Mississippi and paroled at Gainesville, Alabama May 11, 1865, with Prisoner of War card indicating residence as Haywood County, Tennessee; reference slip card in compiled service record referencing Arkansas pension board but no Arkansas pension record found for Collier but notation concerning Andy Paschell or A. W. Paschal Company G 12 Kentucky Cavalry who's compiled service record has a letter from War Department to Arkansas Pension Board at Batesville, Arkansas that references both; per sketch in Mathes book, enlarged edition page 13: born February 12, 1847, (note year difference with grave stone below) in Haywood County, Tennessee, first joined Confederate 1 Cavalry Company I and served throughout the campaigns of 1862 and 1863, discharged in spring 1863, near Columbia, Tennessee because of ill health, made way through federal lines to get home in west Tennessee, fall 1863, when health restored joined Tennessee 7 Cavalry Regiment Company B, member of General Vaughan's staff as commander of Confederate Veterans of Tennessee and was an early and active member of the Confederate Historical Association of Memphis, becoming a charter member as reorganized in May, 1884; article in *Confederate Veteran* Volume XXXVII, November 1929, page 412, with same information and statement that "General Collier" had served as commander of Forrest's Cavalry Association and would be missed; extensive biography in *Confederate Military History*, *Extended Edition*, Volume X Tennessee, page 424; "Wm Armistead Collier" on large stone in lot and on small grave stone with dates February 12, 1846 (note year difference with Mathes sketch) August 18, 1929; died age 83 per Daily Burial Record Book.

Collins, Nathaniel Dixon   Buried January 20, 1874   Fowler 171, #2

Tennessee Collins' Cavalry Regiment (Partisan Rangers) Colonel; Lieutenant Colonel of Regiment which organized Fall 1863 and broken up February 5, 1864, per *Tennesseans in the Civil War* Part 1, pages 106-107; no compiled service record found but may have served in Tennessee 13 Infantry Regiment as Lieutenant Company I and 1 Lieutenant Company E Tennessee 2 (Robison's) Infantry; listed in Elmwood 1874 Book as Confederate soldier buried in Elmwood who was citizen of Memphis or vicinity with rank of Colonel; first initial "W" in Cemetery computer index; Colonel died pneumonia age 41 per Cemetery record; originally buried Chapel Hill 535; born September 19, 1830, and died January 19, 1874, on grave stone; death notice in the January 20, 1874, *Memphis Daily Appeal* stating that "Colonel N. D. Collins" died at Forrest City, Arkansas January 19, 1874, aged 41 years.

Cooper, Lunsford Pitts   Buried August 19, 1902   Chapel Hill 54, #9

Mississippi 42 Infantry Regiment, F&S Captain Quartermaster, enlisted May 14, 1862, Grenada, MS, Private AQM, appointed acting QM May 17, 1862, assigned to duty with Brigade QM July 1864; per sketch in Goodspeed's Shelby County History, page 943, after Regiment reached Richmond made Quartermaster with rank of Captain, after the Quartermasters were abolished retained as Assistant Brigade Quartermaster under Major Reid where served until end of War, returned to Mississippi after the War, later moved to Memphis where practiced law and became a Criminal Court judge; per sketch in Mathes book enlisted in Captain Meek's Company, Mississippi 42 Regiment, with command all the time except about 60 days in 1863 when returned home to attend wife's funeral; large upright grave stone: Born Rutherford County, Tennessee January 8, 1830 Died August 19, 1902.

Copeland P. C.   Buried April 26, 1862   Chapel Hill 659

Texas 3 (Greer's) Cavalry Regiment Corporal Company C; enlisted June 3, 1861 Cherokee County, Texas; per November and December 1861, muster roll enlisted June 3, 1861, Rusk County, Texas; per June to August 1861, muster roll remarks: slightly wounded, in hospital; per report of operations & casualties dated August 12, 1861: wounded at Battle of Wilson Creek, Missouri August 10, 1861; per May and June 1862, muster roll remarks: present or absent not stated; no later information in record; died from caiuf(?) congestion of brain in Daily Burial Record Book; name spelled "Coupland" in Daily Burial Record Book and computer index; "Stone" written in grave # column in Daily Burial Record Book; "lot full of single grave" per note written in Chapel Hill Book Lot 659; original grave stone inscription died aged 21 years; upright CSA marker 1841 April 25, 1862.

Cousins, Peter Robinson   Buried June 1, 1904   Turley 1040, #4

Tennessee 1 Heavy Artillery 1 Lieutenant Company L; first served in Tennessee Johnston's Heavy Artillery Company (Memphis Southern Guards, aka Southern Guards Artillery, see Notes of Interest) Captain James Hamilton's Company (12 Months 1861-62 enlistment); per the Company Muster-in Roll dated August 20, 1861, enlisted April 21, 1861, Memphis age 27; name appears as signature to an Oath of Allegiance to the United States, subscribed and sworn to at Fort Warren, Boston Harbor, Massachusetts, June 12, 1865 and indicated residence as Memphis, Tennessee; sketch in *Confederate Military History, Extended Edition*, Volume X Tennessee, page 431, "Lieutenant Peter Robinson Cousins, of Memphis, a gallant artillery officer, was born in Nottaway county, Va., June 16, 1832, son of Capt. William H. Cousins, a prosperous planter. Coming to Memphis in 1856, he was employed as a mercantile clerk until in the spring of 1861 he entered the Confederate service with the Memphis Southern Guards, of which he had previously been a member, and served with it in the One Hundred and Fifty-fourth (senior) infantry until, a few months later, it was transferred to the artillery service at Columbus. As private, second lieutenant, first lieutenant, and commander of the battery he served throughout the course of the war. Escaping with his command from Island No. 10 before the surrender, he was on duty at Corinth, then at Vicksburg during the siege, and was there surrendered. Being exchanged soon afterward, he was sent to Richmond to negotiate the exchange of his battery, and succeeding in this, he served at Fort Morgan, Mobile bay, during the attack by Farragut. Again surrendered at the fall of that stronghold, he was imprisoned at Fort Lafayette, N. Y., and Fort Warren, Mass., for eleven months. After the close of hostilities he was for many years an active business man of Memphis."; sketch in Mathes book page 244.

Cox, Robert B.
Listed in Elmwood 1874 book as Confederate soldier buried in Elmwood who was citizen of Memphis or vicinity; possibly Robert B. Cox, buried November 14, 1864, Chapel Hill 37, #5, who was killed age 18 per Daily Burial Record Book; possibly Tennessee 41 Infantry Regiment Private Company H; not found in the Official Memorial Roll for the Tennessee 41 Infantry Regiment in Lindsley's Annals; possibly the Bob Cox mentioned by Dr. S. H. Ford in his address on the occasion to commemorate (Confederate Memorial Day) Confederates buried at Elmwood on April 26, 1866, (see articles "The Confederate Dead" in the *Public Ledger* (Memphis), April 27, 1866, page 3, column 2, and "Honors To The Memory Of The Hero Dead" in the April 27, 1866, *Memphis Daily Appeal*, page 3, column 1); mentioned in General W. B. Bates' speech printed in the article "Elmwood" (Grand and Imposing Ceremonies of Commemoration Day), in *Memphis Sunday Appeal*, May 8, 1870, page 4, column 2 ("Near by sleeps young Bruce Rogers, Creighton, Robert Cox, Walter Harris....").

Craft, Judge Henry Kirk   Buried June 25, 1894   Lenow Circle 31-32, #11
Captain, General and Staff Officer, Provisional Army of Confederate State (P. A. C. S.), appointed Assistant Adjutant General (A.A.G.) March 18, 1862, to the staff of Brigadier General James R. Chalmers; submitted resignation June 10, 1862, with reason given as ill health, which wholly disqualifies him for the discharge of the duties if his position; resignation accepted July 19, 1862; was a lawyer prior to the War having attended law school at Princeton, New Jersey; admitted to the bar in 1848, in Holly Springs, Mississippi; came to Memphis in 1858; after the war returned to the practice of law and became a judge; died age 71 years, 2 months and 1 day per Daily Burial Record Book.

Craft, James H.   Buried April 30, 1876   Lenow Circle 5, #1
Tennessee 3 (Forrest's) Cavalry Regiment Private Company A "Bluff City Grays"; only a card in record is name appears on Roll of Prisoners of War paroled at Gainesville, Alabama May 11, 1865, resident of Memphis, Tennessee; no record found Tennessee 154 Senior Infantry Regiment 1st Company B; listed in the June 6, 1878, *Memphis Daily Appeal*, page 4, column 3, article "OUR DEAD HEROES" covering the unveiling of the Confederate Monument and Decoration of Graves at Elmwood as then one of twenty-eight members of the Bluff City Grays, Company B of the 154 Senior Infantry Regiment and Company A of Forrest's Old (Third) Cavalry Regiment buried at Elmwood; listed as one of the "comrades who sleep at Elmwood cemetery " in the article "Veterans in Council" in *Memphis Daily Appeal*, May 12, 1881, page 4, column 4, concerning the meeting of the surviving members in the city of the old Bluff City Grays to appoint the necessary committees for the purpose of making special decoration on the graves of their dead comrades at Elmwood and Calvary cemeteries on Sunday next, Memorial Day; see Notes of Interest - Bluff City Grays; listed ("Jas. H.") in "A COMPLETE ROSTER OF THE BLUFF CITY GREYS" located in the Memphis Room of the Memphis/Shelby County Public Library and Information Center Central Library with note enlistment May 1, 1864, and buried in Elmwood in Turley Section which is incorrect; listed ("Jos. H") as member of Bluff City Grays in *Reminiscences of the Civil War* by John Hallum, Tunnah & Pittard printers, 1903; died consumption age 44 per Daily Burial Record Book.

Creighton, John R. J.   Buried February 10, 1867   Chapel Hill 112, #6
Tennessee 3 (Forrest's) Cavalry Regiment Lieutenant Company A "Bluff City Grays"; first enlisted in the Tennessee 154 Senior Infantry Regiment Lieutenant 1st Company B, per Company Muster-in Roll dated August 13, 1861, at New Madrid, Missouri, enlisted on May 14, 1861, at Randolph, Tennessee age 27; per Tennessee 3 (Forrest's) Cavalry Regiment Company Muster Roll for January 1 to July 1, 1862 enlisted May 4, 1861, at Randolph, Tennessee; appears on a list (not dated) of casualties at the battle before Murfreesboro, Tennessee, December 31, 1962, with note "severely wounded, since died"; death reported in the January 14, 1863, *Memphis Daily Appeal*, page 2, column 1, article "Memphians Killed at Murfreesboro" Captain Jno. R. J. Creighton and listed in January 20, 1863, *Memphis Daily Appeal*, page 1, column 3, article "Report of Killed, Wounded and Missing" in the Battle before Murfreesboro, Tenn., December 31, 1862, Bluff City Grays, acting sharpshooters, Lieut. J. R. J. Creighton. Commanding. - Killed ; funeral notice in *Memphis Daily Appeal*, February 10, 1876, page 2, column 4; burial also mentioned in articles in the *Daily Memphis Avalanche* February 10, 1867, and February 12, 1867; editorial tribute in the *Daily Memphis Avalanche* June 12, 1866, page 2, column 2; killed in battle, adult and removed from Mulfordsville (?), Tennessee per Daily Burial Record Book; mentioned in General W. B. Bates' speech printed in the article "Elmwood" (Grand and Imposing Ceremonies of Commemoration Day), in *Memphis Sunday Appeal*, May 8, 1870, page 4, column 2 ("Near by sleeps young Bruce Rogers, Creighton, Robert Cox, Walter Harris...."); listed in the June 6, 1878, *Memphis Daily Appeal*, page 4, column 3, article "OUR DEAD HEROES" covering the unveiling of the Confederate Monument and Decoration of Graves at Elmwood as then one of twenty-eight members of the Bluff City Grays, Company B of the 154 Senior Infantry Regiment and Company A of Forrest's Old (Third) Cavalry Regiment buried at Elmwood; listed as one of the "comrades who sleep at Elmwood cemetery " in the article "Veterans in Council" in

Memphis Daily Appeal, May 12, 1881, page 4, column 4, concerning the meeting of the surviving members in the city of the old Bluff City Grays to appoint the necessary committees for the purpose of making special decoration on the graves of their dead comrades at Elmwood and Calvary cemeteries on Sunday next, Memorial Day; see Notes of Interest - Bluff City Grays; listed (initials "J. R. J.") in "A COMPLETE ROSTER OF THE BLUFF CITY GREYS" located in the Memphis Room of the Memphis/Shelby County Public Library and Information Center Central Library with note wounded at Murfreesboro and died Chattanooga January 6, 1863, and buried in Elmwood; listed as member of Bluff City Grays in *Reminiscences of the Civil War* by John Hallum, Tunnah & Pittard printers, 1903; also per Hallum's book 2 Lieutenant, promoted to Captain, killed at Murfreesboro leading his company as sharpshooters December 31, 1862; no grave stone.

Culpepper, Joseph A.   Buried May 2, 1862   Chapel Hill 659, #70
Arkansas 9 Infantry Regiment Lieutenant/Captain Old Company I; mustered into state service July 27, 1861; no other information in compiled service record; per Irving Hospital record admitted April 16, 1862 with complaint of right leg and died May 1, 1862; listed in Elmwood 1874 book as Confederate soldier buried in Elmwood who was citizen of Memphis or vicinity with second initial "H"; wounded per Daily Burial Record Book; original grave stone illegible but appears died aged 25 years; upright CSA marker May 1, 1862, with inscription "HE FOUGHT LIKE A HERO AND DIED LIKE A CHRISTIAN."

Currin, David Maney, Sr.   Buried September 24, 1868   Chapel Hill 301, #2
Confederate Congressman (Tennessee); see sketch in Warner's Confederate Congress book page 67; born in Murfreesboro, Tennessee November 11, 1817, graduated from Nashville University at age 17, studied law and ran for state legislature, came to Memphis in 1849, after Tennessee seceded elected to the Provisional Congress and to two regular terms, died suddenly in Richmond, Virginia on March 25, 1864, before taking his seat in the Second Congress; per Daily Burial Record Book removed from Virginia time unknown; sketch in the PoliticalGraveyard.com; sketch in Elmwood Cemetery 1874 book; name spelled "Curren" in Daily Burial Record Book and computer index; large family monument with birth and death dates.

Dashiell, George T.   Buried February 21, 1906   Chapel Hill 158, #37
Captain and Pay Quartermaster on staff of Lieutenant General N. B. Forrest; first enlisted in the Tennessee 154th Senior Infantry Regiment as Private 1st Company B ("Bluff City Grays") at Randolph, Tennessee, age 34; October 22, 1861, appointed Assistant Quartermaster of the Tennessee 154th Senior Infantry Regiment; Captain and Pay Quartermaster in General Cheatham's Division to July 1863, then assigned to duty with General N. B. Forrest, then assigned to 4 Mississippi Infantry Regiment November 30, 1863, but never reported and relieved of that assignment July, 1864, January 24, 1864, assigned to General N. B. Forrest staff and was paroled May 9, 1865; per sketch in Mathes book (both editions) enlisted as Private in Company B, Tennessee 154 Senior Infantry Regiment April 28, 1861, became Paymaster of Cheatham's Division until spring 1863, then ordered to report by War Department to General Forrest, served as Chief Paymaster until end of War and early member of Confederate Historical Association; per enlarged edition born January 10, 1828, at Elk Ridge near Baltimore, Maryland, at start of War as a clerk of W. B. Miller & Company, Memphis, sent to New York to buy equipment for Army of Tennessee after Governor Harris had ordered goods from the firm, after return to Memphis joined Company B, 154 Senior Infantry Regiment, October, 1861, General Polk promoted him to Captain of Cavalry and assigned him to Pay Department of his Corps where remained until January, 1863, when General Forrest had him assigned to his command where he served until end of War as Chief Paymaster, became a member of Confederate Historical Association in 1869, was member of Company A, United Confederate Veterans, July 10, 1897, commissioned Lieutenant Colonel and Paymaster on the staff of General A. J. Vaughan, commanding the Tennessee Division of UCV; biography in *Confederate Military History, Extended Edition,* Volume X Tennessee, page 439; listed in "A COMPLETE ROSTER OF THE BLUFF CITY GREYS" located in the Memphis Room of the Memphis/Shelby County Public Library and Information Center Central Library with remarks that 'Promoted Captain & Paymaster'; listed as member of Bluff City Grays in *Reminiscences of the Civil War* by John Hallum, Tunnah & Pittard printers, 1903; see Notes of Interest - Bluff City Grays; Captain and died age 78 per Daily Burial Record Book; grave stone illegible.

Davie, Patrick Henry   Buried September 20, 1872   Fowler 278, #3
Tennessee 3 (Memphis Battalion) Infantry Battalion Corporal (Captain John B. Weld) Company A; per Company Muster Roll dated March 12, 1862, enlisted March 12, 1862, Memphis; see Notes of Interest "Memphis Battalion - Tennessee 3rd (Memphis) Infantry Battalion"; death notice in the September 21, 1872, *Memphis Daily Appeal,* page 1, column 4; cause of death Congestive Chill age 48 per Daily Burial Record Book.

Davis, Charles B.   Buried April 23, 1883   Chapel Hill 381, #4
Tennessee 3 (Forrest's) Cavalry Regiment Private Company A Musician; Company A and 1 Company B Musician 154 Senior Infantry Regiment ('Bluff City Grays'); enlisted May 14, 1861, at Randolph age 23; per 154 Senior Infantry muster roll dated August 13, 1861, transferred from Company A July 1, 1861; per 3 Cavalry records detailed 4 months as musician July 19, 1862; paroled May 11, 1865 at Gainesville, Alabama; sketch in *The Southern Bivouac,* Volume I, September 1882 - August 1883 (Broadfoot Publishing Company 1992), page 394 that indicates he was member of Fire Company 1 and killed by a tumbling wall at a fire in Memphis; article in *Memphis Daily Avalanche* April 22, 1883, page 4, "Deplorable Accident" concerning fire accident where he was killed when wall fell; article on funeral *Memphis Daily Avalanche* April 24, 1883, page 4, indicating that four pallbearer each from Fire Department and former soldiers of Bluff City Greys of Forrest's Regiment of cavalry; listed in "A COMPLETE ROSTER OF THE BLUFF CITY GREYS" located in the Memphis Room of the Memphis/Shelby County Public

Library and Information Center Central Library; listed as member of Bluff City Grays in *Reminiscences of the Civil War* by John Hallum, Tunnah & Pittard printers, 1903; see Notes of Interest - Bluff City Grays; circle grave stone: Born July 2, 1837 Died April 21, 1883; died by accident age 45 per Daily Burial Record Book.

Dawson, John Francis   Buried December 19, 1895   Turley 1391, #1
Confederate Soldier (no unit identified); per obituary in the December 19, 1895, *The Commercial Appeal* Memphis, page 5, column 6, Capt. John T. (sic) Dawson died from heart disease, at the time of his death was assistant superintendent of the citizens Street Railway Company, was in the Confederate Army and was a faithful and valiant soldier, after the war was for some years connected with the sheriff's office in this county and was for a long time jailer, and leaves a wife and six children; spouse Kathryn Myers Dawson died in 1947 in Houston, Harris County, Texas; residing in Nashville, Davidson County, Tennessee during 1870 census and Memphis, Shelby County, Tennessee during the 1880 census.

Dean, Joseph S.   Buried April 24, 1862   Chapel Hill 407, #1
Missouri 1 Infantry Regiment Company C Lieutenant Aide de Camp; enlisted July 3, 1861, Memphis age 24 per muster roll dated August 28, 1861; per undated historic roll age 22 when enlisted June 27, 1861 at Memphis, Tennessee, a resident of St. Louis, Missouri when enlisted, native of Kentucky, a merchant and elected 1 Lieutenant Company C 1 Missouri Infantry at New Madrid August 27, 1861, and assigned to General Bowen's staff September 1861, wounded Battle of Shiloh and died a few days after at Memphis; per September and October 1861 muster roll remarks: detached as Aide de Camp General Bowen's staff September 30, 1861; at Camp Beauregard, Kentucky in September 1861; severely wounded Battle of Shiloh; per Battle of Shiloh casualty list for unit reported in the April 23, 1862 *Memphis Daily Appeal* was wounded severely in battle; per obituary in the April 26, 1862, *Memphis Daily Appeal* died April 23, 1862 age 22 (note age difference) and native of Kentucky; wounded Battle of Shiloh and from St. Louis, Missouri per Daily Burial Record Book; first was Second Lieutenant Missouri State Guard Company H ("Southern Guard") 2nd Regiment, 1st Brigade Volunteer Militia of Missouri, under command of Colonel John S. Bowen at Camp Jackson, Missouri, after capture took Oath of Allegiance to U.S. and was released, then followed Colonel Bowen to Memphis where enlisted in Missouri 1 Infantry Regiment.

DeGraffenried, Henry E.   Memorial Stone   Fowler 116
Tennessee 154 Senior Infantry Regiment Captain 2 Company B; enlisted May 16, 1862; per January & February 1863, muster roll remarks: wounded at the Battle of Murfreesboro and since died at Chattanooga March 21, 1863; per report of deaths dated December 12, 1863, born South Carolina and died March 22, 1863, at Chattanooga, Tennessee from wounds received in the Battle of Murfreesboro December 31, 1862; buried at the Chattanooga Confederate cemetery per *The history of Hamilton County and Chattanooga, Tennessee Volume I*, by Zella Armstrong, Lookout Publishing Company; 1st Edition (1931), Appendix page 507.

DeSaussure, Charles Alfred   Buried May 4, 1935   Fowler 187, #11
South Carolina Stuart's Artillery (Beaufort Volunteer Artillery) Captain; originally enlisted April 1863, Company C 6 South Carolina Provisional Regiment; April 1863, transferred to Beaufort Volunteer Artillery which became Stuart's Artillery; enlisted South Carolina 8 Regiment March 23, 1864, Camp Beaufort, South Carolina; born McPhersonville, Prince William Parrish, South Carolina September 21, 1846; per Tennessee Death Certificate died in Memphis May 35, 1935, age 88; member Confederate Historical Association, Camp 28, Bivouac 18, Memphis and served as commander of Camp 28 United Confederate Veterans, Memphis; sketch in Mathes book; completed Tennessee 1914/1915 Questionnaire of Civil War Veterans; see Paul R. Coppock's Mid-South Volume III, pages 362-366 and pages 412-416; in 1921, wrote about war experiences in "The Story of my Service in the Army of the Confederacy in the War Between the States."

Devlin, James Calvin   Buried April 24, 1900   Chapel Hill 521, #3
Tennessee 3 (Forrest's) Cavalry Regiment Private Company B; per Company Muster Rolls for September 1 to December 21, 1862, enlisted March 10, 1862, at Memphis; appears on Roll of Prisoners of War paroled at Gainesville, Alabama May 11, 1865, resident of Memphis, Tennessee; per Register of Deaths in the City of Memphis, Tennessee died April 23, 1900, from pneumonia age 62; there are two bronze markers on the grave; one marker reads: James D. (painted out) Devlin Company B Forrest Tenn Cavalry 1838 1900, which dates would seem correct based on age at death; second grave stone: James C. Devlin Company B Tennessee 15 Cavalry (no record found that unit) 1840 1900 (based on Census records 1840 would be correct); there is only one "James C. Devlin" in Cemetery records and one "J. C. Devlin" 3 Cavalry in *Tennesseans in the Civil War Part 2*; per April 24, 1900, *The Commercial Appeal* Memphis died April 23, 1900; widow (second spouse) Bettie Brister Devlin received Tennessee pension (file #W5998); on pension application states did not know where he was born; widow born May 3, 1862, in Tate County, Mississippi; they were married May 16, 1882, in Tate County, Mississippi, and she died February 10, 1943.

Dill, Benjamin Franklin   Buried January 14, 1866   Turley 118, #1
Memphis Daily Appeal Business Manager and Co-Partner; "The Dills of *Memphis Daily Appeal*" and "Part of the Appeal staff in its great run in the deep south 1862-1865" inscribed on double grave stone with wife America Carolina Walker Dill, which stone also includes details on *Appeal* association; honored along with John R. McClanahan (who is buried in Elmwood Cemetery - see sketch herein) and wife America Carolina Walker Dill (who wrote editorials for the *Appeal* during the War and who died at Oxford, Mississippi April 10, 1888 and was buried April 13, 1888 age 60 Turley #2 per Cemetery record) October 11, 1998 - see *The Commercial Appeal* Memphis October 12, 1996, and Ceremony program on file in Cemetery Office; sole proprietor June 29, 1865,

after death of John R. McClanahan; see "One Hundred Years of The Commercial Appeal" The Story of the Great Romance in American Journalism 1840 to 1940 (Printed at *The Commercial Appeal*1940 by The Memphis Publishing Company) for story of "Great Civil War Run"; Born in Augusta, Georgia July 5, 1814 and Died in Forest Hill, Tennessee January 4, 1866 inscribed on grave stone; obituaries in *Memphis Daily Appeal* January 5, 1866, page 2, column 1, and January 7, 1866, page 2, columns 1-2; see sketch in Elmwood book; referred to as "W. F. Dill" in Goodspeed's Shelby County History, page 904.

Dillard, John W.   Buried October 26, 1912   Miller Circle 192, #3
Mississippi 2 Infantry Regiment, Lieutenant Company G, originally Private, later Sergeant; enlisted March 2, 1861, Pontotoc, MS, age 23, promoted 2 Lt August 2, 1861, elected 1 Lt April 13 or 21, 1862, Captain July 8, 1863 (?), wounded in battle at Gettysburg July 3, 1863, and made prisoner July 3, 1863, captured Green Castle, PA July 5, 1863, forwarded to Johnson's Island, OH July 18, 1863, per Roll of POW paroled at Johnson's Island and forwarded to City Point, VA from Fort Delaware for exchange February 24, 1865, signed Parole of Honor May 17, 1865 at Columbus, MS; biography in *Confederate Military History, Extended Edition*, Volume X Tennessee, page 446; per *Elmwood 2002: In The Shadows of the Elms*, Perre Magness, Elmwood Cemetery, Memphis, Tennessee, 2001, page 308, born in South Carolina 1837, wounded and captured at Gettysburg, spent 18 months in prison at Johnson's Island, discharged as a captain, after War burned his uniform saying that the Civil War was the "silliest ever fought", 1865 formed cotton firm T. B. Dillard & Brothers which became Dillard & Coffin in 1871, and one of the original incorporators of the Memphis Cotton Exchange (1875); March 2, 1876, elected as a director of the Memphis Gas Light Company; sketch in *Who's Who in Tennessee, A Biographical Reference Book of Notable Tennesseans To-Day*, Paul & Douglass Publishers, Memphis, 1911, page 300; circle stone Born Dec. 12, 1837 Died Oct. 24, 1912; died age 75 per Daily Burial Record Book.

Dillard, Thomas Bonds   Buried September 22, 1883   Turley 612 (Masonic Lot) D2, #59
Mississippi 1 Cavalry Regiment Captain A.Q.M. and Lieutenant Company K; first enlisted in Mississippi 1 (Miller's) Cavalry Battalion Cole's Company ("Pontotoc Dragoons") Private April 1, 1861, Pontotoc, age 33 (a number of the men from the Battalion after it disbanded about June 1862, joined the Mississippi 1 Cavalry Regiment); per Company Muster Roll for April 30 to October 30, 1862, remarks: Appointed Quarter Master 15 June 1862; per Field and Staff Muster Roll for July & August 1864, remarks: On detached service as Qr. Ms. of Recruiting, Eufaula, Ala.; appears on a Roll of Prisoners of War surrendered at Citronelle, Alabama May 4, 1865, and paroled at Jackson, Mississippi May 15, 1865; death notice (died September 21, 1883, age 54) and Masonic Funeral Notice (DeSoto Lodge F. and A.M.) in the September 22, 1883, *Memphis Daily Appeal*, page 1, column 6; per article "A Brief Sketch of His Life—Resolutions of Respect to His Memory." on page 4, column 3, born in Newbury district, S.C., September 13, 1829, 1855 engaged in planting near Pontotoc, Mississippi, where he continued up to the outbreak of the war, served as captain in Colonel Pinson's celebrated First Mississippi regiment of cavalry, and came to Memphis in 1865; died age 53 Dysentery per Register of Deaths in the City of Memphis; died age 53 Flux per Daily Burial Record Book.

Dillon, Charles R.
Listed ("C. R. Dillon") in the June 6, 1878, *Memphis Daily Appeal*, page 4, column 3, article "OUR DEAD HEROES" covering the unveiling of the Confederate Monument and Decoration of Graves at Elmwood as then one of twenty-eight members of the Bluff City Grays, Company B of the 154 Senior Infantry Regiment and Company A of Forrest's Old (Third) Cavalry Regiment buried at Elmwood; listed as one of the "comrades who sleep at Elmwood cemetery" in the article "Veterans in Council" in *Memphis Daily Appeal*, May 12, 1881, page 4, column 4, concerning the meeting of the surviving members in the city of the old Bluff City Grays to appoint the necessary committees for the purpose of making special decoration on the graves of their dead comrades at Elmwood and Calvary cemeteries on Sunday next, Memorial Day; see Notes of Interest - Bluff City Grays; listed in "A COMPLETE ROSTER OF THE BLUFF CITY GREYS" located in the Memphis Room of the Memphis/Shelby County Public Library and Information Center Central Library with notation that enlisted February 1, 1864, Prisoner of War and Died in Memphis Fall of 1877, and buried in Elmwood, which is incorrect; Tennessee 3 (Forrest's) Cavalry Regiment Private Company A ("Bluff City Grays"); per Company Muster Roll dated May 14, 1864, enlisted February 19, 1864, in the field; first enlisted in the Tennessee 154th Senior Infantry regiment Private Company G, per Company Muster-in Roll dated August 13, 1861, at New Madrid, Missouri, enlisted June 3, 1861, at Memphis age 37, per Company Muster Roll for January 1 to July 1, 1862, remarks Discharged July 16, 1862, per Company Muster Roll dated May 5, 1863, remarks Discharged overage; possibly the "Thos. R. Dillon" listed as member of Bluff City Grays in *Reminiscences of the Civil War* by John Hallum, Tunnah & Pittard printers, 1903; not found in Cemetery records; see Masonic Jewel, Volume VII, Number 5, June 1877, page 159: "Dillon - in Columbia, Tennessee, May 16, 1877, Bro. Charles R. Dillon, a member of Desoto Lodge No. 299, and Memphis Chapter No. 59, of Memphis, aged fifty-six years. Bro. Dillon was well and favorably known in Memphis and had resided here for many years. He died of an abscess in the side caused by a wound during the late war and was sick for many weeks. His lodge finally sent him to his old home, Columbia, with his loving mother, that he might die at the old homestead. He was buried with Masonic honors."; the following article printed in the May 20, 1877, *Memphis Daily Appeal*, page 4, column 3: The Columbia (Tennessee) Herald and Mail, of the eighteenth instant, contains the following: "Mr. Charles Robert Dillon, son of Mrs. Dillon, of this place, died last Wednesday morning. He took sick in Memphis, where he has lately resided, and came home with his mother a few weeks since. He was born in Columbia on the twenty-sixth day of June, 1824. He has been a citizen of Memphis for many years, in the cotton houses of Porter, Taylor & Co., and Hill, Fontaine & Co. At the beginning of the late war he joined the One Hundred and Fifty-Fourth Tennessee regiment, commanded by General Preston Smith. At Corinth he was transferred to General Forest's escort. He was taken sick at Memphis last February with an abscess in the right side, of which he died. His mother went to Memphis some seven weeks ago, and attended his sick bedside. She brought him here May 6th. His funeral services were conducted in the Presbyterian church, by Rev. J. C. Mitchell. The burial

service took place in Greenwood cemetery by the Masonic fraternity and the Knights of Honor. His life was insured for two thousand dollars, the policy made payable to his devoted mother. He was a kind and affectionate son and brother, and had a large circle of friends in Memphis and Columbia."

Dixon, Leonida V.   Buried January 24, 1879   South Grove 156, #4
Memphis Legion (Tennessee 3 Infantry Battalion) Colonel; Memphis Legion was the forerunner of the Tennessee 3 (Foute's) Infantry Battalion; only records found in Tennessee miscellaneous compiled service rolls which are copies of letters from Colonel Dixon transmitting muster rolls and asking to be mustered into service with last dated March 18, 1862; Memphis Legion, D. V. Dixon, Colonel, mentioned in July 18, 1861, *Memphis Daily Appeal*; *Memphis Daily Appeal* August 7, 1861, carries an announcement calling for the companies of the Memphis Legion, D. V. Dixon, Colonel, to gather; per *Memphis Daily Appeal*, September 26, 1878, page 1, column 4, Judge L. V. Dixon of Memphis aged 63 died September 17, 1878, in Abington, Virginia of yellow fever, citizen of Memphis past 22 years; per *Memphis Daily Appeal*, January 24, 1879, page 1, column 7, his remains will arrive today and will be interred at Elmwood Cemetery; 1816-1878 on grave stone; was a law partner of General Charles Adams.

Dockery, James Marshall   Buried March 31, 1919   Miller Circle 44, #2
South Carolina 32 Regiment of Volunteers per obituary and service sketch in *Confederate Veteran*, Volume XXVIII, August 1920, page 307, which also indicates second name "Marshall"; there was not a South Carolina 32 Infantry Regiment and not found listed in Confederate index books for any South Carolina unit; article also indicates was member of Confederate Historical Association and was on the staff of the Commander in Chief of the United Confederate Veterans; obituary in March 30, 1919, *The Commercial Appeal* Memphis indicating died at Hot Springs, Arkansas Saturday March 29, 1919, and article on page 7 referred to him as "Colonel" and that he was a Confederate veteran but no unit indicated; grave stone: born November 11, 1843 died March 29, 1919; died age 75 per Daily Burial Record Book.

Dominico, Frank   Buried August 20, 1870   Fowler 605, #33
Not found in any Confederate soldier indexes; no record found in any Missouri compiled service records rolls; per sketch in Elmwood book born in Saxoney, Altenburg, in 1827, educated mainly in Weimar, but spent some time at the University of Jena, got caught up in revolution of 1848, escaped to Switzerland, and thence to America, he finally made home in Missouri when War began, became a Confederate soldier, winning the unlimited confidence of General Price, and in his secret service was arrested within the Federal lines, and condemned to death as a spy, a doctor who recognized him and who was a classmate and member of the German Revolutionary Club of 1848 effected his escape, went to Pittsburgh, taught music, drawing and the German, and came to Memphis, where died August 19, 1870, the forty-third year of his age; not listed in Elmwood 1874 Book as Confederate soldier buried in Elmwood who was a citizen of Memphis or vicinity; *Memphis Daily Appeal*, Tuesday August 23, 1870, page 4, column 2, Local News reported "Professor Frank Dominico died at his residence, on Rayburn Avenue, last Friday evening, and was buried on Saturday. We learned that the deceased was a German by birth, but went into the Confederate army at the breaking out of hostilities, and stuck to it through the war, making a splendid soldier. He leaves a wife and four children in destitute circumstances, and we hope that the Confederate Relief Association will take some steps toward their relief."; died flux age 42 and doubled with wife, B. F. Dominico, per Cemetery records; no grave stone.

Donelson, Daniel S.   Buried May 1, 1864   Fowler 92, #3
Confederate 2 Infantry Regiment (formally known as Mississippi 25 Infantry Regiment and Martin's Regiment of Volunteers) Adjutant; originally enlisted in Tennessee 154 Senior Infantry Regiment Sergeant Company E (Hickory Rifles); per Company Muster Roll dated May 5, 1863, enlisted May 14, 1861, Randolph, Tennessee age 21 and remarks: Transferred to Colonel John D. Martin's regiment as Adjutant; no information in Confederate 2 Infantry Regiment rolls except name appears in a Letter from John D. Martin, Colonel of the organization, to Major General B. Hodge, A.A. Gen., recommending that the 2d Regiment Confederate Infantry be disbanded, which it was on May 2, 1862; Colonel Martin (buried in Elmwood see sketch herein) was next placed in command of the 4 Brigade, 1 Division, Army of the West and was killed on the first day of Battle of Corinth October 3, 1862; no compiles service records found after regiment disbanded May 8, 1862, however, information on his service can be found in a group of letters he wrote to his mother and father and other documents collected for auction (The Life and Death of C.S.A. Lt. Daniel S. Donelson – and His "Gift of the Dead", http://alexautographs.com/shopsite_sc/product510.html); on April 15, 1862, he writes his mother about the battle of Shiloh and that he has been acting Brigade and Regiment Adjutant; fall of 1862, he is in Corinth, Mississippi facing the battle of Corinth; from near Grenada, Mississippi on December 11, 1862, he writes his father saying that General Maury has recommended that he be placed in the Signal Corps and expects to be ordered to do so in a few days but no record of that appointment found; on April 4, 1863, he writes General Samuel Cooper advising that Lieutenant General John Pemberton considered the validity of his commission doubtful and has declined to recognize him as an officer and respectfully desires to know if he is legally a Lieutenant in the service; General Cooper cleared the matter up as evidenced by the next letter in his archive from Lieutenant General Pemberton that addresses him as "Lieutenant"; was in the area of Vicksburg, Mississippi when Lieutenant General Pemberton, commander of the Department of Mississippi, surrendered Vicksburg to Union General Grant on July 4, 1863; sometime between July 6th and September 12th he is paroled from Vicksburg and allowed to go home awaiting the exchange process; in a text written September 12, 1863, he questions whether he should continue to fight for the Confederate States and continues with a six page synopsis weighing the pros and cons, strengths and weakness of both sides of the argument; after raveling approximately 230 miles in eighty days, he takes time on September 20, 1863, to write his mother from Rose Hill, Mississippi advising that "...I am not yet willing to acknowledge our defeat, at the same time, I see no prospect of success - under

these circumstances I have decided that I will leave the army on account of my health and for other reasons..."; four days brings about a total change in his attitude and thought process as evidenced by his next letter on September 24, 1863, from Okolona, Mississippi indicating that after being arrested and imprisoned as a deserter would be sent to a camp of paroled prisoners and if obtain a release will go at once to Bragg's army; on September 25, he receives the news that his brother John (Captain John Samuel Donelson, Tennessee 154 Senior Infantry Regiment Company and A.A.A.G. to General Preston Smith) was killed at the battle of Chickamauga September 19, 1863; in letter penned to his mother he states that General Smith (Preston), Brother John and Mr. Richmond were the only Memphians killed at the battle; October 10, 1863, writes a letter to his father and another to his mother with details of his brother's death and where his body and possessions will remain (location unknow but "In Memory" stone located in the Gallatin City Cemetery, Gallatin, Tennessee); next seven letters in the archive are all written to Brigadier General Mackall and General Samuel Cooper, Adjutant and Inspector General by various officers with whom he had served in which they recommend him for having a good moral character, intelligence, efficience, bravery and with fine business qualifications; last letter on November 20, 1863, to his mother expresses a melancholy mood about the war and that he not yet exchanged; last known letter written to him comes on January 5, 1864, from Colonel W.W. Witherspoon, believed to be back in command of the 36th Miss. Infantry, Headquartered at Enterprise, informing him that he has been exchanged if he will report to the parole camp by November 6, 1863 (sic); next letters concern how his body is found on Camp Creek, DeSoto County, Mississippi; an accompanying document, signed by ten civilian and military witnesses and soldiers, is a medical report, April 29, 1864, bearing a crude map with the location of his body, and a description of the cause of death by gunshot wound; last two letters are summaries of his service, one placing his departure from home for parole camp as January 25, 1864 - making his death about three months before his body would be discovered; (see also Cheathem, Mark R. "The Murder of lt. Daniel Smith Donelson, C.S.A." *Jacksonian America: Society, Personality, and Politics, A historian's view of the Early American Republic*, 17 September 2012, jacksonianamerica.com/2012/09/17/the-murder-of-lt-daniel-smith-donelson-c-s-a/); obituaries in *Memphis Bulletin* April 29, 1864, April 30, 1864 and May 1, 1864, all on page 3, column 2; killed age 21 per Daily Burial Record Book.

Douglass, Henry Lee   Buried January 1, 1907   South Grove 358, #1
Tennessee 9 Infantry Regiment Colonel; Captain of Company A and appointed Colonel May 29, 1861; no enlistment in compiled service record; name spelled "Douglas" and died age 83 per Cemetery record; per small death notice in the *Commercial Appeal*, Memphis, January 1, 1907, died December 31, 1906, age 83; Colonel 9 Tenn. Reg Civil War 1826-1906 inscribed on grave stone.

Douglass, Ila Elmore   Buried October 6, 1897   Chapel Hill 40, #2
Confederate 1 Cavalry Regiment Captain Assistant Quartermaster (A.Q.M.) (record found J. E. Douglass); enlisted age 23 March 7, 1862, at Memphis by Captain M. J. Wicks; no cards for I. E. Douglass in Confederate 1 Cavalry compiled service records rolls; per General and Staff rolls Captain and appointed AQM December 9, 1862, transferred to Colonel Thomas Harrison's Cavalry May 1, 1863, once ordered to Confederate 12 Cavalry Regiment but never did and paroled May 16, 1865, as Captain and AQM Harrison's Cavalry Brigade; per sketch in Mathes book first Private Company I 1 Confederate Cavalry, went out with Captain M. J. Wicks, later under Captain Jackson, then under Captain A. C. Bettis, elected or promoted to 3 Lieutenant April 1862, later promoted to Captain and AQM and assigned to Wharton's Regiment and afterwards Harrison's, then promoted to Major and AQM Wharton's Division, Wheeler's Corps but never received a commission, paroled May 10, 1865, and became a member of the Confederate Historical Association at an early day; also believed to be same J. E. Douglass 2 Lieutenant Confederate 1 Cavalry who per Lindsley's Annals was transferred; per sketch in *Tennessee, The Volunteer State, 1769-1923*, Volume II, pages 388-389 (name spelled "Douglas"), long a leading citizen and successful planter of Shelby county and a Confederate veteran of the Civil war, passed away on the 5th of October, 1897, when fifty-three years of age, born Wilson county, Tennessee, October 12, 1844, his father being Ennis Douglas, left an orphan at the tender age of eight, losing his father at that time, while his mother had died when he was a little lad of but four years, obtained his education in the schools of Dancyville and afterward came to Memphis but had resided in this city for but a brief period when the Civil war broke out, joined the Confederate forces as a private of Company I, First Tennessee Cavalry, and served successively under Captains M. J. Wicks, Jackson and A. C. Bettis, in April, 1862, promoted to the rank of third lieutenant, while subsequently he became captain and assistant quartermaster, being first assigned to duty with Wharton's regiment and later with Harrison's regiment, next won promotion as major and assistant quartermaster of Wharton's division, Wheeler's corps, but never received his commission as major, family still has in its possession the document appointing him to the quartermaster's department, dated Richmond, Virginia, June 6, 1864, and signed R. G. H. Kean, chief of bureau of war, Captain I. E. Douglas, A. Q. M., paroled May 10, 1865, and at an early day became a member of the Confederate Historical Association; died age 56 per Daily Burial Record Book.

Doyle, Decatur John   Buried February 2, 1874   Chapel Hill 347, #3
Listed in Elmwood 1874 book as Confederate soldier buried in Elmwood who was citizen of Memphis or vicinity and sketch; per sketch "...was born in Memphis, and when too young to become a soldier was a volunteer with Gen. Forrest through the three last years of the war between the States. While in this service he was severely wounded in the body, and, never recovering from the effects of the injury, died in Memphis January 31st, 1874, about twenty-eight years of age. He was greatly beloved by his comrades in arms, and no young gentleman has died in Memphis whose untimely fate was more deeply deplored."; name "Dennis J. D. Doyle" in Daily Burial Record Book and computer index and "Dennis John Decatur Doyle" in Chapel Hill book; grave stone: "Decatur John Doyle" January 31, 1874; died age 27 per Daily Burial Record Book; death notice in the February 1, 1874, *Memphis Daily Appeal*, page 1: "Death of Mr. Decatur J. Doyle occurred last night at Peabody Hotel aged 28"; obituary in February 2, 1874, *Memphis Daily Appeal*, page 4: "he was conspicuous as a soldier in Confederate army and bore to his final rest undeniable evidence

of his gallantry - the scars of wounds received in one of the terrible engagements in the western department"; believed to be the "D. J. Doyle" listed in the June 6, 1878, *Memphis Daily Appeal*, page 4, column 3, article "OUR DEAD HEROES" covering the unveiling of the Confederate Monument and Decoration of Graves at Elmwood as then one of twenty-eight members of the Bluff City Grays, Company B of the 154 Senior Infantry Regiment and Company A of Forrest's Old (Third) Cavalry Regiment buried at Elmwood and listed as one of the "comrades who sleep at Elmwood cemetery " in the article "Veterans in Council" in *Memphis Daily Appeal*, May 12, 1881, page 4, column 4, concerning the meeting of the surviving members in the city of the old Bluff City Grays to appoint the necessary committees for the purpose of making special decoration on the graves of their dead comrades at Elmwood and Calvary cemeteries on Sunday next, Memorial Day; not listed as member of Bluff City Grays in *Reminiscences of the Civil War* by John Hallum, Tunnah & Pittard printers, 1903, but his brother W. J. P. Doyle is listed; not listed in the "A COMPLETE ROSTER OF THE BLUFF CITY GREYS" located in the Memphis Room of the Memphis/Shelby County Public Library and Information Center Central Library but his brother W. J. P. Doyle is listed, however, he is listed on the last page as being buried in Elmwood; see also Notes of Interest - Bluff City Grays; no "D. J. Doyle" or "Decatur J. Doyle" found 154 Senior Infantry Regiment or 3 (Forrest's) Cavalry Regiment records, or Confederate index books.

Doyle, Washington Jackson P.   Buried April 3, 1907   Chapel Hill 347, #7
Tennessee 3 (Forrest's) Cavalry Regiment Lieutenant Company A "Bluff City Grays"; first enlisted Sergeant1 Company B Tennessee 154 Senior Infantry Regiment May 14, 1861 Randolph age 22; last card in 154 record is a payment descriptive list as paid March 3, 1863, for October 1, 1862 to February 28, 1863; per 3 Cavalry records enlisted May 4, 1861, Randolph, Tennessee, appointed Lieutenant October 8, 1863, and per descriptive list born Nashville, Tennessee; listed as member of Bluff City Grays in *Reminiscences of the Civil War* by John Hallum, Tunnah & Pittard printers, 1903; listed in the "A COMPLETE ROSTER OF THE BLUFF CITY GREYS" located in the Memphis Room of the Memphis/Shelby County Public Library and Information Center Central Library with notation that "1st Corp. Elected 2d Lt. 1864"; see also Notes of Interest - Bluff City Grays; grave stone: Born Hermitage, Tennessee February 22, 1836 April 2, 1907; died age 68 per Daily Burial Record Book; birth year should be 1839 when comparing age at death and age at enlistment; per widow Minerva Hosbrook (Selden) Doyle Tennessee pension (file #W8196) he was born "Washington Jackson Phif? Doyle" February 22, 1836, in Hermitage (Nashville), Tennessee, General Andrew Jackson was his grandfather, and he died April 2, 1907; she was born April 19, 1849, in Louisiana and they were married August 4, 1865, in Shelby County, Tennessee.

Driver, William T.   Buried July 21, 1866   Chapel Hill Circle 72, #2
Tennessee 2 (Robison's) Infantry Regiment Major; enlisted May 1, 1861, Memphis age 20; 2 Lieutenant Company E and promoted to Adjutant May 6, 1861; elected Major May 1, 1862; per April 30 to August 31, 1864, muster roll remarks: killed in action at Jonesboro, Georgia August 31, 1864; unit also known as Confederate 2 Infantry under which name the unit sketch is found in Lindsley's Annals; listed in Elmwood 1874 book as Confederate soldier buried in Elmwood who was citizen of Memphis or vicinity and sketch; per sketch born Pontotoc County, Mississippi June 15, 1840, and killed on the battlefield at Jonesboro, Georgia August 31, 1864; graduate of the University of Mississippi Class of 1861; elected Captain of "University Blues" that was organized at the University in 1861 (The Oxford Register, January 16, 1861; William B. Lowry listed as Captain in February 23, 1861, issue) and which later became known as "University Greys" and Company A of the Mississippi 11 Infantry Regiment (no record found in this Regiment's compiled service records); member of the Eta Chapter of Sigma Chi Fraternity at the University; signed autograph book of Anthony D. Whitfield, University of Mississippi Class of 1862 (copy in Greenwood, Mississippi Library) and indicated born June 15, 1840, and occupation as agriculturalist; brother-in-law of Colonel William R. Hunt; originally placed in Driver Vault and moved to Chapel Hill Circle; "William T. only son of Eli M. & Julia S. Driver, Late Major of the 2nd Regt Tenn Vol's C.S.A., Born in Pontotoc County, Miss June 15, 1840, Killed at his Post by a shell at the Battle of Jonesboro, GA Aug. 31, 1864, Midst the roar of battle, he yielded his young life which he had consecrated to his Country's Defense" on Driver monument; mentioned in General W. B. Bates' speech printed in the article "Elmwood" (Grand and Imposing Ceremonies of Commemoration Day), in *Memphis Sunday Appeal*, May 8, 1870, page 4, column 2.

DuBose, Julius J.   Buried March 24, 1912   Turley 829, #3
Arkansas 9 Infantry Old Companies I & H; mustered into service July 27, 1861 Pine Bluff, Arkansas; transferred to Company H October 24, 1861; per October 31 to December 31, 1862 muster roll remarks: absent without leave; per January 1 to May 1, 1863, muster roll remarks: absent and returned to Arkansas by order of General Holmes; per General and Staff records (initials "J. G.") Drill Master, Quartermaster Sergeant, Reserve Corps, Davies Brigade, Prisoner of War card indicates (captured) surrendered at LaGrange, Tennessee May 20, 1865, and remarks that had left command at Panolia (sic), Mississippi; per sketch in Mathes book born in Shelby County and studied law at University of Lebanon, early in War joined Arkansas 9 Infantry, after Shiloh transferred to the Trans-Mississippi Department with rank of Lieutenant, promoted to Captain and made chief inspector and ordnance officer for the Department of North Arkansas and the Indian Territory, later with General Magruder and rendered special service, sent into Federal lines several times to gather information with the last time he came out to find that the surrender had taken place, never captured, wounded or paroled, after War came to Memphis, practiced law, edited the *Public Ledger*, took part in local politics, elected to the State Senate and served a year or two, served as Judge of Criminal Court, and became member of the Confederate Historical Association July 1, 1869; per sketch in *Confederate Military History, Extended Edition*, Volume X Tennessee, page 456, born December 13, 1839, enlisted as private in Arkansas Infantry, made color-bearer, transferred to Trans-Mississippi Department with General Hindman, rank of Lieutenant as drill master in Morgan's Arkansas Cavalry Regiment, detailed as ordnance officer at Fort Smith, later appointed chief inspector of the Army of North Arkansas and Indian Territory at rank of Captain, after War made

way to Memphis and engaged in practice of law except two years as editor of Evening Ledger, served seven years upon the bench of the Criminal Court, served as state senator of Shelby and Fayette counties in 1871-72, and 30 years member of Confederate Historical Association; per the *Commercial Appeal*, Memphis March 22, 1912, died March 21, 1912, aged 72 and per article on page 1, column 2, born 1839 in Shelby County near where Millington is now located, same information on War service except indicates was a Lieutenant Colonel, never surrendered, early member of Ku Klux Klan, and once impeached, convicted and driven from the bench; second name may have been "Jesse"; no grave stone; sketch in Goodspeed's Shelby County History, page 954.

Duff, William Lewis   Buried March 16, 1909   Chapel Hill Circle 5, #3
Mississippi 8 Cavalry Regiment Colonel; originally enlisted as 3 Lieutenant Mississippi 17 Infantry Regiment on April 23, 1861, at Sarepta, Mississippi; per muster roll dated June 7 - May 28, 1861, age 21, and student when enlisted; elected Captain April 10, 1862; promoted to Major October 21, 1862; per November & December 1862, muster roll remarks: wounded at Fredericksburg and absent; per January & February 1864, muster roll remarks: commanding cavalry regiment in Mississippi and dropped from rolls January 1, 1864; promoted Lieutenant Colonel 19 Mississippi Cavalry Battalion September 1, 1863; one card in record has Mississippi as where born and another has South Carolina and age 22 when enlisted; on register of General Hospital Richmond, Virginia dated May 12, 1863, with remarks that was transferred May 14, 1863, to Jackson, Mississippi and given permission to raise cavalry; Mississippi 8 Cavalry Regiment was organized September 10, 1863, as the 19 Cavalry Battalion and was increased to regiment February 15, 1864, and known as Duff's Regiment Mississippi Cavalry until designated the 8 Regiment by Special Order 169 dated July 19, 1864; promoted to Colonel February 15, 1864; Parole dated July 8, 1865, at Oxford, Mississippi; per sketch in Mathes book enlisted May 1861, successively Captain, Major and Lieutenant Colonel Mississippi 17 Infantry Regiment, afterwards raised and was Colonel of Mississippi 8 Cavalry in 1863 and became member of Confederate Historical Association May 26, 1870; mentioned in an article in May 19, 1873, *Memphis Daily Appeal*, page 4, on Association meeting to plan attendance at funeral of Colonel Richard Alexander Pinson; died age 64 per Daily Burial Record Book. Per Bruce Allardice died February 2, 1909 in San Francisco, California and first buried Mountain View Cemetery, Oakland and moved to Elmwood.

Dunavant, William Pemberton   Buried June 1, 1891   Lenow Circle 97, #3
Colonel - C.S.A. inscribed on grave stone; no compiled military service record found; may have served as a "volunteer aide" because of his railroad construction business; see sketch on Samuel Tate who was appointed Colonel and Volunteer Aide by General Albert Sidney Johnston, Commander of the Western Department of the Army; per *Railroad Builders: The Dunavant Family of Virginia, North Carolina and Tennessee*. C. H. Robertson, Lulu Press, Inc., Raleigh, NC, 2016 Edition, "By 1856, the Dunavants had begun building Southern railroads and they would eventually be among the South's prominent railroad contractors. They migrated from Southside VA to Western NC and Memphis, TN, adding to those regions new railroads, hotels, golf clubs, dams and tunnels. For 73 years, from 1856 to 1929, the Dunavants' large-scale construction projects contributed substantially to the development of Southside VA, Western NC (Morganton, Charlotte, Statesville, Asheville and Blowing Rock), and the South. In TN, the Dunavants were instrumental in developing Memphis as a railroad hub, and their descendants would build the world's largest privately-owned cotton company."; per History of Dunavant Enterprises (http://www.dunavantenterprises.com/about-us/dunavant-history/) "Colonel William Pemberton Dunavant and General Nathan Bedford Forrest were early pioneers of the first short-line railroads built in Mississippi. These later became part of the Frisco Railroad, used extensively for transporting cotton, freight and other agricultural product."; grave stone: August 28, 1837 May 30, 1891.

Dupuy, A. P.   Buried July 13, 1862   Turley 1, #6
Tennessee 154 Senior Infantry Regiment 2 Lieutenant Company L; enlisted March 7, 1862 Memphis (no age indicated); per register of soldiers who died of wounds: deceased July 1862 Memphis wounds; per May 6, 1863 muster roll remarks for "H. P." (age 28): not re-elected at organization, died from effects of wounds; not found Lindsley's Annals; cards for "H. P. Dupuy" in same unit under "A. P. Dupuy"; listed in Elmwood 1874 book as Confederate soldier buried in Elmwood who was citizen of Memphis or vicinity with first initial "S"; Daily Burial Record Book grave column indicates "Northwest Cor."

Duttlinger, John   Buried September 29, 1873   Chapel Hill 541, #2
Tennessee 3 (Memphis Battalion) Infantry Battalion 1 Lieutenant/Captain F. W. Buttinghaus' Co. F, enlisted March 12, 1862, age 38; see Notes of Interest "Memphis Battalion - Tennessee 3 (Memphis Battalion) Infantry Battalion"; name spelled "Dutlinger" in Daily Burial Record Book and computer index and Register of Death in the City of Memphis; died age 49 of Yellow Fever per Death Register; large/tall grave stone: John Duttlinger, Born in Baden, Germany, Feb. 4, 1826, Died Sep. 28, 1873; wife's, Josepha Duttlinger, birth (March 13, 1832) Baden-Wurttemberg, Germany and death (November 16, 1879) inscribed on the stone; death notice in *Memphis Daily Appeal*, September 29, 1873, page 1, column 7, indicating died September 28, age 50; Biographical Sketch in Elmwood 1874 book but not listed as Confederate soldier buried in Elmwood who was citizen of Memphis or vicinity.

Eanes, John E.   Buried July 30, 1866   Turley 258, #4
Tennessee 3 (Forrest's Old) Cavalry Regiment Sergeant Company A "Bluff City Grays"; first enlisted in 154th Senior Infantry Regiment Private 1st Company B, and per Company Muster-in Roll enlisted May 14, 1861, at Randolph, Tennessee age 24; per 3 Cavalry records Company Muster Roll for January 1 to July 1, 1862, enlisted May 4, 1861, at Randolph, Tennessee, appears on a register of Prisoners of War at Memphis, Tennessee – Deserters from rebel army dated May 19, 1864, with residence as Memphis, Tennessee and age 27, appears on a register of Prisoners of War belonging to the Rebel Army in custody of Provost Marshall, Memphis, Tennessee received May 7, 1864, sent from Bolivar, Tennessee and released on oath May 10, 1864, by Provost Marshall

and remarks deserter, name appears as signature on an Oath of Amnesty subscribed and sworn to at Memphis, Tennessee May 18 to 31, 1864, age 27, appears on Roll of Prisoners of War paroled at Gainesville, Alabama May 11, 1865, resident of Memphis, Tennessee; listed in Elmwood 1874 book as Confederate soldier buried in Elmwood who was citizen of Memphis or vicinity; listed in the June 6, 1878, *Memphis Daily Appeal*, page 4, column 3, article "OUR DEAD HEROES" covering the unveiling of the Confederate Monument and Decoration of Graves at Elmwood as then one of twenty-eight members of the Bluff City Grays, Company B of the 154 Senior Infantry Regiment and Company A of Forrest's Old (Third) Cavalry Regiment buried at Elmwood; listed as one of the "comrades who sleep at Elmwood cemetery" in the article "Veterans in Council" in *Memphis Daily Appeal*, May 12, 1881, page 4, column 4, concerning the meeting of the surviving members in the city of the old Bluff City Grays to appoint the necessary committees for the purpose of making special decoration on the graves of their dead comrades at Elmwood and Calvary cemeteries on Sunday next, Memorial Day; listed in "A Complete Roster of The Bluff City Greys" located in the Memphis Room of the Memphis/Shelby County Public Library and Information Center Central Library with notation Died near Memphis, and buried in Elmwood; listed as member of Bluff City Grays in *Reminiscences of the Civil War* by John Hallum, Tunnah & Pittard printers, 1903; see also Notes of Interest - Bluff City Grays; death and funeral reported July 30, 1866, in both the *Memphis Daily Appeal*, page 3, column 3, and *Public Ledger* (Memphis), page 2, column 4; article "Melancholy Occurrence — A Man Shot and Instantly Killed" in the Monday Evening July 30, 1866, *Public Ledger* (Memphis), page 3, column 3, states that he is shot with his own gun after laying down "apparently to rest" and lived only a couple of minutes and also states that he was about 31 years of age, unmarried, and had served in the Confederate army during the war, being a member of the Bluff City Grays, McDonald's Battalion; Daily Burial Record Book has name "Mr. J. E. Eanes" and pistol shot; Cemetery computer index has name "Eaves, J. C."; grave stone partly illegible: born in Hardeman County, Tennessee (date not clear) and died near Memphis (date not clear).

Edmondson, Edmond Augustus   Buried November 23, 1913   Turley 1007, #5
Tennessee 3 (Forrest's) Cavalry Regiment Adjutant Company A "Bluff City Grays"; first enlisted in 154th Senior Infantry Regiment Private 1st Company B, per Company Muster-in Roll dated August 13, 1861, enlisted May 14, 1861, at Randolph, Tennessee age 22; assigned to extra duty as Clerk in the A.A.G. Office November 27, 1862, to July 15, 1863; per 3 Cavalry records Company Muster Roll for January 1 to July 1, 1862, enlisted May 4, 1861, at Randolph, Tennessee, appointed Adjutant of the battalion March 22, 1864; appears on Roll of Prisoners of War paroled at Columbus, Mississippi May, 1865, resident of Memphis, Tennessee; listed in "A COMPLETE ROSTER OF THE BLUFF CITY GREYS" located in the Memphis Room of the Memphis/Shelby County Public Library and Information Center Central Library with notation "Detailed Ge. Chalmers A.A.G.O."; listed as member of Bluff City Grays in *Reminiscences of the Civil War* by John Hallum, Tunnah & Pittard printers, 1903; see also Notes of Interest - Bluff City Grays; grave stone: March 31, 1839 November 22, 1913.

Edmondson, Isabella Buchanan "Belle"   Buried July 16, 1873   Chapel Hill 162, #12
Confederate Secret Agent; the following narrative is from *Heroines of Dixie: Winter of Desperation*, Katharine M. Jones, editor, Mockingbird Books, St. Simons, Inc., Chapter 11, page 62, "Belle Edmondson - Smuggling from Memphis" *At eighteen Belle Edmondson was living with her family at their plantation house near Nonconnah in Shelby County, Tennessee, where her father had large holdings of land and slaves. A war romance ended sadly when her Confederate soldier boy was transferred to Mobile and transferred his affections. Perhaps because of this unhappy love affair, Belle, according to family tradition, volunteered as a secret agent for the Confederacy. After near-by Memphis was occupied by Federal troops in June 1862, she engaged in the dangerous business of smuggling contraband between the lines. Her father served as a volunteer scout and her two brothers were with General Forrest. During the war years Belle kept a diary which is a lively account of life on the plantation and her activities in occupied Memphis, the center of drug and cotton smuggling.*; see also "A lost heroine of the Confederacy," editors Loretta and William Galbraith, University Press of Mississippi, 1990, transcribed from: Diary of Belle Edmondson January - November, 1864 (transcript), from the manuscript (#1707) in the Southern Historical Collection, University of North Carolina at Chapel Hill; died age 32 per Daily Burial Record Book; listed in "Touring Historic Elmwood Cemetery" Brochure (January 2000) #68.

Edmondson, James Howard   Buried October 21, 1884   Chapel Hill 162/163, #22
Tennessee 11 (Holman's) Cavalry Regiment Colonel; originally Captain 1st Company B ("Bluff City Grays") Tennessee 154 Senior Infantry Regiment, per Company Muster-in Roll dated August 13, 1861, enlisted May 14, 1861, at Randolph, Tennessee age 28; single card in Tennessee 3 Cavalry Regiment records indicating Captain Company A; appointed Colonel Tennessee 11 Cavalry February 25, 1863, by General N. B. Forrest, resigned July 22, 1863; listed in "A COMPLETE ROSTER OF THE BLUFF CITY GREYS" located in the Memphis Room of the Memphis/Shelby County Public Library and Information Center Central Library with notation "Captain Co. Resigned May 1861 Afterwards Col. 11th Tenn. Cav. Died Memphis, October 20, 1884."; listed as member of Bluff City Grays in *Reminiscences of the Civil War* by John Hallum, Tunnah & Pittard printers, 1903; see also Notes of Interest - Bluff City Grays; listed in Mathes book as a member of Confederate Historical Association but no sketch; died congestion age 53 per Daily Burial Record Book.

Elcan, Dr. Joseph John   Buried June 15, 1914   Turley 1279, #3
Tennessee 7 Cavalry Regiment Private Company B; per Company Muster-in Roll dated August 31, 1861, enlisted May 31,1861, Mason Depot, Tennessee age 19; appears on a Roll of Prisoners of War surrendered at Citronelle, Alabama, May 4, 1865, and paroled at Grenada, Mississippi, May 18, 1865; sketch in Goodspeed's 1887 Biographical Sketches, Tipton County, Tennessee, "a practicing physician of Mason, Tipton County, Tennessee, was born in Haywood County, December 27, 1841, and is a son of George H. and Elizabeth H. Elcan, natives of Virginia and North Carolina. Our subject was raised on a farm and received his

education at Covington, Tennessee, and in 1860 commenced the study of medicine under Dr. G. M. Whitthorne, of Bellefonte, Fayette County, Tennessee. In 1861 he entered the Confederate service; was under General Forrest in the Seventh Tennessee Regiment of volunteers until the close of the war, and participated in most of the battles that Forrest's command engaged in. When the war closed he again took up his chosen profession, medicine, and commenced the study of it under Dr. A. D. Clement, and his brother, Dr. A. L. Elcan, of Tipton County, Tennessee, and in 1869-1870 attended the Medical University of Louisville, Ky. Since then he has been constantly engaged in the practice of medicine, and has established the reputation of being a well read and reliable physician. Dr. Elcan was married March 4, 1874, to Kate Green, daughter of Nathaniel and Lucy A. Green, of Virginia, and by this marriage has a son and a daughter: Lizzie R. and Claude V. Dr. and Mrs. Elcan are members of the Episcopal Church; also a K. of H. (Knights of Honor), and in politics is a Democrat. He is highly esteemed both as a citizen and a physician in his community."

Eldridge, Thomas Dillon   Buried December 18, 1912   Chapel Hill Circle 75, #4
Per sketch (submitted by Jeanne E. Cloyes Crawford of Memphis) in file at Elmwood Cemetery Office served as attorney general for Shelby County from 1859 until he was arrested by Federal troops in the occupation of Memphis, escaped and reached Selma, Alabama where served as clerk to the commanding officer of the CSA unit there until his capture at the surrender of Selma and his parole to Memphis; also per sketch born in Pulaski, Tennessee in 1823, attended school there and received appointment to West Point but did not stay and studied law at Pulaski and was appointed assistant attorney general soon after passing the his exams and came to Memphis in 1854 at age 31 to become a partner with his brother-in-law Archibald Wright and opposed to both slavery and secession and never joined the army; per obituary in *The Commercial Appeal* Memphis December 18, 1912, died December 17, 1912, and large article and picture on page 8, column 1 that indicates born April 8, 1822 (sic); grave stone: 1923 – 1912.

Ellett, Henry Thomas   Buried October 17, 1887   Turley 1065½, #1
Per congressional sketch in the PoliticalGraveyard.com a Representative from Mississippi, born in Salem, New Jersey, March 8, 1812, attended the Latin School in Salem and Princeton College, studied law and was admitted to the bar in 1833 and commenced practice in Bridgeton, Cumberland County, New Jersey, moved to Port Gibson, Claiborne County, Mississippi, in 1837 and continued the practice of law, elected as a Democrat to the Twenty-ninth Congress to fill the vacancy caused by the resignation of Jefferson Davis and served from January 26 to March 3, 1847, declined to be a candidate for reelection in 1846 and resumed the practice of law, member of the State senate 1853-1865, member of the State secession convention in 1861 and member of the committee that framed and reported the ordinance of secession of Mississippi, appointed Postmaster General of the Confederacy in February 1861 but declined, elected judge of the State supreme court on October 2, 1865 and served until January 1868 when he resigned, moved to Memphis, Tennessee in 1868 and resumed the practice of law, elected chancellor of the twelfth division of Tennessee in 1886, and died while delivering an address of welcome to President Grover Cleveland in Memphis, Tennessee, October 15, 1887; death mentioned in Past Times article "More famous in death then in life" by Perre Magness, *The Commercial Appeal* Memphis, April 22, 1999, Neighbors Section, page 2; obituary in *Memphis Daily Appeal* October 16, 1887, page 2, column 1; died age 75 years, 7 months, 7 days from heart disease per Daily Burial Record Book; grave stone partly illegible.

Elliott, Leonidas Hooper   Buried February 4, 1866   South Grove 52, #3
Tennessee 154 Senior Infantry Regiment Private Company E; enlisted May 14, 1861, Randolph; record found under first name "Lee"; per May 5, 1863, muster roll remarks: 3 Corporal and age 21; listed in Elmwood 1874 book as Confederate soldier buried in Elmwood who was citizen of Memphis or vicinity and sketch, which indicates that he enlisted May, 1861, wounded six times and twice on November 30, 1864, at Battle of Franklin, Tennessee and died of these wounds at Columbus, Mississippi February 12, 1865, at age 25 with remains brought to Elmwood; mentioned by Dr. S. H. Ford in his address on the occasion to commemorate (Confederate Memorial Day) Confederates buried at Elmwood on April 26, 1866, (see article "Honors To The Memory Of The Hero Dead" in the April 27, 1866, *Memphis Daily Appeal*, page 3, column 1); not found Lindsley's Annals; moved-in per Daily Burial Record Book; grave stone died (date illegible) aged 26 years.

English, Richard Theodore   Buried October 15, 1871   Turley 612 (Masonic Lot), D1 #21
Mississippi English's Company Light Artillery Captain; enlisted August 11, 1862, Fayette, Mississippi age 29; unit organized August 11, 1862, for 2 years or war by officers who formerly belonged to Captain English 1 Company F 1 Regiment Confederate Infantry; per sketch in Mathes book joined Confederate Relief and Historical Association July 1, 1869, and died in this city (Memphis) October 13, 1871, born July 4, 1832 in Chester County, Pennsylvania, removed to Natchez, Mississippi with family in 1852, April 1861, 3 Lieutenant Quitman Artillery, Captain 3 months later, appointed Provost Marshall at Port Hudson, captured in 1863, sent to Camp Chase, Ohio, before capture appointed to Lieutenant Colonel of artillery and was on way to serve under Kirby Smith when taken prisoner and funeral attended by the Masonic Brotherhood; buried Free Mason lot; died heart disease age 39 per Daily Burial Record Book.

Ensley, Edward L.   Buried May 7, 1862   Lenow Circle 13, #3
Tennessee 11 (Gordon's) Cavalry Battalion Captain Company D; no information in compiled service record (all cards undated); originally buried Chapel Hill 58; funeral notice in the May 6, 1862, *Memphis Daily Appeal* indicating died age 24; grave stone indicates died May 5, 1862, aged 28 years.

Erskine, Dr. Alexander O.   Buried December 15, 1913   Chapel Hill Circle 55, #6
Surgeon; per General and Staff record appointed Surgeon May 30, 1863, to rank November 16, 1862; record also found Tennessee

2 (Robison's) Infantry Regiment Assistant Surgeon which compiled service record indicates his date of commission as December 19, 1862; per sketch in Mathes book born in Huntsville, Alabama September 26, 1832, studied four years at the University of Virginia graduating in Chemistry and German, read medicine in his father's office at Huntsville, returned to the University where he took a medical course, went to the University of New York and graduated there in medicine in 1858 and settled in Memphis the same year; further per Mathes sketch when War broke out entered Confederate service and was with Generals Cleburne, Cheatham, Bragg and Polk in Tennessee, Kentucky, Mississippi and Georgia and after War resumed medical practice in Memphis; per sketch in *Who's Who in Tennessee, A Biographical Reference Book of Notable Tennesseans To-Day*, Paul & Douglass Publishers, Memphis, 1911, page 304 first enlisted Tennessee 15 Infantry Regiment under Colonel Tyler but no record found on the same; biography in *Confederate Military History, Extended Edition*, Volume X Tennessee, page 464; brother of Dr. John H. Erskine (see his sketch herein); article on death in *The Commercial Appeal* Memphis December 14, 1913, page 7, indicating died December 13, 1913, age 81; no grave stone.

Erskine, Dr. John Henry   Buried September 17, 1878   Chapel Hill Circle 55, #3
Surgeon; per General and Staff record appointed Assistant Surgeon from Tennessee April 27, 1861, November 29, 1862, appointed Surgeon, March 30, 1862, Medical Director Cleburne's Division, 2 Corps Army of Tennessee, March 1865 Surgeon and Medical Director of Lee's Corps Army of Tennessee, and paroled in North Carolina as Surgeon, Acting Medical Director Army of Tennessee April 1865; record also found Tennessee 2 (Robison's) Infantry Regiment Assistant Surgeon which compiled service record indicates his date of appointment as May 6, 1861; per *Confederate Staff Officers 1861 -1865* by Joseph H. Crute, Jr. (Derwent Books 1982): a) January 1, 1863, Staff Medical Inspector on Staff of Major General Patrick R. Cleburne, Surgeon, 2 Tennessee Infantry Regiment Provisional Army; b) May 2, 1862, Surgeon on Staff of Major General John C. Breckinridge; c) February 18, 1864, Surgeon on Staff of Major General Stephen D. Lee; and d) 1865 Surgeon on Staff of General Joseph E. Johnston; per sketch (with photograph) in Mathes book (see pages 92 and 246) born at Huntsville, Alabama December 23, 1834, and was one of three brothers, Drs. Albert and Alexander (see his sketch herein) being the others, who went through the War as Confederate surgeons, graduated in medicine at the University of New York in 1858 and at once began practice in Memphis, early in 1861 was commissioned as assistant surgeon of Bate's (Robison) Second Tennessee Regiment, served more than a year as such, was promoted to the rank of senior surgeon on the staff of General Cleburne, and was soon chief surgeon of Cleburne's Division, next was medical inspector of Hardee's Corps, became chief surgeon of the corps, and at the close he was acting as medical director of the Army of Tennessee on the staff of General Joseph E. Johnston; further per Mathes sketch after War became member of Confederate Historical Association July 15, 1869, served as Memphis health officer in 1873, 1876 and 1878 and died of yellow fever September 17, 1878; biography in *Confederate Military History, Extended Edition*, Volume X Tennessee, page 465; subject of Past Times article "Library named for heroic physician" by Perre Magness, *The Commercial Appeal* Memphis, March 23, 2000, Section EM, Neighbors, page 2, indicating that the Health Department library was named in honor of one of the martyrs of Memphis medicine when in 1974 the library in the L. M. Graves Building was named the John H. Erskine Memorial Library, " to stand for all to remember with gratitude the supreme sacrifice made by Dr. Erskine when he laid down his life for his fellow men"; Magness article also describes his War service and post War service as Memphis health officer and that he sacrificed his life during the disastrous yellow fever epidemic of 1878; subject of story "Memphis' No. 1 Fighter of Yellow Fever-John H. Erskine" (June 9, 1974) in *Paul R. Coppock's Mid-South*, Volume II, pages 242-246; death reported in *Memphis Daily Appeal*, September 18, 1878, page 1, indicating died September 17, 1878, of yellow fever age 44.

Estes, Zenas Newton, Sr.   Buried September 25, 1904   Chapel Hill Circle 36, #5
Confederate 1 Cavalry Regiment 1 Lieutenant (M. J. Wicks') Company I; per Company Muster-in Roll dated March 7, 1862, enlisted March 7, 1862, Memphis age 27; received gun shot wound through the nose May 21, 1864; paroled at Gainesville, Alabama, May 11, 1865; per Estes Genealogies 1097—1893 (Salem, Massachusetts 1894) born in Burke County, N. C., December 1, 1831, and is senior partner of Z. N. Estes & Co., wholesale grocer and cotton factor, Union street, Memphis, Tennessee; grave stone: 1831 - 1904; died age 72 per Daily Burial Record Book.

Evans, James M.   Buried May 5, 1862   Chapel Hill 659, #71
Missouri 6 Regiment Company C and died Overton Hospital per Daily Burial Record Book; no compiled service record found; not found Confederate general index or any Missouri 6 unit for "J. M." or "James M."

Evans, Joe
Listed as one of the "comrades who sleep at Elmwood cemetery " in the article "Veterans in Council" in *Memphis Daily Appeal*, May 12, 1881, page 4, column 4, concerning the meeting of the surviving members in the city of the old Bluff City Grays to appoint the necessary committees for the purpose of making special decoration on the graves of their dead comrades at Elmwood and Calvary cemeteries on Sunday next, Memorial Day; he was not listed in the June 6, 1878, *Memphis Daily Appeal*, page 4, column 3, article "OUR DEAD HEROES" covering the unveiling of the Confederate Monument and Decoration of Graves at Elmwood as then one of twenty-eight members of the Bluff City Grays, Company B of the 154 Senior Infantry Regiment and Company A of Forrest's Old (Third) Cavalry Regiment buried at Elmwood, which article lists all others that were in the 1881 article; listed in "A COMPLETE ROSTER OF THE BLUFF CITY GREYS" located in the Memphis Room of the Memphis/Shelby County Public Library and Information Center Central Library with notation that "Promoted Captain 10th Tenn. Mch. '62" but not included in list of those buried in Elmwood; note also listed in the Roster is "Evans, J" with no notation or burial indicated but no records found for him; believed to be the "John D. Evans" listed as member of Bluff City Grays in *Reminiscences of the Civil War* by John

Hallum, Tunnah & Pittard printers, 1903; see also Notes of Interest - Bluff City Grays; Tennessee 10 Infantry Regiment Lieutenant Company B, no enlisted information, appears on a Register of Floyd House and Ocmulgee Hospitals, Macon, Georgia, admitted October 17, 1863, and resident of Somerville, Tennessee, no parole indicated in record; first enlisted in the Tennessee 154 Senior Infantry Regiment Private 1st Company B ("Bluff City Grays"), per Company Muster-in Roll dated August 13, 1861, at New Madrid, Missouri, enlisted on May 14, 1861, at Randolph, Tennessee age 18 and present on only other card in record: Company Muster Roll for August 14 to November 1, 1861; Tennessee 3 (Forrest's) Cavalry Regiment Private Company A, per Company Muster Roll for January 1 to July 1, 1862, enlisted June 25, 1861, at Randolph, Tennessee, present on muster rolls dated to December 31, 1862; based on being age 18 when first enlisted in the Tennessee 154 Senior Infantry Regiment Private 1st Company B ("Bluff City Grays") and his residence Somerville, Tennessee indicated in the Tennessee 10 Infantry Regiment record believed to be the J. D. Evans in the Fayette County, Tennessee 1850 census age 8 and 1860 census age 18; not found in Cemetery computer index.

Evans, Russ   Buried October 14, 1868   Fowler 235, #1
Confederate Soldier and 1830-1866 on grave stone; died age 48 and removed from Winchester per Daily Burial Record Book; January 5, 1866, *Daily Memphis Avalanche* death notice: "Died - In this city, yesterday, of erysipelas, Mr. Russ Evans, formerly of Des Arc, Ark."; possibly served in Arkansas 1 Mounted Rifles Private Company B/A, enlisted March 13, 1862, Jacksonport, Arkansas, per January & February 1863, muster roll remarks transferred from Arkansas 25 Infantry Regiment and February 12, 1862, detailed as Brigade Forage Master; same enlistment in Arkansas 25 Infantry Regiment, age 28 (note age may indicate not right soldier) on May & June 1862, muster roll with remarks detailed as Master Sergeant May 8, 1862, and per January & February 1863, muster roll transferred to Company B 1 Arkansas Mounted Rifles February 12, 1863; paroled Greensboro, North Carolina April 30, 1865, with indication that enlisted September 1861, Pocahontas, Arkansas.

Faires, James B.   Buried September 10, 1878   Turley 994, #3
Mississippi 44 (A. K. Blythe's) Infantry Regiment Sergeant Company E (record found Farris, James B. with name "Faires" on several cards in record); per Company Muster-in Roll dated August 7, 1861, enlisted July 3, 1861, Union City age 21; per Company Muster Roll for November and December, 1862, remarks: wounded Murfreesboro and sent to hospital 31 December; per Company Muster Roll for July and August, 1863, remarks: Sent to Hospital by order of Brigade Surgeon from Chattanooga July 6, 1863; per Company Muster Roll for March and April, 1864, remarks: Absent without leave from April 29, 1864; per Company Muster Roll for May 1 to August 31, 1864, remarks: wounded at Chattanooga July 7, 1863. Absent without leave since 29 May 1864. Dropped from the Roll as Deserter; received Medical Certificate of permanent disability May 6, 1864, and detailed in the Quartermaster Department as Grenada, Mississippi; appears on a Special Report of employees on P. & P. Q. M. Department at Grenada, Mississippi as Purchasing Agent with date detailed August 19, 1864; appears on a Roll of Prisoners of War surrendered at Citronelle, Alabama, May 4, 1865, and paroled at Grenada, Mississippi, May 18, 1865; brother, William A. Faires, also served in Mississippi 44 (A. K. Blythe's) Infantry Regiment Private Corporal Company E and is buried in Elmwood (see sketch next below); post War was a partner with his brother and Jesse A. Forrest in the livery stables business (Forrest & Faires - see 1876 *Boyle-Chapman Memphis City Directory*, page 172); died age 40 per Daily Burial Record Book.

Faires, William A.   Buried July 3, 1913   Turley 994, #3
Mississippi 44 (A. K. Blythe's) Infantry Regiment Private Corporal Company E (record found Farris, Wm. A. with name "Faires" on several cards in record); per Company Muster-in Roll dated August 7, 1861, enlisted August 1, 1861, New Madrid age 25; per Company Muster Roll for September and October, 1862, remarks: wounded and left at Munfordville; appears on a Report of the killed and wounded in the engagement near Munfordville, Ky., Sept. 14 and 16, 1862 with nature of wound "In breast by spent ball" (slightly); per Company Muster Roll for September and October, 1863, remarks: wounded at the battle of Chickamauga September 20, 1863, and sent to hospital by order of Brigade Surgeon; there is a compiled service record single card for a W. A. Faires Mississippi 38, 14 and 3 Consolidated Cavalry Regiment Private Company G indicating appears on a Roll of Prisoners of War surrendered at Citronelle, Alabama, May 4, 1865, and paroled at Gainesville, Alabama, May 12, 1865, and residence of Yalobusha County, Mississippi; per his Tennessee Confederate Pension (S13637) application filed July 15, 1912, (Accepted) born Lauderdale County, Alabama in 1837, joined Company E A. K. Blythe's Battalion, which became Mississippi 44 (A. K. Blythe's) Infantry Regiment, in the summer 1861, wounded slightly at Shiloh and right arm broken above elbow at Chickamauga, paroled at Munfordville, Ky being wounded and captured there, and paroled at Gainesville, Alabama with Forrest command in 1865; brother, James B. Faires, also served in Mississippi 44 (A. K. Blythe's) Infantry Regiment Sergeant Company E and is buried in Elmwood (see sketch next above); post War was a partner with his brother and Jesse A. Forrest in the livery stables business (Forrest & Faires - see 1876 *Boyle-Chapman Memphis City Directory*, page 172); died age 79 per Daily Burial Record Book.

Falls, George A.   Buried March 1, 1863   Chapel Hill Circle 68, #3
Tennessee 3 (Forrest's) Cavalry Regiment Private Company A ("Bluff City Grays"), per Company Muster Roll for January 1 to July 1, 1862, enlisted 4 May 1861, at Randolph, Tennessee, per Company Muster Roll for October 31 to December 31, 1862, remarks: wounded at the battle of Murfreesboro; appears on a List of Confederate prisoners who died within the Federal lines, in the Department of the Cumberland, from December 31, 1862, to March 1, 1863, taken prisoner at Stones River, cause of death Gunshot wound, date of death January 11, 1863, at Murfreesboro; first enlisted in the 154th Senior Infantry Regiment Private 1st Company B ("Bluff City Grays"), per Company Muster-in Roll dated August 13, 1861, at New Madrid, Missouri, enlisted May 14, 1861 at Randolph, Tennessee age 19 and present on August 14 - November 1, 1861, Company Muster Roll; killed at

Murfreesboro, Tennessee and originally buried Chapel Hill 90, #5 and moved to Chapel Hill Circle per Daily Burial Record Book; per Cemetery Alpha Book moved to Turley 68 February 20, 1869, but not found in Turley book; found in Chapel Hill Circle book; listed in Elmwood 1874 book as Confederate soldier buried in Elmwood who was citizen of Memphis or vicinity; mentioned by Dr. S. H. Ford in his address on the occasion to commemorate (Confederate Memorial Day) Confederates buried at Elmwood on April 26, 1866, (see article "Honors To The Memory Of The Hero Dead" in the April 27, 1866, *Memphis Daily Appeal*, page 3, column 1); listed in the June 6, 1878, *Memphis Daily Appeal*, page 4, column 3, article "OUR DEAD HEROES" covering the unveiling of the Confederate Monument and Decoration of Graves at Elmwood as then one of twenty-eight members of the Bluff City Grays, Company B of the 154 Senior Infantry Regiment and Company A of Forrest's Old (Third) Cavalry Regiment buried at Elmwood; listed as one of the "comrades who sleep at Elmwood cemetery " in the article "Veterans in Council" in *Memphis Daily Appeal*, May 12, 1881, page 4, column 4, concerning the meeting of the surviving members in the city of the old Bluff City Grays to appoint the necessary committees for the purpose of making special decoration on the graves of their dead comrades at Elmwood and Calvary cemeteries on Sunday next, Memorial Day; listed in "A COMPLETE ROSTER OF THE BLUFF CITY GREYS" located in the Memphis Room of the Memphis/Shelby County Public Library and Information Center Central Library with notation "Killed Murfreesboro, Dec. 31, 1862" and buried in Elmwood; listed as member of Bluff City Grays in *Reminiscences of the Civil War* by John Hallum, Tunnah & Pittard printers, 1903; see also Notes of Interest - Bluff City Grays.

Farris, William Harvey   Buried March 2, 1876   South Grove 28, #2
Tennessee 22 (Barteau's) Cavalry Regiment 2 Lieutenant Company K; enlisted May 1, 1863, Union City, Tennessee and paroled at Memphis for 5 days ending May 25, 1865; promoted from Private Company C Tennessee 7 Cavalry Regiment; per Tennessee 7 Cavalry Regiment records enlisted March 10, 1862, Union City, Tennessee, captured Covington, Tennessee April 4, 1863, first sent to Memphis as Prisoner of War, next to St. Louis, Missouri April 27, 1863, then to Military Prison, Alton, Illinois and paroled April 28, 1863; per family information in the Oliver B. Farris personal file in Cemetery individual files born August 20, 1818, Giles County, Tennessee and half brother of Oliver B. Farris (who is buried in Soldiers Rest - see his sketch for more information on family and unit); per death notice in *Memphis Daily Appeal* March 2, 1876, page 1, "Died - Farris on February 29th near Woodstock after long illness Wm. Farris aged 57 years and 10 days"; no grave stone.

Farrow, George Ferdinand   Buried October 29, 1907   Turley 1085½, #2
Tennessee 13 Infantry Regiment, Private Company C; per sketch in Mathes born 1842 in Marshall County, Mississippi, came to Tennessee at age 11, enlisted at Germantown April 20, 1861, soon after battle of Belmont transferred to McDonald's Battalion, Forrest's Old regiment (Tennessee 3 Cavalry Regiment, Private Company A), captured at Britton's Lane, Tennessee, exchanged ten days later, remained with command to the end and surrendered and paroled at Gainesville, AL in May 1865, and joined Confederate Historical Association June 13, 1894; obituary and sketch (G. Ferd Farrow) in *Confederate Veteran* Volume 16, March 1908 page 131; per sketch born in Marshall County, MS, and was brought to Tennessee when four years of age by his parents, who settled at Germantown, near Memphis; also per sketch "participated in the battle of Belmont, in which his brother, John P. Farrow, was killed in the first volley fired by the enemy (battle of Shiloh per Lindsley's Annals). The noble character of John Farrow, his great gallantry, the prominence of his family, and the fact that he was the first of the sons of the Confederacy to offer up his life upon the alter of his country in the Department of the West created a profound impression. His remains were sent home and buried with the greatest possible civic and military honors."; died age 65 per Daily Burial Record Book; large tall stone, George Ferdinand Farrow Sept 20, 1842 October 29, 1907 "Even So, Father it Seemed Good in Thy Sight."

Finch, William Frank   Buried May 15, 1925   Fowler Public Lot 6, #1286
Mississippi 14 Battalion Light Artillery Private Company B (Ward's Battalion Light Artillery) and Yates Battery (transferred to Captain Yates' Battery by reason of consolidation of the regiments); record found under Frank Finch; enlisted December 25, 1862, Hernando, Mississippi; captured and paroled at Vicksburg July 4, 1863; absent without leave August 23, 1863 to January 26, 1864; last muster roll dated December 1864 and per Roll of Prisoners of War (Yates Battery indicated on card) paroled April 26, 1865 at Greensboro, North Carolina; single card in Yate's Battery rolls indicating enlisted May 6, 1862, Panola, Mississippi; per Tennessee pension file #S13012 born January 12, 1844 Carroll County, Tennessee, joined Company B 14 Battalion November 1862, captured at Vicksburg, and surrendered at Greensboro, North Carolina 1865; per article in *Confederate Veteran*, Volume XXXIX, July 1921, page 268, born in Carroll County, Tennessee December (note month difference with pension file) 12, 1844 and died in Memphis May 14, 1925; article also indicates first joined Mississippi 10 Battalion Field Artillery but no records found for that unit; died age 80 per Daily Burial Record Book.

Finlay, Luke William   Buried January 27, 1908   Lenow Circle 11, #3
Tennessee 4 Infantry Regiment Lieutenant Colonel; per Company Muster-in Roll dated August 16, 1861, enlisted May 15, 1861, at Germantown, Tennessee as 1st lieutenant Company A, age 29; promoted to Major April 24, 1862; promoted to Lieutenant Colonel July 26, 1863; wounded several times including at the battle of Shiloh April 6, 1862, and during the Atlanta Campaign at Ellsbury Ridge May 27, 1864, which disabled him for several months; on detached service recruiting from November 1862 to February 28, 1863; on General A.P. Stewart's staff as V.A.D.C. December 29, 1862, to January 4, 1863; returned to regiment September 20, 1863; was Lieutenant Colonel of regiment final reorganization as 3rd Consolidated Tennessee Infantry Regiment that surrendered in April, 1865, and appears on Muster Roll of Officers and Men paroled at Greensboro, North Carolina, May 1, 1865; listed as member of Company A ("Shelby Greys") 4 Tennessee Infantry in the articles "Military" in the April 18, 1861, *Memphis Daily Appeal*, page 3, column 3 (original members list), "Testimonial of Respect" in the December 7, 1861, *Memphis*

Daily Appeal,, page 4, column 2, and the May 15, 1909, *The Commercial Appeal* Memphis article "Forty=Eight Years Ago Today, The Shelby Greys Entered the Confederate Service—Record of a Famous Memphis Military Company."; per sketch in Mathes book, page 93, born near Brandon, Rankin County, Mississippi, October 8, 1831, graduated at Yale in 1856, had charge of Academy at Brandon a year, settled in Memphis August 1, 1857, January 1, 1860, entered upon the practice of law, appeared in Supreme Court, April term, 1861, April 19, 1861, he enlisted as First Lieutenant of Company A, Fourth Tennessee Infantry and became a member of this Association many years ago; wrote article (includes photograph) "Unfurl The Flag," A Reminiscence of 1865 printed in the *Confederate Veteran* Volume XII, Number 3, March, 1904, pages 110-111, about the unfurling of the battle flag once more when in Ashville, North Carolina, while marching home after the surrender; biography in *Confederate Military History, Extended Edition*, Volume X Tennessee, page 473; died January 26, 1908, age 76 per City Of Memphis Burial Permit; grave stone inscribed with service and rank and dates of birth Oct 8, 1831 and death Jan 26, 1908.

Fiser, John Calvin   Buried June 15, 1876   Chapel Hill Circle 37, #1
Mississippi 17 Infantry Regiment Colonel; enlisted May 27, 1861 Corinth age 23 as Lieutenant Company H; elected Adjutant June 7, 1861; promoted to Lieutenant Colonel April 26, 1862; wounded at Battle of Gettysburg; promoted to Colonel February 26, 1864; per May/June 1864 muster roll remarks retired and assigned to duty as Adjutant General Department Southern Georgia June 12, 1864; lost right arm at Knoxville and retired; June 16, 1864 assigned Savannah, Georgia Invalid Duty; per sketch in *More Generals in Gray* born May 4, 1838 in Dyersburg, Tennessee, at start of War commissioned Lieutenant Mississippi 17 Infantry Regiment and Adjutant June 4, 1861, elected Lieutenant Colonel April 26, 1862, wounded three times at Battle of Gettysburg, arm amputated from wound received at assault on Fort Sanders outside of Knoxville, Tennessee November 23, 1863, promoted to Colonel on February 26, 1864 but having not recovered from loss of arm resigned June 12, 1864, winter of 1864 transferred to South Carolina and assigned to command a brigade of Georgia reservists, listed as Brigadier General in several publications, including *Confederate Veteran*, and per obituary (*Memphis Daily Appeal* June 15, 1876) commission as Brigadier General was issued in the last days of the War but never reached him; not listed in the *Memorandum relative to the General Officers Appointed by the President in the Armies of the Confederate States - 1861-1865* compiled from Official Records by the Military Secretary's Office, U. S. War Department 1905; not listed in *Generals in Gray*; per sketch in Mathes book elected to Confederate Historical Association April 28, 1870, succeeded former Governor Isham G. Harris as President in 1871 and died June 15, 1876; died age 38 from flux per Daily Burial Record Book; grave monument: born Dyersburg, Tennessee May 4, 1838 and died June 14, 1876; also listed in chapter on Generals; listed in "Touring Historic Elmwood Cemetery" Brochure (January 2000) #57 but not listed as General in its predecessor "Touring historic Elmwood Cemetery" (Brochure and Map of Historic Gravesites); sketch #18 in Elmwood *Civil War Tour* booklet (2012).

Fisher, Charles Glover, Jr.   Buried September 26, 1878   Turley 468½, #1
Tennessee 7 Cavalry Regiment Private Company I, enlisted May 15, 1862 at Fort Pillow, Tennessee and paroled May 11, 1865 at Gainesville, Alabama; first enlisted in Tennessee 4 Infantry Regiment Private Company I at age 23 per muster roll dated August 17, 1861, at Fort Pillow; wounded and captured in Mississippi in 1862; also had enlisted (transferred) August, 1861, in Tennessee Heavy Artillery, Captain Johnston's Company L (Southern Guards Artillery), also known as Captain Hamilton's Battery Company L, Tennessee Artillery Corps, (12 Mos. 1861-1862), which per muster roll card dated April 14, 1862, unit mustered out of service by order of General Beauregard, Corinth, Mississippi, April 14, 1862; note enlisted and served with brother Philip Alston Fisher in same units; born January 6, 1837, and one of the five sons and three daughters of Dr. Charles G. Fisher, Sr. and Virginia Dunham Fisher of Covington, Tennessee (Dr. Fisher was the third physician to reside and practice there); in 1868, married Martha W. Smith, and they moved to Memphis; within two years he rose to a partnership in Gage & Fisher Cotton Factors; active in business and civic affairs and served several terms as City Councilman; with the onset of the Yellow Fever Epidemic of 1878, sent his wife and children to Covington, but he remained behind; seeing the need for public services, he and five other concerned citizens organized the Citizens Relief Committee; he was chairman, and on September 20, wrote of "feeding some 10,000 persons sick and destitute in camps and in the city."; shortly after, he fell ill with the fever and died on September 26 with burial that same day leaving his wife and their children, Fred, Ashley and Mamie; per article in *Memphis Daily Appeal* September 27, 1878, page 1, column 1, Mr. Charles G. Fisher, chairman of Citizens Relief Committee died and was buried yesterday, native of Tipton County, a son of Dr. Fisher, of Covington, and served throughout the war in the Confederate army; listed in the May 17, 1881, *Memphis Daily Appeal*, page 2, column 3, article "OUR HEROIC DEAD" reporting on the Memorial Day ceremonies at Elmwood Cemetery on Sunday May 15, 1881, indicating grave was handsomely decorated and located outside the Confederate grounds; originally buried Turley Lot 469 and moved January 10, 1881; circle grave stone with upright Woodsman stone at head with dates of January 6, 1837 September 26, 1878; Memphis Register of Deaths indicates died age 37 of Yellow Fever; died age 37 per Daily Burial Record Book; information primarily from "Once Upon a Time" article by Sara Holmes on him and brother in *Historic Elmwood Cemetery Journal*, Summer 2003, Volume XV, Number 2.

Fisher, Philip Alston   Buried January 16, 1898   Turley 1368½
Tennessee 7 Cavalry Regiment Second Lieutenant Company I, enlisted as a Private May 15, 1862, at Fort Pillow, Tennessee, elected second lieutenant May 12, 1863, a rank he held until the end of the war, signed Parole of Honor May 11, 1865, at Gainesville, Alabama; first enlisted in Tennessee 4 Infantry Regiment, Private Company I, per muster roll dated August 17, 1861, at Fort Pillow; also had enlisted (transferred) August 1861 at age 22 in Tennessee Heavy Artillery, Captain Johnston's Company L (Southern Guards Artillery), also known as Captain Hamilton's Battery Company L, Tennessee Artillery Corps, (12 Mos. 1861-1862), which per muster roll card dated April 14, 1862, unit mustered out of service by order of General Beauregard, Corinth, Mississippi, April

14, 1862; note enlisted and served with brother Charles Glover Fisher, Jr. in same units; born November 18, 1838, and one of the five sons and three daughters of Dr. Charles G. Fisher, Sr. and Virginia Dunham Fisher of Covington, Tennessee (Dr. Fisher was the third physician to reside and practice there); after the War married Katherine Posey Ridgeway; they moved to Missouri, where he taught school; his father died in 1879, and he returned to Covington to take charge of family affairs; he twice served as Superintendent of Public Instruction for Tipton County; in 1889, he and his immediate family moved to Memphis, where he opened the insurance agency of PA. Fisher & Co.; died of pneumonia on January 16, 1898, at his residence at 463 Lauderdale Street; his children were Drury A., Charles Glover, Frances R. Blanker, Virgie D. Williford, Katherine (Kate) A. Terrell, and Philip Allen; circle stone November 18, 1838 January 16, 1898; originally buried Turley Lot 468½ and moved March 8, 1906; Memphis Register of Deaths indicates died age 59 of pneumonia; information primarily from "Once Upon a Time" article by Sara Holmes on him and brother in *Historic Elmwood Cemetery Journal*, Summer 2003, Volume XV, Number 2.

Flournoy, Ryland Hall   Buried November 10,1861   Turley 90, #1
Tennessee 3 (Forrest's) Cavalry Regiment Private Company A ("Bluff City Grays"), only unit envelope in record with only notation to see also "Genl Thompson's Command" and "154 Senior Regt Tenn. Inf."; first enlisted in 154 Senior Infantry Regiment Private 1 Company B, per Company Muster-in Roll dated August 13 1861, enlisted May 14, 1861, at Randolph age 19, per remarks on August 14 - November 1, 1861, Company Muster Roll transferred September 13, 1861, to General Thompson's command, unit card states see also "Mo. State Guard"; Missouri State Guard Captain 1 Division Drill Master; per September 24, 1861, the *Avalanche* (Memphis) Hall Flournoy had been appointed Drill Master of Jeff Thompson's Brigade with the rank of Captain. He was one of the original Zouare Cadets but left here with the Bluff City Grays, Captain Edmondson (originally Company B TN 154 Senior Infantry Regiment), not yet 20 years old; listed as member of Bluff City Grays in *Reminiscences of the Civil War* by John Hallum, Tunnah & Pittard printers, 1903; listed in "A COMPLETE ROSTER OF THE BLUFF CITY GREYS" located in the Memphis Room of the Memphis/Shelby County Public Library and Information Center Central Library with notation "2d Corp. Promoted Mo. Regt. Killed at Frederickstown, Mo. Sept. 1861" and buried in Elmwood; per article in October 29, 1861, *Memphis Daily Appeal*, page 3, column 1, killed in battle at Fredericktown, Madison County, Missouri October 21, 1861; formerly 2 Lieutenant Colonel 1 Division Missouri State Guard, which is on grave stone with dates of October 14, 1842 October 21, 1861; killed in Missouri per Daily Burial Record Book; not listed in Cemetery computer index; brother of William Augustus Flournoy; funeral notice in the November 10, 1861, *Memphis Daily Appeal* (page 4, column 2); listed in Elmwood 1874 book as Confederate soldier buried in Elmwood who was citizen of Memphis or vicinity as "Hall Florney"; mentioned by Dr. S. H. Ford in his address on the occasion to commemorate (Confederate Memorial Day) Confederates buried at Elmwood on April 26, 1866, (see articles "The Confederate Dead" in the *Public Ledger* (Memphis), April 27, 1866, page 3, column 2, and "Honors To The Memory Of The Hero Dead" in the April 27, 1866, *Memphis Daily Appeal*, page 3, column 1); listed in the June 6, 1878, *Memphis Daily Appeal*, page 4, column 3, article "OUR DEAD HEROES" covering the unveiling of the Confederate Monument and Decoration of Graves at Elmwood as then one of twenty-eight members of the Bluff City Grays, Company B of the 154 Senior Infantry Regiment and Company A of Forrest's Old (Third) Cavalry Regiment buried at Elmwood; listed as one of the "comrades who sleep at Elmwood cemetery " in the article "Veterans in Council" in *Memphis Daily Appeal*, May 12, 1881, page 4, column 4, concerning the meeting of the surviving members in the city of the old Bluff City Grays to appoint the necessary committees for the purpose of making special decoration on the graves of their dead comrades at Elmwood and Calvary cemeteries on Sunday next, Memorial Day; see also Notes of Interest - Bluff City Grays.

Flournoy, Thomas Conn   Buried April 7, 1876   Chapel Hill 538½, #8
Tennessee 17 Battalion Cavalry (Sanders') Captain Company A; per Company Muster Roll dated October 31, 1862, enlisted April 26, 1862, in Memphis, age 34, and remarks that breveted Captain September 15, 1862, and commanding Confederate Rangers; originally Colonel, C. D. C. M., Desha County Battalion, Arkansas Militia, per letter dated November 28, 1861, at Laconia to Governor H. M. Rector, Commander-in-chief of Arkansas Militia; record also found Mississippi 9 Cavalry Captain Miller's Regiment; signed Parole of Honor May 20, 1865, at Grenada, Mississippi, Captain Commanding Scouts; per notice in *Memphis Daily Appeal*, Memphis, Tennessee, April 2, 1876, page 2, column 6, - DIED – FLOURNOY – At his residence on Arkansas River, Friday, March 31st; per notice in *Memphis Daily Appeal*, April 7, 1876, page 1, column 6, funeral took place from the residence of his mother-in-law, Mrs. M. A. Rice, 375 Orleans Street, that afternoon; tombstone: T. C. Flournoy Born August 10, 1828 Died March 31, 1876; spouse Lucky Kirby Rice March 28, 1845 January 25, 1923 (Little Rock, Arkansas); married August 9, 1860, Memphis, Tennessee.

Flournoy, William Augustus   Buried January 16, 1866   Turley 90, #2
Tennessee 38 Infantry Regiment Private Company A; single card in compiled service record indicates enlisted September 17, 1861, Memphis (no other information); initials "H. A." and died age 18 colice in Daily Burial Record Book; "H. A." in Cemetery computer index; not listed in the Tennessee 38 Infantry Memorial Rolls in Lindsley's Annals; brother of Ryland Hall Flournoy; 1845 1863 on grave stone; listed in Elmwood 1874 book as Confederate soldier buried in Elmwood who was citizen of Memphis or vicinity as "Willie Florney"; mentioned (Willie Flournoy) by Dr. S. H. Ford in his address on the occasion to commemorate (Confederate Memorial Day) Confederates buried at Elmwood on April 26, 1866, (see articles "The Confederate Dead" in the *Public Ledger* (Memphis), April 27, 1866, page 3, column 2, and "Honors To The Memory Of The Hero Dead" in the April 27, 1866, *Memphis Daily Appeal*, page 3, column 1).

Folkes, William C.   Buried May 18, 1890   Miller Circle 272, #1
Virginia Horse Artillery, Private Shoemaker's Company, "The Beauregard Rifles" Shoemaker's Lynchburg Artillery; enlisted March 31, 1862, Lynchburg; wounded July 1, 1862, Battle of Malvern Hill and leg amputated; per *The Virginia Regimental Histories Series*, 1st Edition, Robert H. Moore, II (1995), page 113, enlisted March 31, 1862, in Lynchburg, wounded July 1, 1862, at Malvern Hill, leg amputated July 2, 1862, and admitted to Charlottesville Hospital November 29, 1864; per *Tennessee, The Volunteer State, 1769-1923*, Volume II, pages 120-121, it was recorded that he joined the Confederate Army in 1861, was severely wounded at 1st Battle of Manassas, recovered in time for fighting at Malvern Hill where lost a foot, remained in active service until end of War, entered Law School at University of Virginia where graduated 1865, next year came to Memphis to practice, married Miss Mary Wright, and was elected to Supreme Court August 1866; per the *Memphis Appeal*, May 18, 1890, page 4, column 6, Judge Folkes is Dead, born in Lynchburg, Virginia in 1844, served in Confederate Army, lost leg at Malvern Hill and came to Memphis in 1866; per Cemetery record born Lynchburg, Virginia June 8, 1845, (note year difference with newspaper) and died in Memphis May 17, 1890.

Foote, Shelby Dade, Jr.   Buried November 2, 2005   Chapel Hill Circle 76
Historian and novelist who wrote *The Civil War: A Narrative*, New York: Random House. 1958–1974, a three-volume history of the Civil War, and seven fictional novels including *Shiloh*. New York: Dial Press, 1952; born November 17, 1916, in Greenville, Washington County, Mississippi, and died June 27, 2005, in Memphis; sketch #16 in Elmwood *Civil War Tour* booklet (2012).

Forrest, Aaron H.   Chapel Hill Circle 47
Lieutenant Colonel Forrest Cavalry C. S. A. engraved on grave marker (1833 1864) in the Forrest Lot but no Cemetery record of actual burial; Captain Mississippi 6 Battalion Cavalry in only compiled service record; Lieutenant Colonel is rank stated in most books on his brother Lieutenant General Nathan Bedford Forrest; Lieutenant Colonel is rank stated in reports (Official Records Serial No. 57, page 349) by brother Major-General Forrest to Lieutenant-General Polk in February 1864; William Hudson Lawrence, Colonel Commanding Post at Columbus, Kentucky in report dated April 15, 1864, (Official Records Serial No. 59, page 374) to Captain J. H. Dolin, Assistant Adjutant-General, Cairo, Illinois, reported that "Col. Aaron Forrest, brother of the general, died at Jackson on Thursday last."; died of pneumonia and in Dresden, Tennessee per most accounts on his death.

Forrest, Jeffery Edward   Buried March 27, 1868   Chapel Hill Circle 47, #4
Alabama Cavalry Forrest's Regiment Colonel; originally enlisted in J. S. White's Company E ("The Tennessee Mounted Rifles") Tennessee 6 (Logwood's) Cavalry Battalion, resigned and joined Tennessee Forrest's Cavalry Battalion that became Tennessee 3 Cavalry Regiment; per Tennessee 3 Cavalry Regiment record enlisted September 1, 1861, in Memphis at age 23, per March 1 to June 30, 1862, muster roll remarks removed by reorganization of Company according to Act of Congress January 17, 1862, per September and October 1862, muster roll remarks elected Captain March 11, 1862, of Company C and discharged June 17, 1862; per Alabama Forrest's Cavalry compiled service record J. E. Forrest, Colonel Commanding, 4 Brigade appears on a list of casualties in Forrest's Cavalry in the engagement (Meridian, Mississippi Expedition) February 20 to 24, 1864, dated at Columbus March 9, 1864, with remarks killed February 22, 1864; killed at Battle of Okolona, Mississippi February 22, 1864; per sketch in *More Generals in Gray* born June 10, 1838 Tippah County, Mississippi, after leaving Tennessee 3 Cavalry Regiment commissioned Major then Lieutenant Colonel Tennessee 8 Cavalry Regiment, in 1864 joined General Forrest in northern Mississippi and put in charge of a Brigade and some sources indicate commissioned Brigadier General but appears died a Colonel; not listed in the *Memorandum relative to the General Officers Appointed by the President in the Armies of the Confederate States - 1861-1865* compiled from Official Records by the Military Secretary's Office, U. S. War Department 1905; not listed in *Generals in Gray*; no records in General and Staff records; listed (Forrest, Maj. Jeffery) in Elmwood 1874 book as Confederate soldier buried in Elmwood who was a citizen of Memphis or vicinity; biography in *Confederate Military History*, *Extended Edition*, Volume X Tennessee, page 475; grave stone: Colonel Alabama Cavalry C.S.A. 1837 1863; Confederate index book: J. E. Forrest Alabama Cavalry Forrest's Regiment Colonel, J. E. Forrest Tennessee 10 (De Moss') Cavalry Regiment Colonel (reference slip only), J. E. Forrest Tennessee 13 (Gore's) Cavalry Colonel (reference slip only) and Jeff E. Forrest Tennessee 3 (Forrest's) Cavalry Captain Company C; brother of Lieutenant General Nathan Bedford Forrest; reburial celebrated during the Commemoration Day (Confederate Memorial Day) ceremony at Elmwood Cemetery on Saturday May 2, 1868, see article "Our Soldier Dead."…"The Last Tribute of Love and Honor to General Preston Smith and Colonel Jeffrey Forrest" in the *Public Ledger* (Memphis), Saturday Evening, May 2, 1868, pages 2 and 3; see also article "Elmwood – Memorial Day Celebration at Elmwood — Funeral of General Preston Smith and Colonel Forrest." In the May 3, 1868, *Daily Memphis Avalanche*, page 1; mentioned by Dr. S. H. Ford in his address on the occasion to commemorate (Confederate Memorial Day) Confederates buried at Elmwood on April 26, 1866, (see article "Honors To The Memory Of The Hero Dead" in the April 27, 1866, *Memphis Daily Appeal*, page 3, column 1); mentioned in General W. B. Bates' speech printed in the article "Elmwood" (Grand and Imposing Ceremonies of Commemoration Day), in *Memphis Sunday Appeal*, May 8, 1870, page 4, column 2; also listed in chapter on Generals; ; listed in "Touring Historic Elmwood Cemetery" Brochure (January 2000) #62 but not listed as General in its predecessor "Touring historic Elmwood Cemetery" (Brochure and Map of Historic Gravesite); included in Forrest Family lot sketch #17 in Elmwood *Civil War Tour* booklet (2012).

Forrest, Jesse Anderson   Buried December 16, 1889   Turley 1010, #9
Tennessee 21 (Wilson's) Cavalry Regiment Lieutenant Colonel; originally enlisted in Tennessee 3 Cavalry Regiment Captain Company D February 27, 1862, at Memphis and per March 26 to June 30, 1862, muster roll remarks dismissed June 27, 1862; appointed Lieutenant Colonel March 7, 1864, at Tupelo, Mississippi; second initial "N" on some compiled service records cards;

brother of Lieutenant General N. B. Forrest; per obituary in December 16, 1889, *Memphis Daily Appeal*, page 4, born Bedford County, Tennessee April 19, 1834, at age 18 married Miss Mayberry, left widow and five children, died age 55 at residence 690 Union; post War was a partner with brothers James B. and William A. Faires (see sketches supra) in the livery stables business (Forrest & Faires - see 1876 Boyle-Chapman Memphis City Directory, page 172); included in Forrest Family lot sketch #17 in Elmwood *Civil War Tour* booklet (2012).

Forrest, William Hezekiah   Buried March 14, 1875   Chapel Hill Circle 47, #5
Tennessee 3 (Forrest's) Cavalry Regiment Major/Captain Company C; enlisted March 10, 1862, Huntsville, Alabama, 1 Lieutenant; discharged June 17, 1862; appointed 1 Lieutenant Tennessee 11 (Holman's) Cavalry Regiment November 14, 1862; Captain March 1 to June 30, 1863; appointed Major 3 Cavalry when Forrest's Regiment increased to full regiment strength November 22, 1864; single card in General and Staff officers compiled service record rolls indicating Captain Provisional Army, Confederate States and surrendered at Citronelle, Alabama May 4, 1865, and paroled May 19, 1965; brother of Lieutenant General N. B. Forrest; died inflammation of stomach age 44 per Daily Burial Record Book; Major Company C 3 Regiment Tennessee Cavalry C.S.A. 1831 1874 on grave stone in Forrest Lot; included in Forrest Family lot sketch #17 in Elmwood *Civil War Tour* booklet (2012); illegible circle grave stone.

Forrest, William Montgomery   Buried February 8, 1908   Chapel Hill Circle 47, #17
Aide de Camp Staff of General N. B. Forrest Lieutenant; per General and Staff officers compiled service record rolls 1 Lieutenant & Aide de Camp to General N. B. Forrest, from State of Tennessee, appointed March 16, 1864, confirmed May 11, 1864, to rank February 19, 1864, accepted May 6, 1864, Department Alabama, Mississippi & East Louisiana and appointment confirmed by Secretary of War J. A. Seddon and per entry in file Lieutenant General N. B. Forrest says entitled to another Aide de Camp and appointed his own son; son of Lieutenant General Nathan Bedford Forrest; born September 26, 1846, at Hernando, Mississippi; died February 7, 1908; sketch in Mathes book; per sketch joined White's Mounted Rifles in June 1861, served on staff of his father Lieutenant General N. B. Forrest as 1 Lieutenant and Aide de Camp and joined Confederate Historical Association October 9, 1894; Captain and died age 61 per Daily Burial Record Book; Captain Forrest Tennessee Cavalry September 26, 1848 February 7, 1908 on grave stone in Forrest Lot; included in Forrest Family lot sketch #17 in Elmwood *Civil War Tour* booklet (2012).

Fowlkes, Sterling, Jr.   Buried January 22, 1863   Chapel Hill 481, #3
Tennessee 154 Senior Infantry Regiment Captain Company D; enlisted May 14, 1861, Randolph age 21; per May and June 1862, muster roll remarks: killed accidentally at Richmond, Kentucky in action; per May 5, 1863, muster roll remarks (age 22): accidentally killed in action at battle Richmond, Kentucky August 30, 1862; per register of soldiers killed in battle: born Memphis, Tennessee, deceased August 30, 1862, Richmond, Kentucky gunshot wound (same information found on report of deaths in Company D 154 Senior Regiment found in compiled service records of J. B. Jennings of the 154 Senior Infantry Regiment); listed in Elmwood 1874 book as Confederate soldier buried in Elmwood who was citizen of Memphis or vicinity and sketch; per sketch fell at Battle of Perryville at age not more than twenty five years; Lindsley's Annals indicates killed at Richmond, Kentucky (August 30, 1862); killed per Daily Burial Record Book; Captain Harris Zouave Cadets 154 Senior Regiment Tennessee Volunteer born April 10, 1840, killed at the Battle of Richmond, Kentucky August 31, 1862 on family monument; "; mentioned by Dr. S. H. Ford in his address on the occasion to commemorate (Confederate Memorial Day) Confederates buried at Elmwood on April 26, 1866, (see articles "The Confederate Dead" in the *Public Ledger* (Memphis), April 27, 1866, page 3, column 2, and "Honors To The Memory Of The Hero Dead" in the April 27, 1866, *Memphis Daily Appeal*, page 3, column 1).

Frayser, Robert Dudley   Buried October 26, 1893   Miller Circle 2682, #1
Tennessee 37 Infantry Regiment Lieutenant Colonel; enlisted as Private Company F September 1, 1861, Knoxville, appointed Adjutant, appointed Lieutenant Colonel May 10, 1862; sketch in Mathes book; per sketch born in Memphis June 4, 1840, joined Company F Tennessee 37 Infantry, appointed Adjutant August 1861, elected Lieutenant Colonel after Battle of Shiloh, retained as Lieutenant Colonel when Tennessee 15 and 37 Infantry Regiments were consolidated in 1863, wounded July 22, 1864, at Atlanta, once Grand Master of IOOF of Tennessee, joined Confederate Historical Association July 15, 1869; sketch in Goodspeed's Shelby County History, page 963; died age 53 per Daily Burial Record Book.

Frazer, Charles Wesley   Buried July 12, 1897   Fowler 727/747, #1
Confederate 5 Infantry Regiment (also called Confederate 9 Infantry) Captain Company B and Major and Assistant Adjutant General (AAG); originally enlisted May 1861, at Memphis as Captain Company I Tennessee 21 Infantry Regiment which consolidated with Tennessee 2 (Walker's) Infantry July 1862, to form Confederate 5 Infantry Regiment; per General and Staff records (record under Frazier, Charles W. but spelled Frazer on most cards) on List of Appointments, from Tennessee, to report to General J. W. Frazer (his brother) July 9, 1863, Adjutant General Department, appointed Brigade Quartermaster August 3, 1863; per list in record: July 8, 1862, Lieutenant Tennessee 21 Infantry, detailed for special duty in Inspector General Department, Army of Mississippi, afterwards Captain Company B 5 Confederate Regiment and resigned June 6, 1863, to accept appointment as Captain AAG Frazer's Command; August 19, 1863, appointed Major and Quartermaster; September 9, 1863, when General Frazer surrendered to Federal forces, listed as Captain AAG; September 9, 1863 - March 10, 1865 no records found as probably prisoner of war as was forwarded to prison at Johnson's Island, Ohio from Louisville, Kentucky September 23, 1863; March 10, 1865, prisoner at Johnson's Island and signs as Captain and AAG with note that captured at Cumberland Gap September 9, 1863; released on oath June 11, 1865, at Depot Prisoners of War, near Sandusky, Ohio; per sketch in Mathes book Major and Adjutant General,

served on staff of his brother Brigadier General John W. Frazer, slightly wounded at Belmont and Murfreesboro, captured September 1863, and confined at Johnson's Island until released June 11, 1865, served as President of Confederate Historical Association and wrote play "Johnson's Island"; per Mathes book enlarged edition joined Confederate Historical Association July 1, 1869, and died Sunday July 11, 1897, after having served as President of Confederate Historical Association from his first election in 1884 to the end of his life; wrote regimental sketch for Confederate 5 Infantry for Lindsley's Annals; subject of article in *Confederate Veteran* Volume V, October 1897, page 505; born near LaGrange, Fayette County, Tennessee July 21, 1834, educated at University of Mississippi, admitted to Memphis bar at age 19, practiced law in Memphis after war; appendix in *More Generals in Gray* indicates that "C. W. Frazier" was called a general in the *Southern Historical Society Papers* list of Confederate generals; per note at the end of the article "Confederate Generals of Tennessee" in *Confederate Veteran*, Volume XVIII (1910), pages 170-172, Governor Isham G. Harris appointed "C. W. Frazier" a brigadier general in the state's provisional army in 1861 but was not appointed when Tennessee became part of the Confederate States; Colonel and died age 65 per Daily Burial Record Book; Captain Company D, born July 21, 1834, and died July 11, 1897, inscribed on "In Memory Of" stone located in walk around Confederate Soldiers Rest Monument; originally buried Chapel Hill 105, #10 and moved April 4, 1901; see Note 1 in chapter on Generals; (father of Virginia Frazer Boyle "Poet Laureate of the Confederacy" see sketch supra); listed as Major in "Touring historic Elmwood Cemetery" (Brochure and Map of Historic Gravesite) #73.

Freeman, Edward T.   Buried July 23, 1878   South Grove 8, #7
Adjutant and Major; Virginia Military Institute (VMI) Class of 1862; per information in VMI library archives file born in Norfolk, Virginia, on September 20, 1841, entered VMI from Baltimore, Maryland, on July 28, 1859, at the age of eighteen, was a cadet for two years and was declared a graduate of the Class of 1862, in 1861 when War began the cadets were ordered to Richmond where they served as drill instructors for Confederate recruits being assembled there, was one of the cadets who left for Richmond in April 1861 and served as a drillmaster until the Corps was ordered to return to Lexington eight months later, was among many of the older cadets who went on to commissioned service with the Confederacy and who were later declared graduates of the Institute, and other records indicate that he was a major on the staff of Major General S. G. French; also per sketch in VMI library archives file appointed Cadet July 1861 and assigned as 1 Lieutenant and Adjutant 40 (Colonel L. M. Walker's) Tennessee (5 Confederate) Infantry, Assistant Adjutant General with forces at New Madrid, Missouri March 1862, captured April 7, 1862, at Island 10, held at Johnson's Island, Ohio, exchanged September 1862, assigned July 1863, as Assistant Inspector General on staff of Major General S. G. French (some records show as 2 Lieutenant, Assistant Adjutant Inspector General), at Allatoona October 5, 1864, "Conspicuous for his gallant conduct," wounded in action (slight foot) by artillery shell at Nashville December 16, 1864, and on staff of Major General E. C. Walthall December 1864 - January 1865; per information in Tennessee 40 (Walker's) Infantry Regiment compiled service record July 19, 1861, appointed Cadet, September 12, 1861, ordered to report to General A. S. Johnston, November 11, 1861, appointed from Tennessee as 1 Lieutenant and Adjutant to report to 40 Tennessee Regiment, July 25, 1863, as 2 Lieutenant assigned by Major General French as Assistant Inspector General on his staff, December 1864 General E. C. Walthall mentioned him as Lieutenant on French's staff, and paroled 1865; per prisoner of war descriptive roll card in compiled service record arrested at Island 10 April 7, 1862, received at Camp Chase April 13, 1862, transferred to Johnson's Island April 24, 1862, and sent to Vicksburg, Mississippi for exchange September 1, 1862; only a reference slip card in General and Staff compiled service record rolls indicating records filed in Tennessee 40 Infantry Regiment records; per *Confederate Staff Officers 1861-1865* by Joseph H. Crute, Jr. (Derwent Books 1982) Cadet, Assistant Adjutant & Inspector General, July 25, 1863, on the staff of Major General Samuel G. French, Provisional Army of Confederate States; death notice in the *Daily Memphis Avalanche* July 21, 1878, "Died - Freeman. At the residence of his father-in-law, Captain Joseph Lenow (Elmwood Cemetery President - see his sketch herein), at 8 p.m. on July 20, Major Edward T. Freeman."; the *Daily Memphis Avalanche* July 23, 1878, page 4, Personal Matters, "Major Edward T. Freeman's death was noticed in the *Avalanche* of Sunday. He was a Virginian by birth and passed from his State's Military Institute to the field of battle. He in turn served with gallantry as Adjutant under Colonel James E. Bailey and on the staffs of Generals French and Walthall. Since the war he has been engaged in commercial life in Memphis."; killed Edward Lumpkin Hamlin (see his sketch herein) in a duel August 26, 1870, that took place just across the Tennessee/Mississippi state line off Highway 51; allegedly they were rivals for a beautiful woman who was as noted below Lou Lenow, his first wife; duel reported *Memphis Daily Appeal* August 27, 1870, page 4; the duel was subject of article "VMI Search Revives Memphis' Last Dueling Victim" by Paul R. Coppock in *The Commercial Appeal* Memphis July 7, 1974, Section 6, page 7; duel also subject of story "Illegal Honor" by Paul R. Coppock in *Memphis Sketches*, page 229 (Friends of Memphis and Shelby County Libraries, 1976); per information in VMI archives married twice, first to Lou Lenow (daughter of Joseph Lenow) who was alleged to have been the beautiful woman loved by both Freeman and Hamlin, and after her death in childbirth December 14, 1871, married her sister Elizabeth (Lizzie) Lenow; died age 36 erysipelas per Daily Burial Record Book; second initial "F" in Cemetery computer index and in Shelby County Funeral Index book; born September 20, 1841 and died July 20, 1878 inscribed on upright grave stone (partially illegible).

Freeman, Dr. Robert J.   Buried October 22, 1873   South Grove 8, #6
Confederate Navy Assistant Surgeon; no enlistment in compiled service record; cards in Hospital and Prison records of Confederate Naval and Marine Personnel - name appears on a roll of surgeons released at Fort Monroe, Va. December 10, 1863, captured on board Ram Atlanta June 17, 1863; listed in Elmwood 1874 book as Confederate soldier buried in Elmwood who was citizen of Memphis or vicinity, Surgeon and sketch; per sketch born Norfolk, Virginia 1837, Surgeon in US Army and resigned to join Confederate Navy in 1861 which served through the war, fell victim of the terrible plague October 22, 1873, and monument on grave put there by his mother who came from Baltimore; Doctor and died yellow fever age 36 per Daily Burial Record Book; born

Norfolk, Virginia April 17, 1837, and died in Memphis, Tennessee of yellow fever October 22, 1873, on grave stone; per obituary in the October 23, 1873, *Memphis Daily Appeal*, page 1, Secretary of Board of Health, died of yellow fever and cites US Army and Confederate services.

Gallaway, John Bell   Buried October 26, 1884   South Grove 278, #1
Mississippi 14 Infantry Regiment Private Company K, per Company Muster-in Roll dated June 8, 1861, at Corinth, Mississippi, enlisted May 25, 1861, at Corinth age 18, regiment surrendered at Fort Donelson, Tennessee February 16, 1862, sent to prison at Camp Douglas, Illinois, sent to Vicksburg, Mississippi September 2, 1862, for exchange and regiment re-organized, name appears as signature to an Oath of Allegiance at Tullahoma, Tennessee with oath administered February 4, 1865, place of residence Lincoln County, Tennessee, indicated deserted November 27, 1864 and no family; born November 12, 1843, in Moulton, Lawrence County, Alabama, per *A Standard History of Oklahoma*, Joseph B. Thoburn, Chicago, New York, The American Historical Society, 1916, he was a railroad executive and worked for Texas & Pacific Railroad in New Orleans, Louisiana and Memphis & Charleston Railroad at the time of his death; died October 24, 1884, in New Orleans, Louisiana.

Gallaway, Matthew Campbell   Buried March 1, 1898   Lenow Circle 97¾, #4
Colonel and Aide-de-Camp, General Nathan B. Forrest Staff; born March 4, 1820, in Huntsville, Alabama and died on February 28, 1898; married Fannie Britton Barker in Huntsville, Alabama in 1842, (per her death certificate in Shelby County, TN, she was buried in Elmwood Cemetery burial permit 603, signed by J.R. Thomas with death at 93 Court Street, her home); moved to Memphis where he was a prominent newspaper man; founder of the Memphis *Avalanche* and later purchased *Memphis Daily Appeal*; the two newspapers combined with the Commercial in 1894, resulting in today's Memphis *Commercial Appeal*; postmaster of Memphis, Tennessee in 1860; Mrs. Galloway gave a portrait of General Nathan Bedford Forrest to the Knights of Pythias Lodge in Forrest City, Arkansas, April 1898, via her son-in-law, Captain James V. Fussell, local bank president in Forrest City; daughter Lucille (Galloway) Fussell (note: per family researchers for Galloway family, they had no children, so Lucille must have been adopted); owner/editor of Memphis *Avalanche*, 1857-1870; co-editor of *Memphis Appeal*, 1870-1887; Postmaster of Memphis, 1859-1862; Staff officer (Colonel) to N. B. Forrest, 1862-1865; State Senator, 1891-1893; sketch in Biographical Directory TN General Assembly (F435.S74 1978 TN State Library); see Harkins, John, Ph.D. "Col. Gallaway: His pen was mightier than the sword." *The Best Times.* October 2012. Print.

Gardiner, Samuel Ephraim   Buried September 5, 1902   Evergreen 156, #1
Tennessee 12 (Green's) Cavalry Regiment Private Company K; per Company Muster Roll for August 22, 1863, to May 11, 1864, enlisted October 2, 1863, Shelby County, Tennessee; appears on a report of men of the 1 Brigade, 1 Division, Forrest's Cavalry, who straggled from their command and otherwise misbehaved in the face of the enemy. Report dated Ellis Bridge September 7, 1864. Remarks: Straggled after fight; appears on a register of Prisoners of War at Memphis, Tennessee—deserters from rebel army, April 1, 186?, Shelby County, Tennessee, age 20; name appears on an Oath of Allegiance sworn to at Memphis, Tennessee from April 1 to 15, 1865, residence Shelby County, Tennessee, age 20; grave stone: Mar. 8, 1845 Sept. 5, 1902 (City of Memphis Burial Permit has Date of Birth 1845 Mch 9); died age 57 per Daily Burial Record Book.

Gardner, William Montgomery   Buried June 17, 1901   Evergreen 189, #2
Brigadier General; appointed from Georgia November 14, 1861, (rank November 14, 1861) per *Memorandum relative to the General Officers Appointed by the President in the Armies of the Confederate States - 1861-1865* compiled from Official Records by the Military Secretary's Office, U. S. War Department 1905; also per remarks in said Memorandum included in the Sherman-Johnston convention of April 26, 1865, but no record of his personal parole found; per Georgia 8 Infantry Regiment records appointed Lieutenant Colonel June 8, 1861, wounded July 21, 1861, at Battle of Manassas, promoted to Colonel July 21, 1861, and promoted to Brigadier General January 28, 1861; per General and Staff records appointed from Georgia as Major of Infantry April 13, 1861, detailed as Assistant Adjutant General May 14, 1861, District of Savannah, May 30, 1861, relieved of duty, June 8, 1861, appointed Lieutenant Colonel Georgia 8 Infantry Regiment, promoted to Colonel then Brigadier General November 14, 1861, and paroled at Augusta, Georgia May 20, 1865; born in Georgia June 8, 1824, graduate of West Point (1846) and spent last years at home of his son in Memphis; per sketch in *Generals in Gray* Lieutenant Colonel Georgia 8 Infantry Regiment and appointed Brigadier General November 14, 1861; name spelled "Gardiner" in Daily Burial Record Book and Computer Index; biography in *Confederate Military History*, *Extended Edition*, Volume VII Georgia, page 417; died 77 years and 9 months per Daily Burial Record Book; sketch, photograph, if available, and grave stone photograph in book *Quiet Places: The Burial Sites of Civil War Generals in Tennessee* by Buckner and Nathaniel C. Hughes, Jr., East Tennessee Historical Society (1992); grave stone: born Augusta, Georgia June 8, 1824 and died June 16, 1901; also listed in chapter on Generals; listed under Generals in "Touring historic Elmwood Cemetery" (Brochure and Map of Historic Gravesites) #7; listed in "Touring Historic Elmwood Cemetery" Brochure (January 2000) #131; sketch #35 in Elmwood *Civil War Tour* booklet (2012).

Gee, John Jamison   Buried May 24, 1862   Chapel Hill 659, #77
Arkansas 25 Infantry Regiment Private Company B (Johnston's Battalion Company A per Daily Burial Record Book), per Company Muster Roll (Co. I, Turnbull's Batt'n of Infantry) for March 1 to May1, 1862 (only card in the record), enlisted March 1, 1862, at Little Rock Arkansas, present but no other information; Arkansas 25 Infantry Regiment, which was re-organized after officers election on May 8, 1862, was formerly 11th Battalion Arkansas Infantry, Colonel C. J. Turnbull's Battalion and Lieutenant Colonel B. G. Johnson's (Johnston's on some compiled service records cards in Colonel Turnbull's and others in the Regiment

records) Battalion, Company I of the Battalion become Company B of the Regiment, James W. Adams was Captain of the Company, which per Company Muster Rolls for March 1 to May 1, 1862, was stationed at Camp McIntosh ("Arrived at a point 2½ miles west of Corinth at 7 a.m. and our baggage train passed on to Corinth and returned at 8 p.m. to this present camp, called Camp McIntosh in honor of General James McIntosh, killed at Elkhorn." Reynolds, Daniel Harris. *Worthy of the Cause for Which They Fight: The Civil War Diary of Brigadier General Harris Reynolds, 1861-1865*. Ed. Robert Patrick Bender. University of Arkansas Press, 2011, page 54.); note most of the other Arkansas 25 (Turnbull's) Infantry Regiment soldiers also buried at Elmwood were left at the Overton Hospital in Memphis in April and May 1862, where they died; grave stone is upright government stone with dates 1836 and May 22, 1862.

Genette, Jones   Buried December 25, 1901   Fowler 120 (IOOF), #E/1
Tennessee 15 Infantry Regiment Captain Company B; originally enlisted 154 Senior Infantry Regiment Captain Company A April 23, 1861, age 39, elected Major July 7, 1861, and left regiment for the 15 Infantry Regiment; appointed/elected Captain October 24, 1861; per Company Muster Roll for May & June, 1862, remarks: captured at the battle of Shiloh; appears on a Roll of Prisoners of War at Depot Prisoners of War, near Sandusky, Ohio, indicating captured Shiloh April 7, 1862 and sent to Vicksburg September 1, 1862; per Company Muster Roll for September & October 1862, remarks: exchanged September 23 at Vicksburg; per Company Muster Roll for September & October, 1863, remarks: Detached Service conscripting by order of General Bragg June 11, 1864; appears on a Roll of Prisoners of War at Johnson's Island, Ohio, applicants for the oath of amnesty, dated April 24, 24, 1865, indicating captured Conyers Station, Georgia, July 22, 1864, remarks: "Is a native of Baltimore and by occupation before the war, a carpenter. Says that he had been a resident of Memphis for over ten years at the breaking out of the Rebellion; that he was Captain of a volunteer Company in Memphis, and was ordered out by the Governor of Tennessee as part of the 154 Regt. Tenn Militia of which he was elected Major: that he resigned and went home in October 1861 but was forced by the state of feeling existing in Memphis at that time to reenter the Army which he did as Captain 15 Tenn Regt; he was not a Secessionist and never voted for it; that he did not desire the dissolution of the Union, has no sympathy with the Rebellion and if permitted to take the oath and return home is determined hereafter to live a loyal citizen of the United States; that he has a dependent family and is anxious to be released to enable him to take care of them."; appears as a signature to an Oath of Amnesty subscribed and sworn to at Johnson's Island, Ohio, May 13, 1865, indicating residence of Memphis, Tennessee and age 41; buried Odd Fellows (IOOF) Section; per Daily Burial Record Book died age 82.

George, Thomas Fletcher   Buried November 17, 1916   Fowler 3043, #1
Tennessee 32 Infantry Regiment Private/Sergeant Company I; enlisted October 18, 1862 Millville; name appears as signature to an oath of amnesty subscribed and sworn to at Pulaski, Tennessee with date of administration of oath January 14, 1865, residence of Lincoln County, Tennessee, entered service October 18, 1862, deserted December 18, 1864 and remarks of no family; on Confederate Historical Association application indicated that went on sick leave December 23, 1864 and never returned; per Tennessee Confederate Pension application #15052 born November 27, 1843 Madison County, Alabama; widow's (Mollie H. Benson) Tennessee Confederate Pension application #6724; per November 17, 1916 *The Commercial Appeal* Memphis died November 16, 1916 age 73; Confederate and died age 72 per Daily Burial Record Book; originally buried Confederate Rest and moved December 1, 1917; member Confederate Historical Association, Camp 28, bivouac 18, Memphis; no sketch in Mathes book; small grave stone partially underground which appears to be same stone that would have been in Confederate Soldiers Rest

Gober, Daniel C.   Buried October 15, 1889   South Grove 182, #6
Louisiana 16 (Gober's) Infantry Regiment Colonel; unit also known as Colonel Gober's Louisiana Mounted Infantry; originally Captain Company K; April 17, 1864 transferred to east Louisiana to command cavalry; doctor and died age 60 per Daily Burial Record Book; circular grave stone with inscription born March 3, 1828 and died October 13, 1889; per 1860 Census 31 year old physician in Opelousas, Louisiana with wife Rosalie Compton Gober and four children; married March 28, 1849 in Shelby County; died in Frankfort, Kentucky.

Goodbar, James Monroe   Buried June 14, 1920   Lenow Circle 2, #4
Tennessee 4 (Murray's) Cavalry Regiment 2 Lieutenant Company D and Quartermaster, Captain and Commissary Department; Tennessee 4 (Murray's) Cavalry Regiment record found as "J. L. Goodbar" enlisted November 11, 1862 Livingston (Overton County, Tennessee) and resigned July 18, 1863; per General and Staff records "Goodbye, J. M." ("J. M. Goodbar" on most cards) Captain and Assistant Quartermaster; "J. M. Goodbar" on one card indicating Adjutant Assistant Quartermaster Murray's 4 Tennessee Cavalry recommended for Assistant Quartermaster August 1862; paroled May 3, 1865 Charlotte, North Carolina; record also found "J. L. Goodbar" Confederate 1 Cavalry 2 Lieutenant 2 Company C (formerly Company D Tennessee 4 Murray's Cavalry Regiment) with same enlistment; per sketch in Shelby County's history in Goodspeed's *History of Hamilton, Knox and Shelby Counties of Tennessee*, page 971, native of Overton County, Tennessee, born in 1839, moved to White County in 1850 and to Memphis in 1860 where entered wholesale boot and shoe trade; enlisted as a private but soon promoted to 2 lieutenant and afterwards to quartermaster; at regiment reorganization transferred to commissary department and continued there until the close of the War; returned to Memphis after War and re-embarked in the wholesale boot and shoe business; per sketch in Mathes book selected regiment quartermaster by Colonel Murray and when regiment reorganized about January 1863 assigned to duty as purchasing agent in the commissary department and served in that capacity the remainder of the War; biography in *Confederate Military History*, *Extended Edition*, Volume X Tennessee, page 506; very prominent businessman in Memphis after the War; referenced and sketches in several publications, including but not limited to, *Who's Who in Tennessee*, *Notable Men of Tennessee*

and *The Mid-South and Its Builders* (see surname cards in Memphis and Shelby County Public Library, History Department); obituary article, with photograph, in *The Commercial Appeal* Memphis June 14, 1920, page 1, column 1; grave stone: May 29, 1839 - June 13, 1920; Goodbar Avenue between Harbert and Central Avenue is named after him (see Ann Meeks' article June 22, 2000, *The Commercial Appeal* Memphis, Section EM, Neighbors, page 2).

Goodloe, James Lockhart   Buried October 19, 1917   Fowler 273-283

Forrest 's Scouts, CSA Private Harvey's Company Scouts; no enlistment in compiled service record; single card that "Appears on a Roll of Prisoners of War of Captain A. Harvey Scouts, CSA, commanded by Lieutenant George Harvey, surrendered at Citronelle, Alabama, by Lieutenant General R. Taylor, CSA, to Major General E. R. S. Canby, USA, May 4, 1865, and paroled at Jackson, Mississippi, May 13, 1865" with residence stated as Madison County, Mississippi; records also found Mississippi 28 Cavalry Regiment compiled service records that include only information about being captured at Spring Creek, Georgia on June 11, 1864, and first sent to Nashville, Tennessee where on the Prisoners of War Rolls dated June 20, 1864, then sent to Military Prison, Louisville, Kentucky on June 21, 1864, then transferred to Rock Island, Illinois where received June 22, 1864, then listed on the Prisoner of War Rolls to be transferred February 25, 1865, then admitted to Jackson Hospital, Richmond, Virginia where admitted March 6, 1865, and given a 30 day furlough March 9, 1865; member Confederate Historical Association and sketch in Mathes book; per sketch: born in Madison county, Miss., September 3, 1840, enlisted in 1861 in Company E, Twenty-eighth Mississippi Cavalry; detailed to Harvey's Scouts; captured June, 1864, at Allatoona, Ga.; imprisoned at Rock Island, Ill; wounded at Cassville, Ga., May, 1864; paroled February, 1865, and sent to Richmond, Va.; practiced law at Memphis, Tenn., since 1867, joining this Association about 1886; name on List of Members of Confederate Historical Association, Camp 28, U. C. V. compiled by Mr. I. M. Rainey, Adjutant, on September 6, 1912 (copy found in the Memphis and Shelby County Room of the Memphis Public Library and Information Center); per narrative for Kizer's Tennessee Cavalry in *Tennesseans in the Civil War, Part I*, on December 2, 1864 General Forrest ordered: "There are four regularly organized and recognized Companies of scouts for this command: Captain Henderson's, Harvey's, Kizer's and Cobb's. None others will be recognized."; the compiled service record card for Forrest 's Scouts, C.S.A. indicated that "The following companies served at various times as part of this command: Capt. Joseph T. Cobb's Company, Capt. Thomas W. Elliott's Company, Capt. Addison Harvey's Company, Capt. Thomas Henderson's Company, Capt. Thomas N. Kizer's Company and Captain _____ Sanders' Company"; died age 78 per Daily Burial Record Book; wrote the article "Harvey's Scouts. Roster of a Famous Confederate Organization." that was cut from a newspaper (paper name and date not shown) and submitted in support of Mattie S. Lorance's application for a Tennessee Confederate Pension (W3571) based on her deceased husband's (John Lorance, Private Harvey Scouts) service; per article in T*he Clarion*, Jackson, Mississippi, September 8, 1886, at an organization meeting of former members of Harvey's Scouts at Canton, Mississippi August 30, 1886, to form the "Harvey's Scout Memorial Association" was elected as a permanent officer (vice president) and its was resolved to remove the remains of Captain Addison Harvey from Columbus, Georgia to Canton, Mississippi at his house as soon as practicable and resolved to approve the movement to erect a monument to Captain Harvey; reported in *Confederate Veteran* Volume II, April, 1894, No. 4, page 117, that the monument would be unveiled at Canton, Mississippi, next August; reported in *Confederate Veteran* Volume II, September, 1894, No. 9, page 273, that the monument was unveiled on September 18, 1894, and that "Miss Georgia Goodloe sung the 'Confederate Song' composed by her father, James L. Goodloe, one of the company, the music of which was written by a "yankee," and all published in the July Veteran." (actually, published *Confederate Veteran* Volume II, August 1894, No. 8, "Confederate Veteran Song," Words by James Lockhart Goodloe, of Harvey's Scouts, and Music by F. Peterson Dunn; per article "The Gallant Goodloe Brothers." *Confederate Veteran* Volume XXII, September, 1914, No. 9, page 419, reported that "James L. Goodloe, a lawyer od Memphis, Tenn., who served with Harvey's Scouts of Forrest's command, is the last one of four brothers."; post war digital photograph in military uniform with hand on the hilt of his sword as if he might draw it out is located in the Hallum W. Goodloe Papers at the Tennessee State Library & Archives, War and Reunion – The Lost Cause in Southern Memory, Tennessee Virtual Archives; circle grave stone: 1840-1917.

Gordon, George Washington   Buried August 12, 1911   Fowler 180, #4

Brigadier General; appointed from Tennessee August 16, 1864 (rank August 15, 1864) per the *Memorandum relative to the General Officers Appointed by the President in the Armies of the Confederate States, 1861-1865*, the Military Secretary's Office U. S. War Department 1905; originally enlisted as Captain Company I Tennessee 11 Infantry Regiment July 31, 1861, elected Lieutenant Colonel May 27, 1862 and promoted to Colonel November 7, 1862; captured in Kentucky August 1862 and exchanged August 15, 1862; wounded in thigh and captured at Battle of Murfreesboro December 31, 1862 and exchanged April 29, 1863 at age 26; captured in action at Franklin, Tennessee November 30, 1864 and released from Fort Warren, Massachusetts July 24, 1865; per General and Staff records appointed August 16, 1864, captured Franklin, Tennessee November 30, 1864, sent to Johnson's Island December 3, 1864, sent to Fort Warren, Massachusetts December 14, 1864, and released July 24, 1865; per biography in *Confederate Military History, Extended Edition*, Volume X Tennessee, page 507: born Giles County, Tennessee, October 5, 1836 (military career briefly described on pages 309 and 310); became a lawyer after the War and later Superintendent of Memphis Schools, then a Member of Congress; per sketch in Mathes book born Giles County, Tennessee and raised in Mississippi and Texas; per sketch in Generals in Gray was Commander-in-Chief of the United Confederate Veterans when died August 9, 1911; died age 74 per Daily Burial Record Book; sketch in Tennessee, The Volunteer State, 1769-1923, Volume II, page 131; sketch in the PoliticalGraveyard.com; sketch, photograph, if available, and grave stone photograph in book *Quiet Places: The Burial Sites of Civil War Generals in Tennessee* by Buckner and Nathaniel C. Hughes, Jr., East Tennessee Historical Society (1992); born October 5, 1836, and died August 9, 1911, inscribed on "In Memory Of" stone located in walk around Confederate Soldiers Rest Monument; also listed in chapter on Generals; listed under Generals in "Touring historic Elmwood Cemetery" (Brochure and Map of Historic

Gravesites) #8; listed in "Touring Historic Elmwood Cemetery" Brochure (January 2000) #10; sketch #3 in Elmwood *Civil War Tour* booklet (2012).

Graham, Albert Kimbrough   Buried January 24, 1951   South Grove 65, #2
Tennessee 7 Cavalry Regiment, Private Company A; per sketch in Mathes (Enlarged Edition) born October 19, 1833 in Shelby County, Tennessee, father was one of the first sheriffs of Shelby County, graduated at the University of North Carolina at Chappel (sic) Hill in the class of 1854, engaged in planting on Arkansas River when War broke out, enlisted in the "Memphis Light Dragoons" (Logwood's cavalry company that became Company A), never wounded or captured, never had a furlough except for twenty days in four years of War though seriously injured (dislocated) shoulder in a railroad accident night before battle of Belmont, summer 1863 before fall of Vicksburg when regiment at Canton, Mississippi detailed to cross Mississippi and convey change of the Confederate secret cipher from Richmond to General Dick Taylor then at Alexandria that was rendered necessary from the fact that Federals had captured key to the cipher used by the Confederates who signaled to each other across the Mississippi River which duty was accomplished in thirty days, at close of War paroled at Gainesville, Alabama, and after War married and settled near Raleigh, Tennessee; death (April 12, 1909) mentioned in *Confederate Veteran* Volume X, October 1909, page 520 in "Death List of Memphis Historical Society" between January 1, 1909 and July 1, 1909; originally buried in family cemetery behind home 877 N. Graham (subdivision bounded by Graham Road, Macon, Wingfield and Given Avenues), Memphis, and six graves moved to Elmwood Cemetery January 24, 1851; died age 78 per Daily Burial Record Book; per Family file in Cemetery office Graham Street and Grahamwood School named after family, Joseph Graham came to Shelby County in 1828 and was first Sheriff of Shelby County, and Sylvester Graham, a doctor and scientist, invented graham cracker in 1829; flat family grave stone (broken); Tennessee Confederate Pension S6490.

Green, H. Dixon   Buried March 22, 1862   Chapel Hill Circle 25, #2
Captain; listed in Elmwood 1874 book as Confederate soldier buried in Elmwood who was citizen of Memphis or vicinity with rank of Captain; funeral invitation notice in the March 22, 1862, *Memphis Daily Appeal*, page 1, column 6; Captain, died pneumonia age 33 per Daily Burial Record Book; originally buried Turley 147, #1 and moved February 7, 1868; not H. D. Green - Tennessee 15 Infantry Regiment, Tennessee 3 Cavalry Regiment, or Mississippi 13 Infantry Regiment.

Green, Solomon P.   Memorial Stone   Fowler 116
Tennessee 4 Infantry Regiment Surgeon; enlisted May 16, 1861, Germantown, Tennessee; records also found in Confederate Officers Rolls; no death indicated in compiled service record; not found in the Official Memorial Roll for the Tennessee 4 Infantry Regiment in Lindsley's Annals; service sketch in the *Southern Historical Society Papers* Volume XXII, 1894, page 206; memorial stone in lot where wife, Sarah Baker Degraffenreid Green (February 21, 1826 December 28, 1900) is buried; Fowler Lot 116 is the Mrs. Sarah B. Green lot per Elmwood 1874 book List of Proprietors; 1820 1864 on stone; no Cemetery record found.

Greene, Colton   Buried October 3, 1900   Fowler 193, #1
Missouri 3 Cavalry Regiment Colonel; per undated muster roll in Missouri 3 Cavalry Regiment compiled service records age 30, appointed November 4, 1862, by the President of C.S.A., born South Carolina and lives in Missouri; per sketch in *More Generals in Gray* listed as general in several publications, often commanded a brigade but the Official Record shows him as Colonel as late as December 31, 1864, petitions for his promotion to general in 1865 were signed by practically all the officers in the Trans-Mississippi army but the Official Record shows no indication of any promotion by either President Davis or General Kirby Smith, and full name appears to be "George Colton Greene"; not listed in the *Memorandum Relative to the General Officers appointed by the President in the Armies of the Confederate States - 1861-1865* compiled from Official Records by the Military Secretary's Office, War Department 1905; not listed in *Generals in Gray*; listed in Mathes book as a member of Confederate Historical Association but no sketch; organized State Savings Bank, Memphis, and the Tennessee Club and proposed a Mardi Gras in Memphis; General Colton Greene and died age 64 per Daily Burial Record Book; biography in *Confederate Military History*, *Extended Edition*, Volume XII Missouri, page 302; see "OUR MOST NOBLE STRANGER": THE MYSTERY, GALLANTRY AND CIVICISM OF COLTON GREENE by Charles Steven Palmer, Master Thesis, University of Oklahoma, 1995, and the Colton Greene collection in the Memphis Room of the Memphis/Shelby County Public Library and Information Center; grave stone: General Colton Greene, 1832-1900, per Bruce Allardice research birth was July 7, 1833, as found on an old passport; First President The Tennessee Club 1875; also listed in chapter on Generals; listed under Generals in "Touring historic Elmwood Cemetery" (Brochure and Map of Historic Gravesites) #10; listed in "Touring Historic Elmwood Cemetery" Brochure (January 2000) #11; sketch #2 in Elmwood *Civil War Tour* booklet (2012).

Greenlaw, Alonzo   Buried September 26, 1875   Turley 250, # 11
Tennessee 3 (Forrest's) Cavalry Regiment Private Company F; appears on a Roll of Prisoners of War paroled at Gainesville, Alabama May 11, 1865, residence Memphis, Tennessee, with notation on card that Company appears to have formerly served as Company C, 2d Regiment Mississippi Partisan Rangers, and to have become a part of Forrest's Old Regiment Tennessee Cavalry, in compliance with S. O. No. 28, Headquarters Cavalry, District of Mississippi and East Louisiana, dated February 13, 1865; name appears on an Oath of Allegiance sworn to at Memphis, Tennessee, from June 1 to 15, 1865, date June 2, 1865, residence Memphis, Tennessee, age 23; appears on a register of Prisoners of War at Memphis, Tennessee — Deserters from the rebel army. The name appears under the following heading: "Administered in lieu of the Amnesty." Date June 2, 1865, residence Memphis, Tennessee, age 23; Mississippi 2 (J. G. Ballentine's Regiment of Cavalry) Partisan Rangers Private (Captain Edward E. Porter's Partisan

Company – see Rev. Edward E. Porter sketch) Company C; enlisted October 1, 1862, Byhalia, Mississippi, by Captain Porter, per Company Muster Roll for May and June, 1863, remarks: Ordnance Sergeant April 20, 1863, per Company Muster Roll for September and October, 1863, remarks: wounded at Strailfence Creek October 16, 1863, and at hospital at Canton, per October 31, 1862, to February 24, 1864, muster rolls absent without leave, and present on September and October 1864, muster roll; appears to have first enlisted Tennessee 2 (Walker's) Infantry Regiment, Brevet 2 Lieutenant Company A April 26, 1861, Memphis, per March/April, 1862, muster roll remarks absent wounded, per undated company muster roll remarks discharged May, 1862, wounded Shiloh, age 18; per *Greenlaw Rediscovered, A History*, pages 4-5, Peggy Boyce Jemison, Metropolitan Inter-Faith Association, Memphis, Tennessee, 1979, "said to have served under General Forrest and to have been sent to recapture the Greenlaw home on Union after the federal forces had commandeered it."; son of William Borden Greenlaw; cadet at Virginia Military Institute (VMI); per information in VMI library archives file reported for duty July 5, 1860, for Class of 1864, age 17, dismissed November 8, 1860, for neglect of duties and studies ("Was an habitual drunkard"); also per letter in VMI library archives file written by nephew, W. B. Greenlaw, dated August 31, 1910, born 1842, died at Memphis at the age of 32 and never married; died September 25, 1875, near Germantown per death notice in the *Memphis Daily Appeal,* September 26, 1875, page 1 (no age indicated); died age 37 per Daily Burial Record Book but actual age was 32; Turley Lot 250 is the Greenlaw Family Lot; number 76 in the "Touring historic Elmwood Cemetery" (Brochure and Map of Historic Gravesites), which was the predecessor of the "Touring Historic Elmwood Cemetery" Brochure (January 2000).

Greenlaw, J. Oliver   Buried April 23, 1864   Turley 250, #5
Per *Greenlaw Rediscovered, A History*, page 4, Peggy Boyce Jemison, Metropolitan Inter-Faith Association, Memphis, Tennessee, 1979 "served bravely in the Confederate Army under General Polk and General Cheatham, and he died in the war."; per sketch in Elmwood book, page 119, "(H)e went aboard a steamer on fire, freighted, as he knew, with many tons of gunpowder, and extinguished the flames. The Confederate forces, under Gen. Polk, had just landed at New Madrid, and many vessels were lying at the wharf. All who saw the flames fled save Greenlaw and Gen. Cheatham. Such is the story told of his daring conduct, by which many lives, and much valuable property, and many steamers were saved."; monument shared with brother, W. B. Greenlaw, description in the "The Monuments." chapter in Elmwood book page 88; see also *West Tennessee Historical Society Papers*, 1957, Volume 11, page 99, which indicates "J. O. (Oliver) Greenlaw and W. B. (Borden) were brothers who shared everything in common ownership.... They share the same tombstone at Elmwood." but this appears not to be incorrect as each has a separate grave stone and records indicates different graves although per note in Daily Burial Record Book "two together marked"; see also Paul R. Coppock's *Memphis Sketches*, pages 103-108; not believed to be Joseph Greenlaw, Confederate Signal Corps, whose record has one card that indicates name appears on a list of officers and privates of the Signal Corps in Richmond and on the Potomac (not dated) and detached in West Moreland County, Virginia, duty: boatman; grave stone Born Westmoreland, County, Virginia March 13, 1812 Died February 19, 1864; Turley Lot 250 is the Greenlaw Family Lot; # 76 in the "Touring historic Elmwood Cemetery" (Brochure and Map of Historic Gravesites), which was the predecessor of the "Touring Historic Elmwood Cemetery" Brochure (January 2000).

Greenwood, Edmund Rice   Buried October 10, 1902   Lenow Circle 47, #3
Tennessee Logwood's Cavalry; no record found; unit per article in *The Commercial Appeal* Memphis October 9, 1902, page 8, column 3, that indicates died October 8, 1902, born Hubbardstown (sic), Massachusetts about 65 years ago, came south at age 14, lived in Memphis about 45 years and served in Logwood's cavalry for whole four years; per sketch in *Greenwood Genealogies, 1154-1924*, by Frederick Greenwood, New York: The Lyons Genealogical Company, 1914, page 368, born December 18, 1837, in Hubbardston, Massachusetts, died October 8, 1902, at Memphis, Tennessee, lived in Ashburnham until 16 years old when he went West where he lived several years, in 1859 settled at Memphis, Tennessee, was in stock business at Memphis and later in cotton commission business there, joined the Confederate Army serving in the 154th Tennessee Regiment (no record found), and married in Memphis November 17, 1861, to Mary Josephine Haning (born at Grand Gulf, Mississippi December 20, 1837 and daughter of Aaron and Nancy (Dickinson) Haning); large family stone with only surname and small stone December 18, 1837 October 8, 1902; died age 66 per Daily Burial Record Book.

Greer, Elkanah Brackin   Buried March 28, 1877   Turley 93, #13
Brigadier General; appointed from Texas October 8, 1862 (rank October 8, 1862) per the *Memorandum relative to the General Officers Appointed by the President in the Armies of the Confederate States - 1861-1865* compiled from Official Records by the Military Secretary's Office, U. S. War Department 1905; also per remarks in said Memorandum included in the Canby-Smith convention of May 26, 1865 but no record of his personal parole found; originally Colonel Texas 3 Cavalry Regiment; no individuals records found Texas 3 Cavalry Regiment records but listed on organization cards as Colonel; per General and Staff records Chief of Bureau of Conscription, Trans Mississippi Department, Provisional Army, Marshall, Texas September 1864 and signed Parole of Honor 24 June 1865 at Marshall, Texas; born October 11, 1825 in Paris, Tennessee, with Jefferson Davis in Mexican War, died at DeValls Bluff, Arkansas March 25, 1877 while visiting sister; sketch in *Generals in Gray*; died Phthisis Pulmonary age 52 per Daily Burial Record Book; grave stone: Brigadier General Texas Confederate States Army October 11, 1825 March 25, 1877; biography in *Confederate Military History*, *Extended Edition*, Volume XV Texas, page 233; sketch, photograph, if available, and grave stone photograph in book *Quiet Places: The Burial Sites of Civil War Generals in Tennessee* by Buckner and Nathaniel C. Hughes, Jr., East Tennessee Historical Society (1992); also listed in chapter on Generals; listed under Generals in "Touring historic Elmwood Cemetery" (Brochure and Map of Historic Gravesites) #9; listed in "Touring Historic Elmwood Cemetery" Brochure (January 2000) #28; sketch #32 in Elmwood *Civil War Tour* booklet (2012).

Greer, Hugh Dunlap   Buried April 29, 1899   Turley 24, #10

Tennessee 38 Infantry Regiment Lieutenant Colonel; enlisted 1 Lieutenant June 13, 1861 Memphis; promoted to Lieutenant Colonel May 10, 1862; captured in Desoto County, Mississippi July 20, 1862, sent to Military Prison in Alton, Illinois and sent to Vicksburg, Mississippi for exchange September 23, 1862; member Confederate Historical Association and sketch in Mathes book, page 111; Colonel indicated in Daily Burial Record Book and Mathes sketch; biography in *Confederate Military History, Extended Edition*, Volume X Tennessee, page 514; per biography born February 4, 1836, Paris, Tennessee and accidentally killed by a passing train at Buntyn Station April 29, 1899; died age 64 per Daily Burial Record Book.

Grice, James W.   Buried December 24, 1867   Fowler 233, #3

Tennessee 3 (Forrest's) Cavalry Regiment Private Company A ("Bluff City Grays"), enlisted May 4, 1861, Randolph, Tennessee and detailed to Ordnance Department December 3, 1861; per General and Staff compiled service record rolls Ordnance Sergeant, Forrest's Cavalry Ordnance Department and paroled May 10, 1865, at Gainesville, Alabama; first enlisted in the Tennessee 154 Senior Infantry Regiment May 14, 1861, at Randolph, Tennessee, age 24 and Property Clerk per receipt for pay for August, 1863, at Selma Arsenal; listed (second initial "H.) in Elmwood 1874 book as Confederate soldier buried in Elmwood who was citizen of Memphis or vicinity; listed in the June 6, 1878, *Memphis Daily Appeal*, page 4, column 3, article "OUR DEAD HEROES" covering the unveiling of the Confederate Monument and Decoration of Graves at Elmwood as then one of twenty-eight members of the Bluff City Grays, Company B of the 154 Senior Infantry Regiment and Company A of Forrest's Old (Third) Cavalry Regiment buried at Elmwood; listed as one of the "comrades who sleep at Elmwood cemetery " in the article "Veterans in Council" in *Memphis Daily Appeal*, May 12, 1881, page 4, column 4, concerning the meeting of the surviving members in the city of the old Bluff City Grays to appoint the necessary committees for the purpose of making special decoration on the graves of their dead comrades at Elmwood and Calvary cemeteries on Sunday next, Memorial Day; listed as member of Bluff City Grays in *Reminiscences of the Civil War* by John Hallum, Tunnah & Pittard printers, 1903; listed in "A COMPLETE ROSTER OF THE BLUFF CITY GREYS" located in the Memphis Room of the Memphis/Shelby County Public Library and Information Center Central Library with notation "Detailed in Odr. Died Memphis, 1867" and buried in Elmwood; see also Notes of Interest - Bluff City Grays; died age 23 consumption per Daily Burial Record Book.

Guess, George W.   Buried July 19, 1868   Fowler 74, #1

Texas 31 Cavalry Regiment Lieutenant Colonel and Good's Company Artillery (Texas State Troops) Private; per information courtesy of John Luckey and Bruce Allardice, who are co-authors of a soon-to-be-published Civil War book on notables of Texas (*Texas Burial Sites of Civil War Notables- A Biographical and Pictorial Field Guide*), born in North Carolina ca 1829 (1860 Dallas County, Texas census, page 3092: age 31, lawyer, born North Carolina, wife Mary B. Guess age 18), lived in Dallas, Dallas County, Texas, lawyer, married Molley Miller, before the war became a widower, was a city alderman of Dallas from August 1860 to August 1862, close friend of Captain John J. Good of Good-Douglas Texas Battery, CSA, for a while serves as a private in this battery, but acted as an assistant to Captain Good most of the time, mentioned many times and listed (page 196) as a Private in Dallas Light Artillery, John J. Good Captain, when tendered to the State of Texas February 22, 1861 in Captain Good's book, *Cannon Smoke: the Letters of Captain John J. Good, Good-Douglas Texas Battery CSA*, Lester Newton Fitzhugh editor, The Hill Junior College Press, Hillsboro, Texas, 1971, after left the battery joined 31st Texas Cavalry Regiment as a Lieutenant Colonel, probate was recorded at the Dallas County Court House on February 1880 and closed in 1883, and had some lands in West Texas; brief War sketch in *Portraits of Conflict, A Photographic History of Texas in the Civil War*, by Carl Moneyhon and Bobby Roberts, Portraits of Conflicts Series, The University of Arkansas Press, Fayetteville 1998, page 303, with *carte de viste* portrait, which sketch indicates captured during battle September 29, 1863 at Stirling's Plantation near Morganza, Louisiana and was confined in New Orleans where he was at first given wide latitude as a prisoner of war, including the right to cross between the lines, but Federal authorities later accused him of "speculating in cotton, the profits to be shared between himself and others within the enemy's lines."; paroled June 10, 1865; per the Appendix, page 350, "George Guess returned to his law practice in Austin (sic Dallas) after the war. He was elected mayor to fill an unexpired term (from 1866 to 1867 and per other sources it appeared that Guess was supplanted by the Federal military (Reconstruction) government at San Antonio, Texas; see also page 54 *History of Dallas County, Texas: From 1837 to 1887*, by John Henry Brown, Dallas, Texas: Milligan, Cornett & Farnham, Printers. 1887, republished 1966 by The Aldredge Book Store: Dallas). On July 18, 1868, Guess was aboard a steamer returning from a trip to Memphis, Tennessee, when he died from sunstroke."; several Memphis newspaper articles concerning his death (note confusion with names and spelling mistakes): the *Sunday Morning Appeal* (the Sunday edition of *Memphis Daily Appeal*), July 19, 1868, page 3, column 7, under Miscellaneous in the River Matters section: "About two years ago a Mr. Robinson (Frank Robberson per grave stone - see below), of Texas, who was on his way with a lot of cattle, died and was buried at Island 35. On the last up trip of the Mollie Able his brother-in-law (married sisters - see below), Mr. Frank Guess, together with Mrs. Robinson and two young ladies, arrived in this city from Texas, on their way to recover the body and bury it in our beautiful Elmwood. Yesterday evening they all started for Island 35 on the Victor, but Mr. Guess was sun struck shortly after leaving our city, and when near Fort Harris the boat was turned about to procure medical aid, but Mr. Guess died just as she reached the wharf. It is a sad story." (the newspaper indicated that the temperature reached 98 "in the shade" on the 18th); *Memphis Daily Appeal*, July 20, 1868, page 3, column 2, "INQUESTS. - Coroner Samelson held inquests on the bodies of two men yesterday. The first of whom was Frank Guess, who died day before yesterday, on the steamer VICTOR as she neared the wharf, having been sunstruck on his way down to Island 35. .... The verdict in both cases was death from sunstroke...."; *Memphis Daily Appeal*, July 21, 1868, page 3, column 2, "CORRECTION. - The gentleman whose death was mentioned in our last, as having occurred by sun stroke on the steamer

VICTOR, was Col. George W. Given, of Dallas, Texas, a prominent citizen of that State, a Mason of eminence, and during the late war a Colonel who won honor in the Confederate service. Coming here to remove the remains of a relative, he lost his own life in performing a duty of love and humanity."; and *Memphis Daily Appeal*, July 25, 1868, page 3, column 6, under Miscellaneous in the River Matters section: A.... 35 Miles Above Town, at Anchor. *Dear Appeal*: .... The Victor No. 2 is now at the landing, and reports the death of Col. Geo. W. Guess, of Texas, who died suddenly on board last evening. She was forced to return with his corpse, where they have been cenotaphed to await the arrival of the remains of A. Frank Roberson, his brother-in-law, who died in the bend of 35 some two years ago. What a melancholy truth do we find in this fearful and heart-rendering picture. His loved wife, a most excellent lady, had come on a pilgrimage of more than a thousand miles to visit the burial place of her husband, who had found a grave amidst strangers in a wild yet hospitable land. She had come to pay love's last tribute at her heart's wedded shrine - to remove to your beautiful Elmwood all that was mortal of him, and immortal with her, that he might rest in this his last slumber, though far away from his loved Lone Star home, above the high waters of the lowland where stranger hands had placed him; that she might plant with her own hands the willow, fit emblem of her sorrow, and the ivy, fit memento of her love. "Two graves," side by side, will hold the two Texan friends. May the turf rest lightly upon them, and may prudence teach this wounded heart to bear the trials of His will. When she returns home with a gulf dividing her from him, may she calmly await till she, too, is called to meet him, where flowers fade not, and death is known no more. We but express her own wishes in thanking her friends. Their kind deeds will be remembered. To Mr. S, of Arkansas, and the urbane hosts of the Overton, S. B. Robbins & Co., her thanks are especially due. More anon, semi occasionally, WHETSTONE, JR.; per *Marriages Dallas County, Texas Volume 1, Books A-E*, compiled and published by Dallas Genealogy Society 1978, page 6, Marriage Book A-B, George W. Guess married Mary B. Miller December 4, 1856, and page 14, Marriage Book C, Frank Robberson married Sue Miller January 8, 1866 (Mary and Sue were sisters and the daughters of William B. Miller per the aforesaid *History of Dallas County, Texas: From 1837 to 1887*, page 83); author of "Civil War Letters of Colonel George W. Guess to Sarah Horton Cockrell"; per Cemetery Daily Book July 19, 1868, G. W. Guest (sic - misspelled in all Cemetery records) died of congestion and first placed in Receiving Tomb 21; per Cemetery Daily Book July 23, 1868, (no first name) Robertson (sic - misspelled in all Cemetery records), age 50, buried Lot 74 Fowler, remarks: "Removed from Arkansas"; per Cemetery Register of Deeds Book Fowler Lot 74 was purchased July 23, 1868, by Sue Robertson; per Fowler Book Lot 74 G. W. Guest buried in grave #1 and Mr. Robertson buried in grave #2; per Shelby County Funeral book Mr. Robberson was buried at Elmwood July 23, 1868, survivor: Robberson, S. (Mrs.) (Wife), CHGS AT LANIES LDG TO P. H. HARRELL - PD BY MR. ROBBINS 7/27/68; upright double grave stone (broken in half below names and inscriptions faded and partially illegible) with Free Mason symbol above each name; left side: The Grave of George W. Guess of Dallas, Texas - Death has given thee one grave, That thou as friends may sleep, Till morn eternal will be again, And then from earth be reclaimed, Sleep on sleep on together sleep, A fond heart here and distant, With a sisters love and wifes prayer, Will await to meet the both again - Died at Memphis, Tenn. July 18, 1868, in his 44 Year; right side: The Grave of Frank Robberson of Dallas, Texas placed here by his devoted wife July 1868 - From my distant love I'm home, To thy grave thy wife has come, To place this stone above thy breast, Sacred spot of final rest. Here flowers from your Praries fair, Shall sweetly bloom without my care, While d__ of ____ so sweetly g__n, Will bless them till we meet in Heaven - Died September 5, 1866, at Bend 35 Ark in his 31 Year; note spelling and ages differences with records and newspapers; sketch in the PoliticalGraveyard.com.

Guy, William Wallace   Buried August 20, 1879   South Grove 54, #1
Johnson's Corps Major; 1861 made Associate Commissary General with rank of Major of Infantry; served under General Lucius Polk; acting commissary for the Army of Tennessee, 1863; surrendered at Montgomery, Alabama in 1865; born in Franklin County, Alabama October 27, 1832; served in the Tennessee General Assembly 1859-61 representing Hardeman County; died in Memphis during the yellow fever epidemic on August 19, 1879; biography in *Biographical Directory of the Tennessee General Assembly*, Volume I, 1796-1861, pages 316-317, Tennessee State Library and Archives, Nashville, 1975; grave stone inscription includes "Major C.S.A"; died age 50 (sic) per Daily Burial Record Book.

Gwynne, Andrew Dunn   Buried July 23, 1909   Lenow Circle 82, #6
Tennessee 38 Infantry Regiment Lieutenant Colonel; enlisted 2 Lieutenant Company A (Captain Lea's Company) August 15, 1861 Memphis age 22; elected 1 Lieutenant 1 Company A January 10, 1862; appointed Lieutenant Colonel June 28, 1862; captured Atlanta, Georgia July 22, 1864; forwarded to Louisville November 21, 1864; sent to Johnson's Island November 22, 1864; transferred to Point Lookout February 16, 1865; record also found "A. D. Gwynn" ("Gywnne" on some cards) Alabama 50 Infantry Regiment Major (first known as Alabama 26 (Coltart's) Infantry Regiment with designation changed June 6, 1863) which record indicates appointed April 4, 1862 and June 28, 1862 appointed Lieutenant Colonel Tennessee 38 Infantry Regiment and wounded severely in arm by shell at Battle of Shiloh (note Major Alabama 26 Infantry Regiment on this record card); per sketch in Mathes book born Londonderry, Ireland January 18, 1839, enlisted in Sumter Grays which became Company A of Tennessee 38 Infantry Regiment, elected Lieutenant and appointed Adjutant of Tennessee Battalion, promoted to Major April 3, 1862 and assigned to Alabama 26 Infantry Regiment, wounded Battle of Shiloh at age 23 and after battle promoted to Lieutenant Colonel and assigned to Tennessee 38 Infantry Regiment, wounded in left arm July 22, 1864 at Battle of Atlanta, taken prisoner and sent to federal hospital at Marietta, Georgia, prisoner at Johnson's Island, February 1865 exchanged and sent to Richmond, Virginia; biography in *Confederate Military History, Extended Edition*, Volume X Tennessee, page 517; died age 70 per Daily Burial Record Book; per grave stone born January 18, 1839 and died July 20, 1909; Gwynne Road in East Memphis was named for him per Ann Meeks' Streetscapes article in *The Commercial Appeal* Memphis, May 23, 2002, Section EM, Neighbors.

Hall, W. A.
Listed in Elmwood 1874 book as Confederate soldier buried in Elmwood who was citizen of Memphis or vicinity; possibly William Adolphus Hall, age 38, buried September 22, 1873, Fowler Public Lot 3, #303, no stone; per death notice in the September 22, 1873, *Memphis Daily Appeal*, page 1, column 7, William Adolphus Hall was born March 25, 1835, in Halifax County, Virginia and died in Memphis September 21, 1873; born Virginia died age 38 yellow fever per Memphis and Shelby County Library Memphis Room funeral index book.

Hamilton, James   Buried September 17, 1861   Turley 90½, #1
Tennessee Johnston's Heavy Artillery Company (Memphis Southern Guards, aka Southern Guards Artillery, see Notes of Interest) Captain James Hamilton's Company (12 Months 1861-62 enlistment) Captain; per Company Muster-in Roll dated April 21, 1861, enlisted April 21, 1861, Memphis age 33; appeared only on August 20, 1861, muster roll; died at Columbus, Kentucky; death reported in September 17, 1861, *Memphis Daily Appeal* Local Matters; September 17, 1861, the *Avalanche* (Memphis) under local matters reported on his death and indicated that he was about 35, native of Columbus, Georgia, resided in Memphis about 2 years and a lawyer; a tribute poem on Hamilton was included in September 19, 1861, the *Avalanche*; identified as brother of S. H. D. Hamilton of same unit when his death was reported in the January 3, 1862, *Memphis Daily Appeal*; listed in Elmwood 1874 book as Confederate soldier buried in Elmwood who was citizen of Memphis or vicinity and sketch; grave stone inscription born Missouri November 14, 1827, and died in Belmont, Missouri September 17, 1861, aged 34 years; sun stoke and Captain Southern Guard per Daily Burial Record Book; mentioned by Dr. S. H. Ford in his address on the occasion to commemorate (Confederate Memorial Day) Confederates buried at Elmwood on April 26, 1866, (see articles "The Confederate Dead" in the *Public Ledger* (Memphis), April 27, 1866, page 3, column 2, and "Honors To The Memory Of The Hero Dead" in the April 27, 1866, *Memphis Daily Appeal*, page 3, column 1); mentioned ("Captain Hamilton—so much loved—one of our earliest dead—placed near the gate, as if on guard over his sleeping comrades.") in General W. B. Bates' speech printed in the article "Elmwood" (Grand and Imposing Ceremonies of Commemoration Day), in *Memphis Sunday Appeal*, May 8, 1870, page 4, column 2.

Hamilton, S. H. D., Jr.   Buried January 2, 1862   Fowler Public Lot 1, #376
Tennessee Johnston's Heavy Artillery Company (Memphis Southern Guards, aka Southern Guards Artillery, see Notes of Interest) Captain James Hamilton's Company (12 Months 1861-62 enlistment) 2 Lieutenant on compiled service record envelope but Captain on several cards and also listed as Captain in the Johnston's Heavy Artillery Company unit history in *Tennesseans in the Civil War Part 1*, page 133; per Company Muster-in Roll dated August 21, 1861, enlisted May 14, 1861, Memphis age 22; per letter of Colonel Marshall, Assistant Adjutant General, in compiled service record died January 1, 1862, at friend's house in Memphis of typhoid pneumonia; brother of James Hamilton of same unit per article on death reported in the January 3, 1862, *Memphis Daily Appeal*.

Hamlin, Edward Lumpkin   Buried August 27, 1870   Chapel Hill 130, #5
Virginia Military Institute (VMI) Cadet (Class of 1867) Company D and Confederate 8 Infantry Battalion (2 Foreign Legion, 2 Foreign Battalion) 2 Lieutenant Company F (two cards in record: company muster roll dated December 24, 1864, and name appears on a Certificate of Election for Commissioned Officers dated December 26, 1864); only record in VMI compiled service record is that name appears on Morning Report Robertson Hospital Richmond, Virginia dated November 14, 1864 and again on November 19, 1864; per information in *Cadets at New Market* in VMI library archives file born Athenia, Marshall County, Mississippi January 24, 1845, matriculated at VMI on July 25, 1863, from Memphis, Tennessee and later in that session served as a cadet private in Company D in the battle of New Market, the following year returned when the corps was stationed at the Alms House in Richmond but left on January 9, 1865, assigned to the staff of General Wright and served until the end of the war; also per sketch in VMI library archives file entered VMI 25 July 1863, Private Company D at New Market, with Corps at Richmond fall 1864, in hospital in Richmond November 1864, identification speculative but may have been the "E. L. Hamlin" whose only record shows that at Florence, South Carolina on 26 December 1864, was elected 2 Lieutenant, Company F, 8 Confederate States Battalion (2 Foreign Legion, 2 Foreign Battalion) and on muster roll 27 December 1864, unofficial source says was on the staff of Brigadier General M. J. Wright but no official record found, at Harvard University 1865-1871, and killed in DeSoto County, Mississippi in duel over "a beautiful woman" by E. T. Freeman (VMI 1862) that was supposed to have been last duel fought between Tennesseans if not VMIers; listed in Elmwood 1874 book as Confederate soldier buried in Elmwood who was citizen of Memphis or vicinity and sketch; per sketch born Marshall County, Mississippi 1845, cadet at Virginia Military Institute September 1863, and joined Confederate service in 1864 with other cadets; graduate of Harvard Law School; died August 26, 1870, from gunshot wound received in a duel with Edward T. Freeman (VMI Class of 1862) that took place just across the Tennessee/Mississippi state line off Highway 51; allegedly they were rivals for a beautiful woman - per information in Edward T. Freeman's VMI archives file Lou Lenow (daughter of Joseph Lenow, Elmwood Cemetery President - see sketch herein) was alleged to have been the beautiful woman loved by both Freeman and Hamlin; duel reported *Memphis Daily Appeal* August 27, 1870, page 4; the duel was subject of article "VMI Search Revives Memphis' Last Dueling Victim" by Paul R. Coppock in *The Commercial Appeal* Memphis July 7, 1974, Section 6, page 7; duel also subject of story "Illegal Honor" by Paul R. Coppock in *Memphis Sketches*, page 229 (Friends of Memphis and Shelby County Libraries, 1976); died age 25 per Daily Burial Record Book; large Hamlin family monument indicating born "Athenia" Marshall County, Mississippi January 24, 1845 and died Desoto County, Mississippi August 26, 1870; killed in duel age 25 per Daily Burial Record Book.

Hamner, Constantine Scales   Buried August 2, 1888   Fowler 279/314, #32

Tennessee 19 Cavalry Regiment Sergeant Company L; enlisted July 11, 1862, Jackson, Tennessee; appears on roll of prisoners of war who surrendered and paroled at Gainesville, Alabama May 10, 1865; per August 2, 1888, *Memphis Daily Appeal* C. S. Hamner, age 54, died July 31, 1888, (no other information); name "C. L. Hamner," age 53, Fowler 279-314 (Memphis Typographical Union Lot) #12 in Cemetery Daily book; name "C. S. Hamner," Grave #32 in Cemetery Fowler book; Sergeant Company L 19 Tennessee Cavalry C.S.A. December 22, 1835 July 31, 1888 on grave stone.

Hanauer, Louis   Buried August 23, 1889   Lenow Circle 30, #7

Arkansas 7 Infantry Regiment Assistant Commissary of Subsistence; name appears on roster of regiment, organized June 16, 1861, and mustered into Confederate service July 26, 1861, resigned July 26, 1861; per sketch in Mathes book born in Bavaria in 1820, came to America 1838, lived in Pocahontas, Arkansas, removed to Memphis 1860, enlisted in Confederate army and served for a time on General Hardee's staff, prominent merchant and died August 1889; sketch in Goodspeed's Shelby County History, page 1037 (Messrs. Schoolfield, Hanauer & Co.); died age 68 years 10 months 21 days per Daily Burial Record Book; born Munich, Bavaria September 30, 1820 and died August 21, 1889 on grave stone; Hanauer Street in South Memphis was named for him (see Ann Meeks' street name article in *The Commercial Appeal* Memphis, Neighbor Section page 2, February 17, 2000).

Hanks, Calvin James   Buried March 22, 1922   Evergreen 470¾, #5

Captain, A.D.C., General and Staff Officer (complied service records in Confederate general and staff officers and nonregimental enlisted men microfilm rolls); first enlisted April 1861, in Company E, 1st Battalion of Arkansas Cavalry (no compiled service records found) and per his Tennessee Confederate Pension (S15423) filed June 13, 1919, and January 9, 1922, was made adjutant of the battalion and discharged April 20, 1862, at Corinth, Mississippi and reenlisted June 10, 1862, at Searcy, Arkansas on staff of Brigadier-General Dandridge McRae; per compiled service record: January 21, 1863, appointed from Arkansas as captain, AD.C. on McRae's staff, April 14, 1864, return shows him as 1st Lieutenant A.A.D.C. General McRae's Brigade, Price's Division, Trans-Mississippi Department, April 30, 1864, General T. J. Churchill commanding Division mentioned Captain C. J. Hanks as volunteer aide on his staff and September 15, 1864, return shows him as 1st Lieutenant A.A.D.C. Colonel Slemons' Brigade, Major General Fagan's Division, Trans-Mississippi Department; per sketch in Mathes book (enlarged edition), pages 55-56, was in the raid into Missouri (1864) and afterwards was assigned to Major General James F. Fagan's staff, serving as A.D.C., until the surrender at Shreveport; gave Parole of Honor on June 7, 1865, in Shreveport, Louisiana signing rank as 1st Lieutenant & A.D.C on staff of Major General Fagan; was a member of Camp 28, United Confederate Veterans, of Memphis, Tennessee and Company A; upon his death the Camp passed a Memorial Resolution honoring him, which was published in the *Confederate Veteran*, Volume XXX, Number 6, June 1922, page 228; born in Dahlonega, Lumpkin County, Georgia December 16, 1834; grave stone: December 16, 1834 March 20, 1922; per Shelby County, Tennessee Marriage Book 6, Page 88, married Miss Mollie E. Graham of Memphis; on May 28, 1867; her grave stone: Mary E. Hanks August 18, 1840 September 18, 1915.

Harris, Cornelius Leroy "Lee"   Buried October 10, 1916   Evergreen 445, #4

Mississippi 2 Infantry Regiment 1 Lieutenant Company D (Beck Rifles or Matthews Rifles); enlisted for one year April 27, 1861, Pine Grove, Tippah County, Mississippi; elected 2 Lieutenant July 26, 1861, by order of Colonel Falker; promoted to 1 Lieutenant November 14, 1861, by order of Colonel Falker; discharged April 23, 1862, by reorganization of company; often referred to as Captain but no record of that rank found; owned a substantial interest in the Gulf & Chicago Railroad, a.k.a. the Ripley Railroad, and served as superintendent of the line; married Frances Lee Craig (1840 – 1908) September 20, 1859, in Tippah County, Mississippi; moved to Memphis prior to the 1910 census; grave stone: March 7, 1841 October 9, 1916.

Harris, Edward R.

Listed in Elmwood 1874 book as Confederate soldier buried in Elmwood who was citizen of Memphis or vicinity; possibly Edward R. Harris, age 31, buried February 3, 1873, Chapel Hill 23, #17 (no stone) and died erysipelas; also, if not John Harris, infra, possibly the "Harris" mentioned by Dr. S. H. Ford in his address on the occasion to commemorate (Confederate Memorial Day) Confederates buried at Elmwood on April 26, 1866, (see articles "The Confederate Dead" in the *Public Ledger* (Memphis), April 27, 1866, page 3, column 2, and "Honors To The Memory Of The Hero Dead" in the April 27, 1866, *Memphis Daily Appeal*, page 3, column 1).

Harris, Eugene T.   Buried July 23, 1876   Chapel Hill 172, #2

1 Lieutenant and Aide de Camp on staff of General Marcus J. Wright; appointed April 23, 1863, to take rank January 20, 1863; served as Volunteer Aide de Camp on the staff of Major General Benjamin F. Cheatham, appointed August 20, 1862; signed Parole of Honor May 17, 1865; son of Governor Isham Green Harris (supra); grave stone: Born August 26, 1844 Died July 22, 1876; age 30 and died from heart disease per Daily Burial Record Book.

Harris, John W.   Buried May 11, 1866   Chapel Hill 239, #14

Captain and Brigade Inspector, Field and Staff Officer; served as Assistant Inspector General on the staff of both General Preston Smith and General Alfred J. Vaughn; record also found in Tennessee 29 Infantry Regiment (Captain Company B) but no enlistment in record, earliest muster roll dated January and February 1863, per January and February 1865, muster roll remarks: killed 27 May 1864, and all cards have remarks that he signed certificates as inspector and muster officer; per Daily Burial Record Book killed at Atlanta May 24, 1864; obituary in the May 31, 1864, *Memphis Daily Appeal* (Atlanta, Georgia) Afternoon Edition, page 2, column

8, "Killed, in a skirmish with the enemy, near Dallas (note Dallas, Georgia is located northwest of Atlanta), on Friday morning May 27, Capt. John W. Harris, inspector general of Vaughan's brigade and son of the late A. O. Harris of Memphis, Tenn., aged twenty-four years. A devoted friend, a brave and gallant soldier, and a noble patriot, his name is but one more that will adorn the roll of those who have offered themselves up on their country's "alter of sacrifice." His loss has created a void that cannot well be filled in the hearts of those who 'knew him but to love him.'"; per the May 10, 1866, *Pubic Ledger* (Memphis, Tennessee), page 3, column 2, "The remains of the late Captain John W. Harris arrived in the city yesterday, and will be interred at Elmwood Cemetery tomorrow. Captain Harris was Inspector General on Pres. Smith's staff, and as gallant and brave soldier as ever drew the breath of life. He fell at the battle Ellerslie Mountain, Ga., in the retreat from Dalton to Dallas."; listed in Elmwood 1874 book as Confederate soldier buried in Elmwood who was citizen of Memphis or vicinity.

Harris, Isham Green   Buried July 13, 1897   Chapel Hill 172, #4
Tennessee Governor at start of War; commander of state troops until transferred to Confederate service April 1, 1861; served with Army of Tennessee to end of War as a Civil Officer and without command; with General Albert Sidney Johnston when he was killed at Shiloh; sketch in Mathes book, page 121; joined Confederate Historical Association July 1, 1869, served as Association President for two years, serve as U. S. Senator; biography in *Confederate Military History, Extended Edition*, Volume X Tennessee, page 526; died in Washington, DC per July 9, 1897, *The Commercial Appeal* Memphis; Senator and died age 79 per Daily Burial Record Book; February 10, 1818 - July 8, 1897 on monument with bust unveiled July 4, 1924, (see July 5, 1924, *The Commercial Appeal* Memphis); see Tennessee Blue Book, 1971-72, page 318; sketch in the PoliticalGraveyard.com; listed under Ex-Governors and U.S. Senators (#52) in the "Touring historic Elmwood Cemetery" (Brochure and Map of Historic Gravesites), which was the predecessor of the "Touring Historic Elmwood Cemetery" Brochure (January 2000), where also listed (#51); sketch #12 in Elmwood *Civil War Tour* booklet (2012).

Hart, Robert A.   Buried August 6,1863   Chapel Hill 186, #1
Arkansas 30 Infantry Regiment Colonel; commissioned November 12, 1862; per July & August 1862, muster roll remarks: died in Memphis August 6, 1863, from wound received at Helena, wounded July 4, 1863; name appears on a roll of prisoners of war captured at Helena, Arkansas July 4, 1863, with note that sent to General Hospital Memphis on U. S. Hospital Steamer R. C. Woods; name appears on a roster of Price's Division indicating commissioned November 12, 1862, appointed from Tennessee, born Ireland, age 25 and killed; name appears on a roll of prisoners of war Inmates of Officers' Hospital Memphis, Tennessee August 31, 1863, with complaint of shell wound right leg, admitted July 7, 1863, captured Helena July 4, 1863, and died August 5, 1863; name appears on a list of casualties of 3 Brigade, Price's Division, Arkansas Infantry at the Battle of Helena, Arkansas July 4, 1863, dated July 14, 1863, with remark flesh wound in left (note difference with hospital record) leg on field; per register of Confederate officers who died of wounds died August 6, 1863; mentioned by Dr. S. H. Ford in his address on the occasion to commemorate (Confederate Memorial Day) Confederates buried at Elmwood on April 26, 1866, (see article "Honors To The Memory Of The Hero Dead" in the April 27, 1866, *Memphis Daily Appeal*, page 3, column 1); listed in Elmwood 1874 book as Confederate soldier buried in Elmwood who was citizen of Memphis or vicinity with rank of Colonel; Colonel in Confederate service, Mason and wounds per Daily Burial Record Book.

Hart, Robert T. G.   Buried May 23, 1877   Turley 180, #3
Tennessee 3 (Forrest's) Cavalry Regiment Private Company B; per Company Muster Roll for November & December 1863, enlisted November 1, 1863, at Dalton, Georgia; name appears on a Roll of Prisoners of War paroled at Gainesville, Alabama May 11, 1865; death notice in the May 23, 1877, *Memphis Daily Appeal*, page 1, column 3; died consumption age 58 per Daily Burial Record Book.

Hart, W. W.   Buried April 13, 1862   Chapel Hill 148, #2
Tennessee 154 Senior Infantry Regiment Private Company L Maynard Rifles; enlisted March 7, 1862, Memphis; per May 6, 1863, muster roll remarks: killed at Battle of Shiloh; per register of soldiers killed in battle died April 1862, Memphis; per report of deaths dated October 30, 1863, enlisted March 8, 1862, Memphis and died April 15, 1862, at Memphis of wound and entitled to $50 bounty, $25 commutation and $20 stoppage; per Battle of Shiloh casualty list for unit reported in April 23, 1862 *Memphis Daily Appeal* wounded in battle; mentioned (Billy Hart) by Dr. S. H. Ford in his address on the occasion to commemorate (Confederate Memorial Day) Confederates buried at Elmwood on April 26, 1866, (see articles "The Confederate Dead" in the *Public Ledger* (Memphis), April 27, 1866, page 3, column 2, and "Honors To The Memory Of The Hero Dead" in the April 27, 1866, *Memphis Daily Appeal*, page 3, column 1).

Hartsfield, William G.
Listed in Elmwood 1874 book as Confederate soldier buried in Elmwood who was citizen of Memphis or vicinity; believed to be W. G. Hartsfield, buried July 29, 1865, Fowler 171, #1, age 32 Cong. Chill, first buried Chapel Hill section and record also indicates as in Donoho Vault (marked out in Alpha Book), grave stone (partly illegible) has name on top and age on face, but not listed in Cemetery computer index; and further believed to be "W. G. Hartsfield," Tennessee 154 Senior Infantry Regiment Private Company L, enlisted March 7, 1862, Memphis, September & October 1862, Muster Roll Remarks detailed in Quartermaster Department by General Kirby Smith, May 6, 1863, Muster Roll Remarks discharged having furnished substitute, Pay Sheet on Discharge dated February 23, 1863, at Shelbyville, Tennessee indicates born Harris County, Georgia age 29.

Haskell, William C.   Buried June 19, 1863   Chapel Hill 1, Vault
Tennessee 3 (Forrest's) Cavalry Regiment Private Company A ("Bluff City Grays"), per Company Muster Roll for January 1 to July 1, 1862, enlisted May 4, 1861, Randolph, Tennessee and remarks that "Apt. Chaplain, 154th Regt July 19/61"; first enlisted in the Tennessee 154 Senior Infantry Regiment Private 1 Company B, per Company Muster-in Roll dated August 13, 1861, at New Madrid, Missouri enlisted June 4, 1861, at Randolph, Tennessee age 20 and remarks elected Chaplain of the regiment; mentioned by Dr. S. H. Ford in his address on the occasion to commemorate (Confederate Memorial Day) Confederates buried at Elmwood on April 26, 1866, (see articles "The Confederate Dead" ("Heiskel, chaplain of the 154th") in the *Public Ledger* (Memphis), April 27, 1866, page 3, column 2, and "Honors To The Memory Of The Hero Dead" ("Capt. W. C. Haskell, of the 154th") in the April 27, 1866, *Memphis Daily Appeal*, page 3, column 1); listed ("W. C. Heiskell") in the June 6, 1878, *Memphis Daily Appeal*, page 4, column 3, article "OUR DEAD HEROES" covering the unveiling of the Confederate Monument and Decoration of Graves at Elmwood as then one of twenty-eight members of the Bluff City Grays, Company B of the 154 Senior Infantry Regiment and Company A of Forrest's Old (Third) Cavalry Regiment buried at Elmwood; listed ("W. C. Haskell") as one of the "comrades who sleep at Elmwood cemetery " in the article "Veterans in Council" in *Memphis Daily Appeal*, May 12, 1881, page 4, column 4, concerning the meeting of the surviving members in the city of the old Bluff City Grays to appoint the necessary committees for the purpose of making special decoration on the graves of their dead comrades at Elmwood and Calvary cemeteries on Sunday next, Memorial Day; listed as member of Bluff City Grays in *Reminiscences of the Civil War* by John Hallum, Tunnah & Pittard printers, 1903; listed in "A COMPLETE ROSTER OF THE BLUFF CITY GREYS" located in the Memphis Room of the Memphis/Shelby County Public Library and Information Center Central Library with notation "Elected Chaplain 154th Sr. Rgt. Died in Memphis, 1863" but not included on the list at the end of the soldiers buried at Elmwood; see also Notes of Interest - Bluff City Grays; "Mr. Haskell" with no other names or initials and remarks "Said in Leatherman Vault" in Daily Burial Record Book and name spelled "Haskele" in Alpha Book.

Haynes, Milton Andrew   Buried October 1, 1867   Turley 423, #6
Tennessee (McCown's) Artillery Corps Lieutenant Colonel; appears on an undated Roll of the Field and Company Officers belonging to the Artillery Corps of the Provisional Army of Tennessee transferred to the Confederate States with date of commission May 1, 1861; wrote the training manual "The Confederate Artillerist: Instruction in Artillery & Foot"; recommended for rank of Brigadier General but never promoted; paroled May 4, 1865, at Charlotte, North Carolina; wrote President Andrews July 24, 1865, requesting a pardon; submitted the list of field officers and captains of Tennessee Artillery Corps appointed by Governor Isham G. Harris and confirmed by the Legislature of Tennessee in Lindsley's Annals, page 878; practiced law prior to and after the War; moved to Memphis from Giles County after the War; 1838 graduate of West Point, served in the Indian (Florida) and Mexican wars; died from inflammation of the lungs at age 58 per Daily Burial Record Book; funeral notice in October 1, 1867, *Memphis Daily Appeal*, page 2, column 4.

Heiskell, Carrick White   Buried July 30, 1923   Turley 1082, #3
Tennessee 19 Infantry Regiment Colonel; enlisted as Private Company H June 4, 1861, at Knoxville; commissioned 1 Lieutenant Company C May 22, 1861; elected Captain Company K May 8, 1862; promoted to Major of the Regiment April 15, 1863; wounded in arm at Battle of Chickamauga September 19, 1863; promoted to Lieutenant Colonel November 25, 1863, after Battle of Missionary Ridge; promoted to Colonel July 22, 1864, when then Colonel Francis M. Walker was killed at Peachtree Creek; per sketch in Mathes book born Fruit Hill, Knox County, Tennessee July 25, 1836; notice in July 30, 1923, *The Commercial Appeal* Memphis indicating was a Lieutenant Colonel Tennessee 19 Infantry and died age 89 (sic); died age 89 (sic) per Daily Burial Record Book; July 25, 1836 July 29, 1923 on grave stone; brother of Joseph Brown Heiskell; completed Tennessee 1914/1915 Questionnaire of Civil War Veterans; sketch in Goodspeed's Shelby County History, page 979; biography in *Confederate Military History*, *Extended Edition*, Volume X Tennessee, page 532; sketch in *Tennessee, The Volunteer State, 1769-1923*, Volume II, page 166.

Heiskell, Joseph Brown   Buried March 8, 1913   Evergreen 225, #6
Confederate Congressman (Tennessee); see sketch in Warner's Confederate Congress book pages 114-115; born Knoxville, Tennessee November 5, 1823, graduated from East Tennessee College (now the University of Tennessee) at age 17, studied law, began practice in Madisonville, Tennessee in 1844, about 1847 moved to Rogersville, Tennessee, ran for state senate in 1858 and was elected representing Hawkins, Hancock, and Jefferson counties, declined to take seat in the Provisional Congress, elected to First Regular Congress and reelected in 1863 both times unopposed, 1864 while temporarily at home in Rogersville was arrested by Federal authorities and confined until the close of the War, because sentiment in east Tennessee being decidedly anti-Confederate he like many others moved to Memphis which was home thereafter, member of the 1870 constitutional convention, same year appointed attorney general which held for eight years, Heiskell Reports became the cornerstone of Tennessee jurisprudence, and died in Memphis March 7, 1913 age 90; biography in *Confederate Military History, Extended Edition*, Volume X Tennessee, page 534; detailed sketch *The Joseph Brown Heiskell Family* (December 17, 1972) in Paul R. Coppock's Mid-South, Volume II, pages 116-120; mentioned in sketch on son Frederick Hugh Heiskell in *Tennessee, The Volunteer State, 1769-1923*, Volume III, page 191; sketch in the PoliticalGraveyard.com; brother of Carrick White Heiskell; grave stone November 5, 1823 March 7, 1913; died aged 89 per Daily Burial Record Books.

Helbing, Adolphus   Buried January 6, 1871   Turley 562, #1
Tennessee 2 (Walker's) Infantry Regiment Sergeant Company E; per Company Muster-in Roll dated September 9, 1861, enlisted

May 11, 1861, Memphis, with remarks: Transferred to Regimental Band July 21, 1861; per undated Company Muster Roll remarks: Specialty detailed to Brigade Commissary; per Company Muster Roll dated July 23, 1863, remarks: Discharged May 5, 1862; Funeral Notice in the Friday January 6, 1871, *Memphis Daily Appeal,* page 1, column 5; died age 48 from consumption per Daily Burial Record Book.

Henderson, John W.   Buried May 15, 1862   Turley 76, #3
Arkansas 20 (King's) Infantry Regiment Private Company K; enlisted March 6, 1862, Lafayette City; per March 6 to May 2, 1862, muster roll remarks: left at Fort Pillow in hospital; per September and October 1862, muster roll remarks: died of disease July, 1862, at hospital age 22; "W. B. M." in Daily Burial Record Book remarks.

Henry, John Flournoy   Buried April 30, 1862   Turley 144, #1
Tennessee 4 (Neely's) Infantry Regiment Major Field & Staff; enlisted May 15, 1861 Germantown, Tennessee; per report of operations and casualties at Battle of Shiloh, Tennessee April 6 & 7, 1862 dated April 10, 1862 at Corinth, Mississippi: wounded severely in side; funeral notice in April 29, 1862, *Memphis Daily Appeal*; listed in Elmwood 1874 book as Confederate soldier buried in Elmwood who was citizen of Memphis or vicinity with rank of Major and sketch; per sketch born 1837 at Clarksville, Tennessee, ball penetrated lung when leading a charge at Shiloh April 6, 1862, survived till April 28, 1862 and died in Memphis; death reported under Local Matters in the *Avalanche* April 29, 1862 which indicated wounded through the right lung at Shiloh while gallantly fighting the Northern invader and funeral to take place today; wounded per Daily Burial Record Book.

Hessen, George A.   Buried March 3, 1909   Fowler Public lot 6, #807
Mississippi Rifles Company D Drummer Boy (no compiled service record found but believed to be Mississippi New 10 Infantry Regiment Company D); per biography in *Confederate Military History, Extended Edition*, Volume X Tennessee, page 536: born Vicksburg, Miss., July 25, 1847, a school-boy during the days of excitement and enlistment for defense of the South in 1861, but when the spring of 1862 arrived he hid his books under a railroad bridge one day, and made his way from Jackson, Miss., then his home, to Pensacola, Fla., and joined Company D, Mississippi Rifles, as a drummer boy, continued with the regiment after its transfer to the north and assignment to General Chalmers' brigade, went into battle with it at Munfordville, September 4, 1862, in the assault upon the Federal works fell with an ugly wound in the forehead caused, presumably, by a fragment of shell, recovery seemed doubtful at the time, and the wound did not in fact heal for five or six years, this put an end to his military service, in 1867 made his home at Memphis, where in his profession as pharmacist, and particularly by his faithfulness to duty in charge of one of the leading drug stores during the terrible yellow fever epidemic of 1878, earned the confidence and esteem of the community, served worthily in public office as a deputy county trustee, city register, and surveyor of customs for the port of Memphis during the first administration of President Cleveland; per City of Memphis Burial Permit Druggist, born July 25, 1849 (note year difference with biography) and died March 2, 1909, age 60.

Hill, Alphonso Bruce   Buried February 1, 1919   Evergreen 66, #5
Tennessee 51 Infantry Regiment Captain Company G; per sketch in Mathes book, page 125: born December 12, 1837, in Tipton county, Tenn., enlisted as a musician in Company C, Ninth Tennessee Regiment, on the 6th of May, 1861, afterward served in the Fifty-first Tennessee Regiment, was discharged in May, 1862, re-enlisted in the Twelfth Tennessee Cavalry and transferred back to the Fifty-first Tennessee, at the close of the war was Captain of Company G of that regiment, never captured or wounded, paroled May, 1865, afterward came from Tipton county to Memphis, and for many years Secretary of the Memphis City School Board; biography in *Confederate Military History, Extended Edition*, Volume X Tennessee, page 537.

Hill, Harry M.   Buried February 22, 1920   Chapel Hill 129
Tennessee 38 Infantry Regiment Sergeant Company L; per Company Muster Roll dated October 7, 1861, enlisted September 7, 1861, Camp Abington, with remarks: made 4 sergeant on 29 September 1861; per Company Muster Roll for May & June 1862, remarks: Discharged May 10, 1862; per Company Muster Roll dated July 23, 1863, remarks: Discharged May 5, 1862; appears on a register of Prisoners of War at Memphis, Tennessee – Deserters from rebel army dated May 10, 1864, with residence as Memphis, Tennessee, age 21; name appears on an Oath of Allegiance and sworn to at Memphis, Tennessee from May 15 to June 1, 1865, resident of Memphis, Tennessee, age 21; died February 20, 1920, Chicago, Cook County, Illinois.

Hodges, Fleming   Buried July 28, 1893   Fowler 692, # 3
Quartermaster Department Major; most often referred to as Colonel; per article "Col. F. Hodges and Sons, Okolona, Miss." *Confederate Veteran*, Volume XIX, 1911, page 17, born in Smith County, Tennessee February 26, 1815, at beginning of War was made purchasing agent for the Confederate States with headquarters in Mobile, in 1862 suddenly stricken with paralysis at the age of 47 but his usefulness did not cease as he cared for and counseled those within his influence, equipped three companies at his own expense and son Captain Tom Pope Hodges, Mississippi 41 Infantry Regiment, was killed at Battle of Atlanta July 28, 1864 at age of twenty-two; son Captain William Hodges buried at Elmwood Cemetery (see sketch next below); no grave stone.

Hodges, William (Buck) W.   Buried October 24, 1886   Fowler 692, # 2
Alabama 16 Infantry Regiment Captain Company F, per Company Muster Roll dated October, 23, 1861, enlisted August 10, 1861, at Courtland, Alabama, transferred from Mississippi 16 Infantry Regiment, recommended for appointment to Colonel but not made; originally enlisted in Mississippi 11 Infantry Regiment Private Sergeant Company C ("Prairie Riflemen"), per Company Muster

Roll for March 2, 1861, enlisted March 2, 1961, at Okolona, age 21, per Company Muster Roll for July & August, 1861, remarks promoted to the rank of captain in the Confederate Army August 19, 1861, per Company Muster Roll for May & June, 1861, remarks furloughed June 19, 1861, at Winchester, Virginia because of appointment from Sergeant to Captain in the regular army; see article "Col. F. Hodges and Sons, Okolona, Miss." *Confederate Veteran*, Volume XIX, 1911, page 17; lawyer by profession, graduate of Georgetown College, D. C.; per obituary in *Memphis Daily Appeal* October 24, 1886, died October 23, 1886, at or near Marion, Arkansas; widow Sue R. Hodges applied for Arkansas Confederate pension (Application #4261) August 9, 1905 while residing in Marion, Crittenden County, Arkansas; son of Fleming Hodges (see sketch next above); no grave stone.

Howard, William Thomas   Buried January 31, 1869   Lenow Circle 95
Tennessee 7 Cavalry Regiment 1 Lieutenant Company A (Logwood's Company, 6 Cavalry Battalion, which became Company A of the Tennessee 7 Cavalry Regiment); per Company Muster-in Roll dated May 16, 1861, enlisted May 16, 1861, Memphis, age 26; per Young's Book on the Tennessee 7 Cavalry Regiment resigned in 1861; note he resigned before Tennessee 7 Cavalry Regiment actually formed April 1, 1862; wrote letter to General G. T. Beauregard dated March 22, 1862, Memphis, requesting bounty funds to help raise a company of cavalry to join Captain Wicks' Regiment but no reply found or that any company was formed; believed to have joined Confederate 1 Cavalry Regiment Private Captain M. J. Wicks' Company (Memphis Mounted Rebels), Confederate 1 Cavalry Regiment Company I; per Company Muster-in Roll dated March 7, 1862, enlisted March 7, 1862, Memphis, age 26, per Company Muster Roll for March 9 to May 1, 1862, remarks: Transferred by V.O. General A. S. Johnston; per family related publications (*The Converse Family and Allied Families*, by Charles Allen Converse, 1905. (Boston) Private printing, 1907) he was a Major in the Confederate service but such not verified with any official records; per Death Notice in the January 31, 1869, *Memphis Daily Appeal*, page 2, column 6, died in Newburg, New York, January 24, 1869, aged 32; article "Mr. Howard's Funeral" in the Monday Evening February 1, 1869, *Public Ledger* (Memphis), page 3, column 2, indicating interment with appropriate Masonic honors.

Hubbard, John Milton   Buried April 3, 1923   South Grove 276, #3
Tennessee 7 Cavalry Regiment Private Company E; enlisted May 24, 1862 Jackson, Tennessee; residence: Hardeman County, Tennessee; author of *Notes of a Private* (1909); Tennessee Confederate Pension application #S12178; widow (Mary) Tennessee Confederate Pension application #W9344; resided in Memphis when died April 2, 1923; per article in *The Commercial Appeal* Memphis April 3, 1923, page 11, born Anson County, North Carolina and died age 91; sketch in Mathes book; died age 90 per Daily Burial Record Book; article by Paul Coppock in Mid-South Memoirs, *The Commercial Appeal* Memphis, June 2, 1974, Section 6, page 7; grave stone: January 17, 1833 April 2, 1923.

Hughes, Bernard   Buried September 5, 1892   Miller Circle 1252, #2
Tennessee Winston's Light Artillery Company Lieutenant; enlisted August 19, 1861, new Madrid, Missouri; appointed 2 Lieutenant 19 August; per statement in compiled service record "records show that Barney Hughes, 2 Lieutenant Keiter's Battery, McCowen's (sic) Artillery Corps Tennessee C.S.A. enlisted August 19, 1861, at New Madrid, Missouri, 1 year" and records further show that he was serving as Military Telegraph Operator, Army of Tennessee in 1862 & 1863 and that September 18, 1864, was elected 2 Lieutenant Company G Alabama 33 C.S.A.; per Alabama 33 Infantry Regiment compiled service record rolls Private/1 Sergeant Company G, enlisted March 8, 1862, age 19 at Daleville, Dale County, Alabama, note in record indicates 2 Lieutenant, also record indicates August 21, 1861, enrolled as 2 Lieutenant in Captain Keiter's Tennessee Battery and left before November 1862, March 1-17, 1862, Acting Adjutant General with General Trudeau and subsequently became government telegraph operator; per sketch in Mathes book native of Louisville, Kentucky, went out to war as Lieutenant with heavy artillery company, at Belmont, served on staff of General Trudeau at Island 10, telegraph operator at Chattanooga, confidential operator for General Bragg, after war went to Salt Lake City, returned to Memphis taking position with Memphis & Charleston Railroad, died September 1892, and monument over remains in Elmwood placed by friends upon which is recorded his virtues; "Barney Hughes," born Louisville, Kentucky and died Memphis September 3, 1892, aged 53 on monument; died age 51 per Cemetery record; per widow's (Witt Eva (Ellis) Hughes) Tennessee Confederate Pension (W7250) file, he was born Louisville, Kentucky 1840 and died September 2, 1892, in Memphis; she was born June 18, 1850, in Morganfield, Kentucky, and they were married at Henderson, Kentucky December 5, 1871; sketch in Goodspeed's Shelby County History, page 986.

Humes, William Young Conn   Buried September 13, 1882   Chapel Hill 299, #8
Brigadier General; appointed from Tennessee November 17, 1863, (rank November 16, 1863) per the *Memorandum relative to the General Officers Appointed by the President in the Armies of the Confederate States - 1861-1865* compiled from Official Records by the Military Secretary's Office, U. S. War Department 1905; also per remarks in the *Memorandum* included in the Sherman-Johnston convention of April 26, 1865, but no record of his personal parole found; originally enlisted as 1 Lieutenant Tennessee Scott's (Bankhead's) Light Artillery May 13, 1861, at age 30 at Memphis; record also found Tennessee Winston's Light artillery as Captain with records indicating enlisted April 17, 1861, at Memphis and up to November 23, 1861, served as 1 Lieutenant Bankhead's Battery and was then transferred as Captain to this Company by order of Lieutenant General Polk; captured Island 10 on April 7, 1862, sent to Johnson's Island April 26, 1862, and then to Vicksburg September 1, 1862, for exchange; detailed on special service and sent to Mobile, Alabama October 16, 1862; promoted to Major of Artillery May 15, 1863; per sketch in Mathes book born Abington, Virginia, chosen 1 Lieutenant Bankhead's Battery April 1861, promoted to Captain and placed in command of Heavy Artillery at Island 10 where captured, confined to Johnson's Island and exchanged summer 1862, then commanded Heavy Artillery at Mobile, Alabama but later served as cavalry leader under General Wheeler and rose to Major General; graduate from

Virginia Military Institute (VMI) Class of 1851 (classmate of General Alfred J. Vaughan, see sketch herein); per sketch in VMI library archives file parents John Newton Humes and Jane Conn White, enrolled at VMI on November 20, 1848, and graduated second in a class of 29 on July 4, 1851, 1861-Captain Artillery, commanded guns at New Madrid, captured at Island 10 and imprisoned at Johnson's Island, after exchange became cavalry officer, appointed Brigadier General November 1863 and led brigade in Wheeler's Corps fought in Tennessee, Georgia the Carolinas, wounded in action at Monroe's Crossroads, North Carolina March 10, 1865, recommended for promotion to Major General early 1865 (maybe late 1864) and promotion known to have been under consideration in War Department January 1865, with unofficial sources indicating promoted March 1865, but if so word did not reach him as on June 6, 1865, referred to himself as a former Brigadier General and died at Huntsville, Alabama September 11, 1882, (note difference with grave stone); joined Confederate Historical Association July 15, 1869; sketch in *Generals in Gray*; biography in *Confederate Military History, Extended Edition*, Volume X Tennessee, page 313; sketch in *Tennessee, The Volunteer State, 1769-1923*, Volume II, page 151; sketch, photograph, if available, and grave stone photograph in book *Quiet Places: The Burial Sites of Civil War Generals in Tennessee* by Buckner and Nathaniel C. Hughes, Jr., East Tennessee Historical Society (1992); grave stone: May 1, 1830 September 12, 1883; also listed in chapter on Generals; listed under Generals in "Touring historic Elmwood Cemetery" (Brochure and Map of Historic Gravesites) #11; listed in "Touring Historic Elmwood Cemetery" Brochure (January 2000) #65; sketch #21 in Elmwood *Civil War Tour* booklet (2012).

Hunt, Casper Wistar   Buried January 9, 1869   Chapel Hill Circle 70, #6
Tennessee 2 (Robison's) Infantry Regiment Captain Company E; enlisted May 1, 1861, Memphis for 12 months; age 23 on Muster Roll dated May 14, 1861, at Lynchburg, Virginia; per February 13, 1862, Muster Roll remarks "has not reenlisted"; per Muster Roll dated October 8, 1863, discharged April 3, 1862; several references to leaves of absences due to being ill; one doctor's certification of being unfit for duty due to illnesses; no information on death in compiled service record; unit also known as Confederate 2 Infantry under which name the unit sketch is found in Lindsley's Annals where he is listed in sketch but not Memorial Roll; inscription on Hunt Family Monument "Casper Wistar, son of Elijah & Eliza T. Hunt, Late Capt. of Co. E 2nd Reg. Tenn. Vol's. C.S.A., Born in Wilkes Co., Georgia June 15, 1836, Died in Autauga Co., Ala. September 24, 1862, Whilst on Furlough, All Honour to the Young Soldier Who fell in Defense of his Native Land"; died 1862, age 24, and "removed from the South" per Daily Burial Record Book; mentioned in General W. B. Bates' speech printed in the article "Elmwood" (Grand and Imposing Ceremonies of Commemoration Day), in *Memphis Sunday Appeal*, May 8, 1870, page 4, column 2.

Hunt, Clarence P.   Buried July 18, 1922   Fowler 168,169, #10
Tennessee 4 Infantry Regiment Private Company A; per Company Muster-in Roll dated August 16, 1861, enlisted May 15, 1861, at Germantown, Tennessee, per Company Muster Roll for August 17, 1861, to January 1, 1862, remarks discharged by Surgeon November 26, 1861, per Certificate of Discharge age 19 when enlisted and reason for discharge ill health; per Tennessee Death Certificate died July 17, 1922, in Memphis age 80 from fracture of skull when in automobile accident and a retired cotton merchant.

Hunt, William Richardson   Buried May 29, 1872   Chapel Hill Circle 71, #8
Confederate Nitre and Mining Bureau War Department Lieutenant Colonel; appointed Major of Artillery November 16, 1861; per sketch in Mathes book born Washington, Georgia; at outbreak of War given charge of arsenal in Memphis; in 1863 became Chief of the Nitre and Mining Bureau; became member Confederate Historical Association September 9, 1869; listed (Hunt, Col. Wm. R.") in Elmwood 1874 book as Confederate soldier buried in Elmwood who was citizen of Memphis or vicinity and sketch with Major William T. Driver, his brother-in-law; per sketch died in Memphis 1873 (sic), about age 50; died congestion of brain age 46 per Daily Burial Record Book; per biography in *Confederate Military History, Extended Edition*, Volume X Tennessee, page 545, born September 25, 1826, Washington, Georgia; born September 23, 1825 and died May 28, 1872 on Hunt monument, which is described in the "The Monuments." chapter in Elmwood book page 89; listed in "Touring Historic Elmwood Cemetery" Brochure (January 2000) #56 and its predecessor "Touring historic Elmwood Cemetery" (Brochure and Map of Historic Gravesites) #81B.

Hunthousen, William   Buried April 21, 1868   Turley 422, #8
Tennessee 3 (Memphis Battalion) Infantry Battalion Private (Captain E. C. Kirk) Company E, per Company Muster Roll for March 12 to May 1, 1862, enlisted March 12, 1862; see Notes of Interest "Memphis Battalion - Tennessee 3 (Memphis Battalion) Infantry Battalion"; cause of death Pistol Shot Wound per Daily Burial Record Book; name spelled "Hunthausen" in Daily Burial Record Book and computer index.

Hutcheson, Booth Brown   Buried July 19, 1873   Chapel Hill 27, #7
Tennessee 154 Senior Infantry Regiment Captain Company G; enlisted June 3, 1861, Memphis; listed in Elmwood 1874 book as Confederate soldier buried in Elmwood who was citizen of Memphis or vicinity with rank of Captain and name spelled "Hutchinson"; died consumption age 41 per Daily Burial Record Book; family monument illegible; death and funeral notice published in *Memphis Daily Appeal*, July 19, 1873, page 1, column 8, indicating died Friday, July 18, 1873, in the forty-first year of his age; a "Tribute of Respect" by the Confederate Relief Association published in *Memphis Sunday Appeal*, August 3, 1873, page 1, column 7.

Hyatt, Charles H.   Buried September 5, 1863   Turley 205, #1
Confederate Cavalry Wood's Regiment Private Company K; listed in Elmwood 1874 book as Confederate soldier buried in Elmwood who was citizen of Memphis or vicinity; born at _____ City June 4, 1840, and died at Memphis September 4, 1863, on

grave stone; wound and died age 23 per Daily Burial Record Book; enlisted May 9, 1862, Yazoo, Mississippi; per February 28 to June 30, 1863, muster roll remarks: wounded and taken prisoner June 5, 1863; per Overton USA General Hospital, Memphis, Tennessee record admitted June 17, 1863, and returned to duty August 4, 1863, by being transferred to citizens house; per September and October 1863, muster roll remarks: died; per Prisoner of War roll: residence of Panola County, Mississippi; note: Colonel Wirt Adam's Regiment of Cavalry also known as 1 Regiment Mississippi Cavalry and subsequently became Wood's Regiment Cavalry.

Jackson, Charles H.   Buried May 2, 1862   Chapel Hill 411, #1
Confederate 2 Infantry Regiment Private (D. F. Jackson's) Company K; single card in compiled service record rolls that indicates that name appears on an official copy of a report dated at Corinth, Mississippi April 11, 1862, of killed, wounded and missing of the 2 Confederate Regiment of Infantry at Battle of Shiloh, Tennessee April 6 & 7, 1862, with remarks that wounded severely in thigh; initials "C. F.," C. F. Jackson's Company, wounded and age fifteen years, eight months per Daily Burial Record Book; unit actually D. F. Jackson's (his father) Worsham Guard (sometimes referred to as Bluff City Guard); grave stone: killed at Battle of Shiloh aged 15; funeral notice in May 2, 1862, *Memphis Daily Appeal*, page 1, column 7, "died yesterday of wounds received at Shiloh, son of David F. and Elizabeth S. Jackson" and article "A BOY HERO" on page 2, column 6, "… right thigh fractured in the battle of Shiloh, while gallantly fighting by the side of his father, Capt. D F. Jackson."; Worsham Guard formerly Company K Mississippi 25 Infantry Regiment, single card in that record for muster roll dated August 1, 1861, indicating enlisted August 1, 1861, Memphis, age 15; record also found Missouri 1 Infantry Regiment Private Company C (the successor company of Company K Confederate 2 Infantry Regiment after disbanding about May 8, 1862) with same enlistment and reference that died from wound received at Battle of Shiloh; grave stone: "Killed at Battle of Shiloh Aged 15 Tears."

Jackson, David F.   Buried November 1, 1894   Chapel Hill 411, #6
Confederate 2 Infantry Regiment Captain Company K; appointed Captain August 6, 1861; Company K "Worsham Guard" formerly Company K Mississippi 25 Infantry Regiment; name appears in a letter dated April 25, 1862, from Colonel John D. Martin to Major General Hodge recommending that regiment be disbanded; regiment disbanded May 8, 1862, and Company K became part of 2 Company C, 1 Missouri Infantry Regiment; Captain and died age 74 per Daily Burial Record Book; grave stone: May 1, 1820 October 31, 1894; Mississippi 25 Infantry Regiment Company K muster roll dated August 1, 1861, at Memphis indicates enlisted August 6, 1861, Memphis age 41; Missouri 1 Infantry Regiment Company I historic roll indicates occupation policeman, resident of Memphis, elected Captain 1861, engaged at Shiloh, resigned by letter dated July 3, 1862, Camp Price, Mississippi indicating elected in his absence and declined as over 35, said to be in Commissary Department in Charleston; per *Memphis Daily Appeal* dated August 9, 1861, Captain D. F. Jackson's Worsham Guard of Artillery ordered mustered into duty and was on duty at the foot of Jefferson Street; grave stone: Capt. D. F. Jackson May 1, 1920 Oct. 31, 1894.

James, Richard P.   Buried February 18, 1910   Turley 612 (Masonic Lot), D4 #13
Tennessee 19 Infantry Regiment, 2 Lieutenant Company A, enlisted as a Private June 1, 1861, elected 2 Lieutenant August 1, 1863, captured at Franklin, Tennessee December 17, 1865, suffered gunshot fracture of right fibula at Franklin November 30, 1864, sent to hospital in Nashville, age 23 noted on transfer card, and paroled at Richmond, Virginia June 2, 1865; died February 19 (sic) per *Confederate Veteran*, Volume XIX, April 1911, page 174 "The Last Roll," Deaths of Confederates in Memphis, Tennessee who died during 1910 and were members of the Confederate Historical Association, Camp 28, U. C. V., Bivouac 18, C. V. of Memphis, Tennessee; Tennessee Confederate Pension (S2663) file indicates that he was born March 1841; died age 66 per Burial Permit and Daily Burial Record Book, so birth year should have been 1844; buried in Masonic Lot (2 down 1st row, west side of division); note there a sketch for Richard P. James in "The Last Roll," *Confederate Veteran*, Volume XVIII, October 1910, page 479, who per quote by Colonel C. W. Heiskell, 19 Tennessee Infantry Regiment, of Memphis, served in the 19 Tennessee Infantry as orderly sergeant of Company A and indication that he was born March 11, 1844, and died March 17, 1910, (no burial for this date found in Cemetery books), possibly same individual but only one Richard P. James found in the Tennessee 19 Infantry Regiment compiled service records rolls.

Jarnagan, John Hampton   Buried June 19, 1910   Chapel Hill 120-21, #10
Confederate 3 Infantry Regiment Captain Quartermaster, appointed Assistant Quartermaster August 30, 1862, and Quartermaster January 1, 1863; per sketch in Mathes book, page 130, born in Cleveland, Tennessee September 18, 1843, at beginning of War living at Austin, Tunica County, Mississippi, joined Confederate Army May 21, 1861, as private in Young Guards, Captain John Cameron, Ninth (sic) Tennessee, Colonel Carroll (per Tennessee 15 Infantry Regiment sketch in *Tennesseans in the Civil War, Part 1*, John F. Cameron, Captain, 1st Company F, "The Young Guard," men from Memphis, detached June, 1861 and became Company B, 18 (Marmaduke's) Arkansas Infantry, subsequently 3 Confederate Infantry Regiment), June 20, 1861, transferred to Hindman's Legion, June 10, 1861, made Second Corporal, September 1861, promoted to Fourth Sergeant, at battles of Green River, Bowling Green, Shiloh, Farmington, Perryville, Mumfordsville (sic), Murfreesboro, Missionary Ridge and in general fights from Dalton to Atlanta, after retreat from Atlanta stationed at Griffin, Georgia, from there ordered to Augusta and camp near Augusta to help Colonel Leroy O. Bridewell in organizing troops to be forwarded to General Joseph E. Johnston in South Carolina where he was until the surrender of General Johnston's army, rode horseback to Meridian, Mississippi and surrendered to Colonel Bertram, 20 Wisconsin in May 1865, thence on horseback home, commissioned captain and acting quartermaster February 1863, and served on the staff with General John S. Marmaduke and General Granberry, after War engaged in cotton planting in Bolivar County, MS and moved to Memphis 1889 and joined the Confederate Historical Association February 12, 1895; biography in *Confederate*

Military History, Extended Edition, Volume X Tennessee, page 548; not listed in *Tennesseans in the Civil War, Part 2*; name spelled "Jarnigan," Captain 9th Tennessee Infantry and died June 18 per *Confederate Veteran*, Volume XIX, April 1911, page 174, "The Last Roll, Death of Confederates in Memphis, Tennessee" who died during 1910 and were members of the Confederate Historical Association, Camp 28, U.C.V., Bivouac 18, C.V., of Memphis, Tennessee; died age 66 per Daily Burial Record Book; grave stone partially illegible.

Jefferson, Joshua Taylor   Buried May 1, 1919   Lenow Circle 114, #8
Tennessee 4 Infantry Regiment Private Company F; per Company Muster-in Roll dated May 14, 1861, enlisted May 15, 1861, Germantown, 19; per Company Muster Roll for January & February, 1863, remarks: Transferred to Company A ("Shelby Greys") January 5, 1863; appears on a Roll of Prisoners of War captured at Nashville, Tennessee, December 16, 1864, and forwarded to Louisville, Kentucky, December 19, 1864; transferred to Camp Douglas, Illinois, December 21, 1864; appears on a Roll of Prisoners of War paroled at Camp Douglas, Illinois, and transferred to Point Lookout, Maryland, for exchange March 23, 1865; released on Oath June 8, 1865; sketch in Mathes book (Enlarged Edition) page 66; name listed as member of the Company in the May 15, 1909, *The Commercial Appeal* Memphis article "Forty=Eight Years Ago Today, The Shelby Greys Entered the Confederate Service—Record of a Famous Memphis Military Company."; per Tennessee Certificate of Death died April 30, 1919, Dysentery, age 77.

Johnston, James Virgil   Buried December 22, 1901   Turley 328, #6
Mississippi 29 Infantry Regiment Private Company I and Ordnance Sergeant; enlisted March 20, 1862, Corinth, Mississippi; appointed Ordnance Sergeant October 30, 1862; paroled May 19, 1865, Grenada, Mississippi; originally enlisted Mississippi 9 Infantry Regiment Private Old Company K March 27, 1861, Hernando, Mississippi age 29 and discharged January 6, 1862; per sketch in Mathes book, pages 133-134 with photograph, born in Adair County, Kentucky and moved to north Mississippi at an early age, in 1861 enlisted in the company "Irrepressibles" under Captain J. R. Chalmers that became part of Ninth Infantry, after twelve month term returned to Hernando and joined a company under Captain J. B. Morgan which became part of the Twenty-ninth Infantry and was appointed ordnance sergeant, wounded and disabled on July 22, 1864, at battle of Atlanta, and paroled at Grenada, Mississippi May 19, 1865; article in *The Commercial Appeal* Memphis December 21, 1901, page 7, which indicates born near Columbus, Adair County, Kentucky May 15, 1831, went to Hernando at age 17, and would have been 71 next May; article also recites Confederate service; died age 70 per Daily Burial Record Book; circle grave stone and headstone with "James V. Johnston" on top and "Born in Adair County, KY May 15, 1831 Died at St. Louis, Mo December 20, 1901 Aged 70 yrs, 7 mo, & 5 dys" on face.

Johnston, John   Buried May 8, 1928   Fowler 537
Tennessee 14 Cavalry Regiment Company H, Tennessee 7 Cavalry Company L, and Tennessee 6 Infantry Private/Sergeant Company K for which per Company Muster-in Roll dated August 12, 1861, enlisted May 15, 1861, Jackson, Tennessee and per Company Muster Roll for January 1 to May 1, 1862, dated August 12, 1862, remarks: Discharged from service July 4 and account paid and received Certificate of Disability; per biography in *Confederate Military History, Extended Edition*, Volume X Tennessee, page 550: born in Madison county, Tenn., March 11, 1842, veteran of Forrest's cavalry, early 1861, enlisted in April in a company organized at Denmark, called the Danes, which became Company K, Sixth Tennessee Infantry Regiment, with which served fourteen months as a private and non-commissioned officer, in Kentucky, Missouri, Tennessee and Mississippi, at Corinth, before the battle of Shiloh, contracted sickness which necessitated his honorable discharge on account of disability, early in 1863, having regained his health, secured a horse, made his way through the Federal lines, and in Mississippi served in Company L, Seventh Tennessee Cavalry Regiment, with the Seventh until January, 1864, taking part in the actions at Salem, Collierville and Senatobia, and then joined Company H, Fourteenth Tennessee Cavalry Regiment until the final operations of 1865, in June, 1865, made his home at Memphis, and began the study of law since admission to the bar in 1869.

Johnston, Thomas N.   Buried October 8, 1878   Fowler 120 (IOOF)
Tennessee 1 Heavy Artillery Captain Company L (subsequently 3 Company A) "Memphis Southern Guards," per Roster of the First (1st) Heavy Artillery Regiment mustered into State service May, 1861, and elected Captain January 1, 1862, Company captured and paroled at Vicksburg, Mississippi July 4, 1863, per register of Prisoners of War at New Orleans, Louisiana captured at Fort Morgan August 23, 1864, and sent to New York October 12, 1864, per record of Prisoners of War at Fort Warren, Massachusetts received at Fort Lafayette, New York Harbor December 21, 1864, and released June 17, 1865, name appears as signature to an Oath of Allegiance subscribed and sworn to at Fort Warren, Boston Harbor, Massachusetts, June 12, 1865, with place of residence indicated as Memphis, Tennessee; death and personal information published in *Memphis Daily Appeal,* October 9, 1878, page 1, column 1 and page 2, columns 3 and 4, indicating was a native of Fredericksburg, Virginia, an active member of the Odd Fellows relief association and worked as a bookkeeper; name spelled "Johnson" in Daily Burial Record Book and computer index; died age 45 yellow fever per Daily Burial Record Book; buried Odd Fellows (IOOF) Section.

Jones, Columbus Franklin   Buried July 14, 1879   Chapel Hill PL2, #510
Mississippi 19 Infantry Regiment Captain Company E, per Company Muster-in Roll dated June 8, 1861, at Old Fair Grounds near Redmond, Virginia (now West Virginia), enlisted May 15, 1861, at Oxford, Mississippi age 27 as 3 Lieutenant, per Company Muster Roll for July & August 1864, remarks promoted to captaincy from the rank of 1 Lieutenant January 20, 1864; died age 40 consumption and From City Hospital per Daily Burial Record Book; grave stone: June 25, 1832 – July 14, 1879.

Jones, Daniel Curd   Buried March 11, 1909   South Grove 162¼, #2

Tennessee Rice's Company Light Artillery 2 Lieutenant; first enlisted in Memphis August 15, 1861, age 25, as a private in Tennessee 38 Infantry Regiment (1st) Company A, Corporal indicated on muster roll dated September 24, 1861, which company was reorganized in April, 1862, as an artillery organization and it subsequently served as Captain Rice's Independent Company, Light Artillery; per unit card information about December, 1864, some of the company transferred to Captain Morton's Company Tennessee Light Artillery; per sketch in Mathes in February, 1865, transferred to heavy artillery and sent to Mobile and remain there until the end of the War; death (March 1,1909) mentioned in *Confederate Veteran* Volume 10, October 1909 page 520 in "Death List of Memphis Historical Society" between January 1, 1909 and July 1, 1909; obituary in *Commercial Appeal* Memphis March 13, 1909, page 6, column 3; Tennessee Widow Confederate Pension W9905 Mattie Gober Jones.

Jones, John Walker   Buried May 25, 1901   South Grove 565, #1

Confederate Soldier Doctor; "Confederate Soldier" and died age 56 per Daily Burial Record Book; per small death notice in May 25, 1901, *The Commercial Appeal* Memphis, page 5, from Collierville, died Friday May 24, 1901, age 56 and to be buried at Elmwood (no other information); family grave stone: "John Walker Jones, MD" died May 24, 1901, aged 57 years.

Jones, Robert C.   Buried May 24, 1862   Chapel Hill 375, #2

Tennessee 3 (Forrest's) Cavalry Regiment Corporal Company A ("Bluff City Grays"), per Company Muster Roll for January 1 to July 1, 1862, enlisted May 4, 1861, Randolph, Tennessee and remarks Died May 22, 1862; first enlisted in the Tennessee 154 Senior Infantry Regiment Private 1 Company B, per Company Muster-in Roll dated August 13, 1861, at New Madrid, Missouri enlisted May 14, 1861, at Randolph, Tennessee age 21; listed in the June 6, 1878, *Memphis Daily Appeal*, page 4, column 3, article "OUR DEAD HEROES" covering the unveiling of the Confederate Monument and Decoration of Graves at Elmwood as then one of twenty-eight members of the Bluff City Grays, Company B of the 154 Senior Infantry Regiment and Company A of Forrest's Old (Third) Cavalry Regiment buried at Elmwood; listed as one of the "comrades who sleep at Elmwood cemetery " in the article "Veterans in Council" in *Memphis Daily Appeal*, May 12, 1881, page 4, column 4, concerning the meeting of the surviving members in the city of the old Bluff City Grays to appoint the necessary committees for the purpose of making special decoration on the graves of their dead comrades at Elmwood and Calvary cemeteries on Sunday next, Memorial Day; listed as member of Bluff City Grays in *Reminiscences of the Civil War* by John Hallum, Tunnah & Pittard printers, 1903; listed in "A COMPLETE ROSTER OF THE BLUFF CITY GREYS" located in the Memphis Room of the Memphis/Shelby County Public Library and Information Center Central Library with notation "Died Memphis / May, 1862" and included on the list at the end of the soldiers buried at Elmwood; see also Notes of Interest - Bluff City Grays.

Jones, Samuel H.   Buried January 22, 1879   Turley 612 (Masonic Lot), #2

Tennessee 2 Battalion (Biffle's) Cavalry Lieutenant Colonel, per Field and Staff Muster-in Roll dated Camp Lee, Tennessee August 10, 1861, enlisted June 5, 1861, at Columbia, Tennessee, originally captain Company D and elected Lieutenant Colonel July 19, 1861, tendered his resignation September 3, 1861, at Nashville, Tennessee, which was accepted by Governor Harris; born 1824, in Maury County, Tennessee; died in Memphis January 20, 1879; died pneumonia age 56 per Daily Burial Record Book.

Jordan, James Pendleton   Buried November 28, 1922   Turley 388

Virginia 17 Infantry Regiment Sergeant Company H (record found under Jordan, Pendleton James); enlisted April 17, 1861, age 17, Alexander, Virginia; signed Parole of Honor April 28, 1865, Winchester, Virginia; per sketch in Mathes book, page 135: admitted to the Confederate Historical Association October, 1894; biography in *Confederate Military History, Extended Edition*, Volume X Tennessee, page 560; died in Lakeland, Florida November 26, 1922, age 79.

Josey, John E.   Buried November 2, 1866   Turley 1067, #1

Arkansas 15 (Josey's) Infantry Regiment Colonel; enlisted July 23, 1861, Camp Hardee, Pittman's Ferry, Arkansas; 1 Lieutenant Company E; elected Major April 14, 1862; indicated as Lieutenant Colonel on November and December 1862, muster roll; promoted to Colonel April 8, 1863; arrested Madison Company, Arkansas February 14, 1864 and sent to Camp Chase where received May 17, 1864; transferred to Point Lookout February 17, 1865; paroled at Memphis June 15, 1865; died jaundice age 35 per Daily Burial Record Book; originally buried Chapel Hill 739, #1 and moved February 12, 1884; Daily Burial Record Book indicates removed to Turley 1064, however, Cemetery Alpha book indicated removed to Turley 1067 and found listed in Lot 1067 in Turley book; no stone found either lot; per obituary in the November 13, 1866, *Memphis Avalanche,* page 2, column 4, died October 31, at Osceola, Mississippi County, Arkansas.

Kehoe, William   Buried February 4, 1872   Fowler 120 (IOOF), #A-19

Captain; listed in Elmwood 1874 book as Confederate soldier buried in Elmwood who was citizen of Memphis or vicinity with rank of Captain and sketch; per sketch captain of the Memphis Fire Department; died dysentery age 40 per Daily Burial Record Book; not found in any Confederate soldiers index thus may not have served and rank only related to fireman service; per death notice in February 3, 1872, *Memphis Daily Appeal*, page 1, column 5, died February 1, 1872, aged 39 years; per death notice in February 2, 1872, *Memphis Daily Appeal*, page 1, column 5, died February 1, 1872, aged 40 years and ex-Chief of the Memphis Fire Department; possibly served in Arkansas 5 Infantry Regiment Musician, enlisted July 18, 1862, Tupelo, Mississippi, captured Spring Hill, Tennessee December 18, 1864, on roll of prisoners of war at Nashville and sent to Louisville January 27, 1865, received at Camp Chase from Louisville February 3, 1865, and took Oath of Allegiance at Camp Chase, Ohio May 11, 1865; buried Odd Fellows (IOOF) Section.

Kelly, Michael   Buried June 19, 1866   Fowler 152, #10
Tennessee 154 Senior Infantry Regiment Private Company C; enlisted May 14, 1861, Randolph age 27; per May 5, 1863, muster roll remarks deserted April 27, 1862; per same muster roll enrolled April 26, 1861, at Memphis age 26 (note difference); per June 19, 1866, *Daily Memphis Avalanche*, page 3, Michael Kelly, alias Michael Rogan, was killed during an argument with a deputy sheriff early morning June 18, 1866; further per same article native of Algiers, Louisiana, came to Memphis at age 12, at outbreak of War joined the Crockett Rangers (Company F Tennessee 154 Senior Infantry Regiment, note record difference), afterwards transferred to 1st Tennessee Regiment (not found in index books for any 1st Tennessee regiments), deserted and returned to Memphis before Federal occupation, wounded by a Confederate, once stabbed a Federal officer, caused woman's death when he threw her down stairs, and a "bad character."

Kelly, William Owen   Buried February 27, 1905   Turley 984, #2
Tennessee 12 Infantry Regiment, Private Company H (records also found under Tennessee 12 Consolidated Infantry); per sketch in Mathes born in Franklin, Tennessee November 2, 1838, and enlisted June 1861; per obituary in *Confederate Veteran*, Volume XIII, July 1905, page 321, born in Franklin, TN, in November 1838, enlisted June 1861, wounded at battle of Belmont, after battle of Shiloh detailed for duty in commissary department under Major Lee M. Gardner, Polk's Division, later aid-de-camp on the staff of the commanding officer in resisting the advance of General Grierson in his famous raid through Mississippi, paroled at Meridian, Mississippi, June, 1865, settled in Trenton, TN where married, moved to Memphis in 1881, member of Confederate Historical Association, and on December 26, 1904, was fatally injured by being thrown from a street car, lingering in a painful illness until February 26, when the summons came; name on top of stone but inscriptions illegible with dates November 2, 1838 February 26, 1905; Tennessee Widow Confederate Pension (W3601), Lucelle Elder Kelly.

Kenneday, Dr. Absolom Early   Buried January 10, 1931   Turley 7
Arkansas 3 Cavalry Regiment Corporal/Private Bugler Company A; per Company Muster Roll for August 31 to November 30, 1861, enlisted July 29, 1861, Pocahontas; per Company Muster Roll for April 30 to June 30, 1862, rank Sergeant; per Company Muster Roll for October 31 to December 31, 1862, rank Sergeant and remarks: Detailed as Regimental Musician November 6, 1862; per Company Muster Roll for May & June, 1863, rank Private; appears on a List of Officers and Men paroled at Chester, South Carolina, May 5, 1865, and remarks: Princeton, Dallas County, Arkansas; sketch in Mathes Book, page 136; per Tennessee Confederate Pension (S15641) application did not take oath of allegiance; brother of Davis Young Kenneday and William Henry Kenneday both buried Elmwood (see sketches next below); per Tennessee Certificate of Death Dentist, died January 8, 1931, Pneumonia, age 87; name spelled "Kennedey" in Cemetery computer index.

Kenneday, David Young   Buried October 30, 1867   Turley 147
Arkansas 3 Cavalry Regiment Private Company A; per Company Muster Roll for August 31 to November 30, 1861, enlisted July 29, 1861, Pocahontas; per Company Muster Roll for January 31 to April 30, 1862 remarks: Returned to Company February 12, 1862, Teamster since April 12; per Company Muster Roll for April 30 to June 30, 1862, remarks: Served as Teamster from April 12 'till May 11, 1862; per Company Muster Roll for July & August, 1862, remarks: Still acting as Teamster; per Company Muster Roll for September & October, 1862, remarks: Detailed as Teamster June 22, 1862; per Company Muster Roll for October 31 to December 31, 1862, remarks: Detailed as musician in Regimental Band November 9, 1862, and indicated as musician on all Company Muster Rolls through January & February, 1864; signed form May 8, 1865, at Greensboro, North Carolina, giving solemn obligation not to take up arms against the Government of the United States; brother of Dr. Absolom Early Kenneday and William Henry Kenneday both buried Elmwood (see sketches next above and below respectively); originally buried in Turley Lot 612 (Masonic Lot) Grave #13 and moved to Turley Lot 7; name spelled "Kennedy" in Cemetery computer index.

Kenneday, William Henry   Buried October 20, 1913   Lenow Circle 58, #1
Arkansas 33 Infantry Regiment Lieutenant Company K (record found "Kennedy, William"); first served in Arkansas 3 Cavalry Regiment Sergeant/Private Company G (record found "Kennady, William") and per Company Muster Roll for August 31 to November 30, 1861, enlisted July 18, 1861, Little Rock, Arkansas, as Sergeant, per Company Muster Roll for January 31 to April 30, 1862, remarks: Detailed to carry horses home. Was Sergeant 'till 18 April 1862, and per Company Muster Roll for May & June 1862, (rank indicated as Private) remarks: Deserted. Was detailed 18 April 1862, on special duty to take horses home when dismounted and failed to return, from what cause unknown; per Arkansas 33 Infantry Regiment Company K Muster-in Roll dated July 4, 1862, enlisted June 23, 1862, Salem, age 34 and remarks: Belongs to 3 Arkansas Cavalry Company G (note this card located in the Arkansas 3 Cavalry Regiment compiled service records rolls); per Company Muster Roll for September & October, 1862, (dated February 14, 1863) remarks: A number of the 3 Arkansas Regiment Detained and attached by order of General Hindman; appears on an undated Roster of Commissioned Officers which indicates age 34, elected June 16, 1862, from state of Arkansas and born in Missouri; appears on a Statement showing name, rank, etc., of Officers of the 5 (Tappan's) Brigade, Price's Division, dated April 6, 1863, which indicates age 35, elected June 16, 1862, from state of Arkansas, County of Ouachita and born in Tennessee; brother of Dr. Absolom Early Kenneday and Davis Young Kenneday both buried Elmwood (see sketches next above); name spelled "Kennedy" in both Daily Burial Record Book and computer index.

King, Morris   Buried April 13, 1862   Chapel Hill 83, #2

Listed in Elmwood 1874 book as Confederate soldier buried in Elmwood who was citizen of Memphis or vicinity; killed Shiloh age 18 per Daily Burial Record Book but no unit identified; possibly M. H. King, Tennessee 4 Infantry Regiment, Private Company H, who per April 25 to June 30, 1862, muster roll enlisted May 15, 1861, at Germantown, Tennessee and killed at Shiloh April 6, no age indicated in compiled service record; M. H. King listed in the April 13, 1862, *Memphis Daily Appeal*, page 1, column 3, in article on the Tennessee 4 Infantry Regiment wounded and killed at the battle of Shiloh on the 6th and 7th April, Company H.

Kirby, John Anderson   Buried November 20, 1929   Lenow Circle 4, #5

Tennessee 4 Infantry Regiment, Private Company A (Shelby Greys), enlisted May 15, 1861, at Germantown, Tennessee at age 21, taken prisoner at Missionary Ridge November 25, 1863, first sent to military prison in Louisville, Kentucky, then sent to Rock Island Illinois where took oath of allegiance May 21, 1865; per sketch in Mathes proposed by J. E. Beasley and T. P. Adams for membership in the Confederate Historical Association and elected March 3, 1869; died age 87 per Daily Burial Record Book; large double stone with wife (Ann Eliza 1848-1926) with inscription Shelby Grays C.S.A. 1842-1929, "Until the Day Breaks and the Shadows Flee Away"; completed Tennessee Questionnaire of Civil War Veterans; born August, 1842, in Virginia and died November 19, 1929, in Germantown, Tennessee.

Kirwan, John W.   Buried January 30, 1862   Chapel Hill 358, #1

Mississippi 25 Infantry Regiment Private (O'Haver's) Company F; name spelled "Kerwin" on compiled service record jacket; per single Company Muster Roll card in record dated August 10, 1861, indicating enlisted August 10, 1861, Memphis age 43; per death notice in the January 29, 1862, *Memphis Daily Appeal*, page 2, column 7, (first initial incorrectly indicated as "I") died January 26, 1862, at Bowling Green, Kentucky, age 42 and was the brother of Colonel A. C. Kirwan of this city; under Local Matters, page 4, column 5, of the January 31, 1862, *Memphis Daily Appeal*, "A Soldier's Funeral," died of consumption, member of the company known as Hardee Grays, Captain O'Havre, raised in Memphis six months ago; Company became Company F Confederate 2 Infantry Regiment but no records found that unit; died age 43 per Daily Burial Record Book; broken grave stone with inscription born October 19, 1919, and died January 26, 1862.

Klinck, DeWitt Clinton   Buried May 17, 1875   Chapel Hill 460, #1

Tennessee 7 Cavalry Regiment, Private J. S. White's Company, 1 Battalion Tennessee Cavalry, Tennessee Mounted Rifles, enlisted May 22, 1861 in Memphis; per note on service record card: "(T)his company was successively designated as Captain White's Company Tennessee Cavalry; Company E, 6th Battalion Tennessee Cavalry, and Captain White's Company, 7th Duckworth's Regiment Tennessee Cavalry. It appears to have been disbanded prior to the re-organization of regiment in June 1862."; Nathan Bedford Forrest began his career as a private in this company; per Young's book Company D with note that "(N)o information could be obtained concerning this company except the roster (listed as Klink, Clinton) which is given below. The company was disbanded in May, 1862, most of the members joining other companies in the same regiment."; obituary in Memphis Daily Appeal, May 19, 1875, page 1, column 7; mentioned as being one of the "sleepy heads" along with Joe Luxton and who "served out every day of their time and never had a day's sickness, or a mark on their escutcheons of good name...." in a letter "To the Editors of the Appeal:" printed in *Memphis Daily Appeal*, April 10, 1887, page 9, column 2-3, submitted by R. B. Miller, who served in the company, providing a roster and early information on the Tennessee Mounted Rifles; also mentioned in the *Memphis Avalanche*, September 19, 1861, report "Daring Exploit of Memphis Boys" when he and others while on detachment scouting in the neighborhood of Bird's Point encountered an enemy detachment and when he and J. York started after a soldier had fled was fired upon by a Federal picket killing his horse which fell on him causing an injury to his thigh and disabling him but they were able to escape and return to the unit although having been reported as captured; listed as Klink, Clinton in both articles; died age 36 per Daily Burial Record Book; VA marker 1840 1875; a dedication of the placing of his grave marker along with the one for his brother, James Monroe Klinck, was held by Klinck family members on May 12, 2012, and assisting in the dedication were members of the N. B. Forrest Camp 215, the Robert E. Lee Camp 1640 and the 51st Tennessee Infantry; special thanks to Kristin Grace Klinck Petersen who provided information on the Klinck brothers and who hosts the blog "Dixie Roots" that is her genealogy research repository with the goal, in part, to provide an online home for her ancestors.

Klinck, Haynes Irby   Buried February 7, 1866   Chapel Hill 429, #3

Tennessee 154 Senior Infantry Regiment, Private Company L; per information in Elmwood Office surname file was a policeman for the City of Memphis before and during the War, married Margaret Ann Robertson in 1856 and they had two children, daughter Emma, born in 1860 and a son, John, July 1864, while serving as a detective, having previously served as patrolman in the City's 11th District, Union Major General C. C. Washburn issued General order #70 which declared the city's government "null & void" and disbanded all city employees, faced with unemployment and torn by his love for his family and his desire to serve his state and his country in its most desperate hour had to make an agonizing decision and after much deliberation, made arrangements for the safety of his family, and went off to North Alabama to enlist in the Army of Tennessee, late October or early November 1864 found the army camped near Florence, Alabama and immediately enlisted in a Shelby County unit, some of the boys made him welcome as they recognized him from his police duties, was described as being tall, with dark hair and being well built, when once again trod upon Tennessee soil felt the stirring of doom, shortly before the Battle of Franklin approached his Brigade Quartermaster, Lieutenant J. R. Flippen, and expressed feelings that would not survive the upcoming battle, not heeding Flippen's assurances that it was needless to worry, entrusted Flippen with his gold watch, a diamond ring, and some money for him to give to Margaret in Memphis after the War, premonition of death came true and buried upon the battlefield with hundreds of others from across the

South, Lieutenant Flippen survived the War and returned to Memphis to deliver entrusted mementos to the widow and her children, perhaps also assisted the family in returning remains back home for burial in Elmwood Cemetery on February 7, 1866, little known of family except that Margaret received a Tennessee Confederate Widow's Pension (W592), Fayette County, in 1905, which pension file includes affidavits from J. R. Flippin and Thomas B. Turley verifying service (joining regiment while camped at Florence, Alabama the latter part of October 1864 or November 1, 1864) and death at Battle of Franklin; son, John F. Klinck, died in 1873 while Chief of the Memphis Fire Department; not found in Tennesseans in the Civil War or Lindsley's Annals; name spelled "Klink" in Daily Burial Record Book and "Capt. H. J. Klinch" in Chapel Hill Book; a dedication of the placing of his grave marker was held by Klinck family members on August 9, 2014, and assisting in the dedication were members of the N. B. Forrest Camp 215 and the Memphis Brigade.

Klinck, James Monroe   Buried January 31, 1898   Chapel Hill 460, #3
Tennessee 21 Infantry Regiment, Private Company D, no enlistment indicated on Muster Roll Card dated November & December 1861 but remark that was discharged 30 September 1861 by order of General Polk; name spelled Klink in compiled service record and *Tennesseans in the Civil War*; VA marker 1844 1898; a dedication of the placing of his grave marker along with the one for his brother, Dewitt Clinton Klinck, was held by Klinck family members on May 12, 2012, and assisting in the dedication were members of the N. B. Forrest Camp 215, the Robert E. lee Camp 1640 and the 51st Tennessee Infantry.

Lake, Lorenzo S.   Buried May 26, 1921   Fowler 77 NE Part, #4
Arkansas 1 (Dobbin's) Cavalry Private Company G; record has only two cards with one indicating name appears on a Roll of Prisoners of War reported at Memphis and received for paroles 5 days ending May 20, 1865 and Oath of Allegiance dated May 30, 1865 with card indicating place of residence as Crittenden County, Arkansas age 20; per this unit's web site he was from Crittenden County, age 20 and paroled at Memphis; originally enlisted in Tennessee 13 Infantry Regiment Private Company C; per biography in *Confederate Military History*, *Extended Edition*, Volume X Tennessee, page 570, fought with regiment (Tennessee 13 Infantry) at battle of Shiloh, slightly wounded, and at reorganization, on account of illness and family duties, withdrew from field and joined 1 Arkansas Cavalry November 19, 1863; per Tennessee 13 Infantry records Private enlisted December 1, 1861 Columbus; per March 1 to July 1, 1862 muster roll remarks deserted at Corinth, Mississippi April 25, 1862; per muster roll dated May 5, 1863 deserted May 10, 1862; per sketch in Mathes book, Part II, enlisted in the Secession Guards, of Germantown, Company C Tennessee 13 Regiment and served until after the battle of Shiloh when he was furloughed on account of sickness, while at home 12 month term expired, forced to move to Arkansas and re-enlisted in the First Arkansas Cavalry, later promoted to assistant adjutant general on General Dobbin's staff but later went back to his company, surrendered under General M. Jeff Thompson, then in command of the Department of Eastern Arkansas, in 1865, and joined Confederate Historical Association at an early day; circle grave stone: July 27, 1844 May 24, 1921 and family memorial upright stone; died age 76 per Daily Burial Record Book.

Lake, Richard Pinkney   Buried September 21, 1921   Miller 4, #1
Mississippi 2 Battalion Cavalry Reserves Company I Senior 2 Lieutenant; record includes Parole of Honor that was signed May 16, 1865; also served in state militia - Mississippi 4 Cavalry Militia Company C 2 Lieutenant which record has one card that indicates name appears on a Roster of Officers elected August 22, 1864 at Grenada, Mississippi; per biography in *Confederate Military History*, *Extended Edition*, Volume X Tennessee, pages 570, "(T)hough too young to enlist when the war of the Confederacy began, Colonel Lake became second lieutenant of a company of boys at Grenada, who were regularly drilled by Capt. (afterward colonel) W. S. Statham. The company was able to do some service of value and furnished many good soldiers to the army, as they gradually dropped out and enlisted. Young Lake enlisted in 1864, being then sixteen years of age, in Capt. R. E. Wynn's company of Col. E. S. Fisher's regiment, State militia, and in the rank of second lieutenant of his company saw active service. Early in 1865 he acted as assistant to the adjutant-general of Denis' brigade, State troops, and afterward as second lieutenant in a company of Maj. H. C. Horton's battalion of cavalry. In command of dismounted men, he was stationed at Scooba and Artesia, and reported to Capt. Virgil Moore, of the staff of General Armstrong, who had lost his command at Selma, and was endeavoring to reorganize. While attached to Armstrong's brigade, and at Columbus on a mission to obtain paroles for his battalion, he finally surrendered."; per sketch in Mathes book, page 139-140, born Grenada, Mississippi July (sic) 10, 1848, moved to Memphis in 1894 and soon became a member of the Confederate Historical Association and Company A, Confederate Veterans and was aide-de-camp with rank of colonel on the staff of General Stephen D. Lee, Commanding the Army of Tennessee Department, United Confederate Veterans; sketch in *Confederate Veteran* Volume VI, Number 11, November, 1898, page 139; sketch in *Who's Who in Tennessee, A Biographical Reference Book of Notable Tennesseans To-Day*, Paul & Douglass Publishers, Memphis, 1911, pages 325-326; death notice in *The Commercial Appeal* Memphis September 20, 1921, page 7, indicating died September 19 and funeral September 21 and large article with photograph on page 1 April 20, 1921; circle grave stone: January 10, 1848 September 19, 1921; died age 73 per Daily Burial Record Book.

Landstreet, Edward   Buried January 27, 1899   Fowler 671, #1
Virginia 1 Cavalry Regiment Private Company A; enlisted September 22, 1861 Fairfax, Virginia; per September/October 1861 muster roll on detail service at General Stuart's Headquarters; detailed since October 10 per November/December 1861 muster roll; present on September/October 1862 muster roll; per May/June 1863 muster roll detailed as courier for Colonel Carter; per September/October 1863 muster roll detailed as courier at Brigade Headquarters; per January/February 1864 muster roll detailed to General Wickham as courier; signed parole form April 21, 1865 age 20; per sketch in Mathes book born Baltimore, Maryland August 26, 1844, enlisted September 15, 1861 in Company A 1 Virginia Cavalry (rank indicated as Lieutenant) then commanded

by Lieutenant Colonel J. E. B. Stuart, detailed as courier with Stuart when Stuart promoted to Brigadier General, captured once but escaped, with General Lee's army at Appomattox but escaped with cavalry and finally surrendered with Mosby's command at Winchester, Virginia, returned to Baltimore after War, became member of the army and navy of Maryland, moved to Memphis in 1888, elected member of Confederate Historical Association and was one of first to join Company A, United Confederate Veterans (UCV), elected 2 Lieutenant of Company September 1895; per introduction to Mathes book enlarged edition died January 25,1899 and was buried with military honors by Company A, UCV, on January 27; died age 54 per Daily Burial Record Book; death reported "The Last Roll" section *Confederate Veteran* Volume VII, March 1899, page 132.

Lathan, Mary Helen Wooldridge   Buried April 12, 1917   Lenow Circle 94, #9
Critical in the erection of the Nathan Bedford Forrest memorial (statute) in Forrest Park, Memphis; was a member of the Daughters of the American Revolution and the United Daughters of the Confederacy (U.D.C.); the Memphis chapter of the United Daughters of the Confederacy was named the Mary Latham Chapter in her honor; according to Francesca Morgan, an Associate Professor of History at Northeastern Illinois University, her leadership position within the U.D.C. gave her an opportunity to anticipate Mary Ritter Beard's feminism as she "celebrated married women's property rights, white women's admission to state universities, women's establishment of "industrial and reform schools" for girls, and their community work that resulted in public libraries, public drinking fountains for man and beast, police matrons, public parks, and clean streets."; married March 7, 1861 in Shelby County, Tennessee to Judge Thomas Jefferson Latham (November 22, 1831 – July 24, 1911) who was an American lawyer and businessman and grew up in rural Weakley County, Tennessee in the Antebellum South, became a lawyer and remained neutral during the American Civil War, in the post-bellum era served as the debt receiver of the City of Memphis, Tennessee and was the president of the Memphis Water Company; large Grave Stone honoring both of them.

Law, Sarah Chapman   Buried June 30, 1892   Fowler 48, #2
"Mother of the Confederacy"; President of Southern Mothers Hospital (see chapters on Hospitals and Notes of Interest) which she founded with Mary E. Pope; sketch in *Dictionary of American Biography*, page 42 - traveled at own expense throughout the War to aid the suffering; recognized by General Joseph E. Johnson at Dalton, Georgia; wrote pamphlet *Reminiscences of the War of the Sixties Between the North and South* (1892) in which "she recounts a few of her many wartime experiences, revealing without ostentation how naturally, lovingly, and gratuitously she gave herself to the Confederacy during the war years and afterward"; obituary in the *Memphis Appeal-Avalanche*, June 30, 1894, which is reprinted in *Southern Historical Society Papers*, Volume XXII, pages 63-64 (1894); see several articles and mentions in *Confederate Veteran*; name often found as "Sallie Chapman Gordon Law" or a variation; died age 89 per Daily Burial Record Book; circle grave stone with full name and birth and death dates; listed in "Touring Historic Elmwood Cemetery" Brochure (January 2000) #21; sketch #9 in Elmwood *Civil War Tour* booklet (2012).

Lawler, James H.   Buried October 1, 1867   Lenow Circle 48/49, #2
Tennessee 154 Senior Infantry Regiment Sergeant Company D; enlisted May 14, 1861 Randolph, Tennessee age 22; wounded Battle of Murfreesboro; captured near Nashville December 16, 1864 and sent to military prison Louisville, Kentucky December 31, 1864; took Oath of Allegiance May 10, 1865 at Camp Chase, Ohio indicating on oath form that Shelby County, Tennessee was place of residence; name spelled "Lawlor" in Cemetery computer index; died yellow fever age 25 per Daily Burial Record Book; born in Lewis County, Mississippi and died September 30, 1867 per obituary in October 2, 1867 *Memphis Daily Appeal*, which also includes description of Confederate service; originally buried Fowler Public Lot 2, #201 and moved December 28, 1880.

Lawrence, James H.   Buried September 2, 1878   Turley 593, #3
Tennessee 154 Senior Infantry Regiment, Private Company E; enlisted May 14, 1861 Randolph, Tennessee; per muster roll dated May 5, 1863 age 29 and absent on detailed duty; per March/April 1863 muster roll remarks absent in Ordnance Department at Columbia, Mississippi; name appears on a report of Prisoners of War paroled at Memphis for the five days ending May 25, 1865; grave stone with unit information: Jun 8, 1834 Sep 2, 1878; also upright stone with illegible inscription; name spelled "Laurence" in Daily Burial Record Book and computer index; died yellow fever age 44 per Daily Burial Record Book.

Leath, Peter M.   Buried June 4, 1875   Turley 134½, #14
Confederate 5 Military District Mississippi Major Quartermaster (QM); per General and Staff compiled service record rolls November 11, 1861, invited by Colonel Walker to take position on his staff as QM, December 24, 1861, appointed Major and QM, September 19, 1862, ordered to Richmond. October 31, 1862, at Oxford, Mississippi, August 17, 1863, captured at Grenada, Mississippi, February 17, 1865, QM General recommended he be dropped from rolls as present duty and location unknown, March 3, 1865, dropped by Special Order #52; tried by US Military Court 16 Army Corps for burning the Steamer "Champion" and found guilty of having accepted parole and not to aid or assist enemy but did violate by telling enemy to fire the "Lancaster" (note wrong boat was set afire); Prisoner of War list indicated residence as Memphis, captured at Grenada August 20, 1863, released on parole August 28, 1863, violated parole and sent to Alton Military Prison then to Johnson's Island December 1863, and at General Hospital Richmond, Virginia October 6, 1864, with wound in left hip; listed in Elmwood 1874 book as Confederate soldier buried in Elmwood who was citizen of Memphis or vicinity with rank of Major; died age 38 and removed from Winchester Cemetery per Daily Burial Record Book.

Lee, Pollock B.   Buried January 29, 1867   Turley 612 (Masonic Lot), #3
Adjutant & Inspector General (AIG) Major; per General and Staff rolls appointed from Tennessee September 2, 1861; May 1861,

Tennessee Governor Harris appointed him Major & Assistant Adjutant General in Tennessee Provisional Army; served with Generals Zellicoffer (August-December 1861), Crittenden (January-October 1862), Bragg (June-December 1863), Hardee (December 1863), Polk (December 1863), Hood (July 1864 to February 1865) and Joseph E. Johnston (November 1862, July 1864 and February-April 1865) with whom paroled as Major & AIG; served Court duty January-April 1863; mentioned in his brother's, David Lee Pollock, biography in *Confederate Military History, Extended Edition,* Volume V North Carolina, page 600; lawyer; believed to have died September 8, 1866 and moved to Elmwood to be interred in the Free Mason Lot (Turley Lot 612); per the Memphis *Daily Argus* September 9, 1866, page 3, column 3, "Funeral of Col. Lee. - The funeral of Col. Pollock B. Lee, a well-known lawyer, and late a distinguished staff officer of the Confederate army, took place from Cavalry Church yesterday afternoon at 4 o'clock, under the auspices of the Masonic Fraternity, Dr. White officiating. He died of consumption." (note: no cemetery indicated); the Shelby County Funeral book indicates that Lee, Pollock B. (Maj.) died September 8, 1866 but no cemetery indicated; died age 35 chronic diarrhea per Daily Burial Record Book.

Lee, Samuel Stacker   Buried April 4, 1890   Evergreen 454, #1
Tennessee 3 (Forrest's) Cavalry Regiment Private Company A, per Company Muster Roll for March 1, 1864, to ____, dated May 14, 1864, enlisted March 15, 1864, at Tupelo, Mississippi, paroled May 11, 1865, at Gainesville, Alabama; son of Captain James Lee, Sr., who started the Lee Line Company (riverboats), and became a riverboat captain and was Vice President of the Lee Line of steamers at his death; per sketch in Mathes, entered the service February 1863, and was proposed for membership in the Confederate Historical Association by Colonel John W. Dawson of the Association and elected January 20, 1870; listed in "A COMPLETE ROSTER OF THE BLUFF CITY GREYS" located in the Memphis Room of the Memphis/Shelby County Public Library and Information Center Central Library; per Register of Deaths in the Taxing District (Memphis) died April 3, 1890, age 42 years, 10 months and 18 days and cause of death: Gastritis, and native of Tennessee; no grave stone.

Lenow, Joseph   Buried September 21, 1889   South Grove 8, #1
President of Elmwood Cemetery Association when Elmwood donated a lot for the Confederate dead; see chapter "Elmwood Cemetery and Confederate Soldiers Rest" supra; sketch in Goodspeed's Shelby County History, page 999, that indicates came to Tennessee in 1837, and located at Hickory Withe, Fayette County, where he followed mercantile pursuits until 1848, when he came to Memphis and began dealing in real estate, in 1852, was instrumental in establishing Elmwood Cemetery, been president for almost last thirty years, and served in war with Mexico when he enlisted and commanded Company A, Tennessee regiment of Cavalry; Daily Burial Record Book: Captain Joseph Lenow, 75y, 8m, 26d, buried South Grove 10 and moved to South Grove 8 March 20, 1956; circle grave stone and large monument: born Southampton County, Virginia December 24, 1813 and died September 19, 1889; listed in "Touring Historic Elmwood Cemetery" Brochure (January 2000) #79 and its predecessor "Touring historic Elmwood Cemetery" (Brochure and Map of Historic Gravesites) #86.

Lewis, George Washington   Buried December 1, 1910   Chapel Hill 836½, #1
Tennessee 4 Infantry Regiment, Sergeant Company D, enlisted May 1861, paroled April 17, 1865; per sketch in Mathes book wounded three times, Shiloh, Perryville, and Franklin, paroled April 17, 1865 at Greensboro, North Carolina, and admitted to Confederate Historical Association October 1894; death (December 9, 1910) reported in *Confederate Veteran*, Volume XIX, April 1911, page 174, "The Last Roll, Death of Confederates in Memphis, Tennessee" who died during 1910 and were members of the Confederate Historical Association, Camp 28, U.C.V., Bivouac 18, C.V., of Memphis, Tennessee; Tennessee Pension #S6113; died age 68 per Daily Burial Record Book; died age 69 November 30, 1910 per Shelby County, Tennessee death record; grave stone April 30, 1842 December 12, 1910 (sic).

Locke, Charles G.   Buried January 15, 1909   Chapel Hill 242, #7
Tennessee 9 Infantry Regiment Private Company A; per sketch in Mathes first served in Arkansas 15 (Josey's) Infantry Regiment, Private Company H, while temporarily in Arkansas in April 1861 joined Rector Guard of Des Arc, a company which became part of the Fifteenth Arkansas Regiment, (per compiled service record enlisted May 15, 1862 Corinth, MS and per one card transferred by order of General Hardee May 14, 1863 and per another card transferred May 8, 1863), July, 1863, transferred to the Tennessee 6 and 9 Consolidated Infantry Regiment (Tennessee 9 Infantry Regiment), was on its rolls to the end of War, served as a private and once declined to be elected as captain, born in Memphis and son of Gardner B. Locke who was mayor of Memphis in 1848, became a member of Confederate Historical Association March 20, 1870, and survivor of four brothers who were all in Confederate army for four years; per Mathes sketch the oldest was James Bowdoin Locke (not found Elmwood), Captain of Company C Tennessee 6 and 9 Regiments (per Tennesseans in the Civil War Tennessee 9 Infantry Regiment Captain Company E in Part Two but Company A per Part One and Lindsley's Annals), William Locke (see sketch below), and Joseph Locke (see sketch below) and all three brothers were all wounded slightly several times each, the only severe wound being received by Captain Locke through the right lung at Franklin; death (January 13, 1909) mentioned in *Confederate Veteran,* Volume X, October 1909, page 520 in "Death List of Memphis Historical Society" between January 1, 1909 and July 1, 1909; per obituary in *Confederate Veteran,* Volume XVII, May 1909, page 238 shortly after War became honorary member of Company A, Confederate Veterans, and an active member of Confederate Historical Association; per article in the *Pensacola Journal*, Pensacola, FL, January 14, 1909, page 2, column 3, "fell on an icy pavement here today and struck on his head, dying shortly after his fall."; only stone in lot is for father, Gardner B. Locke.

Locke, Joseph W.   Buried December 5, 1886   Chapel Hill 242, #5
Tennessee 12 Cavalry Regiment, Sergeant Company A, enlisted October 1, 1862, name appeared on Register of Prisoners of War in the custody of the Provost Marshall, Memphis, Tennessee, indicating received February 2, 1865, and released July 9, 1865; per Mathes sketch on brother, Charles G. Locke (above), first served in the Tennessee 13 Infantry Regiment (J. W. Locke, Private, Company A per *Tennesseans in the Civil War*) and being discharged on account of his youth at Tupelo, Mississippi, joined the cavalry with Richardson (Tennessee 12 Cavalry Regiment) and afterward with Forrest; per Tennessee 13 Infantry Regiment records enlisted June 4, 1861, in Company H at age 15 and discharged July 25, 1862 at age 18.

Locke, William B.   Buried November 16, 1874   Chapel Hill 242, #4
Tennessee 9 Infantry Regiment Private Company A, 1863-64 served as a clerk in hospitals in Georgia and took Oath of Allegiance on March 28, 1865, in Memphis, Tennessee, at age 21; per Mathes sketch on brother, Charles G. Locke (above), was absent through sickness for several months in 1862 but was present and on duty at all other times during the entire war; first served in Arkansas 15 (Josey's) Infantry Regiment, Private Company H Band, enlisted July 23, 1861 Camp Yell, Pittman's Ferry, detailed to Provost's office Knoxville, TN 1862, and transferred to TN 9 Infantry Regiment, which per one card transferred by order of General Hardee May 14, 1863 and per another card transferred May 8, 1863.

Logwood, Thomas Henry   Buried May 25, 1884   Chapel Hill Circle 74, #7
Tennessee 15 Cavalry Regiment Colonel; entered service May 1861, as Captain of "The Memphis Light Dragoons," Company A, Tennessee 6 Cavalry Battalion, which subsequently became Company A Tennessee 7 Cavalry Regiment (that record indicates enlisted May 20, 1861, at Memphis age 31 Captain Company A and Lieutenant Colonel commissioned July 25, 1861, and name appears on regiment Return for part of April 1862, dated April 25, 1862, with remarks that absent under an order from General Polk to raise a regiment of lancers since 7 March 1862); and also appears on return as Lieutenant Colonel Tennessee 6 Cavalry Battalion resigned April 25, 1862); elected Lieutenant Colonel at unit organization at Columbus, Kentucky September 1861; August 27, 1863, organized Tennessee 16 Cavalry Regiment and made Colonel; Lieutenant Colonel Tennessee 15 Cavalry Regiment when 16 Cavalry Regiment consolidated with Tennessee 15 Cavalry Regiment and Mississippi Street's Cavalry Battalion February 5, 1864; per sketch in Mathes book in command of troops when entered Memphis August 21, 1864, promoted to full colonelcy of his regiment for gallant services rendered on that day and became member of Confederate Historical Association April 28, 1870; death notice in the May 25, 1884, *Memphis Daily Appeal*, page 1, column 6, died at Florence, Alabama, May 24, 1884; large monument with inscription born March 2, 1829 and died May 21, 1884.

Long, Reverend Nicholas Matthew   Buried January 6, 1931   Fowler 755
Tennessee Sullivan County Reserves (Local Defense), Private Captain James Witcher's Company Home Guard; per Muster and Descriptive Roll dated June 20, 1863, enlisted June 13, 1863, age 13, born Fayette County, Tennessee and residence Sullivan County, Tennessee; sketch in Mathes book, page 255; per biography in *Confederate Military History, Extended Edition*, Volume X Tennessee, page 585: born Somerville, Fayette county, July 27, 1849, May, 1863, while in his fourteenth year, joined Witcher's company of White's battalion, Home Guards, and with this command was on active duty in east Tennessee, until the close of the war, after the disbandment of the forces in that quarter entered King college, Bristol, Tenn., and was graduated in May, 1871, then after a course of two years in the Presbyterian theological seminary of Columbia, S. C. entered the ministry of the Presbyterian church, chaplain of Company A, Confederate veterans, and for several years chaplain of the Dolly Madison chapter, Daughters of the American Revolution; sketch in *Prominent Tennesseans* (William S. Speers, Nashville 1888) page 172.

Looney, Robert Fain   Buried November 21, 1899   Chapel Hill 146/149, #14
Tennessee 38 Infantry Regiment Colonel; per *Tennesseans in the Civil War* Part 1, originally Captain of Company assigned to Tennessee 22 Infantry Regiment August 18, 1861, but transferred to Tennessee 38 Infantry Regiment; per Tennessee 22 Infantry Regiment record Captain Looney's Company, enlisted June 13, 1861, Memphis and note card indicating about September 23, 1861, this company transferred to Tennessee 38 Infantry Regiment becoming Company B and subsequently Company L; elected Colonel of Tennessee 38 Infantry Regiment at organization September 23, 1861, which he commanded at the Battle of Shiloh but not re-elected at reorganization May 1862; several letters of recommendations in compiled service record to have him promoted to brigadier general of brigade he raised but never confirmed; born Columbia, Tennessee August 5, 1824, and died November 19, 1899, on grave stone; sketch in Mathes book (both editions); per sketch born in Maury County, Tennessee, returned to Memphis after war to practice law, was involved in politics and served as one of the commissioners appointed by the government to make Shiloh a national park; biography in *Confederate Military History, Extended Edition*, Volume X Tennessee, page 587; per article in the October 13, 1861, *Memphis Daily Appeal*, page 2 column 3, "ANOTHER REGIMENT - We have information of the organization of a regiment of Alabamians and Tennesseans, a few days since, designated the 1st Tennessee and Alabama regiment. The officers elected are, R. F. Looney, of Memphis, colonel: E. J. Galady, of Lebanon, Tennessee, lieutenant colonel: D. H. Thrasher, of Alabama, major, and Dr. Geo. D. Gray, of Memphis, surgeon."; Robert F. Looney collection of personal papers is located in Memphis and Shelby County Public Library Memphis Room; per collection married Louisa Crofford of Maury County, Tennessee in 1847; sketch in *Tennessee, The Volunteer State, 1769-1923*, Volume III, page 321; sketch in Goodspeed's Shelby County History, page1001; died age 75 per Daily Burial Record Book.

Loudon, James Arlington   Buried May 18, 1932   Chapel Hill 85, #10
Tennessee 7 Cavalry Regiment Private Company G & Arkansas Carlton's Cavalry Battalion 1 Lieutenant Company F; Tennessee

compiled service record found under "Lowden" with some cards having name spelled "Louden" and Arkansas compiled service record found under "Louden"; Tennessee regiment: enlisted May 22, 1861, Memphis, present on muster roll dated October 2, 1862, with no other information in Tennessee unit compiled service record; Arkansas regiment: 1 Lieutenant Company F with only one card in compiled service record indicating captured Arkansas County, Arkansas January 24, 1865, and released on oath (date not clear); name appears as signature to an Oath of Allegiance subscribed and sworn to May 7, 1865, place of residence Arkansas County, Arkansas and age 23; name spelled "Colonel Jamies A. Louden" and died age 89 per Cemetery record; member Confederate Historical Association, Company A, UCV, and sketch in Mathes book both original (page 141) and enlarged (136) editions; per sketch in Mathes book enlisted in Captain White's Cavalry (Company E, Tennessee 6 Battalion Cavalry) in Memphis May, 1861, when only 15 years old, at Belmont transferred to Captain Jack Stock's Company which later became Company G Tennessee 7 Cavalry Regiment, later became sick and was allowed to pass through the lines to go to his father (John Louden) whose boat "Granite State" was operating on the Arkansas River in the service of the Confederacy where recovered, was not allowed to return to command, then assigned to duty as Assistant Pilot on his father's boat with rank of Captain, when Little Rock evacuated ordered to burn the boat, then elected 1 Lieutenant of Captain Gillespie's Company of Colonel Carleston's (sic) Arkansas Cavalry Regiment (brother Hopkins Loudon also in this unit with name spelled "Lowden" in compiled service record), later captured and imprisoned at Pine Bluff but removed to Military Prison in Little Rock where paroled May 6, 1865, and after war returned to Memphis; son of John Louden and brother of Hopkins (Arkansas Carlton's Cavalry Battalion, name spelled "Lowden") and Milton Boyd Louden; biography in *Confederate Military History, Extended Edition*, Volume X Tennessee, page 589; per biography enlisted at age 15; grave stone: Colonel C.S.A., born January 2, 1844 and died May 18, 1832.

Loudon, John   Buried October 23, 1883   Chapel Hill 468, Vault
Captain of river boat; father of Milton B., James A., and Hopkins Loudon; per sketch in Mathes book (enlarged edition) was a planter and a contractor; also per sketch "this gentleman was not a Confederate soldier or voluntarily even in the civil service, but the fact that he had three sons in the armies of the lost cause and that he was an important factor in some matters pertaining to the Confederacy, justifies his biography in this work;...."; further per sketch died October 19, 1884 (sic), age 84; per death notice in the October 23, 1883, *Memphis Daily Appeal*, page 1, column 7, died at Williamette, Arkansas aged 82 years and 11 months; per Daily Burial Record Book died of old age at age 82 (note age differences); name spelled "Lowden" in Cemetery computer index.

Loudon, Milton Boyd   Buried January 15, 1878   Chapel Hill 468, Vault
Confederate 1 Cavalry Regiment Private (M. J. Wick's) Company I; name spelled "Lowden" in compiled service record; per Company Muster-in Roll dated March 7, 1862, enlisted age 24 at Memphis March 7, 1862, by Captain M. J. Wicks; per November and December 1863, muster roll remarks: absent without leave; with Wiggins Battery December 23 and later Moore's Battalion; sketch in Mathes book both original (259) and enlarged (136) editions; per original edition sketch second son of John Loudon, entered the Confederate service at the age of 23 years, in Captain Wicks' Cavalry Company (M. J. Wicks Captain Company I Confederate 1 Cavalry Regiment), attached to General Wheeler's command, served throughout the war, died of yellow fever on board his boat Keokuk in 1873, (note death year date difference) and buried in the Loudon vault, Elmwood Cemetery; per enlarged edition sketch eldest son of John and Mariam Trowbridge (John's second wife per John's sketch in Mathes book enlarged edition) Loudon, Captain of Steamer Granite State, resigned to join Captain M. J. Wicks Cavalry Company, early in war horse killed and joined an artillery company, later rejoined the cavalry and at end of war was paroled with General Joe Wheeler's command; there is a "M. B. Loudon" in *Tennesseans in the Civil War, Part 2* with unit indicated as 7 Cavalry Private but no Tennessee 7 Cavalry compiled service record found and not found in Young's book; died age 36 complications per Daily Burial Record Book.

Lowry, William J.   Buried April 20, 1896   Chapel Hill 187, #11
Tennessee 3 (Forrest's) Cavalry Regiment Private Company F (name "W. J. Lowery"); appears on a Roll of Prisoners of War paroled at Gainesville, Alabama May 11, 1865, residence Memphis, Tennessee, with notation on card that Company appears to have formerly served as Company C, 2d Regiment Mississippi Partisan Rangers, and to have become a part of Forrest's Old Regiment Tennessee Cavalry, in compliance with S. O. No. 28, Headquarters Cavalry, District of Mississippi and East Louisiana, dated February 13, 1865; Mississippi 2 (J. G. Ballentine's Regiment of Cavalry) Partisan Rangers Private (Captain Edward E. Porter's Partisan Company – see Rev. Edward E. Porter sketch) Company C; enlisted October 1, 1862, Byhalia, Mississippi, by Captain Porter; per Mathes book, page 146: "Wil J. Lowry" served in Mississippi 7 (sic – no record found in 7th records) Cavalry Regiment, Private Company C, under Forrest, enlisted July 1862, paroled May 11, 1865, and admitted to Confederate Historical Association March 15, 1895; *The Commercial Appeal* Memphis April 20, 1896, has small death notice indicating died April 19th age 53 but no other information; Cemetery computer index indicates grave number as #1 but Daily Burial Record and Chapel Hill books indicate grave as #11.

Loyd, Andrew Jackson   Buried December 4, 1880   Evergreen 250
Tennessee 154 Senior Infantry Regiment Private Company H; per Company Muster-in Roll dated May 14, 1861, enlisted April 26, 1861, Memphis, age 22; appears on a Roll of Prisoners of War captured December 16, 1864, near Nashville and forwarded to Louisville, Kentucky, December 31, 1864, then to Military Prison at Louisville, Kentucky January 2, 1865, then to Camp Chase Ohio January 4, 1865, paroled at Camp Chase and transferred to Point Lookout, Maryland February 17, 1865, for exchange and appears on a Report of Prisoners of War paroled at Memphis, Tennessee, for 5 days ending June 20, 1865, date June 19, 1865; per Daily Burial Record Book died age 39, heart disease and originally buried Chapel Hill Public Lot 2, #747 and moved to Evergreen 250 December 30, 1925, (spouse Frances Bakewell Loyd (DOD January 1, 1891, burial January 3, 1891) moved same date) ; death

notice in the December 4, 1880, *Memphis Daily Appeal*, page 1, column 6; grave stone: 1840 — 1880.

Lundy, E. C.   Buried August 23, 1864   Chapel Hill Public Lot 1, #46 Old
Tennessee 3 (Forrest's) Cavalry Regiment 2 Lieutenant Company B; enlisted January 3, 1862, Memphis; per special order dated August 5, 1863, dropped from rolls for prolonged absence from duty, without leave; per single Company Muster Roll card dated August 20, 1861, at New Madrid, Missouri, in Tennessee 7 Cavalry Regiment service records originally enlisted June 1, 1861, in Memphis as a Private in White's Cavalry Company; prisoner in Irving Block Prison in Memphis when released on $3,000 bond July 25, 1864; per statement written by Adjutant General and signed by N. B. Forrest October 7, 1865 "N. B. Forrest states and will verify the statement, if necessary, that by Lieutenant General, of Confederate States Army, commanding the Cavalry of the Department of Mississippi and Louisiana, he led in person, the forces in the attack upon the post of defenses of Memphis. One E. C. Lundy, formerly a member of his command, was brought to his headquarters under arrest by men detailed for that purpose, as an absentee and deserter. Not having time or men to spare, to send him dismounted to Meridian to be attached to the Infantry, as was the rule, he ordered him into ranks, and appointed him as guide. After penetrating the lines, and before reaching the city he was killed. He was forced to come into Memphis---and came not as a volunteer."; per article in August 23, 1864, the *Memphis Daily Bulletin*, page 1, columns 5 and 6, he is referred to as Captain E. C. Lundy and was a spy and had visited the camp of the 137 Illinois regiment a few days before the incident on August 21 and also on page 3 under Local Matters, Additional arrest" includes information concerning his previous arrest and bond and that killed in one of the camps Sunday morning while at the head of an artillery of rebels; name written as "Captain E. C. Lundy," shot, age 25 and buried Chapel Hill Single Grave #46 old in Daily Burial Record Book; listed in Elmwood 1874 book as Confederate soldier buried in Elmwood who was citizen of Memphis or vicinity.

Lyles, Oliver P.   Buried April 18, 1893   Evergreen 121, #2
Arkansas 23 Infantry Regiment Colonel; originally served as Sergeant Company C Arkansas 6 Battalion Cavalry (also known as 1 Phifer's, White's and McNeill's Battalion) in which records name appears on a descriptive list dated July 28, 1861, of members of Crittenden Rangers mustered into the service of the State of Arkansas as volunteer for twelve months on June 3, 1861; also per list born Tennessee 1827, and lawyer by profession; enlisted Arkansas 23 Infantry Regiment March 1, 1862, Marion, Arkansas Captain Company D; per descriptive roll served as Ordnance Sergeant in cavalry company (Arkansas 6 Battalion Cavalry) two months in Arkansas state service at the commencement of the war; captured Port Hudson July 23, 1863; transferred to Point Lookout April 22, 1864; paroled and transferred for exchange April 27, 1864; paroled at Wittsburg, Arkansas May 25, 1865; died age 63 per Daily Burial Record Book; grave stone partly illegible but appears born November 27, 1828 and died April 17, 1893; originally buried Turley 291, #5 and moved March 3, 1899.

Macgowan, Evander Locke   Buried May 19, 1907   Turley 1294, #5
Tennessee 7 Cavalry Regiment Private Company A (record found as McGowan, E. L.); enlisted August 18, 1862, Senatobia, Mississippi; paroled at Gainesville, Alabama, May 11, 1865; per sketch in Mathes book enlarged edition, page 60: joined Confederate Historical Association October, 1894; sketch also in Mathes book 1897 edition, page 154 "McGowan, E. L."; per biography in *Confederate Military History, Extended Edition*, Volume X Tennessee, page 603: born in Rutherford county, August 22, 1835, brought to Shelby county by his parents in 1836, received a collegiate education, at the beginning of the war in 1861 temporarily in Tunica county, Miss., farming with his elder and only brother, David who enlisted at once but Evander remained in care of his father's plantations until the summer of 1862, when volunteered in Company A, Seventh Tennessee cavalry, as a private served with this command until the surrender at Gainesville, Ala., after the close of hostilities engaged in farming until 1878, when elected sheriff of Shelby county, and after holding that office one term was county trustee two years.

Magevney, Michael, Jr.   Buried September 22, 1883   Chapel Hill 350, #4
Tennessee 154 Senior Infantry Regiment Colonel; enlisted as Captain Company C May 14, 1861, Randolph age 26; elected Lieutenant Colonel May 3, 1862; promoted to Colonel August 30, 1862; per roll of Prisoners of War dated December 18, 1864, at Nashville, Tennessee: captured December 16, 1864, at Nashville, sent to Louisville, Kentucky, then to Johnson's Island (Ohio) December 20, 1864; per Oath of Allegiance at Johnson's Island: Memphis, Tennessee place of residence and age 30; released on oath May 22, 1865, at Depot of Prisoners near Sandusky, Ohio; died September 21, 1883, age 48 per Register of Deaths in the City of Memphis, Nativity: Ireland and Cause of Death: Alcoholism.

Maier, Maxmillian   Buried May 3, 1867   Fowler 196, #1
Tennessee Artillery (McCown's) Corps; single card in service record indicating appears on a roll of the field and company officers belonging to the Artillery Corps of the Provisional Army of Tennessee transferred to the Confederate States with remark commissioned May 22, 1861; no other service records found; service and unit per great great grandson, Carl Strand; grave stone: Maximilian Maier, born in Baden, Germany July 28 (23), 1829 died May 1, 1867; died age 37 per Daily Burial Record Book.

Malone, Dr. George Booth   Buried April 14, 1922   Evergreen 450
Tennessee 3 (Forrest's) Cavalry Regiment Private Company H; Tennessee 9 Infantry Regiment Private Company E (under age and discharged); Tennessee 12 (Green's) Cavalry Private Company E; per sketch in Mathes book, page 146: private Company E, Ninth Tennessee Infantry, enlisted June 7, 1861, discharged for being under age in 1862, served with the Twelfth Tennessee Cavalry, Reno's and Morton's batteries, Company H, Forrest's old regiment, rejoined the army, served in artillery as orderly sergeant for one year, then restored to cavalry as private, captured near Somerville, Tenn., March 9, 1863, escaped April 27, 1863, paroled May 11,

1865, and joined this Association June 13, 1894; per biography in *Confederate Military History, Extended Edition*, Volume X Tennessee, page 616: began the study of medicine while working on the farm, in 1872 graduated at the medical department of the Washington university, Baltimore, now College of physicians and surgeons, for fifteen years practiced at Indian Bay, Ark., then removed to Memphis, held the positions of first vice-president of the Arkansas medical society, president of the Monroe county (Ark.) Society, and member of the board of medical examiners of that county, a member of the Tri-State medical society, and surgeon of Company A, Confederate veterans, National guard of Tennessee; received Tennessee Confederate Pension S15616, filed July 29, 1921.

Malone, William Battle   Buried November 27, 1897   Evergreen 447, #1
Kentucky 12 Cavalry Private Company A, enlisted April 29, 1863 in North Mississippi, on January 28, 1864 muster roll as present, with horse valued at $500, on roll of POWs of Company C, 8 & 12 Kentucky Cavalry, CSA, commanded by A. R. Shacklett, surrendered at Citronelle, AL, by Lt. General Taylor, CSA, to Major General Canby, USA, May 4, 1865 and paroled at Columbus, MS May 16, 1865 giving residence Hickman County, KY; died age 55 per Daily Burial Record Book; per descendant Gregory S. Miller born September 16, 1842 in Tippah County, Mississippi and died November 26, 1897 at Memphis and member Confederate Historical Association, Camp 28, U.C.V., Bivouac 18, C.V., of Memphis, Tennessee; grave stone: "William Battle Malone 1842 – 1897."

Marley, Hampton Young   Buried February 3, 1907   Fowler 141, #7
Tennessee 3 (Forrest's) Cavalry Regiment Private Company F; appears on a Roll of Prisoners of War paroled at Gainesville, Alabama May 11, 1865, residence Shelby County, Tennessee, with notation on card that Company appears to have formerly served as Company C, 2d Regiment Mississippi Partisan Rangers, and to have become a part of Forrest's Old Regiment Tennessee Cavalry, in compliance with S. O. No. 28, Headquarters Cavalry, District of Mississippi and East Louisiana, dated February 13, 1865; Mississippi 2 (J. G. Ballentine's Regiment of Cavalry) Partisan Rangers Private (Captain Edward E. Porter's Partisan Company – see Rev. Edward E. Porter sketch) Corporal Private Company C; per Company Muster Roll for April 21 to August 1, 1862, enlisted May 7, 1862, Memphis (Somerville on some muster roll cards) by Captain Porter; per Company Muster Roll for July 31 to October 31, 1862, dated October 31, 1862, Corporal and remarks: Absent without leave since 29 November; per Company Muster Roll for October 31, 1862, to February 28, 1863, Private and remarks: Deserted November 24, 1862; per Company Muster Roll for September & October, 1863, Private and remarks: Joined from desertion October 20. Absent from November 30 to October 20; present on all later company muster rolls with last one for September & October 1864; per Daily Burial Record Book died age 63.

Martin, Hugh Bradford   Buried May 3, 1894   Miller Circle 79, #1
Ordnance Officer General & Staff Officer, Captain & Ordnance Officer General Forrest's Brigade, appointed Chief Ordnance Officer July 15, 1863; Captain on staff of General George W. Dibrell *(Confederate Staff Officers 1861-1865* by Joseph H. Crute, Jr., Derwent Books 1982); per sketch in Mathes book (includes photograph) born August 9, 1838, in Columbia, Tennessee, practicing law in Memphis when joined Forrest's Cavalry, soon promoted to ordnance officer on General Forrest's staff (1862-63), appointed Chief of Ordnance July 15, 1863, latter part of 1863, was transferred to staff of General Starnes who was soon after killed at Shelbyville when General Dibrell succeeded in command where remained to end of War, was part of President Davis escort after War and when left the escort was paid in coin (last disbursement of the Confederate States of America); not found in *Tennesseans in the Civil War*; large Martin Stone and circle grave stone: Born August 7, 1838 Died May 1, 1894; service, birth and death dates inscribed on "In Memory Of" stone located in walk around Confederate Soldiers Rest Monument; died age 56 per Daily Burial Record Book.

Martin, James Henry   Buried March 28, 1897   Lenow Circle 79, #8
Aide de Camp Staff of General William H. Jackson Lieutenant; per General and Staff officers compiled service record rolls 1 Lieutenant & Aide de Camp to William H. Jackson, from State of Tennessee, appointed April 18, 1864, confirmed May 11, 1864, to rank March 1, 1864; Tennessee 7 Cavalry Regiment Private Company A ("Memphis Light Dragoons" Tennessee 6 Cavalry Battalion Company A), per Company Muster Roll dated August 18, 1861, enlisted May 16, 1861, in Memphis, Tennessee age 20; per Company Muster Roll for May 16, 1861, to October 31, 1862, absent, detailed October 14 to assist A.A.G; per sketch in Mathes book "became a member of "Logwood's Light Dragoons" before hostilities began, and on May 16, 1861, almost the entire was mustered into service of the Confederate States Army ...." and "(A)t the reorganization of the army after the ninety-day enlistments expired, the company was reorganized as Company A, Seventh Tennessee Cavalry, under that brilliant commander Colonel W. H. Jackson, and when he became general the company was detached from the regiment to act as his escort. About February 1863, Mr. Martin was promoted upon the recommendation of General Jackson, for meritorious performance of duty, to the rank of first lieutenant, and assigned to duty on his staff. In December 1863, Captain James Crump, aid-de-camp to General Jackson, was killed in battle near Sharon, Miss., and again, at the request of General Jackson, Lieutenant Martin was appointed to succeed him, and still holds his commission as such, and served in that capacity until the close of the war."; joined Confederate Historical Association in 1884; not found in Young's book; Wood Hill & Martin lot stone and large monument with east side inscription: James Henry Martin Born Oct 2, 1840 Died March 26, 1897; died age 56 per Daily Burial Record Book.

Martin, John C.   Buried June 12, 1914   Turley 577, # 9
Tennessee 12 (Green's) Cavalry Regiment Private Company E, per Company Muster Roll dated October 11, 1862, enlisted October 11, 1862, in Shelby County, Tennessee; Company E subsequently became 3rd Company H Tennessee 3 (Forrest's) Cavalry

Regiment when the regiments were consolidated and surrendered with Forrest's Regiment and paroled at Gainesville, Alabama May 11, 1865, indicating residence as Shelby County, Tennessee; filed for Tennessee Confederate Pension (S4579) and indicated on application that was born December 2, 1843, in Shelby County, Tennessee; upon his death his widow, Emma N. Martin, filed for a Tennessee Confederate Pension (W5663 – note file found under his pension file); sketch in Mathes book; small grave stone with name and dates December 2, 1843, and June 11, 1914.

Martin John Donelson   Buried November 19, 1874   Fowler 274, #6
Confederate 2 Infantry Regiment Colonel; first enlisted as Captain Company E ("The Hickory Rifles") Tennessee 154 Senior Infantry Regiment and elected Major May 1861; per 154 Senior Infantry Regiment record May 5, 1863, muster roll remarks: first Captain, then Major 154 Senior Infantry Regiment, Colonel and Brigadier General and killed at Battle of Corinth; recommended for Brigadier General for conduct at Battle of Shiloh and given an appointment as Acting Brigadier General but never commissioned; authorized to raise a regiment which became Mississippi 25 Infantry Regiment and appointed Colonel November 16, 1861; Regiment designated Confederate 2 Infantry Regiment January 31, 1862; Regiment disbanded May 8, 1862; next placed in command of the 4 Brigade, 1 Division, Army of the West; killed on the first day of Battle of Corinth October 3, 1862; no records found General and Staff records and not the John D. Martin in General and Staff records who was an Acting Assistant Surgeon; per sketch in *More Generals in Gray* born Davidson County, Tennessee August 18, 1830, served in Mexican War, earned medical degree in 1852 from University of Pennsylvania and became prominent physician in Memphis, and appointed Brigadier General from Mississippi in 1865 according to *Confederate Veteran*, which was three years after his death, when Major General Hardee promoted him to Acting Brigadier General on April 29, 1862, as indicated in a Telegram in possession of family, however, Major General Price in an October 20, 1862, report on the Battle of Corinth made it clear that he died a colonel; not listed in the *Memorandum relative to the General Officers Appointed by the President in the Armies of the Confederate States - 1861-1865* compiled from Official Records by the Military Secretary's Office, U. S. War Department 1905; not listed in *Generals in Gray*; obituary in the November 4, 1862, *Memphis Daily Appeal,* page 2, column 6; originally buried in Mississippi; doctor, moved-in from Mississippi and died age 32 per Daily Burial Record Book; large grave stone: JOHN DONELSON MARTIN, BORN AUGUST 18, 1830, DAVIDSON COUNTY, TENN. CONF BRIG GEN, KILLED LEADING CHARGE AT BATTLE OF CORINTH, MS OCTOBER 3, 1862. GREAT-GRAND-SON OF COL JOHN DONELSON PIONEER LEADER RIVER EXPEDITION FROM VA TO TN 1779. SERVED IN US ARMY IN WAR WITH MEXICO. 1852 M.D. UNIV PA, CAME TO MEMPHIS AND PRACTICED MEDICINE. SURGEON, MEMPHIS HOSPITAL; PROFESSOR, MEMPHIS MEDICAL COLLEGE. PRESIDENT, MEMPHIS BOARD OF HEALTH, 1858. 1857, MARRIED ROSA A WHITE, DAUGHTER OF COL C C WHITE. 1860 CAPTAIN, HICKORY RIFLES IN FIRST MEMPHIS REGT, CSA., COL 2 CONF REGT. WHILE STILL COL COMMANDED BRIGADES ON NUMEROUS OCCASIONS. COMMANDED BOWEN'S BRIGADE, BATTLE OF SHILOH, AND FOURTH BRIGADE AT IUKA AND CORINTH; not listed in Elmwood 1874 book as Confederate soldier buried in Elmwood who was a citizen of Memphis or vicinity; listed in chapter on Generals; listed in "Touring Historic Elmwood Cemetery" Brochure (January 2000) #7 but not listed as General in its predecessor in "Touring historic Elmwood Cemetery" (Brochure and Map of Historic Gravesites); sketch #1 in Elmwood *Civil War Tour* booklet (2012).

Maury, Richard Brooke   Buried March 18, 1919   Chapel Hill 128, #7
Mississippi 28 Cavalry Regiment, Surgeon; commissioned February 24, 1862; per sketch in Mathes book born in Georgetown, DC February 5, 1834, M. D. degree from University of New York, after hospital career went to Natchez, Mississippi and later Port Gibson, Mississippi, joined Confederate service as Surgeon of Mississippi 28 Cavalry, after one year service transferred (per documents in compiled service record transfer approved December 16, 1862, by Edward P. Jones, Major Commanding, 28 Mississippi Regiment) to hospital duty where remained until close of War, 1867 returned to Memphis, first married in Port Gibson, Mississippi to Jane T. Ellett daughter of Honorable Henry T. Ellett, had a family of six children, she died in Memphis in 1875, and next married Jennie B. Poston and they had seven children; died age 85 per Daily Burial Record Book; stone Feb 1834 Mch 1919.

May, Charles   Buried February 25,1862   Turley 193, #3
Tennessee 3 (Forrest's) Cavalry Regiment Captain Company C; enlisted September 1, 1861, Memphis; per September & October 1862, muster roll remarks: killed at Donelson February 15, 1862; per article in the February 25, 1862, *Memphis Daily Appeal* shot in left hand and left side of chest, which caused death, and body arrived in Memphis February 23, 1862; killed at Fort Donelson, Tennessee per Daily Burial Record Book; originally buried Chapel Hill 110, #5 and moved to Turley 193; funeral notice in February 25, 1862, *Memphis Daily Appeal*; not found in Lindsley's Annals Official Memorial Roll for unit but identified as Captain Company C as first organized in unit narrative; listed in Elmwood 1874 book as Confederate soldier buried in Elmwood who was citizen of Memphis or vicinity with rank of Captain and sketch; per sketch born Rockingham County, Virginia 1818, and came to Memphis 1854, 2 Lieutenant of Charles McDonald's Company in 1861 then Captain of Forrest Rangers, fell while leading charge upon Federal battery at Fort Donelson; mentioned by Dr. S. H. Ford in his address on the occasion to commemorate (Confederate Memorial Day) Confederates buried at Elmwood on April 26, 1866, (see article "Honors To The Memory Of The Hero Dead" in the April 27, 1866, *Memphis Daily Appeal*, page 3, column 1); short history included in the May 12, 1888, *Memphis Daily Appeal*, page 2, column 1, article "Loving Tributes" on that day's "Decorating the Confederate Graves" that includes the inscription on his marble monument: Capt. Charles May, of Forrest's Rangers, Died February 15, 1862, aged 44 years. Fell on the battlefield at Fort Donelson. Brave, generous and firm, he fell while leading a charge on the enemy's battery. His last words were "Onward, my brave boys, Onward to Victory!"; grave stone: born February 10, 1818 and died February 15, 1862, aged 44 years.

May, James   Buried April 25, 1862   Chapel Hill 1, Vault
Battles Regiment Private; believed to be James F. May Tennessee 55 (McKoin's) Infantry Regiment Private Company I and Tennessee 44 Consolidated Infantry Regiment Private Company I (Tennessee 44 Consolidated Infantry Regiment was formed by the consolidation of the 44 and 55 Infantry Regiments about April 18, 1862); per both compiled service records enlisted December 30, 1861 Nashville; per 44 Regiment March 1 to June 30, 1862, muster roll remarks: died of a wound 14 May 1862; per narrative on Tennessee 55 Infantry Regiment in Lindsley's Annals, page 532, "among its killed at Shiloh were James May and Napoleon B. Hyde of Nashville, two as gallant young men as ever shouldered a musket...."; per casualty list in Lindsley's Annals, Tennessee 44 Infantry Regiment Company I died May 14, 1862; Battles Regiment, wounded and in Leatherman's Vault per Daily Burial Record Book; not found Tennessee 20 (Battle's) Infantry Regiment or Alabama 3 (Battle's) Infantry Regiment which has a John May, Company G.

McClanahan, John Reid   Buried July 16, 1865   Fowler Lot 128, #2
Memphis Daily Appeal Editor and Proprietor; eulogized and grave stone dedicated October 11, 1998 - see *The Commercial Appeal* Memphis October 12, 1996, and Ceremony program on file in Cemetery Office (note ceremony also honored Benjamin Franklin Dill (business manager and quarter-partner) and wife Carolina Dill who are both buried in Elmwood Cemetery - see sketch herein); grave stone: Born in Laurens District, SC, Died in Memphis June 29, 1865, aged 46, Leader of the Memphis Appeal's Great Civil War Run 1862-65, Co-Proprietor, Co-Editor, *Memphis Daily Appeal* December 18, 1848 - April 22, 1851, Sole Proprietor Editor in Chief April 23, 1851 - June 29, 1865, "The public actions of public men are public property and those who would censure the Press for a candid scrutiny and a fair criticism of those actions has lost his allegiance to liberty and has a forehead ready for the pressure of the despot's heel (March 30, 1862)." The quote is found in editorial titled "The Revolution, Liberty, and The Press" in *Memphis Daily Appeal* Sunday March 30, 1862; often referred to as "Colonel" but no service record found; see "One Hundred Years of The Commercial Appeal" The Story of the Great Romance in American Journalism 1840 to 1940 (Printed at *The Commercial Appeal* 1940 by The Memphis Publishing Company) for story of "Great Civil War Run"; died from fall from window at the Gayoso House, page 46; fatally beaten behind the Gayoso House on June 29, 1865, per Ceremony program; served in Mexican War; sketch in Elmwood book; sketch #5 in Elmwood *Civil War Tour* booklet (2012).

McCollough, Hugh   Buried February 10, 1872   Fowler 606, #25
Tennessee 1 Heavy Artillery Private Company C, per Company Muster Roll for May and June, 1862, enlisted May 27, 1862, Memphis with remarks detailed to tugboat April 20, 1862, at Fort Pillow and per Company Muster Roll for July and August, 1862, remarks has not been heard of since the regiment formed and should be considered deserter and dropped from the rolls; per death notice in February 10, 1872, *Memphis Daily Appeal*, page 1, column 7, "… was well known in this city, and was one of the oldest steamboatmen on the Arkansas river. At the time of his death he was acting as mate of the Government snagboat S. H. Long."; listed in Elmwood 1874 book as Confederate soldier buried in Elmwood who was citizen of Memphis or vicinity with name spelled "McCullough"; died congestion age 37 per Daily Burial Record Book; no grave stone.

McCormick, Dr. Charles   Buried July 16, 1861   Chapel Hill 15 Ayres Vault, #2
Tennessee 2 (Walker's) Infantry Regiment Assistant Surgeon; appears on a Field and Staff Muster Roll dated July 23, 1863, with remarks: appointed May 1861. Died June 1861; per death article in the July 18, 1861, *Memphis Daily Appeal*, page 2, column 8, died on the 15th aged twenty-five, from Virginia and "A few weeks previous to his illness, he had been at Fort Wright, Tenn., as assistant surgeon to the Second regiment of Tennessee Volunteers. The surgeon-general of the State having offered him a transfer to his staff and a permanent situation during the war, the position would have been accepted had he lived."; died from Dysentery per Daily Burial Record Book.

McCroskey, Hiram Alonzo   Buried April 19, 1910   Turley 1086, #7
Mississippi 9 Infantry Regiment, Private Company B, enlisted March 28, 1861, paroled May 1865; per compiled service record mustered into service February 16, 1861 Holly Springs, MS, age 18, remarks druggist, other card has Jr. and enlisted March 27, 1862 Holly Springs, muster roll card November and December 1861 remarks Nurse at Hospital, last Old Company B on muster roll card October 31, 1861 to March 31, 1862, new Company C on muster roll card May & June 1862, wounded battle of Chickamauga, GA September 20, 1863, muster roll card March & April 1864, detailed by command of General Johnston, clerk in Post Commandant office, Atlanta, GA, POW roll dated Grenada, MS May 17, 1865; per sketch in Mathes book (both editions, large edition includes photograph) born July 9, 1842, in Shelby County, Tennessee, enlisted in Company B 9 Mississippi Infantry Regiment, went to Pensacola and remained twelve months, enlisted in the new Mississippi 9 Infantry Regiment and became first sergeant Company C at Corinth, Mississippi 1862, wounded three times in battles of Murfreesboro and Chickamauga and as General Bragg retreated out of Corinth, Mississippi, at Dalton, Georgia was detailed for office duty with General Marcus J. Wright commanding the post at Atlanta and served as clerk until surrender at Grenada, Mississippi May 17, 1865, when paroled, and joined Confederate Historical Association September 15 1891; died April 18 per *Confederate Veteran*, Volume XIX, April 1911, No. 4, page 174, "The Last Roll, Death of Confederates in Memphis, Tennessee" who died during 1910 and were members of the Confederate Historical Association, Camp 28, U.C.V., Bivouac 18, C.V., of Memphis, Tennessee; died age 67 per Daily Burial Record Book; circle grave stone; July 9, 1842 April 18, 1910.

McDonald, Charles   Buried March 15, 1864   Chapel Hill 480, #7
Tennessee 3 (Forrest's) Cavalry Regiment Major/Captain Company B; enlisted June 3, 1862, Memphis by Colonel N. B. Forrest;

per May and June 1863, muster roll remarks: promoted Major June 15, 1863; per roster card dated May 25, 1864, for McDonald's Battalion (Tennessee 3 Forrest's Cavalry Regiment) killed October 7, 1863; per book *First with the Most* killed at Farmington, Tennessee; per Daily Burial Record Book killed age 39; not found in Cemetery Chapel Hill book - the Charles McDonald in Chapel Hill book Lot 480 died age 30 October 9, 1886, so would have been too young for war (possibly son); listed in Elmwood 1874 book as Confederate soldier buried in Elmwood who was citizen of Memphis or vicinity; Major inscribed on grave stone; mentioned by Dr. S. H. Ford in his address on the occasion to commemorate (Confederate Memorial Day) Confederates buried at Elmwood on April 26, 1866, (see articles "The Confederate Dead" in the *Public Ledger* (Memphis), April 27, 1866, page 3, column 2, and "Honors To The Memory Of The Hero Dead" in the April 27, 1866, *Memphis Daily Appeal*, page 3, column 1).

McDowell, John Hugh   Buried February 21, 1927   Turley 1604-05, #1
Tennessee 12 Infantry Regiment Private Company H; per Company Muster Roll for July 31 to October 31, 1861, enlisted May 28, 1861, Jackson, Tennessee; per Company Muster Roll for March 1 to June 16, 1862, promoted to 1 Corporal May 8, 1862, by reorganization but was discharged 16 June; Mississippi 2 Partisan Rangers, Colonel J. G. Ballentine's Regiment of Cavalry, Sergeant Company E, enlisted August 11, 1862 and served with Hood's Army of Tennessee when it moved into Tennessee in November and December 1864; after Hood's retreat from Tennessee and General Forrest and his troops' withdrawal into Mississippi, Company became Company K of the Tennessee 19 & 20 Consolidated Cavalry Regiment by ordered of General Forrest on February 13, 1865, to consolidate his troops; paroled per Roll of Prisoners of War dated Gainesville, Alabama, May 10, 1865; author of *History of the McDowells, Erwins, Irwins and Connections (Being a compilation from various sources)*. Memphis, C. H. Johnston & Co. Publishers, 1918.; per sketch in his book, page 91, "born at Trenton, Tenn., Dec. 12, 1843. He was educated at Andrew College. On May 10, 1861, at the age of seventeen years, he entered the Confederate army, serving through the war, and was paroled at Gainsville (sic), Ala., May 11, 1865, under Gen. Bedford Forrest. After the war he settled on a farm near Humboldt. In 1877 he removed to a farm three miles west of Union City, Tenn., where he lived for forty years. In 1883 he was elected a member of the Tennessee Legislature. In 1885 he was elected State Senator to represent Lake, Dyer and Obion Counties, and re-elected to the Senate in 1887. In 1905 he was again elected a member of the Tennessee Legislature. He married Mary Emma Sandeford, daughter of Nathan Davis and Frances Maria Sandeford, at Humboldt, Tenn., Nov. 2, 1865. (See Avent Line.) He was three times elected Major General of the Tennessee Division United Confederate Veterans, and is now Brigadier General, Tennessee Division, Forrest Cavalry."; sketch in *Who's Who in Tennessee, A Biographical Reference Book of Notable Tennesseans To-Day*, Paul & Douglass Publishers, Memphis, 1911, page 559, under Farmers.

McDowell, Samuel Irwin   Buried June 19, 1888   Turley 1065, #1
Confederate Cavalry (no compiled service record found) per sketch in brother John Hugh McDowell's book *History of the McDowells, Erwins, Irwins and Connections (Being a compilation from various sources)*. Memphis, C. H. Johnston & Co. Publishers, 1918., page 91, and "born near Trenton, Tenn., Sept. 4, 1848. educated at Andrew College. At the age of fourteen he joined General Bedford Forrest's Confederate cavalry, when the command made a raid into Tennessee to Union City and Paducah, Ky. On the army's return through Tennessee the commanders thought the lad was too young to withstand the hardships of war life, and left him at home. After the war he moved to Memphis and opened an abstract office- A few years later he was chosen Chancery Clerk, which he held until his death, June 7. 1888. On Dec. 12, 1883, he married Miss Bessie McGowan, of Memphis, Tenn. No issue."; brother of John Hugh McDowell and Judger William Wallace McDowell (see sketches herein); sketch in Goodspeed's Shelby County History, page 1007; second initial "J" and died age 38 in Daily Burial Record Book and not found in Cemetery computer index.

McDowell, Judge William Wallace   Buried May 1, 1904   Evergreen 35, #4
Tennessee 12 Infantry Regiment 1 Lieutenant Company H; per Company Muster Roll for July 31 to October 31, 1861, enlisted May 28, 1861, Jackson, Tennessee; elected Captain but was dropped at the reorganization of the Regiment May 8, 1862; commissioned by the Secretary of War May 28, 1862, to raise an independent cavalry company that eventually attached to the Mississippi 2 Partisan Rangers, Colonel J. G. Ballentine's Regiment of Cavalry, as Company E, and served with Hood's Army of Tennessee when it moved into Tennessee in November and December 1864; after Hood's retreat from Tennessee and General Forrest and his troops' withdrawal into Mississippi, he ordered on February 13, 1865, a consolidation of his troops; his company became Company K of the Tennessee 19 & 20 Consolidated Cavalry Regiment; surrendered and signed a Parole of Honor on May 13, 1865, at Gainesville, Alabama; extensive sketch in Mathes book (enlarged edition page 22); brother of John Hugh McDowell, who served with him during the entire War, and Samuel Irwin McDowell (see sketches herein); per sketch in brother John Hugh McDowell's book *History of the McDowells, Erwins, Irwins and Connections (Being a compilation from various sources)*. Memphis, C. H. Johnston & Co. Publishers, 1918., page 87, "born June 26, 1833, near Trenton, Tenn., and died at Memphis, Tenn., April 30, 1904. He was educated at Andrew College, Trenton, and other schools of Gibson County. After graduating at Andrew College he attended the Lebanon Law School, and while there joined the Cumberland Presbyterian Church, of which he was a consistent member until his death. At the outbreak of the Civil War, May 10, 1861, he entered the Confederate Army, joining Company H, of the 12th Tennessee Infantry Regiment, commanded by Col. W. B. Russell. He was in the beginning elected first lieutenant of Capt. Ben H. Sandeford's company. At Belmont, Mo., in a battle between General Polk and General Grant, he was shot down and carried from the battlefield supposed to be fatally wounded. He was sent home, and under the gentle nursing of a noble mother he recovered and returned to the army. After the Battle of Shiloh he was elected captain, and was always found at the forefront leading his men. At the close of the war he was in command of General Bell's escort, Forrest Cavalry. After the war he

resumed the practice of law, locating in Memphis, Tenn., in 1867, where he was county attorney for five years, Chancellor eight years, State Senator two years and was also appointed special Supreme Court judge."

McEllroy, Virginius Albert   Buried May 20, 1891   South Grove 165, #4
Mississippi 21 Infantry Regiment Private Company A; enlisted July 20, 1861, Vicksburg, Mississippi; per July & August 1863 muster roll remarks: taken prisoner Pennsylvania; per organization record enlisted May 15, 1861 Vicksburg age 28, born New York (born Norfolk, Virginia per great great grandson John "Roy" Garrett), occupation of Clerk, residence Edwards Depot, captured Gettysburg, Pennsylvania July 4, 1863, appears on register of Prisoners of War Fort Delaware, Delaware, and discharged January 30, 1864; took Oath of Allegiance at Fort Delaware which record indicates place of residence Brooklyn, New York, very ill with chronic diarrhea and released by order of Secretary of war; grave stone has unit information and dates 1833 1891; originally buried South Grove Lot 116½, #4 and moved March 26, 1903; died age 50 per Daily Burial Record Books but this does not fit dates on grave stone; name spelled "McElroy" in some Cemetery records; not listed in Cemetery computer index.

McFarland, Louis Burchette   Buried March 29, 1926   Turley 1072, #2
Tennessee 9 Infantry Regiment 2 Lieutenant Company A; enlisted May 23, 1861 Jackson, Tennessee; per sketch in Mathes book (both editions) enlisted as Private Company A Tennessee 9 Infantry Regiment May 24, 1861, became Sergeant-Major, appointed 2 Lieutenant in April 1863, served as Volunteer Aide de Camp to General George Maney, wounded in left arm at Shiloh, in all battles of Cheatham's Division except Franklin, captured at West Point, Georgia April 16, 1865, and released the following month, returned to Memphis, practiced law and joined Confederate Historical Association August 13, 1869; per enlarged edition born April 7, 1843, in Haywood County, Tennessee, attending University of Florence, Alabama when war started, promoted to Sergeant-Major on second day of Battle of Shiloh which rank held one year then appointed 2 Lieutenant, after War read law at Memphis, graduated from Cumberland University at Lebanon, Tennessee in 1867, appointed judge August 1895, generally known as Major McFarland among ex-Confederate, joined Confederate Historical Association August 13, 1869, and was orator of the day at Confederate Memorial celebration May 6, 1871, at Elmwood Cemetery; on staff (Assistant Adjutant General) of General Bennett H. Young, Commander in Chief United Confederate Veterans, 1913, see picture in *Confederate Veteran*, Volume XXIII, No. 6, June 1915; sketch in *Tennessee, The Volunteer State, 1769-1923*, Volume III, page 31; died age 82 per Daily Burial Record Book; born April 7, 1843 and died March 28, 1926 on monument.

McGee, Dr. John Preston   Buried February 4, 1890   Turley 1152, #2
Surgeon General & Staff Officers Cheatham's Corps Major; compiled service records found in Officers Field and Staff Muster Rolls; appears on a Register of Appointments, Confederate States Army, appointed Assistant Surgeon October 1, 1861, Tennessee 12 Infantry Regiment, with remarks: Promoted to Surgeon May 26, 1863; appears on a Report of Medical Officers on duty in Receiving Hospital or General Hospital No. 9, Richmond, Virginia dated March 1, 1862, with remarks: Contract $80 per month. On duty; appears on a Register of Appointments, Confederate States Army, with remarks: September 28, 1864, "Floater" to Cheatham's Division; appears on a Register of the Army of Tennessee containing a Roster of Surgeons and Assistant Surgeons with remarks: Appointed by Secretary of War August 25, 1863, to rank from 26 May, 1863. Passed Board May 26, 1863. May 31, 1864, Cheatham's Division Hospital. December 1864, left with wounded at Pulaski, Tennessee; appears on a Register of Prisoners of War, Department of Cumberland, captured Pulaski, Tennessee, December 25, 1864, forwarded to Louisville, Kentucky February 18, 1865, and remarks; to be forwarded to Camp Chase, Ohio in accordance with Telegraphic orders from Commissary General of Prisoners dated July, 28, 1864; appears on a Roll of Prisoners of War paroled at Camp Chase, Ohio, and transferred to Fort Delaware, Delaware, March 17, 1865; appears on a Roll of Prisoners of War at Fort Delaware forwarded to Fortress Monroe, Virginia to be sent through the lines March 10, 1865; appears on a Register of prisoners of war at Military Prison, Camp Hamilton, Virginia, confined March 12, 1865, released March 14, 1865, with remarks: sent to Point of Exchange; appears on a List dated April 30, 1865, of Medical Officers, etc., paroled at Greensboro, North Carolina, May 2, 1865; per sketch in Goodspeed's Shelby County History, page 1010, a native of Henry County, Tennessee and born in 1835 (March 7, 1835), 1861 graduated as M. D. from the Jefferson Medical College, Philadelphia, May, 1861, joined Company F, Twelfth Regiment, Provisional Army of Tennessee, and when the company was organized as regular soldiers of the Confederate Army he was made assistant surgeon, promoted by degrees to the highest ranks in that department, was once captured but remained in prison only a short time, after the war practiced medicine at Hickman, Ky., a short time, and in April, 1867, located at Trenton, Tennessee, September, 1883, came to Memphis, and connected with the Tennessee Medical Association,; died age 56 per Daily Burial Record Book.

McHenry, Eli Bass   Buried December 3, 1918   Turley 1051½, #6
Missouri R. C. Wood's Cavalry Regiment (first known as 14 Cavalry Battalion) Lieutenant Adjutant; signed Parole of Honor June 8, 1865, Shreveport, Louisiana; per biography in *Confederate Military History, Extended Edition*, Volume X Tennessee, page 605: after the surrender in June, 1865, returned home to find anti-Confederate sentiment predominant and promptly removed to Memphis upon being warned to leave his native city, at Memphis served fifteen years as deputy clerk of the chancery court, practiced law from 1882 to 1898, with the exception of six years as clerk and master of chancery, since January, 1898, cashier of the Memphis national bank, held the rank of major on the staff of the late Gen. A. J. Vaughan, major-general commanding the division of Tennessee, United Confederate Veterans; per sketch in Mathes book, page156: was one of the early members of the Confederate Relief and Historical Association, and after dropping out for a time rejoined the organization January 8, 1895.

McKinney, John Fletcher   Buried October 6, 1911   Chapel Hill Circle 38, #9

Tennessee 3 (Forrest's Old) Cavalry Regiment Private 2 Company A; originally enlisted Tennessee 154 Senior Infantry Regiment Private (1st) Company B ("Bluff City Grays") and per Company Muster-in Roll dated August 13, 1861, enlisted May 14, 1861, Randolph age 23; per Tennessee 3 (Forrest's) Cavalry Regiment Company Muster Roll for January 1 to July 1, 1862, enlisted May 4, 1861, Randolph; name appears on Roll of Prisoners of War paroled at Gainesville, Alabama, May 11, 1865, resident of Memphis, Tennessee; sketch in Mathes book (page158); listed in "A COMPLETE ROSTER OF THE BLUFF CITY GREYS" located in the Memphis Room of the Memphis/Shelby County Public Library and Information Center Central Library; listed as member of Bluff City Grays in *Reminiscences of the Civil War* by John Hallum, Tunnah & Pittard printers, 1903; listed with indication "Died suddenly in Memphis, October 5th, 1911" in "Captain Thomas F. Pattison's History of the Bluff City Grays" with names as appeared on First Muster Roll and those who joined after September 1, 1861, to surrender, 1865, which document found in the Tennessee Confederate Pension Application (W10343) of Minnie Swayne Wilkins, widow of William G. Wilkins (see sketch infra); see also Notes of Interest - Bluff City Grays; per Tennessee Confederate Pension (S10695) application filed November 21, 1908, (Accepted) born in Ohio March 21, 1839; brother of William Barkley McKinney – see sketch next below; died age 73 per Daily Burial Record Book.

McKinney, William Barkley   Buried January 21, 1885   Chapel Hill Circle 38, #5

Tennessee 3 (Forrest's Old) Cavalry Regiment Private 2 Company A; per Company Muster Roll dated May 14, 1864, enlisted April 29, 1864, Jackson, Tennessee; name appears on Roll of Prisoners of War paroled at Gainesville, Alabama May 11, 1865, resident of Memphis, Tennessee; appears to have first enlisted in Tennessee 3 (Forrest's Old) Cavalry Regiment Private 1 Company B and per Company Muster Roll dated October 30, 1862, enlisted March 10, 1862, Memphis and present on Company Muster Roll for September 1 to December 31, 1862, but other record cards in file; note that 1 Company B transferred to Alabama 4 (Russell's) Cavalry Regiment to become Company A when Regiment organized November 1862, but no record for him in Regiment compiled service record rolls; listed in "A COMPLETE ROSTER OF THE BLUFF CITY GREYS" located in the Memphis Room of the Memphis/Shelby County Public Library and Information Center Central Library with notation that joined April 2, 1864; not listed as member of Bluff City Grays in *Reminiscences of the Civil War* by John Hallum, Tunnah & Pittard printers, 1903; listed ("William M. McKinney") in "Captain Thomas F. Pattison's History of the Bluff City Grays" with names as appeared on First Muster Roll and those who joined after September 1, 1861, to surrender, 1865, (listed as joining after September 1, 1861) which document found in the Tennessee Confederate Pension Application (W10343) of Minnie Swayne Wilkins, widow of William G. Wilkins (see sketch infra); see also Notes of Interest - Bluff City Grays; brother of John Fletcher McKinney – see sketch next above; member of the Confederate Historical Association but no sketch in Mathes book per NAMES WITHOUT SKETCHES chapter pages 232-233; death reported and K. of H. Funeral Notice in the January 21, 1885, *Memphis Daily Appeal*, page 1, column 8.

McLean, William Love   Buried August 14, 1917   Fowler 684, #7

Arkansas 12 Battalion Sharp Shooters Lieutenant Company B and Arkansas 12 Infantry Regiment Lieutenant Company B (records found McLean, W. C); per Company Muster Roll for January & February 1863, enlisted January 1, 1862, New Madrid, Missouri, with remarks: Detailed as adjutant General of Brigade; appears on a Report of Absent Officers dated December 28, 1862, with remarks: Detailed by order of General Van Dorn November 29. Assigned to signal corps; name appears as signature to a Roll of Prisoners of War paroled at Johnson's Island, O., and forwarded to City Point, Va., for Exchange, Feb. 24, 1865, captured Big Black May 17, 1863; sketch in Mathes book page 158, "left Memphis, Tenn., bound for Pensacola, Fla., to join the Fifteenth Mississippi Regiment, April 1, 1861; found that regiment full and returned. The Twelfth Arkansas Regiment was then camped near his father's house and hundreds were down with the measles. Ladies organized an aid society to nurse them. His mother was elected president. Colonel E. W. Gantt, through gratitude, offered to fill the first vacancy with young McLean if he would join, and he did so near New Madrid, Mo.; was assigned to duty as operator in the signal corps under Captain C. C. Cummings. General Beauregard's staff. In a few weeks he was made lance sergeant and ordered to Corinth, Miss. When the army fell back to Tupelo was recommended to General Maury and appointed First Lieutenant Twelfth Battalion Arkansas Sharpshooters, four companies of fifty picked men in each, W. L. Cabell's Brigade, Maury's Division, Price's Corps, Army Mississippi and East Louisiana. Soon after this Captain Cunningham was promoted to major, and McLean was by him recommended to General Earl Van Dorn and by him recommended to the Confederate War Department; was appointed captain of signal corps and assigned to General Maury's staff. The former captain of Company B, Twelfth Battalion, Jas. A. Ashford, was ordered to Arkansas to recruit. Captain McLean was again assigned to the company. After participating in all the battles from Corinth to Big Black, Miss., Company B was cut down to seven men and one officer, and surrendered May 17, 1863, to General Grant's army, that being the day he invested Vicksburg. Captain McLean was sent to Johnson's Island and arrived there June 5, 1863; occupied room No. 18, block 3, and with his bunk mate, John H. Morgan, slept on the same two-foot bunk, grinding their wallet of straw—filled once—into powder. On the 24th day of February, 1865, left the island on the ice over Sandusky Bay to Sandusky; thence to Pittsburg, Baltimore, down the Chesapeake Bay, Fortress Monroe, Hampton Roads, Norfolk and up the James river to Richmond; paroled there March 1, 1865. Went through Virginia, North and South Carolina, Georgia, to Opelika, Ala.; walked from there to Columbus, Miss., across the entire State of Alabama, and walked most of the way from there to Memphis, arriving May 15, 1865. Went to farming and gardening at once; followed it fourteen years. In 1879 became a commercial traveler, and is engaged in that pursuit now. Joined this Association January 12, 1888, and is an enthusiastic member of Company A, Confederate Veterans."; biography in *Confederate Military History, Extended Edition*, Volume X Tennessee, page 605; per Tennessee Confederate Pension application filed June 20, 1912, (Accepted) born Shelby County, Tennessee and resident of Tennessee since October 4, 1842; per Tennessee Death Certificate born October 4, 1842, birthplace Ky., died August 13, 1917, cause Cystitis, age 74.

McLendon, Andrew J.   Buried June 8, 1904   South Grove 158½, #3
Confederate 8 Cavalry Regiment Private Company C (2 Regiment Mississippi and Alabama Cavalry); enlisted January 10, 1862, Columbus, Mississippi; wounded and captured at Crab Orchard, Kentucky, October 10, 1862, and leg amputated; per biography in *Confederate Military History, Extended Edition*, Volume X Tennessee, page 608: served under Wheeler in the battles and skirmishes of his command until after the battle of Perryville, when his service came to an end when during the retreat from Kentucky following that battle, while the cavalry was daily in action holding back the pursuing foe, regiment was ambuscaded by the Federals, and during the desperate fight which resulted was shot three times and his horse riddled with balls, two of his wounds were scalp injuries of little harm, but the third was made by a ball that struck the left knee, plowed through the leg, shattering the bones as it went, and lodged in his saddle, after falling into the hands of the enemy was carried to a field hospital where the leg was amputated and when able to be moved was carried to Camp Chase, Ohio, where held until June 6, 1863, when taken to City Point for exchange, on reaching home found that his horse had also survived and had been sent home, and from the proceeds of the sale of this animal and two or three others was enabled to attend school at Covington, and prepare for business life went to Memphis in 1866, found employment as bookkeeper and otherwise in the city offices and sheriff's office, and in spite of his crippled condition became so widely known as a useful and honorable citizen was elected sheriff of the county in 1888, and twice re-elected, in 1894 elected county trustee, an office held two years, member of the historical association, and an honorary member of Company A, Confederate veterans, and was born at Houston, Miss., September 10, 1844.

Mellon, Alf M.
Listed in Elmwood 1874 book as Confederate soldier buried in Elmwood who was citizen of Memphis or vicinity; possibly Alf M. Mellon, nervous prostration age 32, buried October 5, 1873, South Grove 237 (originally Lot 39) #6, no stone; no Confederate service information in death notice (died October 4, 1873) in the Sunday October 5, 1873, *Memphis Daily Appeal*, page 1, column 6; no Alf M. Mellon found in Confederate index book but possibly A. Mellon Kentucky 3 Mounted Infantry Private Company K which record has a single card indicating enlisted July 19, 1861, Camp Boone age 24 but no other information.

Miller, George Washington   Buried May 29, 1909   Turley 966½, #1
Tennessee 1 Heavy Artillery, Lieutenant Company D (Company K, second companies C, D & L on compiled service record cards), enlisted August 6, 1861, at Memphis, Tennessee at age 28, per Muster Roll for May & June, 1862, elected Lieutenant from Sergeant May 10, 1862, at reorganization and assigned to duty as Lieutenant in Company D at consolidation June 18, 1862, by order of Brigadier General M. L. Smith, captured at Vicksburg, Mississippi July 4, 1863, swore of allegiance July 8, 1863, and then paroled (exchanged) December 20, 1863, and took Path of Allegiance May 11, 1865, at Meridian, Mississippi; per sketch in Mathes joined Captain William Miller's Company of Light Artillery at Memphis April 1861, as a private and at the reorganization was placed in First Tennessee (Heavy) Artillery, after fall of Vicksburg served as ordnance officer for Batteries Hager, Tracey and Spanish Fort in Mobile Bay until the evacuation by troops, then elected first lieutenant at the reorganization, wounded at Spanish Fort, went to Meridian and was there paroled May 1865, and joined Confederate Historical Association June 13, 1894; death (May 18, 1909) mentioned in. *Confederate Veteran* Volume X, October 1909, page 520 in "Death List of Memphis Historical Society" between January 1, 1909 and July 1,]909; circle grave stone birth date illegible; Tennessee Confederate Pensions S11209 & W2706 (Nora Miller), per pension born April 27, 1827, in Jefferson County, Kentucky.

Miller, William
Listed in Elmwood 1874 book as Confederate soldier buried in Elmwood who was citizen of Memphis or vicinity; possibly William S. Miller, age 37, buried March 3, 1872, Fowler 606, #26, no stone; "William L. Miller" in funeral notice in the March 2, 1872, *Memphis Daily Appeal,* page 1, column 8, but no military service information indicated; also this may be the "Billy Miller" who per sketch in "Historic Elmwood Walking Tour" Volume I, April 22, 1995, pages 12-16, compiled by Malcolm Gary Hood (copy on file in Cemetery Office) was a Private in the "Wigfall Grays, assigned to Company E, Seventh Tennessee cavalry fightin with Generals Forrest and Chalmers," and killed when he tried to rescue his girlfriend (Ginny (spelled Jenny in Daily Burial Record Book.and computer index) McGhee who had died unbeknownst to him January 24, 1864) from the Irving Block Prison during Forrest's Raid on Memphis August 21, 1864 (see Robert Millner listed in chapter "Confederate Soldiers Rest Burials").

Mitchell, Dr. Robert Wood   Buried November 3, 1903   Chapel Hill 34, #8
Tennessee 13 Infantry Regiment Surgeon (appointed October 1, 1861) and Tennessee 154 Senior Infantry Regiment when regiments consolidated about March 1, 1863; Brigade Surgeon after battle of Murfreesboro; per sketch in Mathes book, page 162, born in Madison County, Tennessee and moved to Mississippi when very young, educated at Centenary College, Jackson, read medicine in Vicksburg, graduated at the University of Louisiana, returned to Vicksburg and elected physician of the hospital there in 1857, moved to Memphis in 1858, elected secretary of Board of Health (also president per Past Times article "Library named for heroic physician" by Perre Magness, *The Commercial Appeal* Memphis, March 23, 2000, Section EM, Neighbors, page 2), organized the Memphis City Hospital and made surgeon in charge, 1861 became assistant surgeon in Tennessee 15 Infantry Regiment and in autumn of same year was made surgeon of Tennessee 13 Infantry Regiment, afterward became brigade and then division surgeon, served continuously with Army of Tennessee until end of War, and one of the original incorporators of Confederate Historical Association and his membership dates from July 15, 1869; biography in *Confederate Military History, Extended Edition*, Volume X Tennessee, page 634; per obituary in *Confederate Veteran* Volume XII, March 1904, page 127, born in Carroll (note difference) County, Tennessee August 26, 1831, member of Confederate Historical Association, doctor and in

sketch of prominent Tennesseans in 'Confederate History', prominently mentioned in sketch of Colonel Keating's 'History of the Yellow Fever Epidemic in 1878-79' and died November 2, 1903; sketch and picture in *Tennessee, The Volunteer State,* 1769-1923, Volume II, page 218-219; circle grave stone; Dr. R. W. Wood Aug 26, 1833 Nov 2, 1903.

Mockbee, Robert Theodore   Buried July 28, 1922   Fowler 572-5722, #2
Tennessee 14 Infantry Regiment Sergeant Company B; enlisted 17 May 1861, at Camp Duncan near Clarksville, Montgomery County, Tennessee; age 22 on Muster Roll dated March 30, 1864; unit fought as part of Army of Northern Virginia; received Tennessee Confederate Pension (S12840 and applied May 10, 1911); per pension was at Appomattox Courthouse, escaped with General Rosser's Cavalry and paroled at Washington, Georgia June 14, 1865; completed Tennessee Civil War Veterans Questionnaire; per pension born August 18, 1841, in Stewart County, Tennessee and per Questionnaire born August 1841, and would be eighty years on August 17, 1921 (note difference); per Questionnaire living in Montgomery County, Tennessee when enlisted, discharged at Appomattox, Virginia April 9, 1865, after War went to Chester, South Carolina then to Tennessee but found that mother had moved to Paducah, Kentucky and went there, was a brick mason, married Miss Kate Mobley May 3, 1866, and made home in South Carolina for more than 28 years, elected to a four year term to South Carolina Legislature in 1882, January 1, 1893, sold his possessions and moved to Arkansas and in November 1894, moved to Memphis; per sketch in Mathes book (original edition) became a member of Forbes Bivouac at Clarksville, Tennessee and upon removal to Memphis was transferred upon proper certificate to this bivouac (United Confederate Veterans of Tennessee, Camp 28, Bivouac 18, Memphis) March 15, 1895, and also per that sketch had interesting old papers showing that his ancestors came from Wales to Loudon County, Virginia, and took part in the Revolutionary War on the patriot side; listed as a member Confederate Historical Association, Camp 28, United Confederate Veterans, Memphis, on list prepared from list submitted by Mr. I. N. Rainey, Adjutant, on September 6, 1912 (copy found in Gunter Papers in Mississippi Valley Collection, The University of Memphis); died in Memphis July 27, 1922; obituary in *The Commercial Appeal* Memphis July 28, 1922, page 7 and small article on page 13 which includes information on Confederate Service; circular grave stone with birth (August 17, 184) and death (July 27, 1922) dates inscribed at the bottom and Confederate service inscribed at the top; per Daily Burial Record Book died age 80.

Monsarrat, George Henderson   Buried December 12, 1869   Chapel Hill 685, #4
Confederate Field and Staff Officer Quartermaster Department Agent Major and Captain of Artillery; Tennessee Monsarrat's Light Artillery Battalion Captain; per *Tennesseans in the Civil War Part 1,* page 123, Monsarrat's Tennessee Light Artillery Battalion, appointed to command Harding Artillery and attempted to expand to battalion but only lasted about three months in fall of 1861; Tennessee Artillery (McCown's) Corps Captain Company 11 (record found "Monsarratt") and per roll of the Field and Company Officers date of commission September 17, 1861; listed as Captain, Nashville, in Ordnance Department of Special Corps Army of Tennessee August 23, 1861, in Lindsley's Annals; Provisional Army of Tennessee, District of east Tennessee, Major Acting Assistant Adjutant General staff of Brigadier-General William H. Carroll; listed ("Monsarratt") in Elmwood 1874 book as Confederate soldier buried in Elmwood who was citizen of Memphis or vicinity with rank of Major; article "Death of an Old Citizen" reported in the Sunday, December 12, 1869, *Memphis Daily Appeal,* page 4, column 4, "The death of Col. G.H. Monsarrat will be recognized as a calamity not to be soon forgotten by those with whom he was formerly associated. His clear, pellucid intellect; extraordinary quickness of apprehension; his *bonhommie*; his peculiar exhibitions of inoffensive vanity, which of itself rendered him incapable of petty wrong-doing; the readiness with which, Alcibiades-like, he adapted his manner and language to the temper, character, tastes and acquirements of those with whom he was brought in contact, rendered him, when he sought to please, eminently attractive. Born in Baltimore--he lived in early manhood in Cincinnati; afterwards, for several years, was connected with the press of Louisville. He became a successful banker, grew rich, but was bankrupted in some coal mining speculations. In 1853 he traveled over Europe with the late Gov. Jones, with whom he was afterwards associated in business in Memphis. Here he was known as a shrewd and successful real estate broker. Before the war his firm sold a million dollars worth of real estate per annum. His publications in relation to the resources and undeveloped wealth of Memphis, and of the country adjacent, added greatly to the city's actual wealth and attracted population from all quarters. His firm spent in one year—when half the money paid for twice the work of the present time—six thousand dollars in advertising. The whole city reaped riches from Col. Monsarrat's wise business policy. When the war begun Col. Monsarrat was appointed by Gov. Harris Chief of the Ordinance Bureau of Tennessee. He held this position several months, abandoning it to take command of a battery organized in Nashville. For some months he was Post Commandant at Knoxville, while George Crittenden, Leadbetter and Kirby Smith, at different times, commanded the Department. Gov. Brownlow was incarcerated by Leadbetter, and in charge of Monsarrat, when he surrendered himself on condition that he should be sent North in safety. For a few days only Brownlow was in prison. He was then removed to his residence and subjected to the inconvenience of having sentinels posted with-in and around his home. Col. Monsarrat's personal kindnesses to Brownlow begat a friendship surely honorable to our Senator and illustrative of Monsarrat's generosity. At the close of Monsarrat's term of enlistment he abandoned the service, was married and lived during two years of the war in Montgomery, Ala. He returned, after peace, to Memphis, and, as the times permitted, prosecuted his business as a real estate broker. He leaves a wife and four little children, who surely should have been spared this fearful loss."; died consumption age 48 per Daily Burial Record Book.

Moode, Henry   Buried February 15, 1891   Evergreen 278,279, 301, 302, #1
Mississippi 10 Infantry Regiment Private Company M and New Company D; appears on a Muster Roll of recruits for Company M dated March 28, 1862; Company M subsequently served as New Company D; per Company D Muster Roll for May & June 1862, enlisted February 20, 1862, Jackson, Mississippi; per Company Muster Roll for May 1 to August 31, 1864, remarks: Absent

wounded July 28, 1864, near Atlanta, Georgia; appears on a Roll of Prisoners of War paroled at Jackson, Mississippi, May 19, 1865; per article "ELMWOOD. — Grand and Imposing Ceremonies of Commemoration Day." in the Sunday, May 8, 1870, *Memphis Daily Appeal*, page 4, column 2, deposited mementos under the Confederate Rest Monument corner stone during the laying ceremony on Saturday, May 7, 1870 (see CONFEDERATE MONUMENT, page 3); reported in the May 6, 1880, *Memphis Daily Appeal*, page 4, column 4, at the planning meeting for "Decoration Day" to be held May 16, 1880, that he brought up the matter of the Confederate graves at Elmwood not being taken care of and that the graves should be cared for and decorated by the surviving ex-Confederates and moved that a memorial association be organized for that purpose and the matter was referred to a committee to make a report; member of Confederate Historical Association but no sketch in Mathes book per NAMES WITHOUT SKETCHES chapter page 232; per Memphis Register of Deaths died February 14, 1891, age 47, native of Mississippi, cause Consumption; buried in Memphis Typographical Union Lot; not listed in computer index.

Moon, Robert Anderson   Buried June 15, 1869   Chapel Hill 33, #4
Tennessee 154 Senior Infantry Regiment Sergeant Company G, enlisted June 3, 1861, Memphis age 36; per May 5, 1863, muster roll remarks: discharged, over age; per discharge sheet dated July 22, 1862, at Tupelo, Mississippi: born in the town of Scottsville, Virginia, aged 38; letter of recommendation in record dated July 11, 1862, from merchants of Memphis to President Davis recommending him for the Office of Collector of this Port (Memphis); note in compiled service record to see personal papers of Benj. K. Pullen (no unit indicated) but nothing found in B. K. Pullen's Tennessee 3 Infantry Battalion records or in General and Staff records; listed in Elmwood 1874 book as Confederate soldier buried in Elmwood who was citizen of Memphis or vicinity and sketch; per sketch born 1824, came to Memphis from Virginia and died 1869; died dysentery age 44 per Daily Burial Record Book.

Moon, Virginia Bethel "Ginnie"   Buried November 3, 1925   Chapel Hill 33, #12 Ashes
Confederate Spy; full name "Virginia Bethel "Ginny" Moon"; died age 81 per Daily Burial Record Book; born June 22, 1844, and died September 11, 1925, on one grave stone: "Miss Ginny" Moon"; "Confederate spy who became famous during the late war between the states. She was known as an active and dangerous rebel. At the time of her death, she still retained a fierce pride for her beloved south." on second grave stone; see Chapter 13 "Sister Act" in *Spies for the Blue and Gray* by Harnett T. Kane, Hanover House, Garden City, New York, 1954 that details the lives of Ginny Moon and her sister Lottie Moon Clark and their exploits as spies; see also "A Confederate Woman Spy" in *Confederate Veteran*, Volume XXXIV #2, February 1926, page 45 and Chapter IX "Miss Ginny" Moon: Something Old, Something New" in *Memphis Down in Dixie* by Shields McIlwaine, E. P. Dutton and Company, Inc., New York, 1948, pages 260-265 and photograph opposite inside title page; listed in "Touring Historic Elmwood Cemetery" Brochure (January 2000) #63; sketch #20 in Elmwood *Civil War Tour* booklet (2012); historic marker located in Confederate Park, Memphis, Tennessee.

Moore, Dr. George H.   Buried September 17, 1902   Evergreen 343, #1
Mississippi 6 Cavalry Regiment Assistant Surgeon; listed in officers unit card for Mississippi 6 Cavalry Regiment, however, compiled service records found in Officers Field and Staff Muster Rolls; appears on a Register of Appointments, Confederate States Army, State: Alabama, appointed Assistant Surgeon December 4, 1862, to rank August 2, 1862, with remarks: Resigned September 3, 1864; received Medical Certificate (July 28, 1864) of indefinite disability and recommendation of his resignation; per City of Memphis Burial Permit date of birth April 7, 1821, Alabama, date of death September 6, 1902, age 81 years, cause Old Age.

Moores, James Wilson   Buried May 15, 1905   Chapel Hill 33, #14
Army of Tennessee Forage Master; originally enlisted in Tennessee 4 Infantry Regiment Private Company A ("Shelby Grays"); per Company Muster-in Roll dated May 15, 1861, enlisted May 15, 1861, Germantown, Tennessee; per Company Muster-in Roll for April 25 to June 30, 1862, age 25 and remarks: Discharged May 8, 1862; appears on a Roll of Non-commissioned Officers and Privates employed on extra duty and laborers, in the field, during the month of May, 1865, by W. H. Moores, Major and Quartermaster in charge Supply Train, as paroled at Charlotte, North Carolina, May 5, 1865, residence indicated as Memphis, Shelby County, Tennessee; Major W. H. Moores was his brother and he first was Captain Tennessee 55 (McKoin's) Infantry Regiment Company H (Captain William H. Moores' Company, Ladies Guard), which was consolidated with the Tennessee 44 Infantry Regiment to form the Tennessee 44 Infantry regiment (Consolidated) and he became Acting Quartermaster and subsequently Quartermaster; name listed as member of the Company in the May 15, 1909, *The Commercial Appeal* Memphis article "Forty=Eight Years Ago Today, The Shelby Greys Entered the Confederate Service—Record of a Famous Memphis Military Company." with notations transferred to other service, in Army of Tennessee at surrender and died since the surrender; obituary article in the "The Last Roll" section *Confederate Veteran* Volume XIII, No.8, August, 1905, page 371, "J. W. Moores was born July 25, 1837, at Fayetteville, Tenn. He was reared in that community, but moved to Memphis a few years before the War between the States. He entered the Confederate service in 1861 as a member of Shelby's Grays, and left a sick bed at Memphis for Corinth just before the advent of the Federal troops, where he received an indefinite furlough to await convalescence from inflammatory rheumatism. He remained with the army, rendering the best service he could as assistant quartermaster with Hood and most of the time with Gen. Pat Cleburne, with whose command he was at the battle of Franklin. He surrendered at Greensboro, N. C. After the war Comrade Moores engaged in business in Memphis as commission merchant and cotton factor until 1880, since when his life had been spent in Kentucky, where he operated a coal mine until his health failed. He was married to Miss Virginia Molloy, of Memphis, in 1870. His death occurred on May 13, 1905. A devoted Christian, he bore without reproach the "grand old name of gentleman."; member of Confederate Historical Association but no sketch in Mathes book per NAMES WITHOUT SKETCHES chapter page 232.

Morgan, Robert Jarrell Buried July 25, 1899 Chapel Hill Circle 11, #3
Tennessee 36 Infantry Regiment Colonel and Judge Advocate Colonel; per *Tennesseans in the Civil War, Part 1*, Tennessee 36 Infantry Regiment organized February 26, 1862, and disbanded June 1862 and Colonel Morgan was assigned to staff duty with Lieutenant General Leonidas Polk until Polk's death and later served on a Court of Claims in Georgia; per General and Staff compiled service record rolls Colonel and Judge Advocate, November 4, 1862, applied for appointment to Military Court and with General Polk March 4, 1863; per *The Commercial Appeal* Memphis July 24, 1899, (page 2) born in Georgia where spent boyhood, educated and began practice of law, before the war came to Memphis but when hostilities began cast his lot with the Confederacy and became a Colonel of a Georgia regiment, later transferred to General Leonidas Polk's staff until General Polk was killed then served with distinction until end of war and returned to Memphis; per same issue of *The Commercial Appeal* Memphis special from Aberdeen, Mississippi July 23, 1899, that Judge Robert J. Morgan of Memphis died suddenly of heart failure at 2:30 o'clock this afternoon at his summer residence in this city and remains will be carried to Memphis tomorrow; born Putnam County, Georgia and became a member of Confederate Historical Association September 9, 1869; Chapel Hill Circle Lot 11 is the Robert J. Morgan Lot; Judge and died age 69 per Daily Burial Record Book; sketch in Mathes book; sketch in Goodspeed's Shelby County History, page1014; sketch in *Sketches of Prominent Tennesseans: Containing Biographies and Records of Many of the Families who Have Attained Prominence in Tennessee*. Compiled and edited by Hon. W. S. Speer. Nashville: A. B. Tavel, 1888. page 200.

Morrison, A. D. Buried November 21,1861 Fowler 67, #1
Tennessee 154 Senior Infantry Regiment Private Company G ("The Beauregards"); enlisted June 3, 1861, Memphis age 30; per May 15, 1863, muster roll remarks: died; per register of soldiers killed in battle deceased December 1861 from pneumonia; per report of deaths dated October 30, 1863, enlisted June 3, 1861 Memphis, born Virginia and died December 1861 at Columbus, Kentucky of pneumonia; died November 20, 1861, Columbus, Kentucky pneumonia per Cemetery record; first name "Jake" (possibly nickname) and died November 20, 1861 per Lindsley's Annals; possibly the Jacob Morrison listed in Elmwood 1874 book as Confederate soldier buried in Elmwood who was citizen of Memphis or vicinity but no "Jacob" found in Cemetery records and does not appear to be J. W. Morrison, buried July 7, 1866, Turley 1068.5, #1 (originally buried Chapel Hill 679, #1 and removed February 19, 1886) as name on Tucker family stone is John Welbourn Morrison September 3, 1816 June 26, 1866.

Munch, George P. Buried January 1, 1905 Chapel Hill 446, #10
Tennessee 154 Senior Infantry Regiment 1 Lieutenant Company D; per Company Muster-in Roll dated August 13, 1861, enlisted May 14, 1861 Randolph, Tennessee age 23; per Company Muster Roll dated May 23, 1863, age 23, remarks: Reelected 2 Lieutenant May 1, 1862. Promoted 1 Lieutenant April 30, 1863; appears on an Inspection Report dated September 17, 1864, Jonesboro, Georgia, remarks: Absent wounded; name appears as signature to an Oath of Allegiance June 22, 1865, indicating surrendered May 11, 1865, Augusta, Georgia, residence Shelby County, Tennessee; per City of Memphis Burial permit died January 1, 1905, age 67, cause of death Locomotor Ataxia; name spelled "Munech" in Cemetery computer index; sketch in Mathes book, page 165, "First Lieutenant Company D, One Hundred and Fifty-fourth Tennessee; enlisted April 26, 1861; served through the war; was wounded in front of Atlanta; paroled April 26, 1865. Admitted to the Confederate Historical Association January 8, 1895."

Myers, Daniel Emmett Buried November 30, 1910 Miller Circle 33, #2
Kentucky 5 Cavalry Regiment (Colonel D. Howard Smith) 1 Lieutenant Company I (Captain J. Eugene Barnes); enlisted September 2, 1862, Georgetown, Kentucky; appears on a Report of the 5th Regiment Kentucky Cavalry dated January 6, 1864, at Richmond with remarks: Lieutenant Myers was dismissed service by Court Martial at Tullahoma in 1863; Aide de Camp Staff of General Abraham Buford Lieutenant; per *Confederate Staff Officers 1861 -1865* by Joseph H. Crute, Jr. (Derwent Books 1982): appointed August 11, 1863; Captain, Company E, 9th Kentucky Cavalry Regiment; Captain, Assistant Adjutant and Inspector General, 1864. Resigned February 22, 1865; per biography in *Confederate Military History, Extended Edition*, Volume X Tennessee, page 639: born in Bracken county, February 17, 1842 (note year on Burial Permit below), graduated at Transylvania university at Lexington, in 1860, then studied law under Garret Davis, at Paris, Ky., licensed to practice in April, 1862, in the following month entered the Confederate lines, enlisted in Company F (Captain Barnes), Col. Howard Smith's Kentucky regiment, as a private, but was soon elected second lieutenant, served during the Kentucky campaign, and subsequently elected to the captaincy of his company, but declined that honor and accepted advancement to first lieutenant, fought in the battle of Murfreesboro, and took part in the subsequent operations until detached to command the regular scout of Buford's brigade, then located at Beach Grove, Tenn., served in that capacity for a considerable period, scouting in the vicinity of Murfreesboro and other points in middle Tennessee, until wounded near Readyville, when Gen. Abe Buford was sent to command the infantry brigade before Vicksburg, composed of Scott's Louisiana regiment, and Shacklett's, Crossland's and Thompson's Kentucky regiments, and Captain Myers was transferred to staff duty and ordered to report to Buford, served in Mississippi as aide-de-camp with the rank of first lieutenant until the fall of Vicksburg, when he was promoted to inspector-general of the brigade, when the brigade was again mounted at Demopolis, Ala., after the retreat of Polk's corps to that point before Sherman, and Buford was put in command of a division of cavalry, continued with him as inspector-general of the division, and served as such under General Forrest through the western Kentucky campaign, participating in both fights at Paducah, Ky., Hood's campaign in Tennessee, and until the close of the war, four times wounded, shot through the left leg, and received a sabre wound in the face during a charge, but the most serious was a shot through the right foot which detained him for three months in the hospital at Rome, Ga., after parole with the kindness of a friend went to France, but returned in the fall of 1865, resided in Bloomington, Ill., until February, 1866, when made his home at Memphis, since then engaged in the practice of his profession (law), and for twenty years counsel for the State national bank at Memphis; per City of Memphis Burial Permit born February 17, 1839, and died November 29, 1910; grave stone: 1839 — 1910.

Myers, Henry Clay   Buried August 21, 1917   Evergreen 420-421, #2
Missouri 2 Cavalry Regiment Private Company H; per Historic Roll: native of North Carolina, and enlisted May 1, 1864; paroled May 17, 1865, at Columbus, Mississippi, and indicated residence of Marshall County, Mississippi; per biography in *Confederate Military History, Extended Edition*, Volume X Tennessee, page 640: born in Anson county, N. C., October 17, 1847, paroled at Gainesville, Ala., in May, 1865, resided in Mississippi after the war, elected sheriff of his county, took an active part in politics, and became secretary of state, in 1889, made his home at Memphis and became the general agent of a leading insurance company and was quartermaster-general, with the rank of colonel, on the staff of Gen. Stephen D. Lee, commanding the army of Tennessee, United Confederate Veterans; per sketch in Mathes book, page 167: became a member of the Confederate Historical Association in September, 1891.

Nash, William J.   Buried November 5, 1912   Fowler Public Lot 6, #1084
Tennessee 5 Infantry Regiment Private 2 Company I; enlisted September 20, 1861, Columbus, Kentucky; captured near Nashville December 16, 1864; sent to Military Prison Louisville, Kentucky and then to Camp Chase, Ohio January 2, 1865; took Oath of Allegiance May 14, 1865, indicating residence as Henry County, Tennessee; per Tennessee Confederate Pension (S12342) born Henry County, Tennessee March 14, 1843; died age 67 per Daily Burial Record Book.

Neely, Hugh McDowell   Buried August 15, 1919   Miller Circle 304, #1
Tennessee 38 Infantry Regiment Captain Company I; enlisted as Private March 5, 1862, Morning Sun, Tennessee; elected 1 Lieutenant July 14, 1862; promoted to Captain July 1, 1863; served as Assistant Adjutant General to General M. J. Wright August, 1864, and to General George Maney September, 1864; per sketch in Mathes book, page 169: became a member of the old Confederate Association September 9, 1869; biography in *Confederate Military History, Extended Edition*, Volume X Tennessee, page 643; sketch in *Who's Who in Tennessee* page 343; per State of Tennessee Certificate of Death born November 8, 1833, and died August 13, 1919, and indicates buried in Forest Hill Cemetery, however, Elmwood Cemetery records verify his burial at Elmwood and Forest Hill Midtown Office verified no record of burial there; no grave stone.

Nelson, William Adams   Buried July 22, 1875   Lenow Circle 29, #4
Tennessee 3 (Forrest's) Cavalry Regiment Private Company G, H & E; no enlistment information in compiled service record; appears on a Roll of Prisoners of War captured at Jackson, Tennessee (some records indicate Mississippi) July 13 1863; per report dated July 15, 1865, at Corinth, Mississippi, remarks: forwarded to Memphis for exchange; appears on a Register of Prisoners of War in custody of Provost Marshall, Memphis, Tennessee, with Disposition of prisoner: retained by order of D.P.M. July 23. Sent to Alton Illinois August 11, 1863. Remarks: This man confessed that he was a Lieutenant and so reported after he arrived at St. Louis, Missouri; appears on a Roll of Prisoners of War received at and discharged from Gratiot Street Military Prison, St Louis, Missouri, August 15 to 31, 1863, received August 14, 1863, discharged August 21, 1863, remarks: Camp Morton, Illinois; appears on a Roll of Prisoners of War at Camp Morton, Indianapolis, Indiana, captured Jackson, Mississippi, July 12, 1863, remarks: transferred to Fort Delaware March 19 1864; name appears as signature to an Oath of Allegiance subscribed to at Fort Delaware, Delaware, in the month of May, 1865, released May 14, 1865, residence: Shelby County, Tennessee; per Daily Burial Record Book died age 45 inflammation of the bowels (congestion of brain in mortuary report in the July 25, 1875, *Memphis Daily Appeal*, page 4, column 3); death notice in the July 22, 1875, *Memphis Daily Appeal*, page 1, column 8.

Nolley, Thomas L.   Buried January 23, 1889   Turley 6132, #3
Louisiana 3 (Harrison's) Cavalry 1 Lieutenant Company B; no enlistment in record (regiment organized August 1863 from 5 Battalion that organized January 1863); card in record indicates that name appears as a signature on a petition dated May 21, 1863, at Camp Monroe and addressed to Captain Davis asking the promotion of Major I. F. Harrison to Lieutenant Colonel; signed Parole of Honor June 6, 1865, at Natchitoches, Louisiana which card indicates residence Madison Parish, Louisiana; Captain and died age 50 per Daily Burial Record Book but no unit indicated; unit per sketch in Shelby County's history in Goodspeed's *History of Hamilton, Knox and Shelby Counties of Tennessee*, page 1018; also per sketch native of Paris, Tennessee, at age two went with father to Fayette County, when of age went to Louisiana and engaged in planting and merchandising, in 1862, enlisted in the Confederate service, Third Louisiana Cavalry, and remained in service until end of the war, and in 1880 married Mrs. J. H. (Henning) Saddle, of the city of Memphis; Captain, Confederate Battle Flag and 1835 1889 on grave stone that is double stone with wife Judith H. 1847 1929 with cross; not found in Cemetery computer index.

O'Connor, David   Buried November 4, 1877   Lenow Circle 91, #1
Louisiana 9 Infantry Regiment Private/Corporal Company E; per Company Muster Roll dated July 8, 1861, enlisted July 7, 1861, Camp Moore, Louisiana; per Company Muster Roll for November & December, 1862, rank Corporal and remarks: Promoted from ranks November 1, 1862; per Company Muster Roll for January & February, 1864, remarks: Taken prisoner at the Rappahannock, November 7, 1863; appears on a roll of Prisoners of War at Point Lookout, Maryland, with remarks: Exchanged March 10, 1864; appears on a "Record" from July 7, 1861, to March 20, 1865, indicating born Ireland, farmer, residence Madison Parrish, Louisiana, age 17 when enlisted and single; appears on a register of prisoners received and disposed of by the Provost Marshall General, Army of the Potomac, received March 30, 1865, and remarks: Rebel Deserter; death notice in the November 3, 1877, *Memphis Daily Appeal*, page 1, column 6; per article in the December 2, 1877, *Memphis Daily Appeal* (from the Tipton Weekly Record), page 1, column 5; died at Mason, Tennessee, November 2, 1877, aged 32 years, born in Cork, Ireland, April 25, 1845, came to America when six years old and was turned loose at that tender age to battle with the world alone and provided for himself by hard work,

short time previous to the breaking out of the civil war came south and went to Louisiana, where he volunteered at the age of fourteen, into the Confederate army, Co. A, Ninth Louisiana Infantry, participated in every battle, wounded in battle three times (once very severely in the left side), after the war came to Mason, and settled down; Monument Inscription: D. O'Connor, Born in Cork, Ireland, April 25 1845 Died Nov. 2 1877 At Mason Tenn. Erected by his Affectionate wife Mrs. Nellie O'Connor; died from consumption per Daily Burial Record Book.

Omberg, James A.   Buried May 2, 1920   Miller Circle 280

Tennessee 4 Infantry Regiment Private Company A ("Shelby Grays"); per Company Muster-in Roll dated August 16, 1861, enlisted May 15, 1861, Germantown, Tennessee, age 21; per Company Muster-in Roll for November & December, 1862, remarks: Wounded at Murfreesboro December 31; per Company Muster-in Roll for January & February, 1863, remarks: Wounded at Murfreesboro and returned to duty March 20; appears on a Muster Roll of Officers and Men (Tennessee 3 Consolidated Infantry regiment Company D) paroled at Greensboro, North Carolina, May 1, 1865; listed as member of the Company in the May 15, 1909, *The Commercial Appeal* Memphis article "Forty=Eight Years Ago Today, The Shelby Greys Entered the Confederate Service— Record of a Famous Memphis Military Company; sketch in Mathes book, page 269, "born at Lawrenceville, Ga., in 1839. His paternal ancestors came from Norway in the early part of the present century and settled in Georgia. His mother's ancestors came from the north of Ireland in the eighteenth century and became citizens of South Carolina. He prepared for a university course. Preferring a commercial life, however, he accepted at an early age a position as clerk in the Bank of Chattanooga with his uncle, William Fulton, the cashier, and soon succeeded to the position of teller of the Commercial Bank of Memphis. When the war broke out he promptly enlisted in Company A, Shelby Grays, Fourth Tennessee, from which he was soon transferred to the commissary headquarters of his brigade and division, remaining therein until the surrender with the army in North Carolina in April, 1865. In 1879 he became cashier of the Bank of Commerce, and has held the position ever since. Mr. Omberg was married in 1867 to Miss Eliza Graham, of an old and prominent family of Memphis. They have four children."; per Tennessee Certificate of Death died May 6, 1920, age 81 and cause Organic Heart Disease.

Otey, Dr. Paul H.   Buried September 29, 1878   Chapel Hill 347

Arkansas 2 Infantry Regiment Field and Staff Officer Surgeon; compiled service records also found in Officers rolls; appears on a Field and Staff Muster Roll for April 30 to June 30, 1862, date of appointment March 10, 1862; appears on a Field and Staff Muster Roll for August 31 to October 30, 1863, with remarks: Surgeon in charge of Hospital Marietta, Georgia; see *The Yellow Fever Epidemic of 1878 in Memphis, Tenn.* By J. M. Keating Memphis, Tenn.: Printed for the Howard Association. 1879., page 170, for a description of his life and death; died age 54 Yellow Fever per Daily Burial Record Book.

Owen, Augustus   Buried August 24, 1870   Chapel Hill 8, #3

Listed in Elmwood 1874 book as Confederate soldier buried in Elmwood who was citizen of Memphis or vicinity but no record found that indicates Confederate service; possibly Tennessee 17 (Sander's) Cavalry Battalion (that consolidated with Mississippi 17 Cavalry Battalion December 1864, to form Mississippi 9 Cavalry Regiment) enlisted May 2, 1861, 1 Lieutenant and Adjutant (commissioned May 2, 1863); first name "Gus" in Daily Burial Record Book and computer index (adult); cannot tell if Augustus H. Owens, Alabama 1 Infantry Regiment, Captain Company E who enlisted February 28, 1861, and resigned December 4, 1861, or Aug Owen, Georgia 3 Cavalry who was from Louisville, Alabama and age 31 in 1864.

Owen, Ben Franklin   Buried September 28, 1886   Fowler 314, #9

Mississippi 11 Infantry Regiment Private Company H; per Company Muster-in Roll Dated May 13, 1861, Lynchburg, Virginia, enrolled at Houston, Mississippi March 19, 1861; wounded at Battle of Seven Pines May 31, 1862; given a Certificate of Disability for Discharge October 4, 1862 at age 32; grave stone: 1832 – 1886 with Regiment inscribed on stone; per *Find A Grave*, database and images (https://www.findagrave.com), memorial page for Ben Franklin Owen (1832–13 Sep 1886), Find A Grave Memorial no. 110116213, citing Elmwood Cemetery, Memphis, Shelby County, Tennessee, USA, maintained by Mary & Kent (contributor 47170788), an attorney, originally interred at National Cemetery and moved to Elmwood in 1886 and cause of death: railroad accident.

Paddison, Edward Wilmot, Sr.   Buried February 22, 1880   Turley 482

Florida 1 Infantry Regiment Private Corporal (Old) Company D and (new) Company C; per Company Muster-in Roll dated April 19, 1861, enlisted April 2, 1861, Tallahassee, Florida, age 20; per Company Muster Roll for January & February, 1863, Corporal, remarks: Appointed January 1, 1863; death notice in the February 24, 1880, *Memphis Daily Appeal*, page 1, column 7; per article "A Memphis Printer Gone" in the February 23, 1880, *Public Ledger* (Memphis), page 4, column 4, was a native of North Carolina, a well-known printer and was interred at Elmwood by the Typographical union, which he was a member; died age 38 Softening of brain per Daily Burial Record Book; originally buried Fowler Lot 314, #2, and removed to Turley Lot 482 February 28, 1883.

Park, John   Buried August 8, 1897   Chapel Hill 20, #8

Mayor of Memphis 1861 to 1866 (five terms of one year each); see *History of Memphis*, Volume II, O. F. Vedder, page 28, D. Mann & Co., Publishers, Syracuse, N. Y. 1888 - after the capture of Memphis "(T)he city officers continued to govern the city until July 2, 1864, when by order of General Washburne (sic), the newly elected city officers were not allows to qualify."; Special Order No. 70 was issued by Major General C. C. Washburn appointing military officers as city officials due to the "utter failure of the municipal government of Memphis for the past two years to discharge its proper functions, the disloyal character of that government, its want of sympathy for the government of the United States, and its indisposition to co-operate with the military authorities...."; grave stone: John Park 1812-1896, Born County Tyrone, Ireland, Memphis Mayor 1861-1866 During the War between the States; article in *The Commercial Appeal* Memphis August 8, 1887, page 6, died yesterday, would have been 85 years old if had lived to October 12, called "Honest John," and born County of Tyrone, Ireland in 1812; listed under Former Mayors of Memphis and South Memphis in "Touring historic Elmwood Cemetery" (Brochure and Map of Historic Gravesites) #45; listed in "Touring Historic Elmwood Cemetery" Brochure (January 2000) #50; sketch #9 in Elmwood *Civil War Tour* booklet (2012).

Park, Joseph B.   Buried January 17, 1866   Chapel Hill 10, #9
Tennessee 154 Senior Infantry Regiment Private Corporal Company L ("The Maynard Rifles"); enlisted March 7, 1862, Memphis; per November 1, 1862, to February 28, 1863, muster roll remarks: wounded at Murfreesboro; per January & February 1864, muster roll remarks: killed; name appears on a Register of Officers and Soldiers of the Army of the Confederate States who were killed in battle, or who died of wounds or disease which indicates deceased May 29, 1864, at Marietta, Georgia; per other record remarks died in Hospital in Marietta, Georgia May 28, 1864, cause vulnus sclopeticum (relating to a wound caused by a gunshot wound); believed to be the James B. Park, whose grave was handsomely decorated and located outside the Confederate grounds, in the May 17, 1881, *Memphis Daily Appeal*, page 2, column 3, article "OUR HEROIC DEAD" reporting on the Memorial Day ceremonies at Elmwood Cemetery on Sunday May 15, 1881, (note there is a stone for a James B. Park in the Chapel Hill Lot 10 but date of death on grave stone is April 11, 1846); grave stone (badly broken): Jos. B. Park, Maynard Rifles, 154 Regt. Tenn. Vol., Born April 5, _____, Killed _____, May _____; killed in battle per Daily Burial Record Book.

Park, William H.   Buried January 25, 1865   Chapel Hill 10, #7
Tennessee 3 (Forrest's) Cavalry Regiment Private Company A ("Bluff City Grays"), per Company Muster Roll dated May & June 1863, enlisted May 4, 1861, Memphis, Tennessee; first enlisted in the Tennessee 154 Senior Infantry Regiment Private 1 Company B, per Company Muster-in Roll dated August 13, 1861, at New Madrid, Missouri enlisted May 14, 1861, at Randolph, Tennessee age 21; listed in the June 6, 1878, *Memphis Daily Appeal*, page 4, column 3, article "OUR DEAD HEROES" covering the unveiling of the Confederate Monument and Decoration of Graves at Elmwood as then one of twenty-eight members of the Bluff City Grays, Company B of the 154 Senior Infantry Regiment and Company A of Forrest's Old (Third) Cavalry Regiment buried at Elmwood initial "W"; listed as one of the "comrades who sleep at Elmwood cemetery " in the article "Veterans in Council" in *Memphis Daily Appeal*, May 12, 1881, page 4, column 4, concerning the meeting of the surviving members in the city of the old Bluff City Grays to appoint the necessary committees for the purpose of making special decoration on the graves of their dead comrades at Elmwood and Calvary cemeteries on Sunday next, Memorial Day; listed as member of Bluff City Grays in *Reminiscences of the Civil War* by John Hallum, Tunnah & Pittard printers, 1903; listed in "A COMPLETE ROSTER OF THE BLUFF CITY GREYS" located in the Memphis Room of the Memphis/Shelby County Public Library and Information Center Central Library with notation "Died Memphis, January 25, 1865" and included on the list at the end of the soldiers buried at Elmwood; see also Notes of Interest - Bluff City Grays; grave stone reads Wm. H. Park, Bluff City Grays, 154 Regiment Tenn Vol, born in Nashville, Tenn July 3, 1839, died January 25, 1865; died chronic diarrhea age 25 per Daily Burial Record Book; not found in Cemetery computer index.

Parker, Minter   Buried October 8, 1894   Lenow Circle 85, #4
Tennessee 4 Infantry Regiment Private Company A and Sapper & Miners; enlisted June 30, 1862, Tupelo, Mississippi age 19; per March & April 1863, muster roll remarks: detailed to engineers April 20, 1863; per Confederate Sappers & Miners compiled service record rolls in company of Sappers & Miners, Engineers Department, Polk's Corps, Army of Tennessee, C.S.A. and name appears on 2 receipts: 2 quarter 1863 Draftsman and July 1863 Draftsman; per Confederate engineers rolls acting 2 Lieutenant, name appears on return of officers with General Joseph E. Johnston and paroled at Greensboro, North Carolina May 1, 1865; per sketch in Mathes book born in Memphis October 24, 1842, joined Shelby Greys, after Battle of Murfreesboro promoted to position in Topographical Engineers on staff of General Polk, after Polk's death with Generals Johnston and Hood, surrendered with General Johnston, returned to Memphis and died October 7, 1894; brother of William G. Parker who served in same unit and buried at Elmwood; died age 52 per Daily Burial Record Book; died October 7, 1894 on grave stone (partially illegible).

Parker, Robert Alexander, Jr.   Buried December 30, 1928   Miller Circle 265, #3
Commissary and Ordnance Departments; per answers in Tennessee Civil War Veterans Questionnaire served as Clerk and Storekeeper in Commissary and then for last three years in Ordnance Department, never discharged and quit after Battle of Columbus, Georgia and left there about 1 May 1865 to return home; per sketch in *Tennessee, The Volunteer State, 1769-1923*, Volume IV, pages 182-185 (sketch also in Volume V, Deluxe Supplement, page 489), born at Somerville (Fayette County), Tennessee, on the 19th of November, 1836, a son of Robert A. and Lamira (Minter) Parker, brought to Memphis by his parents in 1841, educated in private schools of Memphis, at the age of seventeen went to work and kept at it steadily until the call to arms in 1861, rendered valiant service to the south, with rank of captain of artillery (no record found) and a keeper of army stores, after the war returned to Memphis and took up the routine of life where he left off when he enlisted, and 25th of May, 1858 married in Tipton County, Tennessee, to Miss Sarah Flowers; brother of Minter and William G. Parker (see sketches herein); grave stone: November 19, 1836 December 29, 1928; died age 92 per Daily Burial Record Book.

Parker, William Garnett   Buried March 9, 1878   Lenow Circle 85, #1
Tennessee 4 Infantry Regiment Corporal Company A; enlisted May 15, 1861, Germantown, Tennessee age 20; per casualty report dated April 10, 1862, at Corinth, Mississippi: wounded slightly in arm at Shiloh; per sketch in Mathes book born May 1, 1841

Somerville, Tennessee, enlisted May 15, 1861 and served with unit throughout war surrendering at Goldsboro, North Carolina April 26, 1865, returned to Memphis after War, joined Confederate Historical Association December 16, 1869, and died at home of mother in Memphis March 8, 1878; died congestion of lung age 37 per Daily Burial Record Book; brother of Minter (who served in same unit) and Robert A. Parker buried at Elmwood.

Patrick, Marsh M.   Buried June 1, 1873   Chapel Hill 370, #5
Tennessee 154 Senior Infantry Regiment Lieutenant Colonel (Major on compiled service record file card) Field & Staff, Captain Company H, per Company Muster-in Roll dated August 13, 1861, at New Madrid, Missouri enlisted April 26, 1861, at Memphis, Tennessee age 31; wounded at Battle of Shiloh April 6 & 7, 1862, promoted to Major August 30, 1862, and promoted to Lieutenant Colonel March 1, 1863, died age 43 deranged per Daily Burial Record Book.

Patrick, William
Captain; listed in Elmwood 1874 book as Confederate soldier buried in Elmwood who was citizen of Memphis or vicinity with rank of Captain but no service record found; not found in Cemetery computer index.

Patterson, Reverend George   Buried December 13, 1901   Evergreen 310, #1
North Carolina 3 Infantry Regiment (State Troops) Chaplin; per Field and Staff Muster Roll for December 31, 1863, to August 31, 1864, commissioned December 30, 1862, at Bunker Hill, Virginia and remarks that absent sick since July 25, 1864, in Chimborazo Hospital Richmond, Virginia; per compiled service records became sick as early as September 18, 1863; relieved of duty by Special Order Number 264/10 dated November 5, 1864; appears on a Register of Chimborazo Hospital, No. 1, (undated) that indicates had disease of Debility (physical weakness, especially as a result of illness), admitted August 18, 1864, and returned to duty November 14, 1864; roster dated January 5, 1865, remarks that transferred to duty at Chimborazo Hospital; appears on a Roll of Prisoners of War captured in Hospitals, Richmond, Virginia, April 3, 1865, at Jackson Hospital, May 28, 1865, captured Richmond, Virginia April 3, 1865 and paroled April 17, 1863; was born George Papathakes in Boston, Massachusetts, son of Petro Papathakes and Louisa Miles; biography in *Confederate Military History, Extended Edition*, Volume X Tennessee, page 661; see articles: Tise, Larry E. "Patterson, George" 1994, *Dictionary of North Carolina Biography: Volume 5 P-S*, edited by William S. Powell, University of North Carolina Press, 2000; Gailor, Thomas F. "The Rev. George Patterson, D.D." *The Sewanee Review* 10, no. 2 (October 1902). 439-449; Brown, John Howard, editor. "Patterson, George." *Lamb's biographical dictionary of the United States* IV. Boston, Mass.: Federal Book Company of Boston. 1903. 160-161; image "Rev. Geo. Patterson, D.D., Chaplain." *Histories of the several regiments and battalions from North Carolina, in the great war 1861-'65.* Raleigh [N.C.]: E.M. Uzzell, printer. 1901. 176; per Daily Burial Record Book 1853-1919 died age 73 and remarks that in Donoho Vault "Buried 4-27-1902"; grave stone: George Patterson July 13, 1828 – Dec. 10, 1901 Rector of Grace Church 1886-1901.

Pattison, Oliver Garnett   Buried April 13, 1862   Turley 82, #6
Tennessee 3 (Forrest's) Cavalry Regiment Private Company A ("Bluff City Grays") and Tennessee 154 Senior Infantry Regiment Private 1 Company B; per 154 Senior Infantry record enlisted May 14, 1861, Randolph, Tennessee age 21; killed per Daily Burial Record Book; killed and name spelled "Patterson" per Battle of Shiloh casualty list for unit reported in April 23, 1862, *Memphis Daily Appeal*; per Tennessee 3 (Forrest's) Cavalry Regiment Private Company A record enlisted May 4, 1861, Randolph, Tennessee and per January to July 1862, muster roll remarks killed at Battle of Shiloh April 6, 1862; listed in Elmwood 1874 book as Confederate soldier buried in Elmwood who was citizen of Memphis or vicinity; found in Lindsley's Annals under McDonald's Battery (sic Battalion) Company A as killed in action at Shiloh April 6, 1862; mentioned (Olie Patterson) by Dr. S. H. Ford in his address on the occasion to commemorate (Confederate Memorial Day) Confederates buried at Elmwood on April 26, 1866, (see article "Honors To The Memory Of The Hero Dead" in the April 27, 1866, *Memphis Daily Appeal*, page 3, column 1); listed in the June 6, 1878, *Memphis Daily Appeal*, page 4, column 3, article "OUR DEAD HEROES" covering the unveiling of the Confederate Monument and Decoration of Graves at Elmwood as then one of twenty-eight members of the Bluff City Grays, Company B of the 154 Senior Infantry Regiment and Company A of Forrest's Old (Third) Cavalry Regiment buried at Elmwood; listed as one of the "comrades who sleep at Elmwood cemetery " in the article "Veterans in Council" in *Memphis Daily Appeal*, May 12, 1881, page 4, column 4, concerning the meeting of the surviving members in the city of the old Bluff City Grays to appoint the necessary committees for the purpose of making special decoration on the graves of their dead comrades at Elmwood and Calvary cemeteries on Sunday next, Memorial Day; listed as member of Bluff City Grays in *Reminiscences of the Civil War* by John Hallum, Tunnah & Pittard printers, 1903; listed in "A COMPLETE ROSTER OF THE BLUFF CITY GREYS" located in the Memphis Room of the Memphis/Shelby County Public Library and Information Center Central Library with notation "Killed Shiloh, April 6, 1862" and included on the list at the end of the soldiers buried at Elmwood; see also Notes of Interest - Bluff City Grays; obituary in the April 18, 1862, *Memphis Daily Appeal*, page 2, age 22, son of Colonel George Pattison, and member Bluff City Grays 154 Regiment; son of George Pattison (interred September 4, 1877, age 75, Turley 82, #15) and brother of Thomas F., Robert T. and Reuben K. Pattison (per Thomas' Elmwood sketch Reuben accidentally killed in Memphis by a rocket fired by a youth when the stick struck the knee joint and died from effects of wound the next day, December 25, 1868 – interred age 19 December 27, 1868, Turley 82, #13).

Pattison, Robert T.   Buried November 13, 1866   Turley 82, #9
Listed in Elmwood 1874 book as Confederate soldier buried in Elmwood who was citizen of Memphis or vicinity; since buried in same Turley lot, believed to be brother of Thomas F. Pattison who's sketch in Elmwood book, page 140, captured in New Orleans

1862 on gunboat holding the river, paroled because of health, sailed to Memphis by way of Boston and died in the latter city in 1862 (note indicated as "younger" and second initial "F." in that sketch); not found in Confederate index books; died consumption per Daily Burial Record Book.

Pattison, Thomas Foster   Buried April 2, 1868   Turley 82, #10
Tennessee 3 (Forrest's) Cavalry Regiment Captain Company A ("Bluff City Grays") and Tennessee 154 Senior Infantry Regiment Private 1 Company B; per 154 Senior Infantry Regiment record (found under name spelled "Patterson") enlisted Sergeant Company B May 14, 1861 Randolph age 19; per August 13, 1861 muster roll (name "T. F. Pattison") elected 2 Lieutenant May 3, 1862; per Tennessee 11 Cavalry Regiment record 2 Lieutenant Company F; per Tennessee 3 Cavalry record enlisted May 4, 1861 Randolph; listed in Elmwood 1874 book as Confederate soldier buried in Elmwood who was citizen of Memphis or vicinity and sketch; per sketch born Des Moines, Iowa 1842, entered service as Orderly Sergeant of Bluff City Grays; listed in the June 6, 1878, *Memphis Daily Appeal*, page 4, column 3, article "OUR DEAD HEROES" covering the unveiling of the Confederate Monument and Decoration of Graves at Elmwood as then one of twenty-eight members of the Bluff City Grays, Company B of the 154 Senior Infantry Regiment and Company A of Forrest's Old (Third) Cavalry Regiment buried at Elmwood; listed as one of the "comrades who sleep at Elmwood cemetery " in the article "Veterans in Council" in M*emphis Daily Appeal*, May 12, 1881, page 4, column 4, concerning the meeting of the surviving members in the city of the old Bluff City Grays to appoint the necessary committees for the purpose of making special decoration on the graves of their dead comrades at Elmwood and Calvary cemeteries on Sunday next, Memorial Day; listed as member of Bluff City Grays in *Reminiscences of the Civil War* by John Hallum, Tunnah & Pittard printers, 1903; listed in "A COMPLETE ROSTER OF THE BLUFF CITY GREYS" located in the Memphis Room of the Memphis/Shelby County Public Library and Information Center Central Library with notation "1st Sgt. Elected May 1862, Promoted Capt. Co. Died Memphis" and included on the list at the end of the soldiers buried at Elmwood; see also Notes of Interest - Bluff City Grays; son of George Pattison (interred September 4, 1877, age 75, Turley 82, #15) and brother of O. G., Robert T. and Reuben K. Pattison (per Thomas' Elmwood sketch Reuben accidentally killed in Memphis by a rocket fired by a youth when the stick struck the knee joint and died from effects of wound the next day, December 25, 1868 - interred age 19 December 27, 1868, Turley 82, #13); died consumption age 26 per Daily Burial Record Book; per widow's (Anna Williamson (Holmes) Pattison) Tennessee Confederate Pension (W5382) he was born in Des Moines, Iowa April 6, 1842, and died April 1, 1868, in Memphis; she was born January 28, 1844, and they were married in Covington, Tennessee October 25, 1866; grave stone: 1842-1868 C.S.A.

Pease, George W.   Buried July 25, 1872   Chapel Hill 12, #14
Tennessee 50 Infantry Regiment Lieutenant Colonel; enlisted October 1, 1861, Fort Donelson, captured Fort Donelson February 16, 1862, and sent to Johnson's Island, sent to Vicksburg September 1, 1862, elected Captain September 23, 1862, confined to hospital in Atlanta from wounds received at Battle of Chickamauga (September 19-20, 1863), age 25 on muster roll dated February 29, 1864, promoted Lieutenant Colonel April 12, 1864; some records also found Tennessee 50 Consolidated Infantry regiment, card on Oath of Allegiance Nashville May 29, 1865 - per card place of residence Fayette County, Kentucky, surrendered Greensboro, North Carolina May 1, 1865, and paroled May 29, 1865; reference card also found Tennessee 2 Consolidated Infantry Regiment; mentioned in sketch on son, S. T. Pease, in *Tennessee, The Volunteer State, 1769-1923*, Volume IV, page 678; funeral notice in July 25, 1872, *Memphis Daily Appeal*, page1, which also referred to him as Colonel; no stone; he is possibly the Colonel William Peace listed in Elmwood 1874 book as Confederate soldier buried in Elmwood who was citizen of Memphis or vicinity, however, there is a William Peace buried at Elmwood Cemetery who was interred August 15, 1873, Fowler Public Lot 3, #254 and per Daily Burial Record Book died from consumption age 63 and who died August 14, 1873 age 63 per death notice in August 15, 1873, *Memphis Daily Appeal* but no information in either the newspaper or Cemetery records on Confederate service.

Pepper, Samuel Alexander   Buried February 29, 1932   Chapel Hill 47, #3
Mississippi 29 Infantry Regiment Corporal Company C; originally enlisted in Virginia 11 Infantry Regiment Private Company F May 29, 1861, at Christiansburg, Virginia at age 18 and after July 1, 1863, records found in Mississippi 29 Infantry Regiment records; casualty report on engagement at Missionary Ridge November 25, 1863, indicates rank as private and was severely wounded; promoted to Corporal February 1, 1864; was admitted to St. Mary's Hospital, West Point, Mississippi January 6, 1865, by reason of gunshot wound and transferred January 7, 1865, place not shown; paroled at Greensboro, North Carolina April 26, 1865; per sketch in Mathes book born in Johnson County, Missouri October 27, 1842, living in Virginia when War broke out enlisted in Virginia 11 Infantry Private Company F and afterwards served in Mississippi 24 (not found listed for this unit in Confederate index books) and 29 Regiments; also per Mathes sketch he was one of the early members of the Confederate Historical Association, for many years an active member of the Chickasaw Guards, and Orderly Sergeant of Company A, Confederate Veterans; biography in *Confederate Military History, Extended Edition*, Volume X Tennessee, page 669; received Tennessee Confederate Pension (S16315) October 1927, and widow, Anna Lee Polk Pepper, received Tennessee Confederate Pension (W10487) April 1932; article in *The Commercial Appeal* Memphis February 29, 1932, page 5, indicating died February 28, 1932, at age 89; grave stone: October 27, 1842 February 28, 1932.

Perkins, Alfred Henry Dashiell   Buried January 7, 1928   Evergreen 182, #8
Tennessee 7 Cavalry Regiment Color Sergeant Company E; enlisted December 12, 1862, Torrence Station; per February 29 to May 11, 1864, muster roll remarks: promoted to Color Sergeant March 18, 1864 (for gallantry on the field); name appears on a register of prisoners of war belonging to rebel army, in the custody of Provost Marshall, Memphis, Tennessee, captured May 25, 1863, and sent to Alton June 3, 1863; name appears on a roll of prisoners of war received at Military Prison, Alton, Illinois indicating captured

Hickory Valley May 29, 1863, and received June 6, 1863, exchanged June 12, 1863, and remarks of violated his oath: paroled Gainesville, Alabama May 11, 1865; sketch in Mathes book (both editions); per enlarged edition born July 29, 1845, Shelbyville, Tennessee, first joined Tennessee 6 Infantry Company H in May 1861, but enlisted November 1862, in 7 Cavalry; promoted Color Sergeant May 18, 1864, for gallantry on field per Young's book; most records found as "A. H. D. Perkins"; received Tennessee Confederate Pension (S16022) and widow, Elizabeth James Perkins, received a Tennessee Confederate Pension (W8999); subject of two newspaper articles: "Rebel Flag the Yanks never captured" by Paul Vanderwood, *Memphis Press Scimitar*, June 8, 1962, page 17 and "Carrying the Rebel Colors into the thick of battle" by Paul R. Coppock, *The Commercial Appeal* Memphis, July 25, 1976, Mid-South Memoirs, Section G, page 7; died age 82 per Daily Burial Record Book; 1845-1928 on grave stone; biography in *Confederate Military History*, *Extended Edition*, Volume X Tennessee, page 670.

Person, Richard J.   Buried October 29, 1909   Turley 568, #17
Confederate 9 Infantry Regiment (also called Confederate 5 (Smith's) Infantry Regiment, which was formed by the consolidation of Tennessee 2 (Walker's) Infantry Regiment and Tennessee 21 Infantry Regiment) Major; enlisted Tennessee 21 Infantry Regiment Captain Company B July 10, 1861; assigned to duty as major Confederate 5 Infantry Regiment by Special Order No. 73 July 21, 1862; recommended for Regiment vacant Colonel position but not confirmed; per Roll of Prisoners of War (undated) captured July 22, 1864, near Atlanta, Georgia and first sent Military Prison, Louisville, Kentucky, than forwarded to Johnson's Island, Ohio July 30, 1864; signed Oath of Alliance at Johnson's Island on July 25, 1865, indicating residence of Memphis, Tennessee and age 23; per sketch in Mathes book, page 175, born February 5,1843, graduated from Kentucky Military Institute at Franklin, after four years attendance in 1861, with rank of captain in the Kentucky State Guard, left college for the camp, and soon became Captain Company B Tennessee 21 Infantry Regiment and afterwards Major of 5 Confederate, captured July 22, 1864, in Atlanta and sent to Johnson's Island where confined until end of War, and joined Confederate Relief and Historical Association in 1869; per obituary in *Confederate Veteran* Volume XVII, December 1909, page 609 died in Nashville and buried in Elmwood Cemetery, honorary member of Camp A, Confederate Veterans, Memphis, and also Confederate Historical Society; died age 68 per Daily Burial Record Book; grave stone: Feb. 5, 1843 Oct. 28, 1909.

Peters, Dr. George Boddie   Buried April 30, 1889   Miller Circle 36, #3
Shot and killed Confederate Major General Earl Van Dorn on May 7, 1863, at Spring Hill, Tennessee because his wife, Jessie Helen McKissack, had an affair with General Van Dorn; sketch #38 in Elmwood *Civil War Tour* booklet indicates born in North Carolina, as a child moved to Maury County, Tennessee, after completing medical school practiced medicine in Bolivar, Tennessee, after death of first two wives married his cousin Jessie McKissack who 23 years his junior, later quit practicing medicine and in 1859 elected to the Tennessee General Assembly, when legislature was in session they lived in Spring Hill, Tennessee in the home Jessie inherited from her father and never convicted of killing General Van Dorn; after brief divorce and remarriage, they moved to Memphis per Elmwood Blog: Earl Van Dorn, the "Terror of Ugly Husbands" March 29, 2016, by volunteer Allison Baily; see also: Tim Kent's Civil War tales (trrcobb.blogspot.com/) "The Terror Of Ugly Husbands" December 13, 2013; Siggurdsson. "Confederate General Earl Van Dorn Murdered by Cuckolded Husband." The American Legion's Burnpit. N.p., 7 May 2013. Web. 29 Feb. 2016; Magness, Perre. "General Lived Wildly until the Last." Commercial Appeal [Memphis] 1996: n. pag. Print; "Earl Van Dorn." Council on Foreign Relations. Council on Foreign Relations, n.d. Web. 29 Feb. 2016; and **Seasons in the South: The Lives Involved in the Death of General Van Dorn**, Linda Gupton, Authorhouse, 2013; sketch #38 in Elmwood *Civil War Tour* booklet (2012); no grave stone.

Peters, Jessie McKissack   Buried July 18, 1921   Miller Circle 36, #4
Wife of Dr. George Boddie Peters (see sketch supra) who killed Confederate Major General Earl Van Dorn on May 7, 1863, after she had an affair with General Van Dorn; she and Dr. Peters had six children and she had another daughter who was the child of General Van Dorn; born in Spring Hill, Tennessee January 3, 1838; sketch 38 in Elmwood *Civil War Tour* booklet (2012).

Phelan, George Richard   Buried September 26, 1882   Chapel Hill Circle 40/70, #10
Mississippi 12 Cavalry Adjutant; letter in file dated May 4, 1864, from Colonel C. G. Armistead to Secretary of War Seddon requesting appointment of George R. Phelan as Adjutant, which indicates currently a Private in Mississippi 24 Regiment Company D; letter dated May 13, 1864, in file from father, James Phelan, to Secretary of War Seddon supporting his son's appointment as Adjutant, which also indicates serving in Mississippi 24 Regiment; no records found in Mississippi 24 Infantry or 24 Cavalry Battalion records; letter in file dated September 12, 1864, to General Cooper from Colonel Armistead recommending appointment as adjutant, which indicates born in State of Mississippi, resides in Aberdeen, Mississippi, 19 years of age and has been in the service for more than two years; parole card dated May 14, 1865, indicates age 19 and residence of Liverpool, England (?), commissioned April 18, 1864; signed Oath of Allegiance May 14, 1865, at Meridian, Mississippi; possibly originally served in Mississippi 11 Infantry Private Company I, enlisted October 21, 1861, Camp Fisher, present on March/April 1862, muster roll and discharged May 13, 1862; served in Tennessee General Assembly 1877-1879 representing Shelby County; per *Biographical Directory of the Tennessee General Assembly*, Volume II 1861-1901, by Robert Martin McBride, Tennessee State Library and Archives, Nashville, 1979, page 723, joined the Confederate Army in Virginia, went back to Tuscaloosa to military school, expelled, and rejoined Army; born 1847 in Tuscaloosa, Tuscaloosa County, Alabama and son of James Phelan, Confederate Congressman from Mississippi (see Notes of Interest); per biographical sketch on Hunt Phelan (son of George R. Phelan), published in *The National Cyclopedia*, second name "Richardson" and "while still in his teens he served in the Confederate army in the Civil War as a captain of cavalry."; circle grave stone: G.R.P. and upright grave stone: George R. Phelan Born in Marion Ala. July 15,

1847, Died in Memphis, Tenn. September 22, 1882; died September 24, 1882 aged 35 per obituary in September 26, 1882, *Memphis Avalanche*, page 1; see narrative of his life and service during the War in the *Proceedings of the Bar Association of Tennessee at the Fourteenth Annual Meeting, held at Lookout Inn, Lookout Mountain, Tenn., July 17, 18, 19, 1895.* Nashville: Cumberland Presbyterian Publishing House. 1895. Pages 100-104.

Phillips, William M.   Buried October 23, 1906   Fowler Public Lot 6, #558
Alabama 19 Infantry Regiment Private Company B; enlisted August 12, 1861, Summit, Alabama; per June 1862, muster roll remarks: discharged June 25, 1862, at Tupelo, Mississippi, Court Martial, June 20, 1862; had been sent to jail December 1861 to January 1862 by order of court martial; no other information in record; government grave stone with unit information and dates February 12 1842 October 22, 1906; died age 65 per Daily Burial Record Book.

Pillow, Alexander H.   Buried December 1, 1863   Turley 106, #3
Tennessee 154 Senior Infantry Regiment Private Company G, per Company Muster-in Roll dated August 13, 1861, at New Madrid, Missouri, enlisted May 14, 1861, Randolph, Tennessee, per Company Muster Roll for January 1, 1862, to July 1, 1862, remarks: absent without leave May 6, 1862, per Company Muster Roll dated May 5, 1863, remarks: deserted May 20, 1862; died age 57 per Daily Burial Record Book.

Pillow, Gideon Johnson   Buried February 14, 1884   Evergreen 217, #1
Brigadier General; appointed from Tennessee July 9, 1861 (rank July 9, 1861) per the *Memorandum relative to the General Officers Appointed by the President in the Armies of the Confederate States - 1861-1865* compiled from Official Records by the Military Secretary's Office, U. S. War Department 1905; best remembered for confrontation with Union General Grant at Fort Donelson in February 1862; per General and Staff records surrendered May 5, 1865 at Montgomery, Alabama; per sketch in Mathes book born 1806 in Williamson County, Tennessee, served in Mexican War as Brigadier General and promoted to Major General, Governor Harris appointed him to command state troops with rank of Major General, when Tennessee seceded commissioned Brigadier General, after surrender at Fort Donelson not given a command in field again, joined Confederate Historical Association July 15, 1869; died October 8, 1878 near Helena, Arkansas; sketch in *Generals in Gray*; biography in *Confederate Military History, Extended Edition*, Volume X Tennessee, page 325; sketch in *Tennessee, The Volunteer State, 1769-1923*, Volume II, page 209; see also collection in Memphis Room in Memphis and Shelby County Public Library; sketch, photograph, if available, and grave stone photograph in book *Quiet Places: The Burial Sites of Civil War Generals in Tennessee* by Buckner and Nathaniel C. Hughes, Jr., East Tennessee Historical Society (1992); large monument that recites military career; born Columbia, Tennessee June 8, 1806 on monument; also listed in chapter on Generals; listed under Generals in "Touring historic Elmwood Cemetery" (Brochure and Map of Historic Gravesites) #12; listed in "Touring Historic Elmwood Cemetery" Brochure (January 2000) #133; sketch #36 in Elmwood *Civil War Tour* booklet (2012).

Pinson, Richard Alexander   Buried May 19, 1873   Miller Circle 352, #2
Mississippi 1 Cavalry Regiment Colonel; Captain Company K and promoted to rank of Colonel June 10, 1862, by election in the field; recommended for promotion to Brigadier General but never received appointment; signed Parole of Honor May 16, 1865, at Columbus, Mississippi as "R. A. Pinson" Colonel 1 Mississippi Cavalry CSA; first enlisted in Mississippi 1 (Miller's) Cavalry Battalion Cole's Company ("Pontotoc Dragoons") 1 Sergeant February 22, 1861, Pontotoc, Mississippi age 32 (men from company after battalion disbanded about June 1862 joined Company I Mississippi 1 Cavalry Regiment); listed in Elmwood 1874 book as Confederate soldier buried in Elmwood who was citizen of Memphis or vicinity with rank of Colonel and sketch; per sketch came to Memphis 1866 and died at his lodgings in Peabody Hotel May 17, 1873, age 45; died inflammation of stomach age 45 per Daily Burial Record Book; death and article on his life and career reported in the May 18, 1873, *Memphis Daily Appeal*, page 2, column 1, indicating born Lincoln County, Tennessee 1831, 1834 moved to Pontotoc County, Mississippi, elected to Congress 1865 but denied seat and moved to Memphis 1868, and member of Pontotoc Masonic Lodge No. 18, Mississippi; funeral reported in the article "Honor To The Dead" in the May 20, 1873, *Memphis Daily Appeal*, page 4, column 6; born Pontotoc County, Mississippi (note difference with other newspaper report) per *Daily Memphis Avalanche* May 18, 1873; see also "Honors to Colonel Pinson" *Memphis Avalanche* May 19, 1873, page 4; April 1829 April 1873 on grave stone; originally buried Chapel Hill Circle,34 and moved November 2, 1911; note Mississippi 1 Cavalry Regiment is not the same as Wirt Adams' Cavalry Regiment, which was also known as 1 Regiment Mississippi Cavalry, and was later officially known as Confederate Wood's Cavalry Regiment (no records found in these units); sketch in *Tennessee, The Volunteer State, 1769-1923*, Volume III, page 461; listed under Other Pioneers, Patriots and Patriarchs in "Touring historic Elmwood Cemetery" (Brochure and Map of Historic Gravesites) #92.

Piper, Oliver Hazzard Perry   Buried November 15, 1927   Miller Circle 39, #3
Tennessee Johnston's Heavy-Artillery Private Hamilton's Company; enlisted April 21, 1861, Memphis age 22; per sketch in Mathes book page 275-276: enlisted April 12, 1861, in Southern Guard; brother of William A. Piper; member Confederate Historical Association; born Somerset County, Maryland; included in biography on the three Piper Brothers (Oliver Hazard Perry, John George, and William Augustus – see sketch next below) in *Confederate Military History, Extended Edition*, Volume X Tennessee, page 672; died age 88 per Daily Burial Record Book; large monument: 1839 Oliver H. P. Piper 1927.

Piper, William Augustus   Buried May 12, 1862   Chapel Hill 173, #1
Tennessee 154 Senior Infantry Regiment Private Company L; enlisted March 7, 1862, Memphis; per May & June 1862, muster

roll remarks: died at Corinth May 8, 1862; per register of soldiers killed in battle born Ohio and deceased May 8, 1862, at Corinth; per report of deaths dated October 30, 1863, enlisted March 8, 1862, Memphis, born Ohio, died May 8 Corinth from sickness and entitled to $50 bounty, $20 commutation and $45 stoppage; enlistment in "Maynard Rifles" reported in the February 25, 1862, *Memphis Daily Appeal*; per death notice in the May 9, 1862, *Memphis Daily Appeal,* page 1, column 7, died May 8, 1862, at Corinth, Mississippi after severe illness and member of Maynard Rifles; obituary in May 11, 1862, *Memphis Daily Appeal,* page 2, column 7; per brother's, O. H. P. Piper, sketch in Mathes book one of three brothers, William A., O. H. P. and John George, born in Somerset County, Maryland (note birth place difference with compiled service records), enlisted age 18, took part in Battle of Shiloh and died May 8, 1862, in Major Frank Gailor's tent after great exposure, bringing on a fatal illness; l; included in biography on the three Piper Brothers (Oliver Hazard Perry – see sketch next above, John George, and William Augustus) in *Confederate Military History, Extended Edition*, Volume X Tennessee, page 672; listed in Elmwood 1874 book as Confederate soldier buried in Elmwood who was citizen of Memphis or vicinity.

Pitman, Warren
Listed in Elmwood 1874 book as Confederate soldier buried in Elmwood who was citizen of Memphis or vicinity but no Cemetery or service record found; not found in Cemetery computer index.

Pittman, William Preston Buried October 19, 1867 Turley 435, #5
Georgia Troup Artillery (company transferred from Cobb's Georgia Legion around November 1861); per Bill Smedlund, who is researching Troup Artillery, born June 30, 1843, enlisted September 5, 1861, in Company D Cobb's Legion Infantry Battalion, private, transferred June 1862 to Troup Artillery, private (brothers James E. and Robert W. T. Pittman also served in Troup Artillery), paroled at Appomattox Court House April 9, 1865, and died October 19, 1867, of yellow fever in Arkansas across river from Memphis; died yellow fever, age 25 per Daily Burial Record Book, government stone with unit and dates of birth and death.

Pitman, William Thornton Buried March 8, 1866 Chapel Hill 23, #3
Tennessee 154 Senior Infantry Regiment Corporal Company G; enlisted June 3, 1861, Memphis age 48 (believed should be 18); per November and December 1863, muster roll remarks: absent wounded since muster; per Daily Burial Record Book killed Battle of Franklin, Tennessee November 30, 1864, moved-in and age 21 years, 6 months; no information as to where originally buried; not found in Lindsley's Annals.

Pointer, Marcellus Buried July 15, 1909 Fowler 315, #9
Alabama 12 Cavalry Regiment Colonel, per only card in compiled service record Report of Prisoners of War paroled at Holly Springs, Mississippi from June 5 to 10,1865, surrendered April 23, 1865, and paroled June 9, 1865, residence Shelby Springs, Mississippi (name spelled Marcelus); may have only been Lieutenant Colonel; per widow's Texas Confederate Pension application 17370, Mrs. Willie A. Pointer, Texarkana, Texas, filed October 6, 1909, originally served 12 months in Mississippi 9 Regiment then served on General Wheeler's staff as 1 Lieutenant Aide de Camp, commissioned Lieutenant Colonel 12 Alabama Regiment April 1, 1865, married October 19, 1865, in Marshall County, Mississippi, and died July 9,1909, in New York County, New York; Mississippi 9 Infantry Regiment Private Old Company B, depending on record enlisted March 27,1861, at Holly Springs, Mississippi, enlisted June 3, 1861, Camp Magnolia, last card in record for October 21, 1861, to March 31, 1862, Present; per General & Staff Officers compiled service record rolls 1 Lt & ADC, Register of Appointment State – MS, report to General Wheeler, date of appointment April 30, 1863, ADC, card in record Pvt Old Co B 9 MS Infantry enlisted June 3, 1861, at Camp Magnolia for 12 months and present on all rolls, January 23, 1863, note in file indicates 1st 10 MS Regiment (no record found) when appointed ADC by General Wheeler and wounded October 19, 1862, paper clip in file The New York Tribune July 12, 1909, "Confederates Arrange Funeral Veterans" will bury Colonel Pointer in their plot in Mount Hope Cemetery; per *Confederate Staff Officers* 1861 -1865 by Joseph H. Crute, Jr., Derwent Books 1982, page 208, appointed Lieutenant A. D. C. July 20, 1862, relieved (wounded) October 31, 1862, Lieutenant A. D. C. January 29, September 19, 20, November and December 1863, on the staff of Brigadier General (Major General January 20,1863) Joseph Wheeler; obituary article in *Confederate Veteran* Volume XVII, No.1, January 1909, page 556, indicating that found dead on July 10 at the old Atlantic Hotel in New York; per great great-niece Zee Porter born April 20, 1841, in either Caswell or Person County, North Carolina, family migrated to Mississippi in 1838, and Marshall County in 1844, enlisted at age 19 in Mississippi 9 Infantry Old Company B, served on General Wheeler's staff, Colonel Alabama 12 Cavalry Regiment, after war refused to sign allegiance to the Union, went to Brazil, South America leaving behind a wife and at least 3 known daughters and a son living in Holly Springs, later returned to United States, went to New York, visited Mississippi and businessman in Texas 1889-1894 in real estate and brick manufacturing; per biography in *Confederate Military History, Extended Edition*, Volume VIII Alabama, page 279, sketch on 12 Alabama Cavalry Regiment succeeded Warren S. Reese as Colonel and was wounded; Lieutenant Colonel per Alabama 12 Cavalry Regiment sketch in Chutes' *Units of the Confederate States Army*; referred to as Colonel in *Commercial Appeal* Memphis articles July 14, 1909, page 1, column 2, July 15, 1909, page 4, and July 16, 1909, page 7, column 4; per Funeral Home Records book Pointer, Marcellus (Col) 65 years, NY, NY, apoplexy, Elmwood; per Shelby County Death Record (Book 9, Page 54) died July 10, 1909, age 65; per Marshal County, Mississippi marriage book married Willie A. (Anna per Zee Porter) Mayer October 19, 1865; listed in Morrison & Fourmy's Directory, of the City of Dallas 1884-85 and 1886-87; grave stone: Marcellus Pointer, Col 12 Ala Cavalry, Confederate States of America, Apr 20, 1841 July 9, 1909.

Pope, Andrew Rembert   Buried October 30, 1925   Chapel Hill 618, #10

Tennessee 4 Infantry Regiment Private Company A; enlisted May 15, 1861, Germantown, Tennessee age 19; detailed for special duty at General Polk's Headquarters per August 17, 1861, to January 1, 1862 muster roll; detailed to Signal Corps per March & April 1863, muster roll but no records found in Signal Corps or General and Staff records; took Oath of Allegiance June 6, 1865, at Memphis indicating age 23 and residence as Shelby County, Tennessee; per widow Mary A. Pope's Tennessee Confederate Pension W9763 he was born December 8, 1841, in Shelby County, Tennessee, she was born Mary Murrell in Fayette County, Tennessee November 4, 1847, and they were married September 10, 1865, in Fayette County, Tennessee; obituary in *Confederate Veteran* Volume XXXIII, December 1925, page 468; sketch in Mathes book enlarged edition; grave stone: Andrew R. Pope, Senior Private 4 Tenn. Infantry C.S.A. December 8, 1842, (note year difference with pension file) October 29, 1925; died age 83 per Daily Burial Record Book; grave stone: December 8, 1842 October 29, 1925.

Pope, Mary E. Foote   Buried March 26, 1905   Fowler 234, #4

Secretary of Southern Mothers Hospital (see chapters on Hospitals and Notes of Interest) which she founded with Sarah C. Law; see Paul R. Coppock's Mid-South, Volume III, page 197, "... there came a day when a federal gunboat was sunk in the harbor and the order came down for everyone to hang drape of mourning on their houses. Instead, Mrs. Pope flew the Stars and Bars. She was arrested and might have been put in prison. But the high command thought banishment would be more appropriate."; she left town and took her school with her and went to Hernando; grave stone: Mary Foote Pope, 1821-1905, "Place at my Head, of Gray Stone Wrought, a Cross. That to the passing eye may tell Oh, sweet and blessed thought! That Christian Ashes 'neath it lie." Mary Foote Pope, Poet and Founder of St. Mary's Episcopal School Memphis, Tennessee 1847; obituary in March 26, 1905, *The Commercial Appeal* Memphis, page 3, died March 25, 1905, born at Huntsville, Alabama, and founded young ladies school about 1850; listed in "Touring Historic Elmwood Cemetery" Brochure (January 2000) #12 sketch #4 in Elmwood *Civil War Tour* booklet (2012).

Pope, William S.   Buried July 18, 1866   Fowler 234, #1

Tennessee 7 Cavalry Regiment Lieutenant Adjutant; per company Muster-in Roll dated May 16, 1861, enlisted as Private May 16, 1861, Memphis age 18; per Rosters of Officers for Regiment appointed Adjutant January 20, 1863; appears on a report of casualties in Major General Forrest's command in the Battle of Tishomingo Creek, Mississippi June 10, 1864, (Brices Cross Roads) with remarks killed; listed in Elmwood 1874 book as Confederate soldier buried in Elmwood who was citizen of Memphis or vicinity with rank of Lieutenant; "Lieutenant Pope" in Cemetery computer index and Daily Burial Record Book and "William S. Pope" in Fowler Book; "brought here from" remark in Daily Burial Record Book; grave stone (partly illegible) died June 10, 1864, aged 21 years; per Lindsley's Annals Adjutant William S. Pope killed Tishomingo Creek, Mississippi June 10, 1864; killed at Tishomingo Creek, Miss. June 10, 1864 inscribed on "In Memory Of" stone located in walk around Confederate Soldiers Rest Monument; mentioned by Dr. S. H. Ford in his address on the occasion to commemorate (Confederate Memorial Day) Confederates buried at Elmwood on April 26, 1866, (see article "Honors To The Memory Of The Hero Dead" in the April 27, 1866, *Memphis Daily Appeal*, page 3, column 1).

Porter, Edward E.   Buried October 8, 1867   Fowler 103, #5

Tennessee 3 (Forrest's) Cavalry Regiment Lieutenant Colonel; signed Parole of Honor May 11, 1865; Mississippi 2 (J. G. Ballentine's Regiment of Cavalry) Partisan Rangers Captain (Captain Edward E. Porter's Partisan Company) Company C; enlisted May 7, 1862; Company C transferred to Tennessee 3 (Forrest's Old) Cavalry Regiment Company F in accordance with S. O. No. 28. Headquarters, Cavalry Division District of Mississippi and East Louisiana, dated February 13, 1865, and Company C Prisoner of War Roll (No. 219) on which prisoners of war were paroled at the close of war at Gainesville, Alabama, shows members of Company C paroled in May 1865, as Company F (3d) Forrest's Old Regiment Tennessee Cavalry with George R. Merritt as Captain and Captain E. E Porter, who was Captain of Company C, was promoted to Lieutenant Colonel of the Tennessee 3 (Forrest's Old) Cavalry Regiment (Colonel D. C. Kelly at end of war); remaining troops of the Mississippi 2 (Ballentine's) Partisan Rangers merged (consolidated) into the Mississippi 7 Cavalry Regiment (also called Mississippi 1 Partisan Rangers) - see Ballentine's Cavalry Regiment (also called 2nd Partisan Rangers) sketch in Chutes' *Units of the Confederate States Army* and *Confederate Military History, Extended Edition*, Volume IX Mississippi, page 224, and Volume XV Texas, page 690); appears to have first served in Tennessee 2 (Walker's) Infantry Regiment Captain Company E, appears on a Company Muster-in Roll dated Fort Pillow, Tennessee, September 9, 1861, indicating enlisted May 11, 1861, and Resigned and resignation received August 9, 1861; per sketch in Mathes book, page 278: born March 28, 1832, Lincolnton, Lincoln County, North Carolina, graduate of the Union Theological Seminary, Hampton-Sydney, Virginia, pastor of the Third Presbyterian Church in Memphis when the war commenced, early in war received a commission from President Davis to raise an independent company, known as Porter's Partisans, after evacuation of Columbus and Fort Pillow mustered into Confederate service in the Department of Memphis, finished war with Forrest's command, and died October 6, 1867; listed in Elmwood 1874 book as Confederate soldier buried in Elmwood who was citizen of Memphis or vicinity with rank of Captain and sketch; per sketch and Daily Burial Record Book died age 36; second initial "C" in *Tennesseans in the Civil War, Part 2*; grave stone: Rev. Ed. E. Porter Born March 27, 1832 Died October 6, 1867.

Porter, John William   Buried September 1, 1943   South Grove Single Grave Section 1, #214

Mississippi 1 Battalion Sharp Shooters Private Company B; article in *The Commercial Appeal* Memphis September 1, 1943, page 13, column 3, indicating that he was the last Confederate Veteran of Shelby County and died August 31, 1943, at age 98; article refers to him as "Colonel" and includes picture taken when he attended the Blue-and-Gray Reunion at Gettysburg in 1938; per article born June 23, 1845, son of Colonel A. A. Porter, when not yet 16 years old joined his father and brother, Captain Robert

Porter, when enlisted in Company B Mississippi 1 Battalion Sharp Shooters, wounded at Battle of Peachtree Creek, the same burst of shrapnel killed his brother, and honorably discharged at Abbeville Courthouse, South Carolina; article also references General R. L. Bullington (believed to be Richard E. Bullington who died January 21, 1943 - see sketch) and Reverend R. P. Smith who had died several months before his death and along with whom had attended the Blue-and-Gray reunion at Gettysburg in 1938, as the last survivors of Memphis' "thin gray line" that once numbered thousands; referred to as "Colonel" in Daily Burial Record Book.

Poston, David Hamill Buried March 13, 1891 Chapel Hill 690, #4
Tennessee 4 Infantry Regiment Sergeant Company A ("Shelby Grays"); enlisted May 14, 1861, Fort Randolph, age 17, per muster roll dated August 16, 1861 at Fort Pillow; per muster roll dated April 25 to June 30, 1862 age 18 and enlisted May 15, 1861 at Germantown and remarks that wounded at Perryville; originally enlisted in Tennessee 154 Senior Infantry Regiment, Private 1 Company B and per August 14 to November 1, 1861 muster remarks transferred to Neely's Regiment (Tennessee 4 Infantry Regiment); single card record in Tennessee 3 Cavalry Regiment, Private Company A which was the designation for the Tennessee 154 Senior Infantry Regiment 1 Company B when it was transferred to the Tennessee 3 Cavalry Regiment (probably just on list with other soldiers when company transferred); per sketch in Mathes book law partner of General W. Y. C. Humes and joined Confederate Historical Association August 12, 1969; death notice in March 12, 1891, *Memphis Daily Appeal*, page 1, indicating died March 11, 1891; article on front page the March 12, 1891, *Memphis Daily Appeal-Avalanche* about being shot by H. Clay King at 11:20 am on March 10, 1891; sketch in Goodspeed's Shelby County History, page 1023; circular grave stone: Died March 11, 1891, aged 47 year 1 month and 2 days on it; not listed in Cemetery computer index but his son's listing (interment February 10, 1891) shows his father's date of death.

Poston, William King, Jr. Buried April 20, 1910 South Grove 571, #4
Tennessee 4 Infantry Regiment Private Company A ("Shelby Grays"); enlisted May 15, 1861, Germantown, Tennessee age 15; per January & February 1864, muster roll remarks: wounded and captured November 25, 1863, Missionary Ridge; per prisoner list at General Field Hospital Bridgeport, Alabama December 1863: gunshot wound left shoulder; forwarded to Louisville, Kentucky for exchange January 10, 1864; sent to Rock Island, Illinois January 17, 1864; prisoner until February 1865; February 25, 1865, sent to General Hospital, Howard's Grove, Richmond, Virginia; transferred to Camp Lee February 28, 1865; per sketch in Mathes book born in Shelby County, Tennessee, served in same command throughout war, wounded twice, Shiloh and Missionary Ridge, and paroled May 23, 1865; biography in *Confederate Military History, Extended Edition*, Volume X Tennessee, page 676; sketch in Goodspeed's Shelby County History, page l023; died age 64 per Daily Burial Record Book; 1845 1910 and Confederate unit information on individual grave stone; "William King Poston, II" October 2, 1845-April 19, 1910 on family grave stone; death reported in *Confederate Veteran*, Volume XIX, April 1911, page 174, "The Last Roll" Deaths of Confederates in Memphis, Tennessee who died during 1910 and were members of the Confederate Historical Association, Camp No. 28, U. C. V., Bivouac 18, C. V., of Memphis.

Prescott, Jesse Pearson Buried March 22, 1896 Fowler 144, #4
Alabama State Artillery Sergeant Company D; appears on a Muster Roll of Co. D, State Artillery, 1st Regiment Mobile Vols., Local Defence, organized and accepted for service solely within the city and county of Mobile and for the Defence of said city and county during the war, for November 25 to December 31, 1863, with remarks on active service from November 25 to December 31, 1863; per Company Muster-in Roll dated August 11, 1864, enlisted August 11, 1864, age 46 and Alabama residence; per Company Muster Roll for June 30 to August 31, 1864, Corporal, remarks: promoted from the ranks August 11, 1864; per Company Muster Roll for August 31, to October 31, 1864, Sergeant, remarks: promoted from 4th Corporal September 1, 1864; appears on a Roll of Prisoners of War surrendered at Citronelle, Alabama, and paroled at Meridian, Mississippi, May 11, 1865, residence Mobile, Alabama; death reported in the March 22, 1896, *Commercial Appeal* Memphis, page 5, column 6; died age 69 per Daily Burial Record Book.

Preston, Thomas W. Buried January 12, 1863 Chapel Hill Circle 52, #2
Assistant Adjutant General, Captain, Staff of General Alexander P. Stewart; per General and Staff record appointed Captain Adjutant General February 13, 1862, and killed April 6, 1862, at Battle of Shiloh; first organized Captain T. W. Preston's Company "The Memphis Grey's" but no records found for this unit per *Tennesseans in the Civil War, Part 1*, however, cards found for T. W. Preston, Captain, T. W. Preston's Company, Memphis Greys in Tennessee compiled service records Miscellaneous roll (see also miscellaneous roll cards on Hart, M. L., 1 Lieutenant of the unit); notice in *Memphis Daily Appeal*, July 31, 1861, "Immediate Active Service Col. Thomas W. Preston and S. M. Hart, purpose to raise a company for immediate service, apply at headquarters in the Adams block"; killed at Battle of Shiloh April 6, 1862, per list in *Confederate Veterans* magazine Volume XXXIV, 1926, page 128; large family monument: "Fell at Shilo (sic) April 6, 1862, Aged 44 Years" and "He Sleeps The Sleep of the Brave"; originally buried Chapel Hill 380, #3 and moved April 17, 1868; mentioned (Colonel Preston) by Dr. S. H. Ford in his address on the occasion to commemorate (Confederate Memorial Day) Confederates buried at Elmwood on April 26, 1866, (see articles "The Confederate Dead" in the *Public Ledger* (Memphis), April 27, 1866, page 3, column 2, and "Honors To The Memory Of The Hero Dead" in the April 27, 1866, *Memphis Daily Appeal*, page 3, column 1).

Pullen, Benjamin King Buried July 17, 1900 Turley 1013, #10
Tennessee 3 (Memphis) Infantry Battalion 2 Lieutenant Company C and Captain, Assistant Commissary of Subsistence; enlisted in Tennessee 3 (Memphis) Infantry Battalion March 12, 1862, at Memphis and last card in record is pay voucher signed July 17,

1862; per General and Staff record Captain and Assistant Commissary of Subsistence with card indicating Captain Colonel Ballentine's Cavalry Regiment on leave of absence and resigned March 1863; per Mathes book enlisted in 1861, was a member of Captain J. T. Begbie's (Captain Company C Tennessee 3 Infantry Battalion) Confederate Home Guard, afterward served with Colonel J. G. Ballentine's Cavalry Regiment with rank of Captain up to January 1864 (note not found listed in any index for this regiment or in unit's compiled service records), transferred to post duty at Grenada, Mississippi under Major J. S. Mellon, Chief of Subsistence until the surrender in 1865, and admitted to Confederate Historical Association October 8, 1895; per article in *The Commercial Appeal* Memphis July 16, 1900, page 5 column 4, referred to as Major, died at Houma, Louisiana July 15, 1900, had been a citizen of Memphis until about five years ago, about 75 years of age and remains will be brought to Memphis for interment; no Confederate service information in newspaper; per Shelby County Funeral Books born November 11, 1821, in North Carolina and died of heart failure; per son's (Benjamin K. Pullen, Jr) sketch in Shelby County's history in Goodspeed's *History of Hamilton, Knox and Shelby Counties of Tennessee*, page 1026, came to Memphis in 1860 and engaged in mercantile business; grave stone: General and Staff Officers, CSA, Nov 9 1821 Jul 15 1900.

Purdy, Charles R.   Buried October 11, 1863   Chapel Hill 491, #1
No unit indicated in Daily Burial Record Book but remarks "Confed Soldier"; possibly Charles Robertson Purdy, Louisiana 4 Infantry Regiment 2 Lieutenant/Captain Company C ("Lake Providence Cadets"), enlisted May 25, 1861, Camp Moore, Louisiana, present on muster rolls to October 1861, and on November and December 1862, muster roll but no other information in compiled service record; per *Guide to Louisiana Confederate Military Units, 1861-1865.* Arthur W. Bergeron, Jr., Baton Rouge: Louisiana State University Press, 1996. when the regiment was at Port Hudson, it received orders on May 1, 1863, to try and intercept Colonel Benjamin Grierson's raiders and a detachment of the regiment, mostly men from Company C, remained behind and participated in the Siege of Port Hudson May 23-July 9, 1863, and Charles R. Purdy of Company C was killed June 26, 1863; interred in Chapel Hill Lot 91per computer index.

Quenichet, John Wesley   Buried December 19,1871   Chapel Hill 136
Tennessee 154 Senior Infantry Regiment Private Company L; per Company Muster-in Roll dated March 8, 1862, enlisted March 7, 1862, Memphis; per Company Muster Roll for May & June 1862, remarks: Discharged July 12, 1862; per Company Muster Roll dated May 6, 1863, remarks: Discharged from disability; submitted letter (petition) dated June 9, 1865, requesting amnesty (pardon) to Governor Andrew Johnson and it was approved; per death notice in the December 19, 1871, *Memphis Daily Appeal,* page 1, column 4, died December 18, 1871, after protracted illness; died age 41 consumption per Daily Burial Record Book.

Rambaut, Gilbert Vincent, Jr.   Buried March 1, 1896   Lenow Circle 36, #2
Major, Chief of Subsistence, Staff of General Nathan Bedford Forrest, appointed January 24, 1864 (*Confederate Staff Officers 1861 -1865* by Joseph H. Crute, Jr., Derwent Books 1982); per sketch in Mathes entered the Confederate States Army as a private in Company H, McDonald's Battalion, Forrest's Old regiment, was promoted from private to major July 20, 1862, and served on the staff of General Forrest through all of his promotions, was wounded twice – once at Shiloh and again on the march from Pontotoc, Miss., to Harrisburg and Tupelo and was one of the early members of this Association (Confederate Historical Association); not listed in *Tennesseans in the Civil War* Part 2; wrote Chapter Two "Forrest At Shiloh" of *As They Saw Forrest,* some recollections and comments of contemporaries, edited by Robert Selph Henry, 1956 McCowat-Mercer Press, Inc.; see chapter prologue for more information on him; article regarding death headlined in March 1, 1896, Memphis's *The Commercial Appeal* newspaper, "Gen. N. B. Forrest's Favorite—It was Maj. G. V. Rambaut, Who Died Yesterday (February 29, 1896)"; per chapter in 1993 manuscript on the Rambauts, et al, entitled *Go West Young Man* by great granddaughter Betty Marie McDade he was married to Susan Apperson, daughter of Edmond Minetree Apperson, patriarch of one of the wealthiest families in Memphis and who was connected with most of the principal banks and insurance companies in Memphis, and was also engaged in planting in Mississippi, Tennessee, and Arkansas; sketch in *Sketches of Prominent Tennesseans: containing biographies and records of many of the families who attained prominence in Tennessee.* Compiled and Edited by Hon. William Speer. Nashville, Albert B. Tavel, 1888. pages 350-353; was active in the Grocery & Cotton business and the Memphis Union Stock Yard & Fertilizer Company, a 12 year member of the Memphis City School Board, and a Director of Planters Insurance Company in Memphis from its organization and until 1882, of which General N. B. Forrest was president right after the War; circle grave stone: Gilbert Vincent Rambaut, Born at St. Petersburg, VA Feb. 13, 1837, Died Feb. 29, 1896; wife's circle grave stone: Mrs. Sue A. Rambaut, Born Feb. 19, 1839, Died February 7, 1923.

Rawlings, James Stokely   Buried October 26, 1902   Fowler 100, #8
Tennessee 3 (Forrest's Old) Cavalry Regiment Private 2 Company A and 1 Company B 154 Senior Infantry Regiment ("Bluff City Grays"); enlisted June 4, 1861, Randolph age 26 per 154 Senior Infantry records and present on August 14 to November 1, 1861, muster roll; per 3 Cavalry records enlisted May 4, 1861, Randolph and paroled May 11, 1865, at Gainesville, Alabama; per Shelby County funeral books died of general debility at age 67 and was born in Tennessee; per the sketch on Richard J. Rawlings in Goodspeed's Shelby County History, page 1029, he was the brother of Richard J. Rawlings and Stokely H. Rawlings; notice in *The Commercial Appeal* Memphis October 26, 1902, that the surviving members of Bluff City Greys Company A Forrest's Old Regiment to attend funeral of comrade James S. Rawlings; listed as member of Bluff City Grays in *Reminiscences of the Civil War* by John Hallum, Tunnah & Pittard printers, 1903; listed in "A COMPLETE ROSTER OF THE BLUFF CITY GREYS" located in the Memphis Room of the Memphis/Shelby County Public Library and Information Center Central Library; see also Notes of Interest - Bluff City Grays; grave stone: Sept. 17, 1835 Oct. 25, 1902: died age 67 per Daily Burial Record Book.

Rawlings, Richard Jackson Buried May 16, 1909 Fowler 79-80, #8

Tennessee 3 (Forrest's Old) Cavalry Regiment Private 2 Company A and Tennessee 2 (Walker's) Infantry Regiment Private Company E; per 2 (Walker's) Infantry records enlisted May 11, 1861, discharged by sergeant July 1, 1861, per muster roll dated September 9, 1861, at Fort Pillow and transferred per muster roll dated July 23, 1863, at Chattanooga; per 3 Cavalry Regiment records enlisted February 4, 1864, Panola, Mississippi and paroled May 11, 1865, at Gainesville, Alabama; ; listed in "A COMPLETE ROSTER OF THE BLUFF CITY GREYS" located in the Memphis Room of the Memphis/Shelby County Public Library and Information Center Central Library with notation enlisted in that company February 4, 1864; per sketch in Mathes book private Company B, Forrest's Old regiment, enlisted May 1861, in Welby Armstrong's Company, 2 Tennessee Regiment Infantry and was afterwards transferred to Forrest Regiment Cavalry, meantime had served in 154 Tennessee (no records found this unit), was captured sick at Perryville, paroled and came home, but subsequently escaped and joined his command at Como, Mississippi, served from that date, December 1863, to end of the war, paroled May 11, 1865, and admitted to this Association (Confederate Historical Association) October 1895; per sketch in Goodspeed's Shelby County History, page 1029, he was the brother of James S. Rawlings and Stokely H. Rawlings; also per Goodspeed's sketch born March 17, 1845, at Jackson, Tennessee; wife, Fannie Venable Rawlings, applied for Tennessee Confederate Pension (W9013 March 27, 1928 and W9174 August 31, 1928); per Coppock, Volume IV, page 205, mayor of Lenox in 1900 when he replaced J. T. Vanhorn after he had served a few months and re-elected 1902-1904 (Lenox was suburb of Memphis, incorporated October 7, 1896, and became part of Memphis September 1, 1909); *The Commercial Appeal* Memphis May 16, 1909, indicates died suddenly May 15, 1909, age 65 and husband of Fannie Venable Rawlings; Shelby County Funerals book indicates died from street car accident; ; death mentioned in *Confederate Veteran* Volume X, October 1909, page 520, in "Death List of Memphis Historical Society" between January 1, 1909, and July 1, 1909; grave stone: March 17, 1845 May 15, 1909; died age 64 per Daily Burial Record Book.

Rawlings, Stokely H. Buried May 13, 1862 Turley 79

Tennessee 3 (Forrest's Old) Cavalry Regiment Private 2 Company A and 154 Senior Infantry Regiment Private 1 Company B ("Bluff City Grays"); per 154 Senior Infantry Company Muster-in Roll dated August 13, 1861, enlisted May 14, 1861, at Randolph age 22; per 3 Cavalry Company Muster Roll for January to July 1, 1862, enlisted May 4, 1861, Randolph and died May 13, 1862; found in Lindsley's Annals under McDonald's Battery (sic Battalion) Company A as died May 13, 1862; under Local Matters, the *Avalanche* May 12, 1862, page 3, column 4, "Died - at home, Sunday night, the 11th instant, Stokely H. Rawlings, a member of the Bluff City Greys, aged 23. ...funeral May 13th inst.....''; not found in any Cemetery record books (Daily Burial Record, Alpha or Turley) or computer index; per the sketch on Richard J. Rawlings in Goodspeed's Shelby County History, page 1029, he was the brother of James S. Rawlings and Richard J. Rawlings; mentioned ("Rawlings") by Dr. S. H. Ford in his address on the occasion to commemorate (Confederate Memorial Day) Confederates buried at Elmwood on April 26, 1866, (see articles "The Confederate Dead" in the *Public Ledger* (Memphis), April 27, 1866, page 3, column 2, and "Honors To The Memory Of The Hero Dead" in the April 27, 1866, *Memphis Daily Appeal*, page 3, column 1); listed in the June 6, 1878, *Memphis Daily Appeal*, page 4, column 3, article "OUR DEAD HEROES" covering the unveiling of the Confederate Monument and Decoration of Graves at Elmwood as then one of twenty-eight members of the Bluff City Grays, Company B of the 154 Senior Infantry Regiment and Company A of Forrest's Old (Third) Cavalry Regiment buried at Elmwood; listed as one of the "comrades who sleep at Elmwood cemetery " in the article "Veterans in Council" in the May 12, 1881, *Memphis Daily Appeal*, page 4, column 4, concerning the meeting of the surviving members in the city of the old Bluff City Grays to appoint the necessary committees for the purpose of making special decoration on the graves of their dead comrades at Elmwood and Calvary cemeteries on Sunday next, Memorial Day; listed as member of Bluff City Grays in *Reminiscences of the Civil War* by John Hallum, Tunnah & Pittard printers, 1903; listed in "A COMPLETE ROSTER OF THE BLUFF CITY GREYS" located in the Memphis Room of the Memphis/Shelby County Public Library and Information Center Central Library with notation that died Corinth, May 18, 1862, and included on the list at the end of the soldiers buried at Elmwood with indication buried Turley Lot 79, #3, however, Turley Book indicates that "S. J. Rawlings" is buried in that grave; see also Notes of Interest - Bluff City Grays; found only on Rawlings family stone in Turley Lot 79 (Sarah J Rawlings Lot): "S H Rawlings 1838-1862."

Rawlings, Virgil A. Buried February 9, 1890 Chapel Hill Cir. 2, #7

Tennessee 3 (Forrest's) Cavalry, Private Company H, only Prisoner of War card in compiled service record dated May 11, 1865, Gainesville, Alabama, indicating residence as Shelby County, Tennessee; originally enlisted Tennessee (Memphis) Battalion March 12, 1862, at Memphis, age 18, listed on March 12 to May 1, 1862 Muster Roll Card with no information, unit disbanded May 1862; 46 Years, Stone 1843 -1890; died February 7, 1890, per the Avalanche February 9, 1890, page 4; lived in Raleigh; per widow's (Edith Rawlings) obituary *Commercial Appeal* Memphis January 24,1944, page 12, column 5, he served with General Forrest.

Reddick, George W. Buried May 6, 1866 Fowler 152, #9

Tennessee 154 Senior Infantry Regiment Private Company A; per Company Muster-in Roll dated August 13, 1861, enlisted May 14, 1861, Randolph; appears on a Register of Sick in Overton General Hospital, Memphis, Tennessee, dated March 31, 1862, admitted November 11, 1861; appears on a List of soldiers, Army of Mississippi, to be discharged because of physical disability dated July 4, 1862, Tupelo, Mississippi, per letter written by Captain J. Koneke dated July 5, 1862, entitled to discharge by reason of physical disability caused by a wound received at the Battle of Belmont; per Company Muster Roll dated May 5, 1863, age 40 and remarks: Discharged July 7, 1862, Surgeon Certificate; was a member of Fire Company No. 5 (The Invincible) and name listed on a marker at Elmwood dedicated in 1991, by the Men and Women of the Memphis Fire Fighters Association Local 1784; died age 44 suicide per Daily Burial Record Book.

Reese, Caleb Cox   Buried July 22, 1924   Chapel Hill PL4, #479
Mississippi 7 Cavalry Regiment Private Company A (name spelled Reece, C. C.); regiment organized August 1, 1862, as the 1 Regiment MS Partisans, disbanded November 15, 1862, and reorganized March 1, 1863 and designation changed August 1, 1864, to 7 Regiment MS Cavalry; originally enlisted Mississippi 1 Partisan Rangers Private Company A August 1, 1862, at Ripley, Mississippi (record found under C. C. Reece per War Department card in pension file); per Tennessee Confederate Pension application S14696 (C. C. Rees), filed May 7, 1915, born in Tippah County, Mississippi 1844, enlisted Mississippi 7 Cavalry Company A fall 1862, and paroled at Selma, Alabama April 13, 1865, wife deceased; application denied because not Tennessee resident for 3 years and also drew (indicated) Mississippi pension (no Mississippi pension record found); second Tennessee Confederate Pension application S15118 (C. C. Reese) filed January 8,1917, accepted; copy of oath in file and letter using name Caleb C. Rees; pension records indicates date of death of July 24, 1924 (actually July 21, 1924); died 80 years per Daily Burial Record Book; buried July 21, 1924, per Cemetery computer index; obituary (name spelled Caleb C. Reese) in July 22, 1924, *Commercial Appeal* Memphis, page 7, indicating died at residence 244 Normal Monday evening; grave stone: July 28, 1844 July 21, 1924.

Rice, Clay   Buried December 12, 1875   Chapel Hill 538½, #7
Tennessee 17 (Sanders') Cavalry Battalion Private Company A and Captain Assistant Quartermaster; per Company Muster Roll dated October 31, 1862, age 27, enlisted July 15, 1862, Grenada, and remarks: Acting as Quartermaster Sergeant to Battalion since September 15, 1862; per Company Muster Roll for August 31 to December 31, 1863, remarks: Promoted to Quartermaster 19 September 1863; appears on a Field and Staff Muster Roll for September 1 to December 31, 1863, Captain and Quartermaster, remarks: Appointment confirmed by Secretary of War to date from 19 October 1863; battalion consolidated with the 17th Battalion Mississippi Cavalry and Captain C.A. Jennings' Independent Company, Mississippi Cavalry, to form the 9th Regiment Mississippi Cavalry, by S.O. No--, Hd. Qrs. Cavalry in Mississippi, dated December 24, 1863; brother of Paul Shirley Rice – see sketch next below; nephew of Captain John T. Shirley – see sketch infra; died age 35 per Daily Burial Record Book.

Rice, Paul Shirley   Buried January 26, 1869   Chapel Hill 538½, #2
Tennessee 17 (Sanders') Cavalry Battalion Private Company A; per Company Muster Roll dated Enlistment to June 30, 1862, enlisted May 20, 1861, Paris, Tennessee, with remarks: Transferred from Captain Carnes Light Artillery (note: per Tennessee Captain Carnes Company Artillery (Captain Marshall's Company Artillery, Steuben Artillery) Company Muster Roll for May and June 1862, enlisted May 20, 1861, with remarks: Transferred to Cavalry June 3, 1862); per Company Muster Roll dated October 31, 1862, age 21, enlisted June 4, 1862, Baldwin, Mississippi, with remarks; Transferred from Carnes Battery; per Company Muster Roll for May 1 to August 31, 1863, remarks: On detail in Naval Construction Office at Selma, Alabama; appears on a Roll of Prisoners of War captured at Salt Springs, Georgia on October 1, 1864, and forwarded to Louisville Kentucky October 27, 1864; appears on a Roll of Prisoners of War at Louisville, Kentucky transferred to Camp Douglass, Illinois October 29, 1864; appears on a Roll of Prisoners of War applying for oath of allegiance in November 1864, with remarks: claims to have been loyal, enlisted through false representations, captured and desires to take the oath of allegiance to the United States and become a loyal citizen; appears on a Roll of Prisoners of War transferred to the Commissioner for Exchange, May 23, 1865, from New Orleans; brother of Clay Rice – see sketch next above; per death notice in the September 27, 1868, *Memphis Daily Appeal*, page 2, column 6, died near Lincoln, Desha County, Arkansas, on Monday evening, September 21st, aged 27 years; note date of death difference with grave stone that inscribed born April 4, 1841 and Died September 14, 1868; based on date of death and Elmwood burial date would have been removed to Elmwood from original burial location; brother of Clay Rice – see sketch next above; nephew of Captain John T. Shirley – see sketch infra; died chronic diarrhea per Daily Burial Record Book.

Richardson, Robert Edwin   Buried June 30, 1895   Chapel Hill 228, #8
Tennessee 12 (Green's-Richardson's) Cavalry Regiment Sergeant Staff of Colonel Richardson; appears on a Roll of Prisoners of War surrendered at Citronelle, Alabama, and paroled at Grenada, Mississippi, May 18, 1865, residence Fayette County, Tennessee; son of General Robert Vinkler Richardson – see sketch next below; per article in the June 30, 1895, *Commercial Appeal* Memphis died DeVall's Bluff, Arkansas, June 29, 1895, after an illness of three months age 48; grave stone inscription appears to be: Born January 23, 1848 Died June 29, 1895.

Richardson, Robert Vinkler   Buried January 10, 1870   Chapel Hill 228, #5
Brigadier General; appointed from Tennessee December 3, 1863 (rank December 1, 1863) per the *Memorandum relative to the General Officers Appointed by the President in the Armies of the Confederate States - 1861-1865* compiled from Official Records by the Military Secretary's Office, U. S. War Department 1905, however, remarks in said Memorandum indicate that the nomination returned by the Senate to the President February 9, 1864; nomination was withdrawn by President Jefferson; originally enlisted as Colonel Tennessee 12 Richardson's-Green's Cavalry Regiment; no information in Tennessee 12 Cavalry Regiment compiled service record rolls other than rank of Colonel and remark that promoted to Brigadier General December 1, 1863; in General and Staff records name appears on a list of Prisoners of War indicating Colonel Provisional Army and paroled Grenada, Mississippi May 8, 1865; born November 4, 1820; a lawyer and levee contractor who took part in obscure border warfare of Tennessee, Missouri and Arkansas; per sketch in *Generals in Gray* born November 4, 1820, Granville County, North Carolina, and

while on railroad project trip stopped to spend night on January 5, 1870, at a tavern in the Village of Clarkton, Dunklin County, Missouri where was mortally wounded by an unknown assailant and died next morning; listed (Richardson, Gen. R. V.) in Elmwood 1874 book as Confederate soldier buried in Elmwood who was a citizen of Memphis or vicinity and sketch that indicates came to Memphis 1845; shot, wound, and age 49 per Daily Burial Record Book; death ("assignation") reported under Local Paragraphs in the January 10, 1870, *Memphis Daily Appeal*, page 4, column 5; biography in *Confederate Military History, Extended Edition*, Volume X Tennessee, page 686; sketch, photograph, if available, and grave stone photograph in book *Quiet Places: The Burial Sites of Civil War Generals in Tennessee* by Buckner and Nathaniel C. Hughes, Jr., East Tennessee Historical Society (1992); grave stone: November 4, 1820 January 6, 1870; also listed in chapter on Generals; listed under Generals in "Touring historic Elmwood Cemetery" (Brochure and Map of Historic Gravesites) #13; listed in "Touring Historic Elmwood Cemetery" Brochure (January 2000) #73; sketch #22 in Elmwood *Civil War Tour* booklet (2012).

Rives, Charles B.   Buried January 27, 1926   Turley 1688, #1
Mississippi 44 Infantry Regiment Private Company H; record found under spelling "Rieves, C. A. B."; enlisted October 24, 1861, Holly Springs; per May 1 to August 31, 1864 muster roll remarks wounded July 28, 1864, near Atlanta and sent to hospital; muster roll card dated November 1864, in record has name as "Charles B. Rives" and indicates served as teamster November 1-20, 1864, with remarks that returned to company 21 November (on extra duty as teamster per September/October 1862, muster roll remarks); per Tennessee Confederate Pension S13510 born Marshall County, Mississippi 1842, enlisted Mississippi 44 Infantry Company H November 1861, General Blythe's command, Captain Brown and surrendered at Holly Springs, Mississippi; War Department card in pension file has name as "C. A. B. Rieves," Private Company H, Mississippi 44 infantry, enlisted October 24, 1861, wounded near Atlanta July 28, 1864, sent to hospital and no further record; affidavit in pension file by comrade, B. C. Gray (not found in Confederate index book but there is a record for Grey, Benjamin C. Kentucky 2 Cavalry Regiment Private Company F with single card in record indicating name appears on undated Roll of Prisoners of War reported at Memphis, Tennessee May 20, 1865, and a reference card only for Gray, Benjamin F. Private but no company indicated), indicating that Rives joined Kentucky 2 Cavalry in January 1865, (not found listed in any index for that unit), and surrendered with regiment at Holly Springs, Mississippi and that he had been wounded in thigh and joined cavalry because of wound; faded grave stone: March 18 1842 January 26, 1926; died age 83 per Daily Burial Record Book.

Rives, John G.   Buried August 1, 1875   Chapel Hill 34, #5
Tennessee 3 (Forrest's Old) Cavalry Regiment Private Company A "Bluff City Grays"; per 3 Cavalry record (second initial "C" in *Tennesseans in the Civil War* Part 1) enlisted May 4, 1861, Randolph and transferred to Jackson's Cavalry June 10 per January to July 1862, muster roll remarks; not found in 154 Senior Infantry Regiment compiled service records; listed in the June 6, 1878, *Memphis Daily Appeal*, page 4, column 3, article "OUR DEAD HEROES" covering the unveiling of the Confederate Monument and Decoration of Graves at Elmwood as then one of twenty-eight members of the Bluff City Grays, Company B of the 154 Senior Infantry Regiment and Company A of Forrest's Old (Third) Cavalry Regiment buried at Elmwood; listed as one of the "comrades who sleep at Elmwood cemetery " in the article "Veterans in Council" in the May 12, 1881, *Memphis Daily Appeal*, page 4, column 4, concerning the meeting of the surviving members in the city of the old Bluff City Grays to appoint the necessary committees for the purpose of making special decoration on the graves of their dead comrades at Elmwood and Calvary cemeteries on Sunday next, Memorial Day; listed in "A COMPLETE ROSTER OF THE BLUFF CITY GREYS" located in the Memphis Room of the Memphis/Shelby County Public Library and Information Center Central Library with notation that died Memphis, 1874 and included on the list at the end of the soldiers buried at Elmwood; not listed as member of Bluff City Grays in *Reminiscences of the Civil War* by John Hallum, Tunnah & Pittard printers, 1903; see also Notes of Interest - Bluff City Grays; died consumption age 35 per Daily Burial Record Book.

Rodgers, E. S.   Buried September 13, 1893   Chapel Hill Public Lot 2, #1914
Tennessee 6 Infantry Regiment Private Company L; enlisted Tennessee 55 (Brown's) Infantry Regiment Ford's Company March 10, 1862, at Jackson, Tennessee which company reorganized May 8, 1862, and assigned to Tennessee 6 Infantry Regiment as Company L; name spelled "Rogers" in Tennessee 6 Infantry Regiment rolls and "Rodgers" on with some cards; discharged January 13, 1863, due to age; per written discharge certificate in compiled service record file born Madison County, Alabama and age 45; grave stone: E. S. Rodgers Private Company L 6 Regiment Tennessee Infantry Confederate States Army 1817 1893; name spelled "Rogers" in Cemetery Daily Burial Record and Turley Section books and "Rodgers" in Cemetery computer index; died age 77 per Daily Burial Record Book; obituary "E. S. Rogers" in the *Memphis Commercial* September 13, 1893, aged 77 years, died September 12, 1893, apoplexy; not the E. S. Rodgers Tennessee Confederate Pension S12381 who served in North Carolina 25 Infantry Regiment.

Rodgers, Volney P.   Buried February 10, 1869   Chapel Hill Circle 66, #4
Listed in Elmwood 1874 book as Confederate soldier buried in Elmwood who was citizen of Memphis or vicinity and biographical sketch (both spell name "Rogers"); per sketch born four miles east of Memphis, "was distinguished for his skill and courage as an officer and a soldier" and died February 16, 1869, age 39; per Daily Burial Record Book name spelled "Rodger," died from typhoid pneumonia, age 40 and buried in Fowler Section Lot 95, #3; "Rodger, Volney P., Estate of" in Elmwood 1874 book List of Proprietors, Chapel Hill Circle Lot 66; no indication in Cemetery records when moved; death reported with name spelled "Rogers" in *Memphis Daily Appeal*, February 10, 1869, page 2, column 4, "At his place of residence, Walnut Bend, Phillips county, Ark., at 7 o'clock, February 6th, in the 40th year of his age, Vol. P. Rogers. The funeral will take place this Wednesday evening ....";

possibly Arkansas 1 (Dobbin's) Cavalry Private Company F, only a single card in compiled service record of muster and descriptive roll of prisoners of war indicating paroled May 25, 1865, Wittsburg, Arkansas, enlisted Langville, born Tennessee and age 36 at surrender; grave stone with initials on top.

Rogers, Henry A. "Hal"   Buried June 12, 1881   South Grove 14, #6
Tennessee 9 Infantry Regiment Major, appointed November 1862 when Major Kelso resigned, originally Captain Company I ("The Memphis Rangers"); only single card in compiled service record; per Daily Burial Record Book remark was brought from Hot Springs, Arkansas; grave stone: Maj. Co I 9 Tenn Infantry Confederate States Army 1832 Jun12, 1881; a "In Memoriam" published in *Memphis Daily Appeal* July 10, 1881, page 1, column 7.

Rogers, Dr. William Egbert   Buried May 23, 1885   Evergreen 5, #2
Tennessee 9 Infantry Regiment Surgeon, appointed May 26, 1861, appointed Surgeon of Provisional Army of the Confederate States September 26, 1861, tendered resignation February 17, 1862 "on account of Mrs. Rogers situation", resignation accepted March 7, 1862 by the President (Special Orders 53/1, Adjutant and Inspector General's Office, Richmond, VA); large grave stone inscribed Wm. E. Rogers, born Hillsboro, NC September 26, 1826, died May 21, 1885; biographical sketch in Hambrecht, F. T. & Koste, J. L., Biographical register of physicians who served in the Confederacy in a medical capacity. 12/13/2012. Updated 7/16/2013. Unpublished database.

Rogers, William Simeon, Sr.   Buried June 14, 1914   Fowler 584, #5
Tennessee 6 (Wheeler's) Cavalry Regiment (also called 1 and 2 Tennessee Cavalry Regiment), Private Company K; compiled service records found under "Rodgers, W. S." but "Rogers" on most cards in record; enlisted December 9, 1861, Nashville; name appears on the 2nd Battalion, Troops and Defenses, Macon, Georgia, Company H November/December 1864, muster roll with remarks that in prison in Macon, Georgia; paroled May 3, 1865, Charlotte, North Carolina and indicated residence Franklin, Williamson County, Tennessee (sic); article in *The Memphis Educator*, January 1, 1906, page 2, indicates born in Memphis 1833, volunteered in 1861, in Company K, First Tennessee Cavalry, first under General N. B. Forrest and then under General Joseph Wheeler, surrendered at Charlotte, North Carolina, and is a faithful and watchful keeper of Forrest Park; Tennessee Confederate Pension S12373 dated February 20, 1911, indicates enlisted May 1, 1861, Company K 1 Tennessee Cavalry but note War Department indicated enlisted December 9, 1861, Company K 6 (Wheeler's) formerly 1 (Wheeler's) Tennessee Cavalry; widow, Eugenia Leon Williams Rogers, applied for Tennessee Confederate Pension (W5482) and indicated born Whiteville, Tennessee 1849, married in Fayette County, Tennessee January 30, 1867; per sketch in Mathes book name spelled "Rodgers, W. S.," enlisted May 1, 1861, as private in Company K, First Tennessee Cavalry, Humes Brigade, paroled May 3, 1865, and joined this Association May 14, 1889; death notice in *The Commercial Appeal* Memphis, page 7, column 4, indicating died age 81; article also found *The Commercial Appeal* Memphis, page 9, column 5, "Old Park Guardian Funeral is Arranged" which indicates in charge of Forrest Park since founded and was a Confederate soldier and member of Forrest's Cavalry; grave stone: Feb 17, 1833 June 12, 1914.

Ross, William Brown   Buried February 28, 1863   Turley 573, #2
Tennessee 2 (Walker's) Infantry Regiment Lieutenant Colonel; no enlistment in compiled service record; elected Major May 12, 1861; promoted to Lieutenant Colonel October 1861; resigned March 12, 1862; served as volunteer on General A. P. Stewart's staff after resignation; wounded at Battle of Murfreesboro December 31, 1862, and died January 2, 1863; listed in Elmwood 1874 book as Confederate soldier buried in Elmwood who was citizen of Memphis or vicinity and sketch; per sketch born 1831, participated with regiment at Belmont and Shiloh, when enlistment expired appointed Inspector General on staff of then Major General A. P. Stewart, wounded at Battle of Murfreesboro December 31, 1862, died January 2, 1863, first interred at Murfreesboro and later reinterred in Elmwood; per Daily Burial Record Book remarks laid in Wheatley's Vault, also note "Moved to Fowler 136" written in by pencil but not found in Fowler book; grave stone: Col. W. B. Ross C.S.A. Fell Battle of Murfreesboro 1832-1863; mentioned ("Major Ross") by Dr. S. H. Ford in his address on the occasion to commemorate (Confederate Memorial Day) Confederates buried at Elmwood on April 26, 1866, (see articles "The Confederate Dead" in the *Public Ledger* (Memphis), April 27, 1866, page 3, column 2, and "Honors To The Memory Of The Hero Dead" in the April 27, 1866, *Memphis Daily Appeal*, page 3, column 1).

Ryan, Charles Roscoe   Buried November 29, 1885   Evergreen 10, #1
Arkansas 18 Infantry Regiment Private Company B; no compiled service record found; unit per sketch in Mathes book; per sketch born Monticello, Jasper County, Georgia January 31, 1845, joined Arkansas 25 Infantry in 1861, at Corinth, Mississippi, captured at Port Hudson and after exchange went to Georgia and became connected to medical department, after war moved to Memphis, died Manitou (Springs), Colorado, remains brought back to Memphis and now lie in Elmwood Cemetery and was one of the early members of the old Confederate Historical Association; believed to be the C. R. Ryan found in Arkansas 18 infantry Regiment who's cards are filed with cards on R. C. Ryan; R. C. Ryan Private Company C enlisted March 8, 1862, Des Arc, Arkansas; R. Ryan Private Company B captured April 16, 1865, West Point, Georgia and transferred to military prison April 23, 1865; name appears on a list of non-commissioned officers and privates, prisoners of war, who have this day (July , 1863) released on their parole, was captured at Port Hudson, Louisiana July 9, 1863; died age 40 per Daily Burial Record Book; died November 25, 1885 and "BRAVE SOLDIER OF THE LOST CAUSE" on Ryan monument.

Sanford, Dr. William Bailey   Buried September 5, 1910   Chapel Hill 906, #5

Mississippi – no official service record found; per biography in *Confederate Military History, Extended Edition*, Volume X Tennessee, page 694: youngest of four brothers who were in the Confederate military service, at the inauguration of war in 1861, he and brother John, age 12, could not enter the army, though saw no little of military operations at their home in Holly Springs, Miss., when General Villepigue's forces passed through that place in 1862, retreating from Fort Pillow, in great need of equipment of every kind, the mother of the Sanford boys tendered the use of her team and wagon to the Confederates, and permitted her sons to go with the troops, fully uniformed and armed as soldiers, they remained with Villepigue's command for six months, after return to Holly Springs, it fell into the hands of Grant's army in the winter of 1862-63, and was made the base for the Federal campaign on the Central rail road against Vicksburg, was the fortune of the two boys to be intimately associated with the attack by Van Dorn, in December, 1862, which resulted in the destruction of the enemy's stores and the retreat of Grant to Memphis, going out one day to carry relief to a starving family, several miles from town, met two Confederates, who advised with them about the best approaches to the Federal position, and it was according to the advice they gave to these scouts of Van Dorn that the famous attack was made on the following morning; died in Colorado Springs, Colorado, September 2, 1910.

Saunders, Dr. Dudley Dunn   Buried February 26, 1908   Turley 28-33

Confederate Surgeon, Field and Staff Officer, appointed April 9, 1862, first assigned to duty by the Surgeon General, afterward placed in charge of hospital posts nearest the army and paroled 1865; after War was professor of medicine at both Medical College of Memphis and Memphis Hospital Medical College; worked to save lives during the yellow fever epidemic in Memphis in 1878; honored at Marty Park; sketch in Mathes book (Part II).

Saunders, Solomon H.   Buried August 6, 1862   Fowler Public Lot 1, #435

Tennessee 2 Regiment Company A and died age 20 per Daily Burial Record Book; no compiled service record found; grave number listed in Single Grave Column along with Federals in Daily Burial Record Book (not found as Federal); in Irving Hospital records there was a soldier by name of S. H. Saunders, Tennessee 40 Infantry Regiment Private Company J, who was admitted April 28, 1862, with complaint of pneumonia and who per remarks deserted May 18, 1862 but compiled service record has name spelled as Sanders, S. H., Private Company I and enlisted September 23, 1861, Madison, Arkansas age 20 and all muster roll remarks (last dated November and December 1861) indicate present.

Scales, Dabney Minor   Buried May 29, 1920   South Grove 200-201, #3

CSS Shenandoah Lieutenant; per sketch in Mathes book was midshipman in US Navy but resigned when native state Mississippi seceded and enlisted May 1861; originally enlisted in Mississippi 17 Infantry 1 Sergeant Company G May 27, 1861, Corinth, Mississippi, age 18, mustered in April 22, 1861, at Holly Springs, Mississippi, occupation: student and appointed midshipman June 4, 1861; served on Steamers Savannah, Charleston and Ram Arkansas; sent to Europe to serve on Cruiser Shenandoah that played havoc with US merchant marines in Pacific coast, and was never captured, but returned to Liverpool in 1866; never paroled; became member of Confederate Historical Association August 12, 1884 (March 12, 1884 per obituary in *Confederate Veteran*, see below); widow Susan Winchester Scales applied for Tennessee Confederate Pension W8283) April 8, 1925; per application he was born June 1, 1841, in Orange County, Virginia, she was born December 9, 1852, in Sumner County, Tennessee, and they were married January 10, 1886, in Nashville, Tennessee; per article in *The Commercial Appeal* Memphis May 27, 1920, page 1, died in Sheridan, Wyoming May 26, 1920, at home of son, George W. Scales; further per newspaper article a student at Annapolis, and after War returned to Holly Spring, Mississippi in fall 1866 after first going to Mexico, graduated 1869 (1868 per bibliography in *Confederate Military History*, see below) in law from the University of Mississippi, served in Spanish American War; commander of Company A, United Confederate Veterans, 1895 served Shelby County in the Tennessee State Senate; newspaper article indicates marriage in 1885; grave stone: June 1, 1841 May 26, 1920; obituary in *Confederate Veteran*, Volume XXVIII, November 1920, page 431, which indicates born June 1, 1841, near Holly Springs, Mississippi, Lieutenant on Gunboat Arkansas and Lieutenant in Navy during Spanish American War; bibliography in *Confederate Military History, Extended Edition*, Volume X Tennessee, page 699, which indicates born June 1, 1842, (note difference with other records and grave stone), appointed to US Naval Academy 1859, assisted in organization of military company at Holly Springs at start of War, received appointment of midshipman, promoted to post midshipman, promoted to 2 Lieutenant while in Paris and made 2 Lieutenant of Shenandoah; served as Lieutenant and executive officer of gunboat Fishhawk in Spanish American War; article in the Spring 1990 Elmwood Journal; sketch in *Who's Who in Tennessee*. Memphis: Paul & Douglass Company, Publishers, 1911, page 353; sketch (August 22, 1982) in Paul R. Coppock's *Mid-South*, Volume IV, pages 350-364.

Selden, Metellus L.   Buried May 11, 1909   Chapel Hill Circle 42, #5

Tennessee 7 Cavalry Regiment, Private Company A, enlisted March 21, 1862, at Humbolt and paroled at Memphis, Tennessee, May 1865; per sketch in Mathes book, page 188: enlisted February 1862, and remained with this company known as "Memphis Light Dragoons" until close of War and paroled May 1865, and joined Confederate Historical Association May 29,1884; per Young's book enlisted March 21, 1862, and on courier duty October 31,1862; biography in *Confederate Military History, Extended Edition*, Volume X Tennessee, page 703; death (May 9, 1909) mentioned in *Confederate Veteran* Volume X, October 1909, page 520 in "Death List of Memphis Historical Society" between January 1, 1909, and July 1, 1909, with first name spelled "Martillus"; president of Bon Aqua Springs Company May 21, 1874, per note in Bygone Days *Commercial Appeal* Memphis; per notice May 10, 1909, *Commercial Appeal* Memphis, page 5, "Old Vet Answers Call," M. L. Selden died Sunday afternoon, age 66, born Louisiana and father was Colonel Churchill Selden; first name spelled "Mettellus" in Daily Burial Record Book.and computer index; died age 66 in Daily Burial Record Book; no grave stone.

Selden, Clarence Churchill   Buried April 18, 1900   Chapel Hill 186, #17
Tennessee 7 Cavalry Regiment, Private Company A, enlisted August 31, 1863, at Canton and paroled May 11, 1865, at Gainesville, Alabama; died April 17, 1900, age 54, apoplexy, per Memphis Register of Deaths; no grave stone.

Sharp, Thomas C.   Buried January 19, 1863   Fowler Public Lot 1, #806
Texas 6 Infantry Regiment Sergeant/Private Company C; per Company Muster-in Roll dated October 3, 1861, enlisted September 21, 1861, at Gonzales, Texas age 23; per Company Muster Roll for November and December 1862, remarks: Resigned as 4th Sergeant and returned to rank November 10, 1862; per Company Muster Roll for May and June 1863, remarks: died in Memphis of a wound received at Arkansas Post; per card for USA Hospital Steamer D. A. January complaint: Vulnus Sclopeticum (gunshot wound) left leg (gangrene), admitted January 13, 1863, died January 16, 1863, and remarks that buried at Memphis; per card for USA Hospital Steamer Louisiana complaint: Wounded left leg and admitted January 11, 1863; on list of wounded of 1 and 2 Divisions, 15 Army Corps, on Hospital Boat Louisiana during engagement at Arkansas Post, January 11, 1863; death mentioned in the sketch on J. F. Cummings. who served in same company, in the *Reminiscences of the Boys in Gray 1861-1865* Volume 1 (Sketches of several hundred Confederate veterans, residing in Texas, giving particulars of their war service) that was compiled by Miss Mamie Yeary and published for the author by Smith & Lamar, Publishing House M.E. Church, South, Dallas, Texas, 1912, pages 165-166, "Tom Sharp, who belonged to my company, was wounded at the same time, but the poor fellow died before we reached Memphis. We were taken prisoner in the same fight, on the 10th day of January, 1863, and were carried to Memphis ..."; grave number listed in Single Grave Column along with Federals in Daily Burial Record Book.

Shelby, Evan J.   Buried February 3, 1866   Turley 571, #2
Mississippi 28 Cavalry Regiment 3 Lieutenant/Captain Company E ("Mayson's Dragoons"), per Company Muster-in Roll dated March 10, 1862, enlisted Prentiss, Mississippi March 10, 1862, age 21, per Company Muster Roll for January & February 1863, remarks: promoted February 6, 1863, name appears on a report of casualties in Major General Forrest's Cavalry Corps during months of November and December 1864, with remarks wounded severely leg but no death indicated; per Daily Burial Record Book Captain, killed in Battle, age 22 and remarks C.S.A.; no indication in Cemetery records on being removed to Elmwood; Cemetery computer index shows lot as 591; stone illegible; son of Colonel Moses Darwin Shelby (see sketch below) and brother of Isaac Shelby (see sketch below); age 18 in the 1860 Bolivar County, Mississippi census, M. D Shelby head of household; per brother Isaac's Obituary in *Memphis Daily Appeal*, October 21, 1883, page 1, column 8, "He (Isaac) commanded company "E" of Starke's Twenty-eighth Mississippi Cavalry in the Confederate army – the same company of which his brother Evan was a former captain, and who was killed at Duck river during Hood's retreat."

Shelby, Isaac   Buried February 20, 1896   Turley 571, #6
Mississippi 28 Cavalry Regiment Private/Captain Company E ("Mayson's Dragoons"), company muster rolls appear to be incorrect in that indicated enlisted August 1, 1861, at Lynchburg, Virginia by Major Clarke (no Major Clarke in Regiment), however, Company Muster Roll for September & October, 1862, remarks "Joined by transfer 5 Sept.", he should have enlisted essentially at the same time and place as his brother, Captain Evan J. Shelby who per Company Muster-in Roll dated March 10, 1862, enlisted Prentiss, Mississippi March 10, 1862; captured Pulaski, Tennessee December 25, 1864, first sent to Nashville, Tennessee, then forwarded to Military Prison, Louisville, Kentucky January 1, 1865, then sent to Fort Delaware, Delaware, January 9, 1865, and subscribed to Oath of Allegiance at Fort Delaware indicating Bolivar County, Mississippi as place of residence and released June 9, 1865; originally enlisted in Mississippi Captain M. D. Shelby's (his father) Company ("Bolivar Greys"), an Independent Company of State Troops, as Sergeant, only record for the Company is one undated muster roll that indicates mustered into service May 4, 1861, at Greenville by William G. Yerger; son of Colonel Moses Darwin Shelby and brother of Evan J. Shelby (see sketches); death reported in the October 19, 1883, *Memphis Daily Appeal*, page 1, column 7, "At Concordia, Miss., October 15, 1883, Capt. Isaac Shelby, aged forty-two years."; per obituary in *Memphis Daily Appeal*, October 21, 1883, page 1, column 8, born in October, 1840, in Claiborne County, County, Mississippi and "He (Isaac) commanded company "E" of Starke's Twenty-eighth Mississippi Cavalry in the Confederate army – the same company of which his brother Evan was a former captain, and who was killed at Duck river during Hood's retreat."; per Daily Burial Record Book Isaac, Ella P., Evan J. and Isaac Jr. were interred "all in 1 box"; Ella P. (DOD January 6, 1884) was his spouse and Evan J. (DOD August 26, 1877) and Isaac Jr. (DOD November 11, 1880) were his sons.

Shelby, Moses Darwin   Buried September 28, 1871   Turley 571, #3
Mississippi Captain M. D. Shelby's Company ("Bolivar Greys"), an Independent Company of State Troops, only record for the Company is one undated muster roll that indicates mustered into service May 4, 1861, at Greenville by William G. Yerger; father of Isaac Shelby and Evan J. Shelby (see sketches above); per death reported in *Memphis Daily Appeal*, September 28, 1871, page 1, column 5, "Shelby – On the 25th instant, in Bolivar county, Miss., Colonel M. D. Shelby, of Memphis."; per "IN MEMORIAM" in *Memphis Daily Appeal*, November 5, 1871, page 1, column 6, Moses Dalwin (sic) Shelby was born September 9, 1814, (Claiborne County, Mississippi) and died September 25, 1871 (Bolivar County, Mississippi); per Daily Burial Record Book died age 58 from pernicious fever.

Shelton, Jack   Buried November 18, 1861   Colored Single Grave #89

Servant Slave of 2 Lieutenant T. J. Shelton Company B (subsequently Captain Company D) Arkansas 13 Infantry Regiment; article in the *Memphis Avalanche*: "In the recent battle of Belmont, Lieut. Shelton, of the 13th Arkansas Regiment, had his servant Jack in the fight. Both Jack and his master were wounded, but not till they had made most heroic efforts to drive back the insolent invaders. Finally, after Jack had fired at the enemy twenty-seven times, he fell seriously wounded in the arm. Jacks' son was upon the field, and loaded the rifle for his father, who shot at the enemy three times after he was upon the ground. Jack's son hid behind a tree, and when the enemy retreated, they took him to Cairo and refused to let him return. Jack was taken from the field in great pain, and brought to the Overton Hospital, where he bore his sufferings with great fortitude till death relieved him of his pains yesterday. His example may throw a flood of light upon the fancied philanthropy of abolitionism. Jack was a brave and obedient servant, and deserves all praise for his heroic conduct upon the bloody field of Belmont." Daily Burial Record Book remarks: "Lieut. T. J. Shelton 13th Ark Regt – owner O. H. (Overton Hospital); per Overton Hospital Register, 1861 – 1862, Memphis, Tennessee, page 5: Shelton, T. J. 2nd Lt 13th Ark Co B; Comp.- neck; Adm. – 15th Nov.; Furloughed- 6th Dec.; see footnote 54 on page 247 in *The Battle of Belmont, Grant Strikes South*. Nathaniel Cheairs Hughes, Jr., The University of North Carolina Press, Chapel Hill, 1991.: "There may have been perhaps forty servants in the fight at Belmont. Most were slaves. … A black father and son, "armed with muskets and knives," fought in the ranks with the 13th Arkansas. "I asked them if they were volunteers, they said they were for that day & looked as cool as the bravest." Jack, the servant of Lieutenant Shelton, fired twenty-seven times before he was incapacitated with three wounds. He was taken to the Overton Hospital in Memphis with the other wounded Confederates and died there of his wounds on November 18. His son, George W. Shelton, was captured "with a musket in his hand, a cartridge box on," and taken to Cairo where he and another servant "Rob" were delivered to Company A, 31st Illinois, to be used for "camp purposes."

Shields, William Samuel   Buried May 27, 1862   Chapel Hill 130, #3

Tennessee 154 Senior Infantry Regiment Private Company G & Tennessee Artillery Corps; enlisted August 12, 1861, New Madrid, Missouri; per August 13, 1861, muster roll remarks: absent sick; per May 5, 1863, muster roll remarks: promoted to Lieutenant, died April 28, 1862; record also found Tennessee Artillery Corps rolls, same enlistment, native of Mississippi, citizen of Tennessee, 2 Lieutenant Lynch's Battery (only reference slip in Lynch's rolls), see also personal papers of Charles G. Rogers (not found); Lieutenant per Daily Burial Record Books; listed in Elmwood 1874 book as Confederate soldier buried in Elmwood who was citizen of Memphis or vicinity with rank of Lieutenant; not found Lindsley's Annals; large monument "William Samuel Shields" born June 27, 1839 and died May 25, 1862 "A Gallant Artillery Officer of the Late Confederate States Army."; mentioned (Willie Shields) by Dr. S. H. Ford in his address on the occasion to commemorate (Confederate Memorial Day) Confederates buried at Elmwood on April 26, 1866, (see articles "The Confederate Dead" in *Public Ledger* (Memphis), April 27, 1866, page 3, column 2, and "Honors To The Memory Of The Hero Dead" in the April 27, 1866, *Memphis Daily Appeal*, page 3, column 1).

Shirley, John T.   Buried September 9, 1873   Chapel Hill 538½, #5

Steamboat Captain and Builder; per the article "The Arkansas Ram" by Martha Goodwin, In the New Orleans Picayune, *Confederate Veterans* Volume 28, July 1920, No. 7, page 263, "In the fall of 1861 the Confederate government ordered the construction of two gunboats by Capt. John B. Shirley at Memphis, Tenn. Both vessels belonged to that formidable class of naval armament known as rams. One of them, the Arkansas, was destined by its exploits to gain a reputation that will last as long as the name of the Confederacy itself."; also built the CSS Tennessee, which was built at Selma, Alabama, where she was commissioned on February 16, 1864; uncle of Clay Rice and Paul Shirley Rice – see sketches supra; died age 50 Congestion per Daily Burial Record Book.

Shover, Felicia Lee Carey Thornton   Buried December 14, 1898   Turley 894, # 4

Confederate Spy and Smuggler; she was an active spy and smuggler in Memphis where drugs and other goods were sometimes concealed in coffins and the carcasses of dead mules for Confederate soldiers to later secure; she was a cousin of Robert E. Lee; *Untold Glory* by Cothburn O'Neal, New York, Crown Publishers (1957) is a biographical novel of her exploits; a brief sketch on her is included in the three part article "Heroines of the Confederacy" by David J. Harkness in *Southern Observer* magazine, January 1961, page 5; death notice and article in *The Commercial Appeal* Memphis, December 13, 1898, page 10, column 5; listed in "Touring Historic Elmwood Cemetery" Brochure (January 2000) #47.

Simpson, James G.   Buried December 8, 1876   Lenow Circle 94, #3

Tennessee 3 (Memphis Battalion) Infantry Battalion Private Company A; per Company Muster Roll dated March 12, 1862, enlisted March 12, 1862, Memphis, age 28; no other information in compiled service record; see Notes of Interest "Memphis Battalion - Tennessee 3 (Memphis Battalion) Infantry Battalion"; death reported in the December 8, 1876, *Memphis Daily Appeal*, page 1, column 6, in 44 years of his age; "Resolution of Respect" adopted in his honor by the Howard Association at its meeting on December 8, 1876, reported in the December 9, 1876, *Memphis Daily Appeal*, page 1, column 6; per Daily Burial Record Book died age 44 of Complicated and interred in Chapel Hill Lot 224, Grave No. 3, with remarks: R. T. (Receiving Tomb) removed to 94 Lenow Circle April 20, 1882; grave stone: James G. Simpson Dec. 7, 1876.

Smith, James Hammond   Buried June 17, 1921   Miller Circle 47

Provost Marshall under General Bragg in the district composed of Western Tennessee, Eastern Arkansas and Northern Mississippi (Allison, John, 1845-1920. *Notable Men of Tennessee: Personal and Genealogical, With Portraits. Volume II.* pages 243-244.

Atlanta: Southern Historical Association, 1905); sketch in *Who's Who in Tennessee*. Memphis: Paul & Douglass Company, Publishers, 1911, pages 356-357; member of Tennessee Legislature 1879 to 1882, Postmaster of Memphis 1882; indicated served in CA (Confederate Army) in the 1910 Memphis, Shelby County, Tennessee Census; grave stone: July 6, 1835 June 16, 1921.

Smith, James N. Buried November 14, 1910 Turley 612 (Masonic Lot), D2 #56
Tennessee Captain Marshall's (Carnes) Company Artillery Private, enlisted May 14 1, 1861, captured at Salisbury, NC April 12, 1862, and sent from Nashville, Tennessee to Military Prison at Louisville, Kentucky April 29, 1865, then transferred to Camp Chase, Ohio May 2, 1865, and swore Oath of Allegiance at Camp Chase June 13, 1865, age 31, indicating residence as Shelby County, Tennessee; per sketch in Mathes book enlisted as private in Harris' Zouave Cadets, Tennessee 154 Senior Infantry Regiment, Private Company D, April 1861, and afterwards transferred to Carnes' Battery, captured at Saulsbury (sic), North Carolina April 12, 1865, paroled June 1865, and joined Confederate Historical Association June 13, 1894; death (November 12, 1910) reported in *Confederate Veteran,* Volume XIX, April 1911, page 174, "The Last Roll" Deaths of Confederates in Memphis, Tennessee who died during 1910 and were members of the Confederate Historical Association, Camp 28, U. C. V., Bivouac 18, C. V. of Memphis, Tennessee; died age 63 per Daily Burial Record Book and buried in Masonic Lot (SE corner, end of 2nd row, near road).

Smith, Preston Buried May 2, 1868 Chapel Hill 146, #3
Brigadier General - appointed from Tennessee October 27, 1862, (rank October 27, 1862) per the *Memorandum relative to the General Officers Appointed by the President in the Armies of the Confederate States - 1861-1865*; originally enlisted as Colonel Tennessee 154 Senior Infantry Regiment May 6, 1861, age 37 at Fort Wright, Randolph, Tennessee; wounded at Battle of Shiloh; ordered to report to Major General Polk by General Bragg May 14, 1862, as Acting Brigadier General; killed at Battle of Chickamauga September 19, 1863, (September 20, 1863 per General and Staff records) and originally buried in Atlanta and removed to Elmwood in 1868; killed in battle age 40 per Daily Burial Record Book; listed (Smith, Gen. Preston) in Elmwood 1874 book as Confederate soldier buried in Elmwood who was a citizen of Memphis or vicinity and sketch; per sketch in *Generals in Gray* born Giles County, Tennessee December 25, 1823; mentioned by Dr. S. H. Ford in his address on the occasion to commemorate (Confederate Memorial Day) Confederates buried at Elmwood on April 26, 1866, (see articles "The Confederate Dead" in the *Public Ledger* (Memphis), April 27, 1866, page 3, column 2, and "Honors To The Memory Of The Hero Dead" in the April 27, 1866, *Memphis Daily Appeal*, page 3, column 1); reburial celebrated during the Commemoration Day (Confederate Memorial Day) ceremony at Elmwood Cemetery on Saturday May 2, 1868, see article "Our Soldier Dead."..."The Last Tribute of Love and Honor to General Preston Smith and Colonel Jeffrey Forrest" in the *Public Ledger* (Memphis), Saturday Evening, May 2, 1868, pages 2 and 3; see also article "Elmwood – Memorial Day Celebration at Elmwood — Funeral of General Preston Smith and Colonel Forrest" in the May 3, 1868, *Daily Memphis Avalanche*, page 1; biography in *Confederate Military History, Extended Edition*, Volume X Tennessee, page 331; sketch in *Tennessee, The Volunteer State, 1769-1923*, Volume II, page 230; sketch, photograph, if available, and grave stone photograph in book *Quiet Places: The Burial Sites of Civil War Generals in Tennessee* by Buckner and Nathaniel C. Hughes, Jr., East Tennessee Historical Society (1992); grave stone: December 25, 1823 September 20, 1864; listed under Generals in "Touring historic Elmwood Cemetery" (Brochure and Map of Historic Gravesites) #14; listed in "Touring Historic Elmwood Cemetery" Brochure (January 2000) #67; sketch #19 in Elmwood *Civil War Tour* booklet (2012); also listed in chapter on Generals.

Smither, Charles Gabriel Buried May 3, 1910 Evergreen 433, #3
Tennessee 7 Cavalry Regiment Private Company A; enlisted August 18, 1862, Senatobia, Mississippi; swore Oath of Allegiance May 5, 1865, at Memphis age 20; originally enlisted in Tennessee 154 Senior Infantry Regiment Private Company G (Captain James S. Moreland's Company) May 27, 1861, at age 16 but was discharged October 8, 1861, after his father, Gabriel Smither, wrote a letter dated October 5, 1861, to General A. S. Johnston requesting his discharge due to his age.

Sneed, John Louis Taylor Buried July 30, 1901 Turley 1398, #1
Provisional Army of Tennessee Brigadier General; records (mostly letters) found in Tennessee miscellaneous compiled service records rolls; per sketch in *More Generals in Gray* born May 12, 1820, Raleigh, North Carolina, during Mexican war was sergeant major, then captain of Company G Regiment of Tennessee Mounted Volunteers, May 9, 1861, appointed Brigadier General of Tennessee state forces by Governor Harris, not appointed to Confederate service when state forces were transferred, in 1862, attempted to raise a regiment of infantry but Federal advance ended those plans, Governor Harris later appointed him to settle accounts between the Tennessee provisional army and the Confederacy, *Southern Historical Society Papers* and *Confederate Veteran* list him as a Confederate General, and died July 29, 1901; not listed in the *Memorandum relative to the General Officers Appointed by the President in the Armies of the Confederate States - 1861-1865* compiled from Official Records by the Military Secretary's Office, U. S. War Department 1905; not listed in *Generals in Gray*; no records in General and Staff records; sketch in Mathes book; died age 81 per Daily Burial Record Book; sketch, photograph, if available, and grave stone photograph in book *Quiet Places: The Burial Sites of Civil War Generals in Tennessee* by Buckner and Nathaniel C. Hughes, Jr., East Tennessee Historical Society (1992); grave stone: "John L T Sneed born Raleigh North Carolina May 12, 1822 and died July 29, 1901 - Mary Ashe Shepperd wife of John L T Sneed born November 26, 1829 and died February 6, 1919"; also listed in chapter on Generals; listed under Generals in "Touring historic Elmwood Cemetery" (Brochure and Map of Historic Gravesites) # 15B; listed in "Touring Historic Elmwood Cemetery" Brochure (January 2000) #32; sketch #33 in Elmwood *Civil War Tour* booklet (2012).

Sneed, J. West   Buried May 6, 1875   Chapel Hill 462, #2
Tennessee 7 Cavalry Regiment Captain Company A ("Memphis Light Dragoons" Tennessee 6 Logwood's Cavalry Battalion Company A); per Company Muster-in Roll dated August 18, 1861, at New Madrid, Missouri enlisted as Corporal May 16, 1861, Memphis, Tennessee, age 32; Company detached to serve as escort to Brigadier General W. H. Jackson October 1862; promoted to Captain March 6, 1864; signed Parole of Honor at Gainesville, Alabama, May 11, 1865; died age 46, Consumption per Daily Burial Record Book.

Snowden, John Hudson   Buried March 31, 1866   Fowler Public Lot 2, #79
Lieutenant Topographical Engineer, Field and Staff Officer (no records found in Confederate Engineer rolls) on staff of Major General Leonidas Polk; July 1, 1861, ordered to report to General Polk for topographical duty; October 7, 1861, General Polk mentioned him in report as Lieutenant Snowden and assigned as Engineer; November 7, 1861, General Polk mentioned him in report as Lieutenant of Topographical Corps and member of his staff; and November 12, 1861, General Polk reports him killed on above date; see the Letter from Columbus (Special Correspondence of the *Memphis Appeal*) Columbus, November 12, 1861, reported in *Memphis Daily Appeal*, November 14, 1861, page 2, column 5, "A most painful accident occurred here late yesterday afternoon, being the explosion of the big pivot gun-the 128-pounder, that has so frequently made the hills and valleys for thirty miles around Columbus re-echo with its portent voice. … killing eight men, among whom were Lieutenant of Artillery SNOWDEN …."; per correspondence dated October 12, 1861, Columbus, Kentucky, from E. D. Blake, Acting Assistant Adjutant-General, to General S. Cooper, Adjutant and Inspector General, C. S. Army, Richmond, Virginia "A large Dahlgren gun bursted. Lieutenant Snowden, C. S. Infantry, Captain Keiter, and seven soldiers killed; …." OR Series I, Volume LII, Part II, page 206; listed on staff of General Leonidas Polk in *Confederate Staff Officers 1861 -1865* by Joseph H. Crute, Jr., Derwent Books 1982, page 155, (no first name) as Lieutenant, Engineering Officer, November 1, 1861, Killed at Columbus; see *The Bursting of the "Lady Polk."*, *Confederate Veteran*, Volume XII, June, 1904, No. 6, pages 277-279; appears from information in The Virginia Regimental Histories Series, (c) Historical Data Systems, Inc. (www.civilwardata.com), that first enlisted on 5/24/1861 at Richmond, Virginia as a Private into "B" Company ("Maryland Guard" men from Baltimore, Maryland) Virginia 21st Infantry Regiment, was accidentally killed on 10/13/1861 at Columbus, Kentucky (Killed by bursting of a Dahigren (sic) gun), promoted 2nd Lieutenant 6/15/1861 (Estimated day) and was born in Princes George's Co., Maryland, however, no compiled service records found but information may possibly be found in The Maryland Historical Civil War Resources: *Description Roll of Company B, Maryland Guard, Maryland Line, Attached to 21st Virginia Infantry, CSA, 1861-62*; oversize (MF185.4D441) (Published Sources) and *Maryland Cadets and Maryland Guard Records*, 1842-6, 1861 (MS2165) (Manuscript Collections); believed to be brother of Major Charles Alexander Snowden, Quartermaster Department Provisional Army of Confederate States, appointed from Maryland and Major Richard N. Snowden, Assistant Adjutant General and Acting Assistant Inspector General, appointed from Maryland and served on the staffs of Major General Arnold Elsey and Major General Leonidas Polk and no record after July 20, 1863, and indication on one compiled service record card "Dead."; believed also to be J. Hudson Snowden who was a civilian topographer who participated in western territory explorations with Lieutenant Gouverneur K. Warren, U.S. Army Corps of Topographical Engineers, 1855-57, and Captain William F. Raynolds' 1859–60 Raynolds Expedition (an expedition into the Yellowstone region of Montana and Wyoming) while serving as a member of the U.S. Army Corps of Topographical Engineers; Lieutenant and killed at Belmont by bursting of cannon but only last name in Daily Burial Record Book; had to have been moved to Elmwood but no indication found in Cemetery record.

Snowden, Robert Bogardus   Buried October 9, 1909   Miller 1, #1
Tennessee 25 Infantry Regiment Lieutenant Colonel; enlisted Tennessee 1 (Field's) Infantry Regiment 1 Lieutenant Company C & Adjutant May 25, 1861, at Camp Cheatham; appointed Lieutenant Colonel June 24, 1863; resigned March 8, 1865, due to disability; appointed from War Department June 24, 1863, with rank of Colonel; age 30 on muster roll dated April 7, 1864; per November & December 1864, muster roll remarks: on detached service at Richmond and Certificate of Disability; retired March 8, 1865, because of disability; Adjutant Tennessee 1 (Field's) and 27 Consolidated Infantry Regiment which compiled service record rolls has single card dated January 14, 1864, at Dalton, Georgia indicating enlisted May 9, 1861, at Camp Harris and with remarks that was Lieutenant Colonel of first organization Tennessee regiment; per sketch in Mathes book born in New York, entered the war early and became 1 Lieutenant and Adjutant Maney's 1 Tennessee Regiment, served first year in Army of West Virginia, next two years in Army of Tennessee and last year in Army of Virginia, after Battle of Murfreesboro promoted to Lieutenant Colonel, wounded three times, became a member of Confederate Historical Association May 12, 1870, and was Commander-in-Chief at inter-state drill in Memphis in 1895 with rank of Major General; biography in *Confederate Military History, Extended Edition*, Volume X Tennessee, page 723; sketch in *Tennessee, The Volunteer State, 1769-1923*, Volume III, page 133; Colonel and died age 73 per Daily Burial Record Book; grave stone: May 24, 1836 October 7, 1909; listed in "Touring Historic Elmwood Cemetery" Brochure (January 2000) #124.

Southall, Randall M.   Buried May 30, 1884   Turley 54, #10
Tennessee 10 Infantry Regiment Brevet 2 Lieutenant Company K; no enlistment in compiled service record; commissioned May 18,1861; captured Fort Donelson, Tennessee February 16, 1862, and sent to Johnson's Island, Ohio then to Vicksburg, Mississippi September 1, 1862; took Oath of Honor September 3,1862, in St. Louis, Missouri; second name/initial "McG." in compiled service record; died age 44 and second initial "J" in Daily Burial Record Book and computer index; per grave headstone: born November 11, 1840, and died May 29, 1884; per Bruce Allardice his mother's name was McGavock and was cousin of Randal McGavock, mayor of Nashville and Colonel Tennessee 10 Infantry, see *Pen and Sword, The Life and Journal of Randal W. McGavock, Colonel*

, *C.S.A.* The Biography — Herschel, The Early Years Journal — 1848-1851, Herschel Gower, Editor, The Political and Civil War Journals — Jack Allen, Editor. Tennessee Historical Commission – Nashville 1959.

Southerland, James   Buried January 11, 1875   Chapel Hill 592, #3
Tennessee 3 (Forrest's) Cavalry Regiment 2 Lieutenant Company A; originally enlisted Tennessee 154 Senior Infantry Regiment Private 1 Company B May 14, 1861 Randolph, Tennessee age 26; per Tennessee 3 (Forrest's) Cavalry record 2 Lieutenant 2 Company A, enlisted May 4, 1861, Randolph, appointed 2 Lieutenant May 7, 1864, and signed oath May 11, 1865 as 2 Lieutenant Company A Forrest Old Regiment; listed in the June 6, 1878, *Memphis Daily Appeal*, page 4, column 3, article "OUR DEAD HEROES" covering the unveiling of the Confederate Monument and Decoration of Graves at Elmwood as then one of twenty-eight members of the Bluff City Grays, Company B of the 154 Senior Infantry Regiment and Company A of Forrest's Old (Third) Cavalry Regiment buried at Elmwood; listed as one of the "comrades who sleep at Elmwood cemetery " in the article "Veterans in Council" in the May 12, 1881, *Memphis Daily Appeal*, page 4, column 4, concerning the meeting of the surviving members in the city of the old Bluff City Grays to appoint the necessary committees for the purpose of making special decoration on the graves of their dead comrades at Elmwood and Calvary cemeteries on Sunday next, Memorial Day; listed in "A COMPLETE ROSTER OF THE BLUFF CITY GREYS" located in the Memphis Room of the Memphis/Shelby County Public Library and Information Center Central Library with notation that "Elected Lt. 1864 Died Memphis June 15, 1875" and included on the list at the end of the soldiers buried at Elmwood with indication that buried in Chapel Hill 610 which is part of same lot as 592; listed as member of Bluff City Grays in *Reminiscences of the Civil War* by John Hallum, Tunnah & Pittard printers, 1903; see also Notes of Interest - Bluff City Grays; member Confederate Historical Association with sketch in Mathes book; widow Imogene (Latham) Southerland received Tennessee Confederate Pension W4421; per pension file he was born December 24, 1836, in Fayette County, Tennessee, they were married December 24, 1867, in Desoto County, Mississippi and he died in Desoto County, Mississippi January 9, 1875; died pneumonia age 50 per Daily Burial Record Book.

Spears, John Henry   Buried July 25, 1872   Fowler Public Lot 12, #154
Missouri 16 Infantry (Van Horn's Battalion) Regiment Private Company A; enlisted August 18, 1862, Jackson, County, Missouri; per June 18 to August 31, 1862, muster roll remarks absent sick since December 11, 1862; per March & April 1863, muster roll remarks left sick at Van Buren, Arkansas December 11, 1862; per April 30 to August 31, 1863, muster roll remarks deserted January 1, 1863, Van Buren; grave stone: Company C Van Hor's Battalion Missouri Infantry 1825 1872.

Spicer, James W.   Buried January 18, 1866   Fowler 99, #2
Tennessee 3 (Forrest's Old) Cavalry Regiment Sergeant 2 Company A "Bluff City Grays"; originally enlisted Tennessee 154 Senior Infantry Regiment Corporal 1 Company B May 14, 1861, Randolph, Tennessee age 22 and present on August 14 to November 1, 1861, muster roll; per Tennessee 3 (Forrest's) Cavalry record enlisted May 4, 1861, Randolph, captured near Athens, Tennessee September 26, 1863, sent to Camp Chase November 14, 1863, transferred to Rock Island, Illinois January 14, 1864, and paroled March 6, 1865, from Rock Island Barracks; listed in Elmwood 1874 book as Confederate soldier buried in Elmwood who was citizen of Memphis or vicinity; listed in the June 6, 1878, *Memphis Daily Appeal*, page 4, column 3, article "OUR DEAD HEROES" covering the unveiling of the Confederate Monument and Decoration of Graves at Elmwood as then one of twenty-eight members of the Bluff City Grays, Company B of the 154 Senior Infantry Regiment and Company A of Forrest's Old (Third) Cavalry Regiment buried at Elmwood; listed as one of the "comrades who sleep at Elmwood cemetery " in the article "Veterans in Council" in the May 12, 1881, *Memphis Daily Appeal*, page 4, column 4, concerning the meeting of the surviving members in the city of the old Bluff City Grays to appoint the necessary committees for the purpose of making special decoration on the graves of their dead comrades at Elmwood and Calvary cemeteries on Sunday next, Memorial Day; listed in "A COMPLETE ROSTER OF THE BLUFF CITY GREYS" located in the Memphis Room of the Memphis/Shelby County Public Library and Information Center Central Library and included on the list at the end of the soldiers buried at Elmwood; listed as member of Bluff City Grays in *Reminiscences of the Civil War* by John Hallum, Tunnah & Pittard printers, 1903; with remarks "Prisoner–Died" and included on the list at the end of the soldiers buried at Elmwood; see also Notes of Interest - Bluff City Grays; died consumption age 20 per Daily Burial Record Book; obituary in *Memphis Daily Appeal*, January 55, 1866, page 1, column 5, include sketch of his War service.

Spicer, John E.   Buried November 3, 1886   Fowler 99, #6
Tennessee 3 (Forrest's Old) Cavalry Regiment Sergeant 2 Company A "Bluff City Grays"; originally enlisted Tennessee 154 Senior Infantry Regiment Sergeant 1 Company B May 14, 1861, at Randolph, Tennessee age 32; per Tennessee 3 (Forrest's) Cavalry record enlisted May 4, 1861, Randolph; listed in "A COMPLETE ROSTER OF THE BLUFF CITY GREYS" located in the Memphis Room of the Memphis/Shelby County Public Library and Information Center Central Library; listed as member of Bluff City Grays in *Reminiscences of the Civil War* by John Hallum, Tunnah & Pittard printers, 1903; see also Notes of Interest - Bluff City Grays; per sketch in Mathes book Private Forrest's Old Regiment, enlisted May 4, 1861, retired at surrender in May 1865 and proposed for membership in Confederate Historical Association by J. A. Loudon and elected January 20, 1870; died age 58 per Daily Burial Record Book.

Spicer, Robert Augustus   Buried July 27, 1905   Turley 1338, #1
Tennessee 3 (Forrest's) Cavalry Regiment Private Company A "Bluff City Grays"; originally enlisted Tennessee 154 Senior Infantry Regiment Private 1 Company B May 14, 1861, Randolph, Tennessee age 28 and present on August 14 to November 1,

1861, muster roll; per Tennessee 3 (Forrest's Old) Cavalry Regiment rolls enlisted May 4, 1861, Randolph, Tennessee, present on all muster rolls to surrender on May 4, 1865, Citronelle, Alabama and paroled May 11, 1865, at Gainesville, Alabama; listed in "A COMPLETE ROSTER OF THE BLUFF CITY GREYS" located in the Memphis Room of the Memphis/Shelby County Public Library and Information Center Central Library; listed as member of Bluff City Grays in *Reminiscences of the Civil War* by John Hallum, Tunnah & Pittard printers, 1903; see also Notes of Interest - Bluff City Grays; per widow's, Martha O. (King) Spicer, Tennessee Confederate Pension (W2911) file he was born Brownsville, Haywood County, Tennessee; she was born September 1841, in Raleigh, Shelby County, Tennessee, they were married September 8, 1868, in Shelby County, Tennessee, and she died October 1910; died age 73 per Daily Burial Record Book.

Spicer, Samuel S.   Buried January 19, 1916   Lenow Circle 101, #5
Tennessee 3 (Forrest's Old) Cavalry Regiment Private 2 Company A "Bluff City Grays"; indicated in Tennessee Confederate Pension Application (S14428) filed June 16, 1914, that first joined Tennessee 154 Senior Infantry Regiment Company B (no records found) and transferred to Forrest Cavalry; per Tennessee 3 (Forrest's Old) Cavalry Regiment Company Muster Roll for October 31 to December 31, 1862, enlisted August 12, 1862, at Knoxville, Tennessee; per Company Muster Roll for May and June, 1863, detailed to QM Department; per Company Muster Roll for March 1, 1864, to May 14, 1864, detailed to Paymaster Department; paroled May 9, 1865, at Gainesville, Alabama and indicated residence as Memphis; not listed as member of Bluff City Grays in *Reminiscences of the Civil War* by John Hallum, Tunnah & Pittard printers, 1903; listed in "A COMPLETE ROSTER OF THE BLUFF CITY GREYS" located in the Memphis Room of the Memphis/Shelby County Public Library and Information Center Central Library with remarks "Detailed in Paymasters Dept."; per pension file born November 14, 1834, in Haywood County, Tennessee; died age 81 per Daily Burial Record Book.

Springfield, Baker Claudius   Buried April 24, 1904   Turley 1294, #4
Tennessee 3 (Forrest's) Cavalry Regiment Private; name appears on an Oath of Allegiance sworn to at Memphis, Tennessee from May 15 to June 1, 1865, dated May 16, 1865, residence Fayette County, Tennessee, age 19; per City of Memphis Burial Permit died April 23, 1904, age 58, cause chronic nephritis.

Steinkuhl, Christain D.   Buried November 11, 1878   Turley 615, #3
Tennessee 3 (Forrest's) Cavalry Regiment Lieutenant Company B; enlisted March 10, 1862, Memphis; elected Lieutenant June 15, 1863; single card in Tennessee 11 (Holman's) Cavalry Regiment record indicating 2 Lieutenant Company A; per sketch in Mathes book enlisted in Company B, Captain James G. Barbour, Forrest's Old Regiment (McDonald's Battalion) and at organization elected Lieutenant, and became member of old Confederate Relief and Historical Association August 13, 1869; died yellow fever age 50 per Daily Burial Record Book.

Steinkuhl, Jacob   Buried July 28, 1896   Chapel Hill 436, #10
Tennessee 3 (Memphis Battalion) Infantry Battalion Private Company D; per Company Muster-in Roll dated March 12, 1862, enlisted March 11, 1862, Memphis, age 88; "Present" indicated on Company Muster Roll dated April 30, 1862; no other information in compiled service record; see Notes of Interest "Memphis Battalion - Tennessee 3 (Memphis Battalion) Infantry Battalion"; died age 71 per Daily Burial Record Book.

Stewart, Charles Pinkey   Buried January 31, 1892   Chapel Hill 300, #5
C.S.A.; died age 43 per Daily Burial Record Book; Stewart family grave stone: "1849 CHARLES PINKNEY CSA 1892"; per Shelby County Funeral index book in Memphis Library Memphis Room died January 29, 1892, age 43 born Tennessee died apoplexy; unit possibly Georgia Pruden's Battery Light Artillery (Light Artillery State Troops), Private/Corporal, per August 31-October 31, 1864, muster roll enlisted August 23 Milledgeville and appointed from Private October 18, 1864, and absent sick.

Stewart, Darwin M.   Buried January 8, 1866   Chapel Hill 300, #3
Tennessee 3 (Forrest's Old) Cavalry Regiment Private 2 Company A "Bluff City Grays"; originally enlisted in Tennessee 154 Senior Infantry Regiment Private 1 Company B May 14, 1861 Randolph, Tennessee age 25 and present on August 14-November 1, 1861, muster roll; per Tennessee 3 (Forrest's Old) Cavalry Regiment rolls enlisted May 4, 1861, Randolph and killed at Somerville per November and December 1863, muster roll remarks; found in Lindsley's Annals under McDonald's Battery (sic Battalion) Company A as killed at Somerville; listed in Elmwood 1874 book as Confederate soldier buried in Elmwood who was citizen of Memphis or vicinity; listed ("D. M. Stewart") as member of Bluff City Grays in *Reminiscences of the Civil War* by John Hallum, Tunnah & Pittard printers, 1903; listed ("D. M. Stewart") in "A COMPLETE ROSTER OF THE BLUFF CITY GREYS" located in the Memphis Room of the Memphis/Shelby County Public Library and Information Center Central Library with remarks "Killed Somerville, Tenn. Dec 25, 1863; shot per Daily Burial Record Book; no mention of being removed to Cemetery in any Cemetery records; January 8, 1865, Chapel Hill 350 in Cemetery computer index; "1841 MAJOR DARWIN CSA 1865" on family grave stone.

Stewart, William Battle   Buried May 5, 1919   Chapel Hill 300, #7
Tennessee 12 (Green's) Cavalry Regiment Lieutenant Company I and Tennessee 154 Senior Infantry Regiment Private Company E; Lieutenant and died age 67 per Daily Burial Record Book but no unit indicated; units per sketch in Goodspeed's Shelby County History, page 1045; per 154 Senior Infantry Regiment Company Muster-in Roll dated August 13, 1861, (William Stewart) enlisted

May 14, 1861, Randolph, discharged "17 day of September" per August 14 to October 31, 1861, Company Muster Roll (W. B. Stewart on this card) and discharged at Columbus, Kentucky in 1861 per Company Muster Roll dated May 5, 1863, (discharged on account of inflammatory rheumatism per Goodspeed's sketch); two records under 12 Cavalry Regiment (organized February 1863 and also known as 1 Tennessee Partisan Rangers) - William B. Stewart, Private Company I, prisoner of war under Provost Marshall in Memphis, received April 18, 1863, captured near Dancyville, Tennessee April 5, 1863, sent to prison at St. Louis and exchanged at City Point, Virginia April 28, 1863; and William Stewart, Corporal/ 2 Lieutenant Company I, enlisted March 6, 1864, Tipton, assigned February 6, 1864, by General Richardson and elected 2 Lieutenant February 4, 1864; per May 5, 1919, *The Commercial Appeal* Memphis died May 4, 1919; native of New Orleans, Louisiana, born in 1843 (note difference) and migrated to Memphis with parents, E. P. and Mary (Battle) Stewart, in 1846 per Goodspeed's sketch; received Tennessee Confederate Pension (S4722) and stated in application born in New Orleans in 1843, enlisted in 154 Infantry in April 1861, discharged on account of rheumatism in October 1861, and was wounded while in cavalry; "1842 WILLIAM BATTLE LT CSA 1919" on Stewart family stone.

Stockdale. George Washington   Buried May 28, 1919   Turley 821¼, #1
Alabama Cavalry Barbiere's Battalion Private Captain A. W. Bowie's Company F Local Defense Troops; the Battalion was organized in 1864 from several independent companies which had themselves been created as supporting forces for the Conscript Reserves; no enlistment information in compiled service records; prior to death drew a pension from the State of Alabama (No. 22455); widow, Alabama Flavio Stockdale, received a Tennessee Confederate Pension (W7328); per application he was born in Talladega, Alabama; per Tennessee Certificate of Death died age 73 from heart disease and senility.

Stockton   Buried July 20, 1868   Turley 423, #12
Captain, chronic dysentery and died age 45 per Daily Burial Record Book and Memphis Register of Deaths (Nativity Delaware); no first name in either record; Confederate per submission to Cemetery office for 1998 Veterans Day activities.

Stone, William Thomas   Buried October 16, 1892   Evergreen 1, #1
Tennessee 13 Infantry Regiment Sergeant Company G; enlisted Private Company E (Captain Dyer) May 28, 1861, Camp Fair (Jackson, Tennessee) age 18; transferred to Company B April 30, 1862, 5 Sergeant; captured near Atlanta and August 3, 1864, sent to Nashville then prison in Louisville, Kentucky August 15, 1864, then Camp Chase; February 12, 1865, transferred to Point Lookout, Maryland; took Oath of Allegiance April 21, 1865, at Memphis, Tennessee and indicted residence of Fayette County, Tennessee age 23; per sketch in Mathes book enlarged edition born December 18, 1840, near Macon, Fayette County, Tennessee, enlisted July 1861, at Moscow, Tennessee in Captain Dyer's Company Dixie Rifles, captured at Battle of Atlanta July 22, 1864, sent to Camp Douglas and exchanged March 1865, after war engaged in mercantile at Rossville, Tennessee, moved to Memphis in 1881 and died October 15, 1892; died age 52 per Daily Burial Record Book; grave stone: "W. Thomas Stone" born 1839 died 1892.

Stovall, George Alexander   Buried September 15, 1906   Chapel Hill Circle 60½
Tennessee 7 Cavalry Regiment Sergeant Company A; per Company Muster Roll for May & June 1864, enlisted August 13, 1862, at Senatobia, Mississippi; issued a Medical Certificate March 16, 1865, that he was unfit for duty in field and ordered to report to camp of disabled officers and enlisted men at Lauderdale Spring, Mississippi; sketch in Mathes book page 283; grave stone: April 11, 1831 September 14, 1906; died age 76 per Daily Burial Record Book.

Strange, John P.   Buried May 19, 1875   Chapel Hill 107, #2
Assistant Adjutant General, Major, staff of General N. B. Forrest; Tennessee 3 (Forrest's Old) Cavalry Regiment Sergeant-Major; no record found 3 Cavalry compiled service record rolls but listed as Adjutant on organization card; per General and Staff records Captain and Assistant Adjutant General, captured at Parker's Crossroads, Tennessee December 31, 1862, sent to Military Prison Alton, Illinois January 21, 1863, sent to Camp Chase, Ohio March 16, 1863, per descriptive roll 5' 4" and age 40, sent to Fort Delaware April 10, 1863, forwarded to City Point for exchange April 29, 1863, per register of appointments appointed October 27, 1862, promoted Major August 30, 1863, with date of appointment September 7, 1863, and paroled May 12, 1865, at rank of Major and Assistant Adjutant General of General N. B. Forrest's staff; see also *Confederate Staff Officers 1861 -1865* by Joseph H. Crute, Jr., Derwent Books 1982, page 63; death notice in *Memphis Daily Appeal*, May 18, 1875, page 5, column 6; funeral notice in *Memphis Daily Appeal*, May 19, 1875, page 1, column 7; large article on funeral and his War service and resolution adopted by his comrades in arms in *Memphis Daily Appeal*, May 20, 1875, page 4, column 4; Major J. P. Strange, born in Virginia May 26, 1823, and died in Memphis May 17, 1875, on grave monument; also on monument Mary J. Strange wife of J. P. Strange, born in Petersburg, Virginia September 24, 1829, married July 2, 1850, died March 17, 1857; died age 52 complications per Daily Burial Record Book; sketch in Mathes book indicating joined Confederate Historical Association March 3, 1870.

Swan, William Graham   Buried April 12, 1869   South Grove 17, #1
Confederate Congressman (Tennessee); see sketch in Warner's Confederate Congress book page 234; per sketch there is a grave stone that indicates born 1821 but stone not found; published sources indicate born in Tennessee but 1860 census for Knox County, Tennessee records his birth place as Alabama, graduated from East Tennessee College (now the University of Tennessee) in 1838, studied law and practiced in Knoxville until outbreak of War, did not own slaves, enlisted as private in Confederate army but November 1861 won election to the first regular Congress, reelected in 1863, after War because of east Tennessee Union sentiment moved to the more congenial atmosphere of Memphis where continued until death April 10, 1869, at age 48; per sketch in

PoliticalGraveyard.com Tennessee state attorney general 1851, mayor of Knoxville 1855-56, served in the Confederate Army during the Civil War, Representative from Tennessee in the Confederate Congress 1862-65, and died April 18, 1869 (sic); Tribute of Respect by the Chickasaw Club and L. A. Rooms (Memphis) in April 15, 1869, *Memphis Daily Appeal*, page 2, Column 4; died consumption age 48 per Daily Burial Record Books.

Swingley, Alfred Lee   Buried May 17, 1873   Chapel Hill 219, #6
Tennessee Newsom's Cavalry Regiment Lieutenant Colonel; captured Bolivar, Tennessee February 20, 1864, sent to Johnson's Island, Ohio then to Camp Chase, Fort Delaware March 25, 1864, and then to Hilton Head, South Carolina June, 1864 and exchanged August 3, 1864; appears on a Roll of Prisoners of War surrendered at Post of La Grange, Tennessee May 17, 1865, that indicates surrendered at La Grange May 17, 1865, and had left his command near Jackson, Tennessee May 16, 1865, and paroled; first served in Missouri State Guard 9 Regiment Cavalry (Alf T. Swingley), 2 Lieutenant Company A, elected July 22, 1861, born Ohio, age 24, from Butler, Bates County, Missouri, and resigned November 6, 1861; per Colonel William H Stephens', Tennessee 6 Infantry Regiment, April 17, 1862, battle report on Shiloh "Capt. A. L. Swingley, of the Army of Missouri, (who) acted as my volunteer aide, … ." but no compiled service records found; per death notice in February 3, 1872, *Memphis Daily Appeal*, page 1, column 5, died February 3, 1872, age 34; was a member of the local bar (lawyer) and per article in February 3, 1872, *Memphis Daily Appeal*, page 4, column 8, that reports local bar members met to acknowledge him and to plan to attend his funeral; the article included a biographical sketch that indicated he was born April 16, 1838, Washington County, Maryland, and before the War moved to Kansas where "(H)e espoused the cause of the South, and was driven from home by the people of his adopted state, narrowly escaping with his life into Missouri, where he found a regiment of State troops. He was captain of a company in the Ninth Missouri State troops, and served through Price's campaign in Missouri, until after the battle of Oak Hill. He then came to the Army of Tennessee, and was present at the battle of Shiloh, where he served as aid-de camp to Col. William H Stephens, and was stunned by a shell bursting near him in that fight. Afterward he joined Forrest's cavalry, and was soon lieutenant-colonel of a regiment, serving in that capacity in several battles. During the latter part of the war he was taken prisoner, and, after remaining in prison some time, was carried to Charleston and placed by the enemy under the fire of our own guns, along with General Duke and other Confederate officers. Near the close of the war he was exchanged. After the close of the war he resumed the practice of law at Jackson, Tennessee. In 1866 he came to Memphis to practice his profession."; removed from Calvary Cemetery per Daily Burial Record Book; died February 2, 1872, aged 35 years on grave stone.

Talbot, John R.
Listed in Elmwood 1874 book as Confederate soldier buried in Elmwood who was citizen of Memphis or vicinity; possibly J. R. Tolbert, buried September 4, 1869, typhoid fever, no age, South Grove 203 (John R. Talbert Lot) #1, no grave stone found; possibly J. R. Talbert Mississippi 29 Infantry Regiment 1 Lieutenant Company E, enlisted March 12, 1862, Grenada and resigned June 19, 1862, because of health.

Talley, Fletcher H.   Buried December 3, 1871   Chapel Hill Circle 18½, # 1
Tennessee 7 Cavalry Regiment Private Company A; enlisted October 18, 1862, Cold Water, Mississippi; per Company Muster Roll for July and August 1863, remarks: Detailed as Transfer Agent January 1, 1863; per sketch in Mathes book, page 284: General Agent for the Memphis & Charleston Railroad Company at Memphis at the beginning of the war, upon the capture of the city in 1862, enlisted in Company A, Seventh Tennessee Cavalry, served continuously until detailed for railroad service at Meridian, Miss., as agent, upon the capture of Meridian by General Sherman moved his office to Selma, Ala., where continued until the capture of that place by General Wilson, and after the war re-employed by the M. & C. R. R. Co. as General Freight and Ticket Agent until his death in 1871; one of four brothers (Foster D., Fletcher H., Richard H. and Wm. F. Talley – see sketches) who entered the Confederate service from Memphis grave stone: Died December 2, 1871, Aged 37 Years.

Talley, Foster Douglas   Buried July 1, 1904   Chapel Hill Circle 44
Tennessee 7 Cavalry Regiment Private Company A; enlisted October 28, 1862, Cold Water, Mississippi; name appears on a Report of Prisoners of War paroled on terms as agreed to for the 5 day period ending May 15, 1865, at Memphis, Tennessee; signed Amnesty Oath August 11, 1865; per sketch in Mathes Book, page 284: one of four brothers (Foster D., Fletcher H., Richard H. and Wm. F. Talley – see sketches) who entered the Confederate service from Memphis; saw much active service and lived through the war, while two brothers-in-law, who married their sisters, never returned, left the railroad service and enlisted in Company A, Seventh Tennessee Cavalry, was in the movement against Corinth in October, 1862, was with Van Dorn at Holly Springs, and under him when he was killed, under General Joseph E. Johnston around Jackson, Miss., and afterward on the Georgia campaign and after several days hard fighting on the New Hope Church and Dallas line detailed for railroad duty and stationed at Selma, Ala., until run out by Wilson's raid, parole dated Memphis, May 11, 1865, joined the C. H. A. in October, 1896; only brother with a biography in *Confederate Military History, Extended Edition,* Volume X, page 733, but biography does describe each of their service; per City of Memphis Burial Permit Date of Birth February 6, 1832, and Date of Death June 6, 1914, age 72 years.

Talley, Richard H.   Buried November 18, 1895   Chapel Hill Circle 18½, #5
Tennessee 38 Infantry Regiment Private/1 Sergeant Company D; enlisted August 20, 1861, Camp Abington (located in Fayette County just east of Collierville, Tennessee); promoted to 1 Sergeant August 1, 1863; per sketch in Mathes Book, page 198: the youngest of four sons of Mrs. Emily B. Talley, all of whom went into the Confederate army, as well as two sons-in-law, the other brothers were Foster D., Fletcher H. and Wm. F. Talley (see sketches), at the age of 16 years left his widowed mother and enlisted

in the Thirty-eighth Tennessee, served throughout the war, paroled May 1, 1865, at Macon, Ga., then took service with the M. & C. R. R. at Collierville, having his office and station in a boxcar, a few years after transferred to Memphis, where employed in the treasurer's office, after fourteen years' service became ticket agent of the C. O. & S. W. R. R. Co., and afterward represented other railroads, secretary of the Memphis Passenger Association when died in 1895, and joined the C. H. A. March 10, 1885; grave stone: Died November 13, 1895; died age 50 per Daily Record Burial Book.

Talley, William F.   Burial Unknown
Mississippi 2 (J. G. Ballentine's Regiment of Cavalry) Partisan Rangers Private (Captain Edward E. Porter's Partisan Company – see Rev. Edward E. Porter sketch) Company C (name Tally); per Company Muster Roll for October 31, 1862, to February 28, 1863, enlisted September 7, 1862, at Cold Water and remarks that taken prisoner December 2 at Oxford; Company C transferred to Tennessee 3 (Forrest's Old) Cavalry Regiment Company F in accordance with S. O. No. 28. Headquarters, Cavalry Division District of Mississippi and East Louisiana, dated February 13, 1865, and soldiers paroled as part of Company F at Gainesville, Alabama May 11, 1865, but no record found in Tennessee 3 (Forrest's Old) Cavalry Regiment Company F rolls; per sketch in Mathes book, page 284: enlisted in Shelby county, Tenn., in 1861, in Captain Porter's independent company (Edward E. Porter's Partisans, which became Company C), captured near Oxford, Miss., and sent North to prison, then returned to Vicksburg to be exchanged, but before reaching Vicksburg all exchange of prisoners had stopped, and the boat, loaded with prisoners, was sent back up the river, at Memphis escaped and rejoined his command but health and constitution had been destroyed by exposure and want while a prisoner, and died just at the close of the war, aged 36 years; one of four brothers (Foster D., Fletcher H., Richard H. and Wm. F. Talley – see sketches) who entered the Confederate service from Memphis.

Tate, Samuel   Buried July 28, 1892   Chapel Hill 12, #19
Colonel and Volunteer Aide as appointed by order No. 2 on September 26, 1861, by General Albert Sidney Johnston, Commander of the Western Department of the Army; "volunteer aides" were made chiefly to secure intelligent advice on the political affairs of the department, each State of which was represented on the staff (see *The Life of General Albert Sidney Johnston: His Service in the Armies of the United States, the Republic of Texas, and the Confederate States*, William Preston Johnston, D. Appleton and Company, New York, 1879.); headed the Demopolis-based construction company contracted to build the South & North Alabama railroad from Montgomery to Decatur but not completed and contract for the uncompleted line was sold to the Louisville & Nashville Railroad in 1871; took Oath of Allegiance and granted a pardon May 31, 1865, (Oath for Application Presidential Pardons Amnesty Papers 186567); requested and received return of ownership of the Memphis and Charleston Railroad from Federal military authorities after the War; payment of claims against the government for damages to the railroad, which he had agreed not to pursue if ownership returned in an agreement with General Edward Bouton, Provost Marshall of Memphis (see *Bouton's Battery in the Civil War (Annotated),* Big Byte Books, 2016), ordered by President Andrew Johnson, who was a friend before the War, was investigated during impeachment of President Johnson, as some claimed that President Johnson received some financial benefit but not proven; worked with General N. B. Forrest in 1866 to build the Memphis and Little Rock Railroad; a shareholder in the Elyton Land Company which founded Birmingham at the crossing of the L&N with the Alabama & Chattanooga Railroad in Jones Valley and went on to help organized the Birmingham Coal and Iron Company in 1880; born November 27, 1817, in Middle Tennessee, during his childhood family moved to Fayette County, Tennessee, where he was educated and became a merchant in Somerville, Tennessee around 1840; lived in several places in his later life including Florida and the Little Rock, Arkansas area; grave stone: Born November 27, 1817 Died July 26, 1892; spouse Mary Augusta Tate who per grave stone born in Hardeman County, Tennessee July 30, 1826, and died at Niagara Falls, New York August 6, 1864.

Tate, Thomas Galen   Buried June 18, 1910   Turley 1412, #1
Tennessee 7 Cavalry Regiment, Private Company A, enlisted October 18, 1862, at Cold Water, Mississippi, and swore Oath of Allegiance at Memphis, Tennessee May 10, 1865, at age 24 and residence indicated as Hernando, Mississippi; per sketch in Mathes book (enlarged edition), page 56, enlisted April 1861 in the Seventh Tennessee Cavalry and served in both Seventh Mississippi (no record found) and Seventh Tennessee Cavalry as first lieutenant, captured at Fort Donelson and escaped the same day, paroled May 1865, and joined Confederate Historical Association January 12, 1897; biography in *Confederate Military History, Extended Edition*, Volume X Tennessee, page 736; per *Confederate Veteran,* Volume XIX, April 1911, page 174, "The Last Roll" Deaths of Confederates in Memphis, Tennessee who died during 1910 and were members of the Confederate Historical Association, Camp No. 28, U. C. V., Bivouac 18, C. V., of Memphis, Tennessee, enlisted April, 1861, paroled May 11, 1865, and at the time of his death, June 18, was sheriff elect of Shelby County, Tennessee; died age 69 per Daily Burial Record Book; grave stone: Capt. C.S.A. "He stood foursquare to all the winds that blew."

Taylor, Archibald Henderson   Buried July 13, 1866   Fowler 24, #6
Tennessee 21 Infantry Regiment 2 Lieutenant Company H and Adjutant, per Company Muster Roll for November & December 1861, enlisted May 15, 1861, at Memphis, appointed Lieutenant May 15, 1861, and appointed Adjutant November 1, 1861, on Report of Prisoners of War paroled by Provost Marshall at Memphis for 5 days ending May 20, 1865; brother of Nathaniel Chapman Taylor (see sketch infra) Captain Company H and Julius Alexander Taylor (see sketch infra) Brevet 2 Lieutenant Company H; Listed in Elmwood 1874 book as Confederate soldier buried in Elmwood who was citizen of Memphis or vicinity; "shot in duel," age 32 per Daily Burial Record Book; no grave stone; killed in a duel with Alonzo Greenlaw (see sketch supra) on July 12, 1866 (see obituary in the July 13, 1866 edition of the *Memphis Daily Post* and article "Duel Yesterday – One Man Killed" in the *Public Ledger* (Memphis), Friday Evening, July 13, 1866, page 3, column 2).

Taylor, Arthur Kennon   Memorial   Chapel Hill 24
Louisiana 16 Infantry Regiment Private Company E; enlisted April 9, 1862, Corinth, Mississippi; present on all rolls to October 1862; per November & December 1862, muster roll dated January 21, 1863, remarks killed in action at Murfreesboro December 31; no Cemetery record of burial at Elmwood; memorial on family stone: "in sacred memory Arthur Kennon Taylor who fell at the Battle of Murfreesboro December 31, 1862, age 16 years, 5 months, 29 days"; brother of William V. Taylor (see sketch infra); Lot 24 is Arthur K. Taylor lot; Dr. Arthur K. Taylor, 68 years, buried June 22, 1886, Chapel Hill 24, # 20.

Taylor, James H. R.   Buried October 31, 1867   Chapel Hill 24, #12
Tennessee 15 Infantry Regiment Lieutenant Colonel; enlisted June 7, 1861, at Jackson, Tennessee at age 40; appears on a Register containing Rosters of Commissioned Officers, Provisional Army Confederate States, that indicates date of appointment as June 17, 1861, resigned November 26, 1861, and a remark that elected Lieutenant Colonel December 4, 1861; subject of court martial November 3, 1861, by Special Order #275; per letter in file resignation accepted by President, CSA, December 26, 1861; died of yellow fever at age 47 per Daily Burial Record Book; listed as General (Taylor, Gen. James H. R.) in Elmwood 1874 book as Confederate soldier buried in Elmwood who was a citizen of Memphis or vicinity; not listed in the *Memorandum relative to the General Officers Appointed by the President in the Armies of the Confederate States - 1861-1865* compiled from Official Records by the Military Secretary's Office, U. S. War Department 1905; no sketch in *Generals in Gray* or *More Generals in Gray*; article in November 1, 1867, *Memphis Daily Appeal* Local Matters: "Death of General Taylor - General James H. R. Taylor of Holly Springs, Mississippi, died at the residence of his father, Dr. W. V. Taylor, in this City on Wednesday afternoon. He was about fifty years of age, and had filled many positions of honor and emolument in his State. His remains were interred at Elmwood yesterday with Masonic Honors."; family monument in lot partly illegible (cannot tell if on monument); died of yellow fever at age 47 per Daily Burial Record Book; full name James Henderson Roberts Taylor; also listed in chapter on Generals; sketch #15 in Elmwood *Civil War Tour* booklet (2012); not listed in Cemetery tour brochures.

Taylor, Julius Alexander   Buried August 2, 1895   Miller Circle 25
Tennessee 21 Infantry Regiment Brevet 2 Lieutenant Company H, per Company Muster Roll for November & December 1861, enlisted May 15, 1861, at Columbus, Kentucky, elected 2 Lieutenant November 1861, on Report of Prisoners of War paroled by Provost Marshall at Memphis for 5 days ending May 20, 1865; brother of Nathaniel Chapman Taylor (see sketch infra) Captain Company H and Archibald Henderson Taylor (see sketch supra) 2 Lieutenant Company H; per sketch in Mathes book (enlarged edition), page 145, born in LaGrange, Tennessee; sketch in Goodspeed's Shelby County History, page 1047; originally buried in South Grove Lot 193 and removed to Miller Circle Lot 25 August 16, 1895; circle grave stone: Born Feb. 6, 1840 Died Aug. 1, 1895.

Taylor, Nathaniel Chapman   Buried February 27, 1904   Miller Circle 25, #25
Tennessee 21 Infantry Regiment Captain Company H, per Company Muster Roll for November & December 1861, enlisted May 15, 1861, at Memphis, appointed Captain May 15, 1861, signed Parole of Honor May 18, 1865, at Grenada, Mississippi; brother of Archibald Henderson Taylor (see sketch supra) 2 Lieutenant Company H and Julius Alexander Taylor (see sketch supra) Brevet 2 Lieutenant Company H; second initial "P" on Memphis Burial Permit, age 79 and Gastritis cause of death.

Taylor, William Fletcher   Buried July 4, 1917   Chapel Hill Circle 33, #2
Tennessee 7 Cavalry Regiment Lieutenant Colonel; enlisted 2 Lieutenant Company A May 16, 1861, age 26 Memphis; promoted Captain September 20, 1862; promoted Major March 31, 1864, by order of General Forrest then Lieutenant Colonel it appears on same date; sketch in Mathes book (both editions); per original edition sketch, page 198, Lieutenant Colonel and Colonel of Tennessee 7 Cavalry Regiment and elected to Confederate Historical Association in 1869 or 1870; per enlarged edition sketch, page 100, born near Huntsville, Alabama July 11, 1835, enlisted in Memphis Light Dragoons early 1861 and elected Lieutenant, elected Captain and Company became part of 7 Tennessee Cavalry, became Lieutenant Colonel at Jackson, Tennessee early 1864, twice wounded, in command of Regiment at surrender, charter member under reorganization of Confederate Historical Association on May 22, 1884; born July 9, 1835 and died July 3, 1917 on grave stone; died age 82 per Daily Burial Record Book; per widow Sallie Shelby (Ford) Taylor Tennessee Confederate Pension W8137 file born July 11, 1835, at Huntsville, Alabama, and died July 3, 1917, at Monteagle, Tennessee; she was born April 15, 1843, in Memphis and they were married December 13, 1866, in Shelby County, Tennessee.

Taylor, William V.   Buried March 1, 1872   Chapel Hill 24, #14
Tennessee 154 Senior Infantry Regiment Private Company G; enlisted June 3, 1861, Memphis age 17; per July and August 1863, muster roll remarks: absent sick wounded Shiloh (to be dropped); listed in Elmwood 1874 book as Confederate soldier buried in Elmwood who was citizen of Memphis or vicinity; funeral notice in March 1, 1872, *Memphis Daily Appeal*, page 1, column 6; Masonic Funeral Notice follows funeral notice; obituary in *Memphis Daily Appeal* March 2, 1872, Local Paragraphs, page 4, column 2, indicating only surviving son of Dr. A. K. Taylor, one of the oldest citizens and leading physicians of Shelby county (note: other son A. K. Taylor had been killed at Battle of Murfreesboro December 31, 1862, see sketch supra); died consumption age 28 per Daily Burial Record Book; born March 1, 1844 and died February 28, 1872 on family monument.

Temple, John H.   Buried October 30,1869   Chapel Hill 427, #4

Tennessee 154 Senior Infantry Regiment Private/Corporal Company L; per Company Muster Roll dated March 8, 1862, enlisted March 7, 1862, Memphis; per Company Muster Roll for May & June 1862, dated October 27, 1862, Corporal; per Company Muster Roll for March and April 1863, remarks: Discharged and statement rendered April 29, over forty years old; per Company Muster Roll dated May 6, 1863, age 43, with remarks: Discharged having served his term and being over forty years of age; death notice in the October 30, 1869, *Memphis Daily Appeal,* page 1, column 4; died age 46 consumption per Daily Burial Record Book.

Thomas, James F.   Buried February 25, 1876   Fowler 120 (IOOF), #51

Confederate Cavalry Private per submission to Cemetery office for 1998 Veterans Day activities; possibly Tennessee 8 (Smith's) Cavalry, 11 Cavalry, 16 Cavalry or 21 Wilson's Cavalry; pneumonia and died age 43 per Daily Burial Record Book; buried in Independent Order of Odd Fellows Lot Space #52 per Fowler Section book but #51 per computer index; IOOF Funeral notice in the February 24, 1876, *Public Ledger*, page 2, column 4; small death notice in the February 25, 1876 *Memphis Daily Appeal*, page 1, column 7, indicating died "yesterday morning" but no information on any Confederate service; buried Odd Fellows (IOOF) Section.

Thompson, Jacob   Buried March 26, 1885   Lenow Circle 116, #3

Inspector General Major on the staff of General John C. Pemberton; per General and Staff compiled service record rolls April 3, 1862, announced as Colonel and Voluntary Aide de Camp Army of Mississippi on the staff of General G. T. Beauregard, about August 12 - December 12, 1862, ordered to report as Lieutenant Colonel of Ballentine's Cavalry Regiment but resigned before confirmed (no individual records found Mississippi 2 (Ballentine's Regiment of Cavalry) Partisan Rangers records), December 29, 1862, appointed as Major Adjutant Department and to report to General Pemberton, February 6, 1864, resignation accepted as Major Assistant Adjutant General; per sketch in Mathes book born in Caswell County, North Carolina in 1810 and died in Memphis March 24, 1885, life epitomized on a tablet dedicated to him in Memorial Hall, Chapel Hill University of North Carolina: "Class of 1831; member of faculty, 1831; representative in congress, 1839-1853; Secretary of the Interior, 1857-1861; Lieutenant-Colonel and Inspector-General C.S.A., 1862-1863; Confidential Agent of Confederate States to the dominion of Canada, 1864-1865.", at Battle of Shiloh, became Lieutenant Colonel of Ballentine's Regiment of Cavalry and subsequently sent on a mission to Canada, name proposed for Membership in Confederate Historical Association by Jefferson Davis, late President of the Confederacy and Reverend J. Carmichael and elected April 28, 1870; sketch in the PoliticalGraveyard.com; monument indicates born May 10, 1810, in Caswell County, North Carolina and died March 24, 1885; died old age (age 75) per Daily Burial Record Book; listed under Other Pioneers, Patriots and Patriarchs in "Touring historic Elmwood Cemetery" (Brochure and Map of Historic Gravesites) #102; listed in "Touring Historic Elmwood Cemetery" Brochure (January 2000) #43; sketch #30 in Elmwood *Civil War Tour* booklet (2012).

Thompson, Joseph Newton   Buried June 21, 1929   Miller Circle 239

Mississippi 44 (Blythe's) Infantry Regiment Private Company E and Regimental Musician, per Company Muster-in Roll dated August 7, 1861, enlisted July 3, 1861, at New Madrid, Missouri at age 20, Musician Field and Staff on March and April 1862, Company Muster Roll, per Company Muster Roll for March & April 1864, transferred from Regimental Band to Company E by order of Colonel Sharp, wounded March 25, 1864, and sent to hospital by order of Brigade Surgeon, suffered partial paralysis of right side and arm; per Tennessee Confederate Pension Application (S16445 filed August 20, 1928) wounded in battle of New Hope Church, Georgia, with part of his skull being taken off leaving no bone protection and also wounded in hand, wound resulted in paralysis of right side and the ball from his head wound was not removed until after close of the war and in Memphis; per Parole (not original but Certificate of Authentication) in pension application file paroled in Granada, Mississippi May 19, 1865; stated in Pension application that was born in Granada, Yallobashia (sic) County, (then) Mississippi in 1843; per sketch in Mathes book, page 202, born September 22, 1841, in Yallabusha (sic) County. Mississippi, enlisted April 27, 1861, as a private in Company E, Blythe's Forty-fourth Mississippi Regiment, was wounded twice in the battle of New Hope Church, Georgia, on the 27th of May1864, served to the end of the war, joined the Confederate Historical Association September 13, 1893, and a member of Company A, Confederate Veterans; gravestone: Sep. 22, 1842 – June 21, 1929; Date of Death on Death Certificate: June 21, 1929 and age 89.

Thornton, Gustavus Brown   Buried May 15, 1914   Turley 582, #6

Tennessee Artillery Corps Johnston's Company Assistant Surgeon; per Tennessee Johnston's Company records (Southern Guards Captain Hamilton's Battery Company L) enlisted April 21, 1861, Memphis; per Tennessee Artillery Corps rolls Assistant Surgeon, enlisted June 29, 1861 Nashville, appointed by governor and confirmed by senate, and per June 29, 1861, muster roll remarks arrived at rendezvous April 21, mustered into service May 21 as Private in Captain Hamilton's (Artillery) and appointed Surgeon June 29; per General and Staff compiled service record rolls from Tennessee, June 29, 1861, Assistant Surgeon McCown's Corps Artillery, January 4, 1862 appointed Surgeon, Major and Chief Surgeon, Walthall's Division, Army of Tennessee, appointed February 17, 1862, and paroled at Greensboro, North Carolina May 1, 1865; per sketch in Mathes book, page 202, born February 22, 1835, Bowling Green, Caroline County, Virginia, came to Memphis 1847, graduated from Memphis Medical College 1858, at University of New York Medical Department 1860, practiced medicine in Memphis one year before joining Southern Guards (part of pre-war organization of the regiment that withdrew and formed an artillery company) Captain James Hamilton Tennessee 154 Senior Infantry regiment, served three/four months then commissioned Assistant Surgeon of State troops and subsequently transferred to Confederate service, assistant Surgeon at battles through Battle of Shiloh, appointed Surgeon and served as Chief

Surgeon in Brigadier General John P. McCown's and General A. P. Stewart's Division, when Stewart promoted placed in command of General H.D. Clayton of Alabama, spring 1865 assigned to Walthall's Division where remained to surrender, returned to Memphis after war and practiced medicine and became member of Confederate Historical Association September 9, 1869; biography in *Confederate Military History, Extended Edition*, Volume X Tennessee, page 749; sketch in *Who's who in Tennessee; a biographical reference book of notable Tennesseans of to-day*. Memphis, Paul & Douglas Co., 1911. page 362; brother of Dr. James Bankhead Thornton III (sketch next below); article on death and photograph in *The Commercial Appeal* Memphis, May 14, 1914, page 4; died age 79 per newspaper and Daily Burial Record Book; grave stone: born Caroline County, Virginia February 22, 1835, and died Culpeper County, Virginia May 13, 1914.

Thornton, Dr. James Bankhead III   Buried February 13, 1917   Turley 894, #8
Tennessee 3 (Forrest's) Cavalry Regiment Private Company B, per Company Muster Roll for January 1 to April 30, 1864, enlisted April 30, 1861, at Jackson, Mississippi, name on monthly report of Gratiot Street Military Prison (St. Louis, Mississippi) January 31, 1863, dated February 12, 1863, indicating captured at Parker's Cross Roads, Tennessee December 31, 1862, and received at prison January 22, 1863 (some other records indicate received February 28, 1863), one report remark: Burnett House Hospital, so may have been injured; name appears on a Roll of Prisoners of War paroled at Gainesville, Alabama May 11, 1865, and name appears on an Oath of Allegiance sworn at Memphis, Tennessee June 6, 1865, indicating resident of Memphis age 25; brother of Dr. Gustavus Brown Thornton (sketch next above); died age 79 per Daily Burial Record Book; gravestone: Jan. 24, 1838 Feb. 11, 1917.

Thrall, James C.   Buried September 8, 1878   Turley 413, #5
Arkansas Captain Thrall's Battery Jackson's Light Artillery (3rd Arkansas Light Artillery) Captain; Company Muster Roll for January and February, 1862, 1 Lieutenant, enlisted July 25, 1861, Pitman's Ferry, Arkansas; elected/commissioned/promoted Captain May 12, 1862, on several records; died age 45 Yellow Fever per Daily Burial Record Book; "Tribute of Respect" by the Office of the Memphis City Fire and General Insurance Company, 19 Madison Street, Memphis, Tennessee, December 10, 1878, reported in the December 15, 1878, *Memphis Daily Appeal*, page 1, column 6.

Thurmond, W. W.   Buried May 12, 1862   Fowler 120 (IOOF), #B-4
Tennessee 154 Senior Infantry Regiment Private Company G; enlisted June 3, 1861 Memphis age 28; per January to July 1862, muster roll remarks: died; per May 5, 1863, muster roll remarks: died of wounds received (second card missing indicating where); per register of soldiers killed in battle, born Ohio, deceased December 31, 1862 (sic) and wounded in the Battle of Shiloh; per report of deaths dated October 30, 1863, (filed under records of D. Morrison) died May 1861, (sic) at Memphis from wounds received at Battle of Shiloh; per Battle of Shiloh casualty list for unit reported in April 23, 1862, *Memphis Daily Appeal* was wounded in battle; two Odd Fellows (IOOF) notices on funeral in the *Avalanche* May 12, 1862, page 3, which indicate that he died from wounds received at the Battle of Shiloh; buried Odd Fellows (IOOF) Section.

Titus, James T.   Buried February 12, 1865   Chapel Hill 159, #8
Tennessee 3 (Forrest's Old) Cavalry Regiment Corporal/Private 2 Company A; originally enlisted Tennessee 154 Senior Infantry Regiment Corporal 1 Company B, per Company Muster-in Roll dated August 13, 1861, enlisted as Corporal May 14, 1861, Randolph, Tennessee age 24, appears on Rolls indicating on extra duty in Signal Corps with General Polk March to November, 1863, and per Descriptive List and Account of Pay and Clothing Sergeant, age 24, born Shelby County, Tennessee and a merchant; per Tennessee 3 (Forrest's Old) Cavalry record enlisted Corporal May 4, 1861, at Randolph, Tennessee, records also indicate was a Sergeant when detailed to Signal Corps September 1862, to December 1863, records report him detailed in General Forrest's Acting Adjutant General March 1, 1864, to May 14, 1864, General Forrest in report for June 1-13, 1864, mentioned him as Lieutenant Titus of his staff, per Casualties List for November and December 1864, dated December 6, 1864, wounded dangerously December 4, 1864, leg amputated and died from extreme prostration, some cards in record has second initial as "F" including a Payments Register indicating Sergeant Sharpshooters (Captain P. T. Allin's Company, Sharp Shooters of General Preston Smith's Brigade, which this company was once identified (see Notes of Interest - Bluff City Grays) that may indicate that his and his brother's records were sometimes mistaken for the other); no records found in Confederate Signal Corps compiled service record rolls; mentioned by Dr. S. H. Ford in his address on the occasion to commemorate (Confederate Memorial Day) Confederates buried at Elmwood on April 26, 1866, (see article "Honors To The Memory Of The Hero Dead" in the April 27, 1866, *Memphis Daily Appeal*, page 3, column 1); listed in the June 6, 1878, Memphis Daily Appeal, page 4, column 3, article "OUR DEAD HEROES" covering the unveiling of the Confederate Monument and Decoration of Graves at Elmwood as then one of twenty-eight members of the Bluff City Grays, Company B of the 154 Senior Infantry Regiment and Company A of Forrest's Old (Third) Cavalry Regiment buried at Elmwood; listed as one of the "comrades who sleep at Elmwood cemetery " in the article "Veterans in Council" in Memphis Daily Appeal, May 12, 1881, page 4, column 4, concerning the meeting of the surviving members in the city of the old Bluff City Grays to appoint the necessary committees for the purpose of making special decoration on the graves of their dead comrades at Elmwood and Calvary cemeteries on Sunday next, Memorial Day; listed as member of Bluff City Grays in *Reminiscences of the Civil War* by John Hallum, Tunnah & Pittard printers, 1903; listed in "A COMPLETE ROSTER OF THE BLUFF CITY GREYS" located in the Memphis Room of the Memphis/Shelby County Public Library and Information Center Central Library with remarks killed Nashville, December 4, 1864 and buried Chapel Hill 160 which part of same lot as 159; see also Notes of Interest - Bluff City Grays; listed in Elmwood 1874 book as Confederate soldier buried in Elmwood who was citizen of Memphis or vicinity; killed age 27 and buried Grave #8 per Daily Burial Record Book and buried Grave #9 in Chapel Hill book;

born December 4, 1836 and died December 4, 1864 on grave stone with some illegible inscription; initials "J. T." in Daily Burial Record Book and "J. F" in computer index.

Titus, John Frazier   Buried September 28, 1873   Chapel Hill 160, #13

Tennessee 3 (Forrest's Old) Cavalry Regiment Private 2 Company A; originally enlisted Tennessee 154 Senior Infantry Regiment Private 1 Company B, per Company Muster Roll for August 14 to November 1, 1861, enlisted May 13, 1861, New Madrid, Missouri; per Certificate of Disability for Discharge in 154 Senior Infantry Regiment record enlisted August 14, 1861, New Madrid, Missouri age 20, born Memphis, Tennessee, and discharged December 31, 1862, due to disability; per Tennessee 3 (Forrest's Old) Cavalry record enlisted August 18, 1861, New Madrid, Missouri (some record cards have second initial as "T" that may indicate that his and his brother's records were sometimes mistaken for the other); per Company Muster Roll for September 1 to November 1, 1862, dated January 20, 1863, remarks: Discharged at Knoxville on account of ill health; name appears on a Roll of Prisoners of War as being paroled at Columbus, Mississippi, May ,1865; some records found as Private Captain P. T. Allin's Company, Sharp Shooters of General Preston Smith's Brigade, which this company was once identified (see Notes of Interest - Bluff City Grays); listed in the June 6, 1878, Memphis Daily Appeal, page 4, column 3, article "OUR DEAD HEROES" covering the unveiling of the Confederate Monument and Decoration of Graves at Elmwood as then one of twenty-eight members of the Bluff City Grays, Company B of the 154 Senior Infantry Regiment and Company A of Forrest's Old (Third) Cavalry Regiment buried at Elmwood; listed as one of the "comrades who sleep at Elmwood cemetery " in the article "Veterans in Council" in Memphis Daily Appeal, May 12, 1881, page 4, column 4, concerning the meeting of the surviving members in the city of the old Bluff City Grays to appoint the necessary committees for the purpose of making special decoration on the graves of their dead comrades at Elmwood and Calvary cemeteries on Sunday next, Memorial Day; listed in "A COMPLETE ROSTER OF THE BLUFF CITY GREYS" located in the Memphis Room of the Memphis/Shelby County Public Library and Information Center Central Library with remarks Discharged, Died Memphis, October 1873; see also Notes of Interest - Bluff City Grays; not listed as member of Bluff City Grays in *Reminiscences of the Civil War* by John Hallum, Tunnah & Pittard printers, 1903; listed in Mathes book as a member of Confederate Historical Association but no sketch; listed in Elmwood 1874 book as Confederate soldier buried in Elmwood who was citizen of Memphis or vicinity; died yellow fever age 31 per Daily Burial Record Book; died September 27, 1873 on grave stone.

Townsend, George S.   Buried June 10, 1862   South Grove 11, #2

Tennessee 4 Infantry Regiment Private Company A; per Company Muster-in Roll dated August 16, 1861, at Fort Pillow, Tennessee enlisted May 15, 186, at Germantown, Tennessee age 17; per casualty report dated April 10, 1862, wounded slightly in hand at battle of Shiloh; per Company Muster Roll for April 25 to June 30, 1862, age 18 and remark: Died June 10, 1862; per Daily Burial Record Book died comp (?) fever, age 19 and originally buried South Grove 17, #2; listed in Elmwood 1874 book as Confederate soldier buried in Elmwood who was citizen of Memphis or vicinity; stone: Born September 30, 1843 Died June 9, 1862.

Trezevant, Edward Butler   Buried May 7, 1870   Chapel Hill 512, #4

Tennessee 10 (DeMoss') Cavalry Regiment Lieutenant Colonel; limited information in Tennessee 10 Cavalry records - appears on report of casualties at Battle of Thompson's Station, Tennessee March 5, 1863, with remarks wounded mortally since died; record found Tennessee 7 Cavalry Regiment 3 Lieutenant Company A and enlisted May 16, 1861, Memphis age 23; record also found General and Staff rolls as Adjutant Forrest Regiment Tennessee Cavalry; listed in Elmwood 1874 book as Confederate Soldier buried in Elmwood who was citizen of Memphis or vicinity with rank of Major and sketch (Lieutenant Colonel Ed Butler Trezevant page 159) which is largely from the footnote in Jordan, Thomas and J. P. Pryor, *The Campaigns of Lieut.-Gen. N.B. Forrest, and of Forrest's Cavalry*. Blelock & Co., 1868. page 235 and fully quoted in the Saturday Evening, May 7, 1870, Public Ledger, page 3, column 3; per sketch born 1838 (July 24, 1838) in Shelby County, Tennessee, originally enlisted in Memphis Light Dragoons 3 Lieutenant (Tennessee 6 Logwood's Cavalry Battalion Company A, which subsequently became Company A Tennessee 7 Cavalry Regiment), after battle of Belmont health failed and went to Texas, returned May 1862, and joined General Forrest's Cavalry at Corinth, made Sergeant Major and became Adjutant in June, regiment dissolved and several companies formed a battalion and became Major, February 1862, (sic) entered Tennessee after being made Lieutenant Colonel and placed in command of Tennessee 10 Cavalry and mortally wounded March 5, 1864 (sic); reported in the Friday May 6, 1870, *Memphis Daily Appeal*, page 4, column 4, article "Confederate Soldiers Meeting" that members of the Confederate Relief and Historical Association met "to make all necessary arrangements for the interring of Major Trezevant's remains in Elmwood Cemetery tomorrow; also to confer with the Ladies Monumental Association in making the same part of the proceeding in the decoration of graves."; note the May 7, 1870, "Grand and Imposing Ceremonies of Commemoration Day" was also to lay the corner stone of the Monument (see May 8, 1870, *Sunday Morning Appeal*, page 4, column 2 and the "Confederate Monument" chapter supra); mentioned also by General William B. Bates in his Oration at the May 7, 1870 Ceremony; per Trezevant sketch in Mathes book (enlarged edition page 144) enlisted in Logwood's Company May 16, 1861, became brevet 2 Lieutenant and served with Tennessee 7 Cavalry Regiment for some time and killed at Thompson's Station March 5, 1863; killed in battle age 25 and "moved from" per Daily Burial Record Book.

Trezevant, John Pollard   Buried September 25, 1878   South Grove 559, #1

Commissary of Subsistence Major (Wrights', Maney's, and Carter's Brigades); originally enlisted in Tennessee 154 Senior Infantry Regiment Corporal Company L March 7, 1862, Memphis; per Company Muster Roll dated May 6, 1863, remarks: discharged from wounds received at Battle of Shiloh; appears on a list dated July 4. 1862, at Tupelo, Mississippi of soldiers to be discharged because of physical disability; per "Certificate To Be Given A Soldier" given at Tupelo, Mississippi July 5, 1862, born in Dinwiddie County,

Virginia, aged 45, Clerk of the County Court of Shelby County, Tennessee, and enlisted March 8, 1862, at Memphis; first appointed to Commissary of Subsistence January 20, 1863, to rank April 11, 1863; name appears on a Parole List dated Greensboro, North Carolina, April 23, 1863; notice about death and article in the Thursday September 26, 1878, *Memphis Daily Appeal*, page 1, columns 2 & 4; per Daily Burial Record Book died age 48 (sic) and originally buried in Turley Lot 221, #7 and moved January 28, 1882; per Trezevant sketch in Mathes book (enlarged edition page 144) Private Company A (actually Company L) Captain E. A. Cole, Maynard Rifles, Tennessee 154 Senior Infantry Regiment; son Rembert Trezevant served in the same Company.

Trezevant, John Timothy   Buried May 27, 1887   South Grove 20 & 21, #7
South Carolina Charleston Ordnance Battalion Major; only information in the Battalion compiled service record is that name "J. T. Trezevant" appears on a report; per General and Staff rolls 1 Lieutenant/Major, Captain commanding Charleston Arsenal South Carolina, appointed Major artillery from Mississippi June 23, 1863; may have served in Confederate Tucker's Regiment of Infantry 2 Lieutenant, which record indicates name as J. T. Trezevant, Jr. and contains Certificate of Election dated November 7, 1864, Columbia, South Carolina, appointed October 26, 1864; monument: J. T. Trezevant Born in South Hampton County, Virginia October 8, 1814 Died in Memphis May 25, 1887; per Trezevant sketch in Mathes book (enlarged edition page 144) Major of Ordnance and father of T. B., M. B., and William H. Trezevant; died age 73 per Daily Burial Record Book; South Grove lots 20 & 21 are the J. T. Trezevant lot; per death notice in the Thursday May 26, 1887, *Memphis Daily Appeal*, page 1, column 5, died May 25, 1887, aged 73; Mayor of South Memphis 1847-1848; listed under Former Mayors of Memphis and South Memphis in "Touring historic Elmwood Cemetery" (Brochure and Map of Historic Gravesites) #49; listed in "Touring Historic Elmwood Cemetery" Brochure (January 2000) #80; see The Trezevant Family Papers collection of personal papers located in Memphis and Shelby County Public Library Memphis Room and the Trezevant file in the Elmwood Cemetery Office

Trezevant, Lewis Cruger   Buried June 8, 1871   Chapel Hill 49, #11
Tennessee 4 Infantry Regiment Private Company A; per Company Muster-in Roll dated August 16, 1861, enlisted May 15, 1861, Germantown age 16; per Company Muster Roll for August 17, 1861, to January 1, 1862, remarks: Discharged by Surgeon November 26, 1861; per death notice in the Thursday June 8, 1871, *Memphis Daily Appeal*, page 1, column 5, died at Little Rock, Arkansas June 5, 1871, aged 26 years, youngest son of Brooks R. Trezevant; listed as "Lieu. Louis Cruger Trezevant" in Elmwood 1874 book as Confederate soldier buried in Elmwood who was citizen of Memphis or vicinity; monument: Born February 10, 1845 and Died June 6, 1871; "Louis" in Cemetery computer index; mentioned in Trezevant sketch in Mathes book (enlarged edition page 144).

Trezevant, Marye Beattie   Buried March 16, 1915   South Grove 20, #1
Tennessee 42 Infantry Regiment 2 Lieutenant 2 Company E; originally enlisted Tennessee 4 Infantry Regiment, Private Company A, May 20, 1861, Randolph age 15 and per April 25 to June 30, 1862, muster roll remarks promoted to Lieutenant in Colonel Walker's Infantry (Tennessee 40 Infantry Regiment); per Tennessee 40 Infantry Regiment records 3 Lieutenant Company C but no enlistment indicated, present on January 1 to August 5, 1861, muster rolls and card indicating see J. T. Trezevant Ordnance Officer papers; one card in General & Staff rolls indicating Lieutenant and that records filed with Tennessee 42 Infantry Regiment; per Tennessee 42 Infantry Regiment records 2 Lieutenant 2 Company E (formerly Company C Tennessee 40 (L. M. Walker's) Infantry Regiment, which was officially designated Confederate 5 Infantry Regiment), enlisted January 1, 1862, Memphis, promoted Brevet 2 Lieutenant January 1863, and promoted to Ordnance Department Charlotte, South Carolina May 20, 1863, per Special Order 92 dated April 21, 1863, and signed by Lieutenant General Pemberton; letter in file dated February 16, 1863, in support of his application for transfer to Ordnance Department from father, J. T. Trezevant, Captain Commissary Adjutant, later Major, to Lieutenant General Pemberton requesting that son, not yet 17 and in bad health, be transferred; sketch in *Who's who in Tennessee; a biographical reference book of notable Tennesseans of to-day*. Memphis, Paul & Douglas co., 1911. page 363; died age 69 per Daily Burial Record Book; monument: Born Memphis, Tenn. August 28, 1846 Died March 13, 1915; mentioned in Trezevant sketch in Mathes book (enlarged edition page 144); see The Trezevant Family Papers collection of personal papers located in Memphis and Shelby County Public Library Memphis Room and the Trezevant file in the Elmwood Cemetery Office.

Trezevant, Theodore Brooks   Buried November 19, 1906   South Grove 21, #12
Assistant Adjutant General (AAG) Captain; single card in General and Staff rolls indicating name appears only as signature to muster roll for September/October 1863, of Company H Texas 9 (Young's) Infantry Regiment but no records found for that unit; served on several different staffs and was on staff of General M. D. Rector (per *Confederate Staff Officers 1861-1865* by Joseph H. Crute, Jr., Derwent Books 1982, appointed Engineering Officer and Assistant Inspector General November 2, 1862) when captured September 1864; captured Tensas Parish, Louisiana September 27, 1864, and eventually was sent to Fort Warren, Boston Harbor, Massachusetts where and signed Oath of Allegiance indicating residence Memphis, Tennessee, and released June 12, 1865; large stone and circle grave stone with dates 1844-1906; mentioned in Trezevant sketch in Mathes book (enlarged edition page 144) with indication was Captain and Inspector General on the staff of General Eaton.

Trezevant, Nathaniel Macon   Buried October 18, 1911   Turley 221, #10
Mississippi State Troops; no compiled service record found; information based on his letter dated August 25, 1865, to President 00Andrew Johnson requesting a pardon, which was granted August 28, 1865 (see Confederate Applications for Pardons and Amnesty, Mississippi, file 1838, Record Group 94: Records of the Adjutant Generals Office, 1762-1984); per his letter he stated "That my personal military service in the Rebellion was as follows: In the year 1863 under a regulation of the authorities requiring

military service either in person or by substitute, I furnished a substitute for the Mississippi State service for the term of 4 months, and at the expiration of that time, as an alternative to personal service in the Confederate army, I served as a soldier with the Mississippi State troops for about one month. In the year 1864 under a State militia draft I served as a soldier in the Mississippi militia for the period of two weeks. This is a full statement of my connection with the military service of the rebellion. The above is a full and true account of my connection with the rebellion. I desire to add to the foregoing, that on or about the 15th day of May 1865 I made application to Charles Johnson, United States Commissioner at Memphis Tenne. for the benefit of amnesty oath under President Lincoln's amnesty proclamation then in force, and that the Commissioner then refused to administer to me said oath."; continued to farm during the War and made claims to the Confederate Subsistence Department for items sold and confiscated by Confederate authorities and troops; per sketch in *Yale's Confederates: A Biographical Dictionary.* Nathaniel Cheairs Hughes, Jr., University of Tennessee Press, Knoxville, 2008. page 210, when five years old the family moved from Virginia to Fayette County, Tennessee, when graduated from Yale College studied law but not interested in law and became planter operating one plantation near Memphis, and others in northern Mississippi (Panola County) and in Arkansas, although primary home remained in Memphis, sold his Tennessee cotton lands and moved to California in 1880 where lost most of his money and returned to west Tennessee about 1900 and died at the "Old Mens Home"; City of Memphis Burial permit (24477) indicates date of birth as 1826 and died October 17, 1911.

Trice, Nathan W.   Buried December 8,1861   Fowler 151, #1

Tennessee Captain Thomas G Woodward's Cavalry Company Private; per Company Muster-in Roll dated August 25, 1861, enlisted August 25, 1861, at Camp Trousdale, Tennessee; company organized in Oak Grove, Kentucky about April 9, 1861, and was also known as "The Oak Grove Rangers"; after muster into service of the Confederate States August 25, 1861, divided into two companies, which became Companies A and B of Kentucky 1 (Helm's) Cavalry Regiment, which disbanded June 25, 1862, after enlistment term expired; no records found Kentucky 1 (Helm's) Cavalry or any other Kentucky units; family grave stone: Doctor, Born March 31, 1836 and Died December 7, 1861.

Triplett, William P.   Buried February 24, 1874   Fowler Public Lot 4, #127

Tennessee 2 (Walker's) Infantry Regiment Captain Company B; enlisted May 11, 1861, Memphis (no other information in compiled service records); per sketch in Mathes book (Enlarged Edition page 62); born Stevensburg, Culpeper County, Virginia 1828, 1861, raised a company (B) in Memphis which became part of 2 Tennessee Regiment, at Battles of Belmont and Shiloh, after fall of Memphis went to Virginia and joined General Jackson's army, participated in second Battle of Manassas, sent to Mobile and aided in building gunboats in Tombigbee River that were in Battle of Mobile, returned to Memphis after war and in charge of dry docks at time of death in 1874; died debility per Cemetery record; died of chronic diarrhea aged 48 per death notice in the Tuesday February 24, 1874, *Memphis Daily Appeal*, page 1, column 4.

Trout, William Walter, Sr.   Buried August 28, 1874   Turley 190, #1

Tennessee 1 Heavy Artillery Private Company L and 3 Company A; first served in Tennessee Captain T. N. Johnston's Heavy Artillery Company (Memphis Southern Guards, aka Southern Guards Artillery, see Notes of Interest) Captain James Hamilton's Battery (12 Months 1861-62 enlistment); per the Company Muster Roll dated April 14, 1862, volunteered for unexpired term of this Company; Tennessee Johnston's Heavy Artillery Company (L) was mustered out of service on April 14, 1862, after the surrender of Island 10; Captain Johnston became Captain of Company L of the Tennessee 1 Heavy Artillery (Artillery Corps of Tennessee) and some of the men from his battery re-enlisted with him; Company L was at Vicksburg during the siege and was surrendered there July 4, 1863; Captain Johnston and most of his men from Company L then became 3rd Company A that was then moved to Fort Morgan, Alabama on April 30, 1864, and was surrendered there August 23, 1864; appears on a Roll of Prisoners of War dated January 31, 1865, at Elmira, New York, desirous of taking the Oath of Allegiance, captured Fort Morgan August 23, 1864, and remarks: volunteered November 20, 1863, to avoid conscription, has no interest at the south, his wife and child and fathers family reside at Memphis and are in a destitute and suffering condition and he earnestly desires to be released from confinement so that he may contribute to their support; appears on a Roll of Prisoners of War dated March 31, 1865, at Elmira, New York, released during the month of March, 1865, on their taking the Oath of Allegiance, captured Fort Morgan August 23, 1864; per death notice in the January 4, 1872, *Memphis Daily Appeal*, page 1, column 4, died "suddenly on the 2d inst., in Fayette county, in the thirty-fifth year of his age"; per Daily Burial Record Book removed from Winchester Cemetery along with two children; per Turley Section Book Lot 190 (Thomas Trout Proprietor in 1874 Elmwood book) buried in same grave as daughter Bessie Trout (death notice in the February 22, 1873, *Memphis Daily Appeal*, page 1, column 5); brother of Leland W. Trout who served in same unit and per information submitted to some online ancestry sites, i.e. Ancestry and Find A Grave *(Find A Grave*, database and images (https://www.findagrave.com), memorial page for Leland W. Trout (1841–unknown), Find A Grave Memorial no. 44273506, citing Elmwood Cemetery, Memphis, Shelby County, Tennessee, USA, maintained by Craig H. Trout (contributor 46822921)), he is buried at Elmwood but no Elmwood record found to verify, however, appears he died August 20, 1883, per death notice ("Lee Trout") in the August 22, 1883, *Memphis Daily Appeal*, page 1, column 6, Shelby County, Tennessee Probate File No. 1880-04854 filed by widow, Marietta Trout September 1, 1883, to secure support from his estate assets (remaining salary from the Post Office department) and Memphis Sholes City directories – 1883, page 559, Trout Leland, mail clk P. O., res 83 Tate and 1884, page 529, Trout Marietta, wid. Leland, r 83 Tate; parents (Thomas and Cordelia Trout) are buried at Elmwood in Turley Section Lot 190 (Thomas Trout Proprietor in 1874 Elmwood book).

Turley, Thomas Battle   Buried July 3, 1910   Turley 5, #7
Tennessee 154 Senior Infantry Regiment Private Company L; enlisted March 8, 1862, Memphis; served in Quartermaster Department; captured near Nashville December 16, 1864, and sent to Military Prison at Louisville, Kentucky; paroled at Camp Chase, Ohio February 14, 1865; big monument with "soldier lawyer statesman" and small stone: TBT April 5, 1845 July 1, 1910; subject of Past Times article by Perre Magness in Neighbor Section (EM), page 2, *The Commercial Appeal* Memphis, May 14, 1998, entitled "Civil War Ordeal Left Mark on Turley" that indicates enlisted at age 15, captured December 10, 1864, and freed from Camp Chase in May 1865; sketch in *Tennessee, The Volunteer State, 1769-1923*, Volume II, page 20 with photograph; biography in *Confederate Military History, Extended Edition*, Volume X Tennessee, page 760; sketch in Goodspeed's Shelby County History, page 1049; sketch in the PoliticalGraveyard.com; died age 65 per Daily Burial Record Book; death reported in *Confederate Veteran*, Volume XIX, April 1911, page 174, "The Last Roll" Deaths of Confederates in Memphis, Tennessee who died during 1910 and were members of the Confederate Historical Association, Camp 28, U. C. V., Bivouac 18, C. V. of Memphis, Tennessee; per sketch in Mathes book, page 208, joined Confederate Historical Association October 9, 1894; wrote "A Narrative Of His Capture and Imprisonment During The War Between The States" published by Southwestern at Memphis, 1961, about his captured at the battle of Nashville in December 1864, and imprisonment at Camp Chase, Ohio; widow, Irene R. Turley filed for and received a Tennessee Confederate Pension (W10687 filed January 18, 1933); per letter in Pension file dated November 11, 1932, from Major General C. H. Bridges, The Adjutant General, War Department, " Union Prisoner of War records show that he was captured December 16, 1864, at Nashville, Tennessee, imprisoned at (sic and) paroled at Camp Chase, Ohio, and transferred to Point Lookout, Maryland, February 17, 1865, for exchange. His name appears on an undated Report of Prisoners of War paroled at Memphis, Tennessee, for six days ending May 31, 1865. Parole not stated."

Uhls, John McMurray   Buried May 2, 1862   Chapel Hill 252, #2
Tennessee 24 Infantry Regiment Captain Company C; enlisted August 24, 1861, Camp Trousdale; per February to June 1862, muster roll remarks: died at Memphis, Tennessee April 27, 1862, from wounds received at Shiloh; name spelled "Uhl" in Lindsley's Annals; listed in Elmwood 1874 book as Confederate soldier buried in Elmwood who was citizen of Memphis or vicinity with rank of Captain; Grave #1 in Cemetery Daily Burial Record and Alpha books and computer index but Grave #2 in Chapel Hill Book, Grave #1 is empty; Chapel Hill Book remark indicate "wounded 9 Ark Regt Co I" which is incorrect - see Daily Burial Record Book May 2, 1862, for "Capt Jos. A. Culpepper" listed immediately above "Capt Jno. M. Uhls" with remark "9 Ark. Regt Co I"; so most likely the Chapel Hill Book remark was made from a misreading of the Daily Burial Record Book remarks and there was no "Uhls" found in Arkansas 9 Infantry Regiment records; "wounded" indicated in the Disease column in Daily Burial Record Book; grave stone: unit information and dates May 28, 1823 April 20, 1862.

Unknown   Buried April 9, 1862   Chapel Hill Public Lot 1, #76
Prisoner taken at Shiloh, fell through a scuttle and killed per Daily Burial Record Book; possibly a Union soldier.

Vaccarro, Charles N.   Buried April 18, 1862   Fowler Public Lot 1, #380
Tennessee 154 Senior Infantry Regiment Private Company L; enlisted March 7, 1862, Memphis; per May 6, 1863, muster roll remarks: killed at Shiloh April 7, 1862; per Register of Soldiers Killed in Battle: deceased April 15, 1862, Memphis; per report of deaths dated October 30, 1863, enlisted March 8, 1862, Memphis, died April 15, 1862, Memphis of wound and entitled to $50 bounty, $25 commutation and $20 stoppage; per death notice in the Saturday April 19, 1862, *Memphis Daily Appeal*, page 1, column 7, CHARLES M. VACCARO, late of Louisville, Kentucky, died on the 18th at Irving Hospital, from a wound received at the battle of Shiloh on the 7th April, 1862, and had joined the Maynard Rifles of the 154th regiment Tennessee volunteers; listed as wounded in the battle of Shiloh casualty list for Gen. Polk's Command reported in the Thursday April 24, 1862, *Memphis Daily Appeal*, page 1, column 5; per Irving Hospital record "C. M. Vaccaro" admitted April 11, 1862, with complaint of left shoulder and died April 18, 1862; wounded, 154 Tenn. Regt Maynard Rifles, and Irving Hospital noted in Daily Burial Record Book.

Vance, Rienzi Hobson   Buried December 31, 1916   Miller Circle 285, # 4
Mississippi 29 Infantry Regiment Sergeant Company I; enlisted March 1, 1862, Hernando, Mississippi; per sketch in Mathes book, page 210: born at Bowling Green, Ky., with his parents removed to Hernando at an early age, enlisted in Company I, Captain J. B. Morgan, Twenty-ninth Mississippi Regiment, Walthall's, elected fifth sergeant, and in 1864, made first lieutenant, wounded July 9, 1864, at Chattahoochee river in front of Atlanta, wounded the second time, under General Hood, in front of Nashville, surrendered at Greensboro, N. C, on May 1, 1865, paroled there, returning home and to Memphis, and joined the C. H. A. July 15, 1869, when it was first organized; biography in *Confederate Military History, Extended Edition*, Volume X Tennessee, page 764; per State of Tennessee Certificate of Death born April 12, 1840, and died December 30, 1916; grave stone: April 12, 1839 and December 31, 1916 (note differences with Death Certificate).

Vaughan, Alfred Jefferson, Jr.   Buried October 3, 1899   South Grove 360, #4
Brigadier General; appointed from Tennessee November 21, 1863 (rank November 18, 1863) per the *Memorandum relative to the General Officers Appointed by the President in the Armies of the Confederate States - 1861-1865* compiled from Official Records by the Military Secretary's Office, U. S. War Department 1905; originally enlisted as Captain Company E Tennessee 13 Infantry Regiment May 28, 1861, age 31 at Jackson, Tennessee; elected Lieutenant Colonel June 4, 1861; promoted to Colonel December 4, 1861; had eight horses shot from under him without being injured, then leg was blown off by shell during Atlanta campaign; per Elmwood Newsletter Volume II, Number II, Fall 1987, page 3, his grandson Jack C. Vaughan of Little Rock donated General

Vaughan's desk to Elmwood and now located in the Cemetery Office after being repaired; General and Staff records found mixed with records of Andrew J. Vaughn, Major of Commissary Department, which indicates wounded July 4, 1864, at Atlanta, Georgia and surrendered and took Oath of Allegiance 20 May 1865, at Gainesville, Alabama; per sketch in Mathes book, page 212, born Dinwiddie County, Virginia May 10, 1830; died age 69 per Daily Burial Record Book; not "Jr." but "II" in *Vaughan's Brigade, Volume XVII (1974), Vaughan's American Histories* (copy located in Elmwood Cemetery Office); per sketch in *Generals in Gray* died in Indianapolis, Indiana October 1, 1899; see *The Commercial Appeal* Memphis October 2, 1899; graduate from Virginia Military Institute (VMI) Class of 1851 (classmate of General William Y. C. Humes, see sketch herein); per sketch in VMI library archives file born May 10, 1830, in Dinwiddie County, Virginia, parents Alfred Jefferson Vaughan and Dorothy (nee) Vaughan, enrolled at VMI on July 17, 1848, and graduated 15th in a class of 29 on July 4, 1851, in his final year at VMI he was a cadet captain and company commander, Captain, Lieutenant Colonel and Colonel of the 13th Tennessee Infantry Regiment, in March 1863, Regiment consolidated with Tennessee Senior Infantry Regiment to form 13/154 Tennessee Infantry Regiment with him as Colonel, commissioned Brigadier General, 1863 (Army of Tennessee), led brigade at Missionary Ridge and Atlanta campaign until Vining's Station (4 July 1864), where he was severely wounded (lost leg); sketch and biography in *Confederate Military History, Extended Edition*, Volume X Tennessee, pages 337 and 766; sketch in Goodspeed's Shelby County History, page 1050; sketch in *The National Cyclopedia of American Biography*, Volume 6, page 353; sketch and photograph in *Confederate Veteran*, Volume VI, July 1898, page 336; sketch in *Tennessee, The Volunteer State, 1769-1923*, Volume II, page 245; sketch, photograph, if available, and grave stone photograph in book *Quiet Places: The Burial Sites of Civil War Generals in Tennessee* by Buckner and Nathaniel C. Hughes, Jr., East Tennessee Historical Society (1992); also listed in chapter on Generals; listed under Generals in "Touring historic Elmwood Cemetery" (Brochure and Map of Historic Gravesites) #16; listed in "Touring Historic Elmwood Cemetery" Brochure (January 2000) #84; sketch #27 in Elmwood *Civil War Tour* booklet (2012).

Venn, Frank Hubert   Buried November 1, 1897   Miller Circle 24, #7
Mississippi 19 Infantry Regiment Private Company I; enlisted May 27, 1861, in Mississippi 17 Infantry Regiment Private Company B at Corinth, Mississippi; transferred to Mississippi 19 Infantry Regiment June 3, 1861; per Mississippi 19 Infantry Regiment records enlisted May 25, 1861, Marshall County, Mississippi age 23; appointed 4 Corporal per March & April 1862, muster roll; wounded in the engagement before Richmond, Virginia June 26 to July 1, 1862; per May & June 1864, muster prisoner of war at Point Lookout, Maryland; captured North Anna May 23, 1864, transferred to Union, New York July 8, 1864, released June 14, 1865, from Elmira, New York; per sketch in Mathes book, page 210, enlisted at Holly Springs, Mississippi May 25, 1861, served in Virginia, wounded in one of the battles around Richmond, paroled June 1865, and joined Confederate Historical Association September 9, 1869; per Mathes enlarged edition introduction died of yellow fever October 1897; per sketch in *Tennessee, The Volunteer State, 1769-1923*, Volume II, pages 836-839, born in Cologne, Germany, came to the United States as a lad of fifteen years, spent several years in New York city and there learned the trade of marble cutter, when the Civil War broke out, his sympathies being with the south, enlisted in the Confederate army and served throughout the four years of the war, Company I, Nineteenth Mississippi Regiment, at the close of the war he came to Memphis and resided here until his death, the result of yellow fever in 1897, sixty years of age, was successful as a marble and monument dealer and in 1867 founded the marble works F. H. Venn & Company, which plant was located at the north entrance of Elmwood Cemetery; died age 59 per Daily Burial Record Book; grave stone: 1838 1897.

Vigus, Arthur P.   Buried September 16, 1870   Fowler 605, #36
Tennessee 154 Senior Infantry Regiment Private Company D; per Company Muster-in Roll dated August 13, 1861, enlisted May 14, 1861 Randolph, Tennessee age 20; per Company Muster Roll for July and August 1863, remarks: Detailed. As Draughtsman Engineer Corps by order of General Polk; brother of Frank W. Vigus and James H. Vigus – see sketches below; died age 29, Bilious Fever per Daily Burial Record Book.

Vigus, Frank W.   Buried January 27, 1878   Turley 413-4-5, #1
Tennessee 154 Senior Infantry Regiment Private Company D; per Company Muster-in Roll dated August 13, 1861, enlisted May 14, 1861 Randolph, Tennessee age 19 (sic); father, A. S, Vigus, wrote a letter dated September 17, 1861, to General Polk advising that Frank was underage when he enlisted and did so without his consent, also has a serious health condition and for those reasons that he be discharged; per Company Muster Roll for August 14 to October 31, 1861, remarks: Discharged October 21, special order dated October 21, General Polk, Columbus, Kentucky, however, did remain in the regiment; wrote letter requesting to be appointed Hospital Steward and appears on a Hospital Muster Roll Gilmer Hospital, Marietta, Georgia for January 1 to April 30, 1864, remarks: Extra Duty as Nurse, Hospital Steward; signed parole May 11, 1865; brother of Arthur P. Vigus and James H. Vigus – see sketches next above and below respectively; died age 35, Dropsy of Heart per Daily Burial Record Book; death cause Pericarditis per mortuary report in the February 3, 1878, *Memphis Daily Appeal*, page 4, column 3; buried Knights of Pythias Lot.

Vigus, James H.   Buried January 19, 1883   Turley 278, #3
Tennessee 154 Senior Infantry Regiment Private Company D; per Company Muster-in Roll dated August 13, 1861, enlisted May 14, 1861 Randolph, Tennessee age 21; per Company Muster Roll for March and April 1863, remarks: Detailed. is with Captain E. B. Sayers, Chief Engineer Polk Corps (Sappers and Miners); per Company Muster Roll for July and August 1863, remarks: Detailed Engineers Corps as Clerk; transferred to 3rd Regiment Engineer troops, special order in the field November 3, 1864; brother of Arthur P. Vigus and Frank W. Vigus and– see sketches above; died age 43, Consumption per Daily Burial Record Book.

Volmer, David   Buried November 10,1861   Turley 104, #3

Tennessee 2 (Walker's) Infantry Regiment Private Company K; enlisted April 26, 1861, Memphis age 24; per March and April 1862, muster roll remarks: killed Battle of Belmont November 7, 1861; per funeral notice in the November 10, 1861, *Memphis Daily Appeal*, page 4, column 2, fell in the battle at Columbus, with captured flag (7th Iowa) in his hand; mentioned in the Local Matters article "Soldier's Death" in the November 13, 1861, *Memphis Daily Appeal*, page 4, column 1, stating that Jerry M. Lynch "was killed at the battle near Columbus, when trying with David Vollmer, who was buried Sunday, to seize the colors of the enemy"; incident referenced in Hughes' book *Battle of Belmont*, pages 143-144; listed as "David Vollmer" in the November 13, 1861, *Memphis Daily Appeal*, page 2, column 5, article on the List of the Killed, Wounded and Missing at the battle Belmont; not listed in Cemetery Alpha Book.

Wade, Henry, Jr.   Buried May 5, 1868   Chapel Hill 165, #2

Tennessee 154 Senior Infantry Regiment Sergeant Company G; enlisted May 27, 1861, Union City age 18, elected Sergeant May 6, 1862; listed in Elmwood 1874 book as Confederate soldier buried in Elmwood who was citizen of Memphis or vicinity; died consumption age 22 per Daily Burial Record Book; grave stone partially illegible but part reads Born March __, 1844 and died May 5, 1866 154 Tenn. Regiment.

Walker, Charles John   Buried June 19, 1980   Chapel Hill Circle 77

Tennessee 154 Senior Infantry Regiment Sergeant/Private Company L; per Company Muster-in Roll dated March 8, 1862, enlisted March 7, 1862, at Memphis; February 9, 1865, requested transfer to Forrest Cavalry Company A for reasons including that he was absent on account of wound received at Atlanta 22 July 1864, when command moved into Middle Tennessee and all of Company and greater part of regiment captured near Nashville December last; request forwarded but no record found of being approved; death notice in the Wednesday September 13, 1871, *Memphis Daily Appeal*, page 1, column 6, indicating died Saturday morning, the 9th, in the 29th year of his age; originally buried in the Walker Family Cemetery off Democrat Road, Memphis, Tennessee, on property currently owned by the Airport Authority; the cemetery was removed, and graves interred at Elmwood Cemetery to allow expansion of Federal Express; grave stone: Born January 21, 1843 Died September 9, 1871.

Walker, Creed Taylor   Buried March 13, 1930   Chapel Hill 155

Arkansas 15 (Josey's) Infantry Regiment Private Company B, per Company Muster Roll for July 23 to August 31, 1861, enlisted at Camp Green, Pitman Ferry, Arkansas; Company Muster Roll for March 31 to June 30, 1863 remarks: "wounded at Perryville, Ky October 8, 1862, where abouts not known"; Arkansas; Company Muster Roll for June 30 to August 31, 1863, last roll in file; per Tennessee Confederate Pension Application (S16341) wounded in knee at battle of Perryville, Kentucky, taken prisoner in Harrodsburg, Kentucky and a prisoner until close of War; per his affidavit in Pension file: carried to Lexington, Kentucky by Federals, was paroled under bond to Mercer County, Kentucky, never re-entered the service, under the terms of the bond remained awaiting exchange but no exchange was ever made and after surrender returned to the State of Arkansas where remained until the fall of 1918 when moved to the City of Memphis; died at the home of his daughter in Memphis; per Pension application born in Desha County, Arkansas October 30, 1843; grave stone: October 30, 1843 March 12, 1930.

Walker, James, Jr.   Buried November 12, 1861   Chapel Hill 284-286, #1

Tennessee 2 (Walker's) Infantry Regiment 1 Lieutenant Company I; per Company Muster Roll dated for August 22 to November 1, 1861, enlisted May 12, 1861, Fort Harris; per undated Company Muster Roll remarks: killed at the Battle of Belmont November 1861; father, Samuel P. Walker (brother of Lucius Marshall and J. Knox Walker) made a claim for settlement in the Office of the Confederate States Auditor for the War Department October 28, 1863; not found in Lindsley's Annals; listed as Wounded in the November 13, 1861, *Memphis Daily Appeal*, page 2, column 5, article on the List of the Killed, Wounded and Missing at the Battle Belmont; mentioned by Dr. S. H. Ford in his address on April 26, 1866, on the occasion to commemorate (Confederate Memorial Day) Confederates buried at Elmwood (see article "Honors To The Memory Of The Hero Dead" in the April 27, 1866, *Memphis Daily Appeal*, page 3, column 1); listed in the Elmwood 1874 book as Confederate soldier buried in Elmwood who was citizen of Memphis or vicinity and mentioned in the Sam. P., Marsh, and J. Knox Walker sketch (pages 166-67); mentioned in his uncle's (Colonel Joseph Knox Walker) short history included in the May 12, 1888, *Memphis Daily Appeal*, page 2, column 1, article "Loving Tributes" on that day's "Decorating the Confederate Graves"; mentioned ("Lt. Jimmie Walker") in Hughes' book *Battle of Belmont*, page 123, which references the *Southern Bivouac*, Volume III, No.2, October, 1884, pages 89-90, article "A Young Hero" that appeared in a Southern paper (no citation) indicating that he survived to reach his father's house in Memphis before his death; Chapel Hill 284-286-287 Samuel Polk Walker Lot.

Walker, Joseph Knox   Buried August 23, 1863   Chapel Hill 216, #6

Tennessee 2 (Walker's) Infantry Regiment Colonel; elected Colonel May 13, 1861, resigned May 14, 1862, on account of health; most records found as "J. Knox Walker"; resigned May 14, 1862; short history included in the May 12, 1888, *Memphis Daily Appeal*, page 2, column 1, article "Loving Tributes" on that day's "Decorating the Confederate Graves" and includes information on his brother General Lucius Marsh Walker and mentions his nephew James Walker; nephew of President Polk; listed in the Elmwood 1874 book as Confederate soldier buried in Elmwood who was citizen of Memphis or vicinity with rank of Colonel and sketch (Sam. P., Marsh, and J. Knox Walker sketch pages 166-67); per sketch died at the residence of his sister Mrs. Pickett in Memphis; died age 45 per Daily Burial Record Book; per Bruce Allardice (*More Generals in Gray*) born July 19, 1818, and died August 21, 1863.

Walker, Lucius Marshall   Buried February 19, 1866   Chapel Hill 257, #2

Brigadier General; appointed from Tennessee April 11, 1862 (rank March 11, 1862) per the *Memorandum relative to the General Officers Appointed by the President in the Armies of the Confederate States - 1861-1865* compiled from Official Records by the Military Secretary's Office, U. S. War Department 1905; originally enlisted as Colonel Tennessee 40 (Walker's) Infantry Regiment; no information other than rank of Colonel and remark that promoted to Brigadier General April 11, 1862, in Tennessee 40 Infantry Regiment compiled service record rolls; per sketch in *Generals in Gray* born October 18, 1829, Columbia, Tennessee, nephew of President James K Polk, graduated from West Point 1850 and died September 7, 1863 from wound received in a duel with General J. S. Marmaduke on September 6, 1863 at Little Rock, Arkansas (see *The Commercial Appeal* Memphis for stories on duel - April 27, 1890 and October 7, 1894); short note in the February 11, 1866, *Memphis Daily Appeal*, page 2, column 1, indicating that his remains will be brought back to Memphis for interment Friday next; see also "Confederate Generals Dawn Duel" by J. Carter Watts, *American Civil War* magazine, November 1999, pages 50-56; younger brother of Samuel P. Walker and J. Knox Walker, Colonel Tennessee 2 (Walker's) Infantry Regiment; nephew of President Polk; mentioned in his brother's (Colonel Joseph Knox Walker) short history included in the May 12, 1888, *Memphis Daily Appeal*, page 2, column 1, article "Loving Tributes" on that day's "Decorating the Confederate Graves"; biography in *Confederate Military History, Extended Edition*, Volume X Tennessee, page 341; sketch in *Tennessee, The Volunteer State, 1769-1923*, Volume II, page 246; sketch and grave stone photograph in book *Quiet Places: The Burial Sites of Civil War Generals in Tennessee* by Buckner and Nathaniel C. Hughes, Jr., East Tennessee Historical Society (1992); Daily Burial Record Book indicates Major General and shot; listed (Walker, Gen. Marsh) in Elmwood 1874 book as Confederate soldier buried in Elmwood who was a citizen of Memphis or vicinity and sketch (Sam. P., Marsh, and J. Knox Walker sketch pages 166-67); grave stone: Born October 18, 1829 Died September 7, 1863; also listed in chapter on Generals; listed under Generals in "Touring historic Elmwood Cemetery" (Brochure and Map of Historic Gravesites) #17; listed in "Touring Historic Elmwood Cemetery" Brochure (January 2000) #72; sketch #25 in Elmwood *Civil War Tour* booklet (2012).

Walker, Samuel Polk   Buried November 7, 1870   Chapel Hill 286, #5

Tennessee 40 (Walker's) Infantry Regiment (officially designated Confederate 5 Infantry Regiment) Lieutenant Company I, per Company Muster Roll dated October 31, 1861, enlisted September 3, 1861, at Madison, Arkansas; regiment captured at Island 10 April 8, 1862, released in Vicksburg, Mississippi in September 1862, and declared exchanged November 10, 1862; September 29, 1862, company assigned to Arkansas 15 (Johnson's) Infantry Regiment; brother of J. Knox Walker, Colonel Tennessee 2 (Walker's) Infantry Regiment, and Brigadier General Lucius Marsh Walker; nephew of President Polk; sketch in Elmwood 1874 book (Sam. P., Marsh, and J. Knox Walker sketch pages 166-67); died November 5, 1870, at Baily Springs, Alabama.

Walker, William P.   Buried October 30, 1873   Chapel Hill 284, #11

Tennessee 3 (Forrest's Old) Cavalry Regiment Private 2 Company A ("Bluff City Grays"); per Company Muster Roll for March 1 to May 14, 1864, enlisted April 12, 1864, in the field; name appears on a Roll of Prisoners of War paroled at Gainesville, Alabama May 11, 1865, and resident of Memphis; no record found Tennessee 154 Senior Infantry Regiment; listed (initials "W. P") in the June 6, 1878, *Memphis Daily Appeal*, page 4, column 3, article "OUR DEAD HEROES" covering the unveiling of the Confederate Monument and Decoration of Graves at Elmwood as then one of twenty-eight members of the Bluff City Grays, Company B of the 154 Senior Infantry Regiment and Company A of Forrest's Old (Third) Cavalry Regiment buried at Elmwood; listed as one of the "comrades who sleep at Elmwood cemetery " in the article "Veterans in Council" in Memphis Daily Appeal, May 12, 1881, page 4, column 4, concerning the meeting of the surviving members in the city of the old Bluff City Grays to appoint the necessary committees for the purpose of making special decoration on the graves of their dead comrades at Elmwood and Calvary cemeteries on Sunday next, Memorial Day; listed in "A COMPLETE ROSTER OF THE BLUFF CITY GREYS" located in the Memphis Room of the Memphis/Shelby County Public Library and Information Center Central Library with remarks enlisted April 15, 1864 and Died Memphis; see also Notes of Interest - Bluff City Grays; not listed as member of Bluff City Grays in *Reminiscences of the Civil War* by John Hallum, Tunnah & Pittard printers, 1903, which is probably due to late war enlistment; died age 28 disease of kidney per Daily Burial Record Book; death notice in the October 30, 1873, *Memphis Daily Appeal*, page 1, column 4, indicating died at his plantation in Mississippi and son of late Sam P. Walker; Chapel Hill lots 284-286-287 Samuel Polk Walker lot.

Wallace, Robert Delafield   Buried January 15, 1918   Chapel Hill 108, #6

Tennessee 3 (Forrest's Old) Cavalry Regiment Private 2 Company A; originally enlisted Tennessee 154 Senior Infantry Regiment Private 1 Company B ("Bluff City Grays"), per Company Muster-in Roll dated August 13, 1861, enlisted May 14, 1861, Randolph, Tennessee age 20; per order of General N. B. Forrest Tennessee 154 Senior Infantry Regiment Private 1 Company B was transferred February 22, 1863, to Tennessee 3 (Forrest's Old) Cavalry Regiment as 2 Company A, the first Company A became Company E Woodward's 2 Kentucky Cavalry; per 3 Cavalry early Company Muster Rolls rank is Private but Corporal on 1863 and 1864 Company Muster Rolls and enlistment at Memphis; name and rank of Private appears on a Roll of Prisoners of War paroled at Gainesville, Alabama May 11, 1865, indicating resident of Memphis, Tennessee; Corporal 1845 1918 on grave stone; listed in "A COMPLETE ROSTER OF THE BLUFF CITY GREYS" located in the Memphis Room of the Memphis/Shelby County Public Library and Information Center Central Library; not listed as member of Bluff City Grays in *Reminiscences of the Civil War* by John Hallum, Tunnah & Pittard printers, 1903; see also Notes of Interest - Bluff City Grays; applied for Tennessee Confederate Pension (S6070 February 27, 1904), which was not approved with reasons stated injury sustained or disease contracted not proved satisfactorily and Dr.'s certificate not strong as did not state the extent of disability; per his application he was born in Shelby County, Tennessee June 30, 1844; widow Sarah A. (Nelson) Wallace applied for Tennessee Confederate Pension (W6944 February 26, 1918), which was denied as not being married before 1890, the law at that time, but submitted additional information October

6, 1831, and approved; per her pension application he was born June 30, (she thinks) 1845 in Shelby County, Tennessee and she was born September 7, 1870, in Clayton, England, they were married April 17, 1897, near Hernando, Mississippi and per her Certificate of Death she died September 7, 1962, age 92.

Ward, Charles C.   Buried October 13, 1873   Fowler Public Lot 4, #24
Tennessee 3 (Forrest's Old) Cavalry Regiment Private Company B; enlisted April 7, 1862, Corinth, Mississippi; detailed to General Tilghman November 11, 1862; card for "C. C. Ward" in record indicating Private in Edmondson's Cavalry (Tennessee 11 Holman's Cavalry but no record found) enlisted March 10, 1862, Memphis and took Oath of Allegiance June 5, 1865, indicating resident of Memphis and age 26; listed in Elmwood 1874 book as Confederate soldier buried in Elmwood who was citizen of Memphis or vicinity; died age 34 from yellow fever per Daily Burial Record Book; death notice in the October 13, 1873, *Memphis Daily Appeal*, page 1, column 5, indicating died on the 12th instant in the 34th year of age; died from congestion per Mortuary Report in same paper page 3, column 3.

Ward, John William   Buried April 30, 1889   Turley 612 (Masonic Lot), D6 #62
Mississippi 12 Cavalry Regiment Captain Company F, per Company Muster-in Roll dated May 23, 1861, at Corinth, Mississippi, enlisted as 2nd Lieutenant May 8, 1861, at Corinth at age 23; Captain rank first appears on Company Muster Roll for November and December 1862; wounded severely (gunshot wound of head and paralysis of right side) at battle of Chancellorsville, Virginia May 3, 1863, and sent to hospital; received a Certificate of Retirement November 13, 1864, in accordance with the provisions of an act entitled "An Act to provide an Invalid Corps," approved February 17, 1864; Clara P. Ward, widow, filed for Tennessee Confederate Pension (W4920) May 14, 1913, that was accepted; per her application he was born in Staunton, Virginia, December 6, 1838, they were married November 20, 1880, in Memphis and she died May 31, 1932, and is buried at Elmwood; per death notice in the April 30, 1889, *Memphis Appeal*, page 5, column 4, died on April 29, 1889, age 51; Knights of Honor, Memphis Lodge No. 196, Funeral Notice in *Memphis Appeal* immediately following death notice.

Wardlaw, John Langdon   Buried March 23, 1879   Turley 589, #3
Tennessee Captain's Tobin's Company Light Artillery Sergeant Major; first enlisted Tennessee Captain Johnston's Company (L) Heavy Artillery (Southern Guards Artillery, Captain Hamilton's Battery), 12 month enlistment 1861-1862), Private, April 21, 1861, at Memphis, Tennessee, age 22; records also found Tennessee First Heavy Artillery (Jackson's Regiment) Company L (subsequently 3rd Company A), undated Roll of Prisoners of War at Vicksburg, Mississippi captured and exchanged July 4, 1864; per May and June 1864, Company Muster Roll transferred to the battery (Tobin's) from 1 Tennessee Artillery as sergeant in exchange for private D. T. Flowers by Special Order #163 at HQ District of the Gulf June 11, 1864, promoted to sergeant major on June 15, 1864; appears on a Roll of Prisoners of War as paroled at Meridian, Mississippi, May 10, 1865, with residence Abbeville, South Carolina; record includes correspondence from father, Robert H. Wardlaw, Abbeville, South Carolina, requesting that his son be commissioned in the South Carolina 1st Regular Artillery or 1st Infantry, correspondence stated that his son joined the army in Memphis and that something happened at Island Ten and floated down Mississippi River on a raft, correspondence also indicated had 10 sons; per "Genealogy of the Wardlaw Family" by Joseph P. Wardlaw, "Educated at K.M.M. School and the Citadel. Was in Western Army. Imprisoned at Johnson's Island and escaped by floating down the Mississippi River on a log; rejoined army and served until the surrender. He moved to Memphis, Tenn., and was in the cotton business. He had yellow fever the scrouge of 1878 at Memphis but recovered and died of pneumonia, March 22, 1879. The Confederate Survivor's Association erected a monument to his memory in Elmwood Cemetery at Memphis. Unusually bright, Jolly, handsome and popular. Was unmarried." (note: this sketch may have confused Island Ten with Johnson's Island, which is where with rare exception only officers were imprisoned); per same Wardlaw book, Robert Henry Wardlaw had ten sons in the Confederate Service, nine in actual service and one crippled, as Tax Collector for the Confederacy; per note under Personals section in Sunday March 23, 1879, *Memphis Daily Appeal*, page 1, column 5, "Mr. John L. Wardlaw, well know (sic) in cotton circles, died of pneumonia yesterday at his residence on Vance street. His funeral will take place to-day."; per obituary under Died section in March 23, 1879, *Memphis Daily Appeal*, page 1, column 6, "WARDLAW -Saturday March 22, 1879, 6:30 p.m., J. Langdon Wardlaw, in the forty first year of his age. The funeral will take place this (Sunday) afternoon, at 3:30 o'clock, from the corner of Vance and Avery streets."; per note under Personals section in March 25, 1879, *Memphis Daily Appeal*, page 4, column 3, "Sunday last a meeting of ex--Confederate soldiers was held at the Peabody hotel for the purpose of preparing resolutions with reference to the death of J. Lang. Wardlaw, a former member of the Southern Guards, Confederate States army ....Wardlaw had a severe attack of yellow-fever during the epidemic of 1878, and his constitution was unable to withstand the attack of pneumonia which caused his death. Peace to his ashes."; Shelby County Death Register (file #2160) died March 22, 1879, age 40; large monument stone, John Langdon, Son of Robert H Wardlaw, Born, S. C. Dec 23,1838 Died Mar 22, 1879; all Cemetery records spell name as "Wardlow"; per Daily Burial Record Book died age 41 erysipelas.

Warner, John R.   Buried May 27, 1862   Turley 76, #4
Arkansas 23 (Adams') Infantry Regiment Private (Hillis') Company A; enlisted February 26, 1862, Poinsett County, Arkansas; per February 26 to June 30, 1862, muster roll remarks: died May 4, 1862.

Warren, Archibald   Buried October 3, 1903   Turley 76, #4
Forrest's Cavalry Corps Major and Quartermaster; appointed from Tennessee January 27, 1864, to rank December 21, 1863; paroled as Major Assistant Quartermaster of General A. W. Campbell May 4, 1865; per *Confederate Staff Officers 1861 -1865* by

Joseph H. Crute, Jr., Derwent Books 1982, appointed Major, Quartermaster, April 29, 1864, on the staff of Lieutenant General Nathan Bedford Forrest, page 63, and to the staff of Brigadier General Alexander W. Campbell September 11, 1864, page 31; per sketch in Mathes book (Enlarged edition, page 41) born in County Louth, Ireland, March 22, 1829, came to this country with his father's family in 1831, locating in Wheeling, Virginia, and to Memphis in 1858, engaged in the flouring business on a large scale and "… The Federals took possession of his property, and he went south and served with Generals Polk and price. He was captured and sent to Northern prisons, but was exchanged some months later at Old Point Comfort, and upon his application was assigned to duty as quartermaster with Gen. Forrest, to whom he reported at Oxford, Miss., in 1863, with rank of major. When Maj. Chas. Severson resigned he became chief quartermaster, and served as such to the end of the war. For fifteen months he was in close touch with the "wizard of the saddle," and was witness of and participant in many stirring events. He was paroled at Gainesville, Ala., with General Forrest and staff...."; "Major A. Warren, now (1902) of Memphis, after serving for some time under General Polk, was taken prisoner late in 1863; exchanged at Old Point Comfort; commissioned as quartermaster with rank of major at Richmond; reported to General Forrest early in 1864; succeeded Major Severson, and served actively until the end of the war." *General Forrest.* Capt. J. Harvey Mathes, D. Appleton and company, New York, 1902. (The Great Commanders Series), page 356; per Burial Permit died October 2, 1903, from congestion of lung.

Watkins, Dr. Thomas R.   Buried June 1, 1906   Turley 1397, #2
Tennessee 6 Infantry Regiment, Private Company D, per company muster roll dated January 1 to May 1, 1862, enlisted at Randolph and per muster roll dated July & August, 1862, enlisted May 22, 1861, at Jackson, Tennessee; per sketch in Mathes (1897 edition page 218) enlisted May 18, 1861, wounded at the battles of Perryville and Franklin, captured at Franklin on Hood's retreat from Tennessee, in prison at Columbus, Ohio and Point Lookout, Maryland until June 4, 1865 when paroled, and joined Confederate Historical Association June 30, 1892; per sketch in Mathes (Enlarged Edition page 71) born in LaGrange, Fayette county, Tennessee, November 20, 1840, father, Richard E. Watkins, came from Prince Edward County, Virginia, mother, Lucy N., was a daughter of Stephen K. Sneed, and came to Tennessee from Granville county, N. C., father died in 1848, and the family moved from their country home to Somerville, Tennessee, young Watkins was at the University of North Carolina in 1860, and in 1861 came home and joined a company raised at Somerville, this becoming Company D of the Sixth Tennessee Regiment, and was mustered into service at Union City, the Sixth and Ninth forming Cheatham's Brigade, was in active service from Columbus to Franklin, participating in the battles of Shiloh, Perryville (where he was wounded in the face and right shoulder), Murfreesboro, Chickamauga, Missionary Ridge, Cat's creek, Rocky Face, Resaca, New Hope church, Kennesaw, and on the 20th and 22nd of July in front of Atlanta, Jonesboro, Lovejoy station, and finally at Franklin, where badly wounded in the right thigh and became a prisoner for the rest of the war, paroled at Point Lookout, Maryland on June 7, 1865, reached Memphis on the 28th, read medicine and graduated from the University of Pennsylvania in 1868, practiced ever since near Memphis, married January, 1872, to Miss Sue G. Cannon, and have four children, was a Mason, a Knight of Honor, an Episcopalian, Democrat, a leading man in his populous neighborhood and joined the Confederate Historical Association June 30, 1892; circle grave stone T. R. Watkins, M. D. Nov 20, 1840 May 31, 1906; widow's, Sue Cannon Watkins, Tennessee Confederate Pension application July 27, 1931 (W10064) accepted.

Watson, Elbert Lycurgus   Buried August 3, 1901   Turley 5832, #5
Arkansas 8 Infantry Regiment Quartermaster; enlisted September 10, 1861, Camp Price NE Arkansas age 38; per January 1 to April 30, 1862, muster roll remarks discharged on reorganization May 8, 1862; regiment organized July 13, 1861, and mustered into Confederate service September 10, 1861; some cards has his signature dated August 1861; commissioned July 6, 1861, and resigned May 7, 1862; no records found General and Staff rolls; inscription on grave stone Born at Hawkinsville, Pulaski County, Georgia November 25, 1819 and Died at Newport, Arkansas August 1, 1901; per descendant Tim Watson lived in Jacksonport, Arkansas and age 42 when enlisted in 1861, at Shiloh but furloughed after battle after developing consumption, went to Hot Springs to recover, returned to Jacksonport and became Confederate Commissary Agent, purchased a lot at Elmwood in 1880's as was going to move to Memphis because of business partnership but never did; Colonel and died age 81 per Daily Burial Record Book.

Watson, Ellen M.   Buried May 25, 1906   Chapel Hill Circle 19, #2
Confederate Spy; per Past Times article "Ellen Watson a pillar of the church" by Perre Magness, *The Commercial Appeal* Memphis, May 6, 1999, Section EM, Neighbors, page 2, she was active in Arkansas by selling goods to Union soldiers and using the funds to buy clothes for Confederates and also gathered information to give to the Confederate Army (source "Mrs. Ellen M. Watson," pamphlet printed by the Women's Foreign Missionary Society of the Methodist Church, 1900); born Ellen Maria Anderson in 1844 in Arkansas; her first husband, B. F. Perkins, was killed at the Battle of Murfreesboro; per article in *The Commercial Appeal* Memphis, May 25, 1906, page 7, column 1, she became a nurse at the Southern Mothers Hospital in the Old Irving Block after her first husband's death; married Reverend Samuel Watson after the War; grave stone: December 31, 1842 May 24, 1906; listed in "Touring Historic Elmwood Cemetery" Brochure (January 2000) #59.

Waynesburg, John W.   Buried January 10, 1897   Turley 10332, #3
Tennessee 154 Senior Infantry Regiment Sergeant Company D; enlisted May 14, 1861, age 19 Randolph, Tennessee; per sketch in Mathes book (enlarged edition page 218) joined company at Memphis guarding the magazine latter part of March 1861, mustered into service April 26, 1861, at Randolph as Ordnance Sergeant, wounded at Murfreesboro, Missionary Ridge and Resaca, paroled April 1865, assisted in forming Confederate Relief and Historical Association in Memphis in 1866, member of Company A, United Confederate Veterans, and died January 3, 1897; born June 10, 1842 and died January 3, 1897 on Hamilton/Waynesburg monument.

Weatherford, Pulaski D. "Caesar" Buried February 10, 1897 Evergreen 225, #3
Tennessee 14 Infantry Regiment Sergeant Company H; enlisted May 23, 1861, Clarksville, Tennessee; per muster roll dated March 31, 1864, age 22; took Oath May 1865 indicating residence of Montgomery County, Tennessee; February 11, 1897, *The Commercial Appeal* Memphis, page 5, column 5, refers to him as Major and that two sisters from Clarksville, Tennessee attended funeral; served in the Tennessee General Assembly, Senate 1891-1895, and per sketch in *Biographical Directory of the Tennessee General Assembly*, Volume II 1861-1901, by Robert Martin McBride, Tennessee State Library and Archives, Nashville, 1979, page 962, born Caswell County, North Carolina May 29, 1843, (note difference with grave stone below), came to Tennessee with parents in 1845 near Nashville and later moved near Clarksville, Montgomery County, Tennessee, attending college in Chatham County, North Carolina when War began and joined Tennessee 14 Regiment, captured and imprisoned at Fort Delaware, Delaware, after War graduated from Cumberland University Law School, Lebanon, Tennessee, came to Memphis in 1870 to practice law with brother, married Eliza Heiskell (daughter of Joseph Brown Heiskell, Confederate Congressman from Tennessee) in Memphis December 19, 1870; sketch in Goodspeed's Shelby County History, page 1053, with basically same information and indicates was son of William and Frances G. (Hooper) Weatherford; brother of William Weatherford; grave stone: May 28, 1843 February 9, 1897; buried in J. B. Heiskell Lot.

Weatherford, William Gamaliel Buried December 14, 1898 Evergreen 447¾, #1
Per article in *The Commercial Appeal* Memphis, December 14, 1898, page 6, column 3, referred to as Major, served in the Civil War on the Confederate side, belonged to Joe Johnson command, and was with Forrest a part of the time; also per newspaper article a resident of Memphis since 1869, 65 years of age June 7 of this year, born in Caswell County, North Carolina, moved with family to Nashville at age 12, educated in the law at Cumberland University, Lebanon, Tennessee, and died at residence December 13, 1898; brother of Caesar Weatherford (see sketch next above); died from pneumonia per Daily Burial Record Book; possibly the "William Weatherford" listed in *Tennesseans in the Civil War, Part 2*, as serving in Tennessee 1 Cavalry Battalion (known as 1 (McNairy's) Cavalry Battalion and subsequently 7 Cavalry Battalion and 22 (Barteau's) Cavalry Regiment) Private Company D but no compiled service record found as this appears to be incorrect; per the Confederate index book the "William Weatherford" who was from Tennessee served in the 1 (Colms') Infantry Battalion Company D; record found 1 (Colms') Infantry Battalion as Private Company D, enlisted December 9, 1861, at Sparta, Tennessee and per muster roll dated September 29, 1862, for January 6 to August 1, 1862, remarks discharged at Camp Weakley January 1862; 1 (Colms') Infantry Battalion consolidated with Tennessee 50 Infantry Regiment (temporarily November 1862, and permanently February 1864) to form the 50 Consolidated Infantry but no record found which follows since consolidation formed after his discharge; also there is a "W. G. Weatherford" listed in Confederate index book for Kentucky 8 & 12 Consolidated Cavalry, Captain, Assistant Commissary of Subsistence, who per only card in record signed Parole of Honor May 16, 1865, at Columbus, Mississippi; no record found in the separate compiled service records for Kentucky 8 and 12 Infantry Regiments but there was a "W. M. and A. T. Weatherford" in Company I of the 12 Infantry Regiment who both enlisted in West Tennessee December 1, 1863; not found in General and Staff records; per sketch in *Bench and Bar of Memphis 1833 - 1898*, Memorials, Volume 1, pages 125-126, served under General Lyons whose troops were from Kentucky, and the Tennessee border and during a portion of the war were attached to Forrest, attained the rank of Major, and met future wife, Miss Hitie Watlington, while at Aberdeen, Mississippi.

Webb, John Lewis Buried February 18, 1898 Fowler 115, #10
Tennessee 154 Senior Infantry Regiment Private Company E; enlisted June 3, 1861, Memphis age 23; originally Company C and transferred to Company E August 1, 1862; detailed to Commissary Department; per sketch in Mathes book (both editions) "Cap," born in Haywood County, Tennessee December 2, 1838, enlisted April 28, 1861, Private Hickory Rifles, paroled May 1865, became member Confederate Historical Association February 12, 1895, died in Memphis February 16, 1898, aged 59 years; died age 60 per Daily Burial Record Book; initials "J. L." in Daily Burial Record Book and computer index and "J. S." in Fowler Book; widow Isador (Kitchum) Webb received Tennessee Confederate Pension (W6570); per pension file he was born December 2, 1838, in Haywood County, Tennessee, she was born November 22, 1843, in Somerville, Fayette County, Tennessee, they were married December 2, 1868, in Somerville, Fayette County, Tennessee, and he died February 16, 1898, in Memphis.

Webb, William Buried September 23, 1868 Fowler 115, #3
Tennessee 3 (Forrest's Old) Cavalry Regiment Private 2 Company A ("Bluff City Grays"); per Muster Roll dated May 4, 1864, enlisted May 1, 1864, Verona, Mississippi; wounded slightly in leg August 23, 1864; appears on a Roll of Prisoners of War paroled at Gainesville, Alabama May 11, 1865, indicating resident of Memphis; no record found 154 Senior Infantry records; listed in the June 6, 1878, *Memphis Daily Appeal*, page 4, column 3, article "OUR DEAD HEROES" covering the unveiling of the Confederate Monument and Decoration of Graves at Elmwood as then one of twenty-eight members of the Bluff City Grays, Company B of the 154 Senior Infantry Regiment and Company A of Forrest's Old (Third) Cavalry Regiment buried at Elmwood; listed as one of the "comrades who sleep at Elmwood cemetery " in the article "Veterans in Council" in Memphis Daily Appeal, May 12, 1881, page 4, column 4, concerning the meeting of the surviving members in the city of the old Bluff City Grays to appoint the necessary committees for the purpose of making special decoration on the graves of their dead comrades at Elmwood and Calvary cemeteries on Sunday next, Memorial Day; not listed as member of Bluff City Grays in *Reminiscences of the Civil War* by John Hallum, Tunnah & Pittard printers, 1903; listed in "A COMPLETE ROSTER OF THE BLUFF CITY GREYS" located in the Memphis Room of the Memphis/Shelby County Public Library and Information Center Central Library that indicates enlisted July 1, 1864; see also Notes of Interest - Bluff City Grays; died consumption age 22 per Daily Burial Record Book.

Wheaton, William H.
Listed in Elmwood 1874 book as Confederate soldier buried in Elmwood who was citizen of Memphis or vicinity second initial "N"; possibly William H. Wheaton, yellow fever, age 33, buried September 24, 1873, Chapel Hill 171, #6, no stone; possibly W. H. Wheaton, Tennessee 4 Infantry Regiment Sergeant Company A, enlisted May 15, 1861, Germantown, Tennessee age 19 and took Oath of Allegiance November 5, 1864, indicating residence of Memphis, Tennessee age 21 and oath remarks indicate took deserters oath but *The Commercial Appeal* Memphis, May 15, 1909, article on this company indicates wounded, honorably discharged and died since the surrender.

White, Alphonsus C.   Buried November 19, 1874   Fowler 274, #4
Tennessee 7 Cavalry Regiment Private Company A; single card in service record under name "White" but no information; per Young's Seventh Tennessee Cavalry book enlisted February 1, 1863; within the biographical sketch of A. J. Martin in Goodspeed's Shelby County History, page 63, is information on his father, Colonel Clarke C. White, that indicates that "Alphonsus C., who was aid to Gen. Martin (see sketch supra) during the early part of the war, and afterward a member of Jackson's escort, and died August 12, 1864"; per Cemetery Daily Record Book removed from Mississippi with other family members, age 19.

Whitehead, Henry B.   Buried December 31, 1928   Chapel Hill 937, #3
Tennessee 1 Heavy Artillery Corporal 3 Company A & Stewart's Artillery; enlisted as Private July 18, 1861, Grand Junction, Tennessee; captured at Vicksburg, Mississippi July 4, 1863, and exchanged December 20, 1863; captured at Fort Morgan, Mobile Bay, Alabama August 23, 1864; sent to Fort Columbus, New York where received September 28, 1864, and then sent to Elmira, New York where record indicates received December 5, 1864; only same enlistment card in Stewart's Artillery rolls which company consolidated with 1 Heavy Artillery early in 1862; per Tennessee Confederate Pension file (S14188) born in city of Boston, Lincolnshire, England June 28, 1842, and per letter in file escaped from train on way to Elmira, New York, made way to New York City, then to New Jersey and finally to Pennsylvania where farmed until War was over; died age 86 per Daily Burial Record Book; VA grave stone with service unit and dates June 28, 1842 December 30, 1928; possible wife's grave stone: Clara Rische Whitehead September 1883 July 20, 1915 (same lot).

Whitfield, Edward   Buried January 10, 1869   Turley 17, #3
Ordnance Officer Lieutenant, General Preston's Staff; per General and Staff compiled service record rolls Edwin Whitfield appointed 1 Lieutenant Light Artillery March 26, 1862, to report to Chief of Ordnance, captured Murfreesboro January 5, 1863, sent to City Point for exchange April 29, 1863 and in December 28, 1862 to January 2, 1863 reports General Preston wrote "in the action on 31 Lieutenant Edwin Whitfield of my staff was severely, if not fatally, wounded by my side"; listed in Elmwood 1874 book as Confederate soldier buried in Elmwood who was citizen of Memphis or vicinity with rank of Lieutenant, first name "Edwin" and sketch (page 164); per sketch born Bossier Parish, Louisiana 1841, came to Memphis 1847, when war began a subordinate officer in Stutham's Brigade until at Vicksburg attached to the staff of General W. C. Preston with whom served till both fell wounded at Battle of Murfreesboro, left to die but taken prisoner and after recovery sent to Camp Chase, exchanged and returned to duty with General Preston, when General Preston sent to Mexico as diplomat became an Ordnance Officer, and killed by madman January 8, 1869; January 9, 1869, *Memphis Daily Appeal*, page 3 column 2, "Shocking Tragedy" article on him being killed by a tenant who he had confronted about not paying rent; January 11, 1869, *Memphis Daily Appeal*, page 3 column 2, article on death, slain Friday last (January 8, 1869), and yesterday committed to the tomb, was a member of 154th Senior Regiment (no records found for him in this Regiment's compiled service records) and referred to him as Captain; brother of Francis Eugene Whitfield; grave stone only has information on wife; pistol shot age 28 per Daily Burial Record Book.

Whitfield, Francis Eugene   Buried March 22, 1885   Turley 1048, #1
Mississippi 9 Infantry Regiment Colonel; originally enlisted as Second Lieutenant February 20, 1861, in Corinth, Mississippi at age 21 and lawyer; appointed Adjutant by order of Colonel Chalmers April 11, 1861; when regiment enlistment expired transferred to reorganized regiment December 17, 1861, and appointed Captain Company A; wounded at Battle of Shiloh; appointed Lieutenant Colonel April 16, 1862; per January and February 1863 muster roll remarks: removed by order of General Bragg; per September and October 1863, muster roll remarks: on extra duty Provost Marshall, Polk's Corps; wounded May 14, 1864, at Resaca, Georgia; per sketch in *More Generals in Gray* born Bossier Parish, Louisiana June 22, 1839, at start of War elected Lieutenant of "Corinth Rifles" (later Company A (Company C per Rietti's Mississippi Annals) Mississippi 9 Infantry), later Major of Mississippi 9 Infantry Regiment, wounded in hip at Battle of Shiloh, 1863 Lieutenant Colonel of Regiment, while on sick leave related to the wound received at the Battle of Shiloh General Bragg appointed another officer to fill the colonel's vacancy, when he protested General Bragg had him arrested for being absent without leave which arrest was later voided by the War Department nevertheless this ended his career with the Mississippi 9 Infantry Regiment, at Battle of Chickamauga September 1863 served as Provost Marshall of Polk's Corps of Army of Tennessee, wounded at Battle of Resaca in 1864 which ended field service, after recovery took command of Post of Meridian, Mississippi, paroled May 10, 1865, at Meridian, Mississippi as Colonel Mississippi 9 Infantry Regiment, the *Southern Historical Society Papers* called him General but may have been confused with Brigadier General John W. Whitfield, and on March 18, 1885 died suddenly while on a steamboat on the St. John's River in Florida; not listed in the *Memorandum relative to the General Officers Appointed by the President in the Armies of the Confederate States - 1861-1865* compiled from Official Records by the Military Secretary's Office, U. S. War Department 1905; not listed in *Generals in Gray*; not listed in Cemetery tour brochures; grave stone: born June 22, 1839, and died March 18, 1885; died heart disease at age 45 per Daily Burial Record Book; originally buried Turley 17, #4 and moved February 19, 1886; also listed in chapter on Generals.

Whitmore, Edwin   Buried December 4, 1898   Turley 5622, #1

Tennessee 7 Cavalry Regiment Private Company L; enlisted July 7, 1861, Senatobia age 21; paroled at Gainesville, Alabama May 11, 1865; per sketch in Mathes book (both editions) original sketch (page 220) born September 25, 1833, Fayette County, Tennessee, enlisted Company A Foute's (Memphis) Battalion of Infantry (Tennessee 3 Infantry Battalion) early 1861 (enlisted March 12, 1862, Memphis Private Company A per unit compiled service record) and served one year, sworn into 7 Tennessee Cavalry Company L August 1862, wounded at Medon, had three horses shot from under him, served throughout War except two months in 1864 when had pneumonia, after War founded *Memphis Public Ledger*, joined Confederate Historical Association in 1895 and member Company A; per enlarged edition (page 102) introduction and sketch died December 2, 1898.

Wilkerson, Dr. William North   Buried November 6, 1921   South Grove 157, #3

Tennessee 9 Infantry Regiment Captain Company A; originally enlisted Tennessee 13 Infantry Private Company A May 28, 1861, at Jackson, Tennessee; age 28 on May 8, 1863, muster roll with remark that transferred to the 9 Regiment Tennessee Volunteers at New Madrid, Missouri July 1862; same enlistment card in Tennessee 9 Infantry Regiment rolls; appointed Captain August 13, 1861; subject of court martial November 3, 1861 (no disposition indicated); per pay card in file dated May 7, 1862, residence of Somerville, Fayette County, Tennessee and discharge took effect May 27, 1862; per obituary in "The Last Roll" section of *Confederate Veteran* Volume XXIX, November-December 1921, page 435, born in Montgomery County, Tennessee February 2, 1828, studied medicine at medical school in Cincinnati, Ohio, was one of the organizers of Tennessee 30 Regiment (no record found that regiment), commanded a company that he surrendered so might aid wounded, and was transferred to different commands as the need of his services grew greater; sketch in Goodspeed's Shelby County History, page 1059; circle grave stone: 1829 1921; died November 5, 1921, age 93 per Death Certificate.

Wilkins, Charles W.   Buried September 23, 1870   Fowler 3, #2

Tennessee 3 (Forrest's Old) Cavalry Regiment Corporal 2 Company A and Tennessee 154 Senior Infantry Regiment Private 1 Company B "Bluff City Grays"; per Tennessee 154 Senior Infantry Regiment Company Muster-in Roll dated August 13,1861, enlisted July 28, 1861, New Madrid, Missouri age 20; per Tennessee 3 (Forrest's) Cavalry Regiment Company Muster Roll for September 1 to November 1, 1862, enlisted May 4, 1861, Memphis, Tennessee; wounded at Battle of Murfreesboro, December, 1862; per cards in Tennessee 3 (Forrest's Old) Cavalry Regiment compiled service records was captured at Athens, Alabama, September 24, 1864, first sent to Nashville, Tennessee then to Military Prison at Louisville, Kentucky January 3, 1865, then to Camp Chase Ohio January 9, 1865, paroled at Camp Chase and transferred to Point Lookout, Maryland February 17, 1865, for exchange; per cards in Tennessee 154 Senior Infantry Regiment appears on a register of Prisoners of War at Memphis, Tennessee and name appears on an Oath of Allegiance sworn at Memphis, Tennessee May 11, 1865, at age 24 and residence indicated as Memphis, Tennessee; funeral notice in the September 23, 1870, *Memphis Daily Appeal*, page 1, column 5, wherein "members of the 154th Tennessee regiment are respectfully invited to attend"; listed (C. W. Wilkins") in the June 6, 1878, *Memphis Daily Appeal*, page 4, column 3, article "OUR DEAD HEROES" covering the unveiling of the Confederate Monument and Decoration of Graves at Elmwood as then one of twenty-eight members of the Bluff City Grays, Company B of the 154 Senior Infantry Regiment and Company A of Forrest's Old (Third) Cavalry Regiment buried at Elmwood; listed as one of the "comrades who sleep at Elmwood cemetery " in the article "Veterans in Council" in Memphis Daily Appeal, May 12, 1881, page 4, column 4, concerning the meeting of the surviving members in the city of the old Bluff City Grays to appoint the necessary committees for the purpose of making special decoration on the graves of their dead comrades at Elmwood and Calvary cemeteries on Sunday next, Memorial Day; listed as member of Bluff City Grays in *Reminiscences of the Civil War* by John Hallum, Tunnah & Pittard printers, 1903; listed in "A COMPLETE ROSTER OF THE BLUFF CITY GREYS" located in the Memphis Room of the Memphis/Shelby County Public Library and Information Center Central Library with notation Died at Memphis and buried in Elmwood with location noted; see also Notes of Interest - Bluff City Grays; per sketch in Mathes book (page 228) enlisted in the same company as his brother (William G. Wilkins, see sketch next below) served as corporal, wounded at Murfreesboro and wounded and captured at Athens, Alabama, in September, 1864, sent to Camp Chase, Ohio and paroled just before close of war, returned to Memphis, never married and died in 1870; died bilious fever age 29 per Daily Burial Record Book; grave stone: born November 14, 1840, Booneville, Missouri and died September 22, 1870, Memphis.

Wilkins, William Goodwin   Buried May 13, 1912   Fowler 3, #6

Tennessee 3 (Forrest's Old) Cavalry Regiment Private 2 Company A and Tennessee 154 Senior Infantry Regiment Private 1 Company B "Bluff City Grays"; per Tennessee 154 Senior Infantry Regiment Company Muster-in Roll dated August 13,1861, enlisted June 22, 1861, New Madrid, Missouri age 18; per Tennessee 3 (Forrest's Old) Cavalry Regiment Company Muster Roll for January 1 to July 1, 1862, enlisted May 4, 1861, Randolph, Tennessee; name appears on Roll of Prisoners of War paroled at Gainesville, Alabama May 11, 1865, resident of Memphis, Tennessee; per sketch in Mathes book (page 287-288) took conspicuous part in the battle Chickamauga September 18, 1863, (see Lindsley's Annals, p. 693); brother of Charles W. Wilkins (see sketch next above); listed in "A COMPLETE ROSTER OF THE BLUFF CITY GREYS" located in the Memphis Room of the Memphis/Shelby County Public Library and Information Center Central Library; listed as member of Bluff City Grays in *Reminiscences of the Civil War* by John Hallum, Tunnah & Pittard printers, 1903; see also Notes of Interest - Bluff City Grays; widow, Minnie Swayne Wilkins, received a Tennessee Confederate Pension (W10343), which application file includes "Captain Thomas F. Pattison's History of the Bluff City Grays" with names as appeared on First Muster Roll and those who joined after September 1, 1861, to surrender, 1865, that was submitted by Dr. D. L. Manire, Surgeon Dentist, Memphis, Tennessee; per her pension file he was born August 9, 1842,which is inscribed on his circle grave stone, in Booneville, Mississippi; died age 70 per Daily Burial Record Book.

Williams, Dr. John Joseph   Buried October 24, 1873   Turley 1, #11
Doctor; listed in Elmwood 1874 book as Confederate soldier buried in Elmwood who was citizen of Memphis or vicinity "Dr. J. Joseph Williams"; per grave stone born in Maury County, Tennessee 1827, and died in Memphis, Tennessee 1873; per October 24, 1873, *Memphis Daily Appeal* death notice died yellow fever age 47; doctor and died yellow fever age 45 per Daily Burial Record Book; mentioned ("Joseph J. Williams") in sketch on son Joseph J. Williams in *Tennessee, The Volunteer State, 1769-1923*, Volume III, page 253; possibly J. J. Williams, Captain/Lieutenant Colonel Tennessee 24 Infantry Regiment, mustered into service July 24, 1861, elected Major August 6, 1861, elected Lieutenant Colonel May 2, 1862 but refused to accept, member of Tennessee legislature, per letter in compiled service record dated February 20, 1865, to President Davis recommended for appointment to military court and a lawyer, from Hickman County, Tennessee, badly wounded and not able to serve since but member of Tennessee legislature (no full name in record).

Willins, John T.   Buried January 31, 1892   Turley 1002, #1
Trans-Mississippi Department Assistant Quartermaster (QM) Captain; per sketch in Mathes (page 224) born Brooklyn, NY July 5, 1841, came to Memphis February 1858, enlisted Tennessee 154 Senior Infantry April 1861, (no record found) and served two years, transferred to Trans-Mississippi Department and served as Chief Clerk with Major John N. Norris, Chief QM under Major General S. B. Maxey commanding the District of the Indian Territory, August 9, 1864, ordered by General E. Kirby to duty with Major Norris at Doaksville, Cherokee Nation where served until surrender, paroled at Shreveport, Louisiana August 1, 1865, returned to Memphis after war, early member Confederate Relief and Historical Association and died January 28, 1892, at aged 50 years and six months; died age 50 per Daily Burial Record Book; July 5, 1841 January 28, 1892 on grave stone; possibly J. T. Willins, Private Company H, Tennessee 4 Infantry Regiment who enlisted May 15, 1861, at Fort Pillow and discharged November 5, 1861; General and Staff rolls QM Agent, on QM list dated February 13, 1865, District Indian Territory, appointed August 1, 1864, John T. Willins on one card).

Wills, William A.   Buried June 15, 1866   Chapel Hill 708, #1
Mississippi 2 (J. G. Ballentine's Regiment of Cavalry) Partisan Rangers Private (Captain Edward E. Porter's Partisan Company – see Rev. Edward E. Porter sketch) Company C; per Company Muster Roll for April 21 to August 1, 1862, enlisted May 7, 1862, Somerville (Memphis on some muster roll cards) by Captain Porter; per Company Muster Roll for July and August 1864, remarks: died August 7, 1864, from the effects of gunshot wound; Company C transferred to Tennessee 3 (Forrest's Old) Cavalry Regiment Company F in accordance with S. O. No. 28. Headquarters, Cavalry Division District of Mississippi and East Louisiana, dated February 13, 1865, and soldiers paroled as part of Company F at Gainesville, Alabama May 11, 1865, but no record found in Tennessee 3 (Forrest's Old) Cavalry Regiment Company F rolls; listed in Elmwood 1874 book as Confederate soldier buried in Elmwood who was citizen of Memphis or vicinity; age 22, killed and brought from Atlanta per Daily Burial Record Book.

Winston, Dr. William Benjamin   Buried August 13, 1900   Turley 1151, #4
Tennessee 7 Cavalry Regiment 1 Lieutenant Company C; enlisted July 15, 1861, Memphis; promoted 1 Lieutenant September 25, 1862; name appears on a Report of Prisoners of War paroled on terms as agreed to for the 5 day period ending May 20, 1865, at Memphis, Tennessee; per sketch in Mathes book, page 226: after the wound at Columbia, was disabled completely, the shot being through the head and was not recovered from until six months after the war, and admitted to the C. H. A. April 9, 1895; per biography in *Confederate Military History, Extended Edition*, Volume X Tennessee, page 792, born in Haywood County, Tennessee, October 2, 1836, and graduated from the medical department of the university of Nashville in the spring of 1861.

Wood, Jacob Mabie   Buried February 4, 1900   Fowler 193½
Tennessee 154 Senior Infantry Regiment 1 Sergeant Company L (Maynard Rifles); enlisted March 7, 1861; appears on a Muster Roll of Officers and Men paroled at Greensboro, North Carolina, May 1, 1865; per sketch in Mathes book, page 290: senior officer in command of the One Hundred and Fifty-fourth Tennessee Regiment with twenty-three men at the surrender and arrived in Memphis May 26, 1865; per biography in *Confederate Military History, Extended Edition*, Volume X Tennessee, page 794: born in New York City January 21, 1845, and Mrs. Sallie Chapman Gordon-Law, the "Mother of the Confederacy," in her little book written in 1892, paid him a beautiful compliment on pages 13 and 14, one of which he and his family may ever feel justly proud.

Woodlock, Henry P.   Buried September 6, 1885   Evergreen 19, #1
Tennessee 7 Cavalry Regiment Private Company C; enlisted June 6, 1861, in Captain J. G. Ballentine's Company, in Memphis, age 24; the Company became Company F ("The Shelby Light Dragoons") Tennessee 6 (Logwood's) Cavalry Battalion (also known as Tennessee 1 Cavalry Battalion); Tennessee 7 Cavalry Regiment organized April 1862; December 1, 1861, detailed on detached service on Brigadier General Pillow's staff where promoted to Ordnance Sergeant; death notice (page1 ,column 1) and Obituary (page 4, column 4) in the September 5, 1885, *Memphis Daily Appeal;* per Obituary he was an employee of the Appeal, was born in Ireland in 1835, came to this country with his parents while still young, settled in St. Joseph, Missouri, where learned the art of printing, and came to Memphis in 1857, and began working for the *Eagle and Enquirer*, when the War broke out, he enlisted in Ballentyne's company of cavalry, from which, at Columbus, in October, 1861, detailed by General Pillow, and served on his staff until the close of the war, and worked at the Appeal since 1868; per death notice died age 49 from heart disease.

Woodson, Henry Morton   Buried November 23, 1917   Evergreen 19, #1
Tennessee 13 Infantry Regiment Private Company H (no compiled service records found for this unit); originally enlisted in Mississippi 34 Infantry Regiment Private Company E and name appears on a Roll of the organization mustered into the service of the Confederate States of America on April 14, 1862, at age 17; record indicates transferred to Company H, 13th Tennessee Regiment by Special Ordered 94/6 dated April 5, 1864; per General A. J. Vaughan's book PERSONAL RECORD OF THE THIRTEENTH REGIMENT, TENNESSEE INFANTRY. BY ITS OLD COMMANDER, presented by him to the New York Public Library, he transferred from Company E, Thirty-Fourth Mississippi Regiment, to Company H, Thirteenth Tennessee Regiment; per sketch Mathes book (page 227) he enlisted March 10, 1862, at the age of 17 years, while attending school in Mississippi, and was transferred to Company H, Thirteenth Tennessee Regiment. Vaughan's Brigade, about February or March, 1864; was paroled at Montgomery, Alabama, May 10, 1865, returned to Germantown, married there, but has lived in Memphis many years and became a member of this Association (Confederate Historical Association) about the year 1891; note there is a H. M. Woodson record found in Tennessee 14th Infantry Regiment, Private Company H, with record that name appears on a record of Confederate Soldiers paroled at Montgomery, Alabama May 10, 1865; per Tennessee Certificate of Death died November 22, 1917, age 72 from Apoplexy and was born April 6, 1845; birth and death dates on his grave stone.

Woodward, Henry P.   Buried August 11, 1869   Turley 212, #3
Tennessee 7 Cavalry Regiment Sergeant Company A; enlisted May 16, 1861 Memphis age 33; paroled May 11, 1865 at Gainesville, Alabama; listed in Elmwood 1874 book as Confederate soldier buried in Elmwood who was citizen of Memphis or vicinity with name spelled as "Woodard"; died apoplexy age 41 per Daily Burial Record Book.

Wooldridge, Charles P.   Buried October 5, 1876   Turley 92, #11
Tennessee 3 (Forrest's Old) Cavalry Regiment Private 2 Company A ("Bluff City Grays") and Tennessee 154 Senior Infantry Regiment Sergeant/Private Company E; per Tennessee 154 Senior Infantry Regiment Company E Muster Roll dated August 31, 1861, enlisted May 21, 1861, Randolph, Tennessee, wounded at Murfreesboro December 31, 1862, age 24 on Company Muster Roll dated May 5, 1863, absent without leave on January & February 1864, Company Muster Roll and no other information in record; per Tennessee 3 (Forrest's Old) Cavalry Regiment Company A Company Muster Roll dated May 14, 1864, enlisted May 4, 1861, Memphis and name appears on Roll of Prisoners of War paroled at Gainesville, Alabama May 11, 1865, resident of Memphis, Tennessee; listed in the June 6, 1878, *Memphis Daily Appeal*, page 4, column 3, article "OUR DEAD HEROES" covering the unveiling of the Confederate Monument and Decoration of Graves at Elmwood as then one of twenty-eight members of the Bluff City Grays, Company B of the 154 Senior Infantry Regiment and Company A of Forrest's Old (Third) Cavalry Regiment buried at Elmwood; listed as one of the "comrades who sleep at Elmwood cemetery " in the article "Veterans in Council" in the May 12, 1881, *Memphis Daily Appeal*, page 4, column 4, concerning the meeting of the surviving members in the city of the old Bluff City Grays to appoint the necessary committees for the purpose of making special decoration on the graves of their dead comrades at Elmwood and Calvary cemeteries on Sunday next, Memorial Day; listed in "A COMPLETE ROSTER OF THE BLUFF CITY GREYS" located in the Memphis Room of the Memphis/Shelby County Public Library and Information Center Central Library with notation that joined Company March 1, 1864, and buried in Elmwood Cemetery, Turley 92; listed in "Captain Thomas F. Pattison's History of the Bluff City Grays" with names as appeared on First Muster Roll and those who joined after September 1, 1861, to surrender, 1865, as having joined after September 1, 1861, which document found in the Tennessee Confederate Pension Application (W10343) of Minnie Swayne Wilkins, widow of William G. Wilkins (see sketch supra); not listed as member of Bluff City Grays in *Reminiscences of the Civil War* by John Hallum, Tunnah & Pittard printers, 1903; see Notes of Interest - Bluff City Grays; referred to as "Charles W. Woodridge," whose grave was handsomely decorated and located outside the Confederate grounds, in the May 17, 1881, *Memphis Daily Appeal*, page 2, column 3, article "OUR HEROIC DEAD" reporting on the Memorial Day ceremonies at Elmwood Cemetery on Sunday, May 15, 1881; small round grave stone: C. P. Wooldridge; per small death notice in the October 4, 1876, *Memphis Daily Appeal*, page 1, column 6, died October 3, 1876, in the 38th year of his age; Masonic Funeral Notice in the October 5, 1876, *Memphis Daily Appeal*, page 1, column 7; died congestion age 37 per Daily Burial Record Book; cousin of Egbert and Oscar Wooldridge (see sketches herein).

Wooldridge, Egbert   Buried May 27, 1875   Lenow Circle 40, #6
Tennessee 154 Senior Infantry Regiment Private Company L; per Company Muster-in Roll dated March 8, 1862, enlisted March 7, 1862, Memphis, Tennessee, per discharge certificate dated May 3, 1863, born in Louisville, Kentucky, age 18 and paid on May 2, 1863; per sketch in Mathes book (page 229) "enlisted March, 1862, in Company L, Maynard Rifles, One Hundred and Fifty-fourth Tennessee Regiment, for twelve months; was very young, a mere lad, and was under conscriptive age at the expiration of the time for which he was mustered into the service; he was then entitled to and received an honorable discharge and enlisted in the cavalry, joining the Bluff City Grays, Captain James Edmondson (no record found in any of the "Bluff City Grays" companies, books or lists – see Notes of Interest - Bluff City Grays). His first captain, E. A. Cole, says of him: "If such a thing be possible, he was brave to a fault, always ready to meet the enemy and went into battle cheerfully and with alacrity; in other words, he was a good soldier and never shirked his duty; he was very companionable, with unexceptionable habits and noted for his extreme modesty. With credit and honor to himself he participated while in my command in the battles of Shiloh, Richmond, Ky., Perryville and Murfreesboro." After the surrender returned to Memphis, engaged in business and joined the C. R. and H. A. September 1, 1870; died several years ago."; bother of Oscar Wooldridge and cousin of Charles. P. Wooldridge (see sketches herein); large grave stone: Egbert Wooldridge died May 26, 1875, Aged 29 Years; death notice in the May 27, 1875, *Memphis Daily Appeal*, page 1, column 6; died from congestion age 29 per Daily Burial Record Book.

Wooldridge, Oscar   Buried March 22, 1883   Lenow Circle 94, #4
Tennessee 7 Cavalry Regiment Private Company A; per Company Muster Roll for May 16, 1861, to October 31, 1862, enlisted September 22, 1862, at Davis Mills; per Company Muster Roll dated November 1, 1863, remarks: Absent on special detail 25 days from November 9; name appears on Roll of Prisoners of War paroled at Gainesville, Alabama May 11, 1865, resident of Memphis, Tennessee; per sketch in Mathes book (page 228) "enlisted in the Memphis Light Dragoons, Company A, Seventh Tennessee, September 25, 1862, just in time to take part in the furious attack at Davis' Bridge, Miss. He was in the battles of Corinth, October 4 and 5, 1862, Ripley, Old Lamar, Oxford and Coffeeville, and took part in the capture of Holly Springs, December 20, 1862, and was in the engagements at Davis' Mills and Bolivar December 21 and 24, 1862. In the spring of 1863 the company was engaged in the Vicksburg campaign; from thence it went to Georgia and was actively engaged in front of Sherman in the Atlanta campaign; from Georgia it went to Middle Tennessee with Hood, and the young soldier saw further severe fighting at Lawrenceburg, Campbellsville, Rally Hill, Hurt's X Roads, Mount Carmel, Spring Hill, Franklin, Murfreesboro, Lynnville, Richland Creek, Anthony's Hill and Sugar creek, and in the engagements during the Wilson raid; he surrendered with his company at Gainesville, Ala., May 11, 1865. In all these trying days the young trooper bore himself as a hero. Cool, brave and determined, he was a very type of the Confederate veteran of that day; clean of life, proud, generous to a fault, he was an ideal messmate, and as a soldier worthy the race from which he sprang. He quitted the camp without an enemy, and though long since gone to a better home, his memory lingers green in the hearts of those who knew and loved him best in time of war. He joined the Confederate R. and H. A. September 1, 1870, and died several years afterward."; bother of Egbert Wooldridge and cousin of Charles. P. Wooldridge (see sketches herein); grave stone: Oscar Wooldridge Feb. 20, 1883 A Confederate Soldier; per death notice in the February 21, 1883, *Memphis Daily Appeal*, page 1, column 6, died February 20, 1883, aged forty-six years; died from congestion per Daily Burial Record Book.

Word, Charles Sullivan   Buried May 11, 1913   Fowler Public Lot 6, #1186
Mississippi 22 Infantry Regiment 1 Lieutenant Company H; enlisted August 10, 1861, Oxford, Mississippi age 37; resigned September 19, 1863; signed letter of resignation August 6, 1863; unit per article in *The Commercial Appeal* Memphis, Sunday Morning, May 11, 1913, page 13; death notice on page 7 of the same paper; small article and photograph in *The Commercial Appeal* Memphis, May 12, 1913, page 2; applied for Mississippi Confederate pension in 1909 while living in Lafayette County, Mississippi per Mississippi Confederate Pension Index Book; served in Mexican War in 1846 with Mississippi 1 Infantry Regiment and received a federal pension; died age 90 per newspaper articles and Daily Burial Record Book; found as "Wood, Charles S." in Cemetery computer index but name spelled correctly in Cemetery Daily Burial Record and Alpha books.

Wormeley, Ralph   Buried May 9, 1886   Chapel Hill 241, #5
Tennessee 3 (Memphis Battalion) Infantry Battalion 2 Lieutenant (Captain John B. Weld) Company A; per Company Muster Roll dated March 12, 1862, enlisted March 12, 1862, Memphis; see Notes of Interest "Memphis Battalion - Tennessee 3rd (Memphis) Infantry Battalion"; per death notice in the May 8, 1886, *Memphis Daily Appeal*, page 1, column 5, died May 7, 1886, aged sixty-six; cause of death Heart Disease per Daily Burial Record Book.

Wright, Eldridge E.   Buried April 1, 1863   Miller Circle 272, #2
Tennessee Phillips' Company (Captain E. E. Wright's Company) Light Artillery 1 Lieutenant/Captain; per Company Muster Roll dated January 23, 1863, remarks: elected Captain December 3, 1862, and killed at Murfreesboro January 2, 1863; per *Tennesseans in the Civil War, Part 1*, company organized October 15, 1861, with J. Wesley Eldridge as Captain, reorganized on December 3, 1862, at Murfreesboro with E. E. Wright as Captain and Wright killed in fighting around Murfreesboro (December 31, 1862-January 2, 1863); listed in Elmwood 1874 book as Confederate soldier buried in Elmwood who was citizen of Memphis or vicinity and sketch (page 165); per sketch born in middle Tennessee, graduated from University of North Carolina, came to Memphis to read law in father's office, age not more than twenty when war began, rapidly promoted as an artilleryman, commanded a light artillery at Battle of Murfreesboro and fell (killed); grave stone: born August 22, 1840, killed at the Battle of Murfreesboro January 1, 1863; "Death of Capt. E. E. Wright" reported in the January 7, 1863, *Memphis Daily Appeal*, page 2, column 1, "... the death of Captain Eldridge E. Wright, son of Hon. Archibald Wright, of Memphis. He was killed in battle of Murfreesboro on the 1st inst. ....."; mentioned by Dr. S. H. Ford in his address on the occasion to commemorate (Confederate Memorial Day) Confederates buried at Elmwood on April 26, 1866, (see articles "The Confederate Dead" in *Public Ledger* (Memphis), April 27, 1866, page 3, column 2, and "Honors To The Memory Of The Hero Dead" in the April 27, 1866, *Memphis Daily Appeal*, page 3, column 1); originally buried Chapel Hill Circle 75 and moved March 30, 1899.

Wright, Jesse Clay   Buried May 27, 1907   Miller Circle 43, # 1
Mississippi 17 Infantry Regiment Corporal/Captain Company H; per Company Muster-in Roll dated June 7, 1861, enlisted May 27, 1861, at Corinth, Mississippi, age 20; elected 2nd Lieutenant April 26, 1862, promoted to 1st lieutenant May 1, 1862, and promoted to captain July, 12, 1863; captured at Sailors Creek, Virginia April 6, 1865; signed Oath of Allegiance at Johnson's Island, Ohio, June 20, 1865, age 24 and indication residence as Panola, Mississippi; per Mathes book sketch (page 229) "Captain Company H, Seventeenth Mississippi Regiment, Army of North Virginia, enlisted May 27, 1861; started out as corporal of Company H; was captured at Farmville, Va., April 6, 1865; released at the end of the war. Joined the C. H, A. October 1894."; widow, Frederica O. Wright, applied for Tennessee Confederate Pension (W10505) March 31, 1932, which was accepted; grave stone: January 9, 1842 May 26, 1907.

Young, Hiram Casey   Buried August 18, 1899   Turley 13422, #1

Lieutenant Colonel; per *Confederate Staff Officers 1861-1865* by Joseph H. Crute, Jr., Derwent Books 1982, appointed December 27, 1861, as Captain and Assistant Adjutant General on staff of Brigadier General William H. Carroll (H. C. Young, Captain, appointed A. A. G. October 26, 1861) and appointed July 21, 1863, as Lieutenant Colonel and Acting Assistant Inspector General on staff of Brigadier General James R. Chalmers (H. C. Young, Lieutenant Colonel, appointed A. A. I. G. March 1864); per information in story on Captain Philip Maroney, a Revolution War veteran and an ancestor of Young, in Paul R. Coppock's Mid-South Volume II, pages 262-263, (original newspaper story September 15, 1974), Young was the member of Congress (Tennessee 10th District) who obtained authority for the original Memphis bridge and for the first Custom House on the bluff, usually called the Federal Building, his law career was interrupted by the Civil War, became a Confederate Lieutenant Colonel of cavalry and served with General N. B. Forrest; per congressional sketch in the PoliticalGraveyard.com a Representative from Tennessee, born in Tuscaloosa, Tuscaloosa County, Alabama, December 14, 1828, moved with his parents to a farm near Byhalia, Marshall County, Mississippi, in 1838, attended the local schools and was tutored by his father and also attended Marshall Institute in Marshall County, Mississippi, studied law and was admitted to the bar in 1859 and commenced practice in Memphis, Tennessee, served in the Civil War 1861-1865 as lieutenant colonel of Cavalry and on the brigade staff, Assistant Inspector General, First Division of Cavalry in 1864, elected as a Democrat to the Forty-fourth, Forty-fifth, and Forty-sixth Congresses (March 4, 1875-March 3, 1881), unsuccessful candidate for reelection in 1880, elected to the Forty-eighth Congress (March 4, 1883-March 3, 1885), chairman of Committee on Expenditures in the Department of the Interior (Forty-eighth Congress), not a candidate for renomination, resumed the practice of law and died in Memphis, Tennessee, August 17, 1899; sketch in *Tennessee, The Volunteer State, 1769-1923*, Volume II, pages 362-364; orator at the May 15, 1881, Confederate Memorial Day at Elmwood Cemetery (see *Memphis Daily Appeal*, May 17, 1881, page 2, column 3); died age 50 per Daily Burial Record Book; grave stone has engraved crossed Confederate Battle Flags and name but no dates.

Young, John Preston   Buried June 8, 1934   Chapel Hill 379, #8

Tennessee 7 Cavalry Regiment Private Company A; enlisted November 10, 1864, age 17; author of *The Seventh Tennessee Cavalry* (1890) and *Standard History of Memphis, Tennessee* (1912); circuit court judge; sketch in Mathes book (both editions); per original edition (page 231) first served several months of War with Company A ("Shelby Greys") 4 Tennessee Infantry but being under age never sworn into infantry service (no compiled service record found and not listed as member of Company A ("Shelby Greys") 4 Tennessee Infantry in the articles "Military" in the April 18, 1861, *Memphis Daily Appeal*,, page 3, column 3 (original members list), "Testimonial of Respect" in the December 7, 1861, *Memphis Daily Appeal*,, page 4, column 2, or the May 15, 1909, *The Commercial Appeal* Memphis article "Forty=Eight Years Ago Today, The Shelby Greys Entered the Confederate Service—Record of a Famous Memphis Military Company."); and first regularly enlisted 7 Tennessee Cavalry Regiment November 4, 1864, admitted Confederate Historical Association 1884, elected secretary 1894; per enlarged edition (page 140) born Chulahoma (Marshall County), Mississippi April 18, 1847; died June 6, 1934, age 87 per Cemetery record; biography in *Confederate Military History*, *Extended Edition*, Volume X Tennessee, page 803; sketch in *Tennessee, The Volunteer State, 1769-1923*, Volume II, page 114.

CONFEDERATES REMOVED FROM ELMWOOD CEMETERY

This is a list of known Confederate soldiers and veterans who were originally buried at Elmwood Cemetery as well as other individuals, although not serving in the Confederate military, who served an important part in the Confederate Cause but were later removed from the Cemetery. They were identified primarily from review of Elmwood records. Obviously, there may be others.

Barnes, Robert Weakley   Buried January 22, 1885   Chapel Hill Public Lot 2, #990
Arkansas 1 (Monroe's) Cavalry Captain Company A; enlisted as a Private June 20, 1861, Brownsville; promoted to Captain April 14, 1863, (elected) by reorganization; captured Lynn County, Kansas October 25, 1864; received at Gratiot Street Military Prison at St. Louis, Missouri during 5 days ending November 5, 1864; transferred to Johnson's Island, Ohio (near Sandusky) November 12, 1864; took Oath of Allegiance at Johnson's Island June 16, 1865, indicating residence of Little Rock, Arkansas and age 33; per sketch in Mathes boo, page 234, born near Nashville, Tennessee August 4, 1832, enlisted with father and two brothers in Monroe's Arkansas Cavalry June 1861, made Captain July 1863, captured before Battle of Kansas City, sent to Johnson's Island, released June 16, 1865, died January 20, 1885, leaving wife and nine children, a tenth child had died of yellow fever in 1878; died age 52 per Daily Burial Record Book; removed to Forest Hill Cemetery October 1897.

Bell, William, Jr.   Buried May 3, 1862   Chapel Hill 248, #2
Kentucky 9 Infantry Regiment Adjutant; enlisted October 1861, Bowling Green, Kentucky, Kentucky 5 Infantry; unit designation changed to Kentucky 9 Infantry by order dated October 4, 1861; appointed Adjutant January 28, 1862; per muster roll remarks: mortally wounded Battle of Shiloh April 6, 1862, and died April 29, 1862, Memphis; death reported in the April 30, 1862, *Memphis Daily Appeal,* page 1, column 6, with unit identified as Kentucky 5 Adjutant; per Daily Burial Record Book raised and sent to Louisville, Kentucky (date not indicated).

Dunnico, Parker   Buried April1 5, 1862   Confederate Rest D1, #451
Missouri 1 Infantry Regiment Private Company F; enlisted November 30, 1861, Memphis; per muster roll remarks: wounded Battle of Shiloh and died April 14, 1862, Memphis; per Battle of Shiloh casualty list for unit reported in the April 23, 1862, *Memphis Daily Appeal* wounded in battle; per Overton Hospital record name spelled "Dunnica," admitted April 11, 1862, with complaint of right thigh and wrist and died April 14, 1862; per Daily Burial Record Book "taken to St. Louis May 4, 1867"; name spelled "Dunnica" in Daily Burial Record Book and computer index.

Forrest, Nathan Bedford   Buried October 31, 1877   Chapel Hill Circle 47, #9
Lieutenant General; removed to Forrest Park, Memphis, Tennessee with body of wife, Mary A. Forrest, November 11, 1904; see sketch in chapter on Generals.

Fugue, L. A.   Buried March 27, 1871   Confederate Rest D2, #12A
Confederate Soldier, age 32, no charge and "taken away" (date and where not indicated) per Daily Burial Record Book; burial location not indicated in Daily Burial Record Book but in Alpha Book.

Hamilton, Alexander Samuel   Buried November 15, 1863   Chapel Hill 42, #2
Mississippi 1 (Johnston's) Infantry Regiment Captain Company K, Lieutenant Colonel; enlisted August 24, 1861, age 38; elected Lieutenant Colonel September 9, 1861; captured at Fort Donelson February 16, 1862; died in prison at Johnson's Island, Ohio November 3, 1863, and body sent home for burial; statement by major of regiment indicates that wife Martha Hamilton resides in Mooresville, Itawamba County, Mississippi; per Daily Burial Record Book removed to Mississippi February 24, 1864.

Haynes, Landon Carter   Buried February 18, 1875   South Grove 3, #1
Confederate Senator (Tennessee); sketch in Warner's *Confederate Congress* book pages 113-114; born Elizabethton, Tennessee December 2, 1816, graduated from Washington College as valedictorian, studied law but began career as Methodist preacher, later farmed and practiced law at Jonesboro and elected to the legislature in 1845, 1847 won election to the state senate, 1849 was Speaker of House, October 1861, Tennessee General Assembly chose him a Confederate Senator on the first ballot for a term of six years, after War felt himself at a distinct disadvantage in east Tennessee, many of whose residents had been bitter Union partisans, and made his home in Memphis thereafter and continued his practice of law, died in Memphis February 17, 1875, and first buried in Elmwood Cemetery, twenty-seven years later remains were moved to the Cemetery in Jackson, Tennessee, the home of his eldest son; sketch in the PoliticalGraveyard.com; per Daily Burial Record Book first died from apoplexy, aged 58 and removed to Jackson, Tennessee March 27, 1902.

Mathes, James Harvey   Buried December 17, 1902   Turley 377, #3
Tennessee 37 Infantry Regiment 1 Sergeant Company C and Adjutant; enlisted September 1, 1861, Knoxville, Tennessee; paroled at Memphis May 15, 1865; served as a postmaster, clerk for General Crittenden, and on detached recruiting duty; wounded once; known as Captain; author of *The Old Guard in Gray,* Press of S. C. Toof & Co., Memphis, 1897. Part II, Enlarged Edition 1899; per sketch in his book early member of Confederate Historical Association and honorary member of Company A, Confederate Veterans; sketch in Goodspeed's Shelby County History, page 976; sketch in *Tennessee, The Volunteer State, 1769-1923*, Volume III, page 148; biography in *Confederate Military History, Extended Edition*, Volume X Tennessee, page 624; per notes from *The*

Mathews (Mathes) Family in America, by I. C. Van Deventer, Alexander Printing Company, Publishers, Kansas City, Missouri, 1925, pages 87-88, born near Dandridge, Jefferson County, Tennessee, June 29, 1841, educated at a neighboring academy at Westminster, and at the outbreak of the Civil War he was teaching a flourishing school and reading law in Atlanta, returned to Tennessee and was elected captain of a company of Confederates, but later joined another company as a private, and was soon appointed Sergeant-Major of the Tennessee 37 Regiment, C.S.A., organized under Colonel William H. Carroll at Knoxville, and in which he afterwards became Adjutant, followed the fortunes of his regiment nearly all through the war, was frequently detached for special service and staff duty, was staff officer in General Bates' Brigade and participated in some hard service, was in many of the bloodiest engagements of the west, from Fishing Creek, Kentucky, January 19, 1862, to the campaign from Dalton to Atlanta in 1864, and lost a leg and had a horse shot from under him, July 22, 1864, in front of Atlanta, Georgia, which ended his active military career, for some time previous to this he had corresponded for the *Memphis Appeal*, over the nom de plume of "Harvey", and after the surrender regularly engaged in journalism in Memphis, in 1867, was on the staff of the old *Louisville Courier*, a year later was with the *Memphis Avalanche*, and in 1869, became editor of the *Memphis Public Ledger*, which he ably conducted for twenty years, in 1893, severed his connection with the press, served two terms in the state legislature, attended various state and national Democratic conventions, traveled abroad several times, first as Commissioner appointed by Governor Marks of Tennessee to the Paris exposition in 1878, was elector on the Cleveland and Hendricks ticket, in 1902, published a life of General Forrest, for twelve years was on the State Board of the University of Tennessee at Knoxville, and filled other positions of honor and trust, was a Mason and a member of Knights of Honor, he and his family were members of the Congregational church, and collected material for a Mathes history but did not complete it; United Daughters of the Confederacy in Memphis named "The Harvey Mathes Chapter"; a bust statue of him was placed in the Confederate Park, Memphis, in 1908; per Daily Burial Record Book died age 66 and removed to Forest Hill Cemetery February 16, 1918.

McLean, Albert   Buried October 16, 1861   Confederate Rest D1, #35
Arkansas 12 Infantry Regiment (no compiled service record found), died camp measles age 23 and removed to Arkansas per Daily Burial Record Book; date removed not indicated but had to be before John Holden buried in grave November 15, 1861.

Pickard, H. B.   Buried May 31, 1862   Confederate Rest D2, #276
Tennessee 51 (Consolidated) Infantry Regiment Private Company G; no enlistment in compiled service record; per March to June 1862, muster roll remarks: died May 29, 1862; name crossed out in Daily Burial Record Book which indicates died Overton Hospital typhoid fever and removed (date and where not indicated); not listed in Alpha Book; may not have been buried in Cemetery as "C. Weldon" was buried in same grave on same date.

Standridge, J. M.   Buried May 3, 1862   Confederate Rest D2, #31
Arkansas 18 (Carroll's) Infantry Regiment Private Company D; enlisted March 1, 1862, Pine Bluff, Arkansas; per March to June 1862, muster roll remarks: died June 16, 1862; per Daily Burial Record Book died Overton Hospital pneumonia and remarks "taken up" but no date and where indicated.

Vickers, Benjamin Clothier   Buried May 4, 1862   Chapel Hill 293, #1
Tennessee 4 Infantry Regiment Private Company A ("Shelby Greys"); enlisted May 15, 1861, Germantown, Tennessee age 24; per April to June 1862, muster roll remarks: died May 2, 1862, from wounds received at Shiloh; per casualty report dated April 10, 1862, at Corinth: wounded severely in thigh; death reported under Local Matters "Death of a Wounded Soldier" in the May 7, 1862, *Memphis Daily Appeal*, page 2, column 6; moved to Chestertown, Kent County, Maryland March 10, 1863; name listed as member of the Company in the articles "Military" in the April 18, 1861, *Memphis Daily Appeal*, page 3, column 3 (original members list), "Testimonial of Respect" in the December 7, 1861, *Memphis Daily Appeal*, page 4, column 2, and the May 15, 1909, *The Commercial Appeal* Memphis article "Forty=Eight Years Ago Today, The Shelby Greys Entered the Confederate Service—Record of a Famous Memphis Military Company." With second initial "R" in the 1909 article.

Williamson, Robert C.   Buried January 24, 1886   Turley 612 (Masonic Lot), D6-33
Tennessee 6 Infantry Regiment Major, Lieutenant/Captain Company D; per sketch in Mathes book, pages 222-223, born November 4, 1836, Covington, Tipton County, Tennessee, enlisted in Company D 6 Infantry Regiment and elected 2 Lieutenant, elected Captain when company reorganized in May 1862, wounded at Battle of Atlanta, promoted to Major last days of War and in command of a consolidated regiment at surrender at Greensboro, North Carolina, practiced law after War, became a member of Confederate Historical Association July 15, 1869, and died January 23, 1886; per compiled service record 1 Lieutenant/Captain Company D, enlisted May 21, 1861, Jackson, Tennessee, age 24, 2 Lieutenant and elected 1 Lieutenant August 12, 1861, detailed to recruiting service, appointed Captain May 8, 1862, per report dated September 17, 1864, near Jonesboro, Georgia and wounded August 31, 1864, and paroled at Greensboro, North Carolina; died age 49 years, 2 months and 19 days per Daily Burial Record Book; obituary in *Daily Memphis Avalanche* January 24, 1886, page 7 and article on page 3 which indicates that Captain R. C. Williamson, a Mason, was born November 4, 1836, in Fayette County, Tennessee, joined Confederate Army, rose from private to captain, after War came to Memphis, studied and practiced law, served a term as alderman, and married Miss Delia M. Talbot; originally buried in Mason Lot (Turley 612, #33) and removed to Calvary Cemetery March 26, 1889; service and birth and death dates inscribed on "In Memory Of" stone located in walk around Confederate Soldiers Rest Monument.

This is a list of those Confederate soldiers and veterans buried at Elmwood Cemetery who were either officially appointed to General rank or referred to as "General" in at least one of the following: *Elmwood: Charter, Rules, Regulations, and Bylaws of Elmwood Cemetery Association of Memphis* (1874), the Elmwood Cemetery records, "Touring Historic Elmwood Cemetery" Brochure (January 2000) and its predecessor "Touring historic Elmwood Cemetery" (Brochure and Map of Historic Gravesites), *Memorandum relative to the General Officers Appointed by the President in the Armies of the Confederate States - 1861-1865* compiled from Official Records by the Military Secretary's Office, U. S. War Department 1905, Official Records, compiled service records, *The Old Guard in Gray* (Mathes, 1st Edition 1897 & Enlarged Edition 1899), *Generals in Gray* (Warner, 1959), *More Generals in Gray* (Allardice, 1995), *Confederate Military History, Extended Edition,,* (Broadfoot Publishing Company, Wilmington, NC 1987) and Memphis newspapers.

Union generals William Jay Smith and Milton T. Williamson are buried at Elmwood Cemetery. See Note 2 at end of this chapter.

Adams, Charles W.   Buried September 10, 1878   South Grove 156, #5
Colonel Arkansas 23 (Adams') Infantry Regiment - listed as General in Cemetery tour brochures and per sketch in *More Generals in Gray* from 1864 to early 1865 served as Commander of Northern Subdistrict of Arkansas with rank of Acting Brigadier General; not listed in the *Memorandum relative to the General Officers Appointed by the President in the Armies of the Confederate States - 1861-1865*; not listed in *Generals in Gray*; per undated descriptive roll in compiled service record originally entered service as Colonel April 25, 1862, age 45 and born s; per June 30 - August 31, 1862 Field and Staff muster roll: commissioned (elected) April 25, 1862 at Memphis; he wrote General Smith on February 6, 1864, and asked for promotion to Brigadier General; in June 24, 1864, report from Northern Arkansas General Shelby mentions Adams as General Adams; no records found in General and Staff records; per sketch in *More Generals in Gray* born August 16, 1817, in Boston, Massachusetts, first served as Major and Quartermaster of Arkansas State Troops, after dissolution of the Army of Arkansas in late 1861 raised Arkansas 23 Infantry Regiment and elected Colonel April 23, 1862, Regiment disbanded in July 1863, and joined staff of Major General Thomas Hindman, in December 1863, returned to Arkansas, from 1864 to early 1865 served as Commander of Northern Subdistrict of Arkansas with rank of Acting Brigadier General, died of yellow fever on September 9, 1878; grandfather of Helen Keller; sketch, photograph, if available, and grave stone photograph in book *Quiet Places: The Burial Sites of Civil War Generals in Tennessee* by Buckner and Nathaniel C. Hughes, Jr., East Tennessee Historical Society (1992); grave stone (bronze): Brigadier General 23 Ark Regiment C.S.A. August 16, 1817 September 10, 1878; listed under Generals in "Touring historic Elmwood Cemetery" (Brochure and Map of Historic Gravesites) #1; listed in "Touring Historic Elmwood Cemetery" Brochure (January 2000) #82; sketch #28 in Elmwood *Civil War Tour* booklet (2012).

Anderson, James Patton   Buried September 22, 1872   Fowler 469, #1
Major General - appointed from Florida as Brigadier General February 10, 1862, (rank February 10, 1862) and promoted to Major General February 17, 1864 (rank February 17, 1864) per the *Memorandum relative to the General Officers Appointed by the President in the Armies of the Confederate States - 1861-1865*; December 1860, elected delegate from Jefferson County to a general convention of the State of Florida that passed the ordinance of secession on January 10, 1861; also served as Confederate Congressman (Florida) when as a member of the Florida convention of January 1861 was appointed delegate and attended sessions of the Provisional Congress for about three weeks when resigned April 8, 1861 to accept the colonelcy of the First Florida Infantry (see sketch in Warner's Confederate Congress book pages 5-6); elected Colonel 1 Florida Infantry Regiment March 26, 1861 per some records and April 5, 1861 per compiled service record and autobiography; Florida 1 Infantry Regiment record found under Anderson, J. Patton and General and Staff record found under Anderson, Patton; almost killed by bullet in jaw at Chickamauga; listed (Anderson, Gen. J. Patton) in Elmwood 1874 book as Confederate soldier buried in Elmwood who was a citizen of Memphis or vicinity and sketch; died of pneumonia age 50 per Cemetery record; born Winchester, Franklin County, *Extended Edition*, Tennessee February 16, 1822; February 16, 1822 September 20, 1872 on grave stone; biography in *Confederate Military History*, *Extended Edition*, Volume XVI Florida, page 195; see Mrs. J. P. Anderson (transcriber), "Autobiography of Gen. Patton Anderson, C.S.A.," *Southern Historical Society Papers*, Volume XXIV (1896), pages 57-70, and Anderson's autobiography in the *Biography Directory of the American Congress*; sketch in the PoliticalGraveyard.com; sketch, photograph, if available, and grave stone photograph in book *Quiet Places: The Burial Sites of Civil War Generals in Tennessee* by Buckner and Nathaniel C. Hughes, Jr., East Tennessee Historical Society (1992); listed under Generals in "Touring historic Elmwood Cemetery" (Brochure and Map of Historic Gravesites) #2; listed in "Touring Historic Elmwood Cemetery" Brochure (January 2000) #15; sketch #11 in Elmwood *Civil War Tour* booklet (2012).

Bankhead, Smith Pyne   Buried April 1, 1867   Chapel Hill 67, #2
Colonel Trans-Mississippi Department Artillery - listed as General in Cemetery tour brochures and per sketch in *More Generals in Gray* assigned to command the Northern Sub-District of Texas as Acting Brigadier General on May 30, 1863, but after assignment rank reverted to Colonel which rank was not confirmed until January 14, 1865 to rank from June 15, 1864; not listed in the *Memorandum relative to the General Officers Appointed by the President in the Armies of the Confederate States - 1861-1865*; not listed in *Generals in Gray*; originally enlisted as Captain Tennessee Light Artillery Bankhead's/Scott's Company May 13, 1861 in Memphis at age 37; record also found Tennessee Artillery Corps (McCown's) Captain Company 6 with commission dated May 17, 1861; served as Colonel of Texas Cavalry Mann's Regiment which records has only one card that indicates name

appears on a Return of Captain Peel's and Captain Bond's Detachment, Mann's Regiment, Texas Cavalry at Headquarters of Bankhead's Brigade dated June 21, 1864; per sketch in *More Generals in Gray* born August 28, 1823 at Fort Moultrie near Charleston, South Carolina, served in Mexican War, served as Captain of Artillery at Columbus, Kentucky, New Madrid and Fort Pillow, promoted Major of Artillery April 1, 1862, at Battle of Shiloh Chief of Artillery of Polk's Corps, after Shiloh served in Trans-Mississippi Department, promoted to Colonel November 13, 1862, Spring 1863 commanded San Antonio, Texas Post, assigned to command the Northern Sub-District of Texas as Acting Brigadier General on May 30, 1863, after assignment rank reverted to Colonel which rank was not confirmed until January 14, 1865 to rank from June 15, 1864; not listed in Elmwood 1874 book as Confederate soldier buried in Elmwood who was a citizen of Memphis or vicinity but sketch; called Acting Brigadier General in Official Record and General in Lindsley's Annals; murdered on Main Street March 30, 1867; died age 43 from effects of a blow on head per Cemetery record; grave stone: born Fort Moultrie, South Carolina August 28, 1823 and died March 31, 1867; listed under Generals in "Touring historic Elmwood Cemetery" (Brochure and Map of Historic Gravesites) #3; listed in "Touring Historic Elmwood Cemetery" Brochure (January 2000) #71; sketch #24 in Elmwood *Civil War Tour* booklet (2012).

Bradley, Thomas H.   Buried October 3, 1864   Chapel Hill 305, #1
Brigadier General Arkansas State Forces - per sketch in *More Generals in Gray* was named brigadier general of Arkansas state forces by the secession convention, Arkansas Military Board relieved him of duty in July 1861,took no further part in the War, and relocated to Memphis where died on September 30, 1864; not listed in the *Memorandum relative to the General Officers Appointed by the President in the Armies of the Confederate States - 1861-1865*; not listed in *Generals in Gray*; not found Confederate index books and no records found in General and Staff records; not listed in Elmwood 1874 book as Confederate soldier buried in Elmwood who was a citizen of Memphis or vicinity but sketch that indicates born Williamson County, Tennessee July 25, 1808, in 1842 became a citizen of Crittenden County, Arkansas, made a Brigadier General of the Confederacy but age and physical infirmities prevented very active service, and died September 1864; died age 62 per Daily Burial Record Book; sketch, photograph, if available, and grave stone photograph in book *Quiet Places: The Burial Sites of Civil War Generals in Tennessee* by Buckner and Nathaniel C. Hughes, Jr., East Tennessee Historical Society (1992); not listed in "Touring Historic Elmwood Cemetery" Brochure (January 2000) but listed as General in its predecessor "Brochure and Map of Historic Gravesites" #3B; sketch #26 in Elmwood *Civil War Tour* booklet (2012).

Carnes, James Alexander   Buried March 28, 1867   Chapel Hill 13, #1
Brigadier General Tennessee State Militia - listed as General in "Touring Historic Elmwood Cemetery" Brochure and per sketch in appendix in *More Generals in Gray* was Brigadier General of Tennessee Militia and his brigade was ordered into service to protect the City of Memphis in 1862 (see February 22, 1862 *Memphis Avalanche*); not listed in the *Memorandum relative to the General Officers Appointed by the President in the Armies of the Confederate States - 1861-1865*; not listed in *Generals in Gray*; no compiled service record found; not listed in Elmwood 1874 book as Confederate soldier buried in Elmwood who was a citizen of Memphis or vicinity but sketch that indicates made Major general of the State Militia in the first year of the late war, died during the war in Georgia (sic - see grave stone note), about age 50, and remains were transferred to Elmwood; died age 47 per Daily Burial Record Book; placed in personal vault Chapel Hill Lot 535 and moved September 17, 1867; father of William W. Carnes, Tennessee Carnes' Artillery; grave stone: Born Humphreys County, Tennessee March 9, 1818 and Died in Columbia, South Carolina May 14, 1864; listed in "Touring Historic Elmwood Cemetery" Brochure (January 2000) #53 but not listed as General in its predecessor "Brochure and Map of Historic Gravesites"; sketch #14 in Elmwood *Civil War Tour* booklet (2012).

Carroll, William Henry, Sr.   Buried September 7, 1869   Lenow Circle 57, #1
Brigadier General - appointed from Tennessee October 26, 1861 (rank October 26, 1861) and resigned February 1, 1863, per *Memorandum relative to the General Officers Appointed by the President in the Armies of the Confederate States - 1861-1865*; originally Brigadier General Provisional Army of Tennessee and entered Confederate service as Colonel Tennessee 37 Infantry Regiment; no compiled service record found but listed on first organization card in Tennessee 37 Infantry Regiment compiled service record rolls; per Elmwood "Brochure and Map of Historic Gravesites" #4 son of governor, brother of mayor, postmaster before War and went to Canada after War where died; per sketch in *Generals in Gray* born in Nashville probably 1810 (sic see below), son of Tennessee Governor William Carroll, operated plantation in Panola County, Mississippi, moved to Memphis 1848 where was postmaster, entered Confederate service as Colonel Tennessee 37 Infantry Regiment, promoted to Brigadier General October 26, 1861, arrested on order of General Bragg, after Court of Inquiry resigned commission February 1, 1863, and went to Canada where family had migrated after occupation of Memphis by Federals, died in Montreal May 3, 1868, and remains moved to Elmwood the following years with headstone inaccurate as to years of his birth and death (1813-1866); per Bruce Allardice's article "In Search of ... General William Henry Carroll" in *West Tennessee Historical Society Papers,* XLVIII (1994), pages 60-72, he was actually born 1816 or 1817 based on ages listed in 1850 and 1860 U.S. Census returns for Shelby County, Tennessee; listed (Carroll, Gen. Wm. H.) in Elmwood 1874 book as Confederate soldier buried in Elmwood who was a citizen of Memphis or vicinity and sketch; per Lindsley's Annals, page 596, was Colonel and incorporator of Tennessee 154 Tennessee Infantry (Senior) when incorporated by Act of the Legislature March 22, 1860; biography in *Confederate Military History, Extended Edition*, Volume X Tennessee, page 300; removed from Canada per Daily Burial Record Book; originally buried Chapel Hill 215, Grave #3; see Carroll file in the Elmwood Cemetery Office; sketch, photograph, if available, and grave stone photograph in book *Quiet Places: The Burial Sites of Civil War Generals in Tennessee* by Buckner and Nathaniel C. Hughes, Jr., East Tennessee Historical Society (1992); listed under Generals in "Touring historic Elmwood Cemetery" (Brochure and Map of Historic Gravesites) #4; listed in "Touring Historic Elmwood Cemetery" Brochure (January 2000) #41; sketch #29 in Elmwood *Civil War Tour* booklet (2012).

Chalmers, James Ronald Buried April 10, 1898 Evergreen 448, #1
Brigadier General - appointed from Mississippi February 13, 1862 (rank February 13, 1862) per *Memorandum relative to the General Officers Appointed by the President in the Armies of the Confederate States - 1861-1865*; first served in Mississippi 9 Infantry Regiment as Captain Old Company K and Colonel; enlisted February 17, 1861, Hernando, Mississippi age 30; elected Colonel April 11, 1861; assigned to command of brigade April 15, 1861; relieved of brigade command September 9, 1861 and resumed command of Regiment; prominent in Forrest command; grave stone: born Halifax County, Virginia January 11, 1831 and died April 9, 1898, Memphis; per sketch in Mathes book born Halifax County, Virginia January 11, 1831, March 1861, elected Colonel Mississippi 9 Infantry Regiment, February 12, 1862, made Brigadier General, ordered to North Mississippi in 1863 to command cavalry until Forrest arrived and then commanded First Division of Forrest's Cavalry which he held until end of War; per General and Staff record surrendered at Gainesville, Alabama May 10, 1865; elected to four terms of Congress (1876, 1878, 1880 and 1882); resident of Mississippi and had law office in Memphis; sketch in *Generals in Gray*; died age 67 per Daily Burial Record Book; biography in *Confederate Military History, Extended Edition*, Volume IX Mississippi, page 244; sketch in the PoliticalGraveyard.com; sketch, photograph, if available, and grave stone photograph in book *Quiet Places: The Burial Sites of Civil War Generals in Tennessee* by Buckner and Nathaniel C. Hughes, Jr., East Tennessee Historical Society (1992); listed under Generals in "Touring historic Elmwood Cemetery" (Brochure and Map of Historic Gravesites) #5; listed in "Touring Historic Elmwood Cemetery" Brochure (January 2000) #127; sketch #34 in Elmwood *Civil War Tour* booklet (2012).

Fiser, John Calvin Buried June 15, 1876 Chapel Hill Circle 37, #1
Colonel Mississippi 17 Infantry Regiment; per sketch in *More Generals in Gray* listed as Brigadier General in several publications, including *Confederate Veteran*, and per obituary (*Memphis Daily Appeal* June 15, 1876) commission as Brigadier General was issued in the last days of the War but never reached him; not listed in the *Memorandum relative to the General Officers Appointed by the President in the Armies of the Confederate States - 1861-1865*; not listed in *Generals in Gray*; per Mississippi 17 Infantry Regiment records enlisted May 27, 1861, Corinth age 23 as Lieutenant Company H; elected Adjutant June 7, 1861; promoted to Lieutenant Colonel April 26, 1862; wounded at Battle of Gettysburg; promoted to Colonel February 26, 1864; per May/June 1864, muster roll remarks retired and assigned to duty as Adjutant General Department Southern Georgia June 12, 1864; lost right arm at Knoxville and retired; June 16, 1864, assigned Savannah, Georgia Invalid Duty; per sketch in *More Generals in Gray* born May 4, 1838, in Dyersburg, Tennessee, at start of War commissioned Lieutenant Mississippi 17 Infantry Regiment and Adjutant June 4, 1861, elected Lieutenant Colonel April 26, 1862, wounded three times at Battle of Gettysburg, arm amputated from wound received at assault on Fort Sanders outside of Knoxville, Tennessee November 23, 1863, promoted to Colonel on February 26, 1864, but having not recovered from loss of arm resigned June 12, 1864, and winter of 1864 transferred to South Carolina and assigned to command a brigade of Georgia reservists; per sketch in Mathes book elected to Confederate Historical Association April 28, 1870, succeeded former Governor Isham G. Harris as President in 1871 and died June 15, 1876; died age 38 from flux per Daily Burial Record Book; grave monument: born Dyersburg, Tennessee May 4, 1838 and died June 14, 1876; listed in "Touring Historic Elmwood Cemetery" Brochure (January 2000) #57 but not listed as General in its predecessor "Touring historic Elmwood Cemetery" (Brochure and Map of Historic Gravesites); sketch #18 in Elmwood *Civil War Tour* booklet (2012)).

Forrest, Jeffery E. Buried March 27, 1868 Chapel Hill Circle 47, #4
Colonel Alabama Cavalry Forrest's Regiment; per sketch in *More Generals in Gray* some sources indicate commissioned Brigadier General but appears died a Colonel; not listed in the *Memorandum relative to the General Officers Appointed by the President in the Armies of the Confederate States - 1861-1865*; not listed in *Generals in Gray*; originally enlisted in J. S. White's Company E ("The Tennessee Mounted Rifles") Tennessee 6 (Logwood's) Cavalry Battalion, resigned and joined Tennessee Forrest's Cavalry Battalion that became Tennessee 3 Cavalry Regiment; per Tennessee 3 Cavalry Regiment record enlisted September 1, 1861 in Memphis at age 23, per March 1 to June 30, 1862 muster roll remarks removed by reorganization of Company according to Act of Congress January 17, 1862, per September and October 1862 muster roll remarks elected Captain March 11, 1862 of Company C and discharged June 17, 1862; per Alabama Forrest's Cavalry compiled service record J. E. Forrest, Colonel Commanding, 4 Brigade appears on a list of casualties in Forrest's Cavalry in the engagement (Meridian, Mississippi Expedition) February 20 to 24, 1864 dated at Columbus March 9, 1864 with remarks killed February 22, 1864; killed at Battle of Okolona, Mississippi February 22, 1864; per sketch in *More Generals in Gray* born June 10, 1838 Tippah County, Mississippi, after leaving Tennessee 3 Cavalry Regiment commissioned Major then Lieutenant Colonel Tennessee 8 Cavalry Regiment, in 1864 joined General Forrest in northern Mississippi and put in charge of a Brigade; no records in General and Staff records; listed (Forrest, Maj. Jeffery) in Elmwood 1874 book as Confederate soldier buried in Elmwood who was a citizen of Memphis or vicinity; biography in *Confederate Military History, Extended Edition*, Volume X Tennessee, page 475; grave stone: Colonel Alabama Cavalry C.S.A. 1837 1863; Confederate index book: J. E. Forrest Alabama Cavalry Forrest's Regiment Colonel, J. E. Forrest Tennessee 10 (De Moss') Cavalry Regiment Colonel (reference slip only), J. E. Forrest Tennessee 13 (Gore's) Cavalry Colonel (reference slip only) and Jeff E. Forrest Tennessee 3 (Forrest's Old) Cavalry Captain Company C; brother of Lieutenant General Nathan Bedford Forrest; mentioned in General W. B. Bates' speech printed in the article "Elmwood" (Grand and Imposing Ceremonies of Commemoration Day), in *Memphis Sunday Appeal*, May 8, 1870, page 4, column 2; listed in "Touring Historic Elmwood Cemetery" Brochure (January 2000) #62 but not listed as General in its predecessor "Touring historic Elmwood Cemetery" (Brochure and Map of Historic Gravesites); included in Forrest Family lot sketch #17 in Elmwood *Civil War Tour* booklet (2012).

Forrest, Nathan Bedford   Buried October 31, 1877 (Moved)   Chapel Hill Circle 47, #9

Lieutenant General - appointed from Tennessee as Brigadier General July 21, 1862, (rank July 21, 1862), promoted to Major General December 4, 1863 (rank December 4, 1963) and promoted Lieutenant General March 2, 1865, (rank February 28, 1865) per the *Memorandum relative to the General Officers Appointed by the President in the Armies of the Confederate States - 1861-1865*; originally enlisted June 14, 1861, as a private in Captain (Dr.) Josiah S. White's Company ("The Tennessee Mounted Rifles") Cavalry which became Company E Tennessee 6 (Logwood's) Cavalry Battalion which disbanded May 1862, prior to formation of Tennessee 7 Cavalry Regiment in which regiment records this Company is often identified as Company D; about July 10, 1861, Tennessee Governor Harris asked him to raise a cavalry regiment; October 1861, organized a cavalry battalion and was elected Lieutenant Colonel; March 1862, battalion increased to regiment strength to became Tennessee 3 Cavalry Regiment (also known as Forrest's Old Cavalry Regiment and McDonald's Cavalry Battalion) and elected Colonel; born July 13, 1821, at Chapel Hill, Bedford (now Marshall) County, Tennessee; died October 29, 1877. in Memphis; died from chronic diarrhea at age 56 per Daily Burial Record Book; body moved to Forrest Park in Memphis, Tennessee along with body of wife, Mary A. Forrest, on November 11, 1904; sketch in Mathes book and *Generals in Gray*; biography in *Confederate Military History, Extended Edition*, Volume I, page 699; sketch, photograph, if available, and grave stone photograph in book *Quiet Places: The Burial Sites of Civil War Generals in Tennessee* by Buckner and Nathaniel C. Hughes, Jr., East Tennessee Historical Society (1992). Forrest Avenue, south of North Parkway or Summer Avenue, runs east from Ayers Street and, in several sections, extends beyond North Graham, is named after him (see Ann Meeks' article July 23, 2000, *The Commercial Appeal* Memphis, Section GC, Neighbors, page 2, column 4); not listed in "Touring Historic Elmwood Cemetery" Brochure (January 2000) but listed as under Generals in predecessor "Touring historic Elmwood Cemetery" (Brochure and Map of Historic Gravesites) #6; included in Forrest Family lot sketch #17 in Elmwood *Civil War Tour* booklet (2012).

Gardner, William Montgomery   Buried June 17, 1901   Evergreen 189, #2

Brigadier General - appointed from Georgia November 14, 1861 (rank November 14, 1861) per *Memorandum relative to the General Officers Appointed by the President in the Armies of the Confederate States - 1861-1865*; also per remarks in said Memorandum included in the Sherman-Johnston convention of April 26, 1865, but no record of his personal parole found; per Georgia 8 Infantry Regiment records appointed Lieutenant Colonel June 8, 1861, wounded July 21, 1861, at Battle of Manassas, promoted to Colonel July 21, 1861 and promoted to Brigadier General January 28, 1861; per General and Staff records appointed from Georgia as Major of Infantry April 13, 1861, detailed as Assistant Adjutant General May 14, 1861, District of Savannah, May 30, 1861, relieved of duty, June 8, 1861, appointed Lieutenant Colonel Georgia 8 Infantry Regiment, promoted to Colonel then Brigadier General November 14, 1861, and paroled at Augusta, Georgia May 20, 1865; born in Georgia June 8, 1824, graduate of West Point (1846) and spent last years at home of his son in Memphis; per sketch in *Generals in Gray* Lieutenant Colonel Georgia 8 Infantry Regiment and appointed Brigadier General November 14, 1861; name spelled "Gardiner" in Daily Burial Record Book and Computer Index; biography in *Confederate Military History, Extended Edition*, Volume VII Georgia, page 417; died 77 years and 9 months per Daily Burial Record Book; sketch, photograph, if available, and grave stone photograph in book *Quiet Places: The Burial Sites of Civil War Generals in Tennessee* by Buckner and Nathaniel C. Hughes, Jr., East Tennessee Historical Society (1992); grave stone: born Augusta, Georgia June 8, 1824 and died June 16, 1901; listed under Generals in "Touring historic Elmwood Cemetery" (Brochure and Map of Historic Gravesites) #7; listed in "Touring Historic Elmwood Cemetery" Brochure (January 2000) #131; sketch #35 in Elmwood *Civil War Tour* booklet (2012).

Gordon, George Washington   Buried August 12, 1911   Fowler 180, #4

Brigadier General - appointed from Tennessee August 16, 1864, (rank August 15, 1864) per the *Memorandum relative to the General Officers Appointed by the President in the Armies of the Confederate States, 1861-1865*; originally enlisted as Captain Company I Tennessee 11 Infantry Regiment July 31, 1861, elected Lieutenant Colonel May 27, 1862, and promoted to Colonel November 7, 1862; captured in Kentucky August 1862, and exchanged August 15, 1862; wounded in thigh and captured at Battle of Murfreesboro December 31, 1862, and exchanged April 29, 1863, at age 26; captured in action at Franklin, Tennessee November 30, 1864, and released from Fort Warren, Massachusetts July 24, 1865; per General and Staff records appointed August 16, 1864, captured Franklin, Tennessee November 30, 1864, sent to Johnson's Island December 3, 1864, sent to Fort Warren, Massachusetts December 14, 1864, and released July 24, 1865; born October 5, 1836; became a lawyer after the War and later Superintendent of Memphis Schools, then a Member of Congress; per sketch in Mathes book born Giles County, Tennessee and raised in Mississippi and Texas; per sketch in *Generals in Gray* was Commander-in-Chief of the United Confederate Veterans when died August 9, 1911; died age 74 per Daily Burial Record Book; sketch in the PoliticalGraveyard.com; sketch, photograph, if available, and grave stone photograph in book *Quiet Places: The Burial Sites of Civil War Generals in Tennessee* by Buckner and Nathaniel C. Hughes, Jr., East Tennessee Historical Society (1992); born October 5, 1836, and died August 9, 1911, inscribed on "In Memory Of" stone located in walk around Confederate Soldiers Rest Monument; listed under Generals in "Touring historic Elmwood Cemetery" (Brochure and Map of Historic Gravesites) #8; listed in "Touring Historic Elmwood Cemetery" Brochure (January 2000) #10; sketch #3 in Elmwood *Civil War Tour* booklet (2012).

Greene, Colton   Buried October 3, 1900   Fowler 193, #1

Colonel Missouri 3 Cavalry Regiment; per sketch in *More Generals in Gray* listed as general in several publications, often commanded a brigade but the Official Record shows him as Colonel as late as December 31, 1864, and petitions for his promotion to general in 1865 were signed by practically all the officers in the Trans- Mississippi army but the Official Record shows no indication of any promotion by either President Davis or General Kirby Smith; not listed in the *Memorandum Relative to the*

General Officers appointed by the President in the Armies of the Confederate States - 1861-1865; not listed in *Generals in Gray*; per undated muster roll in Missouri 3 Cavalry Regiment compiled service records age 30, appointed November 4, 1862 by the President of C.S.A., born South Carolina and lives in Missouri; per sketch in *More Generals in Gray* full name appears to be "George Colton Greene"; listed in Mathes book as a member of Confederate Historical Association but no sketch; organized State Savings Bank, Memphis, and the Tennessee Club; General Colton Greene and died age 64 per Daily Burial Record Book; biography in *Confederate Military History, Extended Edition*, Volume XII Missouri, page 302; see "OUR MOST NOBLE STRANGER": THE MYSTERY, GALLANTRY AND CIVICISM OF COLTON GREENE by Charles Steven Palmer, Master Thesis, University of Oklahoma, 1995, and the Colton Greene collection in the Memphis Room of the Memphis/Shelby County Public Library and Information Center; grave stone: General Colton Greene, 1832-1900, , per Bruce Allardice research birth was July 7, 1833, as found on an old passport; First President The Tennessee Club 1875. listed under Generals in "Touring historic Elmwood Cemetery" (Brochure and Map of Historic Gravesites) #10; listed in "Touring Historic Elmwood Cemetery" Brochure (January 2000) #11; sketch #2 in Elmwood *Civil War Tour* booklet (2012).

Greer, Elkanah Brackin   Buried March 28, 1877   Turley 93, #13
Brigadier General - appointed from Texas October 8, 1862, (rank October 8, 1862) per the *Memorandum relative to the General Officers Appointed by the President in the Armies of the Confederate States - 1861-1865*; also per remarks in said Memorandum included in the Canby-Smith convention of May 26, 1865, but no record of his personal parole found; originally Colonel Texas 3 Cavalry Regiment; no individuals records found Texas 3 Cavalry Regiment records but listed on organization cards as Colonel; per General and Staff records Chief of Bureau of Conscription, Trans Mississippi Department, Provisional Army, Marshall, Texas September 1864 and signed Parole of Honor 24 June 1865, at Marshall, Texas; born October 11, 1825, in Paris, Tennessee, with Jefferson Davis in Mexican War, died at DeValls Bluff, Arkansas March 25, 1877 while visiting sister; sketch in *Generals in Gray*; died Phthisis Pulmonary age 52 per Daily Burial Record Book; grave stone: Brigadier General Texas Confederate States Army October 11, 1825 March 25, 1877; biography in *Confederate Military History, Extended Edition*, Volume XV Texas, page 233; sketch, photograph, if available, and grave stone photograph in book *Quiet Places: The Burial Sites of Civil War Generals in Tennessee* by Buckner and Nathaniel C. Hughes, Jr., East Tennessee Historical Society (1992); listed under Generals in "Touring historic Elmwood Cemetery" (Brochure and Map of Historic Gravesites) #9; listed in "Touring Historic Elmwood Cemetery" Brochure (January 2000) #28; sketch #32 in Elmwood *Civil War Tour* booklet (2012).

Humes, William Young Conn   Buried September 13, 1882   Chapel Hill 299, #8
Brigadier General - appointed from Tennessee November 17, 1863, (rank November 16, 1863) per the *Memorandum relative to the General Officers Appointed by the President in the Armies of the Confederate States - 1861-1865*; also per remarks in the *Memorandum* included in the Sherman-Johnston convention of April 26, 1865, but no record of his personal parole found; originally enlisted as 1 Lieutenant Tennessee Scott's (Bankhead's) Light Artillery May 13, 1861 at age 30 at Memphis; record also found Tennessee Winston's Light artillery as Captain with records indicating enlisted April 17, 1861, at Memphis and up to November 23, 1861, served as 1 Lieutenant Bankhead's Battery and was then transferred as Captain to this Company by order of Lieutenant General Polk; captured Island 10 on April 7, 1862, sent to Johnson's Island April 26, 1862, and then to Vicksburg September 1, 1862, for exchange; detailed on special service and sent to Mobile, Alabama October 16, 1862; promoted to Major of Artillery May 15, 1863; per sketch in Mathes book born Abington, Virginia, chosen 1 Lieutenant Bankhead's Battery April 1861, promoted to Captain and placed in command of Heavy Artillery at Island 10 where captured, confined to Johnson's Island and exchanged summer 1862, then commanded Heavy Artillery at Mobile, Alabama but later served as cavalry leader under General Wheeler and rose to Major General; graduate from Virginia Military Institute (VMI) Class of 1851 (classmate of General Alfred J. Vaughan, see sketch herein); per sketch in VMI library archives file parents John Newton Humes and Jane Conn White, enrolled at VMI on November 20, 1848 and graduated second in a class of 29 on July 4, 1851, 1861-Captain Artillery, commanded guns at New Madrid, captured at Island 10 and imprisoned at Johnson's Island, after exchange became cavalry officer, appointed Brigadier General November 1863, and led brigade in Wheeler's Corps fought in Tennessee, Georgia the Carolinas, wounded in action at Monroe's Crossroads, North Carolina March 10, 1865, recommended for promotion to Major General early 1865 (maybe late 1864) and promotion known to have been under consideration in War Department January 1865, with unofficial sources indicating promoted March 1865, but if so word did not reach him as on June 6, 1865, referred to himself as a former Brigadier General and died at Huntsville, Alabama September 11, 1882, (note difference with grave stone); joined Confederate Historical Association July 15, 1869; sketch in *Generals in Gray*; biography in *Confederate Military History, Extended Edition*, Volume X Tennessee, page 313; sketch in *Tennessee, The Volunteer State, 1769-1923*, Volume II, page 151; sketch, photograph, if available, and grave stone photograph in book *Quiet Places: The Burial Sites of Civil War Generals in Tennessee* by Buckner and Nathaniel C. Hughes, Jr., East Tennessee Historical Society (1992); grave stone: May 1, 1830 September 12, 1883; listed under Generals in "Touring historic Elmwood Cemetery" (Brochure and Map of Historic Gravesites) #11; listed in "Touring Historic Elmwood Cemetery" Brochure (January 2000) #65; sketch #21 in Elmwood *Civil War Tour* booklet (2012).

Martin, John Donelson   Buried November 19, 1874   Fowler 274, #6
Colonel Confederate 2 Infantry Regiment; per sketch in *More Generals in Gray* appointed Brigadier General from Mississippi in 1865 according to *Confederate Veteran*, which was three years after his death, when Major General Hardee promoted him to Acting Brigadier General on April 29, 1862, as indicated in a Telegram in possession of family, however, Major General Price in an October 20, 1862 report on the Battle of Corinth made it clear that he died a colonel; not listed in the *Memorandum relative to the General Officers Appointed by the President in the Armies of the Confederate States - 1861-1865*; not listed in *Generals in Gray*;

first enlisted as Captain Company E ("The Hickory Rifles") Tennessee 154 Senior Infantry Regiment and elected Major May 1861; per 154 Senior Infantry Regiment record May 5, 1863 muster roll remarks: first Captain, then Major 154 Senior Infantry Regiment, Colonel and Brigadier General and killed at Battle of Corinth; recommended for Brigadier General for conduct at Battle of Shiloh and given an appointment as Acting Brigadier General but never commissioned; authorized to raise a regiment which became Mississippi 25 Infantry Regiment and appointed Colonel November 16, 1861; Regiment designated Confederate 2 Infantry Regiment January 31, 1862; Regiment disbanded May 8, 1862; next placed in command of the 4 Brigade, 1 Division, Army of the West; killed on the first day of Battle of Corinth October 3, 1862; no records found General and Staff records and not the John D. Martin in General and Staff records who was an Acting Assistant Surgeon; per sketch in *More Generals in Gray* born Davidson County, Tennessee August 18, 1830, served in Mexican War, earned medical degree in 1852 from University of Pennsylvania and became prominent physician in Memphis; obituary in the November 4, 1862, *Memphis Daily Appeal,* page 2, column 6; originally buried in Mississippi; doctor, moved-in from Mississippi and died age 32 per Cemetery record; large grave stone: JOHN DONELSON MARTIN, BORN AUGUST 18, 1830, DAVIDSON COUNTY, TENN. CONF BRIG GEN, KILLED LEADING CHARGE AT BATTLE OF CORINTH, MS OCTOBER 3, 1862. GREAT-GRAND-SON OF COL JOHN DONELSON PIONEER LEADER RIVER EXPEDITION FROM VA TO TN 1779. SERVED IN US ARMY IN WAR WITH MEXICO. 1852 M.D. UNIV PA, CAME TO MEMPHIS AND PRACTICED MEDICINE. SURGEON, MEMPHIS HOSPITAL; PROFESSOR, MEMPHIS MEDICAL COLLEGE. PRESIDENT, MEMPHIS BOARD OF HEALTH, 1858. 1857, MARRIED ROSA A WHITE, DAUGHTER OF COL C C WHITE. 1860 CAPTAIN, HICKORY RIFLES IN FIRST MEMPHIS REGT, CSA., COL 2 CONF REGT. WHILE STILL COL COMMANDED BRIGADES ON NUMEROUS OCCASIONS. COMMANDED BOWEN'S BRIGADE, BATTLE OF SHILOH, AND FOURTH BRIGADE AT IUKA AND CORINTH; not listed in Elmwood 1874 book as Confederate soldier buried in Elmwood who was a citizen of Memphis or vicinity; listed in "Touring Historic Elmwood Cemetery" Brochure (January 2000) #7 but not listed as General in its predecessor "Touring historic Elmwood Cemetery" (Brochure and Map of Historic Gravesites); sketch #1 in Elmwood *Civil War Tour* booklet (2012).

Pillow, Gideon Johnson   Buried February 14, 1884   Evergreen 217, #1
Brigadier General - appointed from Tennessee July 9, 1861, (rank July 9, 1861) per the *Memorandum relative to the General Officers Appointed by the President in the Armies of the Confederate States - 1861-1865*; best remembered for confrontation with Union General Grant at Fort Donelson in February 1862; per General and Staff records surrendered May 5, 1865, at Montgomery, Alabama; per sketch in Mathes book born 1806 in Williamson County, Tennessee, served in Mexican War as Brigadier General and promoted to Major General, Governor Harris appointed him to command state troops with rank of Major General, when Tennessee seceded commissioned Brigadier General, after surrender at Fort Donelson not given a command in field again, joined Confederate Historical Association July 15, 1869; died October 8, 1878, near Helena, Arkansas; sketch in *Generals in Gray*; biography in *Confederate Military History, Extended Edition*, Volume X Tennessee, page 325; sketch in *Tennessee, The Volunteer State, 1769-1923*, Volume II, page 209; see also collection in Memphis Room in Memphis and Shelby County Public Library; sketch, photograph, if available, and grave stone photograph in book *Quiet Places: The Burial Sites of Civil War Generals in Tennessee* by Buckner and Nathaniel C. Hughes, Jr., East Tennessee Historical Society (1992); large monument that recites military career; born Columbia, Tennessee June 8, 1806, on monument; listed in "Touring Historic Elmwood Cemetery" Brochure (January 2000) # 12; listed in "Touring Historic Elmwood Cemetery" Brochure (January 2000) #13; sketch #36 in Elmwood *Civil War Tour* booklet (2012).

Richardson, Robert Vinkler   Buried January 10, 1870   Chapel Hill 228, #5
Brigadier General - appointed from Tennessee December 3, 1863, (rank December 1, 1863) per the *Memorandum relative to the General Officers Appointed by the President in the Armies of the Confederate States - 1861-1865*, however, remarks in said Memorandum indicate that the nomination returned by the Senate to the President February 9, 1864; nomination was withdrawn by President Jefferson; originally enlisted as Colonel Tennessee 12 Richardson's-Green's Cavalry Regiment; no information in Tennessee 12 Cavalry Regiment compiled service record rolls other than rank of Colonel and remark that promoted to Brigadier General December 1, 1863; in General and Staff records name appears on a list of Prisoners of War indicating Colonel Provisional Army and paroled Grenada, Mississippi May 8, 1865; born November 4, 1820; a lawyer and levee contractor who took part in obscure border warfare of Tennessee, Missouri and Arkansas; per sketch in *Generals in Gray* born November 4, 1820, Granville County, North Carolina, and while on railroad project trip stopped to spend night on January 5, 1870 at a tavern in the Village of Clarkton, Dunklin County, Missouri where was mortally wounded by an unknown assailant and died next morning; listed (Richardson, Gen. R. V.) in Elmwood 1874 book as Confederate soldier buried in Elmwood who was a citizen of Memphis or vicinity and sketch that indicates came to Memphis 1845; shot, wound, and age 49 per Daily Burial Record Book; death ("assignation") reported under Local Paragraphs in the January 10, 1870, *Memphis Daily Appeal*, page 4, column 5; biography in *Confederate Military History, Extended Edition*, Volume X Tennessee, page 686; sketch, photograph, if available, and grave stone photograph in book *Quiet Places: The Burial Sites of Civil War Generals in Tennessee* by Buckner and Nathaniel C. Hughes, Jr., East Tennessee Historical Society (1992); grave stone: November 4, 1820 January 6, 1870; listed under Generals in "Touring historic Elmwood Cemetery" (Brochure and Map of Historic Gravesites) #13; listed in "Touring Historic Elmwood Cemetery" Brochure (January 2000) #73; sketch #22 in Elmwood *Civil War Tour* booklet (2012).

Smith, Preston   Buried May 2, 1868   Chapel Hill 146, #3
Brigadier General - appointed from Tennessee October 27, 1862, (rank October 27, 1862) per the *Memorandum relative to the General Officers Appointed by the President in the Armies of the Confederate States - 1861-1865*; originally enlisted as Colonel

Tennessee 154 Senior Infantry Regiment May 6, 1861, age 37 at Fort Wright, Randolph, Tennessee; wounded at Battle of Shiloh; ordered to report to Major General Polk by General Bragg May 14, 1862, as Acting Brigadier General; killed at Battle of Chickamauga September 19, 1863, (September 20, 1863 per General and Staff records) and originally buried in Atlanta and removed to Elmwood in 1868; killed in battle age 40 per Daily Burial Record Book; listed (Smith, Gen. Preston) in Elmwood 1874 book as Confederate soldier buried in Elmwood who was a citizen of Memphis or vicinity and sketch; per sketch in *Generals in Gray* born Giles County, Tennessee December 25, 1823; mentioned by Dr. S. H. Ford in his address on the occasion to commemorate (Confederate Memorial Day) Confederates buried at Elmwood on April 26, 1866, (see articles "The Confederate Dead" in the *Public Ledger* (Memphis), April 27, 1866, page 3, column 2, and "Honors To The Memory Of The Hero Dead" in the April 27, 1866, *Memphis Daily Appeal*, page 3, column 1); reburial celebrated during the Commemoration Day (Confederate Memorial Day) ceremony at Elmwood Cemetery on Saturday May 2, 1868, see article "Our Soldier Dead."..."The Last Tribute of Love and Honor to General Preston Smith and Colonel Jeffrey Forrest" in the *Public Ledger* (Memphis), Saturday Evening, May 2, 1868, pages 2 and 3; see also article "Elmwood – Memorial Day Celebration at Elmwood — Funeral of General Preston Smith and Colonel Forrest" in the May 3, 1868, *Daily Memphis Avalanche*, page 1; biography in *Confederate Military History, Extended Edition*, Volume X Tennessee, page 331; sketch in *Tennessee, The Volunteer State, 1769-1923*, Volume II, page 230; sketch, photograph, if available, and grave stone photograph in book *Quiet Places: The Burial Sites of Civil War Generals in Tennessee* by Buckner and Nathaniel C. Hughes, Jr., East Tennessee Historical Society (1992); grave stone: December 25, 1823 September 20, 1864; listed under Generals in "Touring historic Elmwood Cemetery" (Brochure and Map of Historic Gravesites) #14; listed in "Touring Historic Elmwood Cemetery" Brochure (January 2000) #67; sketch #19 in Elmwood *Civil War Tour* booklet (2012).

Sneed, John Louis Taylor   Buried July 30,1901   Turley 1398, #1
Brigadier General Provisional Army of Tennessee; per sketch in *More Generals in Gray* May 9, 1861 appointed Brigadier General of Tennessee state forces by Governor Harris, not appointed to Confederate service when state forces were transferred, in 1862 attempted to raise a regiment of infantry but Federal advance ended those plans, Governor Harris later appointed him to settle accounts between the Tennessee provisional army and the Confederacy, and *Southern Historical Society Papers* and *Confederate Veteran* list him as a Confederate General; not listed in the *Memorandum relative to the General Officers Appointed by the President in the Armies of the Confederate States - 1861-1865*; not listed in *Generals in Gray*; no records in General and Staff records; per sketch in *More Generals in Gray* born May 12, 1820 Raleigh, North Carolina, during Mexican war was sergeant major, then captain of Company G Regiment of Tennessee Mounted Volunteers, and died July 29, 1901; records (mostly letters) found in Tennessee miscellaneous compiled service records rolls; sketch in Mathes book; died age 81 per Daily Burial Record Book; sketch, photograph, if available, and grave stone photograph in book *Quiet Places: The Burial Sites of Civil War Generals in Tennessee* by Buckner and Nathaniel C. Hughes, Jr., East Tennessee Historical Society (1992); grave stone: "John L T Sneed born Raleigh North Carolina May 12, 1822 and died July 29, 1901 - Mary Ashe Shepperd wife of John L T Sneed born November 26, 1829 and died February 6, 1919."; listed under Generals in "Touring historic Elmwood Cemetery" (Brochure and Map of Historic Gravesites) #15B; listed in "Touring Historic Elmwood Cemetery" Brochure (January 2000) #32; sketch #33 in Elmwood *Civil War Tour* booklet (2012).

Taylor, James H. R.   Buried October 31, 1867   Chapel Hill 24, #12
Lieutenant Colonel Tennessee 15 Infantry Regiment - listed as General (Taylor, Gen. James H. R.) in Elmwood 1874 book as Confederate soldier buried in Elmwood who was a citizen of Memphis or vicinity; not listed in Cemetery tour brochures; not listed in the *Memorandum relative to the General Officers Appointed by the President in the Armies of the Confederate States - 1861-1865*; no sketch in *Generals in Gray* or *More Generals in Gray*; article in November 1, 1867 *Memphis Daily Appeal* Local Matters: "Death of General Taylor - General James H. R. Taylor of Holly Springs, Mississippi, died at the residence of his father, Dr. W. V. Taylor, in this City on Wednesday afternoon. He was about fifty years of age, and had filled many positions of honor and emolument in his State. His remains were interred at Elmwood yesterday with Masonic Honors."; enlisted in Tennessee 15 Infantry Regiment June 7, 1861 at Jackson, Tennessee at age 40; appears on a Register containing Rosters of Commissioned Officers, Provisional Army Confederate States, that indicates date of appointment as June 17, 1861, resigned November 26, 1861 and a remark that elected Lieutenant Colonel December 4, 1861; subject of court martial November 3, 1861 by Special Order #275; per letter in file resignation accepted by President, CSA, December 26, 1861; family monument in lot partly illegible (cannot tell if on monument); died of yellow fever at age 47 per Daily Burial Record Book; full name James Henderson Roberts Taylor; sketch #15 in Elmwood *Civil War Tour* booklet (2012).

Vaughan, Alfred Jefferson, Jr.   Buried October 3, 1899   South Grove 360, #4
Brigadier General - appointed from Tennessee November 21, 1863, (rank November 18, 1863) per the *Memorandum relative to the General Officers Appointed by the President in the Armies of the Confederate States - 1861-1865*; originally enlisted as Captain Company E Tennessee 13 Infantry Regiment May 28, 1861, age 31 at Jackson, Tennessee; elected Lieutenant Colonel June 4, 1861; promoted to Colonel December 4, 1861; had eight horses shot from under him without being injured, then leg was blown off by shell during Atlanta campaign and his desk is in Elmwood Cemetery Office; General and Staff records found mixed with records of Andrew J. Vaughn, Major of Commissary Department, which indicates wounded July 4, 1864, at Atlanta, Georgia and surrendered and took Oath of Allegiance 20 May 1865, at Gainesville, Alabama; per sketch in Mathes book born Dinwiddie County, Virginia May 10, 1830; died age 69 per Daily Burial Record Book; not "Jr." but "II" in *Vaughan's Brigade, Volume XVII (1974), Vaughan's American Histories* (copy located in Elmwood Cemetery Office); per sketch in *Generals in Gray* died in Indianapolis, Indiana October 1, 1899; see *The Commercial Appeal* Memphis October 2, 1899; graduate from Virginia Military Institute (VMI)

Class of 1851 (classmate of General William Y. C. Humes, see sketch herein); per sketch in VMI library archives file born May 10, 1830, in Dinwiddie County, Virginia, parents Alfred Jefferson Vaughan and Dorothy (nee) Vaughan, enrolled at VMI on July 17, 1848 and graduated 15th in a class of 29 on July 4, 1851, in his final year at VMI he was a cadet captain and company commander, Captain, Lieutenant Colonel and Colonel of the 13th Tennessee Infantry Regiment, in March 1863, Regiment consolidated with Tennessee Senior Infantry Regiment to form 13/154 Tennessee Infantry Regiment with him as Colonel, commissioned Brigadier General, 1863 (Army of Tennessee), led brigade at Missionary Ridge and Atlanta campaign until Vining's Station (4 July 1864), where he was severely wounded (lost leg); biography in *Confederate Military History, Extended Edition*, Volume X Tennessee, page 337; sketch and photograph in *Confederate Veteran* Volume VI, 1898, page 336; sketch in Goodspeed's Shelby County History, page 1050; sketch in *The National Cyclopedia of American Biography*, Volume 6, page 353; sketch in *Tennessee, The Volunteer State, 1769-1923*, Volume II, page 245; sketch, photograph, if available, and grave stone photograph in book *Quiet Places: The Burial Sites of Civil War Generals in Tennessee* by Buckner and Nathaniel C. Hughes, Jr., East Tennessee Historical Society (1992); listed under Generals in "Touring historic Elmwood Cemetery" (Brochure and Map of Historic Gravesites) #16; listed in "Touring Historic Elmwood Cemetery" Brochure (January 2000) #84; sketch #27 in Elmwood *Civil War Tour* booklet (2012).

Walker, Lucius Marshall   Buried February 19, 1866   Chapel Hill 257, #2
Brigadier General - appointed from Tennessee April 11, 1862, (rank March 11, 1862) per the *Memorandum relative to the General Officers Appointed by the President in the Armies of the Confederate States - 1861-1865*; originally enlisted as Colonel Tennessee 40 (Walker's) Infantry Regiment; no information other than rank of Colonel and remark that promoted to Brigadier General April 11, 1862, in Tennessee 40 Infantry Regiment compiled service record rolls; per sketch in *Generals in Gray* born October 18, 1829 Columbia, Tennessee, nephew of President James K Polk, graduated from West Point 1850 and died September 7, 1863, from wound received in a duel with General J. S. Marmaduke on September 6, 1863, at Little Rock, Arkansas (see *The Commercial Appeal* Memphis for stories on duel - April 27, 1890, and October 7, 1894); see February 21, 1866, *Memphis Daily Appeal* for story on remains being buried in Memphis; see also "Confederate Generals' Dawn Duel" by J. Carter Watts, American Civil War magazine, November 1999, pages 50-56; sketch in Elmwood Book; younger brother of Sam P. Walker and J. Knox Walker, Colonel Tennessee 2 (Walker's) Infantry Regiment; Daily Burial Record Book indicates Major General and shot; listed (Walker, Gen. Marsh) in Elmwood 1874 book as Confederate soldier buried in Elmwood who was a citizen of Memphis or vicinity and sketch; per *The Commercial Appeal* Memphis, September 15, 1915, wife, Mrs. Celestine Stockton, died; biography in *Confederate Military History, Extended Edition*, Volume X Tennessee, page 341; sketch in *Tennessee, The Volunteer State, 1769-1923*, Volume II, page 246; sketch, photograph, if available, and grave stone photograph in book *Quiet Places: The Burial Sites of Civil War Generals in Tennessee* by Buckner and Nathaniel C. Hughes, Jr., East Tennessee Historical Society (1992); grave stone: October 18, 1820 September 7, 1863; listed under Generals in "Touring historic Elmwood Cemetery" (Brochure and Map of Historic Gravesites) #17; listed in "Touring Historic Elmwood Cemetery" Brochure (January 2000) #72; sketch #25 in Elmwood *Civil War Tour* booklet (2012).

Whitfield, Francis Eugene   Buried March 22, 1885   Turley 1048, #1
Colonel Mississippi 9 Infantry Regiment - per sketch in *More Generals in Gray* the *Southern Historical Society Papers* called him General but may have been confused with Brigadier General John W. Whitfield; not listed in Cemetery tour brochures; not listed in the *Memorandum relative to the General Officers Appointed by the President in the Armies of the Confederate States - 1861-1865*; not listed in *Generals in Gray*; originally enlisted as Second Lieutenant February 20, 1861 in Corinth, Mississippi at age 21 and lawyer; appointed Adjutant by order of Colonel Chalmers April 11, 1861; when regiment enlistment expired transferred to reorganized regiment December 17, 1861, and appointed Captain Company A; wounded at Battle of Shiloh; appointed Lieutenant Colonel April 16, 1862; per January and February 1863 muster roll remarks: removed by order of General Bragg; per September and October 1863 muster roll remarks: on extra duty Provost Marshall, Polk's Corps; wounded May 14, 1864, at Resaca, Georgia; per sketch in *More Generals in Gray* born Bossier Parish, Louisiana June 22, 1839, at start of War elected Lieutenant of "Corinth Rifles" (later Company A (Company C per Rietti's Mississippi Annals) Mississippi 9 Infantry), later Major of Mississippi 9 Infantry Regiment, wounded in hip at Battle of Shiloh, 1863 Lieutenant Colonel of Regiment, while on sick leave related to the wound received at the Battle of Shiloh General Bragg appointed another officer to fill the colonel's vacancy, when he protested General Bragg had him arrested for being absent without leave which arrest was later voided by the War Department nevertheless this ended his career with the Mississippi 9 Infantry Regiment, at Battle of Chickamauga September 1863, served as Provost Marshall of Polk's Corps of Army of Tennessee, wounded at Battle of Resaca in 1864 which ended field service, after recovery took command of Post of Meridian, Mississippi, on March 18, 1885 died suddenly while on a steamboat on the St. John's River in Florida, and paroled May 10, 1865, at Meridian, Mississippi as Colonel Mississippi 9 Infantry Regiment; grave stone: born June 22, 1839 and died March 18, 1885; died heart disease at age 45 per Daily Burial Record Book; originally buried Turley 17, #4 and moved February 19, 1886.

Note 1: Charles Wesley Frazer, Major and Assistant Adjutant General and Captain Company B Confederate 5 Infantry Regiment, (also known as 9 Confederate infantry) buried July 12, 1897, in Fowler 727, #1. Sketch in appendix in *More Generals in Gray* indicates that "C. W. Frazier" was called a general in the *Southern Historical Society Papers* list of Confederate generals. Per note at the end of the article "Confederate Generals of Tennessee" in *Confederate Veteran*, Volume XVIII (1910), pages 170-172, Governor Isham G. Harris appointed "C. W. Frazier" a brigadier general in the state's provisional army in 1861 but was not appointed when Tennessee became part of the Confederate States. Charles W. Frazer enlisted in May 1861, at Memphis as Captain

Company I Tennessee 21 Infantry Regiment which consolidated with Tennessee 2 (Walker's) Infantry Regiment in July 1862, to form Confederate 5 Infantry Regiment. See his sketch supra for more information. Listed as Major in Cemetery "Touring historic Elmwood Cemetery" (Brochure and Map of Historic Gravesites) #73. Father of Virginia Frazer Boyle "Poet Laureate of the Confederacy" (see her sketch supra).

Note 2: There are two known Union generals buried at Elmwood Cemetery.

William Jay Smith is buried in the Chapel Hill Section, Lot 59, Grave #12. He was interred on December 1, 1913. He was age 90 per the Daily Burial Record Book. Inscribed on his Monument is: September 24, 1823 - November 29, 1913, Veteran Mexican War 1847, Brig-General U. S. Volunteers 1861-1865, His Wife Mary Ann Ross, September 20, 1829 - June 16, 1921. He enlisted in Union Tennessee 6 Cavalry Regiment Company G as a Private September 18, 1861, at Bethel, Tennessee; promoted to Lieutenant and Regimental Quartermaster November 11, 1862; promoted to Major February 4, 1863; promoted to Lieutenant Colonel October 16, 1863; promoted to Colonel March 13, 1865; and appointed Brevet Brigadier General July 16, 1865, for faithful and meritorious services. Note: Union brevets were largely honorary and rarely carried any authority and on March 13, 1865, the US War Department gave one brevet and sometimes two to nearly every officer on duty with the army. Per compiled service record born Orange County, New York and merchant, however, all other records and accounts has his birth in Birmingham, England. Per article in *The Memphis Educator*, January 1, 1906, pages 1-2, born Birmingham, England, came to United States when very young, learned the painter's trade in Goshen, Orange County, New York, moved to the south in 1846, joined a Tennessee regiment (James Wheat's Mounted Rangers) at the commencement of the war with Mexico, engaged in painting in Memphis after that war for ten years, then moved to Hardeman County, Tennessee, and joined 1st West Tennessee Cavalry, afterwards 6th Tennessee Cavalry, as a private at start of Civil War. Sketch in Coppock, Volume IV, pages 139-143. Served in the Tennessee General Assembly (see sketch in Biographical *Directory of the Tennessee General Assembly*, Volume II 1861-1901, by Robert Martin McBride, Tennessee State Library and Archives, Nashville, 1979, page 844). Served one term as a Republican in the U. S. House of Representatives, Forty-First Congress, March 4,1869-March 3,1871, (see sketch in *Biographical Directory of the American Congress 1774-1961*, United States Government Printing Office, 1961, page 1626). Sketch and photograph in *Brevet Brigadier Generals in Blue* by Roger D. Hunt and Jack R. Brown, Olde Soldier Books, 1990, revised 1997, page 571. Sketch in Goodspeed's Shelby County History, page 1041. Sketch in the PoliticalGraveyard.com. Sketch, photograph, if available, and grave stone photograph in book *Quiet Places: The Burial Sites of Civil War Generals in Tennessee* by Buckner and Nathaniel C. Hughes, Jr., East Tennessee Historical Society (1992). Listed under Generals in "Touring historic Elmwood Cemetery" (Brochure and Map of Historic Gravesites) #15; listed in "Touring Historic Elmwood Cemetery" Brochure (January 2000) #70; sketch #23 in Elmwood *Civil War Tour* booklet (2012)

Milton T. Williamson is buried in the Turley Section, Lot 595, Grave #2. He was interred on June 3, 1912. Per the *Historic Elmwood Cemetery Journal*, Spring 1999, Volume XII, Number 4, he was an Ohio native and became a Memphian after serving with the occupation forces in Memphis. Further per the Journal, he served in the state legislature (see sketch in Biographical *Directory of the Tennessee General Assembly*, Volume II 1861-1901, by Robert Martin McBride, Tennessee State Library and Archives, Nashville, 1979, page 985), as city registrar, as U.S. Marshall and published the most accurate City of Memphis maps of the time. Inscribed on his grave stone are his birth date (April 26, 1822) and death date (June 1, 1902) but no service information. Enrolled and mustered-in October 29, 1861, age 33, as 2 Lieutenant Company C Ohio 72 Infantry Regiment at Cincinnati, Ohio, promoted to 1 Lieutenant Company C February 13, 1862, served as Aid de Camp for part of service, and mustered out October 29, 1864, at expiration of three-year enlistment. Ohio 72 Infantry Regiment was stationed in Memphis in 1863 and 1864. Per compiled service record appears on General Order No. 67, dated War Department, Adjutant General's Office, July 16, 1867, appointed to be Captain by Brevet in the Volunteer Force of the United States, for faithful and meritorious services to date from March 13, 1865. Official Record Series 1, Volume XLVIII/1, page 1028, shows him as Brigadier General of Enrolled Militia, Post and Defenses of Memphis (E.M.D.M.), District of West Tennessee, Department of Mississippi, Division of the West, February 28, 1865. Per article under Local News February 10, 1865, M*emphis Daily Bulletin*, page 3, Colonel Williamson of the 3rd Regiment, E.M.D.M., was proffered the commission of Brigadier General in place of General Dustan and he declined. Per article under Local News February 12, 1865, *Memphis Daily Bulletin*, page 3, "General Dustan's Resignation Accepted - Colonel Williamson Promoted - The resignation of Brigadier General Dustan was accepted yesterday, and, by order of General Roberts, Colonel Williamson, senior colonel of the militia, is promoted to the vacancy, to rank of Brigadier General from date of the order." The Enrolled Militia of the District of Memphis was organized September 14, 1863, (see *Tennesseans in the Civil War, Part 1*, pages 412-413) to serve as home guards under the militia laws of the state. See sketch on Frederick W. Buttinghaus supra and *Colonel in Blue—Indiana, Kentucky and Tennessee: A Civil War Biographical Dictionary*. Roger D. Hunt. McFarland & Company, Inc., Publishers, Jefferson, North Carolina, and London, 2014., page 199, that outlines the commanding officers of the 3rd Regiment, Enrolled Militia of the District of Memphis, which disbanded May 8, 1865. Listed in "Touring Historic Elmwood Cemetery" Brochure (January 2000) #36; sketch #31 in Elmwood *Civil War Tour* booklet (2012).

UNIT/REGIMENT LISTING

This is a listing of the soldier/veteran's unit/regiment either as indicated in the Cemetery records or as research determined as their official unit/regiment under which compiled service records were found. Many soldiers/veterans served in more than one unit/regiment. Therefore, soldiers/veterans may be listed under more than one unit/regiment. Generals are also listed herein under full rank as well as the regiment where they served as colonel and in some cases at lower ranks. Additionally, listed are individuals, although not serving in the Confederate military, who served an important part in the Confederate Cause. (Note: * indicates buried outside of Confederate Soldiers Rest and ** indicates originally buried at Elmwood Cemetery but later removed.)

Adams' Regiment	Carle, Everett
Adams' Regiment Company I	Harper, T J
Adjutant, Major, Virginia Military Class of 1862	*Freeman, Edward T
Adjutant & Inspector General, Major	*Lee, Pollock B
Aide de Camp Staff of General N. B. Forrest Lieutenant	*Forrest, William M
Aide de Camp Staff of General Otho F. Strahl, Captain	*Beasley, James E
Aide de Camp Staff of General William H. Carroll	*Carroll, William H
Aide de Camp Staff of General Dandridge McRae & General James F. Fagan	*Hanks, Calvin J
Aide de Camp Staff of General William H. Jackson	*Martin, James H
Aide de Camp Volunteer Staff of General G. T. Beauregard, Colonel	*Thompson, Jacob
Assistant Adjutant General (AAG) Captain	*Trezevant, Theodore B
Alabama Cavalry Forrest's Regiment Colonel (see sketch for other units)	*Forrest, Jeffery E
Alabama Cavalry Barbiere's Battalion Private Company F Local Defense Troops	*Stockdale, George W
Alabama State Artillery, 1 Regiment Mobile Volunteers, Private Sergeant Company D	*Prescott, Jesse P
Alabama 1 Infantry Regiment Private Company C	Stewart, Jerry F
Alabama 1 Regiment Company B	Merrit, B
Alabama 4 Infantry Regiment Captain Quartermaster	Jones, George W
Alabama 11 Cavalry Regiment Company H	Patterson, Martin D
Alabama 11 Cavalry Regiment Private Company K	Lambert, Joel
Alabama 13 Infantry Regiment Private Company A	Demuth, George
Alabama 16 Infantry Regiment Captain Company A	Dickson, Barton
Alabama 16 Infantry Regiment Captain Company F	*Hodges, William (Buck)
Alabama 17 Infantry Regiment Assistant Surgeon	*Blount, Dr Benjamin F
Alabama 19 Infantry Regiment Private Company B	*Phillips, William M
Alabama 21 Infantry Regiment Private Company I	Palmer, John
Alabama 26 Infantry Regiment	*Gwynne, Andrew D
Alabama 26 Regiment (Hutto's) Company	Swindle, William
Alabama 27 Infantry Regiment Corporal Company I	Lambert, Joel
Alabama 33 Infantry Regiment 2 Lieutenant Company G	*Hughes, Bernard
Alabama 34 Infantry Regiment Private Company F	Kimbrough, James P
Alabama 34 Infantry Regiment Private Company K	Florrence, J H
Alabama 37 Infantry Regiment Company A	Hutto, James
Alabama 50 Infantry Regiment Major (first known as Alabama 26 (Coltart's) Infantry Regiment)	*Gwynne, Andrew D
Appeal Battery Bryan's Company (Arkansas 5 Battery Light Artillery, Appeal Battery)	Scherbe, A
Arkansas Colonel Adams' Regiment	Stacy, L
Arkansas Adams Regiment Company C	Ball, J N
Arkansas Captain Holmes' Company G	Prince, John
Arkansas Captain Murray's Company Green's Company	Williams, Thomas
Arkansas Captain Rice's Artillery	Jeffery, Jesse L
Arkansas Carlton's Cavalry Battalion 1 Lieutenant Company F	*Loudon, James A
Arkansas Carroll's Regiment	Halton, James R
Arkansas Keep's Regiment Company G	Halley, A B
Arkansas King's Regiment Company B	Williams, J J
Arkansas King's Regiment Wheeler's Company	Shadrick, J M
Arkansas McRae's Infantry Regiment Company B	Pratt, Stephen
Arkansas McRae's Battalion Company B	Truite, Lafayette
Arkansas McRae's Regiment Company G	Neighbours, Thomas J
Arkansas Miller's Battalion	Blockman, S W
Arkansas Miller's Battalion (Jones') Company	Gibson, Samuel
Arkansas Miller's Battalion (Wilson's) Company	Gowans, Daniel
Arkansas Miller's Battalion Company D	Waldrop, William L
Arkansas Miller's Battalion Company E	Lee, Jessee
Arkansas Miller's Battalion Company E	Brown, John F

Arkansas Miller's Battalion (Murray's) Company I	Whitney, George
Arkansas Morgan's Cavalry Regiment	*DuBose, Julius J
Arkansas Regiment	Posten, William
Arkansas Regiment (not clear in Cemetery record; possibly Art CSA)	Rodgers, R B
Arkansas Regiment Company I	Robinson, Wallace
Arkansas Rivers' (Provence's/Arkansas First Light Artillery Company) Battery Private	Aldrige, Thomas H
Arkansas Rivers' (Provence's/Arkansas First Light Artillery Company) Battery Private	Richardson, James
Arkansas Thrall's Battery Jackson's Light Artillery (3rd Arkansas Light Artillery) Captain	*Thrall, James C
Arkansas Volunteers Captain Gray's Company	Rhine, George
Arkansas 1 (Colquitt's) Infantry Regiment Private Company B	Crawford, Charles M
Arkansas 1 (Colquitt's) Infantry Regiment Private Company D	Doherty, James
Arkansas 1 (Colquitt's) Infantry Regiment Private Company G	Lax, Joseph G
Arkansas 1 (Dobbins') Cavalry Regiment Private Company C	*Brown, Alfred H
Arkansas 1 (Dobbins') Cavalry Regiment Captain Company E	*Bateman, Morgan M
Arkansas 1 (Dobbins') Cavalry Regiment Private Company F	Rodgers, Volney P
Arkansas 1 (Dobbins') Cavalry Regiment Private Company G	*Lake, Lorenzo S
Arkansas 1 (Dobbins') Cavalry Regiment Private Company H (Walker's Brigade)	Macon, Richard T
Arkansas 1 (Monroe's) Cavalry Captain Company A	**Barnes, Robert W
Arkansas 1 Infantry Regiment Company D	Mitchell, William
Arkansas 1 Infantry Regiment Company E	Macomb, N
Arkansas 1 Infantry Regiment Company E	Sherman, S B
Arkansas 1 Infantry Regiment Company H	Willis, W L
Arkansas 1 Mounted Rifles (Harper's) Regiment Private Company A	Raney, Marcus G
Arkansas 1 Mounted Rifles (Harper's) Regiment Private Company H	Neal, William
Arkansas 1 Mounted Rifles (Harper's) Regiment Private Company K	Richardson, John S
Arkansas 2 Infantry Regiment Lieutenant Colonel	Patterson, Charles E
Arkansas 2 Infantry Regiment Field & Staff Surgeon	*Otey, Dr Paul
Arkansas 2 Infantry Regiment Private Company B	Moore, William
Arkansas 2 (Hindman's) Infantry Regiment Private Company B	Cohn, Harvey H
Arkansas 2 Infantry Regiment Company D	Thompson, W M
Arkansas 2 (Hindman's) Infantry Regiment Private Company F	Quinn, William
Arkansas 2 (Hindman's) Infantry Regiment Private Company G	Giles, Franklin M J
Arkansas 2 Infantry Regiment Private Company I	Castlebury, Joel
Arkansas 2 Infantry Regiment Private Company K	Mullins, Albert A
Arkansas 2 Infantry Regiment	Giles, G Y
Arkansas 2 Infantry Regiment	Johnson, Morgan
Arkansas 2 Infantry Regiment	Irwin, Thomas
Arkansas 2 Infantry Regiment Private Company A	Rasor, John W
Arkansas 2 Mounted Rifles Regiment Private Company A	Lynn, Thomas
Arkansas 2 Mounted Rifles Regiment Private Company A	Saddler, C G
Arkansas 2 (Locke's) Mounted Rifles Private (Hemby's) Company C	Arrington, Edmund A
Arkansas 2 Mounted Rifles Regiment Private Company I	Jones, Willis
Arkansas 2 Regiment Hindman Legion	McCulloch, James
Arkansas 2 Regiment Company B	Burk, John H
Arkansas 2 Regiment	Irwin, G W
Arkansas 3 Cavalry Regiment Corporal/Private Bugler Company A	*Kenneday, Dr. Absolom E
Arkansas 3 Cavalry Regiment Private Company A	*Kenneday, David Y
Arkansas 3 (Borland's) Cavalry Regiment Private (Blackwell's) Company B	Morris, John
Arkansas 3 Cavalry Regiment Sergeant Company G	*Kenneday, William H
Arkansas 3 Infantry Regiment Corporal/Sergeant Company D	Phillips, David P
Arkansas 4 Infantry Battalion Private Company E	Downs, E G
Arkansas 4 Infantry Battalion Private Company E	Nowell, A J
Arkansas 4 (McNair's) Infantry Regiment Private (Tyson's) Company D	Sheffield, Mark
Arkansas 4 Infantry Regiment Private Company F	Weldon, Columbus
Arkansas 4 Regiment	Sanders
Arkansas 5 Battery Light Artillery (Appeal Battery) Captain	*Bryan, William C
Arkansas 5 Battery Light Artillery (Appeal Battery)	*Brooks, Albert J
Arkansas 5 Infantry Regiment Private (Green's) Company C	McCammon, Columbus D
Arkansas 5 Infantry Regiment Private Company B	Pitts, James F M
Arkansas 5 Regiment	Reeves, M L
Arkansas 6 Cavalry Battalion (1 Phifer's, White's and McNeill's Battalion) Sergeant Company C	*Lyles, Oliver P
Arkansas 6 Infantry Regiment Private Company C	Woody, J M

Arkansas 6 Infantry Regiment Private Company D Old	Burch, A D
Arkansas 6 Regiment Company F	Dean, Issac A
Arkansas 6 Regiment Captain Jones' Company	Parton, D L
Arkansas 6 Regiment	Wallace, Robert
Arkansas 7 Infantry Regiment Assistant Commissary of Subsistence	*Hanauer, Louis
Arkansas 7 Infantry Regiment Private Company A	Martin, Henry R
Arkansas 7 Infantry Regiment Private Company B	Clay, T G
Arkansas 7 Infantry Regiment Private Company D	Wirt, William
Arkansas 7 Infantry Regiment Private Company F	Perkins, G W
Arkansas 7 Infantry Regiment Private Company H	Holcombe, William H
Arkansas 7 Infantry Regiment Private Company H	Trimble, M R
Arkansas 7 Regiment Company B	Perkins, T J
Arkansas 7 Regiment Company H	Hyman, S C
Arkansas 7 Regiment Lieutenant	Ferguson, William B
Arkansas 8 (Miller's) Infantry Battalion Private Company C	Smith, William S
Arkansas 8 (Miller's) Infantry Battalion Private Company C	Trammell, George W
Arkansas 8 (Miller's) Infantry Battalion Private (Franklin's) Company C	Winters, James C
Arkansas 8 Infantry Regiment Quartermaster	*Watson, Elbert L
Arkansas 8 Infantry Regiment Private New Company A	Callahan, David
Arkansas 8 Infantry Regiment Private New Company B	Everett, Francis M
Arkansas 8 Infantry Regiment Private New Company C	Mauldin, Jesse A
Arkansas 8 Infantry Regiment Private New Company D	Davidson, W M
Arkansas 8 Infantry Regiment Private New Company E	Reeves, Stephen C
Arkansas 8 Infantry Regiment (Desha's Battalion) Sergeant/2 Lieutenant New Company H	Denton, Frank D
Arkansas 8 Infantry Regiment (Desha's Battalion Company E) Private New Company K	Myers, J A
Arkansas 8 Infantry Regiment Private New Company K	Woodson, J M
Arkansas 8 Regiment	Burton, J B
Arkansas 9 Infantry Regiment	Faust, J
Arkansas 9 Infantry Regiment	Wells, G L
Arkansas 9 Infantry Regiment 1 Sergeant Company A	Long, Adam L
Arkansas 9 Infantry Regiment Corporal (Hawley's) Company A	Sledge, Washington M
Arkansas 9 Infantry Regiment Private Company A	Bradley, Mitchell
Arkansas 9 Infantry Regiment Private Company A	Crow, John M
Arkansas 9 Infantry Regiment Private Old Company B	Tribble, Alfred L
Arkansas 9 Infantry Regiment Private (Isom's) Old Company B	Whitaker, Alfred H
Arkansas 9 Infantry Regiment Private (Thomasson's) New Company B	Bonds, T S
Arkansas 9 Infantry Regiment Private (Thomasson's) New Company B	Goodwin, J H
Arkansas 9 Infantry Regiment Private (Thomasson's) New Company B	Patrick, Dan
Arkansas 9 Infantry Regiment Private (Thomasson's) New Company B	Sackett, James
Arkansas 9 Infantry Regiment Private (Thomasson's) New Company B	Shanks, M C
Arkansas 9 Infantry Regiment Private (Thomasson's) New Company B	Young, Thomas
Arkansas 9 Infantry Regiment Private Company C	Davis, W G
Arkansas 9 Infantry Regiment Private Company C	Evans, Crawford L
Arkansas 9 Infantry Regiment Private (Henry's) Company C	Hudson, Henry
Arkansas 9 Infantry Regiment Private (Henry's) Company C	Rhodes, William H
Arkansas 9 Infantry Regiment Private (Henry's) Company C	Saunders, William H
Arkansas 9 Infantry Regiment Sergeant (Dunlap's) Company D	Akins, Jasper L
Arkansas 9 Infantry Regiment Corporal Company D	Evans, Ezekiel
Arkansas 9 Infantry Regiment Private Company D	Black, William E
Arkansas 9 Infantry Regiment Private Company D	Robertson, Augustus
Arkansas 9 Infantry Regiment Private Company D	Thompson, Andrew J R
Arkansas 9 Infantry Regiment Private Company E	Callaway, Levi A
Arkansas 9 Infantry Regiment Private Company E	McKinney, John
Arkansas 9 Infantry Regiment Private (Blankenship's) Company E	Sheppard, James H
Arkansas 9 Infantry Regiment Private Company E	Thompson, John F
Arkansas 9 Infantry Regiment Private Company F	Brooks, Kosisco
Arkansas 9 Infantry Regiment Private (Haseslip's) Company F	Emmerson, Thomas J
Arkansas 9 Infantry Regiment Ordnance Sergeant Company G	Palmer, Green M
Arkansas 9 Infantry Regiment Private (Wallace's) Company G	Carter, Robert D
Arkansas 9 Infantry Regiment Private (Wallace's) Company G	Culpepper, John W
Arkansas 9 Infantry Regiment Private Company G	Adams, William J
Arkansas 9 Infantry Regiment Private Company G	Varnell, William P

Arkansas 9 Infantry Regiment Private Company G	May, William H
Arkansas 9 Infantry Regiment Private Company G	Culpepper, Henry J
Arkansas 9 Infantry Regiment 2 Lieutenant Company H	Rigney, Henry
Arkansas 9 Infantry Regiment Corporal (Armstrong's) Company H	Walker, John T
Arkansas 9 Infantry Regiment Private Company H	Lindsay, John H
Arkansas 9 Infantry Regiment Private Company H	Lowe, Samuel C
Arkansas 9 Infantry Regiment Private Company H	Womac, John A
Arkansas 9 Infantry Regiment Old Companies H & I	*DuBose, Julius J.
Arkansas 9 Infantry Regiment Lieutenant/Captain Old Company I	*Culpepper, Joseph A
Arkansas 9 Infantry Regiment Private (Gantt's) Old Company I	Edwards, William B
Arkansas 9 Infantry Regiment Private Old Company I	Copeland, Thomas W
Arkansas 9 Infantry Regiment Private Old Company I	Woodward, William F
Arkansas 9 Infantry Regiment Private Company K	McCurdy, William P
Arkansas 9 Infantry Regiment Private Company K	Aust, L F
Arkansas 9 Regiment	Gerris, David
Arkansas 10 Infantry Regiment (Jenning's) Company G	Guyton, T B
Arkansas 10 Infantry Regiment Company C	Curtic, J R
Arkansas 10 Infantry Regiment Private Company C	Jones, William D
Arkansas 10 Infantry Regiment Sergeant Company D	Sanders, John B
Arkansas 10 Infantry Regiment Private Company D	Dunn, W O
Arkansas 10 Infantry Regiment Company D	Leggett, William T
Arkansas 10 Regiment Company B	Brown, Benjamin
ARKANSAS 11 INFANTRY REGIMENT RECORDS ALSO FOUND ARKANSAS 11/17 CONSOLIDATED INFANTRY	
Arkansas 11 Infantry Regiment Private Company A	Dunn, T J
Arkansas 11 (Smith's) Infantry Regiment Private Company A	McCool, Andrew J
Arkansas 11 Infantry Regiment Private Company A	Russel, Oliver
Arkansas 11 Infantry Regiment Private Companies B/I	Grimmett, Robert W
Arkansas 11 Infantry Regiment Private Company B	Hollinsworth, A W
Arkansas 11 Infantry Regiment Private Company B	Miller, H
Arkansas 11 Infantry Regiment Company B	Shanault, A S
Arkansas 11 Infantry Regiment Company C	Sarat, William
Arkansas 11 Infantry Regiment Private Company D	Capps, Thomas J
Arkansas 11 Infantry Regiment Private Company D	Hawthorn, Augustus
Arkansas 11 Infantry Regiment Private Company D	Williams, William
Arkansas 11 Infantry Regiment Wagoner Company E	Cothran, Samuel M
Arkansas 11 Infantry Regiment Private Company E "Falcon Guards"	Adams, Anderson
Arkansas 11 Infantry Regiment Private Company E	Cook, James
Arkansas 11 Infantry Regiment Company E	Gray, Columbus
Arkansas 11 Infantry Regiment Private Company E	McLure, R H
Arkansas 11 Infantry Regiment Company F	Holbert, F S
Arkansas 11 Infantry Regiment Company F	Loomis, J J
Arkansas 11 Infantry Regiment Private Company G	Jeffus, Needham H
Arkansas 11 Infantry Regiment Private Company I	Blakely, John W
Arkansas 11 Infantry Regiment Private Company I	Christopher, Matthew
Arkansas 11 Infantry Regiment Private Company I	Godwin, B F
Arkansas 11 Infantry Regiment Private Company I	Irwin, G W
Arkansas 11 Infantry Regiment Private Company I	Odell, James
Arkansas 11 Infantry Regiment Private Company K	Johnston, James J
Arkansas 11 Infantry Regiment Private Company K	Jones, Andrew J
Arkansas 11 Infantry Regiment Private Company K	Julian, John R
Arkansas 11 Infantry Regiment Private Company K	McCance, R M
Arkansas 11 Infantry Regiment Private Company K	Palmer, J M
Arkansas 11 Infantry Regiment Private Company K	Webb, T S
Arkansas 11 Infantry Regiment Private Company K	Workman, Amos
Arkansas 11 (Smith's) Infantry Regiment	Baker, Daniel
Arkansas 11 Infantry Regiment	Hannberger, Wiley W
Arkansas 12 Battalion Sharp Shooters Lieutenant Company B	*McLean, William
Arkansas 12 Infantry Regiment Adjutant	Dupuy, John J
Arkansas 12 Infantry Regiment Company A	Dozier, D M
Arkansas 12 Infantry Regiment Company A	Rose, M K
Arkansas 12 Infantry Regiment Company A	Shackleford, L A
Arkansas 12 Infantry Regiment Company A	Tate, J L

Arkansas 12 Infantry Regiment Company A	Welch, William
Arkansas 12 Infantry Regiment Lieutenant Company B	*Mclean, William L
Arkansas 12 Infantry Regiment Company B	Buckner, Jasper W
Arkansas 12 Infantry Regiment Private Company B	Collins, John J
Arkansas 12 Infantry Regiment Company B	Crittenden, E A
Arkansas 12 Infantry Regiment Company B	Hill, M H
Arkansas 12 Infantry Regiment Company C	Cobb, H J
Arkansas 12 Infantry Regiment Company C	Coggin, B F
Arkansas 12 Infantry Regiment Company C	Owens, T L
Arkansas 12 Infantry Regiment Company C	Pryor, W J
Arkansas 12 Infantry Regiment Company D	Pope, Riley
Arkansas 12 Infantry Regiment Private Company D	Tomlinson, Felix G
Arkansas 12 Infantry Regiment Private Company E	Benson, Joseph N
Arkansas 12 Infantry Regiment Private Company E	Benton, William
Arkansas 12 Infantry Regiment Private Company E	Brooks, Jackson
Arkansas 12 Infantry Regiment Private Company E	Clark, Simpson H
Arkansas 12 Infantry Regiment Sergeant Company F	Baker, T R
Arkansas 12 Infantry Regiment Private Company F	Adams, W J
Arkansas 12 Infantry Regiment Private Company F	Bledsoe, T G
Arkansas 12 Infantry Regiment Private Company F	Bryant, Jackson J
Arkansas 12 Infantry Regiment Private Company F	Elliott, Mark L
Arkansas 12 Infantry Regiment Private Company F	Jones, George P
Arkansas 12 Infantry Regiment Private Company F	Wiginton, W J
Arkansas 12 Infantry Regiment Private Company G	Biggs, David
Arkansas 12 Infantry Regiment Private Company G	Broombly, David T
Arkansas 12 Infantry Regiment Private Company G	Cone, Elijah M
Arkansas 12 Infantry Regiment Private Company G	Hulsey, H C
Arkansas 12 Infantry Regiment Private Company G	Jackson, A M
Arkansas 12 Infantry Regiment Private Company G	Hill, Benjamin
Arkansas 12 Infantry Regiment Private Company G	Shields, S J
Arkansas 12 Infantry Regiment Company H	Conn, John S
Arkansas 12 Infantry Regiment Private Company H	Jackson, Salathiel P
Arkansas 12 Infantry Regiment Private Company H	Jackson, William S
Arkansas 12 Infantry Regiment Private Company H	Lendwell, William D
Arkansas 12 Infantry Regiment Private Company H	Miller, Robert
Arkansas 12 Infantry Regiment Private Company H	Rhodes, Morgan G
Arkansas 12 Infantry Regiment Private Company J	Dier, Andrew J
Arkansas 12 Infantry Regiment Private Company K	Ward, Isaac L
Arkansas 12 (Gantt's) Infantry Regiment	Dawes, John
Arkansas 12 (Gantt's) Infantry Regiment	Galbreath, James
Arkansas 12 (Gantt's) Infantry Regiment Private (Jones') Company E	Fink, John W
Arkansas 12 (Gantt's) Infantry Regiment (Wyatt's) Company F	McMaury, Hezekiah
Arkansas 12 Infantry Regiment	Knox, William M
Arkansas 12 Infantry Regiment	**McLean, Albert
Arkansas 12 Infantry Regiment	Shanks, M O
Arkansas 12 Infantry Regiment	Whitehead, William
Arkansas 13 (Tappan's) Infantry Regiment Private Company A	Hankins, William W
Arkansas 13 Infantry Regiment Private Company B	Clements, Augustus
Arkansas 13 Infantry Regiment Servant Slave of 1st Lieutenant T. J. Shelton Company B	*Shelton, Jack
Arkansas 13 Infantry Regiment Company B	Taylor, G W
Arkansas 13 Infantry Regiment Company C	Goforth, William
Arkansas 13 Infantry Regiment Company C	Henson, John
Arkansas 13 Infantry Regiment Company C	Prince, James
Arkansas 13 Infantry Regiment Company D	Phillips, G W
Arkansas 13 Infantry Regiment Company E	Caldwell, John
Arkansas 13 Infantry Regiment Company E	Cooper, Thomas
Arkansas 13 Infantry Regiment Company E	Gregory, Edward
Arkansas 13 Infantry Regiment Company F	Cummins, Isaac A
Arkansas 13 Infantry Regiment Private Company F	Pittman, P P
Arkansas 13 Infantry Regiment Company G	Smith, W S
Arkansas 13 Infantry Regiment Company G	Vandever, G W
Arkansas 13 Infantry Regiment Company H	Neely, Huron

Arkansas 13 Infantry Regiment Company I	Ros, A W
Arkansas 13 Infantry Regiment Company I	McGuire, Rufus
Arkansas 13 Infantry Regiment (Gand's) Company	Pickering, J E
Arkansas 13 Infantry Regiment (Johnson's) Company	Blackwell, J T
Arkansas 13 (Tappan's) Infantry Regiment	Broom, William
Arkansas 13 Infantry Regiment	Davidson, J F
Arkansas 13 Infantry Regiment	Goodman, C B
Arkansas 13 Infantry Regiment	Hackleburn, L D
Arkansas 13 Infantry Regiment	Henley, J
Arkansas 14 (McCarver's) Infantry Regiment Private Company C	Evans, Caleb J
Arkansas 15 (Johnson's) Infantry Regiment Private Company C	Johnekin, John E
Arkansas 15 (Johnson's) Infantry Regiment Private Company F	Bull, Cicero B
Arkansas 15 (Josey's) Infantry Regiment Colonel	*Josey, John E
Arkansas 15 (Josey's) Infantry Regiment Private Company B	*Walker, Creed T
Arkansas 15 (Josey's) Infantry Regiment Private Company C	*Barksdale, Robert E
Arkansas 15 (Josey's) Infantry Regiment Private Company C	Moore, Peter
Arkansas 15 (Josey's) Infantry Regiment Private Company E	Burkett, Andrew J
Arkansas 15 (Josey's) Infantry Regiment Private Company H	Avery, Jesse N
Arkansas 15 (Northwest/McRae's Battalion) Infantry Regiment Private Company I	Turner, G W
Arkansas 15 (Northwest) Infantry Regiment Private Company K	Blunt, Thomas E
Arkansas 15 Infantry Regiment Company B	Friar, John
Arkansas 15 Infantry Regiment	Baldin, J
Arkansas 17 (Griffith's) Infantry Regiment Private Company G	Blackburn, Marion
Arkansas 17 (Griffith's) Infantry Regiment Private Company G	Johnson, Thomas S
Arkansas 17 (Griffith/Rector's) Infantry Regiment Company G	Joyce, T S
ARKANSAS 17 (LEMOYE'S) INFANTRY REGIMENT - SEE ALSO ARKANSAS 21 INFANTRY REGIMENT	
Arkansas 17 (Lemoyne's) Infantry Regiment Private Company A	Adams, A J
Arkansas 17 (Lemoyne's) Infantry Regiment Private Company A	Lackey, William
Arkansas 17 (Lemoyne's) Infantry Regiment Private Company A	Music, Richard
Arkansas 17 (Lemoyne's) Infantry Regiment Private Company B	Collins, John W
Arkansas 17 (Lemoyne's) Infantry Regiment Private Company C	Hill, Allen L
Arkansas 17 (Lemoyne's) Infantry Regiment Private (Perry's) Company C	Terry, James G
Arkansas 17 (Lemoyne's) Infantry Regiment Private Company E	Brewton, James J
Arkansas 17 (Lemoyne's) Infantry Regiment Private Company E	Hall, Jesse H
Arkansas 17 (Lemoyne's) Infantry Regiment Private Company E	Hall, Lucilius M
Arkansas 17 (Lemoyne's) Infantry Regiment Private Company E	Jones, William P
Arkansas 17 (Lemoyne's) Infantry Regiment Private Company E	Pearce, Andrew J
Arkansas 17 (Lemoyne's) Infantry Regiment Private Company E	Roberts, John S B
Arkansas 17 (Lemoyne's) Infantry Regiment Private Company F	Mathis, Andrew J
Arkansas 17 (Lemoyne's) Infantry Regiment Private Company H	Golding, John
Arkansas 17 (Lemoyne's) Infantry Regiment Private Company H	Thrailkille, James M
Arkansas 17 (Lemoyne's) Infantry Regiment Private Company H	Wagnon, Clarence
Arkansas 17 Infantry Regiment Company A	Hardin, Powell
Arkansas 17 Infantry Regiment Company E	Riley, William
Arkansas 17 Infantry Regiment Company E	Wheeler, John
Arkansas 17 Infantry Regiment Company F	Barnes, William
Arkansas 17 Infantry Regiment Company H	Knowles, Hardy
Arkansas 17 Infantry Regiment Bonner's Company	Rayburn, M
Arkansas 17 Infantry Regiment	Mineace, J J
Arkansas 17 Regiment	Watkins, J W
Arkansas 18 (Carroll's) Infantry Regiment Sergeant (Peel's) Company A	Parks, John
Arkansas 18 (Carroll's) Infantry Regiment Private Company A	Letlow, Isham H
Arkansas 18 (Carroll's) Infantry Regiment Private Company A	Sorralls, James R
Arkansas 18 (Carroll's) Infantry Regiment Sergeant Company B	Benson, Frederick A
Arkansas 18 (Carroll's) Infantry Regiment Private Company B	Adams, William J
Arkansas 18 (Carroll's) Infantry Regiment Private Company B	Chadwick, P Frank
Arkansas 18 (Carroll's) Infantry Regiment Private Company B	Crouse, Franklin
Arkansas 18 (Carroll's) Infantry Regiment Private (McLenders') Company B	Loftin, William
Arkansas 18 (Carroll's) Infantry Regiment Private Company C	Bradberry, James
Arkansas 18 (Carroll's) Infantry Regiment Private Company C	Love, Nathan
Arkansas 18 (Carroll's) Infantry Regiment Private Company C	McKinney, L R
Arkansas 18 (Carroll's) Infantry Regiment Private Company D	Collins, James

Arkansas 18 (Carroll's) Infantry Regiment Private Company D	**Standridge, J M
Arkansas 18 (Carroll's) Infantry Regiment Private Company G	Cole, Porter
Arkansas 18 (Carroll's) Infantry Regiment Private (Lynch's) Company G	Cook, T H
Arkansas 18 (Carroll's) Infantry Regiment Private (Lynch's) Company G	Gowns, William
Arkansas 18 (Carroll's) Infantry Regiment Private (Lynch's) Company G	Howell, W B
Arkansas 18 (Carroll's) Infantry Regiment Private (Lynch's) Company G	Swink, Drew L
Arkansas 18 (Carroll's) Infantry Regiment Private Company H	Barclay, James
Arkansas 18 (Carroll's) Infantry Regiment Private (Parrish's) Company H	Blevins, Jasper
Arkansas 18 (Carroll's) Infantry Regiment Private Company H	Dorrough, John G
Arkansas 18 (Carroll's) Infantry Regiment Private (Parrish's) Company H	Haley, David G
Arkansas 18 (Carroll's) Infantry Regiment Private Company H	Simmons, John C
Arkansas 18 (Carroll's) Infantry Regiment Private Company H	Smith, George B
Arkansas 18 (Carroll's) Infantry Regiment Private (Parrish's) Company H	Waymack, Joel S
Arkansas 18 (Carroll's) Infantry Regiment Private Company I	Barnes, William C
Arkansas 18 (Carroll's) Infantry Regiment Private Company I	Woodward, Jason
Arkansas 18 (Carroll's) Infantry Regiment Private Company K	Pearcy, C C
Arkansas 18 (Carroll's) Infantry Regiment Private Company K	Rhodes, Charles C
Arkansas 18 (Carroll's) Infantry Regiment Company A	Nearce, H J
Arkansas 18 (Carroll's) Infantry Regiment Company B	Gowen, William
Arkansas 18 (Carroll's) Infantry Regiment (Lynch's) Company G	McKay, Michael
Arkansas 18 (Carroll's) Infantry Regiment (Parrish's) Company H	Lynch, R
Arkansas 18 (Carroll's) Infantry Regiment Company H	Scrouse, J
Arkansas 18 (Carroll's) Infantry Regiment Private (Owen's) Company K	Dardenno, Andrew
Arkansas 18 (Marmaduke's) Infantry Regiment Captain Company B	*Cameron, John F
Arkansas 18 (Marmaduke's) Infantry Regiment Corporal/Sergeant Assistant Quartermaster Company B	*Jarnagin, John H
Arkansas 18 (Marmaduke's) Infantry Regiment Private (Robertson's) Company K	Null, John B
Arkansas 18 Infantry Regiment Private Company B	*Ryan, Charles R
Arkansas 18 Infantry Regiment Private Company C	Gish, H H
Arkansas 19 (Dockery/Smead's) Infantry Regiment Lieutenant Company A	Garlington, W H C
Arkansas 19 (Dockery/Smead's) Infantry Regiment Corporal Company A	Bland, James W
Arkansas 19 (Dockery/Smead's) Infantry Regiment Private Company A	Erkridge, George C
Arkansas 19 (Dockery/Smead's) Infantry Regiment Private Company A	Matheus, Samuel
Arkansas 19 (Dockery/Smead's) Infantry Regiment Private Company A	Mathews, John W
Arkansas 19 (Dockery/Smead's) Infantry Regiment Private (Johnson's) Company A	Sewell, John
Arkansas 19 (Dockery/Smead's) Infantry Regiment Private Company A	Wallace, A M
Arkansas 19 (Dockery/Smead's) Infantry Regiment Sergeant Company B	Stephens, J J
Arkansas 19 (Dockery/Smead's) Infantry Regiment Private Company B	Smith, C C
Arkansas 19 (Dockery/Smead's) Infantry Regiment Private Company C	Wilson, J R
Arkansas 19 (Dockery/Smead's) Infantry Regiment Lieutenant Company D	Keith, John T
Arkansas 19 (Dockery/Smead's) Infantry Regiment Private Company D	Laird, Miles F
Arkansas 19 (Dockery/Smead's) Infantry Regiment Private Company D/E	Moore, William H
Arkansas 19 (Dockery/Smead's) Infantry Regiment Private Company D/E	Reams, Levi E
Arkansas 19 (Dockery/Smead's) Infantry Regiment Private Company E	Comstock, Joseph L
Arkansas 19 (Dockery/Smead's) Infantry Regiment Private (Clayton's) Company E	Edwards, James J
Arkansas 19 (Dockery/Smead's) Infantry Regiment Private Company E	Garner, John L
Arkansas 19 (Dockery/Smead's) Infantry Regiment Sergeant Company G	Dobbs, Benjamin O
Arkansas 19 (Dockery/Smead's) Infantry Regiment Private Company G	McAnulty, S H
Arkansas 19 (Dockery/Smead's) Infantry Regiment Private Company G	Pate, Wiley A
Arkansas 19 (Dockery/Smead's) Infantry Regiment Private Company G	Saunders, J C
Arkansas 19 (Dockery/Smead's) Infantry Regiment 4 Sergeant Company H	Greer, A Sidney
Arkansas 19 (Dockery/Smead's) Infantry Regiment Private Company H	Cook, J E
Arkansas 19 (Dockery/Smead's) Infantry Regiment Private Company H	Hare, Elijah L
Arkansas 19 (Dockery/Smead's) Infantry Regiment Private Company H	Permenter, J R
Arkansas 19 (Dockery/Smead's) Infantry Regiment Private (Cook's) Company H	Trible, C B
Arkansas 19 (Dockery/Smead's) Infantry Regiment Private Company I	Baker, Alex F
Arkansas 19 (Dockery/Smead's) Infantry Regiment Private Company I	Camper, John M
Arkansas 19 (Dockery/Smead's) Infantry Regiment Private Company K	Pope, J J
Arkansas 19 (Dockery/Smead's) Infantry Regiment Private (Perry's) Company K	Ray, Mark R
Arkansas 19 (Dockery/Smead's) Infantry Regiment Company B	Sewell, J B
Arkansas 19 (Dockery/Smead's) Infantry Regiment Company C	Hartsfield, W H
Arkansas 19 (Dockery/Smead's) Infantry Regiment Company E/F	Jackson, J C
Arkansas 19 (Dockery/Smead's) Infantry Regiment Company F	Reeves, E L

Arkansas 19 Infantry Regiment Company B	Hardeman, Elbert
Arkansas 19 Infantry Regiment Company B	Hollinsworth, Matthew
Arkansas 19 Infantry Regiment	Snead, Thomas
Arkansas 19 Infantry Regiment	Warner, W E
Arkansas 20 (King's) Infantry Regiment Private Company C	McCarty, William E
Arkansas 20 (King's) Infantry Regiment Private (Lindsey's) Company D	Buggs, William C
Arkansas 20 (King's) Infantry Regiment Private Company D	Fitzhugh, John M
Arkansas 20 (King's) Infantry Regiment Captain Company E	Cottingham, Jeff
Arkansas 20 (King's) Infantry Regiment Private Company E	Hyden, Matthew H
Arkansas 20 (King's) Infantry Regiment Private Company E	Nolan, David C
Arkansas 20 (King's) Infantry Regiment Private Company E	Pitman, W Thomas
Arkansas 20 (King's) Infantry Regiment Private Company E	Porter, E V
Arkansas 20 (King's) Infantry Regiment Private (Beebe's) Company F	Connor, Z M
Arkansas 20 (King's) Infantry Regiment Private Company G	Hawkins, James J
Arkansas 20 (King's) Infantry Regiment Private Company G	Ortner, D M
Arkansas 20 (King's) Infantry Regiment Private Company G	Shanberger, George W
Arkansas 20 (King's) Infantry Regiment Private (Swaggerty's) Company G	Simpson, Thomas P
Arkansas 20 (King's) Infantry Regiment Private Company H/B	Williamson, J J
Arkansas 20 (King's) Infantry Regiment Private (Kelly's) Company K	Adams, A H
Arkansas 20 (King's) Infantry Regiment Private (Kelly's) Company K	Adams, W T
Arkansas 20 (King's) Infantry Regiment Private Company K	*Henderson, John W
Arkansas 20 (King's) Infantry Regiment Private Company K	King, Andy
ARKANSAS 21 INFANTRY REGIMENT - SEE ALSO ARKANSAS 17 (LEMOYNE'S) INFANTRY REGIMENT	
Arkansas 21 Infantry Regiment Private Company C	Cupp, Nathan J
Arkansas 21 Infantry Regiment Private Company G	Golding, John
Arkansas 21 Infantry Regiment Private Company I	Pearce, Andrew J
Arkansas 21 Infantry Regiment Private Company I	Roberts, John S B
Arkansas 21 Infantry Regiment Private Company K	McDonnel, John C
Arkansas 21 Infantry Regiment	Evans, Caleb J
Arkansas 23 Infantry Regiment Colonel	*Adams, Charles W
Arkansas 23 Infantry Regiment Colonel	*Lyles, Oliver P
Arkansas 23 Infantry Regiment Private Company A	Akers, John E
Arkansas 23 Infantry Regiment Private Company A	Hampton, Wade
Arkansas 23 Infantry Regiment Private Company A	James, Isaacs
Arkansas 23 Infantry Regiment Private (Hillis') Company A	Shelton, George B
Arkansas 23 Infantry Regiment Private Company A	Shelton, Jesse F
Arkansas 23 Infantry Regiment Private (Hillis') Company A	*Warner, John R
Arkansas 23 Infantry Regiment Private Company A	Williams, Samuel J
Arkansas 23 Infantry Regiment Private Company C	May, Leander
Arkansas 23 Infantry Regiment Private Company C	Newman, B S
Arkansas 23 Infantry Regiment Private Company E	Bonner, Benjamin F
Arkansas 23 Infantry Regiment Private (Black's) Company E	Breuer, Martin V
Arkansas 23 Infantry Regiment Private (Harris') Company F	Chapman, William F
Arkansas 23 Infantry Regiment Private (Harris') Company F	Davis, Nathan
Arkansas 23 Infantry Regiment Private (Harris') Company F	Martin, John
Arkansas 23 Infantry Regiment Private (Harris') Company F	Meek, Joseph C
Arkansas 23 Infantry Regiment (Hughes' Battalion) Private (Robinson's) Company G	Thornton, William
Arkansas 23 Infantry Regiment (Hughes' Battalion) Private (Robinson's) Company G	Waits, Dempsey
Arkansas 23 Infantry Regiment Private (Pennington's) Company H	Barentine, William
Arkansas 23 Infantry Regiment Private (Pennington's) Company H	Brumley, Joseph
Arkansas 23 Infantry Regiment Private (Pennington's) Company H	Colloway, Nathaniel C
Arkansas 23 Infantry Regiment Private Company H	Easley, James C
Arkansas 23 Infantry Regiment Private (Pennington's) Company H	McCollum, John W
Arkansas 23 Infantry Regiment Company H (no rank in record)	Steaphuns, John M
Arkansas 23 Infantry Regiment 1 Lieutenant Company I	Neely, Calvin H
Arkansas 23 Infantry Regiment Private Company I	Cottrell, George
Arkansas 23 Infantry Regiment Private Company I	Honeycutt, Francis M
Arkansas 23 Infantry Regiment Private Company I	Potter, Pleasant B
Arkansas 23 Infantry Regiment Private Company I	Simmons, John B
Arkansas 23 Infantry Regiment Private Company I	Southerland, Peter
Arkansas 23 Infantry Regiment Private Company K	Boggs, Caldwell
Arkansas 25 Infantry Regiment Private Company B	Gee, John J

Arkansas 25 Infantry Regiment Private Company C	Rains, William J
Arkansas 25 Infantry Regiment Private Company D	Griffith, Silvester
Arkansas 25 Infantry Regiment Private Company D	Harper, William H
Arkansas 25 Infantry Regiment Private (Peirs') Company D	Lamb, Samuel F
Arkansas 25 Infantry Regiment Private Company D	Loyd, Wiley H
Arkansas 25 Infantry Regiment Private Company E	Dumas, John C
Arkansas 25 Infantry Regiment Private Company E	Mathis, B B
Arkansas 25 Infantry Regiment Private Company E	Newman, Martin
Arkansas 25 Infantry Regiment Private Company G	Parsley, Amsi
Arkansas 25 Infantry Regiment Private Company G	Smutherman, Green A
Arkansas 25 Infantry Regiment Sergeant (McKay's) Company I	Miller, Van
Arkansas 25 Infantry Regiment Private Company K	Washburn, John M
Arkansas 30 Infantry Regiment Colonel	*Hart, Robert A
Arkansas 30 Infantry Company C	Dickinson, Henry
Arkansas 31 (McCray's) Infantry Regiment Private Company B	Holsonback, John R
Arkansas 31 (McCray's) Infantry Regiment Private Company G	Luther, Calvin
Arkansas 31 (McCray's) Infantry Regiment Private Company G	Luther, Jackson
Arkansas 31 (McCray's) Infantry Regiment Private (Barnes') Company H	Jewerls, J W
Arkansas 31 (McCray's) Infantry Regiment Private Company H	Neighbors, Thomas J
Arkansas 30 Infantry Regiment Captain Company B	Borum, Joseph B
Arkansas 33 Infantry Regiment Lieutenant Company K	*Kenneday, William H
Artillery Corps Vol. Company M	Dorr, Frederick
Assistant Adjutant General, Major, Staff of General N. B. Forrest	*Strange, John P
Assistant Adjutant General, Captain, Staff of General James R. Chalmers	*Craft, Henry
Assistant (Acting) Adjutant General, Captain, Staff of General James R. Chalmers	*Carroll, William H
Assistant Adjutant General, Captain, Staff of General Alexander P. Stewart	*Preston, Thomas W
Assistant Adjutant General, Captain	*Trezevant, Theodore B
Assistant Inspector General, Lieutenant Colonel, Staff of General James R. Chalmers	*Young, H Casey
Assistant Inspector General, Captain, Staffs of General Preston Smith and A. J. Vaughn	Harris, John W
Avery's Regiment	Owen, E
Baker's Alabama-Tennessee-Mississippi Regiment	Martin, M M
Baker's Regiment Company F	Beard, P L
Barrett's Battery Van Dorn's Division	Lamb, Asa
Battles Regiment Private	*May, James
Brigadier General	*Carroll, William H
Brigadier General	*Chalmers, James R
Brigadier General	*Gardner, William M
Brigadier General	*Gordon, George W
Brigadier General	*Greer, Elkanah B
Brigadier General	*Humes, William Y
Brigadier General	*Pillow, Gideon J
Brigadier General	*Richardson, Robert V
Brigadier General	*Smith, Preston
Brigadier General	*Vaughan, Jr Alfred J
Brigadier General	*Walker, Lucius M
Brigadier General Arkansas State Forces	*Bradley, Thomas H
Brigadier General Provisional Army of Tennessee	*Sneed, John L
Brigadier General Tennessee State Militia	*Carnes, James A
Bruce's Battalion Company A	Smith, James
Campbell's Battalion (Wright's) Company	Owens, D F
Captain	Dalton, Daniel W "Kit"
Captain	Gray, A B
Captain	*Green, H D
Captain	Jones, R S
Captain	*Kehoe, William
Captain	*Patrick, William
Captain	*Shelby, E J
Captain	*Stockton
Captain Barbiere's Company	Leary, D
Captain Barbiere's Company	Mowatt, James
Captain Gregory's Company	Galey, Oliver
Captain Gregory's Company	Graves, Riley

Captain Jones' Company	Johnson, R B
Captain Jones' Company	Jones, J W
Captain Jones' Heavy Artillery	Jones, N L
Captain Warren's Company Price's Division	Henderson, Thomas
Captain Wood's Company	Thompson, William
Captain Wood's Company	Wynn, Newton M
Carroll's Regiment	Watson, William J
Carver's Regiment	White, S W
Claiborne's Regiment	Ellis, William
Colonel	Cole, J C
Colonel and Volunteer Aide to General Albert Sidney Johnston	*Tate, Samuel
Colonel	*Peace, William
Colonel Adams' Regiment Company A (Confederate Cavalry Wood's Regiment)	Baker, Charles W
Commissary and Ordnance Departments	*Parker, Robert A
Commissary of Subsistence, Major	*Trezevant, John P
Commissary of Subsistence (Assistant) Captain	*Pullen, Benjamin K
Company B	Adams, James
Confederate Cavalry	*McDowell, Samuel I
Confederate Cavalry Private	*Thomas, James E
CONFEDERATE CAVALRY WOOD'S REGIMENT ALSO KNOWN AS MISSISSIPPI 1 CAVALRY AND ADAMS' CAVALRY	
Confederate Cavalry Wood's Regiment Sergeant Company E	Embry, Mitchell A
Confederate Cavalry Wood's Regiment Private 1 Company G	Baker, Charles W
Confederate Cavalry Wood's Regiment Private Company K	*Hyatt, Charles H
Confederate Congress	*Chambers, Henry Cousins
Confederate Congress	*Clapp, Jeremiah W
Confederate Congress	*Currin, David Maney Sr
Confederate Congress	**Haynes, Landon Carter
Confederate Congress	*Heiskell, Joseph Brown
Confederate Congress	*Swan, William Graham
Confederate Corps of Topo Engineers, Captain staff of General Leonidas Polk	Gray, A B
Confederate Corps of Topo Engineers, Lieutenant staff of General Leonidas Polk	*Snowden, John H
Confederate Johnson's Corps Major	*Guy, William Wallace
Confederate Marine Corps Captain Hays Company	Sheridan, Michael
Confederate Navy Assistant Surgeon	*Freeman, Dr Robert J
Confederate Nitre and Mining Bureau War Department Lieutenant Colonel	*Hunt, William R
Confederate Quartermaster Department Agent Major and Captain of Artillery	*Monsarrat, George H
Confederate Sapper & Miners	*Parker, Minter
Confederate Sapper & Miners	*Vigus, James H
Confederate Secret Agent	*Edmondson, Isabella B
Confederate Soldier	*Dawson, John F
Confederate Soldier	*Evans, Russ
Confederate Soldier	James
Confederate Soldier	*Jones, Dr John W
Confederate Soldier	*Purdy, Charles R
Confederate Surgeon Cheatham's Corps	*McGee, Dr John P
Confederate Surgeon & Medical Director McGown's Corps	*Bell, Dr William S
Confederate Surgeon	*Avent, Dr Benjamin W
Confederate Surgeon	*Erskine, Dr Alexander O
Confederate Surgeon	*Erskine, Dr John H
Confederate Surgeon	*Saunders, Dr Dudley D
Confederate Assistant Surgeon	*Armstrong, Dr William J
Confederate Assistant Surgeon	Buford, Dr Smith
Confederate Assistant Surgeon	*Moore, Dr George H
Confederate Spy	*Moon, Virginia B
Confederate Spy	*Watson, Ellen M
Confederate Spy and Smuggler	*Shover, Felicia Lee Carey Thornton
Confederate 1 Cavalry Regiment Captain Assistant Quartermaster	*Douglass, J E
Confederate 1 Cavalry Regiment 2 Lieutenant 2 Company C	*Goodbar, James M
Confederate 1 (King's Battalion) Cavalry Regiment Private (Gray's) 2 Company F	Burks, William
Confederate 1 (King's Battalion) Cavalry Regiment Private (Gray's) 2 Company F	Carrick, George
Confederate 1 (King's Battalion) Cavalry Regiment Private (Gray's) 2 Company F	Carrick, John

Confederate 1 (King's Battalion) Cavalry Regiment Private (Gray's) 2 Company F	Grooms, J C
Confederate 1 (King's Battalion) Cavalry Regiment Private (Gray's) 2 Company F	Hatton, W H
Confederate 1 (King's Battalion) Cavalry Regiment Private (Gray's) 2 Company F	Noonan, John
Confederate 1 (King's Battalion) Cavalry Regiment Private (Gray's) 2 Company F	Roark, W T
Confederate 1 (King's Battalion) Cavalry Regiment Private (Gray's) 2 Company F	Thomas, W H
Confederate 1 (King's Battalion) Cavalry Regiment Private (Gray's) 2 Company F	Thompson, Thomas
Confederate 1 Cavalry Regiment Company I	*Collier, William A
Confederate 1 Cavalry Regiment Company I	*Howard, William T
Confederate 1 Cavalry Regiment 1 Lieutenant (M J Wick's) Company I	*Estes, Zenas N
Confederate 1 Cavalry Regiment Private (M J Wick's) Company I	*Loudon, Milton B
CONFEDERATE 2 INFANTRY REGIMENT ORIGINALLY MISSISSIPPI 25 INFANTRY REGIMENT	
Confederate 2 Infantry Regiment Colonel	*Martin, John D
Confederate 2 Infantry Regiment Adjutant	*Donelson, Daniel S
Confederate 2 Infantry Regiment Private Company G	Nelson, Irvin
Confederate 2 Infantry Regiment Private Company I	Tucker, Adolphus F
Confederate 2 Infantry Regiment Captain Company K	*Jackson, David F
Confederate 2 Infantry Regiment Private (D F Jackson's) Company K	*Jackson, Charles H
Confederate 3 Infantry Regiment Lieutenant Colonel	*Cameron, John F
Confederate 3 Infantry Regiment Captain Quartermaster	*Jarnagin, John H
Confederate 3 Infantry Regiment Private Company B	*Bourne, Edward
CONFEDERATE 4 (BAKER'S) INFANTRY REGIMENT (ALSO KNOWN AS 1 ALABAMA, TENNESSEE AND MISSISSIPPI INFANTRY REGIMENT)	
Confederate 4 Infantry Regiment Lieutenant Colonel (Colonel Tennessee 39 Avery's Infantry)	*Avery, William T
Confederate 4 Infantry Regiment Private (Griffin's Rifles) Company B	Henderson, John W
Confederate 4 Infantry Regiment Private (Griffin's Rifles) Company B	Mims, John T
Confederate 4 Infantry Regiment Private (Griffin's Rifles) Company B	Smith, Armstrong B
Confederate 4 (Baker's) Infantry Regiment Private Company B	Wallace, R J
Confederate 4 Infantry Regiment Private (Alabama 1 Infantry Griffin's Rifles) Company B	Yearger, Elias
Confederate 4 (Baker's) Infantry Regiment Private Company D	Hendricks, Daniel
Confederate 4 (Baker's) Infantry Regiment Private Company D	Lewis, Jacob
Confederate 4 (Baker's) Infantry Regiment Private Company F	Harwell, Washington
Confederate 4 Infantry Regiment Private (Andy Moore's Guards, Alabama) Company F	Holden, John
Confederate 4 Infantry Regiment Private Company F	Lassiter, Amos A
Confederate 4 (Baker's) Infantry Regiment Private Company K	Brown, John H
Confederate 5 Infantry Regiment (also known as 9 Infantry Regiment) Assistant Adjutant General	*Freeman, Edward T
Confederate 5 Infantry Regiment (also known as 9 Infantry Regiment) Captain Company B	*Frazer, Charles W
Confederate 5 Military District Mississippi Major Quartermaster	*Leath, Peter M
Confederate 8 Cavalry Regiment Private Company C	*McLendon, Andrew J
Confederate 8 Infantry Battalion (2 Foreign Legion, 2 Foreign Battalion) 2 Lieutenant Company F	*Hamlin, Edward L
Confederate 9 Infantry Regiment (also known as Confederate 5 Infantry Regiment) Major	*Person, Richard J
Confederate 9 Infantry Regiment (also known as Confederate 5 Infantry Regiment) Surgeon	Carlin. Dr. Robert F
CSA	*Stewart, Charles P
CSS General Beauregard Seaman	Conn, William
CSS General Bragg	Welsh, John
CSS Colonel Lovell	Malin, John
CSS Colonel Lovell Clerk/Purser	Steiner, J P
CSS Steamer Ponchatrain	Lane, Morris
CSS Shenandoah Lieutenant	*Scales, Dabney M
DeShea's Battalion Company F	Graham, A H
Doctor	*William, Dr J Joseph
Elmwood Cemetery President	*Lenow, Joseph
Flannery's Company	Smith, N D
Flarney's Company	Mitchell, John
Florida 1 Infantry Regiment Colonel	*Anderson, James P
Florida 1 Infantry Regiment Private/Corporal (Old) Company D & New Company C	*Paddison, Edward W
Florida 6 Infantry Regiment Private Company B	Tomberland, William H
Florida 7 Regiment	Higgins, S S
Forrest's Cavalry Corps Major and Quartermaster	*Warren, Archibald
Forrest's Scouts Private (Harvey's Company Scouts)	January, W W
Gallimard's Company Sappers & Miners 2 Sapper	Ehretsman, Joseph
General Steins' Bodyguard (Cooper's) Company	Embree, William
General Polk's Staff	*Greenlaw, J Oliver

Georgia Cobb's Legion Cavalry Battalion Company D	High, Edward D
Georgia 1 Local Troops Infantry Private Company D	Farris, Miles H
Georgia 8 Infantry Regiment Colonel	*Gardner, William M
Georgia 8 Infantry Regiment	Harper, John
Georgia 34 Infantry Regiment Private Company D	Harper, John
Georgia 56 Infantry Regiment Private Company E	Golden, George W
Harmon's Regiment (Sherman's) Company	Strussell, Thomas
Heth's Division Captain & Assistant Quartermaster	Cage, John F
Hindman's Regiment	Dierman, Daniel
Homers Artillery Price's Division	Nicholson, Daniel R
Inspector General Staff of General Joseph Wheeler, Lieutenant	*Cochran, John W
Inspector General Staff of General John C Pemberton, Major	*Thompson, Jacob
J B Clark's Battalion (Steven Casper's) Company	Davis, Clarence W
Jeff Thompson's Command (McDonald's) Company	Dowdy, John T
Jeff Thompson's Brigade Lieutenant Kelsey's Company	Gentry, J A
Johnson's (Major) Battalion	McFarland, J
Johnson's Corps Major	*Guy, William Wallace
Jones' Battalion (Love's) Company	Reynolds, E
Jones Battery of Memphis	Elam, W S
Judge Advocate Colonel	*Morgan, Robert J
Kentucky 1 Cavalry Regiment Private Company B	Hamilton, Isiah
Kentucky 2 Cavalry Regiment (2 Battalion Mounted Riflemen) Private Companies A/I	Elam, W S
Kentucky 2 (Duke's) Cavalry Regiment 3 Lieutenant Company K	Cole, John B
Kentucky 2 (Duke's) Cavalry Regiment Private Company C	Patton, Lucius E
Kentucky 2 (Woodward's) Cavalry Regiment Sergeant (Boone Rangers) Company E	Overton, William G
Kentucky 3 Mounted Infantry Regiment Private Company D	Husbands, Henry L
Kentucky 5 Cavalry Regiment 1 Lieutenant Company I	*Myers, Daniel E
Kentucky 5 Infantry Regiment	**Bell, William Jr
Kentucky 5 Mounted Infantry Regiment 2 Lieutenant 3rd Company I	*Anderson, Abram K
Kentucky 7 Mounted Infantry Regiment Private (Stubblefield's) Company G	Holden, G W
Kentucky 7 Mounted Infantry Regiment Private Company K	Gregory, Edward
Kentucky 7 Mounted Infantry Regiment Private Company K	Pentecost, F J
Kentucky 9 Infantry Regiment Adjutant (Kentucky 5 Infantry)	**Bell, Jr William
Kentucky 9 Infantry Regiment Adjutant (Kentucky 5 Infantry)	*Anderson, Abram K
Lieutenant General	**Forrest, Nathan B
Lieutenant	*Snowden
Louisiana Captain Cole's Company Cavalry (Louisiana Mounted Rangers)	Bazar, Jacob
Louisiana Volunteer (Dreper's) Company	Fox, Peter
Louisiana 1 Cavalry Regiment Private Company C	*Brady, James H
Louisiana 1 Regiment Company G	Sharpling, Lemuel
Louisiana 3 (Harrison's) Cavalry Regiment 1 Lieutenant Company B	*Nolley, Thomas L
Louisiana 5 Battalion Company G	Simpson, John F
Louisiana 9 Infantry Regiment Private/Corporal Company E	*O'Connor, David
Louisiana 11 Infantry Regiment Private Company B	McCormic, Patrick
Louisiana 12 Infantry Regiment Private Company A	McCaghren, James
Louisiana 12 Infantry Regiment Private Company C	Peoples, John W
Louisiana 12 Infantry Regiment Private Company C	Rogers, Oliver G
Louisiana 12 Infantry Regiment Private Company D	Curry, James D
Louisiana 12 Infantry Regiment Private Company D	Walker, James A
Louisiana 12 Infantry Regiment Private (Steven's) Company F	Andrews, H J
Louisiana 12 Infantry Regiment Private (Steven's) Company F	Pearson, N D
Louisiana 12 Infantry Regiment Private Company I	Anderson, Eli
Louisiana 12 Infantry Regiment Private Company I	Lambright, Lewis T
Louisiana 12 Infantry Regiment Private Company K	Smith, B A
Louisiana 12 Regiment Company K	Hardee, George W
Louisiana 12 Regiment	Henson, W H
Louisiana 12 Regiment (Not Organized)	Land, William T
Louisiana 12 Regiment	Lee, Richard
Louisiana 12 Regiment	Vevers, J
Louisiana 13 Infantry Regiment Private Company B	Brown, George
Louisiana 13 Infantry Regiment Private Company G	Haifleigh, Augustus
Louisiana 13 Regiment Company H	Collins, Thomas

Louisiana 16 (Gober's) Infantry Regiment Colonel	*Gober, Daniel C
Louisiana 16 Infantry Regiment Private Company E	*Taylor, Arthur K (Memorial)
Louisiana 18 Regiment Company K	*Adams, Reuben B
Louisiana 19 Regiment	Bostick, Samuel
Louisiana 21 (Kennedy's) Infantry Regiment Private Company E	Clair, John
Louisiana 21 Regiment Company A	Nelson, C
Louisiana 21 Regiment Company D	McClanahan, W P
Louisiana 21 Regiment Company D	McClusky, W P
Louisiana 21 Regiment Company G	Pyburn, John
Louisiana 21 Regiment Company H	Gantron, Jack
Louisiana 21 Regiment Company I	Hunter, James
Louisiana 25 Infantry Regiment Private Company E	Smith, Robert
Louisiana 25 Infantry Regiment Private Company E	Whitescarver, Frederick W
Louisiana 25 Infantry Regiment Private Company H	Peak, T J
Louisiana 25 Infantry Regiment Private Company H	Hutto, Thomas
Louisiana 25 Infantry Regiment Private Company H	Sims, G W
Louisiana 25 Infantry Regiment Private Company H	Daly, William L
Louisiana 25 Infantry Regiment Private (Scarborough's) Company K	Lefebere, John
Major General	*Anderson, James P
Major	*Weatherford, William G
Mayor of Memphis	*Park, John
Martin's Regiment Company G	Morris, Richard
Martin's Regiment Ray's Company	Martin, Alfred
McCown's Brigade Company H	Woods, S K
McNair's Regiment Company E	Schinon, E H
Memphis Legion (Tennessee 3 Infantry Battalion) Colonel	*Dixon, Leonida V
Memphis Appeal Battery (Arkansas 5 Battery Light Artillery)	Morfels, Henry
Memphis Daily Appeal Editor and Proprietor	*McClanahan, John R
Memphis Daily Appeal Business Manager and Co-Partner	*Dill, Benjamin F
Miller's Battalion (Harris') Company	Bagley, Humphrey
Miller's Battalion (Holmes') Company	Finley, C M
Miller's Battalion (Holmes') Company	Hardin, William
Miller's Regiment Company G	Lingo, George
Mississippi Ballentine's Cavalry Regiment Lieutenant Colonel	*Thompson, Jacob
Mississippi Blythe's Rifles	Thompson, W J
Mississippi English's Company Light Artillery Captain	*English, Richard T
Mississippi Graves' Company Light Artillery (Issaquena Battery)	Matthews, John B
Mississippi Hoole's Company Light Artillery (Hudson's) (Pettus Flying Artillery)	Montjoy, P T
Mississippi Montgomery's Company of Scouts	Roden, George
Mississippi Rifles Company D Drummer Boy	*Hessen, George A
Mississippi Soldier	*Sanford, Dr William B
Mississippi Soldier	Spencer, Benjamin
Mississippi State Troops & Militia	*Trezevant, Nathaniel W
Mississippi Volunteers Captain Dockery	Teufel, Fred
Mississippi Captain J. J. Gage's Company ("Wigfall Guards") State Troops	*Bill, Nelson, A
Mississippi Captain M. D. Shelby's Company ("Bolivar Greys" Independent Company of State Troops)	*Shelby. Isaac
Mississippi Captain M. D. Shelby's Company ("Bolivar Greys" Independent Company of State Troops)	*Shelby. Moses D
Mississippi 1 Battalion Sharp Shooters Private Company B	*Porter, John W
Mississippi 1 (Miller's) Cavalry Battalion 1 Sergeant Cole's Company	*Pinson, Richard A
Mississippi 1 (Miller's) Cavalry Battalion Private Cole's Company	*Dillard, Thomas D
Mississippi 1 (Miller's) Cavalry Battalion Private Company A	Roden, George
Mississippi 1 (Miller's) Cavalry Battalion Private Company K	Carter, Thomas J
Mississippi 1 Cavalry Regiment Colonel	*Pinson, Richard A
Mississippi 1 Cavalry Regiment Captain AQM & Lieutenant Company K	*Dillard, Thomas D
Mississippi 1 Cavalry Regiment Private Company A	Carter, Thomas J
Mississippi 1 Cavalry Regiment Private Company E (Captain George Polk's Rangers)	Foster, John T
Mississippi 1 Cavalry Regiment Sergeant Company H	*Anderson, William L
Mississippi 1 Cavalry Regiment Private Company H	Roden, George
Mississippi 1 Infantry Battalion Company A	Tucker, Adolphus F
Mississippi 1 (Johnston's) Infantry Regiment Captain Company K, Lieutenant Colonel	**Hamilton, Alexander S
Mississippi 1 (Johnston's) Infantry Regiment Private Company K	Morris, Thomas
Mississippi 2 Battalion Cavalry Reserves Company I Senior 2 Lieutenant	*Lake, Richard P

Mississippi 2 Cavalry Regiment Company D	Tucker, Adolphus F
Mississippi 2 (Ballentine's Regiment of Cavalry) Partisan Rangers Captain Company C	*Porter, Edward E
Mississippi 2 (Ballentine's Regiment of Cavalry) Partisan Rangers Corporal Private Company C	*Marley, Hampton Y
Mississippi 2 (Ballentine's Regiment of Cavalry) Partisan Rangers Private Company C	*Greenlaw, Alonzo
Mississippi 2 (Ballentine's Regiment of Cavalry) Partisan Rangers Private Company C	*Lowry, William J
Mississippi 2 (Ballentine's Regiment of Cavalry) Partisan Rangers Private Company C	*Talley, William F
Mississippi 2 (Ballentine's Regiment of Cavalry) Partisan Rangers Private Company C	*Wills, William A
Mississippi 2 (Ballentine's Regiment of Cavalry) Partisan Rangers Captain Company E	*McDowell, William W
Mississippi 2 (Ballentine's Regiment of Cavalry) Partisan Rangers Sergeant Company E	*McDowell, John H
Mississippi 2 Infantry Regiment Private Company C	Pettigrew, James L
Mississippi 2 Infantry Regiment 1 Lieutenant Company D	*Harris, Cornelius L
Mississippi 3 Cavalry (E Q Withers) Company	Boyd, Carter M
Mississippi 3 Regiment Company E	Wilkerson, George
Mississippi 4 Cavalry Militia Company C 2 Lieutenant	*Lake, Richard P
Mississippi 4 Regiment Company K	Pringle, W
Mississippi 5 Cavalry Regiment Captain Company D	Scales, William M
Mississippi 6 Cavalry Assistant Surgeon	*Moore, Dr George H
Mississippi 6 Infantry Regiment Private Company B	Fortune, Asa J
Mississippi 7 Cavalry Regiment Private Company F	Carter, Thomas J
Mississippi 7 Infantry Regiment Private Company A	Gunter, John F
Mississippi 8 Cavalry Regiment Colonel	*Duff, William L
Mississippi 8 Cavalry Regiment Private Company C	Murphree, Anderson
Mississippi 9 Infantry Regiment Colonel	*Chalmers, James R
Mississippi 9 Infantry Regiment Colonel	*Whitfield, Francis E
Mississippi 9 Infantry Regiment Private (Old) Company K & Sergeant (New) Company K	Cotton, James R
Mississippi 9 Infantry Regiment Private Old Company K	*Johnston, James V
Mississippi 10 Infantry Regiment (Crook's) Company	Wilder, H H
Mississippi 10 Infantry Regiment Private Company M & New Company D	*Moode, Henry
Mississippi 11 (Perrin's) Cavalry Regiment Private Company C	*Carson, Orval
Mississippi 11 Infantry Regiment Company G	*Chilton, Thomas H
Mississippi 11 Infantry Regiment Private Company H	*Owen, Ben H
Mississippi 11 Infantry Regiment Private Company K	Jennings, John W
Mississippi 11 Regiment	Arnold, William
Mississippi 12 Cavalry Regiment Adjutant	*Phelan, George R
Mississippi 12 Cavalry Regiment Captain Company F	*Ward, John W
Mississippi 14 Battalion Light Artillery & Yates Battery Private Company B	*Finch, William F
Mississippi 14 Infantry Regiment Private Company K	*Gallaway, John B
Mississippi 15 Infantry Regiment Private Company F	Buford, Smith
Mississippi 17 (Steede's) Cavalry Battalion Assistant Surgeon	Buford, Dr Smith
Mississippi 17 Infantry Regiment Colonel	*Fiser, John C
Mississippi 17 Infantry Regiment 3 Lieutenant	*Duff, William L
Mississippi 17 Infantry Regiment Sergeant Major Company F	Cloud, Joseph F
Mississippi 17 Infantry Regiment 1 Sergeant Company G	*Scales, Dabney M
Mississippi 17 Infantry Regiment Private Company B	*Venn, Frank H
Mississippi 17 Infantry Regiment Corporal/Captain Company H	*Wright, Jesse C
Mississippi 17 Regiment Company B	Bronhors, A
Mississippi 18 Cavalry Regiment Private Company F	*Bullington, Richard E
Mississippi 18 Cavalry Battalion Captain Company C	*Carroll, William H
Mississippi 19 Cavalry Battalion Lieutenant Colonel	*Duff, William L
Mississippi 19 Infantry Regiment Captain Company E	*Jones, Columbus F
Mississippi 19 Infantry Regiment Private Company F	Strickland, William V
Mississippi 19 Infantry Regiment Private Company I	Harris, Andrew J
Mississippi 19 Infantry Regiment Private Company I	*Venn, Frank H
Mississippi 21 Infantry Regiment Private Company A	Adams, Walter W
Mississippi 21 Infantry Regiment Private Company A	*McEllroy, Virginius A
Mississippi 22 (Bonham's) Infantry Regiment Private Company C	Hanrahan, James
Mississippi 22 (Bonham's) Infantry Regiment Private Company C	Taylor, William
Mississippi 22 (Bonham's) Infantry Regiment Private Company E	Dunn, John C
Mississippi 22 Infantry Regiment 1 Lieutenant Company H	*Word, Charles S
Mississippi 22 (Bonham's) Infantry Regiment Private Company I	Walton, Tilman
Mississippi 22 (Bonham's) Infantry Regiment Private Company K	Harrison, Thomas
Mississippi 22 (Bonham's) Infantry Regiment Private (Lester's) Company K	Jones, James L

Mississippi 22 (Bonham's) Infantry Regiment Private Company K	Leverett, Martin M
Mississippi 23 Infantry Regiment Private Company E	Smith, James
Mississippi 23 Infantry Regiment Private/Corporal Company E	Thomas, John P
Mississippi 24 Regiment	Shaw, C M
Mississippi 25 (Martin's) Infantry Regiment Colonel	*Martin, John D
Mississippi 25 (Martin's) Infantry Regiment Private Company F	Hamilton, Isiah
Mississippi 25 Infantry Regiment Private (O'Haver's) Company F	*Kirwan, J W
Mississippi 25 Infantry Regiment Private Company H "Wigfall Guards"	Bryant, J W
Mississippi 25 Infantry Regiment Private Company I	Tucker, Adolphus F
Mississippi 26 Infantry Regiment Private Company A	Barnett, Miles R
Mississippi 26 Infantry Regiment Private Company C	Ricketts, John C
Mississippi 26 Infantry Regiment Private/Musician Company F	Smith, Joel H
Mississippi 28 Cavalry Regiment 3 Lieutenant/Captain Company E ("Mayson's Dragoons")	*Shelby, Evan J
Mississippi 28 Cavalry Regiment Private/Captain Company E ("Mayson's Dragoons")	*Shelby, Isaac
Mississippi 29 Infantry Regiment Corporal Company C	*Pepper, Samuel A
Mississippi 29 Infantry Regiment Ordnance Sergeant Company I	*Johnston, James V
Mississippi 29 Infantry Regiment Sergeant Company I	*Vance, Rienzi H
Mississippi 31 Infantry Regiment Company I	Johnson, Jack
Mississippi 34 Infantry Regiment Private Company E	*Woodson, Henry M
Mississippi 44 (Blythe's 1 Battalion) Infantry Regiment Private Company B	Boyle, Robert
Mississippi 44 (Blythe's 1 Battalion) Infantry Regiment Private (Humphries') Company B	Owen, F M
Mississippi 44 (Blythe's 1 Battalion) Infantry Regiment Private (Du Berry's) Company C	Davis, Samuel T
Mississippi 44 (Blythe's 1 Battalion) Infantry Regiment Sergeant Company E	*Faires, James B
Mississippi 44 (Blythe's 1 Battalion) Infantry Regiment Private/Corporal Company E	*Faires, William A
Mississippi 44 Infantry Regiment Private Company H	*Rives, Charles B
Mississippi 44 Infantry Regiment Company K	Gunter, John F
Mississippi 44 (Blythe's 1 Battalion) Infantry Regiment Private Company K	McDaniel, Daniel
Missouri Clark's Infantry Regiment Private (Wright's) Company C	Jones, R
Missouri Farris' Battery Light Artillery (Clark Artillery) Sergeant/Private	Ing, Richard
Missouri Gaines Artillery	Bradburg, Thomas R
Missouri Goram's Artillery	Webb, George
Missouri H M Bledsoe's Company Light Artillery Private	Brown, Benjamin
Missouri Landis' Company Light Artillery	Sheffield, William
Missouri Priest's Regiment (Hughes') Company	Tippet, Zachariah
Missouri R C Wood's Cavalry Regiment	*McHenry, Eli B
Missouri Ross' Regiment (Waddell's) Company	Ward, Isaac N
Missouri Snider's Cavalry Battalion Company E	Hefferon, Thomas
Missouri State Guard Captain & Drill Master	*Flournoy, R Hall
Missouri State Guard 9 Regiment Cavalry	*Swingley, Alfred L
Missouri State Guard (Gant's) Company	Hart, C F
Missouri Windsor Guards, General Price's Escort (Missouri 2 Cavalry Regiment 3 Company K)	Bellows, John W
Missouri 1 Cavalry Regiment Private Company D	Fletcher, John N
Missouri 1 NE Cavalry (Missouri Porter's Cavalry)	Hefferon, Thomas
Missouri 1 Infantry Battalion Brevet 2 Lieutenant Company B (Thompson's Brigade)	Carman, Samuel M
Missouri 1 Infantry Battalion Corporal Company C	Kelly, James A
Missouri 1 Infantry Battalion Private Company C	Bullard, St Clare
Missouri 1 Infantry Battalion Private Company C	Melton, John
Missouri 1 Infantry Battalion Private (Kelsey's) Company C	Saxon, Irving
Missouri 1 Infantry Battalion Private (Kelsey's) Company C	Stephens, Felix
Missouri 1 Infantry Battalion Private Company C	Wood, Edward
Missouri 1 Infantry Regiment Company C Lieutenant Aide de Camp	*Dean, Joseph S
Missouri 1 Infantry Regiment Captain (New) Company C	*Jackson, David F
Missouri 1 Infantry Regiment Private (New) Company C	*Jackson, Charles H
Missouri 1 Infantry Regiment (New) Company C	Hamilton, Isiah
Missouri 1 (Bowen's) Infantry Regiment Sergeant Company D	Phillips, James
Missouri 1 Infantry Regiment Private Company F	**Dunnico, Parker
Missouri 1 Infantry Regiment Sergeant Company H	Langford, Jordan H
Missouri 1 Infantry Regiment Private Company I	Henly, James M
Missouri 1 Infantry Regiment Private (Phillip's) Company I	Pinnell, A N
Missouri 1 Infantry Regiment Private Company K	Ashley, James D
Missouri 1 Infantry Regiment Private Company K	Marcus, G M
Missouri 1 Infantry Regiment Private Company K	Wheeler, George

Missouri 1 Regiment Company B	Jackson, J A
Missouri 1 Regiment Company C	Northup, A J
Missouri 1 Regiment Company H	Harris, Joseph
Missouri 1 Regiment Company I	Arondale, Anthony
Missouri 1 Regiment Volunteer	McCardy, George R
Missouri 2 Cavalry Regiment Private Company A	Eubank, R P
Missouri 2 Cavalry Regiment Sergeant Company E	Horn, D W
Missouri 2 Cavalry Regiment Private Company G	Nash, Abner W
Missouri 2 Cavalry Regiment Private Company G	Romine, Henry
Missouri 2 Cavalry Regiment Private Company H	*Myers, Henry C
Missouri 2 Regiment Company C	Ditchler, G W
Missouri 3 Cavalry Regiment Colonel	*Greene, Colton
Missouri 4 Infantry Regiment (Missouri 1 Brigade) Private (Walker's) Company A	Antrim, Henry
Missouri 4 Infantry (Major Johnson's Battalion) Regiment Private Company H	McFarland, Andrew J
Missouri 5 (McCown's) Infantry Regiment Private Company A	Cooper, James A
Missouri 6 (Hedgpeth's Battalion) Infantry Regiment Corporal (Kelsey's) Company K	Kelley, James A
Missouri 6 Infantry Private Company K (Jeff Thompson's Command)	Stephens, Felix
Missouri 6 Regiment Company C	*Evans, James M
Missouri 6 Regiment Company H	Donnell, A L
Missouri 14 Cavalry State Guard Company C	Warwick, W L
Missouri 16 Infantry (Van Horn's Battalion) Regiment Private Company A	*Spears, John H
Mother of the Confederacy	*Law, Sarah C
Mounted Battalion (Foot's) Company	White, J F
North Arkansas and Indian Territory Chief Inspector and Ordnance Officer	*DuBose, Julius J
North Carolina 3 Infantry Regiment (State Troops) Chaplin	*Patterson, Reverend George
North Carolina 17 Infantry Regiment (1 Organization) Private Company D	Williford, Sr David J
Ordnance Department, Charlotte, South Carolina	*Trezevant, Mayre B
Ordnance Officer, Lieutenant, General Preston's Staff	*Whitfield, Edward
Pheister's Battalion Company E	McClintock, Edwin M
Phressen's Battalion Company D	Graden, John
Price's Division	*Dominico, Frank
Price's Division	Redding, Benjamin J
Provost Marshall (Western Tennessee, Eastern Arkansas and Northern Mississippi)	*Smith, James H
Quartermaster, Captain, Commissary Department	*Goodbar, James M
Quartermaster, Major	*Hodges, Fleming
Quartermaster, Major, Polk's Corps Army of Tennessee	*Beecher, Edward A
Quartermaster, Major, Stewart's Corps Army of Tennessee	*Beard, William D
Quartermaster, Major, Staff of Brigadier General William H. C. Whiting	Jones, George W
Riverboat Captain	*Loudon, John
Servant Slave of 1st Lieutenant T. J. Shelton Company B Arkansas 13 Infantry Regiment	*Shelton, Jack
Sharpshooter	Stocks, James
Smead's Regiment Company F	Bell, G W
South Carolina 1 Cavalry Regiment Private Company I	Blocker, James A R
South Carolina 3 Infantry Battalion Private Company C	Culberson, John H
South Carolina 6 Provisional Regiment	*De Saussure, Charles A
South Carolina 8 Regiment	*De Saussure, Charles A
South Carolina 10 Regiment Private Company F	Broach, Redding
South Carolina 10 Regiment Private (Miller's) Company F	Evans, N
South Carolina 32 Regiment of Volunteers (Note: no such Regiment)	*Dockery, James M
South Carolina Charleston Ordnance Battalion Major	*Trezevant, John T
South Carolina Stuart's Artillery (Beaufort Volunteer Artillery) Captain	*De Saussure, Charles A
Southern Mothers Hospital	*Law, Sarah C
Southern Mothers Hospital	*Pope. Mary Foote
Steamboat Captain & Builder	*Shirley, John T
Telegraph Operator Army of Tennessee	*Hughes, Bernard
Tennessee & Alabama 1 Regiment (Heath's) Company	Johnson, Matthew
Tennessee Artillery Corps	*Shields, William S
Tennessee Artillery (McCown's) Corps	*Maier, Maxmillian
Tennessee Artillery (McCown's) Corps Captain Company 6	*Bankhead, Smith P
Tennessee Artillery (McCown's) Corps Captain Company 11	*Monsarrat, George H
Tennessee Artillery Corps Johnston's Company Assistant Surgeon	*Thornton, Gustavus B
Tennessee Bankhead's Battery (Tennessee Scott's Light Artillery) Captain	*Bankhead, Smith P

Tennessee Bankhead's Battery (Tennessee Scott's Light Artillery) 1 Lieutenant	*Humes, W Y C
Tennessee Bankhead's Battery (Tennessee Scott's Light Artillery)	Bradshaw, A
Tennessee Bankhead's Battery (Tennessee Scott's Light Artillery) Harris' Company	Carwile, Flemuel
Tennessee Bankhead's Battery (Tennessee Scott's Light Artillery) Harris' Company	Castinere, Antonio
Tennessee Bankhead's Battery (Tennessee Scott's Light Artillery)	Hill, James
Tennessee Bankhead's Battery (Tennessee Scott's Light Artillery)	Josey, William H
Tennessee Bankhead's Battery (Tennessee Scott's Light Artillery)	Keller, Wesley M
Tennessee Bankhead's Battery (Tennessee Scott's Light Artillery)	Ludlow, S
Tennessee Bankhead's Battery (Tennessee Scott's Light Artillery) Harris' Company	Nall, William
Tennessee Bankhead's Battery (Tennessee Scott's Light Artillery)	Ragland, J W
Tennessee Bankhead's Battery (Tennessee Scott's Light Artillery) Harris' Company	Rodgers, John
Tennessee Bankhead's Battery (Tennessee Scott's Light Artillery)	Wallace, J
Tennessee Bibb's Company Artillery Corporal (Hailman's)	Graydon, G W A
Tennessee Bibb's Company Artillery Private (Memphis Guerillas)	Brewster, J J
Tennessee Bibb's Company Artillery (Hailman's)	Evans, John B
Tennessee Bibb's Company Artillery (Hailman's Guerillas)	King, S M
Tennessee Cavalry (Private Company H on grave stone)	Erwin, J C
Tennessee Cavalry Private Company I	Jones, William R
Tennessee Collins' Cavalry Regiment (Partisan Rangers) Colonel	*Collins, Nathaniel D
Tennessee Carnes' (Marshall's & Steuben's) Artillery	*Rice, Paul S
Tennessee Crain's Artillery	Hopkins, Henry
Tennessee Forrest's Cavalry Regiment Adjutant	*Trezevant, Edward B
Tennessee Governor	*Harris, Isham G
Tennessee Johnston's Heavy Artillery Company Captain	*Hamilton, James
Tennessee Johnston's Heavy Artillery Company 2 Lieutenant/Captain	*Hamilton, Jr S H D
Tennessee Johnston's Heavy Artillery Private Hamilton's Company	*Cousins, Peter R
Tennessee Johnston's Heavy Artillery Private Hamilton's Company	*Fisher, Charles G
Tennessee Johnston's Heavy Artillery Private Hamilton's Company	*Fisher, Philip A
Tennessee Johnston's Heavy Artillery Private Hamilton's Company	*Piper, Oliver H
Tennessee Johnston's Heavy Artillery Private Hamilton's Company	*Trout, William W
Tennessee Johnston's Heavy Artillery Private Hamilton's Company	*Wardlaw, John L
Tennessee Judge Advocate, Captain of Cavalry	*Brown, Thomas W
Tennessee Logwood's Cavalry	*Greenwood, Edmund R
Tennessee Monsarrat's Light Artillery Battalion Captain	*Monsarrat, George H
Tennessee McCown's Artillery Corps Lieutenant Colonel	*Haynes, Milton A
Tennessee Artillery (McCown's) Corps Captain Company 11	*Monsarrat, George H
Tennessee Harding Artillery	*Monsarrat, George H
Tennessee Newsom's Cavalry Regiment Lieutenant Colonel Forrest Command	*Swingley, Alfred L
Tennessee Phillips' Company Light Artillery Captain	*Wright, Eldridge E
Tennessee Phillips' Company Light Artillery Sergeant	*Brown, Joseph J
Tennessee Phillips' Company Light Artillery Private	Wheeler, James W
Tennessee Preston's Company "The Memphis Greys" Captain	*Preston, Thomas W
Tennessee Rice's Company Light Artillery 2 Lieutenant	*Jones, Daniel C
Tennessee Shelton's Company Volunteer	Duffo, Stephen M
Tennessee Sullivan County Reserves (Local Defense), Captain Witcher's Company Home Guard	*Long, Rev Nicholas M
Tennessee Tobin's Company Light Artillery Sergeant Major	*Wardlaw, John L
Tennessee Unassigned (Machinist and Pistol Factory)	Farris, Miles H
Tennessee Winston's (Keiter's Battery) Light Artillery Company 2 Lieutenant	*Hughes, Bernard
Tennessee Woodward's Cavalry Company Private	*Trice, Nathan W
Tennessee 1 Heavy Artillery Corporal 3 Company A & Stewart's Artillery	*Whitehead, Henry B
Tennessee 1 (Jones') Heavy Artillery Private Company D/F	Baird, Felix
Tennessee 1 Heavy Artillery (Rucker's Battery) 2 Lieutenant	Clark, William M
Tennessee 1 Heavy Artillery 1 Lieutenant Company L	*Cousins, Peter R
Tennessee 1 Heavy Artillery Private Company L & 3 Company A	*Trout, William W
Tennessee 1 (Field's) Infantry Regiment Adjutant/1 Lieutenant Company C	*Snowden, Robert B
Tennessee 2 (Robison's) Infantry Regiment Major	*Driver, William T
Tennessee 2 (Robison's) Infantry Regiment Surgeon	*Erskine, Alexander O
Tennessee 2 (Robison's) Infantry Regiment Assistant Surgeon	*Erskine, John H
Tennessee 2 (Robison's) Infantry Regiment Captain Company E	*Hunt, Casper Wistar
Tennessee 2 (Walker's) Infantry Regiment Colonel	*Walker, Joseph Knox
Tennessee 2 (Walker's) Infantry Regiment Lieutenant Colonel	*Ross, W B
Tennessee 2 (Walker's) Infantry Regiment Assistant Surgeon	*McCormick, Dr Charles

Tennessee 2 (Walker's) Infantry Regiment Brevet 2 Lieutenant Company A · *Greenlaw, Alonzo
Tennessee 2 (Walker's) Infantry Regiment Private Company A · Shea, Michael
Tennessee 2 (Walker's) Infantry Regiment Captain Company B · *Triplett, William P
Tennessee 2 (Walker's) Infantry Regiment Private Company B · Jackson, Reuben
Tennessee 2 (Walker's) Infantry Regiment Private Company B · Wicks, George D
Tennessee 2 (Walker's) Infantry Regiment Private Company D · Cahill, Edward
Tennessee 2 (Walker's) Infantry Regiment Private Company D · Dempsey, John J
Tennessee 2 (Walker's) Infantry Regiment Private Company D · Ferguson, Terrence
Tennessee 2 (Walker's) Infantry Regiment Private Company D · Gleason, Michael
Tennessee 2 (Walker's) Infantry Regiment Private Company D · Norton, Peter
Tennessee 2 (Walker's) Infantry Regiment Captain Company E · *Porter, Edward E
Tennessee 2 (Walker's) Infantry Regiment Sergeant Company E · *Helbring, Adolphus
Tennessee 2 (Walker's) Infantry Regiment Private Company E · Doyle, Wiley
Tennessee 2 (Walker's) Infantry Regiment Private Company E · *Rawlings, Richard J
Tennessee 2 (Walker's) Infantry Regiment Private Company F · Wren, Thomas
Tennessee 2 (Walker's) Infantry Regiment Private Company G · Worsham, John
Tennessee 2 (Walker's) Infantry Regiment 1 Sergeant Company H · Boyle, Thomas
Tennessee 2 (Walker's) Infantry Regiment Private Company H · Edgecomb, Melvin
Tennessee 2 (Walker's) Infantry Regiment 1 Lieutenant Company I · *Walker, James
Tennessee 2 (Walker's) Infantry Regiment Private Company I · Donohoe, Thomas
Tennessee 2 (Walker's) Infantry Regiment Private Company I · Lyons, Frank
Tennessee 2 (Walker's) Infantry Regiment Private Company K · *Volner, David
Tennessee 2 Regiment · Fount, James
Tennessee 2 Regiment Company A · *Saunders, Solomon H
Tennessee 2 Regiment Volunteer · Shean, John
Tennessee 3 (Forrest's) Cavalry Regiment Colonel · **Forrest, Nathan B
Tennessee 3 (Forrest's) Cavalry Regiment Lieutenant Colonel · *Allin, Philip T
Tennessee 3 (Forrest's) Cavalry Regiment Lieutenant Colonel · *Porter, Edward E
Tennessee 3 (Forrest's) Cavalry Regiment Major/Lieutenant Colonel and Private C · *Balch, Robert M
Tennessee 3 (Forrest's) Cavalry Regiment Major · *Forrest, William H
Tennessee 3 (Forrest's) Cavalry Regiment Major · *McDonald, Charles
Tennessee 3 (Forrest's) Cavalry Regiment Sergeant-Major · *Strange, John P
Tennessee 3 (Forrest's) Cavalry Regiment 1 Company A "Boone Rangers" · Overton, William G
TENNESSEE 3 (FORREST'S OLD) CAVALRY REGIMENT 2ND COMPANY A — ORIGINALLY TENNESSEE 154 SENIOR INFANTRY REGIMENT 1 COMPANY B ("BLUFF CITY GRAYS"), 11 (HOLMAN'S) CAVALRY REGIMENT COMPANY F, AND MCDONALD'S BATTALION COMPANY A — SEE CHAPTER "NOTES OF INTEREST"
Tennessee 3 (Forrest's) Cavalry Regiment Captain Company A · *Edmondson, James H
Tennessee 3 (Forrest's) Cavalry Regiment Captain Company A · *Pattison, Thomas F
Tennessee 3 (Forrest's) Cavalry Regiment Lieutenant Company A · *Creighton, John R
Tennessee 3 (Forrest's) Cavalry Regiment Lieutenant Company A · *Doyle, Washington J P
Tennessee 3 (Forrest's) Cavalry Regiment 2 Lieutenant Company A · *Southerland, James
Tennessee 3 (Forrest's) Cavalry Regiment Adjutant Company A · *Edmondson, Edmond A
Tennessee 3 (Forrest's) Cavalry Regiment Sergeant Company A · *Eanes, John E
Tennessee 3 (Forrest's) Cavalry Regiment Sergeant Company A · *Spicer, James W
Tennessee 3 (Forrest's) Cavalry Regiment Sergeant Company A · *Spicer, John E
Tennessee 3 (Forrest's) Cavalry Regiment Corporal Company A · *Jones, Robert C
Tennessee 3 (Forrest's) Cavalry Regiment Private/Musician Company A · *Davis, Charles B
Tennessee 3 (Forrest's) Cavalry Regiment Private Company A · *Bailey, Thomas F
Tennessee 3 (Forrest's) Cavalry Regiment Private Company A · *Anderson, George W
Tennessee 3 (Forrest's) Cavalry Regiment Private Company A · *Anderson, Isaac M
Tennessee 3 (Forrest's) Cavalry Regiment Private Company A · *Anderson, Julius C
Tennessee 3 (Forrest's) Cavalry Regiment Private Company A · *Craft, James H
Tennessee 3 (Forrest's) Cavalry Regiment Private Company A · *Dashiell, George
Tennessee 3 (Forrest's) Cavalry Regiment Private Company A · *Dillon, Charles R
Tennessee 3 (Forrest's) Cavalry Regiment Private Company A · Drake, John B
Tennessee 3 (Forrest's) Cavalry Regiment Private Company A · *Falls, George A
Tennessee 3 (Forrest's) Cavalry Regiment Private Company A · *Flournoy, Ryland H
Tennessee 3 (Forrest's) Cavalry Regiment Private Company A · *Grice, James W
Tennessee 3 (Forrest's) Cavalry Regiment Private Company A · *Haskell, William C
Tennessee 3 (Forrest's) Cavalry Regiment Private Company A · *McKinney, John F
Tennessee 3 (Forrest's) Cavalry Regiment Private Company A · *McKinney, William B

Tennessee 3 (Forrest's) Cavalry Regiment Private Company A	*Park, William H
Tennessee 3 (Forrest's) Cavalry Regiment Private Company A	*Pattison, Oliver G
Tennessee 3 (Forrest's) Cavalry Regiment Private Company A	*Poston, David H
Tennessee 3 (Forrest's) Cavalry Regiment Private Company A	*Rawlings, James S
Tennessee 3 (Forrest's) Cavalry Regiment Private Company A	*Rawlings, Richard J
Tennessee 3 (Forrest's) Cavalry Regiment Private Company A	*Rawlings, Stokely H
Tennessee 3 (Forrest's) Cavalry Regiment Private Company A	*Rives, John G
Tennessee 3 (Forrest's) Cavalry Regiment Private Company A	*Spicer, Samuel S
Tennessee 3 (Forrest's) Cavalry Regiment Private Company A	*Spicer, Robert A
Tennessee 3 (Forrest's) Cavalry Regiment Private Company A	*Stewart, Darwin M
Tennessee 3 (Forrest's) Cavalry Regiment Private Company A	*Titus, James T
Tennessee 3 (Forrest's) Cavalry Regiment Private Company A	*Titus, John F
Tennessee 3 (Forrest's) Cavalry Regiment Private Company A	*Walker, William P
Tennessee 3 (Forrest's) Cavalry Regiment Private Company A	*Wallace, Robert D
Tennessee 3 (Forrest's) Cavalry Regiment Private Company A	*Webb, William
Tennessee 3 (Forrest's) Cavalry Regiment Private Company A	Wehrle, Fred
Tennessee 3 (Forrest's) Cavalry Regiment Private Company A	*Wilkins, Charles W
Tennessee 3 (Forrest's) Cavalry Regiment Private Company A	*Wilkins, William G
Tennessee 3 (Forrest's) Cavalry Regiment Private Company A	*Wooldridge, Charles P
Tennessee 3 (Forrest's) Cavalry Regiment Captain Company B	*Barbour, James G
Tennessee 3 (Forrest's) Cavalry Regiment Lieutenant Company B	*Steinkuhl, Chris D
Tennessee 3 (Forrest's) Cavalry Regiment 2 Lieutenant Company B	*Lundy, E C
Tennessee 3 (Forrest's) Cavalry Regiment Sergeant Company B	*Cochran, Francis T
Tennessee 3 (Forrest's) Cavalry Regiment Corporal Company B	Palmer, Edward G
Tennessee 3 (Forrest's) Cavalry Regiment Private Company B	*Ammon, D C
Tennessee 3 (Forrest's) Cavalry Regiment Private Company B	*Devlin, James C
Tennessee 3 (Forrest's) Cavalry Regiment Private Company B	*Hart, Robert T G
Tennessee 3 (Forrest's) Cavalry Regiment Private Company B	Kearney (Kerney), J R
Tennessee 3 (Forrest's) Cavalry Regiment Private Company B	*Thornton, Dr. James B
Tennessee 3 (Forrest's) Cavalry Regiment Private Company B	*Ward, Charles C
Tennessee 3 (Forrest's) Cavalry Regiment Private 1 Company B	*McKinney, William B
Tennessee 3 (Forrest's) Cavalry Regiment Private 2 Company B	*Apperson, John W
Tennessee 3 (Forrest's) Cavalry Regiment Captain Company C	*May, Charles
Tennessee 3 (Forrest's) Cavalry Regiment Private Company C	*Barton, David H
Tennessee 3 (Forrest's) Cavalry Regiment Private Company C	Hall, James O
Tennessee 3 (Forrest's) Cavalry Regiment Captain Company D	*Forrest, Jesse A
Tennessee 3 (Forrest's) Cavalry Regiment (McDonald's Battalion) Private Company D	Crofford, John A
Tennessee 3 (Forrest's) Cavalry Regiment Private Company D "May's Avengers"	Harper, James J
Tennessee 3 (Forrest's) Cavalry Regiment Private 3 Company E	*Martin, John C
Tennessee 3 (Forrest's) Cavalry Regiment Private Company F	*Capers, Richard S
Tennessee 3 (Forrest's) Cavalry Regiment Private Company F	*Greenlaw, Alonzo
Tennessee 3 (Forrest's) Cavalry Regiment Private Company F	*Lowry, William J
Tennessee 3 (Forrest's) Cavalry Regiment Private Company F	*Marley, Hampton Y
Tennessee 3 (Forrest's) Cavalry Regiment Private Company G	*Nelson, William A
Tennessee 3 (Forrest's) Cavalry Regiment Private Company H	*Malone, Dr George B
Tennessee 3 (Forrest's) Cavalry Regiment Private Company K	*Anderson, Butler P
Tennessee 3 (Forrest's) Cavalry Regiment Private	*Springfield, Baker C
Tennessee 3 (Forrest's) Cavalry Regiment	Sanders, George H
Tennessee 3 (Memphis Battalion) Infantry Battalion 2 Lieutenant Company A	*Wormeley, Ralph
Tennessee 3 (Memphis Battalion) Infantry Battalion Corporal Company A	*Davie, Patrick H
Tennessee 3 (Memphis Battalion) Infantry Battalion Private Company A	*Simpson, James G
Tennessee 3 (Memphis Battalion) Infantry Battalion Private Company A	*Whitmore, Edwin
Tennessee 3 (Memphis Battalion) Infantry Battalion Private Company B	Baker, Peter
Tennessee 3 (Memphis Battalion) Infantry Battalion 2 Lieutenant Company C	*Pullen, Benjamin K
Tennessee 3 (Memphis Battalion) Infantry Battalion Private Company D	*Steinkuhl, Jacob
Tennessee 3 (Memphis Battalion) Infantry Battalion Sergeant Company E	*Bridges, William H
Tennessee 3 (Memphis Battalion) Infantry Battalion Private Company E	*Hunthousen, William
Tennessee 3 (Memphis Battalion) Infantry Battalion Captain Company F	*Buttinghaus, Frederick W
Tennessee 4 (Murray's) Cavalry Regiment 2 Lieutenant Company D	*Goodbar, James M
Tennessee 4 Infantry Regiment Lieutenant Colonel	*Finlay, Luke W
Tennessee 4 (Neely's) Infantry Regiment Major	*Henry, John F
Tennessee 4 Infantry Regiment Surgeon	*Green, Solomon P (Memorial)

Tennessee 4 Infantry Regiment Private/Lieutenant Company A   Dupuy, John J

Tennessee 4 Infantry Regiment Private/Sergeant Major Company A   *Beasley, James E

Tennessee 4 Infantry Regiment Sergeant Company A   *Poston, David H

Tennessee 4 Infantry Regiment Corporal Company A   *Parker, William G

Tennessee 4 Infantry Regiment Private Company A   Hawkins, William L C

Tennessee 4 Infantry Regiment Private Company A   *Hunt, Clarence P

Tennessee 4 Infantry Regiment Private Company A   *Moore, James W

Tennessee 4 Infantry Regiment Private Company A   *Omberg, James A

Tennessee 4 Infantry Regiment Private Company A   *Parker, Minter

Tennessee 4 Infantry Regiment Private Company A   *Pope, Andrew R

Tennessee 4 Infantry Regiment Private Company A   *Poston, Jr William K

Tennessee 4 Infantry Regiment Private Company A   *Townsend, George S

Tennessee 4 Infantry Regiment Private Company A   Seabrook, John T

Tennessee 4 Infantry Regiment Private Company A   *Trezevant, Lewis C

Tennessee 4 Infantry Regiment Private Company A   *Trezevant, Marye B

Tennessee 4 Infantry Regiment Private Company A   **Vickers, Benjamin C

Tennessee 4 Infantry Regiment Private Company A/F   Jefferson, Joshua T

Tennessee 4 Infantry Regiment Private Company B   Shivers, James N

Tennessee 4 Infantry Regiment Private Company D Musician Drummer   Wells, Julius T

Tennessee 4 Infantry Regiment Private Company E   Smith, John F

Tennessee 4 Infantry Regiment Lieutenant Company G   Nixon, William C

Tennessee 4 Infantry Regiment Private Company G   Chapman, Thomas

Tennessee 4 Infantry Regiment Private Company G   Dyal, G W

Tennessee 4 Infantry Regiment Private (Sutherland's) Company G   Roof, William C

Tennessee 4 Infantry Regiment Drummer Company H   Leland, Charles F

Tennessee 4 Infantry Regiment Private Company I   *Fisher, Charles G

Tennessee 4 Infantry Regiment Private Company I   *Fisher, Philip A

Tennessee 5 Infantry Regiment Sergeant Company A   Bradshaw, J W

Tennessee 5 Infantry Regiment Private Company A   Nairon, Green V

Tennessee 5 Infantry Regiment Private Company C   Charles, John H

Tennessee 5 Infantry Regiment Private Company C   Maynard, John H

Tennessee 5 Infantry Regiment Corporal 2 Company C   Hall, John W

Tennessee 5 Infantry Regiment Private Company F   Reynolds, E T

Tennessee 5 Infantry Regiment Private 2 Company I   *Nash, William J

Tennessee 5 Infantry Regiment Private Company K   Taylor, Joseph

Tennessee 5 Regiment Company M   Thornton, W B

Tennessee 6 (Logwood's) Cavalry Battalion Lieutenant Colonel   *Logwood, Thomas H

Tennessee 6 (Logwood's) Cavalry Battalion Private (White's) Company E "Tennessee Mounted Rifles"   **Forrest, Nathan B

Tennessee 6 (Logwood's) Cavalry Battalion Private (White's) Company E "Tennessee Mounted Rifles"   *Forrest, Jeffrey

Tennessee 6 (Logwood's) Cavalry Battalion Private (White's) Company E "Tennessee Mounted Rifles"   *Forrest, William

Tennessee 6 (Wheeler's) Cavalry Regiment Private Company K   *Rogers, Sr William Simeon

Tennessee 6 Infantry Regiment Major   **Williamson, Robert C

Tennessee 6 Infantry Regiment, Private Company D   *Watkins, Dr. Thomas R

Tennessee 6 Infantry Regiment Company H   *Perkins, Alfred H D

Tennessee 6 Infantry Regiment Private/Sergeant Company K   *Johnston, John

Tennessee 6 Infantry Regiment Private Company L   *Rodgers, E S

Tennessee 7 Cavalry Regiment Lieutenant Colonel   *Taylor, William F

Tennessee 7 Cavalry Regiment Lieutenant Adjutant & Private Company A   *Pope, William S

Tennessee 7 Cavalry Regiment Captain Company A ("Memphis Light Dragoons")   *Sneed, J West

Tennessee 7 Cavalry Regiment 1 Lieutenant Company A   *Howard, William T

Tennessee 7 Cavalry Regiment 2 Lieutenant Company A   *Trezevant, Edward B

Tennessee 7 Cavalry Regiment Sergeant Company A   *Woodward, Henry P

Tennessee 7 Cavalry Regiment Sergeant Company A   *Stovall, George A

Tennessee 7 Cavalry Regiment Private (Taylor's) Company A   Barnes, John P

Tennessee 7 Cavalry Regiment Private Company A   *Buntyn, Dr Geraldus O

Tennessee 7 Cavalry Regiment Private Company A   *Macgowan, Evander L

Tennessee 7 Cavalry Regiment Private Company A ("Memphis Light Dragoons")   *Martin, James H

Tennessee 7 Cavalry Regiment Private Company A   Patterson, William S

Tennessee 7 Cavalry Regiment Private Company A   *Selden, Clarence C

Tennessee 7 Cavalry Regiment Private Company A   *Selden, Metellus L

Tennessee 7 Cavalry Regiment Private Company A   *Smither, Charles G

Tennessee 7 Cavalry Regiment Private Company A   *Talley, Fletcher H

Tennessee 7 Cavalry Regiment Private Company A	*Talley, Foster D
Tennessee 7 Cavalry Regiment Private Company A	*Tate, Thomas G
Tennessee 7 Cavalry Regiment Private Company A	*White, Alphonsus
Tennessee 7 Cavalry Regiment Private Company A	*Wooldridge, Oscar
Tennessee 7 Cavalry Regiment Private Company A	*Young, John P
Tennessee 7 Cavalry Regiment Brevet 2 Lieutenant Company B	*Black, Robert J
Tennessee 7 Cavalry Regiment Private/Corporal Company B	*Collier, William A
Tennessee 7 Cavalry Regiment Private Company B	*Elcan, Dr Joseph J
Tennessee 7 Cavalry Regiment Private Company B/K	Mason, Frank Y
Tennessee 7 Cavalry Regiment 1 Lieutenant Company C	*Winston, Dr William B
Tennessee 7 Cavalry Regiment Private Company C	*Farris, William H
Tennessee 7 Cavalry Regiment Private Company C	*Woodlock, Henry P
Tennessee 7 Cavalry Regiment Color Sergeant Company E	*Perkins, Alfred H
Tennessee 7 Cavalry Regiment Private Company E	*Hubbard, John M
Tennessee 7 Cavalry Regiment Private Company G	*Loudon, James A
Tennessee 7 Cavalry Regiment Private Company I	*Fisher, Charles G
Tennessee 7 Cavalry Regiment Private Company I	*Fisher, Philip A
Tennessee 7 Cavalry Regiment Private Company I (6 Logwood's Cavalry Battalion)	Read, A E
Tennessee 7 Cavalry Regiment Private Company I	Ross, Francis M
Tennessee 7 Cavalry Regiment Private Company L	*Whitmore, Edwin
Tennessee 7 Cavalry Regiment Company L	*Johnston, John
Tennessee 7 Cavalry Regiment Private (White's) Company (Logwood's 6 Cavalry Battalion)	*Bayliss, William H
Tennessee 7 Cavalry Regiment Private (White's) Company (Logwood's 6 Cavalry Battalion)	Dickson, James R
Tennessee 7 Cavalry Regiment Private (White's) Company (Logwood's 6 Cavalry Battalion)	McClure, Jere
Tennessee 7 Infantry Regiment Private Company E	Cage, John F
Tennessee 8 Infantry Regiment Private Company H	*Atkinson, Vanburen B
Tennessee 8 Regiment	Hogan, John
Tennessee 9 Infantry Regiment Colonel	*Douglass, Henry L
Tennessee 9 Infantry Regiment Captain Company A	*Wilkerson, W N
Tennessee 9 Infantry Regiment 2 Lieutenant Company A	*McFarland, Louis B
Tennessee 9 Infantry Regiment Private Company E	Massey, George
Tennessee 9 Infantry Regiment Private Company H	Bell, Henry F
Tennessee 9 Infantry Regiment Private Company K	Warren, J H
Tennessee 10 (DeMoss') Cavalry Regiment Lieutenant Colonel	*Trezevant, Edward B
Tennessee 10 Infantry Regiment Brevet 2 Lieutenant Company K	*Southall, Randall M
Tennessee 11 (Gordon's) Cavalry Battalion Captain Company D	*Ensley, Edward L
Tennessee 11 (Holman's) Cavalry Regiment Colonel	*Edmondson, James H
Tennessee 11 (Holman's) Cavalry Regiment 1 Lieutenant Company A	*Barbour, James G
Tennessee 11 Infantry Regiment Colonel	*Gordon, George W
Tennessee 11 Infantry Regiment Private Company A	Cooley, Robert N
Tennessee 11 Regiment	Tate, R H
Tennessee 12 (Richardson's-Green's) Cavalry Regiment Colonel	*Richardson, Robert V
Tennessee 12 (Richardson's-Green's) Cavalry Regiment Sergeant Staff of Colonel Richardson	*Richardson, Robert E
Tennessee 12 Cavalry Regiment Private Company C	Perkins, Enos S
Tennessee 12 (Green's) Cavalry Regiment Private Company E	*Martin, John C
Tennessee 12 (Green's) Cavalry Regiment Lieutenant Company I	*Stewart, William B
Tennessee 12 Cavalry Regiment Private Company K	*Gardiner, Samuel E
Tennessee 12 Infantry Regiment Assistant Surgeon	*McGee, Dr John P
Tennessee 12 Infantry Regiment 1 Lieutenant Company H	*McDowell, William W
Tennessee 12 Infantry Regiment Private Company H	*Kelly, William O
Tennessee 12 Infantry Regiment Private Company H	*McDowell, John H
Tennessee 13 Infantry Regiment Colonel	*Vaughan, Alfred J Jr
Tennessee 13 Infantry Regiment Private Company A	*Wilkerson, W N
Tennessee 13 Infantry Regiment Private Company B	*Brown, Alfred H
Tennessee 13 Infantry Regiment Private Company B	Owen, Thomas H
Tennessee 13 Infantry Regiment Private Company C	*Farrow, George F
Tennessee 13 Infantry Regiment Private Company C "The Secession Guards"	Harris, John W
Tennessee 13 Infantry Regiment Private Company C	*Lake, Lorenzo S
Tennessee 13 Infantry Regiment Private Company F	Middleton, C H
Tennessee 13 Infantry Regiment Private Company G	Downey, J M
Tennessee 13 Infantry Regiment Sergeant Company G	*Stone, William T
Tennessee 13 Infantry Regiment Private Company H	Marshall, William A

Tennessee 13 Infantry Regiment Private Company H	*Woodson, Henry M
Tennessee 13 (Wright's) Infantry Regiment Private Company I	Barham, John A
Tennessee 13 Infantry Regiment Private (Ross') Company I	Bell, John K
Tennessee 13 Infantry Regiment Private (Crook's) Company I	Waggoner, Hugh N
Tennessee 14 Infantry Regiment Sergeant Company B	*Mockbee, Robert T
Tennessee 14 Cavalry Regiment Company H	*Johnston, John
Tennessee 14 (Neely's) Cavalry Regiment Private/Corporal Company D	Bass, S H
Tennessee 14 Infantry Regiment Sergeant Company H	*Weatherford, Caesar
Tennessee 15 Cavalry Regiment Colonel	*Logwood, Thomas H
Tennessee 15 Cavalry Regiment (Consolidated) 2 Sergeant Company I	Owen, Thomas H
Tennessee 15 Infantry Regiment Colonel	*Carroll, Charles M
Tennessee 15 Infantry Regiment Lieutenant Colonel - General	*Taylor, James H R
Tennessee 15 Infantry Regiment Private Company A	McFarland, John N
Tennessee 15 Infantry Regiment Captain Company B	*Genette, Jones
Tennessee 15 Infantry Regiment (Genette's) Company B	Guard, William
Tennessee 15 Infantry Regiment Private Company C	Collins, Dennis
Tennessee 15 Infantry Regiment Private Company D	Blake, Garret
Tennessee 15 Infantry Regiment Captain 1 Company F	*Cameron, John F
Tennessee 15 Infantry Regiment Private 1 Company F	*Jarnagin, John H
Tennessee 15 Infantry Regiment Corporal Company G	Corder Sr, Phillip T
Tennessee 17 (Sanders') Cavalry Battalion Captain AQM & Private Company A	*Rice, Clay
Tennessee 17 (Sanders') Cavalry Battalion Private Company A	*Rice, Paul S
Tennessee 18 Cavalry Regiment Private Company K	Miller, R B
Tennessee 19 Cavalry Regiment Sergeant Company L	*Hamner, Constantine S
Tennessee 19 (Biffle's) Cavalry Regiment Private Company L	Rutherford, Felix
Tennessee 19 Infantry Regiment Colonel	*Heiskell, Carrick W
Tennessee 19 Infantry Regiment 2 Lieutenant Company A	*James, Richard P
Tennessee 19 Infantry Regiment Private Company D	Beard, Thomas
Tennessee 19 & 20 Consolidated Infantry Regiment Captain Company K	*McDowell, William W
Tennessee 19 & 20 Consolidated Infantry Regiment Private Company K	*McDowell, John H
Tennessee 20 Company K	Seton, William
Tennessee 21 (Wilson's) Cavalry Regiment Lieutenant Colonel	*Forrest, Jesse A
Tennessee 21/22 Cavalry Regiment Private Company G	Martin, James
Tennessee 21 Infantry Regiment Private Company A	Kearney, J R
Tennessee 21 Infantry Regiment Captain Company B	*Person, Richard J
Tennessee 21 Infantry Regiment Sergeant Company B	Kearns, Thomas
Tennessee 21 Infantry Regiment Private Company C	McMullen, John
Tennessee 21 Infantry Regiment Private Company F	O'Day, Roger
Tennessee 21 Infantry Regiment Private Company G	McGowen, John
Tennessee 21 Infantry Regiment Private Company G	Philip, Lewis
Tennessee 21 (Pickett's) Infantry Regiment Private Company H ("Advance Guard")	Chamberland, Rufus
Tennessee 21 Infantry Regiment Captain Company I	*Frazer, Charles W
Tennessee 21 Regiment	Christenham, Peter
Tennessee 22 (Barteau's) Cavalry Regiment Colonel	Barteau, Clark R
Tennessee 22 (Barteau's) Cavalry Regiment Major/Captain Company K	Farris, Oliver B
Tennessee 22 (Barteau's) Cavalry Regiment 2 Lieutenant Company K	*Farris, William H
Tennessee 22 (Barteau's) Cavalry Regiment Private Company K	Brown, Hiram R
Tennessee 22 Infantry Regiment Captain Looney's Company	*Looney, Robert F
Tennessee 22 Infantry Regiment Private Company E	Sherwood, Jonathan
Tennessee 24 Infantry Regiment Captain Company C	*Uhls, John M
Tennessee 24 Infantry Regiment Private Company C	*Black, H M
Tennessee 25 Infantry Regiment Lieutenant Colonel	*Snowden, Robert B
Tennessee 26 Infantry Regiment Private Company C	Osborne, William W
Tennessee 27 Infantry Regiment 2 Lieutenant Company C	Farris, Oliver B
Tennessee 29 Infantry Regiment Captain Company B	*Harris, John W
Tennessee 30 Infantry Regiment Private Company G	Porter, William C
Tennessee 31 (Bradford's) Infantry Regiment Private Company D	Powell, Thomas J
Tennessee 31 Infantry Regiment Company I	Rodgers, C M
Tennessee 32 Infantry Regiment Private/Sergeant Company I	*George, Thomas F
Tennessee 35 Infantry Regiment Private Company A	Womack, W D
Tennessee 36 Infantry Regiment Colonel	*Morgan, Robert J
Tennessee 37 Infantry Regiment Colonel	*Carroll, William H

Tennessee 37 Infantry Regiment Lieutenant Colonel	*Frayser, Robert D
Tennessee 37 Infantry Regiment 1 Sergeant Company C and Adjutant	**Mathes, James H
Tennessee 37 Infantry Regiment	*Carroll, William H
Tennessee 38 Infantry Regiment Colonel	*Looney, Robert F
Tennessee 38 Infantry Regiment Lieutenant Colonel	*Greer, Hugh D
Tennessee 38 Infantry Regiment Lieutenant Colonel	*Gwynne, Andrew D
Tennessee 38 Infantry Regiment Private Company A	*Flournoy, William A
Tennessee 38 Infantry Regiment Corporal 1 Company A	*Rice, Daniel C
Tennessee 38 Infantry Regiment Private 2 Company A	Clinton, Alexander M
Tennessee 38 Infantry Regiment Private/Sergeant Company D	*Talley, Richard H
Tennessee 38 Infantry Regiment Private/Corporal Company D	Eckles, Benjamin E
Tennessee 38 Infantry Regiment Captain Company I	*Neely, Hugh M
Tennessee 38 Infantry Regiment Private Company K	Barker, James L
Tennessee 38 Infantry Regiment Sergeant Company L	*Hill, Harry M
Tennessee 40 (Walker's) Infantry Regiment Colonel	*Walker, Lucius M
Tennessee 40 (Walker's) Infantry Regiment Adjutant 1 Lieutenant	*Freeman, Edward T
Tennessee 40 (Walker's) Infantry Regiment 3 Lieutenant Company C	*Trezevant, Marye B
Tennessee 40 (Walker's) Infantry Regiment Private Company C	Dixon, Claiborne
Tennessee 40 (Walker's) Infantry Regiment Private Company C	Pilcher, S C
Tennessee 40 (Walker's) Infantry Regiment Private Company D	Ross, William R
Tennessee 40 (Walker's) Infantry Regiment Private (Bush's) Company D	Sims, William H
Tennessee 40 (Walker's) Infantry Regiment Private Company D	Stokes, James E
Tennessee 40 (Walker's) Infantry Regiment Private (Bush's) Company D	White, William
Tennessee 40 (Walker's) Infantry Regiment Private (Bibb's) Company E	Collier, T W
Tennessee 40 (Walker's) Infantry Regiment Private Company E	Latham, Charles
Tennessee 40 (Walker's) Infantry Regiment Private Company F	Morgan, Charles A
Tennessee 40 (Walker's) Infantry Regiment Private Company G	Harrington, William J
Tennessee 40 (Walker's) Infantry Regiment Private Company G	Shelton, John
Tennessee 40 (Walker's) Infantry Regiment Corporal (Aaron's) Company G	Tidwell, John L
Tennessee 40 (Walker's) Infantry Regiment Private Company H	Cameron, John S
Tennessee 40 (Walker's) Infantry Regiment Private Company H	Marsh, William
Tennessee 40 (Walker's) Infantry Regiment Private Company H	McIntush, King
Tennessee 40 (Walker's) Infantry Regiment Private Company H	Simmons, T J
Tennessee 40 (Walker's) Infantry Regiment Private Company H	Thompson, Maston
Tennessee 40 (Walker's) Infantry Regiment Lieutenant Company I	*Walker, Samuel P
Tennessee 40 (Walker's) Infantry Regiment Private Company I	Creason, William R
Tennessee 40 (Walker's) Infantry Regiment Private Company I	Foulk, Adam
Tennessee 40 (Walker's) Infantry Regiment Private Company I	Skinner, John
Tennessee 40 (Walker's) Infantry Regiment Corporal Company K	Hunter, John P
Tennessee 40 (Walker's) Infantry Regiment Private Company K	Clinch, John E
Tennessee 40 (Walker's) Infantry Regiment Private Company K	Southerland, James M
Tennessee 40 (Walker's) Infantry Regiment Private Company K	White, John H
Tennessee 42 Infantry Regiment 2 Lieutenant 2 Company E	*Trezevant, Marye B
Tennessee 42 Regiment	Earwin, J C
Tennessee 42 Infantry Regiment Company G	Ivy, J C
Tennessee 42 Infantry Regiment Private Company G	Nicholson, John D
Tennessee 42 Infantry Regiment Private (Barbiere's) 2 Company I	Jackson, William
Tennessee 50 Infantry Regiment Lieutenant Colonel	*Pease, George W
Tennessee 51 Infantry Regiment Captain Company G	*Hill, Alphonso B
Tennessee 51 Infantry Regiment Private Company G	Flanigan, John D
Tennessee 51 (Consolidated) Infantry Regiment Private Company G	**Pickard, H B
Tennessee 55 (Brown's) Infantry Regiment Ford's Company	*Rodgers, E S
Tennessee 154 Senior Infantry Regiment Colonel	*Magevney, Michael
Tennessee 154 Senior Infantry Regiment Colonel	*Smith, Preston
Tennessee 154 Senior Infantry Regiment Lieutenant Colonel	*Patrick, Marsh M
Tennessee 154 Senior Infantry Regiment Major/Captain Company H	*Genette, Jones
Tennessee 154 Senior Infantry Regiment Private Company A	McCullough, Alexander
Tennessee 154 Senior Infantry Regiment Private Company A	*Reddick, George W

TENNESSEE 154 SENIOR INFANTRY REGIMENT PRIVATE 1ST COMPANY B "BLUFF CITY GRAYS" —
SUBSEQUENTLY BECAME TENNESSEE 3 (FORREST'S OLD) CAVALRY REGIMENT 2ND COMPANY A —
SEE THAT LIST SUPRA AND CHAPTER "NOTES OF INTEREST"

Tennessee 154 Senior Infantry Regiment Captain 2 Company B	*Degraffenried, Henry E (Memorial)

Tennessee 154 Senior Infantry Regiment Private 2 Company B	Clarke, Robert J
Tennessee 154 Senior Infantry Regiment Private Company C	Hackett, John
Tennessee 154 Senior Infantry Regiment Private Company C	*Kelly, Michael
Tennessee 154 Senior Infantry Regiment Captain Company D	*Cannon, Wynne G
Tennessee 154 Senior Infantry Regiment Captain Company D	*Fowlkes, Jr Sterling
Tennessee 154 Senior Infantry Regiment 1 Lieutenant Company D	*Munch, Charles P
Tennessee 154 Senior Infantry Regiment Sergeant Company D	*Lawler, James H
Tennessee 154 Senior Infantry Regiment Sergeant Company D	*Waynesburg, John W
Tennessee 154 Senior Infantry Regiment Corporal/Private Company D	Beasley, John R
Tennessee 154 Senior Infantry Regiment Private Company D	*Vigus, Arthur P
Tennessee 154 Senior Infantry Regiment Private Company D	*Vigus, Frank W
Tennessee 154 Senior Infantry Regiment Private Company D	*Vigus, James H
Tennessee 154 Senior Infantry Regiment Major/Captain Company E "The Hickory Rifles"	*Martin, John D
Tennessee 154 Senior Infantry Regiment 1 Lieutenant/Corporal Company E	Stockton, George M
Tennessee 154 Senior Infantry Regiment Sergeant Company E	*Donelson, Daniel S
Tennessee 154 Senior Infantry Regiment Sergeant Company E	*Wooldridge, Charles P
Tennessee 154 Senior Infantry Regiment Private Company E	*Ball, John H
Tennessee 154 Senior Infantry Regiment Private Company E	*Claridge, John M
Tennessee 154 Senior Infantry Regiment Private Company E	*Elliott, Leonidas H
Tennessee 154 Senior Infantry Regiment Private Company E	Gunn, Charles H
Tennessee 154 Senior Infantry Regiment Private Company E	*Lawrence, James H
Tennessee 154 Senior Infantry Regiment Private Company E	*Stewart, William B
Tennessee 154 Senior Infantry Regiment Private Company E	*Webb, John L
Tennessee 154 Senior Infantry Regiment Corporal Company F	*Cameron, D W
Tennessee 154 Senior Infantry Regiment Private Company F	Bruce, T M
Tennessee 154 Senior Infantry Regiment Captain Company G	*Hutcheson, Booth B
Tennessee 154 Senior Infantry Regiment Sergeant Company G	*Moon, Robert A
Tennessee 154 Senior Infantry Regiment Sergeant Company G	*Wade, Jr Henry
Tennessee 154 Senior Infantry Regiment Corporal/Private Company G	*Brett, James
Tennessee 154 Senior Infantry Regiment Corporal Company G	*Pitman, William T
Tennessee 154 Senior Infantry Regiment Private Company G	*Anderson, Isaac M
Tennessee 154 Senior Infantry Regiment Private Company G	*Browne, William H
Tennessee 154 Senior Infantry Regiment Private Company G	Green, Joseph
Tennessee 154 Senior Infantry Regiment Private Company G "The Beauregards"	Lowe, G H
Tennessee 154 Senior Infantry Regiment Private Company G	*Morrison, A D
Tennessee 154 Senior Infantry Regiment Private Company G	*Pillow, Alexander H
Tennessee 154 Senior Infantry Regiment Private Company G	*Shields, William S
Tennessee 154 Senior Infantry Regiment Private Company G	*Taylor, William V
Tennessee 154 Senior Infantry Regiment Private Company G	*Thurmond, W W
Tennessee 154 Senior Infantry Regiment Private Company H	*Anderson, George W
Tennessee 154 Senior Infantry Regiment Private Company H	Cowan, Samuel S
Tennessee 154 Senior Infantry Regiment Private Company H "The Crockett Rangers"	Gallagher, Thomas
Tennessee 154 Senior Infantry Regiment Private Company H	*Loyd, Andrew J
Tennessee 154 Senior Infantry Regiment Private Company H	McLellan, William
Tennessee 154 Senior Infantry Regiment Captain Company L	*Cole, Edmund A
Tennessee 154 Senior Infantry Regiment 1 Lieutenant Company L	*Cochran, John W
Tennessee 154 Senior Infantry Regiment 2 Lieutenant Company L	*Dupuy, A P
Tennessee 154 Senior Infantry Regiment 1 Sergeant Company L	*Wood, Jacob M
Tennessee 154 Senior Infantry Regiment Sergeant/Private Company L	*Walker, Charles J
Tennessee 154 Senior Infantry Regiment Corporal/Private Company L	*Temple, John H
Tennessee 154 Senior Infantry Regiment Corporal/Private Company L	*Trezevant, John P
Tennessee 154 Senior Infantry Regiment Private Company L	Brownelle, E L
Tennessee 154 Senior Infantry Regiment Private Company L "Maynard Rifles"	*Hart, W W
Tennessee 154 Senior Infantry Regiment Private Company L "Maynard Rifles"	*Park, Joseph B
Tennessee 154 Senior Infantry Regiment Private Company L	*Piper, William A
Tennessee 154 Senior Infantry Regiment Private Company L	*Quenichet, John W
Tennessee 154 Senior Infantry Regiment Private Company L	Spillman, Robert B
Tennessee 154 Senior Infantry Regiment Private Company L	*Turley, Thomas B
Tennessee 154 Senior Infantry Regiment Private Company L	*Vaccarro, Charles M
Tennessee 154 Senior Infantry Regiment Private Company L	*Wooldridge, Egbert
Texas Good's Company Artillery (State Troops) Private	*Guess, George W
Texas Mann's Cavalry Regiment Colonel	*Bankhead, Smith P

Texas Morgan's Cavalry Regiment Private Company I	*Cocke, John H
Texas Watts Cameron's Company Infantry	Price, Haisten T
Texas 2 (Moore's) Infantry Regiment Private Company C	Dutton, Peter
Texas 2 (Moore's) Infantry Regiment Private Company G	Johnson, Isaiah W
Texas 2 (Moore's) Infantry Regiment Private Company K	French, J G
Texas 2 (Moore's) Infantry Regiment Private Company K	Whittington, C M
Texas 3 Cavalry Regiment Colonel	*Greer, Elkanah B
Texas 3 (Greer's) Cavalry Regiment Corporal Company C	*Copeland, P C
Texas 3 (Greer's) Cavalry Regiment Private (Chisum's) Company F	Jordan, John
Texas 3 Cavalry Teamster	Van Horn, J W
Texas 3 Regiment Company K	Cook, Joseph
Texas 4 Regiment	Shik, John
Texas 6 (Stone's) Cavalry Regiment Company C	Montgomery, G W
Texas 6 (Stone's) Cavalry Regiment Private Company G	Smith, Robert J
Texas 6 Infantry Regiment Sergeant/Private Company C	*Sharp, Thomas C
Texas 6 Rangers	Unknown
Texas 9 Regiment Company H	Williams, J W
Texas 9 (Sim's Rangers) Cavalry Regiment Private Company A	Parker, William L
Texas 9 (Sim's) Cavalry Regiment Private Company E	Boliner, Patrick M
Texas 9 (Sim's) Cavalry Regiment Private Company E	Coffman, Warren
Texas 9 (Sim's) Cavalry Regiment Private Company E	Matthews, Daniel S
Texas 9 (Sim's) Cavalry Regiment (Duncan's) Company F	Alexander, S R
Texas 9 (Sim's) Cavalry Regiment Private Company I	Hays, William A
Texas 9 (Young's/Maxey's) Infantry Regiment Company A	Moore, Frank
Texas 9 (Young's/Maxey's) Infantry Regiment Private Company A	Moore, Edward
Texas 9 (Young's/Maxey's) Infantry Regiment Private Company A	Scott, Alfred M
Texas 9 (Young's/Maxey's) Infantry Regiment Private Company C	Hall, James
Texas 9 (Young's/Maxey's) Infantry Regiment Company D	Cook, S P C
Texas 9 (Young's/Maxey's) Infantry Regiment Private Company E	Brownfield, J G
Texas 9 (Young's/Maxey's) Infantry Regiment Private Company E	Skeggs, James M
Texas 9 (Young's/Maxey's) Infantry Regiment Corporal Company G	Woodward, J A
Texas 9 (Young's/Maxey's) Infantry Regiment Private Company G	Connor, M E
Texas 9 (Young's/Maxey's) Infantry Regiment Private Company G	Davis, William M
Texas 9 (Young's/Maxey's) Infantry Regiment Private Company G	Henderson, Jesse M
Texas 9 (Young's/Maxey's) Infantry Regiment Private Company G	Horton, Thomas A
Texas 9 (Young's/Maxey's) Infantry Regiment Captain Assistant Adjutant General Company H	*Trezevant, Theodore B
Texas 9 (Young's/Maxey's) Infantry Regiment Private Company H	Smedley, Henry H
Texas 9 (Young's/Maxey's) Infantry Regiment Musician Company I	Barnes, Joseph
Texas 9 (Young's/Maxey's) Infantry Regiment Private Company K	Bryan, James
Texas 9 (Young's/Maxey's) Infantry Regiment Private Company K	Horton, A J
Texas 9 (Young's/Maxey's) Infantry Regiment Private Company K	Tuder, Benjamin F
Texas 10 (Locke's) Cavalry Regiment Private Company A	Lindsey, W P
Texas 10 (Locke's) Cavalry Regiment Private Company B	Greer, James
Texas 10 (Locke's) Cavalry Regiment Private Company C	Black, Henry L
Texas 10 (Locke's) Cavalry Regiment Private Company C	Coffman, John H
Texas 10 (Locke's) Cavalry Regiment Private Company C	Maddox, L H
Texas 10 (Locke's) Cavalry Regiment Private Company C	Thomas, George
Texas 10 (Locke's) Cavalry Regiment Private Company D	Harrison, W B
Texas 10 (Locke's) Cavalry Regiment Private (Redwine's) Company E	Redwine, Dr Rufus E
Texas 10 (Locke's) Cavalry Regiment Private Company F	Freeland, W J
Texas 10 (Locke's) Cavalry Regiment Private Company G	Stone, M F
Texas 10 (Locke's) Cavalry Regiment Private Company H	Smith, Levi
Texas 10 (Locke's) Cavalry Regiment Private (Martin's) Company I	Mansell, James
Texas 10 Cavalry Regiment Private Company I	Timmons, Jordan
Texas 10 (Locke's Rangers) Cavalry Regiment (Winston's) Company	Newberry, William
Texas 11 (Young's) Cavalry Regiment Company E	Mahaffie, H Alexander
Texas 14 (Johnson's) Cavalry Regiment Sergeant (Hamilton's) Company D	Phillips, John C
Texas 27 (Whitfield's Legion) Cavalry Regiment Private Company A	Beavers, Levi J
Texas 27 (Whitfield's Legion) Cavalry Regiment Private Company D/M	Wicklin, Louis W
Texas 27 (Whitfield's Legion) Cavalry Regiment Private Company F	Cunningham, D C
Texas 27 (Whitfield's Legion) Cavalry Regiment Company F	Wray, T J
Texas 27 (Whitfield's Legion) Cavalry Regiment Private Company H	McGill, J T

Texas 27 (Whitfield's Legion) Cavalry Regiment Company I	Gentry, G
Texas 27 (Whitfield's Legion) Cavalry Regiment Sergeant/Private Company K	Rowan, G W
Texas 27 (Whitfield's Legion) Cavalry Regiment Private Company K	Bradshaw, J H
Texas 27 (Whitfield's Legion) Cavalry Regiment Private Company K	Denton, John B
Texas 27 (Whitfield's Legion) Cavalry Regiment Private Company L	Gilliland, Robert S
Texas 27 (Whitfield's Legion) Cavalry Regiment (Lewis') Company	Bennett, J W
Texas 31 Cavalry Regiment Lieutenant Colonel	*Guess, George W
Texas 32 (Crump's Battalion) Cavalry Regiment Private Company D	Clifton, T J
Texas 32 (Crump's Battalion) Cavalry Regiment Private Company D	Starrett, F C
Texas 32 (Crump's Battalion) Cavalry Regiment Private (Weaver's) Company D	Tuck, W L
Texas 32 (Crump's Battalion) Cavalry Regiment Private Company D	Wright, Henry C
Texas 32 (Crump's Battalion) Cavalry Regiment Private (Bennett's) Company G	Craft, Moses M
Texas 32 (Crump's Battalion) Cavalry Regiment Private (Bennett's) Company G	Fuller, E R
Texas 32 (Crump's Battalion) Cavalry Regiment Private Company H	Baber, W C
Texas 32 (Crump's Battalion) Cavalry Regiment Private Company I	Blackwell, B M
Texas 32 (Crump's Battalion) Cavalry Regiment Private Company I	Davenport, Jesse D
Texas 32 (Crump's Battalion) Cavalry Regiment Private Company I	Davenport, Moses
Texas 32 (Crump's Battalion) Cavalry Regiment Private Company I	Davidson, W C
Transportation Agent	*Talley, Fletcher H
Trans-Mississippi Artillery Colonel	*Bankhead, Smith P
Trans-Mississippi Assistant Quartermaster Captain	*Willins, John T
Trans-Mississippi Department of North Arkansas and the Indian Territory Captain	*DuBose, Julius J
Virginia Horse Artillery Private Shoemaker's Company	*Folkes, William C
Virginia Military Institute (VMI) Cadet Company D	*Hamlin, Edward L
Virginia 1 Cavalry Regiment Private Company A	*Landstreet, Edward
Virginia 11 Infantry Regiment Private Company F	*Pepper, Samuel A
Virginia 17 Infantry Regiment Sergeant Company H	*Jordan, James P
Virginia 19 Battalion Heavy Artillery Private Company A	Barradall, Norborne D
Walker's Regiment Company H	Sullivan, George
Walker's Regiment (Aaron's) Company	Railey, L
Walker's Regiment (McLean's) Company	Pearson, S W
Walker's Regiment	Loud, Curty
Warner's Southern Artillery (Tennessee Sterling's Company Heavy Artillery)	Frail, Henry
Waters' Battery	Elam, W S
Watson's Battery	Mantequis, Jules
Young's Regiment Company D	South, N M

ELMWOOD CEMETERY 1874 BOOK
LIST OF CONFEDERATE SOLDIERS

The following list of Confederate Soldiers buried in Elmwood as printed on pages 177-178 of the *Elmwood: Charter, Rules, Regulations, and Bylaws of Elmwood Cemetery Association of Memphis. Elmwood Cemetery* (Memphis, Tennessee). Boyle & Chapman, Printers, Publishers and Binders, No. 279 Main Street, Memphis, Tennessee, 1874. No changes or corrections were made to spelling, order or punctuation.

NAMES OF CONFEDERATE SOLDIERS,

As far as ascertained, buried in Elmwood, who were Citizens of Memphis or vicinity,

There are, in addition to these, nearly a thousand Confederate soldiers buried in the Cemetery, who generally died in hospitals, and were citizens of Arkansas and other States.

Anderson, Gen. J. Patton
Armstrong, John W.
Alford, J. L.
Adams, W. S.
Ammen, D. C.
Apperson, John W.
Allin, Maj. Phil T.
Andrews, W. N.
Bayliss, William H.
Bryant, William C.
Beecher, Maj. E. A.
Bass, S. H.
Burnett, George W.
Black, H. W.
Beaumont, G. T.
Ball, John H.
Carroll, Gen. Wm. H.
Cochran, Francis T.
Collins, Col. Nathaniel D.
Certon, William
Culpepper, Capt. J. H.
Cox, Robert B.
Cole, John B.
Clark, James R.
Cage, John T.
Dupuy, S. P.
Doyle, Decatur J.
Driver, Maj. Wm. T.
Eanes, John
Elliott, Lee H.
Eubank, R. P.
Freeman, Surgeon Robert J.
Fowlkes, Capt. S.
Ferguson, Lieut. W. B.
Forrest, Maj. Jeffrey
Flornoy, Hall
Flornoy, Willie
Falls, George
Gunn, C. H.
Grice, James H.

Green, Capt. H. Dixon
Hall, W. A.
Hamilton, Capt. J.
Hunt, Col. Wm. R.
Hart, Col. Robert
Hamlin, Edward L.
Harris, Ed.
Hartsfield, William G.
Henry, Maj. John F.
Harris, John W.
Hyatt, Charles
Horne, E. W.
Hutchinson, Capt. B. B.
Johnson, J. R. M.
King, Morris
Kehoe, Capt. Wm.
Kelly, John H.
Leath, Maj. Peter M.
Lundy, Capt. E. C.
McDonald, Maj. Charles
Mellon, Alf. M.
Moon, Robert A.
Morrison, Jacob
May, Capt. Charles
Monsarratt, Maj. George H.
Miller, William
McCullough, Hugh
Nash, Abner
Owen, Augustus
Piper, William A.
Pitman, Warren
Pattison, Capt. Thomas F.
Palmer, Edward G.
Peace, Col. Wm.
Pattison, Oliver G.
Patrick, Capt. Wm.
Pattison, Robert T.
Porter, Capt. Edward
Pinson, Col. R. A.
Patterson, Wm. S.

Pope, Lieut. Wm. S.
Richardson, Gen. R. V.
Ross, Col. W. B.
Rogers, Vol. P.
Rhodes, M.
Rowe, E. A.
Smith, Gen. Preston
Seabrook, John T.
Shields, Lieut. W. S.
Stewart, Darwin
Steiner, Lieut. J. P.
Sledge, Washington
Spicer, James W.
Stockton, George M.
Titus, James T.
Titus, John F.
Trezevant, Maj. Ed. B.
Townsend, George
Talbot, John R.
Taylor, Gen. James H. R.
Taylor, A. H.
Taylor, William V.
Timberlake, William H.
Trezevant, Lieut. Louis Cruger
Uhls, Capt. John
Walker, Gen. Marsh
Walker, Col. J. Knox
Wright, E. Eldridge
Whitfield, Lieut. Edwin
Ward, C. C.
Wheaton, W. N.
Williams, Dr. J. Joseph
Wills, Wm. A.
Walker, James
Woodard, Henry P.
White, Andrew J.
Wade, Henry

MEMORIAL (DECORATION) DAY

There seems to have always been some confusion, and even argument, as to how Memorial Day originated in the United States. The most popular or politically correct version is that Memorial Day began upon the following May 5, 1868, order of John A. Logan, Commander-in-Chief, Grand Army of the Republic:

> *General Order, No. 11.*
>> *I. The 30th day of May 1868 is designated for the purpose of strewing with flowers or otherwise decorating the graves of comrades who died in defense of their country during the late rebellion, and whose bodies now lie in almost every city, village, and hamlet churchyard in the land. In this observance no form of ceremony is prescribed, but Posts and comrades will in their own way arrange such fitting services and testimonials of respect as circumstances may permit.*

Although the above lead to a national observance to honor all soldiers who had fallen in defense of the United States of America, Memorial Day or Decoration Day originated in the South. Most accounts credit the first decorating of graves in Columbus, Georgia and in a few localities in Mississippi. It is most likely that many others localities held ceremonies as well to honor their fallen husbands, fathers, sons and brothers. In actuality ceremonies of honoring the dead are common to mankind and as old as history itself. The Greeks, Romans, Druids plus many other societies held ceremonies to honor their dead.

The following is the origin of Memorial Day as publicized by the U. S. House of Representatives Committee on Veteran's Affairs:

> In 1866, memorial associations were formed in Columbus, Georgia, and Columbus, Mississippi, for the purpose of caring for the graves of both Union and Confederate war dead.
>
> Northern cities also paid respect through special observances. The village of Waterloo, New York, honored its war dead on May 5, 1866, by closing its businesses for the day, flying the flag at half-mast, and decorating the graves of fallen soldiers. In 1967, President Lyndon Johnson issued a proclamation officially recognizing Waterloo as "the birthplace of Memorial Day."
>
> On April 29, 1866, the citizens of Carbondale, Illinois, conducted an all-day observance, including a parade, a barbecue, speeches and the decorating of the graves of some 20 Union soldiers. The principal speaker on this occasion was General John A. Logan.
>
> Undoubtedly drawing from his experiences in Carbondale, General Logan, the first Commander-in-Chief of the Grand Army of the Republic, issued on May 5, 1868, the general order providing for the nationwide observance of Decoration Day on May 30th. This date was chosen in order that, all over the country, there might be flowers in bloom that could be used in decorating the graves.
>
> May 30th remained the official date of the occasion until 1971, when Public Law 90-363 went into effect. It called for uniform annual observances of certain legal public holidays, including Memorial Day. It has since been observed nationally on the last Monday in May.

Memorial Day in Tennessee

Tennessee Code Annotated Section 15-2-101 provides that:
> "(E)ach year it shall be the duty of the governor of this state to proclaim the following as days of special observance; . . .; the third day of June, "Memorial or Confederate Decoration Day . . .; the governor shall invite the people of this state to observe the days in schools, churches and other suitable places with appropriate ceremonies expressive of the public sentiment befitting the anniversary of such dates."

Although the law provides for observance of Confederate Memorial Day to be on June 3rd, it is observed in Memphis on the first Sunday in June with a formal ceremony at Confederate Soldiers Rest in Elmwood Cemetery. It was, however, originally observed on April 26th but was changed and finally designated as noted above. One can research the local newspapers and read a report on the annual ceremony. Although the attendances at the more recent ceremonies have not been as large or elaborate as the past ones, they each have the same meaning and purpose to honor the Confederate veterans.

References and accounts of selected early observances in Memphis

Memphis Daily Argus, April 25, 1866, page 3. "Grand Floral Ceremony" – "The public are very cordially invited to unite with the warm-hearted ladies of the Southern Relief Society to-morrow, in decking the graves of our brave and illustrious dead in Elmwood Cemetery, with garlands of roses." Addresses were given by Rev. S. H. Ford, L.L.D., and Rev. J. W. Rogers.

April 26, 1866 - *Memphis Daily Argus*, April 27, 1866, page 3

"THE FLORAL CEREMONY

"Yesterday was the day appointed throughout the South as a day of sweet remembrance for our brothers who now sleep their last long sleep - the sleep of death.

"That day (the 26th day of April) has and will be set apart annually as a day to be commemorated by all the purely Southern people throughout the country, as that upon which we are to lay aside our usual vocations of life and devote to the memory of our friends, brothers, husbands and sons, who have fallen in our late struggle for Southern independence.

".... proceeded to the Elmwood Cemetery, where is interred all that was mortal of some of the most chivalrous sons of the South."

Note: Elizabeth Avery Meriwether wrote in her book, *Recollections of 92 Years 1824-1916,* published by The Tennessee Historical Commission, Nashville, 1958, Chapter XXIII, pages 193-195, that at the first decoration of graves of Confederate soldiers the Yankee Military Commander forbad the decoration by sending an order to Mrs. Lowe, President of the Southern Society which had organized the plan to put the flowers on the southern graves, commanding her and all other persons to desist from the "disloyal project" She ignored it, not mentioning to the men who perhaps would have heeded the warning. She had not told Dr. Ford who gave the address at the ceremony. Therefore, she had not violated the order. She had not even strewn any flowers on the graves and "thus the military Commander found himself unable to do more than fume and grumble." She states that the next year the Union Commanders made no further effort to prevent the activity, however, see note under April 26, 1867, below.

April 26, 1867 - *Daily Avalanche*, April 27, 1867, page 3

"ELMWOOD.
SOLEMN AND IMPRESSIVE CEREMONY
OVER THE CONFEDERATE DEAD

"The 26th day of April is a day to be hallowed by all Southern hearts, through all time. It is a day which mothers and daughters, wives and sisters, devote to the memory of the dead who fell in battle or perished in their cause. It was held in holy veneration yesterday, and the beautiful grounds of the Elmwood Cemetery, where sleep our heroes who fell at Shiloh and on other fields, were filled with patriotic people intent upon their errand of decorating the graves of the fallen heroes."

Note: It was reported in the April 26, 1867, *Daily Avalanche*, page 3, that the local military authorities in a written correspondence requested the mayor to prohibit or modify the proposed ceremonies at Elmwood indicating that "...the public ceremonies proposed are evidently intended to honor the cause they gave their lives for, and are therefore treasonable and inflammatory to the disloyal element still exiting in our midst, ..." This was, however, withdrawn after assurances were made that the ceremonies were only to be of a religious nature in time-honored custom of all Christian countries. See the letters between the Military official, the Mayor and others concerning this matter in *Memphis Daily Appeal* April 26, 1867, page 3.

May 24, 1875 - *Memphis Daily Appeal* May 25, 1875, page 5

"MEMORIAL DAY

"The Grandest Demonstration Ever
Made in Memphis - The Whole
Population Hearty Participants

"The Graves of the Federal and
Confederate alike Decorated
with Wreaths and Immortelies

"No More Sectional Strife or
Dissension - We Will Live and
Labor for the Union, Its Integrity
and Prosperity

"The curtain is down, the lights are out, the play is over. But there remains to us the sweet aroma of the flowers, the memory of loving words of tribute, of the generous rivalry of victor and vanquished in affectionate revival each of the other's prowess, and the picture of unfolding loveliness, of budding promise, of matured and maturing charms and grace of womanhood - a vision of fair women and brave men, of flowers, of poetry, of rhetoric and all that made up the good pageant, the grand procession, the grander multitude who were lookers - on and witnesses, and without whom even the efforts of the survivors of a hundred well fought fields would be barren of results....Forrest, the "terrible fighter," and always the victorious cavalry raider, marched in the same column with the Federals who fought him, and shared a seat on the same platform with our best representatives of the Union armies. Governor Harris – "the war governor" - who had not even one man to fight against the south, but thousands for her defense, gave his presence to the occasion, and in the few words he uttered of introduction of the Confederate orator, left no doubt of his entire sympathy with the great movement that have reawakened and revitalized the patriotism of our people, and re-established the Union in their affections. Mr. Davis, our foremost statesman did not speak, but he was upon the platform, and by his presence gave endorsement to the re-cementing of the bonds of brotherhood. Tribute was paid to the dead, a loving tribute in words and flowers, but the Union was over it all - was uppermost in all minds - and the day was thus made scared to the highest purpose, and the dead were made to serve the noblest use in a text and day on which to preach peace and love, and date the final close of the war and all its bitter dissensions and contentions."

May 27, 1877 - *Memphis Daily Appeal* May 29, 1877, page 4

"THE OBSERVANCE OF DECORATION DAY
STREWING FLOWERS UPON THE GRAVES
OF THE CONFEDERATE DEAD AT ELMWOOD

"The beautiful custom of strewing flowers on the graves of the Confederate dead at Elmwood Cemetery Sunday last. Unlike former celebrations, there was no music or public speaking, no religious discourses or imposing ceremony. All was quiet and melancholy.... It is to be hoped that the decoration of Confederate graves will take place annually, and will be handed down from generation to generation at a sacred duty - a tribute from the living to the ashes of the gallant dead."

June 5, 1878 - *Memphis Daily Appeal* June 6, 1878, page 4

"OUR DEAD HEROES

"On Fame's Eternal Camping Ground
their Silent Tents are Spread, and
Glory Guards with Solemn
Round the Bivouac of
the Dead"

"The Unveiling of the Confederate Monument
and Decoration of the Graves of the Southern
Soldiers in Elmwood Attended with Imposing
Ceremony

"Yesterday was the day selected by the Confederate relief and historical association for the unveiling of the Confederate monument at Elmwood cemetery, and the decoration of graves....
"By four o'clock the cemetery appeared to be crowded, some four to five thousand people were present....
"The graves of the dead Confederate were decorated with flowers. Not a grave was unrecognized....
"Confederate dead: "Fame shall keep the records of your immortal deeds, and honor point the hollowed spot where your dust so proudly sleeps. The heroic soil of this proud land you baptized with your blood shall ever proudly claim the ashes of her braves as the rich spoils of war. Generations yet unborn shall come in laughing June, with opening flowers, to honor thy tombs. Never shall you lie neglected, forgot, nor your names perish from the lips of love."

See also:

Confederate Veteran Volume I, No. 1, January 1893, pp. 20-21, and Volume II, No. 7, July 1894, p. 208.

"Memorial Day born after Civil War." Perre Magness, Past Times, *The Commercial Appeal* Memphis, Thursday, May 31, 2001, Section EM2.

CONFEDERATE HISTORICAL ASSOCIATION

The Confederate Historical Association, originally known as the Confederate Relief and Historical Association of Memphis, was very instrumental in the care of Confederate Soldiers Rest at Elmwood Cemetery and along with the Ladies Confederate Memorial Association erected the Confederate monument. Many of its members are buried in Confederate Soldiers Rest as well as throughout Elmwood. For that reason, it was felt most appropriate to recognize that organization in this work by including the "Introductory" of J. Harvey Mathes' book *The Old Guard in Gray* (1897), page 17. Readers will note that the Association, without losing its identity, became Camp No. 28, United Confederate Veterans of Tennessee. Also, see brief article on the Association in *The Commercial Appeal* Memphis, May 27, 1906, Art Section, page 4. Additionally, the Confederate Historical Association was a forerunner of The West Tennessee Historical Society. See Notes of Interest.

INTRODUCTORY

The original idea of this work was to get up a complete and reliable list of all the members of the Confederate Historical Association of Memphis under present and former charters and give a brief history of the society. But research into old books and papers, interviews and correspondence with comrades and press notices brought out an unexpected amount and variety of valuable historic material, enough indeed, with the reminiscences of men whose lives were a part of the late war, to fill many volumes. The oral testimony of such men cannot much longer be valuable; some of it, in connection with their records and gleanings from various other sources, has been put together in the pages to follow. Thus, condensed to encyclopedic form and arrangement, it may suggest to others more and better work in the same lines.

It will at least group the names and deeds of many representative ex-Confederates, regardless of rank, who exemplified the highest and best qualities of soldiers and citizens, and were willing to die for their principles, their honest beliefs, and the sanctity of ancestral homes. Such men in defeat or victory, living or dead, need no defense or glowing eulogy. It is sufficient that we preserve the actual facts of their lives, and as to the cause in which they fought to transmit as a heritage to posterity; and it is a proud satisfaction to know that so many men and women, and even children, were faithful even unto death, in times of greatest trials and perils that can come to human hearts, and thus were an honor to their race and generation.

Many of the survivors of the civil war are still in the prime of life, and look back with wonder and thankfulness at the mercy of Providence, which preserved them in the midst of so many and great dangers; and having done their part well in war and in peace from a strict sense of duty, they are content with the results, and have no fear of doubt as to the ultimate verdict of the world.

The Southern people have been too busy since the surrender of the Confederate armies to devote much time to the writing, reading or preservation of their own history. They have been occupied in hard struggles to retrieve untoward fate; in building up homes, schools, churches, factories, reclaiming farms, and planting vineyards, and have made a showing which again excites the surprise if not envy of other sections and the admiration of thinking people everywhere. A few persons at least among us have held that we should write and preserve our own history, and not leave it to tradition as so many of our forefathers did after the Revolutionary war, or to outsiders who have a motive for perverting the facts. We were an agricultural people before the war, with but few great colleges or publishing houses, and permitted others to supply most of our school books, histories and literature. After the war school books again come into the hands of our children that were written in a sectional, partisan, misleading spirit. That some improvement has been made is admitted; more expected and demanded in the interest of truth and justice; simply that and nothing else. The humiliation of defeat passed away with the Southern people long ago, and they are as cheerful, industrious, loyal citizens as can be found in any part of the country, but they none the less respect the deeds and sacrifices of the men who wore the gray, whose names will be honored as long as American valor and true manhood endure. In their minds and hearts the bird's nest has been built in the cannon's mouth, and the bloody chasm of history is now a smiling landscape of teeming industries, waving grain, fairest fruits and fragrant flowers. They vie with their Northern brethren in loyalty to all that is meant, or that can properly cluster in memory, around the stars and stripes; at the same time they owe it to themselves and the generations to come to honor the names of their fallen heroes and to preserve a record of the deeds of those who fought under the stars and bars. For these men were as true to their sense of right as were Washington and Warren and Mad Anthony Wayne, as Marion and Sevier, as the Campbells, the Lees and Greens, the Schoolboys and Robertson and their compatriots, who also were classed as rebels against their government. The Southern States withdrew from the Union one by one, in the hope of escaping from aggressions and policies which violated the spirit of the Federal compact and trampled the constitution and all its traditions under foot. They fought for home rule and constitutional liberty and went down in the unequal struggle. But "time makes all things even" at last. They have been restored to their position in the Union with all disturbing causes removed, have rebuilt their waste places, and have set marvelous examples of thrift, patience and recuperative capacity. The bitter chalice has passed with its dregs, and been replaced by the wassail bowl of good fellowship, around which the veterans of both sides may meet to tell many a long-drawn-out story of weary march, of camp life, of surprise, ambush and shock of battle.

It is not possible in the limits of this book to give more than an outline of the military life of any one man. Where mention is made of the civil life of anyone before or after the war, it is merely put in as a record for posterity and to show what kind of men went out to fight the battles of the South as against the North.

In a few instances no data was found in the books of the Association, as some of these have been lost or mislaid. The sketches are meager enough, but are semi-official and deemed entirely reliable. Great pains have been taken to obtain actual facts.

If any preference is shown, it is in favor of the privates and non-commissioned officers, as nearly all the generals and colonels have long since been given conspicuous places in current and permanent histories.

Just when the Confederate Historical Association of Memphis originated is a matter of doubt, owing to the loss of early minutes; some meetings of returned Confederates for social and relief purposes were held as early as 1866, a later book showing that B.J. Semmes joined in that year. The records in existence begin in 1869 and come on down to the present, being kept in a strict business manner. The first charter was obtained from the legislature under an act passed February 17, 1870, found on page 393, Acts of 1869-70. The incorporators named were W. D. Pickett, W. B. Wiggs, R. W. Mitchell and John H. Erskine, and their associates and successors, with succession for thirty-three years. The name then was the Confederate Relief and Historical Association of Memphis. The old association back of that had been reorganized July 15, 1869, as the minutes show, with Isham G. Harris as President and a membership of 225; the membership now is 245. Gov. Harris served two years, and J. Harvey Mathes as Secretary for one or more years, and Felix W. Robertson was Treasurer. Mathes was succeeded in 1871 by Major Minor Meriwether, who also became Treasurer. At the end of the second term of President Harris in 1871, he was succeeded by General John C. Fizer. It was about this time that Jefferson Davis became a citizen of Memphis and a member of the Association. He attended meetings regularly and was frequently called to the chair, in which he presided with that ease, grace and dignity so characteristic of the man in higher places and under all circumstances. He was in the home of his friends and took a lively interest in their proceedings. Memphis was then a rendezvous for ex-Confederates second only to New Orleans. The following distinguished leaders, all or nearly all, belonged to the Association and attended the meetings:

President Jefferson Davis,
Admiral Raphael Semmes,
Lieutenant-General Richard S. Ewell,
Lieutenant-General N. B. Forest,
Major-General Gideon J. Pillow
Major-General W.Y.C. Humes,
Major-General Patton Anderson,
Brigadier-General Francis A. Shoup,
Brigadier-General A. J. Vaughan,
Brigadier-General Colton Greene,
Brigadier-General E. W. Rucker,
Brigadier-General J. W. Frazer,

Brigadier-General George W. Gordon,
Brigadier-General W. M. Brown,
Brigadier-General James R. Chalmers,
Brigadier-General Marcus J. Wright,
Brigadier-General J. C. Fizer,
    commanding brigade,
Colonel C. R. Barteau,
    commanding brigade,
General Thomas Jordan,
Hon. Jacob Thompson,
Isham G. Harris, the war Governor.

This is believed to be the oldest association of the kind in the South. For some years it maintained a relief fund, but this was finally discontinued. A general meeting was held at the Cotton Exchange, May 23, 1884, when it was determined to effect a reorganization. C. W. Frazer was chosen President and J. Harvey Mathes, Vice President. Major Fazer has continued as President ever since. Mathes was succeeded the next year by R. B. Spillman, who has since filled the position. An application was made for a new charter, omitting the word "relief" from the title. It was signed by the following members, duly granted and recorded:

C. W. Frazer,
John F. McCallum,
J. P. Young,
M. J. Miller,
James E. Beasley,

Daniel S. Levy,
A. J. McLendon,
R. J. Black,
R. B. Spillman,
J. Harvey Mathes,

W. F. Shippey,
John T. Willins,
W. F. Taylor,
J. C. McDavitt,
W. A. Collier,

Charles G. Locke,
G. V. Rambaut,
A. J. Murray,
Jno. W. Waynesburg.

A few years ago this Association, without losing its identity, became Camp No. 28, Bivouac No.18, United Confederate Veterans of Tennessee, and it is therefore part of the general organization of which General John B. Gordon is Commander-in-Chief. An excellent hall for an armory and the collection of war relics was secured in 1893, and is used jointly by the Association and its auxiliary, the Ladies' Confederate Memorial Association, and is an attractive gathering place for Confederates and their friends.

Whilst only scant measure is given the services of many gallant Confederates named, they represent a class and must stand as types of the greater number not mentioned. It will be noticed that some who made the very best soldiers were born north of the Ohio river, and some were from other lands, thus showing that human sympathies and courageous qualities are not exclusive privileges for any particular people. It may be mentioned without partiality or invidious intent that the Hebrews, who claim no country as their own, though usually good citizens wherever found, had many valiant soldiers in the Southern armies, as well as a representative in the cabinet of the Confederacy. Several of them are active and honored members of this Association. One of the oldest members is Comrade David Flannery, the veteran telegrapher, born in Limerick, Ireland, February 16, 1828, who rendered such valuable services during the war in his peculiar line. Another of the oldest is Comrade Daniel S. Levy, the artillerist, born in Prussia in the year 1826, a live, working member of Company A, Confederate Veterans, and was able to carry a gun and march in line many miles at Chattanooga last year and at Richmond this year (1896), when younger men fell by the wayside. There are several others, however, who are full seventy years old. The present organization really dates back only to 1884, but it is practically a continuation of the parent society, and it may be accepted as a fact that few or none ever become members without proper indorsement. The strictest scrutiny has always been exercised with regard to applicants, as a matter of proper precaution. This, however, would hardly seem necessary, as no one unworthy of fellowship would be likely to seek it. It will not be many years before the old soldiers will pass away to their eternal rest; others may come after to take up the threads of reminiscence and history as well as romance and poetry, and weave them into volumes of wider scope, to occupy space in the libraries of the future, and the descendants of Southern men and women will doubtless read in no narrow spirit the annals of their whole country's struggles with patriotic pride and satisfaction.

In a few years the ex-Confederates, still so active and potential in all the affairs of life, will sleep peacefully beneath the sod, and no more be seen than their banner which was furled forever. Many names are yet on the rolls of the living, but the final Appomattox must come to each man, and not far over in the next century. A younger generation is succeeding us if it has not done so already. We hope to transmit a respect for law and order and love of country to stronger arms and buoyant, noble hearts. May the sunset of every comrade leave a halo of soft, mellow light and memories of well-spent lives, worthy to be cherished and emulated in other days, is the sincere wish of

THE AUTHOR.

29 Cynthia Place
Memphis, Tenn., December 12, 1896

HOSPITALS, DISEASES AND ILLNESSES

Hospitals

As noted in the comments on the soldiers, many died while in a local hospital. The soldiers were sent to a Memphis hospital either after being wounded in battle, including Belmont, Island 10 and Shiloh, or after contracting a disease or illness while in camp. This chapter provides a brief description of the hospitals that primarily served the Confederacy in Memphis from the beginning of the War to the surrender of Memphis on June 6, 1862, as indicated in the articles noted below and contemporary newspapers.

Overton Hospital - The Overton Hotel was nearing completion in 1861 when it was opened as a Confederate hospital. The Hospital was located on the northwest corner of Poplar and Main streets. It was also used by the Union Medical Department after the surrender of Memphis. Per an Associated Press dispatch from Washington, D.C. June 15, 1897, the United States Court of Claims awarded $53,333 to the Overton Hotel Company of Memphis, Tennessee, in satisfaction of their claim against the government for the occupation of their building for hospital purposes from January 1, 1863, to September 1, 1865. See also *The Commercial Appeal* Memphis June 16, 1897 "For Using The Overton Hospital."

Southern Mothers Hospital - "The Southern Mothers. - The undersigned ladies of Memphis, in response to a call in the Appeal of Saturday, have formed a society, to be called the Southern Mothers, for the purpose of devoting ourselves to the care of the sick or wounded soldiers of the army of the Confederate States of America, whenever the chances of war shall bring them near to us.... Mrs. S. C. Law, President." *Memphis Daily Appeal*, April 25, 1861, page 3, column 3. In June 1861, the leading ladies of Memphis organized the Southern Mothers Society and set up a small hospital in a building on Second at Union. By late summer the Southern Mothers Hospital had moved to the Irving Block, a large commercial building on Second at Court. In December 1861, the Southern Mothers Society Irving Block Hospital was combined with the Overton Hospital. Per Young's *Standard History of Memphis*, page 340, the Hospital was organized April 28, 1861, for the purpose of nursing the sick and wounded soldiers. Per an article in the May 29, 1861, *Memphis Daily Appeal*, page 3, column 2, S. C. Law was President and Mary E. Pope was Secretary (see sketches in chapter on Confederates buried outside of Soldiers Rest). Per an article in the August 9, 1861, *Memphis Daily Appeal*, page 4, column 1, Southern Mothers moved to Irving Block, north building on Court Square. Per an article in the December 24, 1861, *Memphis Daily Appeal*, page 4, column 5, the Southern Mothers Hospital was "yesterday" joined with that of the Overton, the latter building now containing the whole of the patients of the two by order of the general in command.

Ladies Edgewood Hospital Association - The Edgewood Chapel was converted into a 50 bed facility for the sick under the sponsorship of the Edgewood Hospital Association. Per an article in the September 22, 1861 *Memphis Daily Appeal* the Edgewood Hospital Association adopted rules to serve the sick and provide clothing. Mrs. Charles McLean was named President and Mrs. B. B. Waddell was named Secretary. The Edgewood Chapel was located two miles from the city near the residence of Colonel McLean. Per an article in the November 15, 1861 *Memphis Daily Appeal* (Local Matters) the Ladies Edgewood Hospital Association was taking care of sick of Colonel Gantt's Arkansas Regiment (Arkansas 12th Infantry Regiment). See also Colonel Gantt's letters in "Downeasters in Arkansas: Letters of Roscoe G. Jennings to his Brother," by Eugene A. Nolte, *Arkansas Historical Quarterly*, Volume XVIII, Spring 1959, Number 1, pages 14-19.

Irving Hospital - Special Order No. 231 – "In compliance with instructions from General Johnston, Commanding Department. The building formerly occupied by the "Southern Mother" and known as the "Irving Block" will be taken possession of and arranged for the reception of wounded soldiers. The furniture at the Overton Hospital not indispensable there, will be removed to the Irving Block. This later will be known and designated as the Irving Hospital." John Adams, Captain C.S.A., Commanding, Headquarters, Memphis, Tennessee, 5 April 1862. See also Southern Mothers Hospital. Prison during the Union occupation.

State Hospital - The State Hospital was located outside the city limits and was requisitioned by the State of Tennessee in June 1861 for Confederate troops. This hospital was located where the Forrest Park is now located.

For more detailed information on the medicine and hospitals in Memphis during the War, readers are referred to the following:

Patricia M. LaPointe, "Military Hospitals in Memphis, 1861-1865," *Tennessee Historical Quarterly*, Winter 1983, pages 325-342.

Patricia M. LaPointe, "The Disrupted Years: Memphis City Hospitals 1860-1867," *The West Tennessee Historical Society Papers*, XXXVII (1983), pages 9-29.

Patricia M. LaPointe, *From Saddlebags to Science: A Century of Health Care in Memphis, 1830-1930* (Memphis: The Health Sciences Museum Foundation of the Memphis and Shelby County Medical Society Auxiliary, 1984), pages 13-19.

Darla Brock, "OUR HANDS ARE AT YOUR SERVICE': THE STORY OF CONFEDERATE WOMEN IN MEMPHIS," *The West Tennessee Historical Society Papers*, XLV (1991), pages 19-34.

Perre Magness, "Women played a Vital role in Civil War," *The Commercial Appeal* Memphis, Tennessee, August 3, 1995, Section CG, page 2.

Mrs. S. E. D. Smith, *The Soldiers Friend; being a Thrilling Narrative of Grandma Smith's Four Years' Experience and*

Observations, as Matron, in the Hospitals of the South, during the late Disastrous Conflict in America, Memphis, Tennessee, Printed by The Bulletin Publishing Company, 1867, pages 35 and 52-56.

<u>DISEASES AND ILLNESSES</u>

The various records on the soldiers often indicated a disease or illness as cause of death and are included in the comments on the soldiers.

Obviously, many of these diseases and illnesses rarely cause death today. The primary problem during the War was lack of sanitary conditions as bacterial origin of diseases illnesses was still an unknown. Deaths from disease or illnesses and complications from wounds or injury far exceeded the number of deaths from gunshots.

Diseases accounted for an estimated 66 percent of the Union mortality and more than 75 percent on the Confederate side. The overall death rate for soldiers who reached a hospital was more than 14 percent. (1)

The following is a general definition of the more common diseases during the War:

Affection - a general term indicating a disease or ailment.
Apoplexy - sudden loss, more or less complete, of consciousness and voluntary motion, without the circulation or breathing being suspended, which is produced from pressure on the brain, usually from hemorrhage or the plugging of a vessel in the brain or spinal cord.
Brain concussion - cerebral concussion that is a common result from a blow to the head or a fall on the end of the spine with force sufficient to be transmitted upward.
Brain fever - most likely encephalitis, which is an inflammation of the brain.
Catarrh - inflammation of mucous membranes, especially of the nose and throat. Conjunctivitis catarrhal is the inflammation of the mucous membrane that lines eyelids and is reflected out the eyeball due to a variety of causes such as foreign bodies, various bacteria, or irritation from heat, cold, or chemicals.
Catarrhal - of the nature of or pertaining to catarrh.
Chilblains - painful swelling or inflamed sore on the feet or hands, caused by exposure to cold.
Cholera morbus - a disease characterized by vomiting, purging, violent griping, coldness and cramps of the extremities. This was probably appendicitis.
Concussion - an injury resulting from impact with an object.
Congestion - the presence of an excessive amount of blood or tissue fluid in an organ or in tissue.
Consumption - tuberculosis (infectious disease most commonly affecting the respiratory system) wasting, or the using up of anything.
Continuous chill - continuous (without break, cessation or interruption) attack of shivering accompanied by the sensation of coldness and pallor of the skin. Chills accompany various diseases, especially malaria and pneumonia, and are course or fine; diffuse; trembling; etc.
Diarrhea - frequent passage of watery bowel movements. It is a frequent symptom of gastrointestinal disturbances and is primarily the result of increases peristalses, which is a progressive wavelike movement that occurs involuntarily in hollow tubes of the body, especially the alimentary (digestive tube from mouth to anus) canal.
Dropsy - a condition rather than a disease, such as heart disease, kidney disease, cirrhosis of the liver, and other causes such as excessive sodium retention. Morbid accumulation of serum and watery fluid and edema in the tissues and cavities. Also known as nephrosis: degeneration of the kidney; causes swelling due to lack of fluids not passing through kidney to bladder for disposal.
Dysentery - a term applied to a number of intestinal disorders especially of the colon, characterized by inflammation of the mucous membrane.
Dyspepsia - indigestion or heartburn.
Edema - a condition in which the body tissues contain an excessive amount of tissue fluid. It may be local or general. Generalized edema is sometimes called dropsy or anasarca. Blue edema can occur when one sprains a limb and swells by retaining blood and causes a blush condition of the limb.
Enteritis - inflammation of the intestines, more particularly of the mucous and submucous tissues usually of the small intestines, i.e. gastroenteritis, which is the inflammation of the stomach and intestinal track.
Erysipelas - an acute infectious disease of the skin or mucous membranes, also known as St. Anthony's fire. Also, an acute febrile (fever) disease with localized inflammation and swelling of skin and subcutaneous tissue accompanied by systemic disturbance of various degree. Symptoms include fever, chills, nausea, vomiting, painful and warm skin, face and head lesions that are hot and red usually seen within 24-48 hours. Blisters may develop.
Flux - an excessive flow or discharge from an organ or cavity of the body; diarrhea. Discharge from the bowels. Bloody flux is dysentery.
Gravel - kidney stone or stone in the bladder.
Hydrocele - a collection of watery fluid in a cavity of the body, especially in the scrotum or along the spermatic cord.
Inflammation - tissue reaction to injury. The inflamed area undergoes continuous change as the body repair processes start to heal

273

and replace injured tissue.

Janders - jaundice (yellow discoloration of the skin).

Lockjaw - tetanus.

Mania a potu - an obsolete term for several alcoholic psychoses. Used to indicate delirium tremens (a physic disorder involving visual and auditory hallucinations found in habitual and excessive users of alcoholic beverages) or alcoholic mania.

Marasmus - progressive wasting of body tissue denotes malnutrition (starvation) almost wholly occurs due to a sequence of acute diseases, esp. diarrhea.

Measles - a highly communicable virus disease characterized by catarrhal (inflammation of mucous membranes) symptoms and by a typical eruption on the skin and mucous membranes of the mouth.

Neuralgia - pain in a nerve. In 1890 the term was used quite frequently, and apparently in many cases for distress that had little to do with the nerves themselves. For example, there was "neuralgia of the heart" which, judging from the symptoms, was either a heart attack or angina. "Neuralgia of the stomach" seems to have been what we call heartburn. "Neuralgia of the head" was simply a headache.

Pernio - congestion and swelling of the skin due to cold, i.e., chilblain.

Phthisis - an archaic term used for tuberculosis or any disease characterized by emaciation and loss of strength, especially diseases of the lungs, i.e. a wasting away of the body.

Piles - hemorrhoids.

Pneumonia- inflammation of the lungs caused primary by bacteria, viruses, chemical irritants, vegetable dusts and allergy. There are more than fifty (50) causes. Symptoms include chills, high fever, pain in chest and cough. Mortality today is 30% unless treated with antibiotics.

Prolapsis - the falling or slipping out of place of an organ.

Remittent fever - a fever alternately abating and returning without intervals of afebrility (without fever).

Rubella - German measles: acute infectious disease resembling both scarlet fever and measles, but differing from these in its short course, slight fever and freedom from other complications following the disease.

Scorbutus - a deficiency disease due to lack of vitamin C in fresh vegetables and fruits. Synonym: scurvy.

Scrofula - enlargement of one or more glands, particularly the neck. Goiter was considered scrofula.

Typhoid - resembling typhus or typhus fever, which is one of a group of acute, infectious diseases characterized by great prostration, severe headaches, generalized maculopapular rash sustained high fever, and usually progressive neurologic involvement, ending in a crisis in 10 to 14 days.

Typhoid fever- an acute, infectious disease characterized by definite lesions in Peyer's patches, mesenteric glands, and spleen accompanied by fever, headache, abdominal symptoms.

Varicocele - a varicose vein in the scrotum.

Vulnus sclopeticum - relating to a wound caused by a gunshot wound

(1) Patricia M. LaPointe, *From Saddlebags to Science: A Century of Health Care in Memphis, 1830-1930* (The Health Sciences Museum Foundation, 1984), page 13.

Reference: *McGown on Diseases of the South* (1849), Mississippi Valley Collection, The University of Memphis Libraries, RA 804 M3.

NOTES OF INTEREST

The subjects covered in this chapter are items related to this work and the soldiers buried in Elmwood Cemetery. It is not an exhaustive list but just some items that really started out as simple notes.

Alabama 54th Infantry Regiment – The Regiment was organized on October 9, 1862 under Special Order No. 59 dated September 29, 1862, at Jackson, Mississippi by consolidation of four companies of Alabama troops and two companies Mississippi troops from the Alabama, Tennessee, and Mississippi 1st Infantry Regiment and four companies from Tennessee 40th Walker's Infantry Regiment. Colonel Alpheus Baker Commander.

Appeal Battery (Memphis Appeal Battery and Arkansas 5th Light Artillery) - Per February 26, 1862, *Memphis Daily Appeal,* Local Matters, page 2, column 5: "Memphis Appeal Battery - we would advise our friends and all those desirous of joining a light artillery, to apply at No. 27 Front Row. Captain W. C. Bryan is now engaged in raising a company to be called the "Memphis Appeal Battery." Per article "The Appeal Battery—Artillerists Wanted "in the March 15, 1862, *Memphis Daily Appeal,* page 2, column 8, "Fifty dollars bounty will be paid to each man who is mustered in, and every article of clothing which will add to their comfort will be given." Per article under Local Matters, April 17, 1862, *Memphis Daily Appeal,* page 1, column 2, Appeal Battery recruiting office has been removed to the counting room of the Appeal, the company is almost complete, and is encamped south of State Hospital on Pidgeon Roost Road. Recruit notices regularly appeared in *Memphis Daily Appeal* in March and April 1862. In letter to the Editors Appeal, reported in the April 17, 1862, *Memphis Daily Appeal,* page 2, column 7, C. C. Scott, 1st Lieutenant, responds to a request from the Editors and provides a list of the company proper, and also some who have been assigned to duty from "Haynie's Battery" (Alabama 2 Battalion Light Artillery Company C, which per Company Muster Roll for October 31 to December 31, 1862, serving in the Appeal Battery temporarily) on the 25th September, at Baldwin, Mississippi. Per unit description on the service records cards found under Arkansas 5th Battery Light Artillery "(T)his Battery was organized at Memphis, Tenn., in April, 1862, and designated the Memphis Appeal Battery; in 1864 it was reorganized as the 5th Arkansas Battery. During the same time it was also known as Capt. Bryan's Company Arkansas Light Artillery, Captain Hogg's Company Arkansas Light Artillery and Captain Scott's Company Arkansas Light Artillery." Per Appendix V, *One Hundred Years of The Commercial Appeal, The Story of the Greatest Romance in American Journalism 1840 – 1940* (Robert Talley, Editor, The Centennial Edition, Printed at The Commercial Appeal, 1940, The Memphis Publishing Company) "The Appeal Battery was organized in Memphis in the Spring of 1862 by Colonel John R. McClanahan, one of the paper's editors, and was presented with a silken flag by the ladies of the city when it departed for Corinth and the front on May 6. It took part in the fierce battle there, and later moved on to Vicksburg, where it helped defend the city in the historic siege, several of its members being killed in action. In the shift of war events, it became a part of an Arkansas outfit." The Battery was captured when Vicksburg fell on July 4, 1863, and is honored on five tablets on the Vicksburg Battlefield marking the Battery positions. See also, "The Saga of the Memphis Appeal Battery" by Alan Doyle, *Old Shelby County Magazine,* Issue 54, May, 2003, pages 2-10.

Arkansas 15th (Northwest - McRae's Battalion) Infantry Regiment – The Regiment was organized as McRae's Battalion Arkansas Infantry July 15, 1861. It was reorganized as McRae's Regiment December 3, 1861, and as Hobb's Regiment May 8, 1862. Then the designation was changed to 15th Regiment (Boone's) about October 1862 and finally to Northwest 15th Regiment Arkansas Infantry in February 1863.

Arkansas 17th (Lemoyne's) Infantry Regiment – The Regiment as originally organized consisted of eight companies that were consolidated into six companies and joined with four companies of the 14th Regiment (McCarver's) Arkansas Infantry about May 15, 1862, to form the 21st Regiment Arkansas Infantry.

Arkansas 21st Infantry Regiment - This Regiment was organized about May 15, 1862, by the merger of six companies from the 17th Lemoyne's Infantry Regiment and four companies from the 14th McCarver's Infantry Regiment.

Army Hospital - Per June 15, 1861, *Memphis Daily Appeal,* the State Hospital on eastern suburbs of the city to be cleaned for Army patients.

Battle of Memphis (June 6, 1862) Confederate Gunboats - Colonel Lovell (sank); General Beauregard (sank); General Bragg (captured and taken into the U. S. Navy as General Bragg); General Earl Van Dorn (avoided capture or destruction but destroyed June 26, 1862, to prevent capture); General M. Jeff Thompson (set on fire during battle; blew up; and abandoned); General Sterling Price (run ashore; abandoned; later taken into the U. S. Navy as General Price); General Sumter (run ashore; abandoned; later taken into the U. S. Navy as Sumter); Little Rebel (run ashore and captured; later taken into the U. S. Navy under the same name). See Lee N. Newcomer, "The Battle of Memphis, 1862" *The West Tennessee Historical Society Papers,* XII (1958), pages 41-57. Also see "Battle of Memphis" *Memphis Daily Appeal,* June 7, 1874, which list officers.

Bluff City Grays (Greys) - Tennessee 154 Senior Infantry Regiment 1st Company B and Tennessee 3 (Forrest Old) Cavalry Regiment 2nd Company A. Per description on the unit service record cards in the Tennessee 3 (Forrest's Old) Cavalry regiment this company was successively designated as Captain Edmondson's Company; 1st Company B 154th Regiment Tennessee Volunteers; Captain Allin's Company of Sharp Shooters, General Preston Smith's Brigade; Company F 11th Regiment Tennessee Cavalry; Company A McDonald's Battalion Tennessee Cavalry; Company A Forrest's Regiment Cavalry, and 2nd Company A 3rd (Forrest's) Regiment Tennessee Cavalry. Per order of General N. B. Forrest Tennessee 154 Senior Infantry Regiment 1 Company B was transferred February 22, 1863, to Tennessee 3 (Forrest's Old) Cavalry

Regiment as 2 Company A and the first Company A became Company E Woodward's 2 Kentucky Cavalry. Per article in the April 19, 1861, *Memphis Daily Appeal*, page 3, column 2, Bluff City Grays organized night before last with J. H. Edmondson, Captain. See also the June 6, 1878, *Memphis Daily Appeal*, page 4, column 3, article "OUR DEAD HEROES" covering the unveiling of the Confederate Monument and Decoration of Graves at Elmwood, which article indicates that twenty-eight members of the Bluff City Grays, Company B of the 154 Senior Infantry Regiment and Company A of Forrest's Old (Third) Cavalry Regiment, are buried at Elmwood; article "Veterans in Council" in the May 12, 1881, *Memphis Daily Appeal*, page 4, column 4, concerning the meeting of the surviving members in the city of the old Bluff City Grays to appoint the necessary committees for the purpose of making special decoration on the graves of their dead comrades at Elmwood and Calvary cemeteries on Sunday next, Memorial Day, which lists the "comrades who sleep at Elmwood cemetery"; "A COMPLETE ROSTER OF THE BLUFF CITY GREYS" located in the Memphis Room of the Memphis/Shelby County Public Library and Information Center Central Library; and "Muster Roll or Roll of Honor of the Bluff City Grays" in *Reminiscences of the Civil War* by John Hallum, Tunnah & Pittard printers, 1903, page 359. William G Wilkin's widow, Minnie Swayne Wilkins, received a Tennessee Confederate Pension (W10343) and her application file contains a copy of "Captain Thomas F. Pattison's History of the Bluff City Grays" with names as appeared on First Muster Roll and those who joined after September 1, 1861, to surrender, 1865. The document was submitted by Dr. J. L. Manire, Surgeon Dentist, Memphis, Tennessee.

Camp Abington - This camp was located in Fayette County east of Collierville, Tennessee. Per October 1861 *Memphis Daily Appeal* Colonel Looney's 38th Tennessee Infantry Regiment was camped there. Per *Tennesseans in The Civil War, Part 1*, page 255, Tennessee 38th (Looney's) Infantry Regiment was organized September 23, 1861, at Camp Abington.

Camp Beauregard, Kentucky - This camp was located in Graves County, Kentucky at "Old Feliciana" on ridge line some two miles east of Water Valley, Kentucky, which is south of Mayfield, Kentucky. The camp was organized in September 1861 and was destroyed by retreating Confederate troops in February 1862. Many troops encamped there suffered and died of the diseases that were prevalent during the winter of 1861-62. Per *History of Camp Beauregard* compiled by Mrs. George T. Fuller, Chair, Camp Beauregard Monument Committee, in 1936, it was estimated that between 1200 and 1500 Confederate soldiers died while in camp at Camp Beauregard. Per Mrs. Fuller's book the generals under General Beauregard were General Alcorn, who had mixed troops from Tennessee and Mississippi, General Bowen was in command of two Arkansas regiments, General Jacob B. Biffle, Lieutenant Colonel of the 25th Tennessee, was in command of troops from Mississippi, and Colonel Clay King was commander of Kentuckians, commonly known as "Clay King's Hell Hounds." King's Battalion Kentucky Cavalry composed of Boyd's, Pell's and Swan's companies. Further, per Mrs. Fuller's book the following forces were in camp at Camp Beauregard from September 1861 to March 1862: First Missouri Infantry (Colonel Rich), First 22nd and 28th Mississippi Infantry, Hudson's Mississippi Battery, 9th Arkansas (Colonel Dunlap), 10th Arkansas Infantry (Colonel Merrick), 22nd and 27th Tennessee Infantry, Tennessee Cavalry, part of 7th Tennessee Cavalry, William's Tennessee Battery, Beltzhoover's (Watson's) Louisiana Battery, Alabama troops which were merged into the First Confederate Cavalry, a Mississippi Valley Regiment (Colonel Martin), Colonel Logwood's Battalion of Tennessee Cavalry, a Mississippi regiment (Colonel Burrell Williams), 12th Tennessee (Colonel Russell), and two Kentucky companies (Captain Holt of Murray, Kentucky and Captain Outlaw of Moscow, Kentucky). Additionally, per Mrs.' Fuller's book the troops at Camp Beauregard were commanded by Brigadier General John S. Bowen, First Missouri Infantry, a West Pointer, and formerly a Colonel of First Missouri Infantry, and later a Major General in the Provisional Army of the Confederate States. Per *Tennesseans in The Civil War, Part 1*, page 154, Tobin's (William's see above) Tennessee Light Artillery Company was at Camp Beauregard on November 30, 1861. Per Hubbard's Book, page 18, Haywood's and Neely's companies (Companies D and B respectively of 6th Logwood's Tennessee Cavalry Battalion and subsequently Companies D and E respectively of 7th Tennessee Cavalry Regiment) were ordered to Camp Beauregard to picket and scout for Bowen's Brigade. Per Young's book on 7th Tennessee Cavalry, page 23, "about February 19, 1862, the Battalion made a winter's march to Old Camp Beauregard, destroying the railroad from five miles south of Mayfield, Kentucky, to Fulton Station. They also burned Camp Beauregard after removing a large amount of commissary stores. (Logwood's Report, "Reb. Records," 7, 897.)" Official Record, Series I, Volume 7, pages 897-8. See also *Arkansas Confederates in the Western Theatre,* by James Willis, chapter 2 Belmont and Camp Beauregard, page 73-108, Morningside, 1998.

Camp Dean, Tennessee - This camp was located at Germantown, Tennessee. The Tennessee 3rd Regiment was there per May 18, 1861, the *Avalanche* (Memphis).

Camp Johnson, Tennessee - This camp was near Memphis. Per *Tennesseans in The Civil War, Part 1*, page 262, Tennessee 40th (Walker's) Infantry Regiment, which was organized in Memphis on October 5, 1861, was camped there until November 19, 1861, when it moved to Fort Pillow, Tennessee. Some compiled service records of the Tennessee 40th (Walker's) Infantry Regiment have the name incorrectly spelled "Johnston."

Company A, Confederate Veterans – "Company A, Confederate Veterans, had its inception in the minds of a few Confederates at the time a drill contest was given for some local charity by the Chickasaw Guards-veterans against juniors-at the Auditorium, in Memphis, in April 1894. Most prominent among these Confederates were W. J. Crawford, L. B. McFarland, C. W. Heiskell, W.B. Mallory and J. E. Beasley. These gentlemen being in a group who had witnessed the practice drills of the Chickasaws, were indulging in remarks, complimentary and critical, when someone suggested a doubt as to whether the old soldiers of the war knew much about drill. One of the Confederates, in a bantering spirit, said: "Why, we can get up a company of 'Old Rebs' that will put up a drill to make these boys open their eyes." From this suggestion arose a discussion of the idea, till it was determined that a company of Confederate Veterans should be organized to challenge the winning team in the drill contest then about to take place. A meeting of ex-Confederates was called and held in the hall of the Young Men's Business League, Judge L. P. Cooper being selected to preside as chairman and Edward Bourne as secretary. The company was organized and selected the following officers: Captain, W. W. Carnes; First Lieutenant, W. B. Mallory; Second Lieutenant, C. W. Heiskell; Third Lieutenant, J. E. Beasley; Orderly Sergeant, John W. Waynesburg; Second Sergeant, Edward Bourne. (*The Old Guard in Gray*. Mathes, J. Harvey. Press of S. C. Toof & Co., Memphis, 1897. Part II, Enlarged Edition 1899.) See also *Confederate Veteran* Volume 3, August 1895, page 236.

Confederate 2nd Infantry Regiment - See comments on Mississippi 25th Infantry Regiment, which was organized January 31, 1862, and disbanded about May 8, 1862. This unit should not be confused with Tennessee 2 (Robison's) Infantry Regiment which was also called Confederate 2 Infantry Regiment.

Confederate 9th Infantry Regiment - This regiment was organized July 21, 1862, with 8 companies (A-H). It was formed by the consolidation of the 2nd (Walker's) Regiment Tennessee Infantry and the 21st Regiment of Tennessee Infantry per Special Order 101 dated July 1, 1862, (Companies A, D, E and F from Walker's Regiment and Companies B, C, G and H from 21st Regiment). The remnants of the regiment finally became Company I, 3rd Consolidated Regiment Tennessee Infantry. This regiment was also known as 5th Confederate Infantry and 5th Confederate Regiment Tennessee Infantry.

Confederate Hall - Built specifically for the 1901 reunion of the United Confederate Veterans. See A MEMPHIS RECAPTURED BY CONFEDERATE ARMY: THE ELEVENTH ANNUAL UNITED CONFEDERATE VETERANS REUNION 1901," Chris Armstrong, *The West Tennessee Historical Society Papers,* Volume LII 1998, pages 1-12. Per *Confederate Veteran* Volume IX, April 1901, page 150, the headquarters for the Veterans reunion in Memphis will be in the Barksdale, Denton & Company Building at the corner of Front and Court Streets which is across the street from the Confederate Hall. It was located on Front Street where Confederate Park is now located. Per January 10, 1902, *The Commercial Appeal* Memphis, page 6, Confederate Hall on river front was to come down.

Confederate Military History - a 12-volume series of books written and/or edited by former Confederate Brigadier General Clement A. Evans that deals with specific topics related to the military personalities, places, battles, and campaigns in various Southern United States states, including those of the Confederacy. The books were first published in 1899 in Atlanta, Georgia, by Evans' Confederate Publishing Company. The original title was *Confederate Military History: A Library of Confederate States History, written by distinguished men of the South.* Several reprint extended editions exist, with varying numbers of volumes (Wikpedia Foundation, Inc.). The Tennessee Genealogical Society published in its *"Ansearchin'" News* magazine, Volume 41, #4 (1994), Volume 42, #1-4 (1995) and Volume 43, #1-2 (1996), brief sketches of the biographies of those soldiers and other individuals who had a relationship with Tennessee, which was Volume VIII in the original set and Volume X in the Broadfoot Publishing Company 1987 extended edition set. The brief sketches were compiled by Mary Louise Graham Nazor with only genealogical information abstracted from the biographies. Each man gave his Civil War record in his own words, but when a veteran was deceased, a relative or friend wrote the biography. These personal accounts are very detailed, containing many poignant stories.

Confederate Park - Located on Front Street at the corner of Jefferson Street. The Park was established by the Memphis Park Commission in 1908. It had been part of the Public Promenade, which was the land between Front Street and the Mississippi River from Union to Jackson. Portions of the Promenade had over the years been dedicated for various purposes when the Park was established. It was the site of Confederate Hall (see sketch next above) for the 1901 Veterans reunion. See "Confederate Park" (February 4, 1979) in Paul R. Coppock's *Mid-South,* Volume IV, pages 15-19.

Confederate Relief and Historical Association of Memphis and Confederate Historical Association – See West Tennessee Historical Society, infra, and *Record of Ex-Confederate Soldiers and Sailors, Members of the Confederate Relief and Historical Association of Memphis* - Original Tennessee State Library and Archives holding - Manuscript Microfilm #1276, Reel 5, Oversize Volume 8 and the index of individuals who were members of the Confederate Relief and Historical Association of Memphis found on the Tennessee State library and Archives website.

Confederate Soldiers Rest - Located in the Fowler Section. Per September 25, 1861, *Memphis Daily Appeal,* page 4, column 1, Local Matters: "Elmwood Cemetery. This Company, at the commencement of the War, very liberally donated and set apart a lot of ground for the purpose of burying, free of charge, all soldiers who may die honorably in defense of our liberties. We learn from Captain Lenow, the President of the Company, that he has enlarged the ground by changing one of the drives, which is a great improvement to it, and it is now ample for the purpose. In the center of the lot is a circle of twelve feet in diameter, for the erection of a monument, which our patriotic citizens will no doubt raise to the memory of the brave soldiers who have fallen in defense of our country. The grounds at Elmwood are continually receiving substantial improvements, and they are beautified and adorned in so handsome a manner that it reflects credit upon the taste and untiring industry of the President of the Company, who devotes so much time and attention to it." The Tuesday, June 18, 1861, *Memphis Daily Appeal,* page 3, column 2, printed a report from Mrs. S. C. Law, President, Southern Mothers, that there was an intermit on Sunday (June 16, 1861 sic actually Monday June 17, 1861), at Elmwood Cemetery with the Cemetery donating a lot and Flaherty (Funeral Home) donating a coffin and services. The June 27, 1861, *Memphis Daily Appeal* reported that a lot was donated at Elmwood Cemetery for burial of Thomas Gallagher of the Crockett Rangers who died at the house of friend J. M. Patrick after receiving a gunshot wound accidentally June 14, 1861, at Camp Randolph. Per Cemetery Daily Burial Book William Gallagher was buried in Lot 159 Fowler Section Grave #20 on June 17, 1861, with Remarks: accidentally shot at Randolph. H.S.M. (Southern Mothers Hospital); Lot #159 appears to have become part of Soldiers Rest as there is no Lot 159 Fowler Section in the Fowler Book or on the Cemetery Plat. The Fowler Section lots skip from Lot #152/153 to Lot #162. Thus, he was the first burial in Confederate

Soldiers Rest.

Coppock, Paul R. - Compilation of his historic articles and columns printed in *The Commercial Appeal* Memphis between 1928 and 1983 published in book form: *Memphis Sketches* (1976); *Memphis Memoirs* (1980); and *Paul R. Coppock's Mid-South* editions, edited by Helen M. Coppock (his widow) and Charles W. Crawford, The Paul R. Coppock Publication Trust, West Tennessee Historical Society, Volume I (1985), Volume II 1971-1975 (1992), Volume III 1976-1978 (1993), and Volume IV 1979-1982 (1994).

Crain's Artillery - Per November 19, 1861 *Memphis Daily Appeal* (Local Matters): Captain O. W. Crain, for a number of years belonging to the United States Army, has been authorized by General Polk to raise a company of light artillery for immediate service. The officers are now actively recruiting at different points. Lieutenant John W. Harris stationed here, to whom all applicants for enlistment may be made. Apply at his office, No. 25 Front Row, up stairs, or to Day and Proudfit, No. 33 Front Row. Lieutenant John W. Harris will call upon the citizens for money to aid in enlisting and organizing the company. Per *Tennesseans in The Civil War, Part 1*, no muster rolls were found on the Battery.

Crittenden Rangers - April 14, 1861 *Memphis Daily Appeal* (Local Matters), page 3, column 3 – "Unfortunate Accident - Yesterday the Ladies of Crittenden County, Arkansas presented a Flag to the Crittenden Rangers. At the conclusion of the proceedings several cannon shots were fired. Mr. Angus Greenlaw, who resides in Hopefield, and is brother to the Messrs. Greenlaw of this City, was in the act of ramming a charge down, when the gun went off prematurely. The flesh was almost cleared from the hand, the left was terribly burned, the left thigh is also much burned. We learn that the injuries, although very serious, are not considered dangerous in their character."

First Memphis Military Funeral - In Sunday June 23, 1861, *Memphis Daily Appeal*, Local Matters, it was reported that the first funeral procession ever martialed in Memphis according to full and strict military form was held June 22, 1861, for Logan Burton, a private in Captain J. H. Morgan's Company 7th Tennessee Regiment Volunteers (this regiment actually Tennessee 13th Infantry Regiment), who died on Steamer Ingomer from congestive fever since the steamer had left Fort Wright. Also, per resolution passed by officers on the steamer reported in the newspaper article deceased was a native of Kentucky but for some time a resident of Shelby County, Tennessee and at beginning of war joined Secession Guard, J. H. Morgan, Captain (Company C, 13th Tennessee Infantry Regiment). Captain L. Granberry was also identified in the newspaper article and he was captain Company B, Tennessee 13th Infantry Regiment. Logan Burton died June 1, 1861, per 13th Infantry Regiment memorial roll in Lindsley's Annals.

Forrest Raid into Memphis August 21, 1864 – See "Forrest Raid Into Memphis" by W. B. Stewart, Arlington, Tennessee, *Confederate Veteran*, Volume XI, 1903, pages 503-504; "Forrest's 1864 Raid on Memphis" by Jack D. L. Holmes, *Tennessee Historical Quarterly*, Volume XVIII (December 1959), pages 295-321, "(T)he following day he (Forrest) picked men from Neely's and Bell's Brigades and the 15th Tennessee Cavalry under the command of Colonel Thomas H. Logwood. Other units represented in the Confederate raiding party were the 3rd, 12th, 14th, 16th, 21st, and 22nd Tennessee Cavalry; the 2nd Missouri Cavalry, commanded by Colonel Robert ("Red Rob") McCullough (sic "McCulloch"); and the 18th Mississippi Cavalry, under Colonel Alex Chalmers. A section of Forrest's Artillery, that of Morton's Battery, was also chosen." page 299; Report of Major General Nathan Bedford Forrest, August 21, 1864, in Official Record, Series 1, Volume 39, Part 1, page 484; "The Capture of Memphis by General Nathan B. Forrest - Captain Dinkins Recalls a Thrilling Incident of the Civil War - The Great Confederate Cavalry Leader Out-Generaled an Army Larger than His Own," *Southern Historical Society Papers*, Volume XXXVI (1908), pages 180-196; "An Eye-Witness Account of Forrest's Raid on Memphis" by Juan Rayner, *The West Tennessee Historical Society Papers*, Volume XII (1958), pages 134-137.

Fort Harris - Battery on Mississippi River seven miles from the Memphis landing. Then at the foot of Poplar and adjacent to the Navy Yard (*Paul R. Coppock's Mid-South*, Volume III, 1976-1978, page 82, Helen M. Coppock and Charles W. Crawford, Editors, 1993). Per May 7, 1861, *Memphis Daily Appeal*: six miles north of Memphis.

Fort Wright - Located at Randolph, Tennessee north of Memphis.

Gayoso Independent Guards - Per June 5, 1861, *Memphis Daily Appeal*: 1st Lieutenant Joseph Barbiere.

Hopefield, Crittenden County, Arkansas - Burned by Union soldiers on February 19, 1863. See "The Burning of Hopefield" by David O. Demuth, *Arkansas Historical Quarterly,* Volume XXXVI, Summer 1977, Number 2, pages 123-129.

Issaquena Battery - This Company appears to have been organized in July 1861 as the Issaquena Artillery by men from Issaquena County, Mississippi. It was captured at Fort Donelson, Tennessee in February 1862, and exchanged at Vicksburg, Mississippi in August 1862. Subsequently, it appears to have been organized and credited to the State of Kentucky. Shortly after the Battle of Chickamauga in September 1863, it was consolidated with Cobb's Company, Kentucky Light Artillery.

Irving Block - Located on Second Street across from Court Square. In June 1861, the leading ladies of Memphis organized the Southern Mothers Society and set up a small hospital in a building on Second at Union. By late summer the Southern Mothers Hospital had moved to the Irving Block, a large commercial building on Second at Court. In December 1861, the Southern Mothers Society Irving Block Hospital was combined with the Overton Hospital. Per Young's *Standard History of Memphis*, page 340, the Hospital was organized April 28, 1861, for the purpose of nursing the sick and wounded soldiers. Per an article in the August 9, 1861, *Memphis Daily Appeal* Southern Mothers moved to Irving Block, north building on Court Square. Per an article in the December 24, 1861, *Memphis Daily Appeal*, the Southern Mothers Hospital was "yesterday" joined with that of the Overton, the latter building now containing the whole of the patients of the two by order of the general in command. Special Order No. 231 – "In compliance with instructions from General Johnston, Commanding Department. The building formerly occupied by the "Southern Mothers and known as the "Irving

Block" will be taken possession of and arranged for the reception of wounded soldiers. The furniture at the Overton Hospital not indispensable there, will be removed to the Irving Block. This later will be known and designated as the Irving Hospital" John Adams, Captain C.S.A., Commanding, Headquarters, Memphis, Tennessee, 5 April 1862. Prison during Union occupation - See General Order No. 90 dated October 25, 1862, W. T. Sherman, Major-General Commanding, Headquarters First Division, Army of the Tennessee, Memphis, Tennessee, instructing that the provost guard will be headquartered in the Irving Block and that all soldiers or officers arrested or citizens taken by scout, pickets, or guards will be sent to the Irving Block. See also Official Records, Series II, Volumes 5-8. Forrest troops attacked Irving Block Prison August 21, 1864, during raid on Memphis to free prisoners but was unsuccessful. Tablet on Irving Block located on northeast corner of Court Square, which was erected by Confederate Dames in 1915: Prison-History of Memphis "THE BUILDING OPPOSITE KNOWN AS THE IRVING BLOCK WAS USED AS A PRISON BY THE FEDERAL GOVERNMENT FROM 1862-65. MUCH NEEDLESS SUFFERING WAS IMPOSED UPON THE PRISONERS. SO MUCH SO THAT PRESIDENT LINCOLN ORDERED AN INVESTIGATION OF THE CONDITIONS THERE. BOTH CONFEDERATE SOLDIERS AND CITIZENS OF HIGH RANK WERE CONFINED WITHIN ITS WALLS. AT THE CLOSE OF THE WAR, APRIL 1865, ABOUT 1200 SOLDIERS AND 100 CITIZENS, BOTH MEN AND WOMEN, WERE INCARCERATED THERE." Newspapers - *Memphis Appeal* August 17, 1888 (page 3): That Ball and Chain of 1863; *Memphis Press Scimitar* July 29, 1937: 'Unsafe!' City Now Says of Doomed War Prison; *Memphis Press Scimitar* November 16, 1937: Irving Block —Where Prominent Memphians Languished in Pain; *Memphis Press Scimitar* July 1, 1938: Leo Casts His Cast-Iron Eyes at Sewanee Campus concerning lion that was atop the old Irving Prison being moved to the college; *Memphis Press Scimitar* June 9, 1961: New Bank Building to Rise Over Civil War Dungeon; *Memphis Press Scimitar* July 17, 1961: Mystery Uncovered at Civil War Prison Site. See also *Memphis Chamber of Commerce Journal* May 1919, page 75.

Kentucky 2nd (Woodward's) Cavalry Regiment - There were two 2nd Kentucky Cavalry units, Morgan's/Duke's and Woodward's, and both were known as the 2nd during the War. When the Kentucky Adjutant General's Report was published about 1915, they did not know what to do with the two units that were numbered "2nd." Since Morgan and Duke were so well known, they listed their unit as the 2nd and erroneously stuck Woodward's unit in as the "15th Kentucky Cavalry." Woodward's unit was never known as the 15th. They also did this to Diamond's 10th Kentucky Cavalry, which is listed in the book as the "14th Kentucky Cavalry." Officially, Chenoweth's cavalry was the 15th Kentucky Cavalry. Morgan's/Duke's and Woodward's regiments are both listed in the "Official Records" as 2nd Kentucky Cavalry. Neither Woodward's or Diamond's regiments were ever renamed. They were simply listed incorrectly in the Adjutant General's report. (Information supplied by Steve Lynn for Kentucky GenWeb for Civil War Confederate Links.)

Ladies Edgewood Hospital Association - Per September 22, 1861, *Memphis Daily Appeal*: Edgewood Hospital Association Adoption of Rules, Mrs. Charles McLean, President, Mrs. B. B. Waddell, Secretary, serve sick soldiers and provide clothing. Per November 15, 1861, *Memphis Daily Appeal* (Local Matters): Ladies Edgewood Hospital Association taking care of sick of Colonel Gantt's Arkansas Regiment (12th Infantry).

Maynard Rifles - TN 154 Senior Infantry Regiment Company L - Per May 8, 1861, *Memphis Daily Appeal*: Elected officers May 7, 1861, Captain E. A. Cole. Lists of members in February 25, 1862, and March 6, 1862, *Memphis Daily Appeal*. Per article in the November 22, 1861, *Memphis Daily Appeal*, page 4, column 3, at a meeting held yesterday the company changed its name to "Memphis Independents" and will leave for Columbus on Monday.

McCown Regiment - Louisiana 21st Infantry Regiment. Colonel J. P. McCown promoted to Brigadier General October 24, 1861, to command a division.

Memphis Artillery - Per May 2, 1861, *Memphis Daily Appeal*: Captain F. L. Warner of Memphis Artillery.

Memphis Battalion - Tennessee 3 (Memphis Battalion) Infantry Battalion – per notation on compiled service records cards "The 3d (Memphis) Battalion Tennessee Infantry, Companies A-G, was mustered into the service of the Confederate States March 12, 1862, for one year for local defense and special service in the City of Memphis, Tenn. It appears to have been disbanded in May, 1862, on account of the surrender of Memphis."; per narrative in the *Tennesseans in the Civil War*, Part 1: "This organization was mustered into service at Memphis, March 12, 1862, for one year for local defense and special service in the City of Memphis. Adjutant and Inspector General's Office rosters show it was officially recognized as the 3rd Tennessee Infantry Battalion, but it was known as the Memphis Battalion." and "The battalion was to be subject to the call of the Provost Marshall and the Commandant of the Post. It was disbanded in May 1862, due to the surrender of Memphis to the Federal troops."; Originally known as Memphis Legion, Colonel Leonida V. Dixon Commander, who is buried at Elmwood (see sketch herein).

Memphis Battery - Per May 28, 1861, *Memphis Daily Appeal*, Local matters, page 3, column 1, "The Memphis Battery. - This is to stand at the mouth of the Wolf river, on this side, at the point of the bend. It will face the channel west of the island above. An old shanty and some lumber that occupied the intended site were cleared away yesterday. This morning active operations will commence. The contractor talks of having it completed in six days."

Memphis Daily Appeal – "By McClanahan & Dill" per paper by line; See *One Hundred Years of The Commercial Appeal* The Story of the Great Romance in American Journalism 1840 to 1940 (Printed at *The Commercial Appeal*, Copyright, 1940, by *The Memphis Publishing Co.*) for stories on its "Run" and reporting during the War; also see McClanahan, John Reid, Editor, in the chapter Confederates Buried Outside of Soldiers Rest. See also George Sisler, "The Arrest of a *Memphis Daily Appeal* War Correspondent on Charges of treason, *"The West Tennessee Historical Society Papers*, XI (1957), pages 76-92.

Memphis Southern Guards (aka Southern Guards Artillery) - The Memphis Southern Guards were originally part of the prewar 154th Senior Tennessee Infantry Regiment (Company D) under Captain James Hamilton. Per the 154th Senior Tennessee Infantry Regiment unit history in *Tennesseans in the Civil War Part 1,* page 309, "The Southern Guards," of Memphis, Captain James Hamilton, was part of the prewar organization, but withdrew and formed an Artillery company, and their place was taken by "The Beauregards." The Company formed Johnston's Battery, aka Captain T.N. Johnston's Tennessee Heavy Artillery Company, aka Memphis Southern Guards, aka Southern Guards Artillery (formerly Captain James Hamilton's Company; Captain S. H. D. Hamilton's Company). Per the unit history in *Tennesseans in the Civil War Part 1,* page 133, the company was organized at Memphis, Tennessee, April 21, 1861, with James Hamilton as its first captain. It was mustered into Confederate service at New Madrid, Missouri on August 20, 1861. It was first stationed at Fort Pillow, Tipton County. On August 2, 1861, Brigadier General Gideon J. Pillow requested that Jackson's Company be sent to Fort Pillow to relieve Hamilton's Company, and that Hamilton's Company be sent to New Madrid, Missouri. This was done, and the company mustered into Confederate service at that point. In the organization of the forces at Columbus, Kentucky, in September 1861, Captain Hamilton's Battery, Siege Artillery, was placed under the immediate orders of General Pillow. Captain James Hamilton died September 17, 1861, at Belmont, Kentucky and he was succeeded by his brother, S. H. D. Hamilton, as Captain. On October 24, 1861, in the reorganization of the forces, Captain S. H. D. Hamilton's Siege Battery was attached to Pillow's Division. At the Battle of Belmont, November 7, 1861, Hamilton's Battery, on the Columbus side of the river, fired on the Federal gunboats and drove them up the river. Captain S. H. D. Hamilton died on January 1, 1862, and T. N. Johnston succeeded him as captain. Both James and S. H. D. Hamilton are buried at Elmwood Cemetery (see sketches). In January 1862, still at Columbus, Captain Johnston's Siege Battery was reported in the 3rd Division. The battery remained at Columbus, Kentucky until about March 1, 1862, when it moved to Madrid Bend. Brigadier General J. Trudeau, Chief of Artillery, reported that "Captain Johnston was ordered to place at the Island (No.10) his four guns in battery (three 24-pounder siege guns and one 12-pounder) and to take charge of the four 64-pounder howitzers, with 30 rounds of ammunition for each piece." On March 10, 1862, A. B. Gray, Chief Engineer Island Number Ten, reported "This morning Captain Johnston with two pieces of his siege battery (24-pounders) proceeded to the point opposite the village of Point Pleasant, to endeavor to dislodge the enemy. I am afraid that their works have progressed too far for us, from this side, to do much." Johnston's Battery remained on Island Number Ten during the siege of that place beginning March 18 and ending with the evacuation of the island and the capture of a portion of the garrison on April 8, 1862. At the evacuation of the island, the guns were spiked and lost, but Johnston's Battery was not among the troops surrendered there. Being a twelve months' organization, and its term of enlistment having expired, it was mustered out of service by General Beauregard on April 14, 1862. Captain T. N. Johnston became Captain of Company L of the Tennessee 1 Heavy Artillery (Artillery Corps of Tennessee) and some of the men from his battery re-enlisted with him. Company L was at Vicksburg during the siege, was surrendered there July 4, 1863, and Captain Johnston and most of his men from Company L then became 3rd Company A on February 4, 1864.

Mississippi 1st Blythe's Battalion Infantry - The Battalion was mustered into the service of the State of Mississippi May 25 to July 11, 1861, and on August 8, 1861, it was mustered into the Confederate States service for one year. The Battalion was increased to a regiment and known as Blythe's Regiment Mississippi Infantry. This designation was changed to 44th Regiment Mississippi Infantry by Special Order No. 135, A. and I. G. O., dated June 6, 1863.

Mississippi 25th Infantry Regiment - The Regiment (also known as Colonel John D. Martin's Regiment of Volunteers) was designated the 2nd Regiment Confederate Infantry by Special Order No. 25, A. and I. G. O., dated January 31, 1862. Per the regiment descriptive narrative in the compiled service record, the Confederate 2nd Infantry Regiment appears to have been disbanded about May 8, 1862 and Companies A, H, and I became Companies B, D, and A, respectively, 1st Battalion Mississippi Sharpshooters; Companies B and D became Companies D and A, respectively, 55th Regiment Alabama Infantry; Companies F and K were consolidated and formed (New) Company C, 1st Regiment Missouri Infantry; Company C became Company K, 7th Regiment Kentucky Infantry (Mounted); Company G became (New) Company I, 9th Regiment Arkansas Infantry; and Company E probably became Company E, 2nd Regiment South Carolina Artillery.

Missouri 1 Infantry Battalion – The Battalion was made up of three companies: Company A (Captain Jason H. Hunter), Company B (Captain William L. Watkins) and Company C (Captains E. G. Liles, Alvah G. Kelsey and I. N. Hedgbeth). In August 1862, Companies A and B consolidated to form Company K, Missouri 5 Infantry Regiment, and Company C became Company K, Missouri 6 Infantry Regiment. All three companies were at Fort Pillow in April and May 1862, pursuant to orders by General M. Jeff Thompson to assist in defending the river and while there operated as marines on board the various river defense fleet gunboats. Note that soldiers in Alvah George Kelsey's Company C enlisted in Pocahontas, Randolph County, Arkansas in March 1862 by Major W. F. Rapley, which may explain the confusion of some of the soldiers being in Arkansas Rapley's Battalion Infantry in Daily Burial Record Book. That was not the case and should not be confused with Arkansas 12 (Rapley's) Battalion Sharp Shooters, which was formally organized June 30, 1862.

Missouri 1st Infantry Regiment - Per regimental returns, this regiment was organized June 22, 1861, at Camp Calhoun near Memphis, Tennessee. It was at Camp Beauregard, Kentucky from September to November 1861.

Phelan, James (1821-1873) - Confederate Senator (Mississippi), Colonel of Cavalry and Judge Advocate; General and Staff rolls single card indicating Colonel of Cavalry, State of Mississippi, and to report to P. J. Court of S. D. Lee, appointed April 13, 1864; see sketches in *The National Cyclopedia of American Biography*, Volume 36, page 504, and in Warner's *Confederate Congress* book pages 194-195; elected to the Mississippi state senate in 1860 and fall 1861 chosen to the First Regular Confederate Congress for a two year term; 1863 defeated for reelection and then became a Judge Advocate; per General & Staff compiled service record rolls Colonel of Cavalry from Mississippi, appointed April 13, 1864 and ordered to report to P. J. Court S. D. Lee's Cavalry Division; per sketch in Mathes book Colonel and Judge Advocate of Military Court 1864-65, proposed for membership in Confederate Historical Association by Jefferson Davis and Isham G. Harris and elected May 26, 1870; per several biographical sketches born October 11, 1821, Huntsville, Alabama, son of John Phelan and Priscilla Ford, married Elizabeth Jones Moore September 22, 1846, editor and printer in Alabama and moved to Aberdeen, Mississippi in 1849, lawyer and state senator in Mississippi, Confederate Senator 1861-63, defeated for re-election, appointed Colonel of Cavalry and Chief Judge of the Military Court of S. D. Lee's Corps April 13, 1864, to rank April 6, 1864, and postwar attorney in Memphis; died May 17, 1873, in Memphis; death and information on life reported in the *Memphis Avalanche* May 18, 1873, and tribute reported May 20, 1873; death and article on his life and career also reported in the May 18, 1873, Memphis Daily Appeal, page 2, column 2, indicating born Huntsville, Alabama, October 20, 1821; article "Honor To The Dead" in the May 20, 1873, Memphis Daily Appeal, page 4, column 6, reports on resolution "Tribute of Respect to the Memory of Hon. James Phelan" adopted by the Confederate Relief Association, the bar of Memphis and the citizens assembled in joint meeting. Several sources, including Warner's *Confederate Congress* book, indicate that he and his son, James (1856-1891), are both buried at Elmwood, which is incorrect. Only the son, James Phelan, is buried at Elmwood (February 17, 1892). The son's gravestone has the inscription "James Phelan, Representative Shelby County, United States Congress, 1856-1891." He died in the Bahamas January 30, 1891, and his remains later moved to Elmwood but no verification or date yet found. For the elder James Phelan, it was reported in the *Memphis Avalanche*, May 20, 1873, page 4, column 1, News in Brief section, "Yesterday the remains of Hon. James Phelan were sent to Aberdeen, Mississippi for burial." Another son, George R. Phelan, who served in the Confederate army, is also buried at Elmwood (see sketch supra).

Quinby and Robinson - Per May 31, 1861, *Memphis Daily Appeal*: five 6-pounder cannons for Captain Burn's Independent Company at Greenville, Mississippi. The foundry was located on the river front where the sand bar now extends at the foot of Adams Street per J. P. Young's *History of Memphis, Tennessee* (1912) page 340.

Shelby Grays (Greys) Tennessee 4 Infantry Regiment Company A– Reported in the April 18, 1861, *Memphis Daily Appeal* under Local Matters, page 3, column 2, that "A new military company was formed last in our city, ... They adopt the name of "Shelby Greys." In column 3 article "Military" reports the names of the gentlemen enrolled and "assumed the name of the "Shelby Grays." Note spelling difference. Names of officers elected reported in the April 20, 1861, *Memphis Daily Appeal* under Local Matters, page 3, column 2: James Somerville, captain; Luke W. Finley, first lieutenant; W. Hutchinson, second lieutenant; T. W. Francis, third lieutenant; J. W. Rogan, orderly sergeant. Lists of members also reported in December 7, 1861, *Memphis Daily Appeal* under Local Matters, page 4, column 2, and the May 15, 1909, *The Commercial Appeal* Memphis, page 4, "Forty=Eight Years Ago Today The Shelby Greys Entered the Confederate Service —Record of a Famous Memphis Military Company," which is based on a complete eynoptical history of the company prepared by James E. Beasley, a member of the company, who is buried at Elmwood (see his sketch)..

Shiloh Casualties Reports in *Memphis Daily Appeal* 1862 - 10 April: Shelby County wounded/killed; 11 April: 9th, 12th and 15th Tennessee, 13th Arkansas, Mississippi Blythe's, Irving and Overton Hospital list of wounded and note re Bankhead's Battery; 12 April: Overton Hospital list and 154th Tennessee Senior Infantry Regiment; 13 April: Bluff City Grays, Tennessee 2nd, 4th, 5th and 15th and Martin's Regiment; 15 April: report on Captain O'Haver's Company F of Colonel Martin's Regiment; 16 April: Breckinridge's Brigade (Kentucky 3rd, 4th, 5th and 6th and Cobb's Light Artillery and Lyon's Battery); 18 April: 13th Tennessee; 20 April: 1st Arkansas (Fagan's) and 6th Tennessee; 23 April: General Statham's Brigade (Tennessee 19th, 20th, 28th and 45th; Mississippi 15th and 22nd; Captain A. M. Rutledge's Battery and Captain H. L. McClung's Battery) and 1st Missouri; 24 April: General Polk's command (Tennessee 1st, 9th, 12th, 33rd, 154th Senior, Forrest's Cavalry, Smith's Battery, and Polk's Battery) and Colonel Blythe's Mississippi; 25 April: Wood's Brigade (Arkansas 8th and 9th, Tennessee 27th, 44th and 55th, 3rd Mississippi Battalion), Colonel Blythe's Mississippi Regiment, Companies D and E (Carolina Grays) of Colonel Bates 2nd Tennessee Infantry Regiment.

Southern Mothers Association Hospital – "The Southern Mothers. - The undersigned ladies of Memphis, in response to a call in the Appeal of Saturday, have formed a society, to be called the Southern Mothers, for the purpose of devoting ourselves to the care of the sick or wounded soldiers of the army of the Confederate States of America, whenever the chances of war shall bring them near to us.... Mrs. S. C. Law, President." *Memphis Daily Appeal,* April 25, 1861, page 3, column 3; per Young's Standard History of Memphis, page 340, the hospital was organized April 28, 1861, for the purpose of nursing the sick and wounded soldiers; per an article in the May 29, 1861, *Memphis Daily Appeal*, page 3, column 2, S. C. Law was President and Mary E. Pope was Secretary (see sketches in chapter on Confederates buried outside of Soldiers Rest); per article in the June 1, 1861, *Memphis Daily Appeal*, the rooms of the Southern Mothers (corner of Madison and Second Street) will be open 5-7pm; per article in the August 9, 1861, *Memphis Daily Appeal*, page 4, column 1, Southern Mothers Hospital moved to Irving Block, north building on Court Square; September 10, 1861, *Memphis Daily Appeal,* page 3, column 3: report of deaths at the hospital; December 24, 1861, *Memphis Daily Appeal,* page 4, column 5: The Southern Mothers Hospital was yesterday joined with that of the Overton, the latter building now containing the whole of the patients of the two institutions by order of the general in command; see also Mrs. S. E. D. Smith, *The Soldiers Friend; being a Thrilling Narrative of Grandma Smith's Four Years' Experience and Observations, as Matron, in the Hospitals of the South, during the late Disastrous Conflict in America*, Memphis, Tennessee, The Bulletin Publishing Company, 1867, pages 35 and 52-56.

Tennessee Bibb's Company Artillery (Hailman's) - Per *Tennesseans in the Civil War, Part 1*, pages 125-126, Bibb's Tennessee Artillery Battery was formerly Captain S. F. Hailman's Company, known as "Memphis Guerillas." It was mustered into service at Memphis on August 5, 1861, as Captain Hailman's Company Tennessee Volunteers. It was placed under the command of Captain Bibb about March 25, 1862, and served as Company H Tennessee Artillery Corps. It was captured at Island No. 10 April 8, 1862. After exchange at Vicksburg, Mississippi September 1862, the remnants of the company disbanded by Special Order No. 79, Headquarters Jackson, Mississippi dated October 30, 1862, and the members assigned to various commands. Also, per *Tennesseans in the Civil War, Part 1*, page 126, a report from Camp of Returned Prisoners, Jackson, Mississippi, dated October 3, 1862, gave the following account: "All books and papers belonging to the company were destroyed at the time of capture ...."

Tennessee 3rd Cavalry Regiment 2nd Company A (Bluff City Grays) - Per compiled service record card: this company was successively designated as Captain Edmondson's Company, Tennessee 154th Regiment Volunteers; Captain Allin's Company of Sharp Shooters, General Preston Smith's Brigade; Company F, Tennessee 11th Regiment Cavalry; Company A, McDonald's Battalion Tennessee Cavalry; Company H Forrest's Regiment Cavalry; and 2nd Company A, Tennessee 3rd (Forrest's) Regiment Cavalry. Per *Reminiscences of the Civil War* by John Hallum, Tunnah & Pittard, printers, 1903, pages 363-363, General Smith, the first Colonel of the Tennessee 154th Senior Infantry Regiment, protested when Forrest had the company transferred to his command. See Bluff City Grays supra.

Tennessee 7th Cavalry Regiment - See *West Tennessee Historical Society Papers*, Volume 17 (1963) pages 108-117.

Tennessee Mounted Rifles - Company E of Logwood's Tennessee 6th Cavalry Battalion, J. S. White Captain. It was disbanded before organization of 7th Cavalry Regiment. N. B. Forrest began his military career as a private in this company. A resolution to organize reported in the April 20, 1861, *Memphis Daily Appeal* under Local Matters, page 3, column 3. Roster and early information on the Tennessee Mounted Rifles provided by R. B. Miller, who served in the company, in a letter "To the Editors of the Appeal:" printed in *Memphis Daily Appeal*, April 10, 1887, page 9, column 2.

Union Soldiers Burials - Union soldiers were also buried in the Fowler Section in public lots. In the Daily Burial Record Book a grave number is listed in the "Single Graves" column, indicating burial in the public lot. The first Union burial was March 26, 1862, Single Grave #372. The last Union single grave burial with a number was #931 on January 28, 1863. Beginning January 29, 1863, "Name" was written in the "Single Graves" column. In May 1868 Union soldiers were removed to the Memphis National Cemetery, which was originally known as Mississippi River National Cemetery. See Quartermaster General's Office. *Roll of Honor. Names of Soldiers Who Died in Defence of the American Union. Interred in the National Cemeteries*. Washington, D.C.: Government Printing Office, 1865-1871. Volume XXI, Mississippi River National Cemetery, Near Memphis, Tennessee.

University Greys - Mississippi 11 Infantry Regiment Company A. See William Thomas Driver in chapter "Confederates Buried Outside of Soldiers Rest."

Watson Louisiana (Beltzhoover's) Battery (Louisiana 1 Battery of Artillery) - Per November 8, 1861, *Memphis Daily Appeal* Local Matters: difficulty in the Watson Battery and 40 men had to be transferred to Dick Stewart's Company. Some soldiers will be court martialed. Lieutenant Cage had resigned and returned home. Point Couppee Artillery, Captain Stewart, per St. Joseph (Louisiana) Gazette. Participated in the Battle of Belmont, November 7, 1861, (see references in Hughes, Nathaniel Cheairs, Jr. *The Battle of Belmont: Grant Strikes South* (Chapel Hill, NC: The University of North Carolina Press), 1991.

West Tennessee Historical Society - The Society traces its history back to 1857. It is the successor of four historical societies. The first of these was known as the Old Folks of Shelby County, which met monthly and published a monthly journal called the *Old Folks Record*. Succeeding the Old Folks of Shelby County was the Confederate Historical Association, which came into existence in 1866 as the Confederate Relief and Historical Association of Memphis. This was organized in 1869 (*Public Acts of Tennessee, 1869-70*, Chapter 59, Section 11, Page 393) and again in 1884 reorganized as Camp 28, United Confederate Veterans. Its historian, Captain J. Harvey Mathes, produced an historical volume entitled *The Old Guard in Gray*, Press of S. C. Toof & Co., Memphis, 1897. Part II, Enlarged Edition 1899. The next historical society in the chain of descent was the Memphis Historical Society organized by Judge John Preston Young, who had been a leader in the Confederate Historical Association. In 1935, the Memphis Historical Society changed its name to the West Tennessee Historical Society. The West Tennessee Historical Society was succeeded by the West Tennessee Historical Society, Incorporated, on September 28, 1950, when the incorporators took over the affairs of the unincorporated society and granted memberships of the same charter as held by the former members of the society who were in good standing on September 1, 1950. The incorporated society voted to list as charter members all persons who were members on September 1, 1950, or who had joined the society during the first year of the corporation's existence. The corporation, therefore, is a continuation of, as well as a successor to, the unincorporated West Tennessee Historical Society. The Society annually publishes *The West Tennessee Historical Society Papers*.

Worsham Guards - Captain David F. Jackson's Company. Also, known as Bluff City Guards; Company K Mississippi 25th Infantry Regiment; later Confederate 2 Infantry Regiment; then Missouri 1st Infantry Regiment New Company C (merger of Companies F and K). The company was originally organized as a home guard unit. Per August 9, 1861, *Memphis Daily Appeal* Local Matters: Active Duty - Captain D. F. Jackson yesterday received orders from Captain E. D. Blake, by the direction of General Polk, to enter with his Company of Worsham Guards of Artillery on duty in the Battery at the foot of Jefferson Street, Captain And. Jackson, who had command there, having been allotted duty up the River. The officers of this company, which is now full and made up of the best kind of men are: D. F. Jackson, Captain; A. L. Hill, 1st Lieutenant; John Coleman, 2nd Lieutenant; and G. L. Penn, 3rd Lieutenant. The Company was mustered into the service of the Confederate States on Tuesday last. Captain D. F. Jackson and his son, David H. Jackson, who served with his father and was killed at the Battle of Shiloh, are buried at Elmwood.

PARTIAL BIBLIOGRAPHY AND ONLINE INTERNET RESOURCES

Allardice, Bruce S. *More Generals in Gray*. Baton Rouge and London: Louisiana State University Press, 1995.

Allardice, Bruce S. *Confederate Colonels: A Biographical Register*. Columbia and London: University of Missouri Press, 2008.

Allen, Desmond Walls. *Index to Arkansas Confederate Soldiers*. 3 volumes. Arkansas Research, Conway, AR, 1990.

Booth, Andrew B., Commissioner Louisiana Military Records, comp. *Records of Louisiana Confederate Soldiers and Louisiana Confederate Commands*. 3 volumes. New Orleans, LA,1920.

Bergeron, Arthur W., Jr. *Guide to Louisiana Confederate Military Units 1861-1865*. LSU Press, Baton Rouge, 1989.

Crute, Joseph H., Jr. *Confederate Staff Officers 1861 -1865*. Powhatan, Va.: Derwent Books 1982.

Crute, Joseph H., Jr. *Units of the Confederate States Army*. Midlothian, Va.: Derwent Books, 1987.

Cupples, Douglas W. "The Confederate City of Memphis, 1861-1862." *Confederate Chronicles of Tennessee*, Volume 2 (December 1987), pages 5-20.

Dacus, Dr. Robert H. *...Reminiscence...of Company "H", First Arkansas Mounted Rifles*. Dardanelle, AR, August 1, 1897, Post-Dispatch Print, Dardanelle, AR.

Donnelly, Ralph W. *The Confederate Marine Corps*. 1989, White Publishing Company, Inc.

Douthat, James, ed. Shelby County, Tennessee Works Projects Administration Records, Mountain Press, Signal Mountain, TN, 1993.

Elmwood Cemetery. *Civil War Tour*. A self-guided walking tour that introduces readers to 38 of Elmwood's residents who played vital roles during the American Civil War, with stories, photos and biographical sketches of soldiers, politicians, spies, journalists, and other ordinary citizens who faced war on their own doorstep. Elmwood Cemetery, Memphis, Tennessee, 2012.

Elmwood Cemetery. *Elmwood: Charter, Rules, Regulations, and Bylaws of Elmwood Cemetery Association of Memphis*. Boyle & Chapman, Printers, Publishers and Binders, No. 279 Main Street, Memphis, TN, 1874.

Evans, Clement A., ed. *Confederate Military History: A Library of Confederate States History*. 1899; 17 volume extended edition plus 2 volume index, Broadfoot Publishing Company, Wilmington, NC 1987.

Ferguson, John L., ed. *Arkansas in the War*. Arkansas Historical Commission. Pioneer Press, n. d.

Fuller, Mrs. George T. (Lizzie Lowe). *History of Camp Beauregard*. Graves County, KY. 1936.

Goodspeed Publishing Company, *History of Hamilton, Knox and Shelby Counties of Tennessee*. Reprinted from Goodspeed's History 1887, Published and Distributed by Charles and Randy Elder Booksellers, Nashville, TN, 1974.

Hartman, David W., compiler, and Coles, David, associate compiler. *Biographical Roster of Florida's Confederate and Union Soldiers 1861-1865*. Broadfoot Publishing Company, Wilmington, NC 1995.

Hewett, Janet B., ed. *The Roster of Confederate Soldiers 1861-1865*. 16 volumes Broadfoot Publishing Company, 1996.

Hubbard, John Milton. *Notes of A Private*. Published by E. H. Clarke & Brother, Memphis, TN, 1909.

Hughes, Nathaniel Cheairs, Jr. *The Battle of Belmont: Grant Strikes South*. The University of North Carolina Press, 1991.

Lake Blackshear Regional Library Americus Georgia. *Roster of the Confederate States Soldiers of Georgia 1861-1865*. 6 volumes and index. The Reprint Company Publishers, Spartanburg, SC, 1982.

Lindsley, John Berrien, ed. *The Military Annals of Tennessee: Confederate*. J. M. Lindsley and Company, Publishers: 1886. The Reprint Company, Publishers, Spartanburg, SC, 1974.

Mathes, J. Harvey. *The Old Guard in Gray*. Press of S. C. Toof & Co., Memphis, TN, 1897. Part II, Enlarged Edition 1899.

McCollum, Kimberly and Bearden, Will, compilers. *Images of America Elmwood Cemetery*. Arcadia Publishing, Charleston, South Carolina, 2016.

Moore, John Trotwood, ed. and Austin P. Foster, *Tennessee, The Volunteer State, 1769-1923*, Chicago, Nashville, The S. J. Clarke Publishing Company, 1923, 4 volumes (Volume V, Deluxe Supplement).

Mundie, James A., Jr./ Letzring, Dean E./ Allardice, Bruce S./ Luckey, John H. *Texas Burial Sites of Civil War Notables- A Biographical and Pictorial Field Guide*. Published by Hill College Press, Hillsboro, Texas, 2002.

Paul & Douglass Company, *Who's Who in Tennessee, A Biographical Reference Book of Notable Tennesseans To-Day*. Paul & Douglass Publishers, Memphis, 1911.

Quartermaster General's Office. *Roll of Honor. Names of Soldiers Who Died in Defence of the American Union. Interred in the National Cemeteries*. Washington, D.C.: Government Printing Office, 1865-1871. Volume XXI, Mississippi River National Cemetery, Near Memphis, Tennessee.

Rietti, J. C. *Military Annals of Mississippi*. Jackson, MS, n. d. The Reprint Company, Publishers, Spartanburg, SC,1974.

Talley, Robert, ed., The Centennial Edition. *One Hundred Years of The Commercial Appeal, 1840 - 1940* Printed at the *Commercial Appeal* by The Memphis Publishing Company, 1940.

Tennessee Civil War Centennial Commission. *Tennesseans in the Civil War*. 2 parts. Nashville, TN 1964.

Tennessee State Library and Archives. "Questionnaires of Civil War Veterans." Nashville, TN 1914, 1915 and 1920.

U. S. War Department. *Memorandum relative to the General Officers Appointed by the President in the Armies of the Confederate States - 1861-1865*. (Compiled from Official Records) The Military Secretary's Office, 1905.

U. S. War Department. *War of the Rebellion; Official Records of the Union and Confederate Armies*. 128 parts in 70 volumes. Washington, D.C., 1880-1901. Historical Times, Inc.,1985.

U. S. War Department. Record Group #109, National Archives: Records of Confederate Soldiers Who Served During the Civil War, Microfilmed Indexes and Compiled Service Records for Confederate Army Volunteers; Records Pertaining to Confederate Naval and Marine Personnel (M260); Confederate States Army Casualties: Lists and Narrative Reports,

1861-1865. Roll 7. Undated Return of Killed and Wounded, 1st Brigade, 1st Division, Forrest's Cavalry during the Month of August 1864 (M836); and Medical Department, Chapter VI, Volume 92, Overton General Hospital (Memphis) - Register of Patients, December 31, 1861-March 31, 1962, with a Register of Deaths, March 3-31, 1862, and Southern Mothers Hospital (Memphis) - Undated inventory of furniture, with an undated memorandum regarding the hospital buildings and a roll of the sick men at the State Hospital January 31, 1862.

Warner, Ezra. *Generals in Grays: Lives of the Confederate Commanders*. Baton Rouge, 1959.

Warner, Ezra and Yearns, W. Buck. *Biographical Register of the Confederate Congress*. LSU Press, Baton Rouge, 1975.

Wiefering, Edna, abstractor, and Sherrill, Charles A., ed. *TENNESSEE'S CONFEDERATE WIDOWS and their Families. Abstracts of 11,190 Confederate Widows Pension Applications*. A Publication of the Cleveland Public Library Staff & Volunteers, Cleveland, TN, 1992.

Wright, Marcus J. *Tennessee in the War 1861-1865*. Ambrose Lee Publishing Company, Williamsbridge, New York City, 1908.

Wright, Marcus J. *Texas in the War, 1861-1865*. Ed. Harold B. Simpson. The Hill Junior College Press, 1965.

Young, J. P. *The Seventh Tennessee Cavalry, (Confederate) A History*. M. E. Church, Publisher, Nashville, TN, 1890. Press of Morningside Bookshop, Dayton, OH, 1976.

Young, J. P., ed. *Standard History of Memphis, Tennessee*. Knoxville, TN: H. W. Crew & Company Publisher, 1912.

Ancestry.com is a family history resource home to historical records, family trees and more.

Confederate Veteran was a monthly magazine founded "in the interests of Confederate veterans and kindred topics" that was first published in 1893 and ran until 1932. A serial archive listing can be found on The Online Books Page: onlinebooks.library.upenn.edu/webbin/serial?id=confedvet; and an index is available at the Library of Virginia: lva1.hosted.exlibrisgroup.com/F/?func=file&file_name=find-b-clas65&local_base=CLAS65.

Early Memphis Newspapers indexes, including obituaries, compiled by Joyce McKibben, Research and Instruction Librarian, University of Memphis (umdrive.memphis.edu/mckibben/www/).

FamilySearch.org is a genealogy organization operated by The Church of Jesus Christ of Latter-day Saints and maintains a collection of records, resources, and services designed to help people learn more about their family history.

Find A Grave (FindAGrave.com) allows the public to search and add to an online database of cemetery records and contains listings of cemeteries and graves from around the world. American cemeteries are organized by state and county. Individual grave records may contain dates and places of birth and death, biographical information, cemetery and plot information, photographs (of the grave marker, the individual, etc.), and contributor information. Elmwood Cemetery: findagrave.com/cemetery/11738.

Fold3.com is a collections of original military records, including the Civil War, that include the stories, photos, and personal documents of the men and women who served in the military. Many of the records come from the U.S. National archives.

Library of Congress Chronicling America: Historic American Newspapers - National Digital Newspaper Program is a partnership between The National Endowment for the Humanities and the Library of Congress to create a national digital resource of historically significant states and U.S. territories newspapers published between 1690 and 1963. See specifically: Memphis Daily Appeal 1847-1886 (chroniclingamerica.loc.gov/lccn/sn83045160/issues/1857/), Memphis Daily Appeal 1886-1890 (chroniclingamerica.loc.gov/lccn/sn84024448/issues/) and Public Ledger (Memphis) 1865-1893 (chroniclingamerica.loc.gov/lccn/sn85033673/).

National Park Service Soldiers and Sailors Database (nps.gov/civilwar/soldiers-and-sailors-database.htm).

The Civil War Soldiers and Sailors System (CWSS) is a database containing information about the men who served in the Union and Confederate armies during the Civil War. Other information on the site includes histories of Union and Confederate regiments, links to descriptions of significant battles, and selected lists of prisoner-of-war records and cemetery records, which will be amended over time. The CWSS is a cooperative effort between the National Park Service and several public and private partners whose goal is to increase Americans' understanding of this decisive era in American history by making information about it widely accessible.

Political Graveyard (politicalgraveyard.com/index.html) identifies locations of the graves of American politicians and includes manner of death, and other biographical information.

Shelby County, Tennessee Register of Deeds (register.shelby.tn.us) – As part of its Archives Section on Shelby County records links are provided to Birth Records 1874-1917, Death Records 1848-1967, Memphis Census 1865, Memphis City Directories 1849-1943, Memphis Provost Marshal 1863-1865, Naturalization Records 1856-1906, Probate Court Loose Paper Index 1820-1900, Probate Court Wills 1830-2004, Elmwood Cemetery Daily Burial Record 1853-1919, Old Shelby County Magazine and West Tennessee Historical Society Papers 1947-2015.

Tennessee State Library and Archives Civil War Research (sos.tn.gov/products/tsla/tennessee-civil-war-research-sources) – The site has research sources for Service Records, Pension Records, Biographical Sources, Unit Histories and Manuscripts and includes Name Indexes for TN Confederate Pension Applications: Soldiers & Widows (Name and County Indexes), TN Confederate Physicians: An Annotated List, Members of the Confederate Relief and Historical Association of Memphis, TN Confederate Soldiers' Home: Applications and Ledgers, TN Civil War Veterans' Questionnaires, Union Provost Marshal Records from TN and Southern Claims Commission - TN.

BALLAD OF 1862

by Ruby Hyden Flowers

The year was 1862
And war clouds hovered near
Where a family lived on a homestead claim
Along the old frontier.

Hope was gone that war would cease
And leave their homes secure
For men were marching, marching on
In a struggle to endure.

Matt Hyden heard the war talk
Of battles near and far
And thought to choose most wisely
His part in approaching war.

One morning just at daybreak
His friends came riding by.
Together in this conflict
Their fortunes they would try.

If they waited for conscription
With strangers they might be.
Together they would help one another
Whatever their destiny.

Matt kissed his two small children,
Caressed his young wife Jane
And told her to car a for the young ones
Until he was with them again.

She saw him ride out with the others.
Not for long, she thought, would he stay.
She could not know that the hazards of war
Would keep him forever away.

Letters were few that he wrote her.
Describing the journey they made
Toward Memphis where soldiers were gathering
To learn of the plans that were laid.

He sent her a present - a tintype,
A photograph in a fine case
And wrote of the rumors of fighting,
Maneuvers of soldiers in place.

Then suddenly there were no letters.
Jane could not know of this plight,
She heard he was left by his regiment
As men made their way to the fight.

He was ill. That was all that they told her.
Came war's end and no more could she learn.
Some day he will come, she thought bravely,
As she waited for his return.
It was early spring in '62
When Matt rode away in the dawn.
His fight was a losing battle with death.
He was forever gone.

For the camps in Memphis were crowded
With illness and death so well-known
And many young men were buried there
Away from their loved ones - alone.

A record has since been discovered
Too late for his family to learn:
He was lying in death in Memphis
As they waited for his return. *

* After considerable research, a great-grandson who bore the same name was able to determine that Matthew Hyden died in Memphis in 1862 as his regiment was marching to join other forces, and that he was buried in Elmwood Cemetery along with other Confederate soldiers.

This poem was written by Ruby Hyden Flowers, granddaughter of Matthew Hyden, and was included in a small book of verses by her titled *A Walk in the Garden* (1976). Matthew Hyden is buried in Confederate Soldiers Rest.

Re-printed with the permission of the Hyden family.

REST IN PEACE

DEDICATION TO THE CONFEDERATE DEAD

Sleep on, ye glory wraped heroes
  Of a warm and sunny land,
Whose deeds of true valor compare
  With that brave Spartan band.
Those heroes of old ne'er fought and bled
  For a land that was fairer, which to love
In their hearts' rich blood was glory and joy:
  Then rest in peace ye gallant brave.

The turf presses lightly on your broad breast,
  The winter winds sing you a lullaby song,
And cool summer zephyrs sigh thro' the trees,
  While busy bees hum to you all the day long.
No care, pain, or sorrow belong to you now:
  No grim prison walls before you arise.
Nor sentinel dread on your slumber glares:
  Then rest, for the brave man never dies.

Your memory, enshrined in fond hearts and true,
  Grows fresher as day follows day:
For 'tis watered by tears from gratitude's fount,
  And warmed by affection's ray.
Sleep undisturbed, tho' thunder may roll,
  And lightning's red flash dart over your head
No battle cry will awake you again:
  Then rest in peace, ye honored dead.

The halo of glory which circles your brows
  Was bought in a cause most holy and pure,
And has rendered immortal you sons of the
  South,
Who fought for a land from which naught
  Could allure.
Your slumber is sweet, your strife is now o'er --
  The lark sings a requiem above your green graves,
And the soft summer breezes lull you to sleep:
  Then rest in peace, ye immortal braves.

Daily Memphis Avalanche, August 17, 1866, page 4

www.ingramcontent.com/pod-product-compliance
Lightning Source LLC
Chambersburg PA
CBHW080231270326

41926CB00020B/4209